# Mozambique at a Fork in the Road

Few countries have experienced as many political and economic changes as Mozambique. A vast and diverse country, it faced a particularly difficult start after a long period of colonial dominance followed by a deadly war that formally ended only in 1992. However, despite impressive growth after multiparty elections, Mozambique's pattern of growth is fragmented, not sustainable and non-inclusive. Investigating the deep factors that undermine economic development, *Mozambique at a Fork in the Road* offers an insightful analysis of the historical and political context of Mozambique and its institutional constraints to economic development. It examines sectors that are critical for sustainable growth, such as agriculture, that receive low priority, and the frequent shocks in strategic policy that result in the absence of a clear national development vision. Building on a core set of thematic chapters, this compelling diagnostic tool provides a thorough and structured approach to understanding institutional dimensions of development. This title is also available as Open Access on Cambridge Core.

António S. Cruz is an independent researcher in economics collaborating with the University of Copenhagen Development Economics Research Group (UCPH-DERG). He was Director of Studies at the Ministry of Planning and Development and Director of Studies Centre, at Economics Department, Eduardo Mondlane University, Mozambique.

Ines A. Ferreira is assistant professor in UCPH-DERG. She works on different topics related to inequality and institutions, with a particular focus on Mozambique.

Johnny Flentø has 38 years of experience in international development with the Danish MFA and Copenhagen University. He has done several years of research in institutional and economic development with a focus on international development through bilateral and multilateral frameworks.

Finn Tarp is Professor of Economics, University of Copenhagen, and former Director of United Nations University World Institute for Development Economics Research (UNU-WIDER). He is a leading international expert on development strategy and policy and has published more than 130 articles in internationally refereed academic journals – alongside 6 books, 29 edited book volumes/special journal issues, and 67 book chapters.

# The Institutional Diagnostic Project

A suite of case-study monographs emerging from a large research program on the role of institutions in the economics, and the political economy of development in low-income countries, supported by a synthesis volume of the original case studies. This program was funded by the United Kingdom's Foreign and Commonwealth Development Office during a period of six years, during which program researchers had regular interactions with its staff, either directly or through Oxford Policy Management (the lead managing organisation).

## Books in this collection:

François Bourguignon and Jean-Philippe Platteau *Institutional Challenges at the Early Stages of Development: Lessons from a Multi-Country Study*

Selim Raihan, François Bourguignon and Umar Salam (Eds.) *Is the Bangladesh Paradox Sustainable?*

António S. Cruz, Ines A. Ferreira, Johnny Flentø and Finn Tarp (Eds.) *Mozambique at a Fork in the Road*

François Bourguignon, Romain Houssa, Jean-Philippe Platteau and Paul Reding (Eds.) *State Capture and Rent-Seeking in Benin*

François Bourguignon and Samuel Mwita Wangwe (Eds.) *State and Business in Tanzania's Development*

UNU World Institute for Development Economics Research (UNU-WIDER) was established by the United Nations University as its first research and training centre and started work in Helsinki, Finland, in 1985. The mandate of the institute is to undertake applied research and policy analysis on structural changes affecting developing and transitional economies, to provide a forum for the advocacy of policies leading to robust, equitable, and environmentally sustainable growth, and to promote capacity strengthening and training in the field of economic and social policy-making. Its work is carried out by staff researchers and visiting scholars in Helsinki and via networks of collaborating scholars and institutions around the world.

*United Nations University World Institute for Development Economics Research*
*(UNU-WIDER)*
*Katajanokanlaituri 6B, 00160 Helsinki, Finland*
*www.wider.unu.edu*

# Mozambique at a Fork in the Road

## The Institutional Diagnostic Project

Edited by

**ANTÓNIO S. CRUZ**
*University of Copenhagen*

**INES A. FERREIRA**
*University of Copenhagen*

**JOHNNY FLENTØ**
*University of Copenhagen*

**FINN TARP**
*University of Copenhagen*

# CAMBRIDGE
## UNIVERSITY PRESS

Shaftesbury Road, Cambridge CB2 8EA, United Kingdom

One Liberty Plaza, 20th Floor, New York, NY 10006, USA

477 Williamstown Road, Port Melbourne, VIC 3207, Australia

314–321, 3rd Floor, Plot 3, Splendor Forum, Jasola District Centre,
New Delhi – 110025, India

103 Penang Road, #05–06/07, Visioncrest Commercial, Singapore 238467

Cambridge University Press is part of Cambridge University Press & Assessment,
a department of the University of Cambridge.

We share the University's mission to contribute to society through the pursuit of
education, learning and research at the highest international levels of excellence.

www.cambridge.org
Information on this title: www.cambridge.org/9781009265751

DOI: 10.1017/9781009265799

First published 2023

*A catalogue record for this publication is available from the British Library*

*Library of Congress Cataloging-in-Publication Data*
NAMES: Cruz, António S., 1959– editor. | Ferreira, Ines A., 1989– editor.
| Flentø, Johnny, 1959– editor. | Tarp, Finn, 1951– editor.
TITLE: Mozambique at a fork in the road / edited by António S. Cruz,
University of Copenhagen, Ines A. Ferreira, University of Copenhagen, Johnny Flentø, University
of Copenhagen, Finn Tarp, University of Copenhagen.
DESCRIPTION: Cambridge, United Kingdom ; New York, NY : Cambridge
University Press, 2023. | Includes bibliographical references and index.
IDENTIFIERS: LCCN 2022062035 | ISBN 9781009265751 (hardback) |
ISBN 9781009265799 (ebook)
SUBJECTS: LCSH: Economic development – Mozambique. | Mozambique – Economic conditions – 1975–
| Economic stabilization – Mozambique. | Structural adjustment (Economic policy) – Mozambique.
CLASSIFICATION: LCC HC890 .M639 2023 | DDC 330.9679–dc23/eng/20230113
LC record available at https://lccn.loc.gov/2022062035

ISBN 978-1-009-26575-1 Hardback

# Contents

# Figures

# Tables

# Notes on Contributors

**João Z. Carrilho** works at Observatório do Meio Rural (OMR), collaborating in land policy–related research projects. He is a member of the Commission of the Land National Policy Review. He had served at local, district, and province levels. At national level, Carrilho served as the chairman of the Institute of Rural Development and Deputy Minister of Agriculture and Rural Development. His recent research interest is sustainability in peri-urban territory informal occupation and spatial planning.

**António S. Cruz** is an independent researcher in economics collaborating with UCPH-DERG. He has worked before for the National Directorate of Statistics at the National Commission of Planning, the Ministry of Planning and Finance, the Ministry of Planning and Development and as an Assistant Professor in the Department of Economics at the Eduardo Mondlane University in Mozambique. He has published on industrialisation and related issues, social accounting matrix, and macroeconomic issues.

**Ines A. Ferreira** is assistant professor in UCPH-DERG. She works on different topics related to inequality and institutions, with a particular focus on Mozambique. She was previously engaged in projects on state fragility, aid effectiveness, poverty measurement and the determinants of individual behaviour and preferences.

**Johnny Flentø** has 38 years of experience in international development with the Danish Ministry of Foreign Affairs and Copenhagen University, and several years of research in institutional and economic development. He is a seasoned diplomat with a focus on international development through bilateral and multilateral frameworks. He has significant experience in all aspects of diplomacy with a focus on development programming and policy dialogue. He had spent majority of his career abroad in Mozambique, Benin, Tanzania, and Bangladesh.

**Salvador Forquilha** is assistant professor at the Department of Political Science and Public Administration, Eduardo Mondlane University, and a senior researcher at the Institute for Social and Economic Studies (IESE) in Mozambique. He holds a PhD in political science from the University of Bordeaux in France. His research focuses on state building and political violence in Mozambique.

**Paulo Ivo Garrido** is a retired professor of anatomy and surgery at the Eduardo Mondlane University. He was Minister of Health between 2005 and 2010, and had a long career as a medical surgeon, occupying different leadership positions as well.

**Sam Jones** is a Research Fellow at UNU-WIDER based in Mozambique, on extended leave from his position as an associate professor in the Department of Economics, University of Copenhagen. He is a versatile economist with expertise in macroeconomic analysis, development finance (including foreign aid), microeconomic empirical methods, education and labour markets. Sam's work has been published in leading journals, such as *Journal of Development Economics*, *World Bank Economic Review*, *American Journal of Agricultural Economics*, *Food Policy*, *Social Science & Medicine*, *Journal of Economic Inequality*, *World Development*, *Journal of Development Studies*, *African Development Review*, and *Journal of African Economies*. Much of Sam's academic research has focused on sub-Saharan Africa and he has previously worked extensively in Mozambique, spending seven years as an advisor in the Ministry of Finance.

**José Jaime Macuane** is associate professor at the Department of Political Science and Public Administration, Eduardo Mondlane University, Mozambique. His research interest areas are political institutions, democratisation, state reform, and political economy of development in Africa and Mozambique.

**Mouzinho Mário** is an independent consultant, currently with the Ministry of Science, Technology and Higher Education of Mozambique, after an academic career that spanned over three decades at Eduardo Mondlane University. His research interests include higher education policy and development, faculty development, and teacher education. He has a number of publications in the fields of higher education, teacher education, adult education and literacy, and quality of student learning in primary schools.

**Celso M. Monjane** is a research associate in the Department of International Relations, at the University of the Witwatersrand. His research experience and interest include examining governance in Africa, particularly with regard to business interests of elites and political economy of natural resources, applying also data science and statistical modelling. He has a promising record of scholarly publications in several academic journals on the politics of Development in Mozambique.

**Carlos Muianga** is an associate researcher at IESE in Mozambique, having been a permanent researcher for the last 12 years. He is currently a PhD candidate in development studies at the School of Oriental and African Studies (SOAS), University of London. His PhD research is on the political economy of agrarian capitalism in Mozambique, with focus on the Limpopo Valley His research interests include the political economy of the patterns of accumulation; economic and social transformation in Mozambique; and the agrarian political economy and the agrarian question in Mozambique. He is an editorial assistant of the Journal of Agrarian Change.

**Rui de Nazaré Ribeiro** has an MSc in rural and agricultural development. He is an active member of Observatório do Meio Rural (OMR), providing inputs to research and advocacy work. He has been engaged in rural and agricultural development in Mozambique for more than 40 years. Through his career, Ribeiro has held strategic positions within agriculture public institutions dealing with technical and policy issues. He is a senior consultant, and in the last 25 years, he has been involved in managing major agriculture and rural development programmes and doing studies related to the agriculture institutional environment, agriculture markets systems, seed sub-sector and agribusiness.

**Ricardo Santos** is a UNU-WIDER Research Fellow and a technical advisor to the Centre of Studies in Economics and Management of Eduardo Mondlane University. His research focuses on education and labor economics, poverty and inequality, and institutional economics of aid.

**Leonardo Santos Simão** is a medical doctor, with a master's degree in public health, a former Minister of Health and Minister of Foreign Affairs of Mozambique. He is now the Executive Director of the Joaquim Chissano Foundation, Chairman of the Board of Trustees of the Manhiça Foundation (dedicated to health research), and High Representative for Africa of the European and Developing Countries Clinical Trials Partnership (EDCTP). His main areas of interest are medical research and social development.

**Finn Tarp** is Professor of Economics, University of Copenhagen, and former Director of UNU-WIDER (2009–18). He is a leading international expert on development strategy and policy. In addition to his university posts, he has held senior appointments and advisory positions with international organisations and several national governments and is a member of a series of international committees and advisory bodies. He has led development projects and integrated policy advisory/field-level work in some 35 countries across the world. This includes a long list of duties in Mozambique during more than four decades (with 10+ years in the country). He has published more than 130 articles in internationally refereed academic journals – including *The Economic Journal, Journal of Development Economics, World Bank Economic Review, European Economic Review, American*

*Journal of Agricultural Economics, World Development, Oxford Bulletin of Economics and Statistics, Land Economics, Review of Income and Wealth, Feminist Economics, Economic Development and Cultural Change,* and *Climatic Change* – alongside 6 books, 29 edited book volumes/special journal issues, and 67 book chapters.

**João Carlos Trindade** is a retired judge of the Supreme Court of Mozambique, former dean of the Legal and Judicial Training Centre (1999–2006), and Professor of Criminal Procedural Law and History of Mozambican Law at the Law School of Eduardo Mondlane University (1994–2001). He is also President of the Board of the General Meeting of CTV – Centro Terra Viva, Estudos e Advocacia Ambiental. He has carried out several studies and research activities, with papers published in the areas of sociology of law and the administration of justice.

**Mariam Umarji** is a public finance expert working in Africa. She is currently doing her PhD in global health and development with a focus on the health workforce and public financial management (PFM). She has done PFM work in developing countries for more than 15 years.

# Foreword

The vital importance of institutions for economic development is widely acknowledged in both the theoretical and empirical literature. Institutions matter for growth and inclusive development. However, despite increasing awareness of the importance of institutions on economic outcomes, there is little evidence on how positive institutional change can be achieved. The precise nature of the relationship between the two is unclear: do 'good' institutions produce development, or does development lead to 'good' institutions? The Economic Development and Institutions (EDI) research programme aims to fill this knowledge gap by working with some of the finest economic thinkers and social scientists across the globe. The EDI programme was launched in 2015 and concluded in 2022, made up of four parallel research activities: path-finding papers, institutional diagnostic, coordinated randomised control trials, and case studies. Funded by the UK Foreign and Commonwealth Development Office (FCDO) (for more information, see http://edi.opml.co.uk), the institutional diagnostic component developed a framework that can help us understand better the nature of institutional impediments to development, and identify ways of attenuating them. In this Mozambique case study under the Institutional Diagnostic Project, the Development Economics Research Group at UCPH-DERG, in collaboration with Oxford Policy Management (OPM) and UNU-WIDER, carried out such a diagnostic of Mozambican institutions, which aims to identify weak institutional areas that restrict development and suggest appropriate directions for reform.

Few countries have experienced as many extreme political and economic changes as Mozambique both before and since independence in 1975. Despite an impressive growth performance after multiparty elections in 1994, the pattern of growth in Mozambique is fragmented, not sustainable and non-inclusive. This situation reflects low productivity growth in agriculture, lack of diversification, and a low level and pace of structural transformation. At the same time, the reduction of poverty has, after sharp drops from the mid-1990s, been rather slow and accompanied by increasing inequality. With the discovery of oil and gas in the early 2000s, focus has turned to the future of extraction of natural resources and the challenges of ensuring that it generates a positive impact on the Mozambican economy. The country now finds itself at a fork in the road. Critical choices have to be made as to whether to remain on the present path which will lead to increasing inequality, further regional imbalances, and possibly armed conflict or alternatively use the expected gas revenues effectively for poverty reduction, in a process where agricultural development, agro-industry, and labour-intensive private sector advancement are central.

The diagnostic of institutions in Mozambique proceeds in several stages. We start by compiling an overview of the historical and political context and of the performance of Mozambique in different socio-economic dimensions. We then complement this background with an analysis of institutional indicators from existing datasets, as well as with the implementation of a quantitative questionnaire and a series of key informants' interviews, both aimed at gathering the perceptions of people in Mozambique on the institutional constraints to economic development in the country. This serves as a stepping stone to identifying a series of critical areas for further analysis in eight thematic chapters on which we draw in developing our institutional diagnostic.

Our synthesis shows that the combination of a complex set of deep factors leads to crucial institutional bottlenecks, which have undermined economic development. Sectors that are critical for sustainable and inclusive growth, such as agriculture, receive low priority, and frequent shocks in strategic policy direction result in the absence of a clear national development vision. The lack of separation of powers obstructs effective law enforcement and public financial management. Citizens' trust in government and effective government accountability are negatively affected by lack of voice and a weak political opposition. In parallel, the potential risks associated with a very large extractive sector are beginning to influence socio-economic development. Finally, a process of change from being highly dependent on foreign aid to more complex international interactions, including powerful foreign investors, is unfolding. We end the volume with proposals for reform, which we hope will contribute to national debate and reflection on the way forward in Mozambique.

# Preface

This study of Mozambique is one of four case studies in a research project whose final aim is to devise a methodology that would establish an 'institutional diagnostic' of economic development in a particular country. The objective of such a diagnostic is to identify the institutional factors that may slow down development or reduce its inclusiveness or sustainability, the reforms likely to overcome these weaknesses, but also the political economy that may prevent or facilitate such reforms. These diagnostics must thus rely on a thorough review of economic development and institutional features of countries under analysis, which is the content of this volume on Mozambique. As a preamble, the following pages offer a general description of the whole diagnostic project.

## 'INSTITUTIONS MATTER'

'Institutions matter' became a motto among international development agencies in the late 1990s, when it became clear that structural adjustment policies – themselves based upon the so-called 'Washington Consensus' – and their emphasis on markets were not delivering the growth and development that was expected. The slogan sounded a note of disappointment for those liberalist reformers, sometimes jokingly called the 'marketeers', who promoted the reliance on market mechanisms and the pre-eminence of private actors in order for developing countries to get out of the crises of the 1980s and restore long-run growth. Giving more space to the market was probably justified from a theoretical point of view. Practically, however, it was another story. What the marketeers had not fully realised was that a well-functioning market economy requires regulating institutions, public goods, and non-market services

xix

which most often were missing or deficient in the economies being considered. Under these conditions, liberalising, privatising, and deregulating might in effect prove counterproductive without concomitant institutional changes.

Nowadays, the 'institutions matter' slogan appears as a fundamental truth about development, and it is indeed widely shared by the development community, including international organisations. Equally obvious to all is the complementarity between the market and the state: the economic efficiency expected from the former requires some intervention by the latter through adequate policies, the provision of public services, and, more fundamentally, institutions able to impose rules constraining the activity of various economic actors, whether public and private. Practically, however, the institutions of a country are the outcome of history and specific events or circumstances. Therefore, they are not necessarily well adapted to the current economic context and to the modern development challenge. This raises the issue as to how existing institutions can be reformed.

That 'institutions matter' has also long been evident for those academic economists and political scientists who kept stressing that development is the outcome of the joint and interactive evolution of the economy and its institutional set-up, with the latter encompassing not only state and political agencies but also cultural and social norms. As a matter of fact, the study of the role of institutions has a long history in the development economics literature, from the very pioneers of the discipline in the post–Second World War years and their emphasis on development as a structural and cultural transformation, as for instance in the writings of Peter Bauer, Albert Hirschman, Arthur Lewis, or Hla Myint, to the New Institutional Economics as applied to development issues, in particular with the work of Douglass North, to the Institutional Political Economy approach put forward nowadays by social scientists like Mushtaq Khan, and to the more formalised school of Political Economics pioneered by Daron Acemoglu and James Robinson.

## HOW INSTITUTIONS MATTER IN DEVELOPMENT
## POLICY TODAY: THE ROLE OF 'GOVERNANCE'

Faced with the disappointing performances of the so-called 'Washington Consensus', which governed the market-oriented 'structural adjustment' policies put to work in developing countries at the time of the macroeconomic crisis of the early 1980s, international organisations and bilateral development agencies switched to what was called the 'post-Washington Consensus'. This extended set of principles were seen as a way of compensating for the neglect of institutional considerations in the original set of policies. Market-oriented reforms had thus to be accompanied by other reforms, including the regulation of various sectors, making government more efficient, and improving human capital formation. Most importantly, however, emphasis was put on good governance as a necessary adjuvant to market-led development, especially in its capacity to protect property rights and guarantee contract enforcement. With time, governance then became a key criterion among donors for allocating aid across low-income countries and monitor its use.

It is fair to say that, practically, governance is defined and evaluated in a rather ad hoc manner, based on some expert opinion, firm surveys, and some simple economic parameters like the rate of inflation or the size of budget deficit. The relationship with the actual nature and quality of institutions is thus very indirect. This still seems the case today, even though the recent World Development Report by the World Bank, *Governance and the Law*,[1] intends to go deeper by showing how governance, or policymaking in general including institutional reforms, depends on the functioning of institutions, the role of stakeholders and their relative political power. Practically, however, there remains something rather mechanical and schematic in the way institutions are represented in this report, which is actually more about effective policymaking than on the diagnosis of institutional weaknesses and possible avenues for reform.

If there is no doubt that institutions matter for development, the crucial issue is to know how they matter. After all, impressive economic development achievements have been observed despite clear failures in particular institutional areas. In other words, not all dimensions of governance may be relevant at a given point of time in a given country. Likewise, institutional dimensions that are not included in governance criteria may play a decisive role.

There is admittedly limited knowledge about how institutions affect development, how they form, and how they can be reformed in specific contexts. Despite intensive and increasing efforts over the last few decades, the challenge remains daunting. The difficulty comes from the tight imbrication of the way the quality of existing institutions affects the development process, including policies, the political economy context which conditions possible institutional reforms, and the influence that the pace and structure of development exerts, directly or indirectly, on the dynamics of institutions.

SEARCHING FOR EVIDENCE ON THE RELATIONSHIP BETWEEN
THE QUALITY OF INSTITUTIONS AND DEVELOPMENT

Three approaches have been followed to help in the identification of development-hindering or -promoting institutional features, and of their evolution over time, whether autonomously or through discretionary reforms. All three approaches have their own drawbacks.

The first approach consists of historical case studies. These are in-depth studies of successful, or unsuccessful, development experiences, and their causes and processes as they unfolded in the historical past or in the

---

[1] World Bank (2017).

contemporary world. The formation and success of the Maghribi trading networks in eleventh-century Mediterranean basin, the effects of the Glorious Revolution in Britain, the enactment of effective land reforms in Korea and Taiwan after the demise of the Japanese colonial rule, and the implementation of the Household Responsibility System in rural China – all these are examples of institutional changes that led to vigorous development, whether state-led or resulting from decentralised initiatives triggered by external factors. On the other hand, violent fights for the appropriation of natural resource rents in several post-independence African states illustrate the opposite course of blocked development under essentially predatory states. Studying such events is of utmost interest insofar as they highlight rather precise mechanisms susceptible of governing the transformation of institutions, often under the pressure of economic and other circumstances, sometimes prompting and sometimes hampering development. In their best-selling book *Why Nations Fail*, for instance, Acemoglu and Robinson (2012) masterfully show the role of institutions in several historical and contemporaneous experiences of sustained or failed development. In particular, they stress the critical role of inclusive institutions as compared with predatory ones, and most importantly the role of favourable political conditions in changing institutions and sparking off development. The most serious problem with this approach, however, is that the experiences thoroughly analysed in the history-based empirical literature are rarely transferable in time or in space and are not necessarily relevant for developing countries today.

Under the second approach are cross-country studies pertaining to the contemporaneous era. It relies on indicators that describe the strength of a particular set of institutions or a specific aspect of governance in a country: protection of property rights, nature of legal regimes, extent of democracy, strength and type of controls on the executive, and extent of corruption, the issue being whether there is a correlation between these indicators and gross domestic product (GDP) growth or other development outcomes. These institutional and governance indicators are generally based on the opinion of experts in various areas evaluating, on a comparative basis, countries on which they have specialised knowledge. They are thus based on largely subjective grounds and lack the precision needed for statistical analysis. If correlation with development outcomes is sometimes significant and often fit intuition, the use that can be made of them is problematic as they essentially refer, by construction, to an abstract 'average country' and may be of little use when focusing on a particular country. Most importantly, they say nothing about causality and still less about the policy instruments that could improve institutions under consideration. Corruption is generally found to be bad for development, but in what direction does the causality go? Is it true in all countries and all circumstances? What about the cases where corruption 'greases the wheels' and reintroduces economic efficiency in the presence of too stringent administrative constraints? And, if it is to be curbed, what kind of reform is likely to work?

Cross-country studies are a useful approach provided that it is considered as essentially exploratory. They need to be complemented by more country-specific analyses that can detect causal relationships, shed light on dynamic processes at play in key sectors of the economy as well as on their interactions with institutions and the political arena, and inform on potential ways of conducting reforms.

The third approach exploits the fact that some sorts of institutional weaknesses or strengths are readily observable, such as the delivery of public services like education or healthcare. For instance, the absenteeism of teachers in public schools reveals a breach of contract between civil servants and their employers and/or a monitoring failure by supervisors. There are ways of incentivising teachers so that they show up in school, and numerous experimentations, rigorously evaluated through randomised control trial (RCT) techniques in various community settings, have successfully explored the impact of such schemes in various countries over the last two decades or more. Identification of similar institutional weaknesses at the micro level and experimentation of ways to remedy them have sprouted up in the recent past, so much so that the field has become the dominant subject among researchers in development economics. Inspired by the RCT methodology and its concern with causality, a new economic approach to history has also blossomed in the last decades. This literature exploits so-called 'natural experiments' and intends to assess the impact of institutional changes that exogenously emerged in particular geographic areas in the past, the outcomes of which can still be observed and compared to otherwise similar neighbouring regions today. These outcomes can be of an economic, a social, or a political nature.

A major limitation of the third approach is that it generally addresses simple cases that are suitable for experimentation. Identifying more macro-level institutional failures and testing appropriate remedies through the RCT method is much less easy, if not impossible. In addition, successful testing of reforms susceptible of correcting well-identified micro-level institutional failures does not mean that the political will exists, or an effective coalition of interest groups can be formed, to fully correct the detected inefficiency. Thus, in the above example of teachers' absenteeism, there is no guarantee that the state will systematically implement the incentive scheme whose impact has been shown to be the best way to improve school performances. The institutional weakness may thus not be so much in the breach of contract between teachers and their public employer as in the incapacity of the latter to design and implement the right policy. As this example shows, an in-depth understanding of macro-political factors is needed to reach a proper assessment of the feasibility of reforms and the conditions required for their successful implementation.

The above empirical approaches leave a gap between an essential macro-view of the relationship between institutions and development, whether it consists of stylised historical facts or cross-country correlations between GDP growth and governance or institutional indicators, on the one hand, and a micro-perspective on institutional dysfunction (e.g., the observation of absenteeism of civil servants or corrupt tax inspectors) and possible remedies, on the other hand. Also note that, in most cases, these approaches permit to identify relationships between institutional factor and development outcomes but not the mechanisms responsible for them. In economic modelling parlance, they give 'reduced form' rather than 'structural' evidence about the institution–development nexus. Filling this twofold gap requires a meso-approach based, as much as possible, on structural analysis conducted at intermediate levels of the social and economic structure of a country, including economic or social sectors as well as key groups of actors and official decision-making or monitoring entities.

Awareness of these drawbacks of the standard analysis of the relationship between institutions and development and, therefore, of the need for a more structural, sectoral, and political economy approach to that relationship has motivated the exploratory research undertaken within the present Institutional Diagnostic Project.

## INSTITUTIONAL DIAGNOSTIC AS A NEW APPROACH TO INSTITUTIONS AND DEVELOPMENT

The Institutional Diagnostic Project research programme aims at developing a methodology or, better said, a framework that allows the identification of major institutional weaknesses or dysfunctions that block or slow down economic growth and structural transformation, and/or make them non-inclusive and non-sustainable, in a given country at a given stage of its development process. The diagnostic is also intended to formulate a reform programme and point to the political stakes involved in its implementation. In other words, it should contribute simultaneously to a better understanding of the specific relationship between institutions and development in the country under consideration, to a more complete stocktaking of policies and reforms likely to improve the development context, and to characterising the political barriers that might obstruct these reforms. It is a country-centred approach that differs from historical case studies, in the sense that the focus is not on a particular event, circumstance, or episode in a country but on the overall functioning of its economy and society. It also goes beyond the mere use of governance or institutional indicators that appear much too rough when dealing with a specific economy. On the other hand, it makes use of microeconomic evidence on institutional weaknesses and dysfunction in a country and, when available, on whatever lesson can be learned from experimental works that may have been conducted in the area concerned. It thus makes use of the various methodological approaches to the study of the institution–development relationship but goes beyond them by embedding them in essentially a structural approach adapted to the particulars of a country.

*A priori*, it would seem that institutional diagnostics should resemble the 'growth diagnostics' approach developed by Hausmann, Rodrik, and Velasco[2] some 15 years ago to identify the binding economic constraints to economic growth. The resemblance can only be semantic, however. Practically, if the objective is similar, the difference is huge. Most fundamentally, the growth diagnostics approach relies explicitly on a full theoretical model of economic growth based on the accumulation of means of production and innovation in the private sector, the availability of infrastructure, financial facilities, the control of risk through appropriate insurance mechanisms, and the development of human capital. Constraints in one of these dimensions should logically translate into a high relative (so-called) 'shadow' price paid for that resource or that facility that is the actual cost paid by the user of that resource which may differ from its posted price. The observation of those prices should then allow the analyst to identify the constraints most likely to be binding. No such model is available, even implicitly, in the case of the relationship between institutions and development: there is no shadow price easily observable for the availability of a fair and efficient judiciary, an uncorrupted civil service, an effective regulatory agency, or a transparent budget. Another, more heuristic approach needs to be developed.

In the exploratory attempt of the Institutional Diagnostic research programme, we decided to avoid designing a diagnostic framework *a priori*, testing it through application to various countries, and then revising it progressively in the light of accumulated experience. Instead, our preference went to a more inductive approach consisting of exploring the relationship between existing institutions and the development process in a limited number of countries. On the basis of these in-depth country case studies, the idea is to draw the contours of an institutional diagnostic framework destined to be applied to other countries. The purpose of this framework is to identify pivotal and dysfunctional institutions, understand the causes of the dysfunction, and suggest feasible ways of correcting them in the particular social and political context of a country. In short, the elaboration of the diagnostic methodology has proceeded quasi-heuristically, from a few exploratory yet detailed attempts to understand the role and the dynamic of major institutions in a country, as well as their interactions with the local environment, including the society, the polity, and the geography.

A requirement of the UK Department for International Development, now the Foreign and Commonwealth Development Office, which funded this research project, was to focus on low-income and lower middle-income countries. Accordingly, and in view of available resources, the four following countries were selected: Bangladesh, Benin, Mozambique, and Tanzania. The rationale for this choice will be provided in the individual case studies. At

---

[2] Hausmann et al. (2005).

this stage, it will be sufficient to emphasise that, taken together, these four countries exhibit the diversity that is needed in such an exploratory exercise, diversity being understood in terms of geography, population size, economic endowments, historical and cultural legacy, or development strategy. Despite that diversity, however, the fact that they often face similar economic and institutional challenges in their development suggests that there may be common lessons to be drawn from the in-depth study of these challenges.

## STRUCTURE OF CASE STUDIES

Before presenting the structure of the case studies, it is worth defining more precisely what is meant by 'institutions'. In the present research programme, we use a definition derived from North (1990), proposed by Baland et al. (2020: 3) in the recently published *Handbook of Institutions and Development*:

(Institutions are defined) as rules, procedures or other human devices that constrain individual behaviour, either explicitly or implicitly, with a view to making individual expectations about others' behaviour converge and allowing individual actions to become coordinated.

According to that definition, laws and all that they stipulate are institutions, insofar as they are commonly obeyed. Even though often appearing under the label of governance, democratic elections, the control of the executive, or the functioning of public agencies are institutions too. But this is also the case of customary law, even unwritten, or common cultural habits. Institutional failures correspond to situations where a law or a rule is not operating and contraveners are not punished. Actually, this situation may concern large groups of people such as when, for instance, several laws coexist, or a law cannot be enforced on the whole population for lack of resources. The formal production relationship between employers and employees or between firm managers and the state through tax laws are institutions that govern modern companies in developing countries, but the existence of informal production sectors results from the inability of the state to have labour and tax laws enforced throughout the whole production fabric, especially among micro and small enterprises. Yet, implicit rules govern the relationship between informal managers, their clients, and people who work for them. As such, production informality may thus be considered as an institution in itself, which coexists with formal labour laws. The concept of institution also applies to laws and customs that rule social and family life. Here too, informal institutions are when, for example, religion or tribal tradition dictate behavioural rules that differ from secular laws, for instance in areas like marriage, divorce, or inheritance. However, note that, because the focus is on economic development, most institutions or institutional weaknesses considered in the Institutional Diagnostic Project generally refer to those likely to have a significant impact on the economy.

Equipped with this definition, the in-depth study of the relationship between institutions and development in a country and the identification of institutional impediments to long-term inclusive and sustainable development will proceed in three steps. The first one is 'mechanical'. It consists of reviewing the economic, social, and political development of a country, surveying the existing literature, and querying various types of decision-makers, top policymakers, and experts about their views on the functioning of institutions in their country. The latter can be done through questionnaire surveys or through focused qualitative interviews. Based on this material, some binding 'institutional weaknesses' on economic development may be identified and hypotheses elaborated regarding their economic consequences and, most importantly, their causes.

This direct but preliminary approach to the institutional diagnostic of a particular country is also expected to point to several thematic areas where critical institutions seem to be at play. Depending on the country considered, some of the areas obviously deserving scrutiny are the following: modalities of state functioning, that is the bureaucracy and the delivery of basic public goods like education; tax collection; economic regulation and the relationship between private business and political power; land allocation system and property rights; decentralisation, and so forth.

The second step consists of a thorough analysis of these critical areas in order to precise the *modus operandi* of relevant institutions and the sources of their inefficiencies, the ways of remedying the situation, and the most important challenges posed by the required reforms. Are the observed institutional inefficiencies caused by a lack of competent civil servants, their tendency to shirk or get involved in corrupt deals, the excessively intricate nature of the law or administrative rules or their undue multiplication and their mutual inconsistency, or else the bad organisation of the administration? Moreover, why is it that reforms that seem adequate to correct major institutional inefficiencies have not been undertaken or why important reforms voted in the parliament have not been effectively implemented? Who would be the gainers and the losers of particular reforms, and, consequently, who is likely to promote or oppose them?

Based on these detailed analyses of key thematic areas, the third step of the case studies, and the most challenging task, is to synthesise what has been learned into an articulated view of the main institutional problems hindering progress in various areas, their negative consequences for development and, most importantly, their causes, proximate or more distant, as well as their susceptibility to reforms. This is the essence of the 'diagnostic' that each case study is expected to deliver.

It bears emphasis that the above exercise is a diagnostic, not a reform agenda. Because there are gainers and losers from most reforms, political and economic circumstances will determine whether they can be undertaken or not. This needs to be thoroughly discussed, but it must be clear that no firm conclusion about the political feasibility can be reached without a precise evaluation of the distribution of political power in the society, something that goes beyond the contemplated diagnostic. From the strict standpoint of the diagnosis, however, its critical contribution is to expose the nature of the institutional dysfunction, and highlight possible reforms and the stakes involved. In other words, the diagnostic must eventually make all key actors aware of the implications of the needed reforms, and of the expected collective gains and the possible losses, which they would entail for some groups of the population or some categories of key economic and political actors.

François Bourguignon, Research Director, Institutional Diagnostic Project,
Chair, Scientific Committee – Institutional Diagnostic
Emeritus Professor, Paris School of Economics

Jean-Philippe Platteau, Research Director, Institutional Diagnostic Project
Director, CRED, University of Namur

# Acknowledgements

It was with deep gratitude that we accepted the kind invitation from François Bourguignon and Jean-Philippe Platteau, research directors of the Institutional Diagnostic Project, to lead the Mozambique Institutional Diagnostic, a both challenging and rewarding task. François Bourguignon steered our work throughout, in person and online, and provided excellent guidance, without which this study would not have been possible. Sincere thanks are also due to members of the scientific committee, who accepted to engage with our work. The late Benno Ndulu as well as Celestin Monga provided very helpful advice and reviewer comments that helped sharpen our focus.

Furthermore, we wish to acknowledge the EDI team members at OPM, who contributed valuable insights and provided timely management assistance to the process of producing the Mozambique Institutional Diagnostic. They include Mark Henstridge, Stevan Lee, Umar Salam, Rachel Smith-Phiri, Benjamin Klooss, and Katie Mcintosh. We acknowledge the Inclusive Growth in Mozambique (IGM) programme as well for professional interaction and effective collaboration in relation to the organisation of key events in Maputo. Special thanks are due to Vasco Nhabinde, Enilde Sarmento, Fernando Lichucha, José Guambe, Patricia Justino, Sam Jones, Ricardo Santos, Eva-Maria Egger, Elina Penttinen, and Anette Camorai, as well as the IGM interns. Furthermore, we express our gratitude to UNU-WIDER for institutional interaction and copy-editing and translation support. Particular thanks go to Lorraine Telfer-Taivainen, UNU-WIDER's Editorial and Publishing Associate, for all of her very careful, critically needed, and sustained editorial publication support, including the many exchanges with Cambridge University Press. Special thanks are also due to Siméon Rapin, who supported the production of the working papers. Christel Brink Hansen provided kind programme support at UCPH and colleagues in UCPH-DERG were helpful from beginning to end, including, in particular, Hanna Berkel who produced the country maps in Chapter 2 from publicly available data.

We also wish to thank the many participants who joined our workshops and seminars, and provided insights that helped us come to grips with the many intertwined issues related to the development challenges in Mozambique. They include the key informants who contributed time and insights alongside the respondents to our quantitative questionnaire.

We also thank the panel members in our Project Launch Workshop held on 12 June 2019, Jorge Ferrão, Zélia Menete, Magid Osman, and Laura Torvinen, and the moderator of the session, Julieta Langa. The same goes for Leonardo Santos Simão and António Souto who served as key discussants at the Draft Report Launch that took place on 4 November, where we collected comments and input from a wide range of stakeholders. Denise Malauene, José Chichava, and Paulo Mole, all participated in the panel on this occasion, which was moderated by Sheilla Loforte and Sam Jones, and introduced by Enilde Sarmento and Fernando Lichucha. Particular gratitude is due as well to Tony Addison, João de Barros, Maria Ana Jalles d'Orey, Luis Magaço Júnior, Miguel Niño-Zarazúa, Vincenzo Salvucci, Damiano Stella, Hermínio Sueia, and Rafael Uaiene. Together with colleagues already mentioned and chapter authors, they contributed with helpful written comments on the thematic chapters that are at the core of this volume.

Our most sincere gratitude goes to the chapter authors of this volume for their willingness to participate in this project, during what became a particularly challenging time due to the onset of the COVID-19 pandemic, and for their many insightful contributions. This goes, in particular, for António S. Cruz and Johnny Flentø, who also served as co-editors. Moreover, most helpful reviews and critique of the background and synthesis chapters were received from Tony Addison and Leonardo Santos Simão, as well as Sam Jones and Ricardo Santos. While it is our sincere hope that this final volume accurately reflects the advice and professional input referred to above, all the usual caveats apply.

Finally, a word of thanks for funding from UK Aid, and support to the IGM Programme by Finland, Norway, and Denmark.

Finn Tarp, Principal Investigator of the Mozambique Institutional Diagnostic

Ines A. Ferreira, Research Associate

# Abbreviations

| | |
|---|---|
| ADE | Direct Support to Schools |
| ADLI | Agricultural Development Led Industrialisation |
| AEI | High Authority for the Extractive Industry |
| AU | African Union |
| CAADP | Comprehensive Africa Agriculture Development Programme |
| CE | School Council |
| CEA-UEM | Centre of African Studies at the Eduardo Mondlane University |
| CES | Centre for Social Studies at the University of Coimbra |
| CFJJ | Centre for Judicial and Legal Training |
| CGT | Capital Gains Taxes |
| CIP | Public Integrity Centre |
| CMH | Mozambican Hydrocarbons Company |
| CNP | National Planning Commission |
| CSMJ | Superior Council of Judicial Magistrates |
| DF | Deep Factors |
| DSF | Defence and Security Forces |
| EDI | Economic Development and Institutions |
| EdM | Public Electricity Company |
| EITI | Extractive Industries Transparency Initiative |
| ENH | Hydrocarbons National Company |
| EP1 | Level 1 Primary Education |
| EP2 | Level 2 Primary Education |
| FCA | Municipal Compensation Fund |
| FDI | Foreign Direct Investment |
| FID | Final Investment Decision |
| FPC | Permanent Lending Facility |
| FPD | Permanent Deposit Facility |

| FRELIMO | Mozambique Liberation Front |
| GBS | General Budget Support |
| GCCC | Central Office for Fighting Corruption |
| GDP | Gross Domestic Product |
| GoM | Government of Mozambique |
| GVC | Global Value Chains |
| IMF | International Monetary Fund |
| INAMI | National Mines Institute |
| INP | National Petroleum Institute |
| IPAJ | Institute for Legal Representation and Assistance |
| IW | Institutional Weaknesses |
| KI | Key Informant |
| LNG | Liquefied Natural Gas |
| MADER | Ministry of Agriculture and Rural Development |
| MASA | Ministry of Agriculture and Food Security |
| MDM | Democratic Movement of Mozambique |
| MEF | Mozambican Ministry of Economics and Finance |
| MINEC | Ministry of Foreign Affairs and Cooperation |
| MINED | Ministry of Education |
| MINEDH | Ministry of Education and Human Development |
| MITADER | Ministry of Land, Environment and Rural Development |
| MNC | Multinational Corporations |
| MNR | Mozambican National Resistance |
| MoF | Ministry of Finance |
| MPD | Ministry of Planning and Development |
| MTEF | Medium-Term Expenditure Framework |
| NDS | National Development Strategy |
| NGO | Non-Governmental Organisation |
| O&G | Oil and Gas |
| OAM | Mozambican Bar Association |
| ODA | Overseas Development Assistance |
| OGDP | Decentralised Provincial Governance Bodies |
| OIIL | Local Initiative Investment Budget |
| OREP | State Provincial Services |
| PARPA | Poverty Reduction Strategy Paper |
| PC | Proximate Causes |
| PDR | People's Democratic Republic |
| PED | Decentralisation Policy and Strategy |
| PEDD | District Strategic Development Plans |
| PERPU | Fund for the Reduction of Urban Poverty |
| PESOD | District Economic and Social Plans and Budget |
| PFM | Public Financial Management |
| PIC | Criminal Investigation Police |
| PR | President of the Republic |

| PRE | Economic Rehabilitation Programme |
| PRODEM | Municipal Development Programme |
| Renamo | Mozambican National Resistance |
| SACMEQ | Southern and Eastern Africa Consortium for Monitoring Education Quality |
| SAP | Structural Adjustment Programme |
| SDGs | Sustainable Development Goals |
| SERNIC | National Criminal Investigation Service |
| SISTAFE | State Financial Administration System |
| SME | Small and Medium Enterprises |
| SNE | National Education System |
| SWAP | Sector-Wide Approach |
| TA | Administrative Court |
| USAID | United States Agency for International Development |
| UTRAFE | Technical Unit of the State Finance Administration |
| WHO | World Health Organization |
| ZIP | School Cluster Zones |

PART I

# GENERAL APPROACH TO THE DIAGNOSTIC

I

# Introduction and Overview

## Ines A. Ferreira and Finn Tarp

In 1975, the year in which Mozambique became independent from Portuguese colonialism, Nobel Laureate Bob Dylan recorded a song about this welcoming, picturesque, and troubled country in Southern Africa. He sang about magic in a land where the sunny sky is aqua blue. Indeed, Mozambique is unique, also in the field of development economics.

Definite gains were over the years achieved across many metrics of development. However, since independence the development history of Mozambique is as well crowded with unfulfilled hopes, war and calamities, misguided policies, and continued conflict. No single domestic driver of growth and economic transformation was established – in spite of the natural comparative advantage in agriculture and agro-industry – and there was limited time to build the institutions required to support effectiveness and consistency in policies oriented towards inclusive development.

Finally, the country is now, in 2022, at a fork in the road, grappling with the many opportunities and risks associated with having discovered some of the largest natural gas fields in the world. The option is not whether or not to exploit these resources at this point in the history of modern Mozambique. The challenge is whether Mozambique will be able to use the natural resource revenues effectively for poverty reduction and inclusive development instead of continuing on the present fragmented, not sustainable, and non-inclusive path, reflecting low productivity growth in agriculture, lack of diversification, and a low level and pace of structural transformation.

The main historical and economic events since independence in 1975 began with the almost complete dismantling of colonial institutions with the departure of the Portuguese settlers who had ruled the country. In 1977 a stern Marxist-Leninist regime took over, and the conflict between Frelimo and Renamo began. The war intensified in the early 1980s, engineered in large measure by the apartheid regime in South Africa. At an economic low point in 1986,

Mozambique made a U-turn in economic policy, accepting an orthodox structural adjustment programme imposed by Bretton Woods institutions and other donors in a war-torn economy. Peace followed in 1992, when South Africa moved away from apartheid, which resulted in a process of rapid growth and high hopes for the future. Yet, the much-needed progress essentially reflected the return of millions of peasant refugees and recovery from an extremely low base. Growth started tapering off in the early 2000s in spite of investments in a few megaprojects, and it became increasingly clear that the development path was not inclusive. In parallel, huge gas reserves were discovered, while institutional indicators across a broad range of measures deteriorated. More recently, the rural sector has continued to stagnate, and a critical economic crisis erupted in 2016 due to a combination of corruption (associated with a major hidden debt scandal) and natural calamities, while political violence and military insurgency began escalating once again.

On this background, this volume proposes a reflection on the nature and quality of institutions in Mozambique and their capacity or incapacity to respond to the needs of development, as well as on the deep factors likely to hinder institutional reforms and, more importantly, development. We do this through a general reflection on the economic and political history of Mozambique as well as the institutional performance of the country, and through a series of thematic studies. The volume aims at identifying the way institutional weaknesses are obstacles to sectoral or general development and discusses how to remedy them given the political economy context. This 'institutional diagnostic' of Mozambique is part of a wider set of case studies of low-income countries,[1] whose objective is to elaborate a methodological framework for identifying institutional weaknesses and directions for reform in low-income countries in general, inspired by the Hausmann et al. (2005) growth diagnostic approach.

Our volume is structured in three parts. Part I lays out the general approach to the diagnostic, including this introduction and Chapter 2 that puts Mozambique's development in perspective, while Chapter 3 brings out key insights from existing international databases, a quantitative survey, and a series of key informants' interviews. Part II includes the thematic papers ranging from the relative neglect of agriculture to the uncertain development impact of the extraction sector. Part III contains our synthesis, in which we bring together the insights from previous chapters in our institutional diagnostic and look to the future.

Through the above steps, we uncover and trace the determinants of basic institutional weaknesses in Mozambique to a series of proximate causes and deep factors. They include:

• Mozambique is a vast, diverse country, lacking integration in terms of economic and physical infrastructure as well as a consolidated sense of unity.

[1] See https://edi.opml.co.uk/research-cat/institutional-diagnostic-tool

- Independence came late as compared to other African countries and the socio-economic starting point was extremely low, with a particularly difficult transition after centuries of colonial oppression and neglect. The departure of the educated and trained Portuguese settlers left the country with a severe lack of skills.
- There was no sustained opportunity for building institutions between independence and the war of the 1980s, which had a devastating effect on the country. The polarisation between Frelimo, which has governed Mozambique since independence, and the main opposition, Renamo, continued to the present, and violence has escalated once again with recent armed insurgency in Cabo Delgado.
- Frelimo has been the political 'powerhouse' domestically for more than forty-five years, and the political opposition remains weak. One result is a lack of separation of the executive, legislative, and judicial powers; another is inadequate development strategies and policy choices made by political leaders.
- Mozambique has been critically dependent on geopolitical factors, including its neighbourhood with South Africa, which supported Renamo during the war in the 1980s. This geographic proximity also benefits the elite and urban middle class in southern Mozambique and contributes to the fragmentation of the economy and people between the southern region, on the one hand, and the centre and north on the other.
- The donor community has had a heavy influence in the country. One consequence of the externally imposed market reforms in the late 1980s and the desire to avoid external dominance was that the national elite associated with Frelimo took over state-owned assets leading to a merger of political and economic powers. The entrepreneurial class in Mozambique remains incipient and the political opposition lacks business influence.
- The lack of agency of Mozambique in an international context is a result of the country's dependence on external finance. Continuous domestic and externally imposed changes have contributed to the instability and lack of implementation of development strategies and plans.
- The huge potential from the natural resources sector increases opportunities for rent-seeking and the risk of elite capture in the years to come. Recent events revealing lack of transparency in the natural resources deals and the hidden debt scandal are powerful reminders of the harmful effects of corruption.

From the thematic contributions in this volume, we learn that while the government regularly announces formal pro-poor development strategies and plans, implementation is lacking. This is so in the agriculture sector, in particular, and while the public financial management system was reformed and improved in the 1990s, its performance has weakened more recently. The contributors to this volume also point to different dimensions of low state capacity, for instance, in terms of poor public service delivery, which helps explain the low quality of education and the existing inequality in access to health. Failures in the decentralisation process and the lack of voice at regional and local level also stand out. Judicial power remains dependent on the executive, and the unstable and multifaceted relationship with donors has been at the core of the volatile development path of Mozambique since its independence. Finally, the last thematic chapter provides a detailed account of how the discovery of natural resources and their management have exposed severe institutional problems with the regulatory environment and ineffective auditing.

Our synthesis brings these elements together and focuses on the need for reforms. Different political economic characteristics (fundamentals) that shape all the proximate causes for Mozambique's institutional performance can be highlighted. They include, first, the close link between holders of political office and owners of private firms, which underpins the poor institutional performance in the country. Second, elected officials are held accountable to the governing party rather than the electorate – tying governance to Frelimo at the exclusion of all other parties and independent candidates – embedding as well the perpetual conflict with Renamo. Third, extensive powers allocated to the presidency by the Mozambican Constitution can be used to secure loyalty to the governing party in all three pillars of the state giving rise to the absence of independence among the three branches and indeed removing the basis for checks and balances.

The troubled path of Mozambique has led neither to building strong institutions nor ultimately to sustainable development. However, the fork in the road implies that Mozambique now has a unique opportunity to change. To avoid repeating mistakes from the past and elsewhere in Africa and aggravating socio-economic problems, including inequality and increasing internal conflict, we propose a series of measures that we deem critical for pro-poor structural transformation and broad-based development. We highlight that agriculture and agro-industry must take centre stage. This is essential to address existing poverty and is the only way to tackle fragmentation and spatial inequality and ultimately conflict, on the one hand, and macroeconomic challenges including Dutch disease due to natural resource revenues, on the other. Moreover, such an approach is associated with the added bonus that if gas disappoints – with weak revenues once it comes on stream because the global energy transition to renewables moves fast or a glut of gas develops – then a more dynamic agriculture has been built.

This will require developing a unifying vision for a growth strategy centred on agriculture and agro-industry, labour-intensive private sector dynamics and natural resources. Moreover, reforms in the national health system, the promotion of systematic quality standards on education and the expansion of social protection will be essential to help guarantee a more inclusive Mozambican society. This diagnostic points additionally to the need to level the playing field in terms of political competition, namely with respect to party financing, as well as to ensure the separation between the executive, judicial, and legislative powers through the creation of a president of the judiciary and by pursuing the process of decentralisation effectively. In face of the events over the past few years, the costs of corruption and lack of transparency highlight that active monitoring and auditing are necessary. Finally, changes in the relations with donors and the increasing importance of foreign direct investment call for entities that are suited to deal with foreign nations and for alignment of the foreign investments with a truly national, unifying development strategy and investment plan.

# 2

# Economic Development in Perspective

António S. Cruz, Ines A. Ferreira, Johnny Flentø,
Sam Jones, and Finn Tarp

## I INTRODUCTION

Few countries have experienced as many extreme political and economic
changes as Mozambique both before and after independence in 1975. 'The
combined legacies of colonialism, idealism, socialism, war fuelled by racism,
economic collapse and structural adjustment (inspired by stout liberalism)
have made a lasting impact on the structure of the economy' (Tarp et al.
2002: 1).

The purpose of this chapter is to provide essential historical and socio-
economic background and summarise the key characteristics of the society
and economy of modern Mozambique as a first step towards developing an
institutional diagnostic. The aim is to offer overall framing and draw attention
to the big picture story of Mozambique, including its challenging history, both
pre- and post-independence; post-conflict progress in the 1990s; the increasing
complexity and gradual institutional weakening to the present;[1] and the small
externally dependent economy character and interlinked set of challenges
Mozambique is facing.

Focus is on features that we deem particularly important rather than on
completeness. A key point that serves as a core theme throughout the diagnostic is that the building of modern, efficient institutions reflects history in
intricate ways and is likely to be a long and arduous process that even under
the best of circumstances will take a long time to complete. Escaping from
past legacies and overcoming current constraints require decisive action,
clear goals, consistency, and patience. While Mozambique has seen much
action over the years, goals and strategies have shifted dramatically, and

---

[1] We refer the reader to Chapter 3 for details about the weakening of institutions between 2005
and 2019/20 based on available international comparative data.

the building of the institutions needed for development has received limited attention.

We begin Section II with a historical overview to capture key events that have shaped Mozambique over the centuries and finish with a summary of recent events. Next, in Section III, we turn to a description and interpretation of socio-economic indicators and trends. Section IV concludes.

## II HISTORY

### A Geography and Ethnic Diversity

Mozambique, with a population of around 30 million (INE 2019), covers a total land area of more than 799,380 km² (FAO 2016). It is located on the East Coast of Southern Africa and borders six other countries: Tanzania in the north; Malawi, Zimbabwe, Zambia, and Swaziland to the west; and South Africa to the south (see Figure 2.1).

Mozambique's total border length is around 4,445 km and its approximately 2,515 km of generally sandy coastline to the east faces the Indian Ocean and includes a number of islands (FAO 2016). Some twenty-five main rivers flowing east towards the Indian Ocean cross Mozambique. The largest and

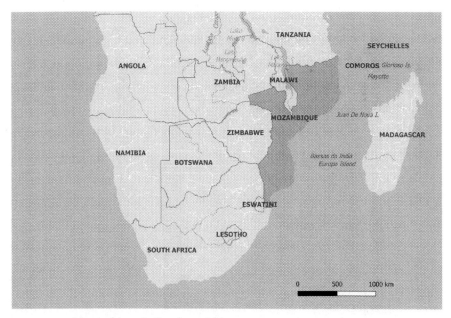

FIGURE 2.1 Mozambique in Southern Africa
Source: Authors' construction based on Natural Earth Data (available at: www .naturalearthdata.com/about/terms-of-use/).

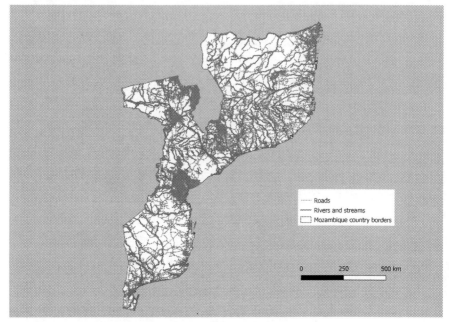

FIGURE 2.2  Road infrastructure and rivers
Source: Authors' construction using © OpenStreetMap contributors (available at: www.openstreetmap.org/, www.opendatacommons.org/) for roads and the Regional Centre for Mapping of Resources for Development (RCMRD) (available at: https://opendata.rcmrd.org/) for waterways.

historically most important river is the Zambezi, whose 820 km Mozambican section is navigable for 460 km. The road infrastructure illustrates the lack of integration in the north–south dimension (see Figure 2.2), a characteristic to which we return in what follows.

The country is made up of eleven provinces, and the major urban centres are generally situated along the coast, the most important being Maputo, the capital, in the far south. Other cities include Beira, in the middle of the country, Quelimane, north of Beira, Nampula, yet further north, and Cabo Delgado in the north-east corner (see Figure 2.3).

Before the arrival of Vasco da Gama in 1498, Bantu-speaking tribes had occupied the territory of modern Mozambique since the first centuries CE. The Arabs started influencing from approximately 1100 CE and, while the effects of the encounter between the local population and Arab traders differed between the existing tribes, the resulting ethnic diversity and Arab influence remain present to this day. Many of the conflicts and contradictions between the different parts of Mozambique that exist today also have deep historical roots – a point to which we will return in what follows.

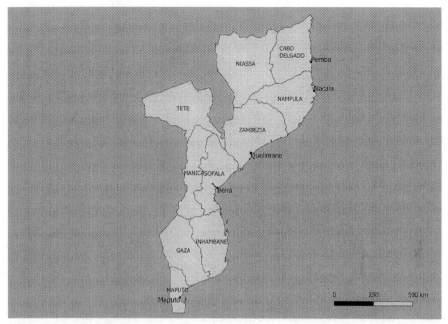

FIGURE 2.3 Administrative map of Mozambique
Source: Authors' construction based on Natural Earth Data (available at www
.naturalearthdata.com/about/terms-of-use/).

The major ethnic groups (and subgroups)[2] in Mozambique, some of which
are linked to ethnic groups in neighbouring countries, are: Yao, Nyanja,
Makonde, Mwani, and Makua-Lomwe in the north and centre; Nsenga,
Pimbwe, Chuwabo, Nyungwe, Maravi, Sena, and Shona-Ndau in the cen-
tre; and Chopi, Bitonga, Tswa, Shangana, and Ronga in the south. To these
must be added Portuguese descendants and a 'mestiço' minority of African/
Portuguese descent. Finally, there is a community of Indian Asian origin from
Pakistan, India, and various Arab countries.

Importantly, these geographic characteristics imply that economic transaction costs are exceedingly large, and regional and ethnic divides have resulted
in both economic fragmentation and differences in access to political power
(for details, see Grobbelaar and Lala 2003). In broad terms, economic as well
as political power concentrated in the south even before independence, and
did so because of the South African economy. The capital was moved from
Ilha de Moçambique to Lourenço Marques (renamed Maputo after independence) in the early 1900s, following the discovery of gold in South Africa. The

---

[2] http://culturamocambicana.blogspot.com/2017/07/principais-grupos-etnicos-de-mocambique
.html

significance of the move of the capital to the extreme south of a very large country because of the important economic links with a much larger neighbouring economy cannot be overemphasised.

## B Colonial Legacy

Historically, Mozambique was particularly attractive for the trade of gold, ivory, and slaves, as well as other metals and hides, and, even though their occupation was limited at first, the Portuguese gradually established commercial influence from 1505, adopting protectionist measures as well as clientelist and corrupt practices. The Portuguese importance grew in the following centuries as the colonial system was progressively developed,[3] and it intensified in the mid-1880s, backed by investments by foreign capital and companies, especially British, Rhodesian, and South African.

The Portuguese colonial presence and the control of private – often foreign, Anglophone – companies over Mozambique's basic infrastructure had tremendous consequences. Portuguese settlers effectively colonised Mozambique,[4] and its administrative and bureaucratic institutions, as well as the army, depended on instructions from Lisbon. Existing infrastructure ran east–west and the country remained not only ethnically but also economically disintegrated in the north–south dimension. Moreover, there was a weak and biased colonial education system, resulting in virtually no training of indigenous people or recruitment of African-Portuguese, though with some prominent exceptions.

Until around the mid-1950s, Mozambique was largely limited to supplying cheap raw materials to Portugal and cheap labour and transport services to neighbouring countries. The traditional rural sector received no government support and remained underdeveloped. Additionally, a series of legal measures aggravated the economic and social differences that divided the population. In the 1960s, there was increasing migration of settlers to Mozambique, expanding the economy and the internal market. By 1964, industrial production for the internal market exceeded production for export (Leite 1989). But despite the fact that the economy had started to become less orientated towards continental Portugal, the struggle for independence began in that same year.

Serious challenges mounted (see Section C) and outright chaos broke out at the time of independence in 1975, when a majority of the Portuguese population left the country. Within weeks, administrative structures had collapsed and become empty shells,[5] and the Mozambique Liberation Front

---

[3] Full colonial military control and occupation of Mozambique occurred after 1895 with the fall of the Gaza Kingdom (Sousa 2018).

[4] The colonial exploitation of the peasants took place through (i) forced cultivation of cash crops, (ii) seasonal and low paid work in the colonial farms and plantations, and (iii) supply of agricultural goods at low prices to the industrial sector through Portuguese traders.

[5] Unlike other European colonies, where natives were already involved in administration, and sometimes politics, before independence.

(FRELIMO), which, although a well organised liberation movement, had no experience of running a country, took over.[6] Its focus was on dismantling colonial institutions.

## C Independence, Geopolitics, and War

The decade before independence was marked by military struggle. Although FRELIMO had been formed in 1962 as a constitutionalist and non-violent movement, it launched a military offensive in 1964 and continued to do so into the 1970s, initially taking control of parts of the north and progressively advancing towards the centre of the country. Largely due to the overthrow of the Portuguese government in April 1974, official talks about Mozambican independence started, and they led in September of the same year to the signing of the Lusaka Agreement, which established a transition government with a majority of FRELIMO members. Formal independence and the foundation of The People's Republic of Mozambique as a one-party socialist state happened on 25 June 1975 under the leadership of Frelimo[7] and President Samora Machel (see Figure A2.1 for a timeline of the main events since independence).

As was the case in Vietnam in the mid-1970s after its defeat of US forces, the atmosphere in Mozambique was 'upbeat' among the Frelimo 'comrades'. Having 'defeated' the Portuguese colonial power, Frelimo ambitiously declared, in jubilant tones, that the coming decade would see victory over under-development. While it was over-optimistic and, in retrospect, naive to compare victories achieved on the battlefield with challenges faced in the development field, it is pertinent to recall that the course of action taken appeared at the time self-evident to many, including the leadership in both Vietnam and Mozambique, with both economies being poor, exploited, and destroyed.[8]

---

[6] FRELIMO was originally a united front of three political parties engaged in the liberation struggle, which put ideological differences aside, at least for a while in pursuit of the common objective of sovereignty, though internal disagreement was common. For example, several leading figures disappeared or died under disputed circumstances. Dissidents came to play a key role in the establishment of the Mozambican National Resistance (MNR), as discussed later in this chapter.

[7] When referring to the Liberation Front pre-independence, this is spelled FRELIMO, while the post-independence party is referred to as Frelimo.

[8] Portuguese colonisation differed from the French and British in at least three distinct ways. The first was the timing and number of colonial settlers (including migrants from Europe), which were earlier and much higher in Portuguese colonies. In Mozambique, more than half a million Portuguese settled and occupied all walks of life, including smallholder farming, lower management positions, and operatives in industry and transport, in an economic structure that was closer to those of South Africa and Rhodesia. Second, and as a result of this, no import of such a labour force occurred, as it did in French colonies, where Lebanese, North African, and British (Indian) labour was imported and stayed when colonisers left at independence. Third, Portugal made little or no attempt to educate the indigenous population and passed laws of assimilation that were not far from apartheid. In relation to institutional strengths and weaknesses, all this meant that the Portuguese colonies started from a lower point in 1974 than most other African countries did in the early 1960s (with noticeable exceptions, like Sudan).

During the immediate post-independence period, national reconstruction and consolidation were in focus. However, a series of factors undermined these efforts. The first was the serious economic challenges that marked this period. As alluded to above, approximately 80 per cent of the Portuguese population had left the country. This created extreme labour shortages in public administration and the secondary and tertiary sectors, as well as having a devastating effect on agriculture, which depended on settlers for input supplies and the marketing of output, including extensive credit provision, often in kind. Consequently, living and educational/managerial standards were dismal to begin with in the newly independent country.

Second, after its transformation into a Marxist-Leninist party in 1977, Frelimo initiated a ten-year plan (1981–90) with the goal of overcoming under-development. Socialist policies were indeed the norm at the time in newly independent African countries and a logical reaction to the past. However, the strategy, conceived in orthodox central planning terms, was out of touch with the reality on the ground. Import substitution, forced mechanisation of agriculture, and resettlement of large numbers of people were at the core of the strategy. Similarly, only scant attention was paid to small farmer needs and their requirements in terms of input supplies and output outlets. Accordingly, misconceived policies were introduced, including a hostile view of the private sector. This bias had long-lasting effects, and rather than winning support among the peasantry, Frelimo was losing it.[9] There was room for voice and participation but only inside the party structures. At the same time, Frelimo developed authoritarian and coercive methods, in large measure in response to the context of a brutal war instigated by outsiders.

Third, independence came suddenly as well as late to Mozambique as compared with other African countries, and regional (Rhodesia and South Africa) and global (Cold War) conflicts left the new country with very little room for manoeuvre, either politically or economically. This turned out to be very costly indeed, illustrated by the heavy economic and military impact of Mozambique's decision to enforce United Nations sanctions against Rhodesia in 1976 (UN 1976).

Mozambique's independence posed threats to Rhodesia and South Africa, which feared a communist onslaught. They therefore supported and financed Renamo (the Mozambican National Resistance, originally designated MNR), which opposed Frelimo's socialist orientation.[10] Renamo gathered Frelimo

---

[9] At the Fourth Congress in 1983, Frelimo recognised the neglect of small peasant farmers and called attention to the role of private sector development, but by then the country was once again at war.

[10] MNR was originally formed by FRELIMO dissidents aided (organised and trained) by a group of Portuguese businessmen, elements of the former Portuguese Secret Police (PIDE), and, not least, Rhodesia. MNR's first leader was succeeded by Afonso Dhlakama in 1980. Renamo members opposed the political and military dominance of Frelimo after 1975 and adopted a right-wing stance, in opposition to the Marxist-Leninist stance adopted by Frelimo in the first

dissidents under the leadership of André Matsangaíssa (1977–79) and Afonso Dhlakama (1979–2018). The Renamo leadership came from the centre of Mozambique, but the movement was also constituted by members from elsewhere in the country. Frelimo has over the years pursued a policy of having representatives from all relevant ethnic groups in high positions in the party and in the government, yet prominent representatives from the centre and the north have felt ostracised.

After the independence of Zimbabwe (former Rhodesia) in 1980, the apartheid regime continued skilfully to exploit both historical and current ethnic contradictions and grievances and turned Renamo into a significant military force capable of disrupting and sabotaging large parts of the country. The Mozambican government responded by increasing repression and by targeting the supply lines of Renamo with a stronger and more sophisticated military presence and firepower. This strategy failed and the war escalated, in the midst of the regional and global Cold War. With the signing of the Nkomati Accord of non-aggression between Mozambique and South Africa in 1984, President Samora Machel hoped for some reprieve, but large-scale sabotage and destruction of infrastructure and killings continued, with support from South Africa.[11] Backed by the military might of South Africa, Renamo's ruthless warfare slowly but surely undermined Frelimo's nation-building efforts. A stubborn but ineffective strategy by Frelimo to criminalise insurgents and Renamo supporters, not recognising the need for political settlements, added to the complexity of the situation.

Fourth, another consequence of the late timing of Mozambique's independence was that the country had no more than a five-year 'settling-in' period before laissez-faire ideological winds of change swept across the world around 1980, including the election of President Ronald Reagan in the US and Margaret Thatcher as Prime Minister in the UK. These changes influenced the policy stance of international financial institutions, including in particular the International Monetary Fund (IMF) and the World Bank, and this turned out to be critical in the mid-1980s in Mozambique (see Tarp 1993).

years of independence. This was the political justification for their military opposition, and for obtaining support from the minority governments of Rhodesia and South Africa and from the US and West German governments, as well as from former Portuguese settlers. In parallel, it must be kept in mind throughout that the Portuguese settlers who fled to Rhodesia and South Africa after losing their assets played a key role in the formation of MNR.

[11] As already alluded to, the Rhodesian Central Intelligence Organization (CIO) funded and organised MNR under the leadership of Matsangaíssa from 1977 to 1980 when Zimbabwe became independent. The South African government took over the CIO's role in 1980. After 1984 and the Nkomati Accord, the South African government support for Renamo became clandestine. Other international supporters of Renamo were the Frontline Fellowship, a missionary group in South Africa, some former Portuguese settlers, the US government, and some West German politicians. Although relations between the US government and the Frelimo government improved from 1983, North American conservatives increased their support for Renamo in 1985.

## D The Bretton Woods Institutions and a U-turn in Economic Strategy

The fragility of former alliances in Eastern Europe and elsewhere in the global arena (including those between the USSR, East Germany, Cuba, and China), the ongoing war, and an economic state of affairs that reached a historical low point in 1986 forced Frelimo to change course. Mozambique had no viable option but to turn increasingly to Western donors (with the Nordics having been present from very early on) for external finance, and the donors came to play a decisive role, imposing free-market policy conditionality on a war-torn economy. The Nkomati agreement, signed by President Samora Machel and the Prime Minister of South Africa, P. W. Botha, signalled the beginning of negotiations for support from the Bretton Woods institutions and the Paris Club creditors,[12] though concrete policy initiatives only materialised after Samora Machel's death in a plane crash in South Africa in 1986. The government launched the five-year Economic Rehabilitation Programme (PRE) in 1987 and in effect turned the economic strategy pursued so far on its head.[13] The implications were wide ranging.

First, the structural adjustment programme (reflecting a standard package of orthodox policy reforms that took no account of local circumstances) was ill conceived for a country at war, as had been the ten-year development plan, and the short-, medium-, and longer-term economic effects were dire. No supply response from agriculture was possible due to the overwhelming effects of the war; and subsidised industries in the cities had to lay off workers, adjust wages, and eventually expect privatisation or closure.

Second, a key element of the PRE was the privatisation of state-owned enterprises. Diogo (2013: 18) notes: 'To make the transition from a centrally planned economy to a market economy, Mozambique privatized more than 4,000 companies, about 80 pct. of them benefitting Mozambicans and on highly advantageous conditions.' This was done presumably over a few years and without a transparent and well-functioning financial market. Moreover, in the longer term, the PRE introduced a deep-seated structural and highly problematic economic imbalance between Frelimo and Renamo as privatisation went ahead while Renamo guerrillas were still in the bush. The drive to avoid foreign takeovers ran as a red thread through the process, instituted through a national ownership requirement. There was, however, no indigenous entrepreneurial class, given the weakness in the domestic politico-judicial system and the private sector. So assets and power transferred instead to a group of

---

[12] Negotiations also included massive amounts of food aid from the US and other donors, which was much needed due to both the war and a series of natural calamities.

[13] For further background and discussion, see Addison (2003), including Chapters 4 and 9 addressing rural livelihoods and social capital and the agrarian question in Mozambique's transition and reconstruction.

individuals in the public service and to Frelimo party officials, who managed to secure favourable bank loans (see Diogo 2013).[14]

Sumich and Honwana (2007: 19) add:

> By taking the initiative and reforming the economic and political structures before the peace agreement had been signed and before Renamo was able to influence the direction of the reforms, Frelimo created a significant advantage for itself (Morier-Genoud 2007). Thus, privatisation, as argued by Pitcher (1996, 2002) and Castel-Branco et al. (2001), was not a neutral, technical measure as the World Bank and the IMF seemed to naively assume, but a deeply political process where Frelimo directed events as much as possible to assure the continuing support of some elements of older constituencies and create new ones.

Thus, as a consequence of policy conditionalities, a 'new' political and business elite (which overlapped in very large measure with the 'old' elite) started emerging that commanded not only political power, as in the early days after independence, but also economic power – and this often without the necessary management training and capacity. Importantly, Renamo associates were in no position to benefit, as they were still in the bush when assets and opportunities were privatised.

## E  Peace and Multiparty Elections

Peace returned with the Rome General Peace Accords in 1992, made possible by the political transition from apartheid in South Africa. In 1994, the first multiparty elections led to the election of President Joaquim Chissano, leader of Frelimo, as President of the Republic of Mozambique. There were signs of economic recovery after peace re-established itself, with impressive growth rates, a significant decline in poverty, and the creation of new infrastructure, particularly in the social sectors, supported by the donor community.

Aid flows surged and Mozambique became widely perceived as a donor darling. However, the external assistance often came with explicit and implicit conditionalities, such as a heavy reliance on external consultants rather than promoting capacity building of nationals. Moreover, the impressive growth, in large measure due to returning refugees, did not lead to a fundamental transformation of economic structures (see Section III). Finally, while some Renamo commanders and soldiers were integrated into the new Mozambican army, no full disarmament took place. Integration into the police force was

---

[14] Banks, for example, financed projects put forward by representatives of the elite in power, which led to major losses. Moreover, this process helped institutionalise an entrepreneurial class that depended on political alliances for business success more than on managerial and technical skills. Importantly, as already noted, the timing of the adjustment programme and the privatisations, large parts of which took place before the peace agreement and demobilisation happened, meant that one of the parties (i.e. Renamo) was not at the table to participate.

especially difficult, and the Renamo leader, Afonso Dhlakama, maintained a strong personal protection force.

On the political front, Sumich and Honwana (2007: 18) stress that

> democracy was introduced when the possibility for actual policy differences between parties was at its lowest. Both Frelimo and Renamo campaigned on similar political (i.e. democracy) and economic platforms (i.e. free markets), therefore much of the campaign centred around interpretations of history, with Frelimo using its credentials as the liberator of the nation and Renamo speaking of villagisation and the attack on tradition.

The polarisation between Frelimo and Renamo continued, and while the ideological differences weakened, regional and ethnic contradictions came more into focus.

## F  Dominance of Frelimo

Frelimo maintained political power in the country after the closely contested general election in 1999. Joaquim Chissano continued as president, and in the Assembly of the Republic, Frelimo held 133 and Renamo 117 seats. Shortly afterwards, Frelimo made an important strategic move 'when the government after six years of debate, in an effort to broaden its social base and weaken Renamo, issued a decree creating "community leaders", which meant that former "régulos" [traditional chiefs] could hold office at the local level' (Sumich and Honwana 2007: 17). Accordingly, the Frelimo government actively sought ways to engage with and remunerate the traditional chiefs by attributing formal duties to them. The system was quite transparent and deliberately visible as chiefs also got uniforms for official occasions and visits. Such relations with traditional authority count a lot in an election, when many voters seek guidance from their local chiefs. While this was a remarkable move considering Frelimo's history as a socialism-inspired liberation movement, it helped Frelimo remain the dominant political power in the subsequent elections.

In 2002, Frelimo elected Armando Guebuza as its Secretary General and presidential candidate. Guebuza moved quickly to strengthen the party structures in all spheres of the public administration and created cells at all levels. He also deliberately chose a government of politicians over technocrats and soon commanded a structure not much different from the one in place under the one-party state. He won a comfortable victory in 2004 and became President in 2005, backed by an overwhelmingly superior financial and organisational machinery amid widespread abstention.

In 2009, a new political party started competing in the parliamentary and presidential elections. The Democratic Movement of Mozambique (MDM) started up as a splinter group of Renamo, led by the mayor in Beira, Daviz Simango, son of one of FRELIMO's first vice-presidents during the liberation war. The Simango family, from the centre of Mozambique, had joined Renamo expecting to create a strong political opposition to Frelimo. But Renamo, dominated by Afonso Dhlakama, was not a democratic party. Young and capable members therefore broke away, aiming to pursue democratic political process. Unlike earlier splinter groups, MDM enjoyed widespread popular support, and expectations were that it would win a significant part of the votes, ending the bipolar impasse in Mozambican politics.

However, in what many observers see as a concerted effort to sabotage MDM by Frelimo and Renamo party members of the electoral commission, MDM's lists of candidates were rejected in 7 of the 11 provinces (including Maputo city), leaving the party with no possibility of winning any significant part of the votes. Among the reasons given were missing details in the candidates' dossiers; the whole provincial list was dropped if just one of the candidates, even if it was a substitute candidate, failed to submit all the necessary documents, such as an original birth certificate. Some candidates' dossiers were even 'lost' in the election commission's offices. Donors protested to President Guebuza before the election but to no avail. Nevertheless, Renamo suffered significantly from MDM's appearance on the political scene and was reduced to only 49 seats in Parliament, while Frelimo was taken by surprise when it lost important areas in Maputo to the new party.

While traditional party politics seemed locked in a Frelimo hegemony, 2008 and 2010 witnessed a surge of demonstrations and popular uprisings in the largest cities. Discontent was ignited by the worsening living conditions among the lower middle class (due, for example, to rising food prices – see Pinstrup-Andersen 2014). Moreover, on both occasions Frelimo and the government underestimated the strength of the reaction. The events, especially in Maputo, had tragic consequences, with police shooting resulting in civilian deaths, including children, and gave rise to a debate within Frelimo about leadership and inclusion. Eventually, President Guebuza controlled the situation partly by force and partly by giving concessions, delaying increases in the price of water, electricity, and public transport (fuel).

The Guebuza regime ended in violent confrontation with Renamo,[15] which no longer believed that the government was willing to give in to its demands, including increased decentralisation. A last-minute peace deal paved the way for an election in 2014, but even within Frelimo, the issue of succession created problems. Guebuza held on to power as long as he could, and although the Frelimo candidate Filipe Nyusi won the election, he faced massive challenges from his first day in office, as discussed below.

---

[15] There are various explanations of why confrontation broke out again. One is that Frelimo had an incentive to attack Renamo's bases before the election to prevent Renamo going back to armed struggle after the election results were announced and to prevent or weaken Renamo's participation in the municipal elections in 2013. Another explanation is that Renamo may have attacked first, the underlying reason being that Dhlakama's 'hidden fighters' were getting older and knew that the 2014 election was their last chance to get a piece of the peace dividend that they had been promised since 1992. Moreover, Renamo felt that Frelimo was systematically committing election fraud and that the only way to force Frelimo to play the democratic game was through military action.

## G  Recent Events

The first of Nyusi's challenges was that the settlement with Renamo was short-lived. Renamo argued that all the problems it had pointed to remained, and the hardliners in Frelimo, who had gained strength under Guebuza's ten-year rule, argued that it was better to solve the Renamo challenge militarily and decisively. So violent conflict escalated and soon central parts of the country were at war. Broken power lines, sabotaged railway lines, and army convoys protecting vehicles on the main roads were once again the order of the day in Mozambique in 2016.

The Nyusi government then chose to negotiate with Renamo and give in to some of its main demands. These included decentralisation and the election of provincial governors. This move was sustained even after the death of Renamo's leader, Afonso Dhlakama, in May 2018, which led to a considerable weakening of the party under its new leader, Ossufo Momade. A 14-page constitutional amendment was approved by which elected bodies were created at provincial, district, and municipality levels.

A second challenge was the so-called 'hidden debt' scandal, which had become symptomatic of the increase in corruption Mozambique had experienced over the last couple of decades. While they recognise that the figure is open to contestation, Williams and Isaksen (2016) note in their introduction: 'The average annual cost of corruption to Mozambique was recently estimated to be up to US$4.9 billion for the period 2004–2014.' The authors, who provide a detailed account (on which the following is based),[16] point out that in the final years of Guebuza's second term, three semi-public entities took out over US$2 billion in loans from private foreign banks without submitting them to the Assembly for approval, as required by the Mozambican constitution, even though they greatly exceeded the limit placed on government borrowing by the relevant annual budget appropriation bill. Williams and Isaksen (2016) pointedly note:

It is alleged that in order to secure his [i.e. Guebuza's] economic future three semi-public entities – Ematum, Proindicus and MAM – were established in the period 2012–2014 as vehicles for obtaining foreign private loans, to be raised without the knowledge of key government institutions, of parliament, the Mozambican public, or the country's foreign development partners.

The sources of the loans included Credit Suisse and the VTB Bank, and it is clear that Ematum, Proindicus, and MAM (Mozambique Asset Management) were owned and controlled by a very small group of individuals and that they were very closely linked to the security sector. When the existence of the loans became public, the IMF suspended its support to Mozambique, and much foreign aid, including all direct support to the state budget (already on

---

[16] See also MNRC (2017a, 2017b) and Behuria et al. (2017).

a downward trajectory), was frozen or significantly reduced. This drastically restricted the fiscal space of the government and led to an economic crisis that lasted throughout the first term of President Nyusi, and which continues to impact.[17] The subsequent legal process led in 2019 to the US indictment of former Minister of Finance Manuel Chang and others (see MNRC 2019). While the case continues in the courts, Mozambique's relations with the donor community have started to normalise. A central element in this has been the re-establishment of relations with the IMF,[18] illustrated in the approval on 19 April 2019 of IMF emergency assistance following Cyclone Idai, which hit Mozambique earlier in the month, causing massive damage in the centre of the country, including the city of Beira.

A third challenge has been the deteriorating security situation and armed insurgency in the north-eastern province of Cabo Delgado, where Islamic militants have attacked key towns, killing or uprooting well over 100,000 people. The roots of the conflict are still debated, but seem to include a series of local grievances related to social exclusion, combined with interventions from international groups involved in criminal activities such as ivory and heroin trafficking. The conflict is dangerous in itself but also has the potential to spill over to other parts of the country. Importantly, Cabo Delgado is close to the major gas fields.

The fourth challenge, the discovery of huge gas resources after the turn of the millennium, is also an opportunity to turn the country around, provided appropriate institutions and policies are put in place. The aforementioned hidden debt deals undertaken by the Guebuza regime were likely associated with the decision to start developing Mozambique's massive oil and gas reserves at a time when institutions that provide for various checks and balances were still weak. The creditworthiness of Mozambique stemming from the hype of the gas resources was enough to nourish fraudulent deals, and long before gas exploitation was to begin, speculation and rent seeking was rife. As history and experiences elsewhere in Africa and beyond document, benefiting from natural resources is a most challenging political exercise (see Roe 2018). Meanwhile, on the economic front, Mozambique has started engaging with some of the world's largest companies to find the best way of developing the oil and gas sector to the benefit of the country's mostly poor people.

---

[17] For an assessment of what happened to multidimensional poverty see Egger et al. (2020).

[18] The IMF does not impose conditionalities regarding peace; this happens indirectly via the bilateral donors in the IMF board, who officially blocked both general budget support and programme aid due to the debt scandal. It would appear that this decision also relates to the advances of the security forces in central Mozambique and extra-judicial killings and assaults on Renamo officials. Accordingly, progress was made on ceasefire agreements with Renamo, on the one hand, and foreign assistance and oversight of negotiations, on the other, reactivating cooperation with the IMF after the hidden debt crisis.

Finally, Mozambique has, like the rest of the world, struggled to address the impact of the COVID-19 pandemic. The first COVID-19 case was reported on 22 March 2020 and a state of emergency was declared on 31 March. The COVID-19 crisis and its associated economic effects came on top of the hidden debt scandal and the impacts of Cyclones Idai and Kenneth, highlighting that Mozambique remains highly vulnerable to climatic and policy-induced shocks.

## III PATTERNS OF SOCIO-ECONOMIC CHANGE

Until recently, the donor community generally considered Mozambique a development success story (see Arndt et al. 2007). Since the end of conflict in 1992, real Gross Domestic Product (GDP) growth (per capita) has been strong, easily outstripping the global average and surpassing many other countries in the region. However, while Mozambique certainly contributed to the 'Africa Rising' narrative (Addison et al. 2017), as indicated in Figure 2.4, the pace of real aggregate growth peaked at the millennium, slowing moderately during the 2000s. Today, Mozambique is no longer a star growth performer and lags behind its peers in the region, most notably Ethiopia.

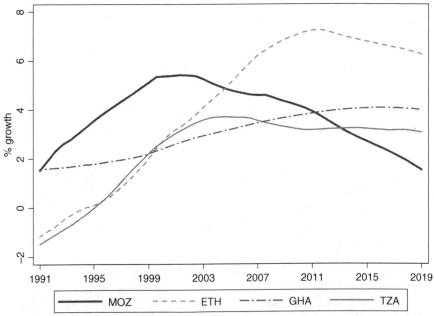

FIGURE 2.4  Real GDP growth per capita, smoothed (1991–2019)
Note: Series are smoothed using a Kernel-weighted local polynomial smoothing algorithm; growth is based on GDP in constant 2011 international prices; countries are as follows: Mozambique = MOZ, Ethiopia = ETH, Ghana = GHA, Tanzania = TZA.
Source: Authors' estimates based on data from WDI (World Bank 2020).

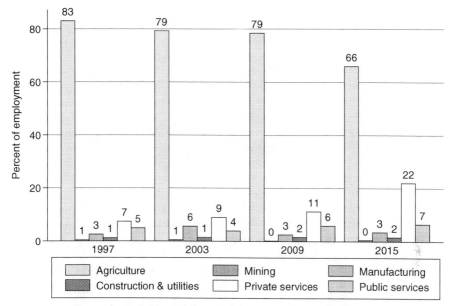

FIGURE 2.5 Sectoral trends in employment (1997–2015)
Source: Authors' estimates based on household survey data series 1996/97, 2002/03, 2008/09, and 2014/15 (see MEF/DEEF 2016); private services include finance; public services include health, education, and public administration.

This section discusses how the country's economic structure has evolved during this period, as well as the changing pattern of aggregate economic growth. Overall, in the following, we highlight the absence of a consistent domestic engine of inclusive growth, a chronic dependence on external savings, and slowing progress across a range of social indicators, which is also symptomatic of an inefficient and low-capacity public sector.

## A Structural Shifts

On the return of peace in the early 1990s, Mozambique was predominantly an agricultural economy. As shown in Figure 2.5, in 1996/97 more than 80 per cent of the workforce identified agriculture as their primary occupation, virtually all of which was smallholder or peasant agriculture, not larger-scale commercial activities.

At the same time, whilst important in terms of total production, agriculture has never represented more than half of aggregate real value-added. Figure 2.6 shows that even in the early 1990s, agriculture contributed only about 40 per cent to GDP, while service activities (public and private) contributed approximately another 40 per cent. As we discuss below, this clearly indicates that agriculture has been and remains a very low productivity activity on average.

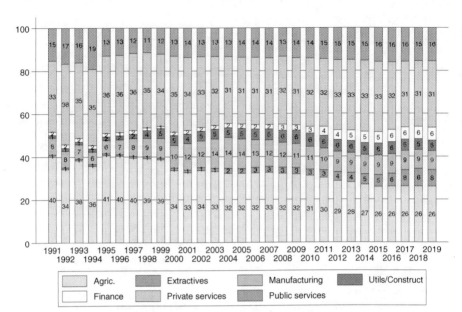

FIGURE 2.6 Sectoral contributions to levels of real value added (1991–2019)
Note: Figure refers to the percentage contribution to production value-added in constant
2014 prices; public services include health, education, and public administration.
Source: Authors' estimates based on unpublished data from National Institute for
Statistics.

Over time, there has been a limited shift in the structure of the economy away
from agriculture. According to the most recent household survey (2014/15),
which constitutes the most reliable source of data on the labour force, around
two-thirds of workers were primarily involved in agriculture and the sector contributed around one-quarter of total value-added. Labour movements out of agriculture have been largely towards the private services sector, including commerce
and transport, which now represents 22 per cent of all employment. However, the
value-added of private services has remained flat over time, indicating that new
workers in this sector tend to be less productive than existing workers. Figure 2.7
clarifies this insight, showing labour productivity differentials across sectors relative to the economy-wide average. Labour productivity in agriculture has been
about half (-.8 log points) that of the average worker, while the productivity of
workers in private services declined over the two decades from 1991 to 2019
from nearly 5 times to just 1.5 times that of the average worker.

As discussed in detail by Jones and Tarp (2015), who provide a full decom-
position of within- and between-sector productivity changes over the same
period, the shift of workers has been largely out of very low-productivity agriculture to informal services activities. Thus, the contribution of the services
sector to growth since 2003 has been dominated by a sectoral reallocation

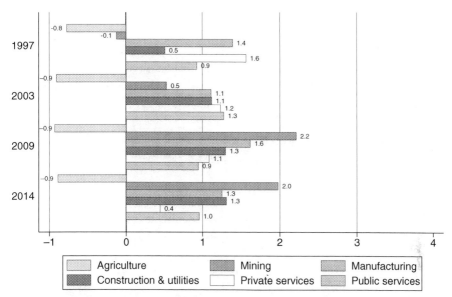

FIGURE 2.7 Labour productivity differences by sector (1997–2015)
Note: X-axis is the natural logarithm of the ratio of labour productivity of the indicated sector to aggregate labour productivity; thus, values below 0 show lower than average productivity; private services include finance.
Source: Authors' estimates based on household survey data series 1996/97, 2002/03, 2008/09, and 2014/15 (see MEF/DEEF 2016).

effect, as even informal services are more productive than agriculture, but not a within-sector productivity effect. In contrast, agriculture has shown fairly robust moderate within-sector productivity increases (over 1 percentage point per year), despite losing workers in relative terms.

The same figures also point to a 'missing middle'. Looking over the full time period, secondary sectors (manufacturing, construction) have remained small, both in terms of their contribution to GDP and in terms of employment. For example, in both 1997 and 2015, just 3 per cent of workers were in the manufacturing sector, and the value-added of the sector was equal to 8 per cent of GDP at the start and 9 per cent at the end of the period. In contrast, mining (extractive industries) has achieved very rapid growth of output, expanding to 8 per cent of real GDP, but with almost no change in its employment share. We return to this point below.

## B Changing Growth Drivers

The changing structure of the Mozambican economy, in terms of both output and employment, hints at how a series of *different* drivers of growth have been operative over the post-war period. Three main growth phases are apparent.

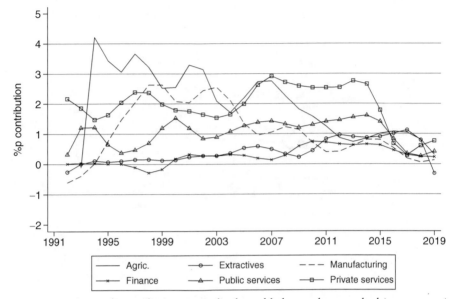

FIGURE 2.8 Sectoral contributions to real value-added growth, smoothed (1991–2019)
Note: Manufacturing includes construction and utilities; growth refers to production
value-added in constant 2014 prices; non-linear five period filter used.
Source: Authors' estimates based on unpublished data from National Institute for Statistics.

First, as further supported by Figure 2.8, from the mid-1990s onwards,
Mozambique successfully took advantage of the peace dividend, achieving
post-conflict stabilisation and recovery (see Tarp et al. 2002). In this period,
strong rates of growth across multiple sectors, including agriculture, reflected
a combination of a return of displaced people to their homes, the rebuilding of
private and public infrastructure, supported by foreign aid and private investment
(domestic and foreign).

A second phase, starting around the turn of the millennium, is associated with strong growth in the manufacturing sector, dominated by large-
scale capital-intensive investments, particularly in the Mozal aluminium
smelter.[19] This period, which lasted until the late 2000s, also saw robust
service sector growth, alongside a sustained and substantial contribution
of agriculture (at 2 percentage points), or more than a quarter of aggregate
growth per annum.

The late 2000s, however, saw a shift to a third phase, characterised by an
emphasis on the natural resources sector (mining), driven by large increases in
foreign direct investment (FDI) into coal and then natural gas field developments.

[19] This investment took advantage of cheap energy and may in some senses be seen as an 'energy'
rather than a manufacturing investment in economic terms.

TABLE 2.1 *Expenditure components and sources of funds, 1999–2019 (as % shares of GDP)*

|  | 1999–2004 | 2005–2009 | 2010–2014 | 2015–2019 | Change |
|---|---|---|---|---|---|
| Consumption | 0.88 | 0.90 | 0.94 | 0.90 | *0.01* |
| Public | 0.16 | 0.17 | 0.21 | 0.24 | *0.08* |
| Private | 0.72 | 0.73 | 0.72 | 0.65 | *−0.06* |
| Investment | 0.31 | 0.18 | 0.40 | 0.40 | *0.10* |
| Public | 0.10 | 0.10 | 0.14 | 0.08 | *−0.01* |
| Private | 0.21 | 0.09 | 0.26 | 0.32 | *0.11* |
| Savings | 0.31 | 0.18 | 0.40 | 0.40 | *0.10* |
| National | 0.12 | 0.10 | 0.06 | 0.10 | *−0.01* |
| Domestic public | −0.08 | −0.10 | −0.11 | −0.04 | *0.03* |
| Domestic private | 0.20 | 0.20 | 0.17 | 0.15 | *−0.05* |
| Foreign | 0.19 | 0.08 | 0.34 | 0.30 | *0.11* |
| External public grants | 0.07 | 0.07 | 0.06 | 0.02 | *−0.05* |
| External public credits | 0.03 | 0.03 | 0.05 | 0.03 | *0.00* |
| External private | 0.09 | −0.03 | 0.23 | 0.25 | *0.16* |

*Note:* Private investment and savings components are calculated as residuals; total foreign savings are derived from the current account deficit plus changes in reserves.
*Source:* Authors' estimates compiled from National Statistics Institute, Central Bank of Mozambique, and Ministry of Economy and Finance (internal).

This coincided with an expansion of the finance (banking sector), which increased in size from 2 per cent of GDP in the mid-2000s to over 6 per cent in the latest period (see Figure 2.6). The same period also saw a trend decline in the contribution of agriculture to growth, but strong private services growth.

To get a sense of the magnitude of the recent shift in the sectoral emphasis of growth towards extractives, which has also arguably become a focus of public policy, Table 2.1 provides a summary of changes in consumption and investment components (reported as shares of GDP), as well as sources of investment funds.

Overall, we note that Mozambique has always been a consumption-heavy economy. Total consumption has consistently equalled around 90 per cent of GDP and, as discussed below, the public sector has accounted for an increasing share of total consumption. This is not to say that investment has been low; on average it has been sustained at about 30 per cent of GDP, with public investment comprising roughly one-third of total investment.

Critically, investment has been financed largely from abroad, indicated by the very large volume of foreign savings (which is the mirror of the current account deficit). During the first period shown in the table (1999–2004), which roughly reflects the beginning of the second growth phase, private foreign investment and foreign aid to the public sector (grants and loans) amounted to nearly 20 per cent of GDP, both in equal measure. In the second half of the 2000s, foreign investments in the manufacturing sector tailed off but aid remained strong. In the last decade, however, FDI jumped to over

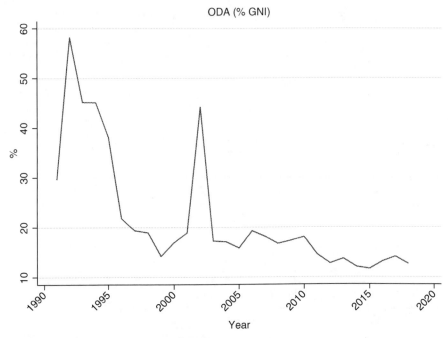

FIGURE 2.9  ODA as percentage of GNI, 1990–2018
Source: Net ODA received (% of GNI) from World Bank (2020) data.

20 per cent of GDP as Mozambique opened up to investment in natural resources extraction, and these flows quickly came to overshadow the contribution of foreign aid, which has declined substantially in relative terms (see Figure 2.9).

Three conclusions can be drawn. First, much of Mozambique's growth has been fuelled by significant inflows of foreign exchange, both public and private, which have generated spillovers either directly into consumption or indirectly into income through investment. Second, however, the pattern of these inflows has shifted increasingly towards capital-intensive natural resource investments, which provides a proximate explanation for the widening labour productivity deficits across sectors (Figure 2.7) and which by definition also suggests that the growth process has lacked 'inclusivity'. Third, Mozambique has not discovered a consistent (sustained) domestic engine of growth. Rather, not only have growth drivers shifted depending on the dominant source of foreign savings, but also the economy seems to have become less diversified over time. This is evident from Figures 2.10 and 2.11, which show the composition of exports and Mozambique's export complexity, respectively. Figure 2.10 reveals that manufacturing exports (aluminium) plateaued by the later 2000s; but, starting roughly in 2010, natural resources exports (mainly coal) have quintupled in value and now account for around 50 per cent of all exports.

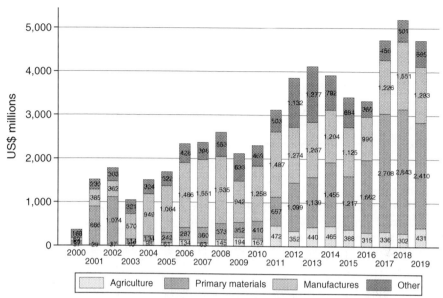

FIGURE 2.10 Major exports in US$ millions (2000–2019)
Notes: Primary materials include energy exports; agricultural goods include fisheries.
Source: Authors' estimates based on unpublished data from Central Bank of Mozambique.

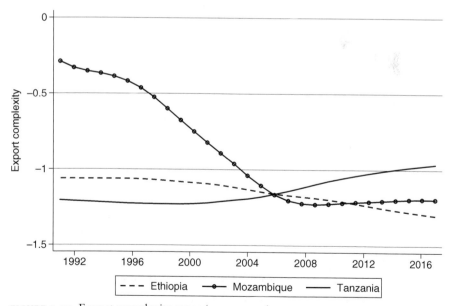

FIGURE 2.11 Export complexity score (1991–2017)
Notes: Lower scores mean less complex exports.
Source: Smoothed estimates from The Growth Lab at Harvard University (2020) data.

Correspondingly, the relative shift towards lower value-added exports (which are lower in complexity) is evident in Figure 2.11.

These three conclusions are reinforced by trends in the final period, as shown in Table 2.1, which merit special attention. As discussed in Section II, in 2016 a series of hidden (illegal) debts taken out since 2013 from overseas commercial banks by publicly guaranteed enterprises came to light. The funds were premised on discoveries of large natural gas fields in the country, but (ex post) appear to have been squandered, various members of the ruling elite and overseas backers being implicated in corruption. Critically, this prompted a major freeze in foreign aid and, correspondingly, a sharp depreciation of the exchange rate. As plotted in Figure 2.8, growth rates simultaneously declined across multiple sectors and public sector investment approximately halved as a share of GDP (see Table 2.1) – that is the sudden lack of foreign inflows outside the natural resources sector, combined with significant macroeconomic uncertainty, had drastic growth consequences, revealing the fragile nature of the earlier growth and the economy's dependence on foreign savings.

Another way of making sense of these trends is to note that Mozambique has been and remains a highly segmented economy. A large share of the population remains engaged in informal rural economic activities, predominantly smallholder agriculture. In comparative terms, productivity in these activities is low and is strongly associated with high rates of poverty (see below). The substantial FDI over the post-war period has focused on enclave-type industries, with few linkages via employment or provision of inputs to domestic productive sectors. Therefore, as Arndt et al. (2012a) and others have formally quantified, inter-sectoral linkages in the economy have been weak and are highly compromised by poor infrastructure and large transport distances between areas of highest agricultural potential and population mass (rural centre and north) and areas of greatest effective demand (urban south). Furthermore, economy-wide benefits from natural resource development have proven elusive, especially as many investments have not reached the production (profitability) phase. In sum, the pattern of employment creation suggests that the infrastructure and business environment remain weak and skewed against labour-intensive manufacturing.

## C  Competent Macroeconomic Management

Despite the most recent period of crisis, the tail end of which has coincided with the COVID-19 pandemic, macroeconomic management has been competent. Broadly speaking, inflation has been well controlled and fiscal deficits have been almost fully covered by substantial foreign inflows (foreign aid) rather than domestic debt. Tax revenues have also steadily increased, from a low level, via a combination of sensible reforms and relatively rapid growth of specific formal segments of the economy (e.g., finance, natural resources).

TABLE 2.2 *Macroeconomic and fiscal indicators (2002–2019)*

|  | 2002 | 2005 | 2010 | 2015 | 2019 |
|---|---|---|---|---|---|
| Macro economy |  |  |  |  |  |
| Real GDP per capita (US$) | 323.7 | 376.2 | 466.4 | 572.6 | 571.0 |
| Inflation rate (%) | 17.3 | 7.0 | 12.4 | 3.6 | 2.8 |
| RER index | 1.1 | 1.0 | 1.1 | 1.1 | 1.5 |
| Trade balance (% GDP) | −11.8 | −5.8 | −18.8 | −37.4 | −26.0 |
| Public sector |  |  |  |  |  |
| Tax revenue (% GDP) | 8.7 | 10.7 | 16.8 | 24.4 | 28.9 |
| Current expenditure (% GDP) | 16.2 | 12.3 | 16.3 | 17.3 | 24.5 |
| Investment expenditure (% GDP) | 8.7 | 8.2 | 11.6 | 13.0 | 7.5 |
| Deficit (% GDP) | −16.2 | −9.8 | −11.1 | −5.9 | −3.1 |
| Domestic public debt (% GDP) | 3.0 | 9.6 | 6.1 | 13.4 | 28.4 |
| External public debt (% GDP) | 72.8 | 60.5 | 37.3 | 74.8 | 96.1 |

*Source:* Ministry of Economy and Finance database, unpublished.

Table 2.2 supports this narrative, summarising a range of macroeconomic and public expenditure figures for selected years since 2002.[20]

Until around 2015, the combination of increased tax revenue and sustained (although relatively smaller) foreign aid allowed both government consumption and investment to expand. However, most recently we observe that consumption spending now accounts for almost 25 per cent of GDP, while public investment spending has fallen back below 10 per cent of GDP. This is explained by large cuts in foreign aid in reaction to the hidden debts and the ensuing rapid build-up of public debt, external *and* internal, entailing much higher recurrent servicing costs.

Thus, as compared with the mid- to late-2000s, when Mozambique benefitted from highly favourable debt write-offs, the government is now in a considerably more fragile fiscal position, with debt at distressed levels. Furthermore, the build-up of public debt has not been matched by any boost in investment spending that could be expected to yield future dividends.

## D  Steady but Slowing Social Progress

Table 2.2 confirms that the real pace of growth on a per capita basis is hardly phenomenal. Since 2000, the average real per capita growth rate equals just 3.4 per cent per annum, implying that it will require more than twenty years to double real incomes. Thus, Mozambique remains a very poor country by any measure. In 2017, Mozambique ranked 180 of 186 countries in terms of real

[20] The effects of monetary policy and of the limited credit expansion to the productive parts of the private sector, including farmers and SMEs, remain the subject of debate.

TABLE 2.3 *Metrics of poverty and inequality in Mozambique, 1996/1997–2014/2015*

|  | 1996/1997 | 2002/2003 | 2008/2009 | 2014/2015 | Growth (%) |
|---|---|---|---|---|---|
| No. consumption baskets | 0.7 | 1.0 | 1.0 | 1.1 | 2.1 |
| Poverty headcount (%) | 68.8 | 52.7 | 51.5 | 46.3 | -2.2 |
| Poverty gap (%) | 28.7 | 19.3 | 19.0 | 16.7 | -3.0 |
| Squared poverty gap (%) | 15.3 | 9.5 | 9.7 | 8.3 | -3.4 |
| Gini (x100) (%) | 40.5 | 41.5 | 41.7 | 46.8 | 0.8 |

*Note:* 'No. consumption baskets' reports the number of baskets that the median household can purchase, a value of 1 being equivalent to the Cost of Basic Needs poverty line; the poverty gap and its square are expressed as a proportion of the poverty line; growth is annualised over the full period.
*Source:* Authors' calculations from household survey microdata (see MEF/DEEF 2016).

GDP per capita (IMF 2018); and 180 of 189 on the UN's human development index (UNDP 2018: 22–25).

The post-war period has shown progress on a range of social indicators, including consumption and multidimensional poverty. Data from a series of household surveys, undertaken approximately every five years since 1996, show particularly strong gains in poverty reduction in the immediate post-conflict period, but less impressive gains since then (see Table 2.3).

This is also consistent with the narrative, outlined above, of a weak connection between specific sources of aggregate demand (sectoral) growth and employment. Over the entire period, we estimate that the consumption poverty headcount fell by 2.2 per cent per year, well below the aggregate rate of growth. In turn, inequality has increased, again suggesting that growth has not been broadly shared,[21] and this tendency has worsened since 2015 (Egger et al. 2020).

Table 2.4 summarises progress in a range of other socio-economic dimensions, including household ownership of assets or capital (economic and human) (see MEF/DEEF 2016).

These are all dummy variables that take a value of one if the household head is literate, has access to electricity, has access to clean water, has clean sanitation, has a robust roof, owns some means of transport, has access to information technology (e.g., telephone), and owns some durable goods (e.g., bed). Throughout the period, all indicators have shown progress. Even so, absolute deprivations are widespread – only about half of adults are literate, half of all

---

[21] For a comprehensive set of analyses of the experience of stagnating poverty between 2002/03 and 2008/09, when inequality remained the same and growth per capita occurred, see Arndt et al. (2012b). Essentially, the terms of trade shock due to the food price crises helped drive aggregate consumption down as a share of GDP.

TABLE 2.4 *Household-level indicators of access/ownership of key assets*

| Indicator | 1996/1997 | 2002/2003 | 2008/2009 | 2014/2015 | Change |
|---|---|---|---|---|---|
| Literacy | 52.3 | 54.4 | 55.4 | 58.4 | 6.2 |
| Electricity | 6.1 | 8.9 | 15.2 | 27.1 | 20.9 |
| Clean water | 27.0 | 41.4 | 42.5 | 52.3 | 25.3 |
| Sanitation | 4.5 | 14.0 | 18.0 | 28.4 | 23.9 |
| Roofing | 21.8 | 29.2 | 32.7 | 42.0 | 20.2 |
| Transport | 17.6 | 34.4 | 45.3 | 44.4 | 26.8 |
| Information | 36.9 | 57.2 | 62.6 | 75.4 | 38.5 |
| Durables | 12.7 | 20.5 | 31.3 | 50.4 | 37.6 |
| Mean | 22.4 | 32.5 | 37.9 | 47.3 | 24.9 |

*Notes:* Indicators are percentages of the total number of households.
*Source:* Authors' calculations from household survey microdata (see MEF/DEEF 2016).

households have access to clean water, and less than a third have adequate sanitation. So, despite twenty-five years of steady growth in the post-war period, plus sustained access to large volumes of foreign savings, a lot remains to be done to ensure that all Mozambicans enjoy a decent standard of living.

## E Public Sector (in)Efficiency

The foregoing raises the important question: how efficient or cost-effective is the public sector in delivering core public services? As already noted, the *relative* size of the public sector in the economy has grown substantially. Table 2.1, for instance, shows that total government current expenditures have increased by almost 10 percentage points in relation to GDP, implying far more rapid expansion than in the private sector as a whole. However, according to Figures 2.5 and 2.6, the employment share of the public sector has increased only moderately, while the real value-added of public services (which includes privately provided health and education) has been almost flat over time. In this sense, there is no clear indication (in aggregate statistics) of any significant real economic impacts of the increased spending.

Table 2.5 compares budget allocations to outcomes in education and health for a range of sub-Saharan African countries. It shows that on a per capita basis, social sector spending in Mozambique is comparable to elsewhere (in the middle). Yet outcomes in Mozambique are considerably poorer – for example while more than 90 per cent of children attend primary school, the primary school completion rate is only around 40 per cent versus 80 per cent in neighbouring Tanzania, and under 5 mortality is 74.2 per 1,000 live births versus 53.0 in Tanzania.

Of course, Mozambique's troubled history explains part of this gap, but other sub-Saharan African countries, such as Ethiopia, also entered the 1990s

TABLE 2.5  *Comparison of social sector spending and outcomes*

| | Education | | Health | |
|---|---|---|---|---|
| | Spend | Primary completion | Spend | Under 5 mortality |
| Ethiopia | 9.44 | 47.0 | 3.83 | 55.2 |
| Ghana | 22.57 | 66.0 | 10.58 | 47.9 |
| Malawi | 3.59 | 47.0 | 1.68 | 49.7 |
| Mozambique | 13.28 | 41.0 | 6.56 | 74.2 |
| Tanzania | 15.55 | 80.0 | 5.97 | 53.0 |

*Note:* Spend indicates budget allocations in 2019, in real US$ per capita (for the population as whole); 'primary completion' indicates the primary school completion rate.
*Source:* Government Spending Watch (2020); UNICEF (2020).

in dire circumstances and would seem to have made stronger progress and at a lower fiscal cost. Additionally, evidence in Mozambique points to extreme and persistent spatial disparities in access to public services (see Egger et al. 2020). The more urban south of the country tends to enjoy not just better quality services but also much higher effective public spending than elsewhere. Thus, overall, the public sector would seem to be not cost-effective and marred by inequities in allocations that fail to benefit the poorest.

## F  Demographic Dynamics

According to INE (2019), summarising the results from the 2017 Population Census, 39 per cent of the rapidly growing Mozambican population lives in Nampula and Zambézia as compared to 21.5 per cent for the provinces in the south. The remaining almost 40 per cent live in the provinces of Tete, Cabo Delgado, Sofala, Manica, and Niassa. The distribution between urban and rural areas shows that two thirds live in rural areas. The overall annual rate of growth of the population between 2007 and 2017 was 2.8 per cent, increasing from 1.7 to 2.5 per cent in the previous decades. Maputo province saw the largest relative increase in its population (60.7 per cent) between 2007 and 2017 while the population of the city of Maputo stagnated. Large increases of more than 40 per cent were experienced in Niassa, Tete, and Nampula, whereas increases of around 30 per cent were experienced in Manica, Sofala, Zambézia, and Cabo Delgado.

Reflecting the steady but slowing social progress discussed in Section D, life expectancy increased from 50.9 years in 2007 to 53.7 years in 2017. However, the population dynamics imply high dependency ratios that will continue at burdensome levels for well more than a generation (Jones and Tarp 2012, 2013, 2016) as nearly half of the population is under fifteen years of age (INE 2019). A critical implication is that the working age population will grow rapidly over the next thirty years. This dynamic is essentially 'locked in' as it reflects past

fertility decisions. Some 34 per cent of the total labour force is concentrated in
the north, 41.9 per cent in the centre and 24.1 per cent in the south (MITSS,
2020), reflecting the regional distribution of the general population.

The majority (60.8 per cent) of the young labour force (15–34 years) is
between fifteen and twenty-four years old and, according to MITSS (2020)
based on the IV General Population Census 2017, it is estimated that between
2020 and 2024, the labour force will increase by 2.26 million, including 1.62
million young people (15–34 years). How can the labour market absorb this
magnitude of new entrants? While it is impossible to make firm predictions,
there is an internal logic to what is feasible, even in the best of policy environ-
ments. This derives from the existing structure of employment – sectors with
large existing employment shares must be the principal sources of 'new' jobs.
Put differently, even if sectors with small employment shares were to grow at
an annual rate of 10 per cent or even 15 per cent, this would be insufficient to
absorb all new entrants (Jones and Tarp 2012, 2013, 2016).

Informal non-farm enterprises, the second largest category of jobs, are both
substantially smaller than agriculture and much bigger than formal employment. The latter constitutes a minor share – less than 15 per cent of all workers
report receiving a wage, of which the large majority is in informal employment. This share configuration dictates that most new entrants into the labour
market must seek work in agriculture or informal enterprises. This has very
much been the situation for the past twenty-five years and will remain the case
in the near future. Indeed, under a high-growth scenario of 8 per cent growth
in formal sector jobs, the informal sector will continue to increase in absolute
size until at least 2030 (Jones and Tarp 2012, 2013).

These facts inescapably imply that future dynamics in smallholder agriculture and the informal sector will be of fundamental importance to achieving
inclusive growth. This is the core policy challenge facing the Mozambican government and its people over the next decades.

## G Taking Stock

The evolving pattern and complexity of Mozambique's growth trajectory, as
well as the sheer scope of the challenges the country continues to face, limit the
value of attempting to reduce this experience to a few well-defined underlying
causes. We would argue that many of the conventional factors identified as
constraints to growth may well be symptomatic of a deeper malaise, namely
the lack of a clear (vision for a) domestic engine of growth and an excess reliance on external savings to finance demand.

While no formal comprehensive growth diagnostic in the spirit of Hausmann
et al. (2005) has been undertaken for Mozambique to date, a range of less formal 'diagnostics' point to weaknesses across multiple domains. These include
low private returns to economic activity as well as the high costs of finance (the
two distinct primary branches of the growth diagnostics framework). These

exercises frequently end up documenting a long list of symptoms and do not identify specific 'deep' causes or reform priorities.

Lledó (2007), for instance, notes that in both 2002 and 2006 firms identified the high cost of finance as a primary concern. However, on top of this, he notes that median returns to manufacturing firms are near zero, which reflects the 'combined impact of low social returns and limited private appropriability' (p. 344). In a more recent exercise, the World Bank (2016) echoes a similarly wide range of key challenges: 'Inadequate physical and logistical infrastructure, excessive bureaucracy, weak public institutions, credit constraints and a complicated land-tenure system continue to discourage investment and narrow the range of economic opportunities available to domestic firms' (p. 35).

The point is not that these diagnostics are necessarily wrong. Rather, it is that it is difficult to isolate unique growth constraints/opportunities or untangle causes from symptoms given the range of challenges and the segmented nature of the economy.

In the same spirit, it can be highlighted that previous diagnostic exercises for Mozambique have placed wildly different interpretations on the direction of public reform efforts. Ten years ago, improvements in the business environment were seen as impressive and indicative of a strong and coordinated government commitment:

Progress in reforming business registration has been remarkable. New regulations simplifying the start-up of commercial and industrial activities were issued in 2004. [...] As a result, the start-up time for new firms in Mozambique decreased by almost three months, from, on average, 113 days to 29 days. (Lledó 2007: 337)

Nonetheless, a 2017 diagnostic of the business environment suggests that these reforms have been cosmetic, that there is 'a lack of political will to implement reforms because the status quo benefits politicians and the politically-connected [... and] business registration reform [...] has resulted in little improvement of the process for entrepreneurs' (Franco and Katiyo 2017: 19–20).

Put differently, views change as to where priorities lie and where genuine progress has been made. And, as yet, there does not seem to be a strong politically independent domestic constituency for deeper reforms.

In our view, what this amounts to is not a specific set of distinct technical growth constraints per se but a more general failure to prioritise the upgrading of domestic competencies in either the public or the private sector beyond that of servicing international demands. A vision of a self-sustaining process of growth and development has been absent, and in its place, a fragmented and shifting external orientation has dominated, most recently degenerating into growth-damaging rent-seeking. Many of the growth challenges represent symptoms of this failed vision and corresponding growth engine.

Looking ahead, a key risk is that this lacuna will only expand as natural resource extraction (natural gas) plays a stronger role, cementing rentier elements in the public and private sectors and undermining competitiveness elsewhere in the economy. In the short-to-medium term, significant public finance gains from these industries are likely to be lacking, while exposure to commodity price volatility is likely to become more acute.

Avoiding an Angola-style scenario of deepening inequality and a bloated public sector that fails to deliver quality public services must be the priority. And this is especially important in Mozambique given political and spatial tensions that have already boiled over into military conflict, as discussed in Section II. Sadly, with public investment weakening and high debt obligations, the capacity of the government to support inclusive structural transformation has weakened since the late 2000s. Thus, decisive action must be taken.

## IV CONCLUSION

In this chapter, we have laid out the historical, political, and economic context that puts development challenges in Mozambique in perspective. We have drawn attention to the big picture story – the deterioration in the comparative institutional performance of Mozambique between 2005 and 2019/20, which we explain in detail in Chapter 3. Overall, we have argued, in Section II, that contemporary Mozambique and its development challenges cannot be understood without reference to the troubled history of the country. On the political side, this includes the continued confrontation between the dominant political party, Frelimo, and the opposition in Renamo, which remains extremely tough, affecting state as well as institutional reform capacity.

In Section III, we highlighted that, while the 1990s saw recovery from war and political conflict, there has not been a consistent domestic engine of inclusive growth in spite of a comparative advantage in agriculture and agro-industry. A vision of a self-sustaining and inclusive process of growth and development has been absent. In its place, a fragmented and shifting external orientation has dominated, most recently degenerating into growing rent-seeking and corruption following the discovery of major gas deposits in the Rovuma basin and elsewhere.

The core messages, which the reader should keep in mind throughout the remainder of this volume, are:

- Historical roots go deep and include regional fragmentation and ethnic diversity. Colonial exploitation left Mozambique at a very low level of living standards to begin with and whatever institutions had existed, collapsed with independence in 1975.
- Independence came late to Mozambique at a time when the Cold War was unfolding and the anti-apartheid struggle was intensifying. Rhodesia and South Africa decided to support Renamo and inflicted massive damage on Mozambique from the early 1980s onwards.
- The Marxist-Leninist regime that prevailed from 1977 impacted greatly on socio-economic development in the early years of independence.

Misconceived policies were forcibly introduced, and influential members of the Frelimo leadership opposed private sector development.

- For some fifteen of the forty-five years since independence in 1975, Mozambique has been engulfed by violent conflict and political instability. The political and economic legacy of this is far from negligible and, when combined with frequent changes in policy direction, explains why Mozambique remains close to the bottom of the scale in terms of GDP and human development.

- The succession of crises – the Renamo/MNR war, the Rhodesian and South African military aggressions, droughts followed by floods, and donor-prompted reforms in 1986/87 – imply that Mozambique has not been a 'normal' country, with time to settle and look into itself, to project and build its future in an environment of tranquillity.

- The international donor community responded to the PRE in 1987 and peace in 1992 with significant amounts of foreign assistance in the form of humanitarian aid and soft loans. Economic recovery took place but a growth engine for sustained inclusive development remained absent. Moreover, Mozambique did not exploit the potential advantages of being a late starter to independence in terms of learning from other countries and avoiding rent-seeking and elite capture.

- The liberalisation and privatisation inherent in the structural adjustment programme was not a simple technical measure in a context where no entrepreneurial class existed and where Renamo was still operating in the bush. This resulted in assets and income being transferred to people associated with Frelimo and public administration, and in the merging of political and economic power. This opened up possibilities for rent-seeking and elite capture and stands out as a major institutional challenge.

- An underlying assumption of the PRE was that, by getting prices right, agriculture would excel. This quickly proved unrealistic in wartime conditions. Agriculture's progress in the 1990s seemed due, in large measure, to the return of refugees. Subsequently, Frelimo has failed to implement the measures necessary for agricultural development, which is critical for structural transformation, poverty reduction, and inclusive development, both vertically and horizontally between different groups of people and different regions of the country.

- The collapse of credit institutions, including the de facto (in kind) credit provision provided by settler farmers to indigenous peasants before independence, and the devastating mining of assets in commercial banking during the structural adjustment programme, left Mozambique with a very non-inclusive banking sector.

- We stress that Mozambique was born into a violent conflict with two of Africa's strongest countries in terms of economic and military power (South Africa and Rhodesia) and these were the exact two countries Mozambique's own economy and infrastructure had been developed to serve and do business with. That old systems took hold again in the mid-nineties form part of the explanation that there is no domestic growth engine, as noted above.

- Looking at the period starting in the 2000s and focusing on the public sector, it is clear that efficiency and effectiveness are well below capacity in spite of the relatively large size of the public sector. While social spending is comparable to that of neighbouring countries, outcomes in Mozambique are considerably poorer and the more urban southern part of the country enjoys not just better quality services but much more effective public spending than elsewhere.

- Solid macroeconomic management played a key role in addressing the economic crisis that erupted following the hidden debts scandal in 2016, even if the costs to the economy in terms of growth due to the stabilisation measures needed were significant. Importantly, continued sound macroeconomic management will be crucial when revenues from the huge gas resources start flowing. Macro management will have to pursue policies that promote the supply side of the economy. This must involve a focus on offsetting Dutch disease by investing in tradeable exportable sectors, implying a very strong role of agriculture, agro-industry, and light manufacturing, which is labour intensive and can absorb workers with limited skills, in national plans and strengthening institutional delivery. The same goes for the promotion of labour-intensive private sector development.

- Foreign aid flows and the role of donors have been of critical importance throughout the modern history of Mozambique, and will continue to be significant, as public revenue from the development of the natural resources sector will lag by at least a decade. While foreign financing has been hugely important for the funding of public expenditures, including critical investment in human capital and infrastructure and much needed humanitarian relief, aid has also been associated with the side effects of aid dependence, including Dutch disease, lack of agency, and undermining of local institutions.

- As already alluded to, Mozambique has experienced violent conflicts at different stages since independence. Among the most recent is the military insurgency in Cabo Delgado. The causes of this conflict are still debated, but likely include local discontent caused by limited socio-economic development and activities of both local and international Islamic groups in an area where illegal trade has been prevalent. If these tensions are not effectively addressed, they may spill over to other parts of northern and central Mozambique.

These insights motivated the selection of eight thematic areas, which are explored in Chapters 4 to 11, with a view to furthering our understanding of current development challenges and existing institutional weaknesses. Accordingly, these chapters delve more deeply into issues related to: the importance of agriculture and the potential and risks of natural resources exploitation; the management of public finances and the provision of education and healthcare; the challenges in the legal sector and in the process of decentralisation; and, finally, the evolving relationship between Mozambique and the donor community. Before we turn to the thematic chapters, we discuss the institutional performance and the perceptions of institutional constraints in Chapter 3.

## APPENDIX

| Presidents | Samora Machel | Joaquim Chissano | | Armando Guebuza | Filipe Nyusi |
|---|---|---|---|---|---|
| Economic system | Central planning economy | Market economy | | | |
| | PPI | PRE | PRES | PARPA I | PARPA II | PARP | |
| Political system | One-party system (Frelimo) | | Multiparty system | | |
| | | | | One party dominance | |
| War/Peace | Wars (Rodhesia, South Africa, Renamo) | | Peace period | | Civil war | +North war |

**Events/Decisions**

- 1975 Independence
- 1975 1st Constitution
- 1976 War with Rodhesia started
- 1977 Marxist-Leninist ideology
- 1977 3rd Frelimo Congress; War with Renamo started
- 1980 1st Multi racial and democratic elections in Zimbabwe
- 1981 PPI; USSR blocked Mozambique's accession to COMECON
- 1981 Mozambique joined Lomé Convention
- 1983 4th Frelimo Congress
- 1984 Mozambique joined IMF and the World Bank
- 1986 Perestroika in USSR
- 1987 Economic Reform Program
- 1987 PRE + social dimension; Decision on privatizations
- 1990 1990 Constitution revision; Mandela freed from prison
- 1990 Severe drought
- 1991 Severe drought
- 1992 Peace Agreement with Renamo
- 1994 1st multiparty elections
- 1994 1st Multi racial and democratic elections in South Africa
- 1998 1st Municipal elections (33)
- 1998 1st investment in Mozal aluminium smelter
- 1999 2nd multiparty elections
- 2000 Big floods; Maputo-Witbank corridor started operating
- 2000 PARPA 1
- 2001 2nd investment in Mozal
- 2002 Chinese trade accelerated
- 2003 2nd Municipal elections (33)
- 2004 3rd multiparty elections
- 2004 2004 Constitution revision; Sasol exports natural gas to SA
- 2006 PARPA 2; Granted rights to explore hydrocarbons (Rovuma)
- 2006 Started ivestment in Mozatize mineral coal
- 2007 China became 2nd largest investor, after South Africa
- 2008 3rd Municipal elections (43)
- 2009 4th multiparty elections
- 2010 Natural gas reserves confirmed (Rovuma)
- 2011 PARP; Companies export mineral coal from Tete in 2011
- 2013 4th Municipal elections (53)
- 2013 EMATUM Bonds issued; War with Renamo re-started
- 2014 5th multiparty elections
- 2016 Proindicus and MAM debt guarantees discovered
- 2017 Started armed conflict in Cabo Delgado
- 2018 5th Municipal elections (53)
- 2019 6th multiparty elections
- 2020 COVID-19; Insurgent attacks intensified (Cabo Delgado)

FIGURE A2.1 Mozambique timeline for an institutional analysis of socio-economic development

Source: Authors' compilation based on Castel-Branco et al. (2001); Andersson (2002); AfDB and OECD (2004); Jansson and Kiala (2009); Intellica (2015); Orre and Rønning (2017); Cruz et al. (2018); Brito (2019); and Simão (2020).

# 3

# Institutional Performance

*Perceptions of Institutional Constraints –*
*Quantitative and Qualitative Insights*

António S. Cruz, Ines A. Ferreira, Johnny Flentø,
and Finn Tarp

## I INTRODUCTION

Having taken stock of the development performance of Mozambique in a historical and socio-economic perspective in Chapter 2, we introduce in Section II of this chapter a series of institutional indicators comparing Mozambique with neighbouring and peer countries using data from existing international databases. We then proceed in Sections III and IV to bring together the results of, respectively, a quantitative survey and a series of key informant (KI) interviews. The aim of these two tools was to gather the perceptions of key politicians, business people, academics, and liberal professionals in Mozambique with regard to institutional challenges and constraints to development.

## II WHAT DO INTERNATIONAL DATABASES SHOW?

### A Overview

This section presents selected trends of the performance of Mozambique in different institutional indicators in comparison with two groups of selected countries: neighbouring – Tanzania, Malawi, and Zambia – and peer – Uganda, Ethiopia, Vietnam, and Lao People's Democratic Republic (PDR). The criteria used in selecting the comparator countries were, on the one hand, geographic and, on the other hand, level of income and similarity in terms of historical and economic characteristics, either past or present.

The discussion of the indicators is not exhaustive, and it is important to keep in mind the limitations of some of these measures (e.g., see Kaufmann and Kraay 2007; Gisselquist 2014; González et al. 2017). However, they were selected based on data availability and relevance for the present study. The different indicators were obtained from a variety of well-established data sources, namely, Varieties of Democracy (Coppedge et al. 2020; Pemstein et al. 2020),

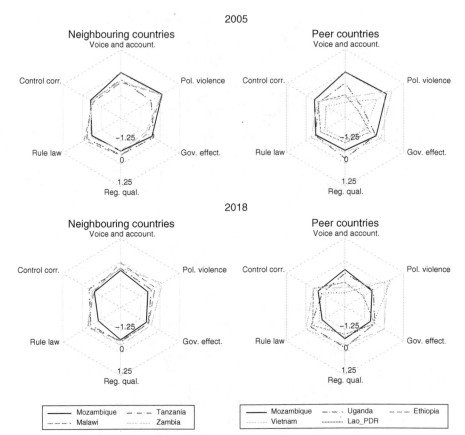

FIGURE 3.1 Worldwide Governance Indicators, 2005 and 2018
Note: Centre is at −2.5; lines further away from the centre correspond to *better* outcomes. The scores range from −2.5 to 2.5, with higher values representing better outcomes. Key: Voice and account, voice and accountability; Pol. violence, political violence; Gov. effect., government effectiveness; Reg. qual., regulatory quality; Rule law, rule of law; Control corr., control of corruption.
Source: Authors' compilation based on Worldwide Governance Indicators (World Bank 2020).

Afrobarometer (2020), World Economic Forum (2020), Worldwide Governance Indicators (WGIs; World Bank 2020), and Bertelsmann Stiftung (BTI 2020).[1]

First, we provide an overview of the scores for Mozambique in the six dimensions of governance suggested by the WGIs – voice and accountability, political violence, government effectiveness, regulatory quality, rule of law, and control of corruption – in comparison to neighbouring and peer countries in 2005 and in 2018 (Figure 3.1).

---

[1] We stress a caveat that has to be kept in mind throughout. Confidence intervals are often quite wide. Thus, statements about the ranking of countries, which are close to each other by a given

In 2005, Mozambique was the best performer in terms of voice and accountability and control of corruption in both groups of countries. The graph for neighbouring countries shows similar performances for the countries considered, but there are noticeable differences when comparing Mozambique with its peers. While it has higher scores than Ethiopia and Lao PDR in all dimensions, Mozambique's score in regulatory quality, for instance, is lower than those of Uganda and Vietnam.

It is tempting to compare the same indicators over time for 2005 and 2018 to get a sense of the institutional dynamics in specific countries. However, the norm of indicators in the WGI database changes from year-to-year. Bearing this in mind, the main point emerging from the graphs is that while Mozambique was doing better than the other countries in 2005, it did worse in 2018. Even though Mozambique remains the best performer in voice and accountability among the peer countries, its scores are lower than all the other four countries in terms of government effectiveness and rule of law. We return to some of these indicators in what follows.

## B Rule of Law and Judicial Independence

The first institutional dimensions we address here relate to confidence in, and abidance by, the known rules to government actors and citizens as well as to the independence of the judicial system. In Figure 3.1, we observed that while in 2005 Mozambique's score in rule of law was already low in comparison to its neighbouring countries, this positioning becomes more apparent in 2018 (even when considering confidence intervals). Compared with its peer countries, Mozambique's score is only lower than that of Vietnam and similar to that of Uganda in 2005, but it is, together with Lao PDR, one of the lowest among the five countries in 2018.[2]

Figure 3.2 represents the perception of respondents of how independent the judicial system is from influences of the government, individuals, or companies. Both graphs in the figure show that the level of independence of the judicial system is perceived as low in Mozambique, the lowest in comparison to the selected countries and across the period. It is also noticeable that there was a decrease from 2008 and a sharp fall after 2017.[3]

---

index, must be interpreted with caution. Similarly, when observations are made about the time dimension, it must be recalled that data sources and country samples vary from year to year.

[2] The data from Varieties of Democracy (Coppedge et al. 2020; Pemstein et al. 2020) confirm that Mozambique did perform worse in terms of rule of law than its neighbouring countries over the 2005–19 period (with the exception of Malawi). However, the Varieties of Democracy data suggest that until 2017 the country's performance was better than that of some of the selected peer countries, namely, Ethiopia, Lao People's Democratic Republic (PDR, and Vietnam, and very similar to that of Uganda.

[3] While the indicator 'independent judiciary' from Bertelsmann Stiftung (BTI) confirms the position of Mozambique as the worst performer among its neighbouring countries in 2020, the data from BTI (2020) suggest that Vietnam and Lao PDR scored lower in this dimension across the period.

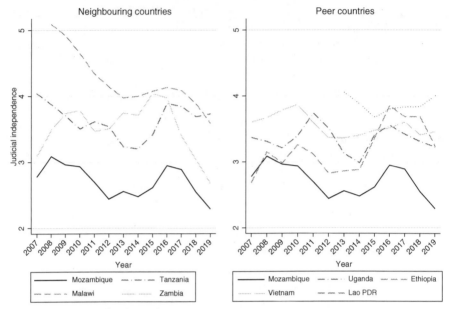

FIGURE 3.2  Judicial independence, 2007–2019
Note: The scores range from 1 to 7, with 1 being 'not independent at all' and 7 'entirely independent'.
Source: Authors' compilation based on the Executive Opinion Survey (World Economic Forum 2020).


## C  Voice, Participation, and Political Accountability

The second group of institutional dimensions recognises the need for citizens to be able to participate politically and hold the executive accountable, as well as the importance of freedom of expression and assembly. The scores for voice and accountability from the WGIs represented in Figure 3.1 pointed to the conclusion that the performance of Mozambique in this dimension seems to have weakened comparing the situation in 2005 with that in 2018, especially in comparison to neighbouring countries.

Figure 3.3 represents the overall level of political participation (represented at the top of the pentagon), which measures the extent to which the populace decides who rules and has other political freedoms. The level of political participation is derived from the BTI scores for the remaining four sub-components represented in the pentagon (clockwise), namely, free and fair elections, effective power to govern, association/assembly rights, and freedom of expression. The graphs for 2006 show that Mozambique was one of the best performers that year among the selected countries in all political participation dimensions. In contrast, according to the assessment in 2020, Mozambique had the worst performance on the overall indicator

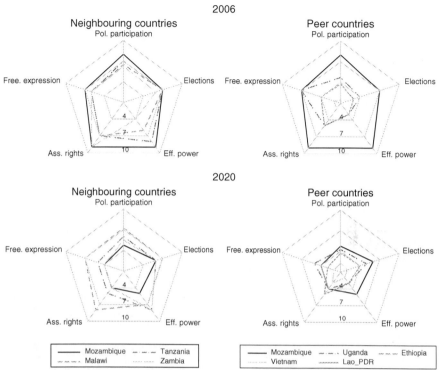

FIGURE 3.3 Political participation and sub-components, 2006 and 2020
Note: Centre is at 1; lines further away from the centre correspond to *better* outcomes. The scale ranges from 10 (best) to 1 (worst). Key: Pol. participation, overall political participation score; Elections, free and fair elections; Eff. power, effective power to govern; Ass. rights, association/assembly rights; Free. expression, freedom of expression.
Source: Authors' compilation based on the transformation index of the Bertelsmann Stiftung (BTI 2020).

of political participation among its neighbouring countries, while its peers show worse scores in all sub-components except freedom of expression and assembly rights.

## D Political Instability, Violence, and State Legitimacy

The third set of dimensions refers to the degree of recognition of the nation as a state, with adequate and differentiated power structures at national and subnational levels, and the likelihood of political instability and of politically motivated violence and terrorism. The scores on political stability and absence of violence motivated by political reasons, including terrorism – represented in Figure 3.1 as 'Pol. violence' – show that Mozambique's relative position

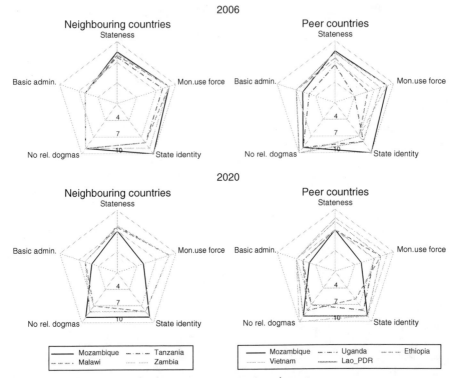

FIGURE 3.4 Stateness and sub-components, 2006 and 2018
Note: Centre is at 1; lines further away from the centre correspond to *better* outcomes. The scale ranges from 10 (best) to 1 (worst). Key: Stateness, overall score; Mon. use force, monopoly on the use of force; No rel. dogmas, no interference of religious dogmas; Basic admin., basic administration.
Source: Authors' compilation based on the transformation index of the Bertelsmann Stiftung (BTI 2020).

compared with neighbouring and peer countries deteriorated over time. It is interesting to note that while Mozambique's score was similar to that of Malawi and Zambia in 2005, it was lower in 2018 (with more certainty in the case of Zambia).

Figure 3.4 represents a measure of political instability, defined as 'stateness', as well as the sub-components used to derive it: monopoly of the use of force, state identity, no interference of religious dogmas, and basic administration. In 2006, Mozambique's performance was similar to that of its neighbours, and it was one of the best among its peer countries. Still, Mozambique's score was relatively much weaker in 2020 compared with the comparator countries, especially concerning the monopoly of the use of force.

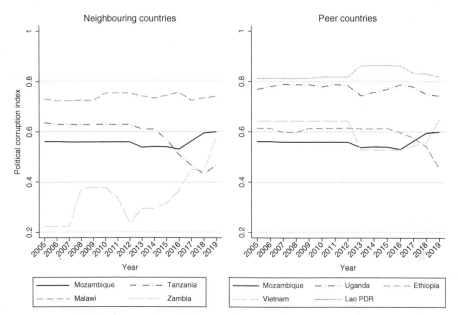

FIGURE 3.5  Political corruption index, 2005–2019
Note: The scale ranges between 0 and 1; the index runs from less corrupt to more corrupt.
Source: Authors' compilation based on Varieties of Democracy data (Coppedge et al. 2020; Pemstein et al. 2020).

## E  State Capacity and Autonomy from Private Interests

The fourth dimensions deal with the capacity of the state to fulfil the social contract and the separation of state power from private interests. Figure 3.1 included the scores for government effectiveness, a measure of perceptions about the quality of public services, civil service, and policy formulation and implementation, as well as the extent to which there is independence from political pressures. The scores for that indicator show that the relative position of Mozambique was quite good in 2005, but depreciated in 2018.

Figure 3.5 shows the level of pervasiveness of political corruption where a high score reflects a high level of corruption. The figure shows that Mozambique's score remained consistently close to that of neighbouring Tanzania (up to 2016), below that of Malawi and above that of Zambia. Compared with its peer countries, the score for Mozambique stayed similar to that of Vietnam and Ethiopia (until 2017) and was lower than the score for Lao PDR and Uganda. Moreover, the hidden debt scandal is reflected in an increase in 2017.

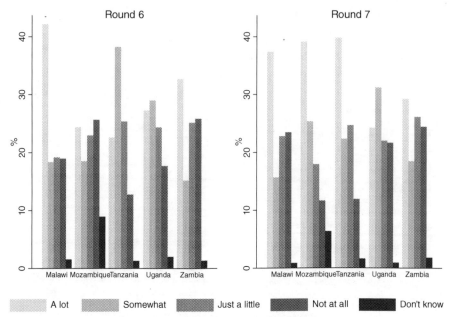

FIGURE 3.6 Trust in police, Rounds 6 and 7 of the Afrobarometer
Source: Authors' compilation based on Afrobarometer Rounds 6 and 7 (Afrobarometer 2020).

Figure 3.6 complements this analysis by asking how much respondents trust one element of the public service, the police. We use data from the two most recent rounds of the Afrobarometer (2020). In 2016, among the selected African countries, the responses for Mozambique show the highest percentage of respondents saying that they do not trust the police at all, and one of the lowest percentages of those who say they trust the police a lot. However, in the latest round the highest percentage corresponds to trusting the police a lot, whereas the response 'Not at all' received a lower percentage of responses.

## F Sovereignty and Independence

The final dimension considered relates to external factors and the degree to which Mozambique has a sovereign position in an international context and whether the political leadership in Mozambique is willing and able to cooperate with external supporters and organisations. Figure 3.7 represents BTI data on international cooperation (the top of the diagram) and its different sub-components, namely, effective use of support, credibility, and regional cooperation (represented clockwise). We note that while Mozambique did well in both 2006 and 2020 in terms of regional cooperation compared with

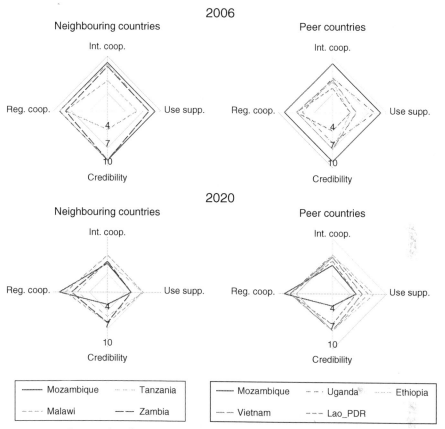

FIGURE 3.7 International cooperation, 2006 and 2020
Note: Centre is at 1; lines further away from the centre correspond to *better* outcomes. The scale ranges from 10 (best) to 1 (worst). Key: Int. coop., overall score; Use sup., effective use of support, which represents the extent to which the political leadership uses the support of international partners to implement a long-term strategy of development; Credibility, represents the extent to which the government acts as a credible and reliable partner in its relations with the international community; Reg. coop., regional cooperation, which represents the extent to which the political leadership is willing and able to cooperate with neighbouring countries.
Source: Authors' compilation based on the transformation index of the Bertelsmann Stiftung (BTI 2020).

all other countries considered, it is clear that the credibility and effective use of support scores, which were both at the top in 2006, were lower than everywhere else in 2020.[4]

---

[4] It is interesting to observe that credibility scores are lower in 2020 than in 2006 for all neighbouring countries and Lao PDR.

III WHAT DO PEOPLE SAY? THE QUANTITATIVE SURVEY

## A Design, Implementation, and Sample of Respondents

### 1 Design and Implementation

The quantitative survey implemented in Mozambique benefited from the implementation experience of the quantitative questionnaires in other countries where the economic development and institutions (EDI) project was implemented (namely, Tanzania and Bangladesh). The survey contained three main parts: The first collected basic demographic questions, including age, province of birth, knowledge of languages, education, etc. The second part asked respondents to select the five biggest constraints to economic development in Mozambique from the following list of fifteen possible constraints and to rank them:

- functioning of the legal sector;
- decentralisation of public power;
- political participation;
- common vision of national strategy;
- agriculture and access to and use of land;
- management of public administration;
- management of macroeconomic and sectoral policy;
- management of natural resources;
- business environment;
- regulatory quality;
- human capital;
- poverty and inequality;
- gender equality;
- foreign aid;
- autonomy in relation to the exterior.

The third and largest section of the survey included a revision of the quantitative survey implemented in Bangladesh, where the various questions were organised in seven themes. These were carefully revised. Some questions were dropped and others consolidated. This resulted in 136 statements organised in the following 18 thematic areas:

- legal and constitutional matters;
- autonomy and public power;
- freedom and political participation;
- state accounts and statistics;
- politics and national identity;
- political violence;
- discrimination and social support network;
- trade unions and strikes;

- public protection;
- land;
- public goods and services;
- formulation and implementation of public policies;
- business environment;
- regulatory quality;
- banking system;
- recruitment and job promotions;
- international collaboration and autonomy;
- foreign aid.

These eighteen thematic areas relate to the overall organizing theoretical framework of the Mozambique study that identifies five institutional areas: (i) rule of law and judicial independence; (ii) voice, participation, and political accountability; (iii) political instability, violence, and state legitimacy; (iv) state capacity and autonomy from private interests; and (v) sovereignty and independence.

For each of the 136 statements, respondents were asked to indicate the degree to which they agreed with them, using the following Likert scale: 1 = 'Completely disagree', 2 = 'Disagree', 3 = 'Don't agree or disagree', 4 = 'Agree', and 5 = 'Completely agree', or to select the 'I don't know' option, which was also available. Moreover, respondents had to express their degree of agreement with every statement before they could proceed with the survey.

The survey was translated into Portuguese and the company Ipsos was contracted to implement it. Ipsos received the survey in English and Portuguese, as well as a list of contacts obtained for the individuals identified in the sample. In the first stage, each contact received an individual link to the online survey. In the second stage, Ipsos followed up with face-to-face interviews with some of the contacts who had not completed the survey online but accepted to do it in person. The content of the questionnaire was exactly the same in both stages.

## 2 Sample of Respondents

The survey was targeted towards key opinion leaders and decision-makers in different core sectors, including, for example, academia, business, diplomats, international non-governmental organisations (NGOs), judiciary, media, national NGOs and public administration, and unions. We identified a core group of individuals in each of these sectors, and a statistical method known as snowballing was used to establish the group of individuals who were invited to respond to the questionnaire.

In total, we received 149 individual responses, 114 through the online survey and 35 through face-to-face interviews. Table 3.1 provides some basic information about the respondents. National NGOs represent about 20 per cent of the respondents, and the same goes for academia, the business sector, and public administration, respectively. Thus, civil society, academia, government,

TABLE 3.1 *Overview of the sample*

| Sphere of influence | Affiliation sector | Number of respondents | % of respondents |
|---|---|---|---|
| Economics | Business sector | 27 | 18.1 |
| | Trade unions | 8 | 5.4 |
| Politics | Public administration | 26 | 17.5 |
| Law and order enforcement | Judiciary system | 3 | 2.0 |
| | Legislative system | 1 | 0.7 |
| | Military | 0 | 0 |
| Civil society | Academia | 30 | 20.1 |
| | National NGOs | 33 | 22.2 |
| | Media | 3 | 2.0 |
| | Religious organizations | 1 | 0.7 |
| International stakeholder | Diplomacy | 7 | 4.7 |
| | International NGOs | 10 | 6.7 |
| Total | | 149 | 100 |

*Source:* Authors' calculations based on quantitative survey.

TABLE 3.2 *Composition of the sample*

| Main characteristics | Number of respondents (%)/ number of years (SD) |
|---|---|
| Male | 117 (79) |
| Average age in years (standard deviation) | 48.2 (12.5) |
| Born in Mozambique | 136 (91) |
| Speaks English | 132 (89) |
| Education: university degree | 139 (93) |
| Studied abroad | 94 (63) |
| Studied in the United Kingdom | 16 (11) |
| Occupied a position in the government | 38 (26) |
| Retired | 19 (13) |
| More than 10 years of professional experience | 116 (78) |

*Source:* Authors' calculations based on quantitative survey.

and business are predominant. In relatively smaller numbers, the sample also included individuals affiliated with international NGOs, trade unions, and diplomats. Additionally, thirty-eight respondents occupied a position in the government at the level of national director or above (see Table 3.2).

Table 3.2 provides more detailed information about the characteristics of the sample. Approximately 79 per cent of the sample consisted of male individuals and the average age was forty-eight years. More than 90 per cent of the respondents were born in Mozambique and have a university degree.

TABLE 3.3 *Geographical origin of the respondents*

| Provinces | Province of birth of respondents born in Mozambique | Province of work of respondents who are not retired |
| --- | --- | --- |
| Cabo Delgado | 4 | 2 |
| Gaza | 8 | 1 |
| Inhambane | 19 | 1 |
| Manica | 6 | 0 |
| Maputo (city) | 49 | 81 |
| Maputo | 17 | 31 |
| Nampula | 5 | 4 |
| Niassa | 3 | 1 |
| Sofala | 11 | 1 |
| Tete | 5 | 5 |
| Zambézia | 9 | 3 |

*Source:* Authors' calculations based on quantitative survey.

Regarding their work situation, 78 per cent of the respondents have more than ten years of experience and 13 per cent are retired. In terms of their international experience, 63 per cent studied abroad (11 per cent in the United Kingdom) and almost 90 per cent of the respondents speak English.

The distribution of respondents according to the provinces in Mozambique is represented in Table 3.3, considering both the location where respondents were born and their main location of work. The great majority of the individuals were born in the province of Maputo (city). Following that, the provinces with the highest numbers of respondents are Inhambane, Maputo, and Sofala. In terms of their main work location, almost all of the respondents work in the provinces of Maputo (city) and Maputo, with a few also in Tete and Nampula.

## B Results

### 1 The Most Important Constraints to Economic Development

This section describes the results obtained when we asked respondents to select and order the biggest constraints to economic development in Mozambique out of the fifteen areas referred in Section I. Figure 3.8 shows in part (a) the number of respondents that selected each of the fifteen areas, without considering their ordering in terms of perceived importance. The areas that were chosen more often among the respondents were human capital and poverty and inequality, followed by management of public administration and common vision of national strategy. Among the areas that were not identified as predominantly as main constraints, one finds foreign aid, gender equality, and autonomy in relation to the outside, followed by regulatory quality.

This is confirmed when one looks at the areas that were selected by the respondents as the main constraint to development; that is, areas that received

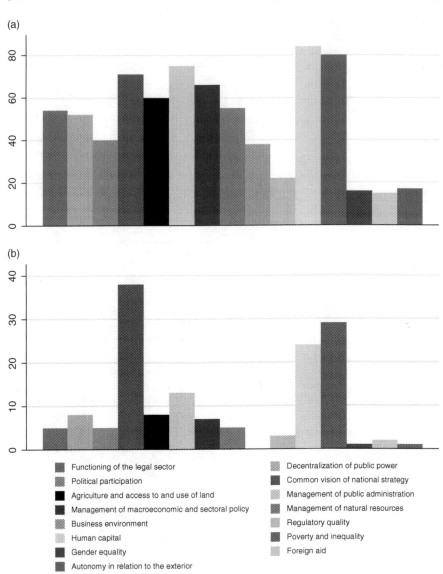

FIGURE 3.8 Choice of main constraints. (a) All ranking positions, number of occurrences. (b) Ranking = 1, number of occurrences
Source: Authors' calculations based on quantitative survey.

a ranking of one more often (Figure 3.8, part (b)). Common vision of national strategy was chosen more often than any of the other areas, in all likelihood reflecting the frequent change of course direction in economic strategy and policy, followed by poverty and inequality and human capital as reasons for the economy and society not working well. Insights from qualitative

TABLE 3.4 *Overview of ranking distribution*

| Areas | Number of occurrences | | | | | |
|---|---|---|---|---|---|---|
| | 1st | 2nd | 3rd | 4th | 5th | Total |
| Functioning of the legal sector | 5 | 8 | 8 | 18 | 15 | 54 |
| Decentralization of public power | 8 | 16 | 10 | 8 | 10 | 52 |
| Political participation | 5 | 5 | 10 | 13 | 7 | 40 |
| Common vision of national strategy | 38 | 12 | 6 | 8 | 7 | 71 |
| Agriculture and access to and use of land | 8 | 6 | 13 | 20 | 13 | 60 |
| Management of public administration | 13 | 22 | 15 | 14 | 11 | 75 |
| Management of macroeconomic and sectoral policy | 7 | 18 | 18 | 13 | 10 | 66 |
| Management of natural resources | 5 | 10 | 12 | 13 | 15 | 55 |
| Business environment | 0 | 6 | 9 | 7 | 16 | 38 |
| Regulatory quality | 3 | 2 | 8 | 5 | 4 | 22 |
| Human capital | 24 | 22 | 18 | 13 | 7 | 84 |
| Poverty and inequality | 29 | 14 | 13 | 11 | 13 | 80 |
| Gender equality | 1 | 4 | 2 | 2 | 7 | 16 |
| Foreign aid | 2 | 1 | 3 | 2 | 7 | 15 |
| Autonomy in relation to the exterior | 1 | 3 | 4 | 2 | 7 | 17 |

*Note:* The three highest numbers of occurrences in each ranking position are highlighted in bold.
*Source:* Authors' calculations based on quantitative survey.

interviews (described in more detail in Section IV) confirm that Mozambique requires a coherent vision and plan to adapt to globalisation and that promoting equality is essential to maintaining a sovereign and united nation. Increasing inequality is likely to undermine social cohesion and stability. In contrast, and maybe somewhat surprisingly, the business environment did not come out at the very top as the main constraint to economic development in Mozambique, and, in line with Figure 3.8 part (a), only a few respondents selected autonomy in relation to the exterior, gender equality, and foreign aid as the main constraint.

Table 3.4 shows the number of occurrences for each area in each position of the ranking. Management of public administration, management of macroeconomic and sectoral policy, and human capital received the highest number of rankings of the second and third most important constraints. In fourth position, most of the respondents selected agriculture and access and use of land, management of public administration once more, and functioning of the legal sector. The last was also one of the most frequently chosen areas in fifth position of the ranking, together with business environment and management of natural resources. This likely reflects that the management of natural resources is understood as a public management/macroeconomic issue and that the constraints associated with the business environment are perceived as less important than agricultural development at this stage and often seen as reflecting the existing lack of human resources.

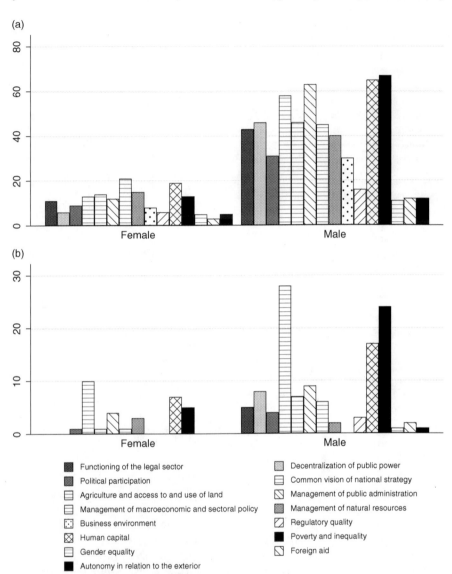

FIGURE 3.9 Choice of main constraints by gender (a) All ranking positions, number of occurrences (b) Ranking = 1, number of occurrences
Source: Authors' calculations based on quantitative survey.

When considering the difference in the choices by gender (Figure 3.9), one observes that female respondents (thirty-two respondents) have selected the management of macroeconomic and sectoral policy as one of the five main constraints more often than any of the other areas (Figure 3.9, part (a)). Still, in line with the male respondents, human capital and poverty and inequality were selected very often. In terms of the area selected as the main constraint

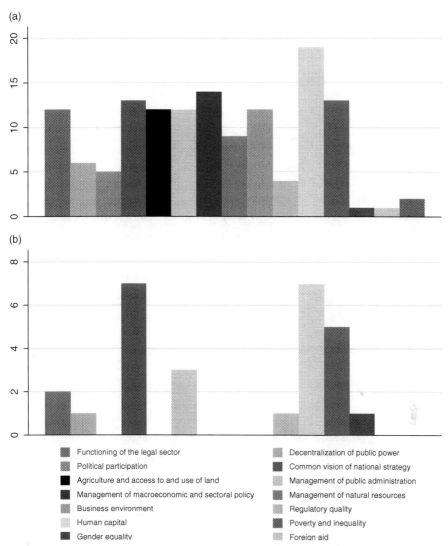

FIGURE 3.10 Choice of main constraints from respondents affiliated with the business sector (a) All ranking positions, number of occurrences (b) Ranking = 1, number of occurrences
Source: Authors' calculations based on quantitative survey.

(Figure 3.9, part (b)), the opinions are similar between male and female respondents, with the lack of a common vision of national strategy being identified as the main constraint more often than the other areas.

In Figures 3.10–3.12, we consider the responses given by respondents affiliated with business, academia, and public administration separately.

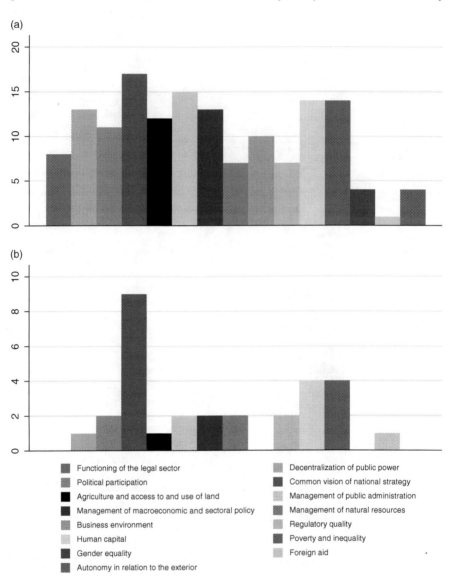

FIGURE 3.11 Choice of main constraints from respondents affiliated with academia (a) All ranking positions, number of occurrences (b) Ranking = 1, number of occurrences
Source: Authors' calculations based on quantitative survey.

Human capital is the constraint that was chosen more often among respondents linked to the business sector, followed by management of macroeconomic and sectoral policy (Figure 3.10, part (a)). When looking at the areas ranked as number one in terms of their importance, both common vision of national strategy and human capital were identified more frequently as the most important constraints (Figure 3.10, part (b)).

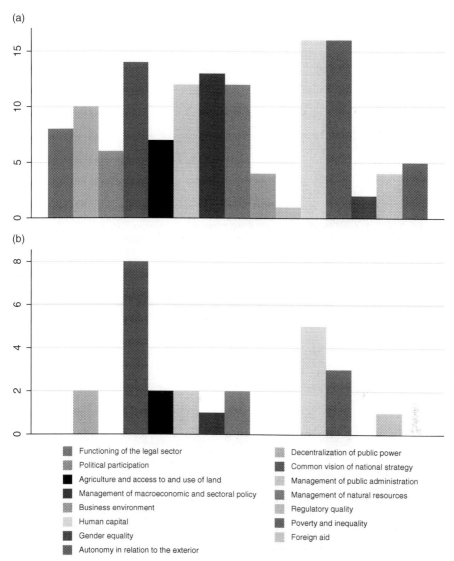

(a)

(b)

Functioning of the legal sector
Political participation
Agriculture and access to and use of land
Management of macroeconomic and sectoral policy
Business environment
Human capital
Gender equality
Autonomy in relation to the exterior

Decentralization of public power
Common vision of national strategy
Management of public administration
Management of natural resources
Regulatory quality
Poverty and inequality
Foreign aid

FIGURE 3.12 Choice of main constraints from respondents affiliated with the public administration (a) All ranking positions, number of occurrences (b) Ranking = 1, number of occurrences
Source: Authors' calculations based on quantitative survey.

Common vision of national strategy is again one of the most selected constraints when we look at the answers from respondents affiliated with academia, followed by management of public administration, human capital, and poverty and inequality (Figure 3.11, part (a)). The last two categories together with common vision of national strategy are also the most commonly ranked as number one in terms of their importance (Figure 3.11, part (b)).

These same three dimensions – common vision of national strategy, human capital, and poverty and inequality – were chosen as important constraints by respondents affiliated with public administration, in both the overall number of occurrences (Figure 3.12, part (a)) and the number of times they were selected as the main constraint (Figure 3.12, part (b)).

### 2 Perceptions of the Quality of Institutions

We now discuss the perceptions of the quality of institutions according to the answers to the 136 statements referred to in Section A. As mentioned, they were grouped in eighteen thematic areas and all respondents expressed their degree of agreement with all of the statements. Figure 3.13 shows the distribution of statements across these eighteen areas.

Before highlighting the main insights from the analysis of the answers, we did a check on the number of respondents that selected 'I don't know' in each statement to identify potential statements that received a lower rate of response. This could be because they were more specific and perhaps required a more in-depth knowledge about the area or because there was some lack of clarity in the formulation. The highest number of 'I don't know' responses (thirty-three responses) referred to the statement 'Auditing of formal firms results in tax adjustments when appropriate'. Three of the other statements with a number of 'I don't know' responses higher than fifteen also belonged

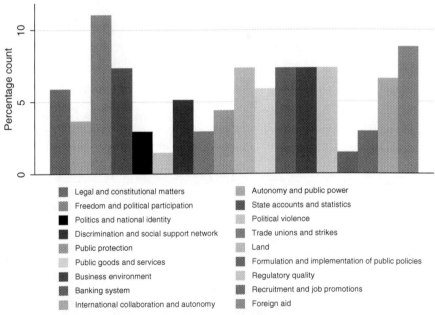

FIGURE 3.13 Distribution of statements by institutional area
Source: Authors' calculations based on quantitative survey.

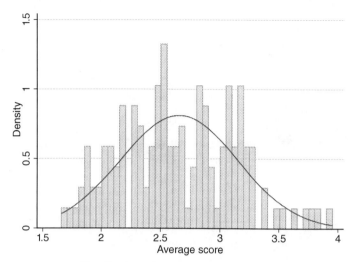

FIGURE 3.14 Distribution of average scores across statements, according to the Likert scores
Source: Authors' calculations based on quantitative survey.

to the group of questions on regulatory quality and required a more detailed knowledge of this area. This might be related also to the fact that regulatory quality was among the areas that were not chosen that often as constraints to economic development. The only other statements with a number of 'I don't know' responses greater than fifteen (eighteen and seventeen responses, respectively) were 'Foreign companies frequently receive support from the state' and 'The unofficial costs (e.g., bribes) of starting a business are high'.

The overall results show an average response of 2.66 across all the statements. This is below the middle level of the scale of score 3, corresponding to 'Don't agree or disagree', suggesting that respondents tend to disagree with positive statements about Mozambican institutions, in line with insights from the qualitative interviews of KIs. Figure 3.14 represents the full distribution of average scores across the statements.

We now describe in more detail the relative frequency of statements within the institutional areas considering their average score. The first group of bars in Figure 3.15 shows the percentage of statements with a score below 2.5 that are related to each institutional area out of all the statements with an average score of 2.5. The second group of bars results from applying the same analysis, but to the statements with an average score above 3. In general, one observes that the opinions regarding the different statements across the institutional areas do not tend to be unanimous, with rather low percentage values even in the areas with higher frequencies.

In terms of the areas where opinions seem to gather one of the more extreme scores, one can mention, for example, legal and constitutional matters, with

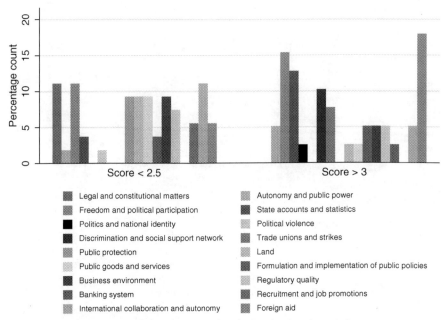

FIGURE 3.15 Frequency of statements under the institutional areas by average scores
Source: Authors' calculations based on quantitative survey.

11.1 per cent of the 54 questions with a score below 2.5 and none of the 39
statements with a score above 3 being related to this institutional area. In
contrast, 17.95 per cent of the statements with a score above 3 are related to
foreign aid and only 5.56 per cent of the statements with a score below 2.5 are
related to this institutional area.

   The institutional areas with a higher frequency of statements with an average score below 2.5 are legal and constitutional matters, freedom and political
participation, and international collaboration and autonomy. These are closely
followed by public protection, land, public goods and services, and business
environment. Freedom and political participation seem to divide the opinion
of respondents, given that there is a high frequency of the statements linked to
this institutional area that have an average score higher than 3. Also showing
high frequencies for statements with average scores higher than 3 are state
accounts and statistics, and foreign aid, as already mentioned.

   Despite these institutional areas being more disaggregated than the institutional constraints analysed in the previous sections, one notices some consistency in the results. Issues related to public protection and to the provision of
public goods and services can be linked to problems of poverty and inequality
and human capital. A link can also be established between a lack of common
vision of national strategy and weaknesses related to legal and constitutional
matters, as well as international collaboration and autonomy.

---

**Box 3.1  Top fifteen major institutional weaknesses**

98. Corruption distorts the business environment. (Yes; 1.66; 99%)

101. Corruption in public administration is prevalent. (Yes; 1.72; 100%)

74. Public services are of an adequate quality. (1.80; 99%)

37. The economic and political influence of the elite class in Mozambique is very strong. (Yes; 1.81; 97%)

76. Coverage of public goods and services is unequal across the country. (Yes; 1.83; 99%)

125. Donors and international organisations are influential with respect to national economic policy. (Yes; 1.86; 99%)

67. Land related conflicts are frequent. (Yes; 1.88; 99%)

3. The judiciary is independent with respect to the state. (1.89; 99%)

1. All citizens are treated equally before the law. (1.90; 99%)

126. Aid is a major contributor to the national budget. (Yes; 1.92; 99%)

2. There is a clear separation of judicial, executive, and legislative powers. (1.95; 99%)

79. Public procurement of goods and services is transparent. (1.96; 98%)

58. Theft is widespread in Mozambique. (Yes; 1.99; 99%)

118. In the past, the country has been affected negatively by political events in neighbouring countries. (Yes; 2.00; 99%)

61. The use of child (below fifteen years old) labour is common in rural areas. (Yes; 2.02; 99%)

Note: The parentheses indicate (i) 'Yes' if the scale was inverted because the statement was phrased in the negative; (ii) the average score obtained according to the following Likert scale: 1 = 'Completely disagree', 2 = 'Disagree', 3 = 'Don't agree or disagree', 4 = 'Agree', and 5 = 'Completely agree'; (iii) the share of the sample giving an opinion on the statement (in percentage).

*Source:* Authors' calculations based on quantitative survey.

---

Next, we focus on the statements that have the lowest and the highest average scores in order to identify what are perceived to be the main weaknesses and strengths, respectively. One should bear in mind that when statements were phrased as negative for the economic development of a country, the Likert scale was inverted so that higher scores reflected better functioning institutions.

Box 3.1 lists the top fifteen major institutional weaknesses according to the lowest average scores. They cover a broad range of institutional areas.

• Corruption seems to affect both the business environment and public administration.

- Three of the statements relate to legal and constitutional matters, highlighting a lack of judicial independence and no separation of judicial, executive, and legislative powers, as well as inequality in the treatment of citizens before the law.
- On average, the respondents agree that there is a very strong economic and political influence of the elite class in Mozambique.
- The scores also indicate some weakness in the provision of public goods and services, which are not of adequate quality and not equally distributed across the country.
- Additionally, respondents agree, on average, that there are frequent conflicts related to land issues.
- There is some suggestion of weak public protection, with the scores pointing to theft being widespread in Mozambique and child labour being common in rural areas.
- Finally, the scores highlight the negative influence of political events in neighbouring countries in the past as well as aid dependence and influence of donors and international organisations in national economic policy.

We now turn to the major institutional strengths, identified based on the highest average scores, which mean agreement with statements that account for positive aspects and disagreement with statements that refer to negative aspects.

Box 3.2 represents the fifteen statements with the highest average scores. Again, they cover a wide range of aspects.

- It is striking to observe that there is agreement in the perception of foreign aid as a strength in Mozambique, given that five of the statements refer to it.
- Three of the statements refer to freedom and political participation. They suggest that people are free to form associations, the media is politically pluralist, and the civil society is able to participate in politics. Related to the latter is the fact that economic policy is actively debated within civil society.
- They also highlight that there is no discrimination and/or segregation on the basis of religion and that traditional solidarity links provide effective support in rural areas.
- Two of the statements relate to public power and autonomy, suggesting that there is political control over the public bureaucracy in Mozambique and that the state is autonomous from religion and traditional norms and values in the formulation and implementation of socio-economic policy and reforms.
- Finally, there is agreement with a strong sense of national identity in Mozambique, together with a significant degree of cooperation with neighbouring countries.

## Box 3.2 Top fifteen major institutional strengths

27. The media is politically pluralist, representing a diversity of viewpoints. (3.25; 98%)
13. The elected political authorities have control over the public bureaucracy. (3.25; 98%)
47. Discrimination and/or segregation by the society on the grounds of religion is prevalent. (Yes; 3.28; 99%)
35. Economic policy is actively debated within civil society. (3.29; 98%)
131. Aid significantly reduces the accountability of government. (Yes; 3.29; 94%)
39. There is a strong sense of national identity in Mozambique. (3.30; 98%)
130. Aid significantly improves the quality of governance institutions. (3.37; 97%)
129. Aid significantly improves the quality of economic policy. (3.38; 98%)
51. Traditional solidarity links (e.g., through family, neighbours, associations, religious groups, etc.) are effective in providing support to those in need in rural areas. (3.47; 94%)
19. Civil society participates in politics, for example, through official commissions, opinion polls, public debates, and op-eds. (3.51; 100%)
88. The state has autonomy in determining and implementing socio-economic policy and reforms independent of religion and traditional norms and values. (3.64; 99%)
120. There is a significant degree of collaboration with neighbouring countries. (3.75; 99%)
25. People are free to form associations to collectively express, promote, pursue, and defend common interests (e.g., religious, ethnic, occupational, political). (3.78; 99%)
127. Aid significantly improves infrastructure development. (3.83; 99%)
128. Aid significantly improves health and education. (3.95; 99%)

Note: The parentheses indicate (i) 'Yes' if the scale was inverted because the statement was phrased in the negative; (ii) the average score obtained according to the following Likert scale: 1 = 'Completely disagree', 2 = 'Disagree', 3 = 'Don't agree or disagree', 4 = 'Agree', and 5 = 'Completely agree'; (iii) the share of the sample giving an opinion on the statement (in percentage).

*Source:* Authors' calculations based on quantitative survey.

TABLE 3.5  *Top issues with significant differences between men and women*

| Statement | Average score female | Average score male | *t*-statistic | *p*-value |
|---|---|---|---|---|
| 110. The Central Bank is managing monetary policy independent of government. | 3.55 | 2.96 | 2.72 | 0.007 |
| 51. Traditional solidarity links (e.g., through family, neighbours, associations, religious groups, etc.) are effective in providing support to those in need in rural areas. | 3.87 | 3.36 | 2.68 | 0.008 |
| 132. Aid significantly increases corruption. | 2.56 | 3.06 | −2.49 | 0.014 |
| 47. Discrimination and/or segregation by the society on the grounds of religion is prevalent. | 2.41 | 2.80 | −2.24 | 0.027 |
| 20. Political corruption, such as vote buying, illegal campaign financing, etc., is prevalent. | 3.43 | 3.90 | −2.15 | 0.033 |
| 66. Land rights are secure in urban areas. | 2.48 | 2.93 | −2.12 | 0.035 |
| 80. Most public policies are guided by a long-term strategic vision. | 2.88 | 2.43 | 2.07 | 0.040 |
| 79. Public procurement of goods and services is transparent. | 2.26 | 1.88 | 2.00 | 0.047 |
| 109. Auditing of formal firms results in tax adjustments when appropriate. | 2.68 | 3.10 | −1.98 | 0.050 |

*Note:* For all the statements, the Likert scale is 1 = 'Completely disagree', 2 = 'Disagree', 3 = 'Don't agree or disagree', 4 = 'Agree', and 5 = 'Completely agree'.
*Source:* Authors' calculations based on quantitative survey.

Lastly, we explore the heterogeneity in respondents' answers according to their gender by listing, in Table 3.5, the nine statements with the largest statistical difference (i.e. largest *t*-statistic derived from two-sample *t*-tests of mean comparisons) between female and male respondents. The main differences in the perceptions of the two groups are related to the independence of the Central Bank in managing the monetary policy and the social support network in rural areas. On average, men tend to agree that aid increases corruption to a stronger degree than women do. The remaining differences are not as big in terms of absolute values, despite being statistically significant.

We repeated the same analysis considering the affiliation of the respondents (Appendix A). Those affiliated with the business sector tend to agree that poverty reduction is a priority for the government, whereas the average response of the remaining respondents is below score 3 (Table A3.1). Additionally, on average, they agree that it is easy for private foreign investors to invest in Mozambique, whereas the average of the remaining responses points to disagreement with this statement (Table A3.1). Academics, on average, seem to be more pessimistic than the remaining respondents in terms of the debate of economic policy within government and parliament, the enforcement of judicial decisions, and the security of land rights in urban areas (Table A3.2). Finally, we find that respondents affiliated with public administration, on average, are more pessimistic than the rest of the respondents in terms of how reactive the public bureaucracy is to changes in the economic and social context (Table A3.3). The same happens for the ability of the opposition to influence political decisions and the predictability of the delivery of government services despite corruption (Table A3.3).

## C  Final Remarks

The overall results of the analysis of the quantitative survey point to the importance of the institutional areas linked to management of public administration and of macroeconomic and sectoral policy, as well as a lack of common vision for a national strategy, as important constraints to economic development. It also seems to be consensual among respondents that problems related to human capital together with poverty and inequality have been impediments to development in Mozambique.

A more detailed analysis of a broad range of institutional areas shows that the answers are spread into different aspects and do not reveal a consensual view on a particular group of constraints. However, there is some indication that there are constraints in the areas of legal and constitutional matters, public protection, and the provision of public goods and services. More specifically, the analysis of the respondents' opinions indicates some weaknesses also in terms of resolution of land issues and of corruption in the business environment and public administration. Some results echo the view that Mozambique has been negatively affected in the past by events in neighbouring countries. However, at the same time, the degree of collaboration with neighbouring countries is highlighted as an institutional strength. Additionally, even though the answers show agreement with a high level of aid dependence, they also suggest that respondents regard development aid as a strength to the economic development process.

IV WHAT DO PEOPLE SAY? KI INTERVIEWS

## A Introduction

This section summarises the views of KIs on major institutional constraints for economic development and their thoughts on possible solutions for the following five fundamental themes:

- rule of law and judicial independence;
- voice, participation, and political accountability;
- political instability, violence, and state legitimacy;
- state capacity and autonomy from private interests;
- sovereignty and independence.

Interviews with 22 KIs – consisting of politicians, business people, academics, and liberal professionals – took place from mid-April to mid-June 2019. During more than 50 hours of interviews, KIs were requested to identify important institutional issues and their perceptions were used to verify the relevance of the five themes and as a basis for further analysis.

Within the framework of the EDI project, 'institutions' were broadly defined as the 'formal or informal rules of the game, which political, social and economic actors are expected to follow, individually and collectively' (EDI 2020).

KIs recognised significant advances in institutional development since Mozambique's independence in 1975, although there were phases when the party in power and government made choices that represented an institutional regression. The country went through periods when institutions were considered as improving and other periods when institutional capacity weakened, and their functions were distorted. Some islands of excellence have been created that seem to persevere, but generally KIs argued that during the past decade some institutions degraded, considering the democratic model as reference and recognising the value of public goods.

As a note on methodology, what is reported in the following sections is a brief set of institutional constraints and proposals for solutions, based on lively KI testimony. Accordingly, this summary is focused more on constraints and less on main institutional advances. Given that many KIs commented on agriculture and education, their views on these sectors are summarised separately. Finally, the conclusion points to a selection of constraints and proposed solutions, which were common to most KI views and seen as relevant for understanding the connections with the economic development.

## B Rule of Law and Judicial Independence

### 1 *Constraints and Causes*

One of the main challenges for the public management in Mozambique is to reinforce a democratic culture. In practice, the country operates under a single-party system. Civil society has been active, but Frente de Libertação de Moçambique (Frelimo) – the Mozambique Liberation Front – finds it difficult to accept criticisms.

The judicial system has been under reform since independence. In the first decade after 1975, there was an attempt to combine the formal justice system, including its courts, with the system of resolution of minor conflicts for the majority of the population. However, after multiparty reforms were implemented, the previous experience was lost. Today, 80 per cent of the population do not solve their conflicts via the courts. The courts serve mainly the wealthy strata of urban centres.

The judicial apparatus is heavy, dispersed in the territory, and inefficient. The aim is that the map of the judiciary should correspond to the administrative map of the territory. However, this correspondence should not be mandatory. A lot has been invested in the 'palaces of justice', but not in the efficient management of the different entities that operate in these buildings. There is also significant inequality in the resources available to the courts in the national and provincial capitals compared with the resources available at district level.

KIs share the perception that there is no independence of the judiciary from the executive. Some KIs believe that the dependence stems from the fact that the judges who lead the Supreme, Administrative, and Constitutional Courts, as well as the Attorney General of the Republic of Mozambique, are appointed by the President of the Republic (PR). This creates an opportunity to demand loyalty, and, therefore, occasionally serious criminal cases are not brought to court.

However, other KIs do not consider this a main factor. They recognise that the appointment systems are quite varied internationally. For example, in the United States of America, the PR appoints the main judges. The important issue is to understand why this system makes the judiciary dependent in Mozambique.

The system of self-governance of the judiciary should be revised. If the Conselho Superior da Magistratura Judicial (CSMJ) – the Superior Council of Judicial Magistrates – has members who accumulate functions of responsibility in the apparatus of the ruling party, this CSMJ is not independent. In the Prosecutor's Office, this failure is even more serious. The Attorney General may instruct a less senior attorney to act under their command.

There are also instances where judges were attacked or killed, allegedly in connection with cases being investigated, but the attackers were not penalised. That is, there are cases of magistrates who made a genuine effort to enforce the law and paid dearly for it. The lack of protection against these incidents and the lack of penalties after the attacks created an environment of fear and legal flaws.

Mozambique had a very small number of lawyers at the time of independence, and for more than a decade, the training of lawyers was neglected when the law school at the only public university was closed. This had a long-term effect on the weakening of the rule of law.

In addition to unsolved criminal cases, which are also of media interest, economic agreements and business contracts are not secure because there are no reliable instruments for orderly conflict resolution in Mozambique. Breaches of contracts and other commercial disputes are often not resolved by the courts in a transparent, impartial, and timely manner.

The police is a complex corporation. Although there are many cases of successfully enforcing the law and discouraging crime, corruption within the police is widespread causing costs and pain to individuals, families, enterprises, and other organisations.

In general, legislation is comprehensive and many laws are being updated. However, owing to the low quality of professionals and the distortions already mentioned, many laws are not being enforced.

The rule of law is not solid enough and the judiciary has a high degree of dependency. Such conditions would pose a threat to any democratic system, impose high costs to society, and create a mistrustful environment towards the judiciary and law-enforcing bodies. There is a link between a fragile rule of law and the declining investment and economic growth.

## 2 Solutions

Some KIs consider that the independence of the judiciary could be strengthened if the presiding judges and the Attorney General were appointed by their peers. Then, the PR could manage the swearing in process for each of them. The annual budget for the judicial system should be approved by the parliament and not be subject to decisions by the executive branch.

However, among KIs there are those who think that it would be more important to understand why the system in Mozambique rewards fidelity and political loyalty to the installed power and does not reward professional merit. The PR has excessive powers, so a constitutional reform is necessary, in combination with a review of the system of self-governance of the judiciary. However, it would be difficult for this proposal to emerge from the executive branch. Civil society could play a dynamic role in reforming the judicial system and the constitution. Attention is needed so that a possible revision of the constitution is not used to alter the positive components of human rights guarantees.

It is necessary to improve the training and qualification of lawyers with the contribution of public funds, as well as in parliamentary procedures, consultations, timely discussions, and the approval of laws.

Arbitration and mediation centres should be combined with the formal judicial system, the commercial sections of the courts, and the tax and customs courts to increase efficiency and ensure justice on the basis of the law and not of the economic power of companies or entrepreneurs.

Better leadership quality in the police, which includes exemplary behaviour regarding law abidance and ethical standards, should help create a trustworthy law enforcement organisation.

## C Voice, Participation, and Political Accountability

### 1 *Constraints and Causes*

Current electoral legislation, regulations, and electoral institutions are designed in such a way that they result in non-transparent, non-free, and unfair elections. Allegations of fraud in presidential, parliamentary, and local elections are recurrent, indicating that they serve the interests of the party in power.

Only 70 out of 250 members of parliament are active in parliamentary committees. They review laws, visit constituencies, and monitor the executive. The remaining members participate in the plenary sessions, but are not engaged in standing or ad hoc committees. As a result, they do not participate in important parliament activities, undermining their oversight role and failing to represent their constituencies.

Mozambique needs more checks and balances in general and one key issue is the presidential powers. They are broadly defined and overarching.

Although KIs did acknowledge that Mozambique has no political prisoners, some indicated that there is political persecution for those individuals who decide to be members of an opposition party. Such individuals can be sacked from high positions in the state apparatus and can be rejected for job positions in civil society organisations and in donor community entities.

The police is also being used to prevent civil society and the opposition parties to exercise freely their advocacy and electoral rights.

Some people who advocate in favour of legal reforms on constitutional and decentralisation matters are intimidated or murdered, and the perpetrators/murderers are never caught or prosecuted.

It was alluded that while both civil society and public institutions have grown in their capacity for action, compared with 1975 or even 1992, in the last decade, the government gradually reduced the space and as a result civil society became weaker. Parliament became less effective, thus weakening the democratic system.

In such a weakened democratic system, individual and family elite interests dominate, including partly capturing the state, which increases the likelihood of distorted economic incentives and slows down poverty reduction. It contributes to low productivity levels in agriculture and related activities, prevents technology advances in smallholder producers, and keeps local and foreign investors demotivated from investing in manufacturing and competitive services.

### 2 *Solutions*

The KIs suggested that the electoral law and institutions need reform to ensure transparent and fair elections and to prevent fraud. Mozambique also needs a constitutional reform that reduces the powers of the presidency. This power reduction should be combined with the diminishing role of the party in power over the state apparatus and with the enforcement of the prohibition law.

The parliament needs reform so its members effectively represent their constituencies, instead of being mostly obliged to follow the top-down party decisions. There is also need for reform in regulations, and parliament members need training, so that all of them participate in standing and ad hoc committees.

Some civil society organisations have good and successful experience in combining advocacy activities with training national public institutions like the police, lawyers, and other judiciary staff members on human rights; gender equality; and the rights of vulnerable and other discriminated citizens.

## D  Political Instability, Violence, and State Legitimacy

### 1  Constraints and Causes

Mozambican history is full of instability and violence related to movements and entities questioning the legitimacy of the state. According to the KIs, recent violence breakouts in the north of Mozambique are caused by exclusion of young people, who do not have access to quality education and good job opportunities. Also, fishermen in the north of Mozambique who were moved from coastal fishing areas to zones without fishing or other job opportunities feel excluded. There is a perception that suppression and violent retaliation from the authorities provoke further violence from a mostly young population. In addition, indiscriminate violence exercised by the authorities towards some communities including innocent people makes recruitment easy for the terrorists.

The creation of good job and business opportunities by the natural gas companies benefited only a limited number of people. This is similar for mineral coal and for other high-value minerals companies. This situation exacerbated the feeling of exclusion and unfairness towards state authorities.

The unequal distribution of government resources between north-central and southern parts of the country also affects state legitimacy in the central and northern parts of Mozambique and undermines nation building.

A higher degree of decentralisation could have a positive or negative impact depending on the way it is done. It can be positive if public funds are used to achieve planned targets with minimum loss/deviation and to improve decision-making and living conditions of local communities. Decentralisation can have negative effects when it is used to channel resources to local elites in the winner parties, buying loyalty and political capital while preventing local communities from benefiting.

Some KIs believe that a deeper political and economic democratic system would allow for an increase in productive investments in Mozambique. A larger aggregate effect on the economic growth would kick in, instead of the current situation where rent-seeking interests seem to dominate the state in a zero-sum game logic. In a free market economy, the strength and potential of a broader democratic system are much larger than a system characterised by abuse of power, inequalities, rent seeking, and corruption.

Resistência Nacional Moçambicana (Renamo) – the Mozambican National Resistance – maintained its army because it did not trust that the ruling party – Frelimo – would allow for an inclusive participation of citizens from all political, social, and territorial groups in public affairs and democratic opportunities. Frelimo would keep control of the defence and security forces (DSF) and use them to marginalise opposition parties. That is, DSF are not non-partisan, failing to observe the constitutional guarantee and key requirements of any modern democratic system.

It was stated that Frelimo aims to keep power at all cost in order to advance the national interest agenda. However, private interests are fused into the national/political party agenda and, through the government, the state gets 'captured'. As such, the elite in Frelimo and many individuals/families affiliated to this political party are profiting from this approach. One direct consequence of this situation and of the widespread corruption around it is the hidden debt equal to 10 per cent of gross domestic product, which was contracted by the government on behalf of a small elite. This provoked an economic and political crisis. The crisis affected the economic growth rate; poverty and inequality increased, whereas social, political, and security conditions deteriorated. Underlying this crisis is a distorted strategy based on the extraction of natural resources – natural gas, oil, coal, and other valuable minerals – which is neglecting mainly smallholder producers in agriculture and related activities as well as youth employment.

KIs perceived that there are Frelimo members who do not agree with the approach above – elite private interests mixed with state interests – and seek alternatives by advocating for a leadership style that will inspire trust from society in the state and the ruling party and will gradually lead to an optimal development of net social welfare.

For a long time, Frelimo has not been receptive to studies and solutions proposed by people who are not party members or who do not enjoy party confidence. There is a strong belief among party members that only those who fought in the liberation war against the colonialists are able to bring change.

## 2 Solutions

State legitimacy can be re-established by applying the principles of separation of the three powers: executive, parliamentary, and judiciary; by enforcing free, transparent, and fair elections; by promoting honest, competent, and strategic leaders; by separating party interests from the DSF; and by allowing an effective and sustainable decentralisation of powers and resources. Different degrees of power alternation or power sharing would contribute to increasing trust between political parties and to opening opportunities for improving the quality of opposition parties within a peaceful framework.

A democratic system with alternation of political parties in power is possible if elites live based on income earned from labour or capital-based activities, or on a developed mechanism of social security. It is not the current opposition but rather the healthy alternation of parties in power that represents opportunities for access to economic productive gains, a larger net social benefit, and a more stable and powerful society. The effective democratic mechanisms will allow for sustainable peace and national reconciliation.

## E  State Capacity and Autonomy from Private Interests

### 1  Constraints and Causes

KIs concur that the number of civil servants and state organisations is too high. There are too many ministries and institutions and too frequent remodelling of government structure. The competences between sector ministries and their subordinating institutions often change for short-term political gains. The lack of clarity on competences blurs responsibility and it implies a heavy burden on the budget. The oversized state apparatus serves the purpose of offering jobs to acquaintances, family members, and the 'comrades', with a view to forming a politically loyal group. The consequence is an ineffective and expensive state, which fails to address the needs of the people for public goods.

For instance, a few KIs indicated that some of these state organisations and positions were not needed, namely, permanent secretaries in the ministries as well as many advisory positions at ministerial cabinets. The positions of the minister and directors would be enough to manage the state affairs in each area. However, this view was not consensual. Other KIs indicated that good-quality and experienced advisers are relevant to the government, including to the PR. In fact, informal and low-profile advisers were viewed as an asset.

The selection of staff and promotions are neither transparent nor based on merit reflecting professional qualifications and results. Many qualified professionals are driven out of state institutions due to low pay or a non-motivating work environment.

Criteria for promotions to the level of national director no longer require experience as provincial director. At the district and local levels, frequently appointed state representatives do not have enough skills to perform their duties. This is so even if this is an essential function. The individual capacity to plan and implement at district level affects the life of many people. Yet, district administrators are nominated based on political loyalty. Most of them are not properly trained and their mission is ambiguous. There is a chronic mismatch between resources and plans and, as district administrators are judged on political affiliation and not on results, the entire planning exercise becomes of secondary importance.

The current proposal to duplicate the role of the provincial governor by appointing a new state secretary may bring additional dysfunction and unnecessary cost at provincial level.

## 2 *Solutions*
The KIs proposed to:

- reduce the size and simplify the structure of the state apparatus;
- keep line ministries for longer periods to ensure institutional stability and quality;
- select and promote staff on professional and merit-based criteria; and
- promote personnel training, supervision, and effective management practices to improve quality performance.

Furthermore, they suggested strengthening training and education of leaders at district level as a *sine qua non* for an effective and efficient application of policies and plans. A specialised training curriculum would be useful, and a non-partisan nomination based on professional qualifications would be necessary.

## F Sovereignty and Independence

### 1 *Constraints and Causes*
Mozambique is a relatively young and low-income country born in the middle of the Cold War where neutrality and de facto sovereignty were rare in Africa. The struggle for independence united the country, and the new leadership enjoyed phenomenal backing and popularity at first. When it tried to become an economic sovereign state after independence under a centrally planned economy, this system failed as the country was torn apart by an internal war, also supported by foreign interests.

The International Monetary Fund (IMF), the World Bank, and the international community contributed positively to the transition to a market economy and a democratic society, through a series of reforms after the war and multiparty and general elections. In this process, it seemed that Mozambique was losing sovereignty. There were many foreign entities trying to influence developments in Mozambique. International financial institutions, donors, and NGOs all wanted policy dialogue and insisted on conditionalities to the point where strong contradictions occurred between the government and the international counterparts.

One result of this transition was that the country developed a system of economic efficiency, which is a major feature to attain economic sovereignty. In this system, the value of inputs has to be lower than the value of outputs. Government cannot consistently spend more than it collects.

Some KIs recognised that today there are signs of reversal of this system of economic efficiency. The proposed labour law over-protects workers, such that it may become extremely difficult to lay them off. The official minimum salary is increasing without a link to productivity. According to an unwritten rule, public companies are expected to run losses in order to feed the 'children of the people'. This goes for job creation as well as pricing of services. When Mozambique bought back the Cahora Bassa Dam and the electricity company, people wondered why they would still need to pay for electricity. An inefficient economic environment most likely will jeopardise the economic sovereignty of the country.

Foreign investors and interests, especially in the natural resources sector, are well connected and use their leverage to shape the rules in their favour. Foreign players need the endorsement and help of national elites for their establishment in the country. This is an ongoing process and once it is done, the scene will be set for decades. Moreover, there are foreign interests also acting in the country in illicit businesses.

Today, some people live in the hi-tech world but the majority of people still live in poor conditions. Inequality is high and a problem.

## 2 Solutions

KIs argued that a sound economic management is the means to ensure economic sovereignty. The labour market should operate in a competitive way, such that both the private and the public sectors have the opportunity of employing the most efficient labour force. These are conditions for companies to prosper in the domestic market and for some of them to compete in the international market. Public enterprises should, at least, be able to cover the costs of operation and, at best, to reinvest in modernisation and expansion.

Mozambique needs a strong leadership with integrity and clear national policies and plans to guide its interaction with foreign interests and to manage globalisation. It must go hand in hand with international treaties enacted through national legislation, which is enforced.

Mozambique has a challenge to adapt to globalisation and will only survive as a truly sovereign nation if it has a coherent plan of its own and strong leadership to manage it. Here, equality is of great importance to keep the nation sovereign and united.

## G Views on Agriculture

### 1 Constraints and Causes

The level of productivity in the main food crops has changed little in the past fifty years. The income of smallholder producers remains at subsistence level. Poverty levels are higher in rural than in urban areas. The dominant technology is still manual. The labour force in agriculture, fisheries, and related activities is still very large, at 70 per cent of total labour force. Large public investments have been directed to various agriculture projects and programmes, national roads, schools and health centres across the entire country, and the electricity national grid. Moreover, agriculture has been defined in the constitution as the basis for national development. Nevertheless, agriculture is still at a low development level.

After independence, the transition to a socialist system of production, central planning, communal villages, and large public companies operating in agriculture helped very little to create incentive mechanisms for smallholder producers.

The network of rural traders – *cantineiros* – disappeared. It was replaced by a public trading company, Agricom. The internal war, also supported by foreign interests, helped destroy trading networks, commercial flows, and infrastructures – roads, bridges, schools, and health centres.

After the war in 1992, there were efforts to reinvest in public infrastructures, on education and health. However, the World Bank and IMF policies prevented the government from defining public policies in support of agricultural production. The argument was that there was a need for reducing the public deficit. As an alternative, there were ad hoc projects like the Mozambique–Nordic Agriculture Programme and donor-funded programmes like ProAgri that were not sustainable and missed the purpose of supporting smallholder producers.

The Ministry of Agriculture went through a period of high instability, frequently changing its denomination: MADER (Ministerio da Agricultura e Desenvolvimento Rural), MINAG (Ministerio da Agricultura), MASA (Ministerio da Agricultura e Seguranca Alimentar). There were excessive changes of ministers and national directors. Many ad hoc document policies were produced, with a low degree of budgetary sustainability. Finally, the '7 million' policy, which was a make-believe agricultural and rural policy, was in fact a mechanism for presidential control and management of local authorities. As a result of this systematic institutional and policy instability and fragility, smallholder producers kept producing at low productivity levels, with mostly manual technology and earning subsistence levels of income.

Smallholder producer organisations were created and dominated by the party in power. Organisations like União Nacional de Camponeses – the Peasants' National Union – were not endogenously created and developed. Therefore, they were not vehicles to defend and promote smallholder producer interests.

KIs recognised that, since independence, efforts were made to train thousands of professionals in agricultural matters. There were also programmes to improve seeds and provide inputs, including machinery and equipment; successful out-grower projects in tobacco[5] and cotton; successful policy in sugar cane plantations; development of financial schemes and institutions dedicated to agriculture activities; various rural development programmes; and new products for exports like soya beans and sesame. In sum, there are also some successes to be told. Unfortunately, the failures outweigh the successes.

### 2 Solutions

According to the KIs, land use rights should serve the purpose of providing income sources for smallholder agriculture producers and for the communities. Land use rights should not be monopolised by state bureaucrats for their own appropriation and transactions, as if the land was owned by the state elite and civil servants.

---

[5] There were KIs who argued that tobacco production cannot be considered a success due to the negative health effects of tobacco.

Smallholder producer unions, associations, and cooperatives should be endogenously created and developed and not created and dominated by the party in power.

The Ministry of Agriculture needs long-term stability in terms of its basic functions. The same applies to public institutions dealing with land, environment, rural development, food security, and forestry matters. It should focus on elaborating and implementing long-term plans for agriculture, which need to have sustainable budgetary and financing components.

Agricultural policies need to be coordinated at central, provincial, district, and local levels. Vertical coordination is also required between central and provincial, provincial and district, and district and local levels. However, there is an underlying assumption: It is the smallholder producer who should decide what to produce rather than the PR, the minister, the national director, the provincial governor, or the district administrator.

Further development of financial and insurance institutions is needed to support agriculture, fisheries, and related production sectors. It was suggested that these institutions should be co-owned by smallholder producers.

There is a need for sustainable investment in research and development as well as in advances in production technology for agriculture and related sectors.

## H  Views on Education

### 1  Constraints and Causes

There has been massive investment in education since independence. Mozambique has achieved significant results in the number of people who have been educated. However, quality in education is lacking at all levels: primary, secondary, higher, and technical–professional.

The policy to allow all students to transit to higher education levels without having minimum quality standards represents a major failure of the education system.

Quality of education in technical and professional schools has been low. For instance, frequently the laboratories in these schools are not properly equipped. When students graduate, most are not sufficiently qualified for tasks in the job market. Many companies have to invest in additional on-the-job training so that newly hired professionals reach the minimum required standards.

It is estimated that about 300,000 young people enter the job market every year. It represents a very high number of people in need of finding employment. At the same time, there is a need for training and qualifying personnel in new areas like cybernetics security, robotics, and artificial intelligence. Universities should be investing in these areas as well. Unfortunately, mainstream national policies still focus on traditional fields, neglecting the new science and technology areas.

The proliferation and subdivision of universities and other higher education institutions go against the objective of improving education quality and represent expensive clientelism.

## 2 *Solutions*

There is a need to introduce quality standards in education, both for teachers and for students. It is important to ensure that students learn how to read and write in primary school. For other education levels, it is also required to ensure minimum qualification standards.

Education policies should be separated from political interests. These interests represent an attempt to obtain parents' votes by allowing students to graduate to higher levels without satisfying minimum required standards.

There is a need to invest sustainably and consistently in fields that the Mozambican economy requires, like agriculture, fisheries, and tourism.

## I Summary of KI Observations

The KIs highlighted the following:

- The judicial system remains weak and not independent of the executive power.
- The rule of law needs reinforcement to prevent/discourage crime and enforce contracts.
- Democratic institutions and regulations need reform to ensure a more inclusive society and bolster it against elite capture and – ultimately – foreign dominance.
- The state apparatus requires better-qualified personnel, downsizing, and a more stable structure, manned by professionals selected and promoted using objective and merit criteria.
- Legislation and institutions should be adapted to further general economic efficiency in the markets, including in public enterprises.
- Decentralisation, including of the public finance system, and a serious reform in agricultural and fisheries policies are required for increased productivity and income levels mostly for smallholder producers.
- There is a need for investment in education quality at all levels, and improvement of technical and professional education.
- Mozambique is a low-income country, and it could make better and more careful use of foreign investments and aid. It is under foreign pressure for its riches, natural resources, and strategic location. It should have its own coherent plan and good quality leadership with integrity, working towards an inclusive Mozambican society to stay independent and peaceful.

## V CONCLUSION

In concluding this chapter, we briefly put together the results from the analysis of existing institutional indicators, the quantitative survey, and the KI interviews, recognizing that these methodological approaches are complementary and not necessarily aligned with each other.

The description of the different institutional indicators points to an overall deterioration of the performance of Mozambique when comparing the early 2000s to the present day. The following institutional constraints were identified as important in both the quantitative survey and the KI interviews:

- agricultural issues and the need for inclusive development;
- human capital/education;
- provision of public goods and services;
- management of public administration and decentralisation;
- legal and constitutional matters and public protection;
- natural resources and corruption.

Finally, the common vision for a national strategy was referred as important in the quantitative survey, and this need appeared as central in the KI interviews in relation to a long-term plan for the agriculture sector. This also relates to the critical importance of donor relations and sovereignty issues. The thematic studies that follow in Chapters 4–11 develop many of these areas.

APPENDIX A

TABLE A3.1 *Top issues with significant differences between respondents affiliated with the business sector and the other respondents*

| Statement | Average score business | Average score non-business | *t*-statistic | *p*-value |
|---|---|---|---|---|
| 120. There is a significant degree of collaboration with neighbouring countries. | 3.85 | 3.30 | 3.36 | 0.001 |
| 81. Poverty reduction is a priority for the government. | 3.19 | 2.37 | 3.27 | 0.001 |
| 34. Economic policy is actively debated within government and parliament. | 3.01 | 2.41 | 2.69 | 0.008 |
| 80. Most public policies are guided by a long-term strategic vision. | 2.62 | 2.08 | 2.37 | 0.019 |
| 97. Firms abide by the minimum wage laws. | 2.98 | 3.48 | −2.19 | 0.030 |
| 102. Despite corruption, government services are delivered in a predictable manner. | 2.78 | 2.30 | 2.16 | 0.032 |
| 60. The use of child (below 15-years-old) labour is common in urban areas. | 3.92 | 3.50 | 2.14 | 0.034 |

TABLE A3.1 *(continued)*

| Statement | Average score business | Average score non-business | *t*-statistic | *p*-value |
|---|---|---|---|---|
| 108. It is easy for private foreign investors to invest in Mozambique. | 3.19 | 2.70 | 2.13 | 0.035 |
| 90. The business environment is an impediment to private sector development. | 3.62 | 4.04 | −2.07 | 0.041 |

*Note:* For all the statements, the Likert scale is 1 = 'Completely disagree', 2 = 'Disagree', 3 = 'Don't agree or disagree', 4 = 'Agree', and 5 = 'Completely agree'.
*Source:* Authors' calculations based on quantitative survey.

TABLE A3.2 *Top issues with significant differences between respondents affiliated with academia and the other respondents*

| Statement | Average score academia | Average score non-academia | *t*-statistic | *p*-value |
|---|---|---|---|---|
| 18. The electoral process is fair. | 2.20 | 2.83 | −2.63 | 0.010 |
| 34. Economic policy is actively debated within government and parliament. | 2.79 | 3.34 | −2.55 | 0.012 |
| 2. There is a clear separation of judicial, executive, and legislative powers. | 1.84 | 2.38 | −2.50 | 0.014 |
| 16. The way in which the executive governs is an impediment to development. | 3.63 | 3.03 | 2.49 | 0.014 |
| 30. Official statistics on poverty and inequality are produced regularly. | 3.00 | 3.50 | −2.37 | 0.019 |
| 7. Judicial decisions are taken in a timely manner once the matter gets to the court. | 1.96 | 2.39 | −2.35 | 0.020 |
| 54. Collective bargaining is prevalent. | 3.08 | 3.52 | −2.18 | 0.031 |
| 8. Judicial decisions are enforced. | 2.77 | 3.20 | −2.16 | 0.033 |
| 66. Land rights are secure in urban areas. | 2.74 | 3.20 | −2.14 | 0.034 |

*Note:* For all the statements, the Likert scale is 1 = 'Completely disagree', 2 = 'Disagree', 3 = 'Don't agree or disagree', 4 = 'Agree', and 5 = 'Completely agree'.
*Source:* Authors' calculations based on quantitative survey.

TABLE A3.3 *Top issues with significant differences between respondents affiliated with the public administration and the other respondents*

| Statement | Average score public administration | Average score non-public administration | *t*-statistic | *p*-value |
|---|---|---|---|---|
| 72. The public bureaucracy is reactive to changes in the economic and social context. | 2.69 | 3.32 | −3.00 | 0.003 |
| 20. Political corruption, such as vote buying, illegal campaign financing, etc., is prevalent. | 3.91 | 3.29 | 2.61 | 0.010 |
| 10. Elected provincial and local authorities have autonomy with respect to the central government regarding local politics. | 2.43 | 3.00 | −2.57 | 0.011 |
| 22. Opposition to the ruling government, from both political parties and civil society, is able to influence political decisions. | 3.15 | 2.64 | 2.57 | 0.011 |
| 119. Today the country is negatively affected by political events in neighbouring countries. | 3.24 | 2.67 | 2.54 | 0.012 |
| 102. Despite corruption, government services are delivered in a predictable manner. | 2.60 | 3.12 | −2.24 | 0.026 |
| 43. The use of violence by political organizations is prevalent. | 3.55 | 3.08 | 2.11 | 0.036 |
| 35. Economic policy is actively debated within civil society. | 3.20 | 3.72 | −2.11 | 0.037 |
| 61. The use of child (below 15 years old) labour is common in rural areas. | 4.05 | 3.65 | 2.03 | 0.044 |

*Note:* For all the statements, the Likert scale is 1 = 'Completely disagree', 2 = 'Disagree', 3 = 'Don't agree or disagree', 4 = 'Agree', and 5 = 'Completely agree'.
*Source:* Authors' calculations based on quantitative survey.

PART II

# THEMATIC PAPERS

# 4

## The Relative Neglect of Agriculture in Mozambique

João Z. Carrilho, Ines A. Ferreira, Rui de Nazaré
Ribeiro, and Finn Tarp

## I INTRODUCTION

The Constitution of the Republic of Mozambique[1] (Article 103) stipulates:
'agriculture shall be the basis for national development', and 'the State shall
guarantee and promote rural development in order to meet the growing and
diverse needs of the people, and for the economic and social progress of the
country'. Moreover, Article 105 about the family sector[2] highlights that 'the
family sector shall play a fundamental role in meeting the basic needs of
the people', and that 'the State shall support and provide incentives for family
sector production, and shall encourage peasants as well as individual workers
to organize themselves into more advanced forms of production'. This reflects
that the large majority of the Mozambican population – about 65 per cent –
lives in rural areas, and rural areas are home to about 75 per cent of the poor
(DEEF 2016).

Moreover, in rural areas, agriculture is by far the most common economic
activity.[3] Yet, those families whose heads work in agriculture present poverty
incidence rates that are substantially higher than for the rest of the population
(Castigo and Salvucci 2017). Importantly, the poverty-growth elasticity for
agriculture is three times higher, compared to that of other sectors (World
Bank 2019). Accordingly, the Mozambican Ministry of Economics and
Finance (MEF) concludes in the Fourth National Assessment of Poverty and
Well-Being that: '[...] the findings in this report inescapably imply that future
dynamics in smallholder agriculture [...] will be of fundamental importance

---

[1] See www.constituteproject.org/constitution/Mozambique_2007.pdf?lang=en.
[2] The small farmer agriculture sector is in Mozambique and in Portuguese referred to as 'o sector
familiar', that is the family sector. We use family sector and family farm sector interchangeably
in what follows.
[3] About 76 per cent of rural household heads declare to be peasants (DEEF 2016).

to achieving continued broad-based progress in welfare enhancement over at least the next decade and likely longer than that' (DEEF 2016).

Nonetheless, the gap in the poverty incidence between rural and urban areas has widened in recent years, from seven to about thirteen percentage points,[4] and regional imbalances between southern, central, and northern Mozambique have developed unfavourably (Egger et al. 2020). Other well-being indicators such as access to safe water sources, quality sanitation, electricity, etc. are also disproportionally concentrated in urban versus rural areas and along regional (north, centre, and south) lines, raising concerns about the model of development followed and the inherent sector prioritiszations.

At a macroeconomic level, agriculture remains among the most important economic sectors, contributing to about a quarter of Mozambican gross domestic product (GDP) and occupying more than three quarters of the population.[5] At the same time, only 6 per cent of the state budget expenditures is allocated to the sector, well below the African Union commitment of 10 per cent (Nova et al. 2019: 6).

Jensen and Tarp (2004) demonstrate the clear socio-economic benefits of following an Agricultural Development Led Industrialisation (ADLI) strategy in the case of Mozambique. The basic arguments are articulated in Adelman (1984) and were successfully pursued in Ethiopia in more recent decades (see Stifel and Woldehanna 2016, and references therein). This strategy views 'agriculture as the engine of growth, based on its potentially superior growth linkages, surplus generation, market creation and provision of raw materials and foreign exchange' (Teka et al. 2013: 947). More specifically, it includes a major public investment programme to shift the supply curve of agriculture as an integral element of an overall growth and employment programme keeping in mind that agriculture is by far the most labour-intensive production sector (Adelman 1984). Simultaneously, the ADLI approach contributes to poverty reduction and increased food security. Jensen and Tarp (2004) bring out these synergy effects from pursuing balanced agricultural and agro-industrial development in a general equilibrium context and show that primary sector export-oriented progress represents a potential significant set of complementary actions.

From a different methodological approach, taking into account both supply- and demand-side factors,[6] Sørensen et al. (2020) confirm that priority should

---

[4] The poverty rate for rural areas was 54 per cent in 2008/09, and it went to 50 per cent in 2014/15, whereas the poverty rate for urban areas was 47 per cent in 2008/09 and went to 37 per cent in 2014/15.

[5] This proportion has hardly moved over time, raising concerns about the process of structural transformation in the country.

[6] In their supply-side analysis, they use network methods to identify a set of target products that are complex, require productive capabilities useful in the export of other products, and are close to Mozambique's existing productive structure, while in their demand-side analysis they rely on gravity models to predict the export potential of target products and markets given product-specific trade resistance and geographically dispersed demand.

be given to agriculture, agro-industry, and metal products, especially when the potential for structural transformation and export growth are considered simultaneously.

Turning to the economic performance of the agriculture sector, broad consensus exists about a few stylized facts.

- First, productivity has been stagnant for most staple crops, both per hectare and per capita, over a very long time period, associated with the fact that the median plot size is only about 0.5 hectares.
- Second, the quality and level of public support services for farmers are far from adequate. Excluding some cash crops like cotton or tobacco, fertilizer and improved seed use is very limited, and access to credit and to extension agents is severely constrained. Moreover, the public institutions in the agriculture sector have delegated the responsibility for direct liaison with small farmers to companies, NGOs, and projects. Thus, by design, the implementation capacity of the public service is limited in scope and coverage and depends on private, other domestic, and foreign interests.
- Third, despite its weight in food production and land use, the family farm sector lacks critical access to inputs and output market outlets. Market access and integration are severely constrained and in many cases non-existent due to the absence of infrastructure (transport and storage, etc.). Moreover, a gamut of market failures is widespread in the family sector, delinking farmers from market processes and access to credit to promote, process, and store production of agricultural products.
- Fourth, exposure to risks and price volatility remains very high. While the concerns with price volatility attracted much attention during the 2007/08 food price crisis (see Nhate et al. 2014), the risks associated with climate shocks and climate change have become increasingly clear and relevant in recent years, as demonstrated by the catastrophic effects of cyclones Kenneth and Idai.

All these elements reflect that Mozambique's agriculture is mostly subsistence agriculture. Commercial agriculture exists, and while expanding in relevance and scope, it remains confined to a few geographic areas and to a limited number of crops.

The aim of this chapter is to put the weak performance of the agriculture sector in perspective and identify underlying factors for this state of affairs, focusing on institutional instability and the inability of the state to provide basic services to small-scale farmers in the family farm sector. One core argument is that frequent organisational changes compromised the ability of key stakeholders to plan, structure, consolidate, and promote dialogue, from central to local levels. Key conclusions include that it is imperative to pursue a concerted reorientation in existing strategies, policies, and priorities. This is so especially in light of the upcoming revenue from natural resource extraction, which offers both socio-economic risks and opportunities (see Page and Tarp 2020).

We organised the chapter as follows.[7] Section II reviews the agriculture economy and its performance in some detail, while Section III discusses existing institutional weaknesses. Section IV brings out the underlying factors, and Section V reflects on future challenges and provides some policy considerations.

## II  THE AGRICULTURE ECONOMY

Mozambique inherited at independence in 1975 a distorted economy characterized by:

- Economic integration with neighbouring countries in which Mozambique was to a large extent a service economy dependent on the provision of transport services and the supply of migrant labour.
- Production of primary commodities for export (cashew, cotton, sugar, copra, and tea), linked to some elementary processing industries.
- A colonial system based on temporary migrant labour to the mines in South Africa and with internal production oriented towards meeting settler needs. A foreign commercial sector had managed this economy through direct production and ownership of modern farms, including marketing control of cash crops produced by the traditional sector and control of food imports.

Concerted efforts took place after independence to transform this system, but the introduction of state farms to take over farms abandoned by the colonial settlers collapsed. More recently, a commercial subsector has started to emerge, characterised by growth in capital-intensive investment, production, and productivity. Private investment is mainly foreign, aimed at export crops and to a lesser extent supplying large urban consumer centres. However, this sector remains incipient and small.

In contrast, the small farmer sector is responsible for 99 per cent of the cultivated area and 95 per cent of food production. It includes two-thirds of the country's working population, who have limited job opportunities outside of agriculture (Jones and Tarp 2012). The family agriculture system is expanding through an increase in the number of farms, which are getting smaller (Mosca and Nova 2019). This reflects demographic dynamics without increasing the total area, low use of technologies to increase productivity, vulnerability to weather variations, and an annual loss of forests estimated at 3 to 4 per cent of the cultivated area. The level of food insecurity remains high as does the number of vulnerable people (Egger et al. 2020), though food insecurity fell from 34.8 per cent in 2006 to 23.7 per cent in 2013 (MASA website[8]). Major food crops in the family sector are cassava, maize,

---

[7] For further background, statistics, and analysis we refer to Carrilho and Ribeiro (2020).
[8] See www.agricultura.gov.mz/estatisticas/san/.

groundnuts, cowpeas, sorghum, and millet, representing an overall majority of the food energy intake at the national level, and with little overall progress over the past two decades.[9]

There are ample water resources in the country especially from the river systems (such as the Zambezi, the Save, or the Limpopo) and from irregular rainfall. The latter is a determinant of the variation in cropping practices and thus a big cause of food insecurity. Due to their more regular rainfall, ample land and fertile soil, the northern and central areas of the country are more suitable for intensive farming. In contrast, rainfall is less predictable and scarcer in the southern regions, where extensive agricultural practices and animal husbandry are more prevalent. Furthermore, the country is abundant in terms of energy, water, forest, mineral and marine resources.[10]

The above lack of progress is highlighted in MASA (2016: 10) where it is noted that 'comparing the economic conditions in 2015 with three years ago, 20.9 per cent of the farms said there had been an improvement, 32.3 per cent believed economic conditions were neither better nor worse, and 46.8 per cent said that they were worse'.

Turning to other recent trends,[11] over the last ten years, while there was an increase in the number of farms, accompanying population growth, the total cultivated area did not increase proportionally (MASA 2015: 22; MASA 2016: 22). While rural–urban migration does indeed occur, the increase in the urban population is mainly driven by natural growth (Hansine and Arnaldo 2019: 307).[12] Moreover, per capita production of food declined, as did productivity per hectare of food crops; total livestock increased, but only for poultry meat, and there was an increase in per capita consumption. In fact, between 2010 and 2017, per capita production of some foodstuffs, such as cereals,

---

[9] See, for example, Amaral et al. (2020) and the annual Agricultural Statistical Yearbooks (MASA 2012, 2015, 2016).

[10] This paragraph relies on Tarp et al. (2004).

[11] Agricultural production performance is measured as an approximation to the function of providing food safety, according to studies carried out by the Rural Environment Observatory (OMR) (Carrilho et al. 2016; Abbas 2017; Mosca and Nova 2019). The main data sources used by these authors are the official statistical yearbooks, based on agricultural surveys (Agricultural Survey Project – TIA; Integrated Agricultural Survey – IAI) (MASA 2012; MASA 2015; MASA 2016; INE 2017), and statistical data from the FAO, some of which are estimated (www.fao .org/faostat/en/#data/QC, accessed 24 October 2019). The statistics published by the Ministry of Agriculture and Food Safety (MASA) are also taken into account (see www.agricultura.gov .mz/estatisticas/, accessed 14 July 2020). The www.agricultura.gov.mz address belongs to the Ministry of Agriculture and Rural Development (MADER), which replaced MASA in February 2020. In June 2020, its website replaced the previous www.masa.gov.mz, which was accessed by the authors in October 2019 in order to prepare this study. Given that the previous address is now inactive, it is the new website that will be referred to throughout the text. Regarding the history of MADER and its predecessors, see Notes in what follows below.

[12] While rural–urban standards of living are different, internal migration is discouraged by limited availability of jobs, high costs of living, low connectivity, and inefficient land markets.

fell to almost half. At national level, the yield per hectare of food crops also declined (see Table 4.1[13]). The reduction in productivity between 2012 and 2015, more pronounced in 2013, was most probably due to floods, pests and lack of rain (MASA 2015: 38; MASA 2016: 46–48), in addition to the general socio-economic context, including the macroeconomic crisis (see Egger et al., 2020). Another element is the increase in deforestation, resulting from the low levels of adoption of sustainable technologies, unsustainable farming practices and the expansion of human settlements.

We highlight that climate change also impacts agricultural performance. In 24 of the last forty-three years, from 1976 to 2019, extreme and moderate climate events were recorded, including cyclones, storms, tropical depressions, floods, and droughts or lack of rain (MICOA 2007: 23; Mandamule 2019: 2). The slow recovery from these events is a clear sign of lack of resilience and of vulnerability of the family farm sector, and it hampers their transition to commercial agriculture as farmers minimise risks.[14] This draws attention to the existing low level of irrigated agriculture and the weak efforts to prevent post-harvest losses.

Productivity did improve in some large and medium-sized farms, and examples of successful contract farming and out-grower schemes between large and medium-sized processing and marketing companies and small farmers do exist in cotton and tobacco (Mucavel 2018: 6, 10). While potentially relevant for future growth and employment creation, these private sector schemes only involve between 10 and 20 per cent of the around 4 million small family farms (MASA 2016: 41, 49). Furthermore, there is evidence that most existing contract farming and out-grower schemes only work for certain commodities in certain markets (Minot 2007) and therefore cannot be generalised across the agriculture sector.

Private investment in agriculture and agro-industry represented 21 per cent of the total private investment between 2001 and 2017 (Mosca and Nova 2019), with 61 per cent of this coming from loans, 32 per cent from direct foreign investment, and 7 per cent from direct national investment, located mainly in Zambézia and Gaza provinces. The proportion of credit to agriculture over total credit to the economy went from around 18 per cent in 2001 to around 3.5 per cent in 2017, 60 per cent of which went to large-scale sugar, cotton, cashew, tea and copra production, as well as livestock and forestry, that is overwhelmingly for un- or semi-processed exports.

In spite of the importance of the agriculture sector in the economy, there is a systematic and increasing trade deficit in food and agriculture products and food production is insufficient to meet the needs of the population (Abbas 2017: 23). The main agricultural exports between 2001 and 2017 were

---

[13] The table includes data on crops generally included in the Agricultural Statistics Yearbook, including roots and tubers. Note that the priority crops in the African Union (AU) are rice, corn, sorghum, millet, vegetables, cassava, cotton, palm oil, beef, dairy products, poultry and fish (AU/NEPAD 2017: 24).

[14] See Salazar-Espinoza et al. (2015), who show that floods and droughts affect cropland decisions.

| | | 2010 | 2011 | 2012 | 2013 | 2014 | 2015 | 2016 | 2017 |
|---|---|---|---|---|---|---|---|---|---|
| | Population (million) | 22.4 | 23.1 | 23.8 | 24.6 | 25.4 | 26.2 | 27.0 | 27.9 |
| Cereal | Maize (000s T) | 2,090 | 2,179 | 2,355 | 1,174 | 1,357 | 1,262 | 1,487 | 1,704 |
| | Rice (000s T) | 258 | 271 | 203 | 114 | 156 | 128 | 108 | 110 |
| | Sorghum (000s T) | 389 | 410 | 139 | 132 | 155 | 82 | 90 | 100 |
| | Millet (000s T) | 49 | 52 | 44 | 20 | 29 | 11 | 12 | 16 |
| | Maize (000s ha) | 1738 | 1,813 | 1,572 | 1,723 | 1,704 | 1,571 | 1,628 | 1,830 |
| | Rice (000s ha) | 227 | 239 | 363 | 404 | 377 | 235 | 182 | 143 |
| | Sorghum (000s ha) | 638 | 639 | 307 | 370 | 295 | 197 | 200 | 210 |
| | Millet (000s ha) | 109 | 114 | 55 | 70 | 51 | 30 | 27 | 35 |
| | Maize (T/ha) | 1.20 | 1.20 | 1.50 | 0.68 | 0.80 | 0.80 | 0.91 | 0.93 |
| | Rice (T/ha) | 1.14 | 1.14 | 0.56 | 0.28 | 0.41 | 0.55 | 0.59 | 0.77 |
| | Sorghum (T/ha) | 0.61 | 0.64 | 0.45 | 0.36 | 0.53 | 0.42 | 0.45 | 0.48 |
| | Millet (T/ha) | 0.45 | 0.45 | 0.80 | 0.28 | 0.58 | 0.37 | 0.44 | 0.45 |
| | Total (000s T) | 2,785 | 2,912 | 2,741 | 1,440 | 1,697 | 1,484 | 1,697 | 1,930 |
| Cereal | Kg/cap. | 124.4 | 126.0 | 115.0 | 58.5 | 66.9 | 56.6 | 62.8 | 69.2 |
| Vegetables | Beans (000s T) | 226 | 228 | 274 | 294 | 284 | 270 | 278 | 292 |
| | Peanuts (000s T) | 158 | 96 | 113 | 121 | 140 | 93 | 85 | 90 |
| | Beans (000s ha) | 698 | 659 | 790 | 1,009 | 833 | 779 | 790 | 800 |
| | Peanuts (000s ha) | 366 | 288 | 389 | 405 | 417 | 382 | 390 | 400 |
| | Beans (T/ha) | 0.32 | 0.35 | 0.35 | 0.29 | 0.34 | 0.35 | 0.35 | 0.37 |
| | Peanuts (T/ha) | 0.43 | 0.33 | 0.29 | 0.30 | 0.34 | 0.24 | 0.22 | 0.23 |
| | Total (000s T) | 384 | 324 | 386 | 415 | 424 | 363 | 363 | 382 |
| Vegetables | Kg/cap. | 17.2 | 14.0 | 16.2 | 16.9 | 16.7 | 13.8 | 13.4 | 13.7 |
| Roots and tubers | Cassava (000s T) | 9,738 | 10,094 | 8,198 | 4,303 | 8,273 | 8,103 | 9,100 | 8,774 |
| | Sweet potato (000s T) | 874 | 916 | 1,173 | 1,469 | 503 | 390 | 644 | 700 |
| | Cassava (000s ha) | 1,254 | 1,294 | 763 | 933 | 870 | 1,016 | 1,165 | 1,070 |
| | Sweet potato (000s ha) | 80 | 78 | 71 | 70 | 72 | 45 | 52 | 66 |
| | Cassava (T/ha) | 7.76 | 7.80 | 10.75 | 4.61 | 9.51 | 7.98 | 7.81 | 8.20 |
| | Sweet potato (T/ha) | 10.96 | 11.75 | 16.46 | 20.98 | 7.03 | 8.72 | 12.31 | 10.67 |
| | Total (000s T) | 10,612 | 11,009 | 9,371 | 5,772 | 8,775 | 8,493 | 9,744 | 9,474 |
| Roots and tubers | Kg/cap. | 474.0 | 476.5 | 393.1 | 234.6 | 345.8 | 324.1 | 360.3 | 339.4 |

*Source:* Authors' elaboration based on data from FAOSTAT, MASA (2015), MASA (2016), INE (2019); FAOSTAT, available at www.fao.org/faostat/en/#data/QC (accessed 24 October 2019).

tobacco, sugar, cotton, cashew, and sesame, representing around 88 per cent of total exports, while maize accounted for 3 per cent of exports during this time. Rice and wheat are the main agricultural imports, representing some 40 per cent of food and agriculture imports in the period since 2001 (Mosca and Nova 2019). Coinciding with a poor harvest and a reactivation of conflict in 2013–2014, the trade deficit for food and agriculture was critical in that year (Mosca and Nova 2019: 16).

In sum, during the 1990s, the return of millions of refugees to agricultural production led to Mozambique's recovery from war and from a very low level of agricultural output. However, the experience of the agricultural sector in the first decade after the turn of the millennium became a disappointing one. With reference to this period, Arndt et al. (2012: 858) highlight that 'agricultural production shows only weak aggregate growth. When adjusted to take into account either the expansion of cultivated area or population growth, the conclusion is that agricultural productivity in the smallholder sector has remained stagnant over time.' Furthermore, the contribution of the agricultural sector to GDP fell by five percentage points between 2010 and 2017.[15] The agricultural sector was neglected and the small peasant farmers were left behind in relative terms.

## III  INSTITUTIONAL WEAKNESSES

Mozambique has, over the past decades, experienced high aggregate economic growth. However, its performance in terms of agriculture progress remains, as noted above, an Achilles heel in relation to aggregate agriculture growth, food security, poverty reduction, inequality, and increasing regional and rural–urban imbalances. We explore in this section a set of key institutional weaknesses that help explain this poor performance, recognising that a variety of underlying factors, to which we turn in Section IV, form part of a more complete picture and comprehensive institutional diagnostic.

## A  Organisational Instability and Incapacity to Implement Plans and Policies

The organisational set-up in the agricultural sector has undergone almost constant change during recent decades in an effort to respond to a plethora of plans and policies. To illustrate, the ten-year period between 1995 and 2005 saw an excessive number of newly approved policies, strategies, and structuring laws, particularly in the area of natural resources, both renewable and non-renewable, including land, forests and wild fauna, land use planning, the environment, conservation, mines, and oil acts (Chiziane 2015: 29), some with provisions conflicting with existing structures and ways of operating.

---

[15] See www.ine.gov.mz/estatisticas/estatisticas-economicas/contas-nacionais/anuais-1/pib-na-optica-de-producao/pib-na-optica-de-producao-2020/view (accessed 14 July 2020).

Furthermore, from 2005 to 2013, a long series of plans and strategies for sectoral development were formulated and approved to bring about change in focus and priorities in the agriculture sector. They include:

- the Rural Development Strategy (EDR);
- the Green Revolution Strategy;
- the Strategic Development Plan for the Agricultural Sector (PEDSA) (MINAG 2011);
- the National Investment Plan for the Agricultural Sector (PNISA) (MINAG 2013; MASA 2018);
- the Support Plan for Intensification and Diversification of Agriculture and Livestock (IDAP),
- the Action Plan for Food Production (PAPA);
- the Agricultural Marketing Strategy;
- the Integrated Agricultural Marketing Plan (PICA), described as an instrument for the implementation of PEDSA;
- the Master Plan for the Development of Agribusiness (PDDA); and
- many others (Mosca 2011: 239–269; Granheim 2013: 47).

Along with these changes, government responsibilities and authority were frequently moved around among ministries and agencies, particularly in the areas of land, marketing, light industry, as well as food, irrigation, and promotion. The instability, often inconsistency, and overlapping or competing mandates cascaded down to the lower levels, with the set-up, closure, and transformation of commissions or national boards, state secretariats, and autonomous funds. Similarly, the duties of agricultural marketing, land and forest administration, and the promotion of rural development were regularly transferred between ministries.[16] A parallel process took place in the areas of domestic and foreign trade, industry, and tourism.[17]

---

[16] The different earlier 'versions' of the ministry responsible for the agricultural sector were successively created by Decree No. 1/1975, of 27 July, Presidential Decree No. 2/1994, of 21 December; Presidential Decree No. 1/2000, of 17 January; Presidential Decree No. 13/2005, of 4 February; Presidential Decree No. 1/2015, of 16 January. The duty of supervision of agricultural marketing was transferred to the Ministry of Internal Trade in 1978 and, in 1981, AGRICOM EE (state agricultural trade company) was set up. In 1994, this gave way to the newly created Institute of Cereals of Mozambique and the Agricultural Marketing Fund (MIC 2013: 12). In 1994, the Ministry of Agriculture and Fisheries (MAP) was also set up. In 2000, MAP gave way to the newly created MADER, which also absorbed the Rural Development Institute (INDER). The Ministry of Agriculture (MINAG) returned in 2005 and was followed by the MASA in 2015. The Ministry of Land, the Environment and Rural Development (MITADER), set up at the same time as MASA, took over responsibility from the Ministry of Agriculture for the management of Land and Geomatics, Forests and Wild Fauna and Rural Development, this last being reintegrated into MADER, set up again in 2020.

[17] See www.mic.gov.mz/por/pocas/HISTORIAL-DO-MIC (accessed 24 October 2019). The Ministry of Industry and Trade became the Ministry of Industry and Energy and the Ministries of Domestic Trade and Foreign Trade in 1983, the Ministry of Trade in 1986, the Ministry of Industry, Trade and Tourism in 1995, and, again, the Ministry of Industry and Trade in 2000, with readjustments every five years.

These vicissitudes totally overburdened the existing human and organisational capacity, and detracted attention away from the provision of core public support services for agricultural development at local level. In addition, there was deconcentration and decentralisation of powers and responsibilities, particularly at provincial, municipal, and district levels, from 2004, with the approval of the regulations[18] for the Local Government Act (LOLE)[19] and other legal documents (Mosca and Bruna 2016: 23–31).

The functioning of the agriculture sector has, as well, been influenced by favouritism and economic interests (Bruna, 2017) linked to powerful social groups. Indications are that this favouritism takes place through protected public officials who establish links between the central state and the regional law, on the one hand, and customary local and general rules, which are not always written down or democratic, on the other.

The Ministry of Agriculture and Rural Development (MADER)[20] is the main public organisation responsible for the agricultural sector. The Ministry of Land, Environment and Rural Development (MITADER) coexisted with the Ministry of Agriculture and Food Security (MASA) until the new government took office in 2020. At this point in time rural development became the responsibility of MADER, while land and environment came under a separate ministry. While both MASA and MITADER were represented at provincial level, representation at district level has not been uniform, and there has been no direct subordination relationship in the ongoing decentralisation process in the country. The organisational changes in the agricultural sector reflect a bewildering combination of underlying factors, to which we return below.

In spite of all of the above, the state budget allocation to the agricultural sector has for decades hovered around 4 per cent, moving up to 6 per cent in 2019, which is well below the African Union commitment of 10 per cent (Nova et al. 2019: 6).[21] Apart from the allocation being below the goal, the same authors (GdM and NEPAD 2017: 8–9) show that the investment aimed at institutional support and production support has been declining since 2012.

## B Competing Approaches to Agricultural Transformation

We have already discussed the frequent restructuring of ministerial organisations and their policies. This has led to a sense of randomness that is associated with the existence of competing approaches to agricultural transformation. While there is widespread consensus around the desire to see rapid

[18] Decree No. 11/2005, of 10 June.
[19] Law No. 8/2003, of 19 May.
[20] The new MADER was set up in 2020. The Ministry of Land and the Environment (MITA) was also set up at this time. This study began in 2019 when the Ministry of Agriculture and Food Safety (MASA), which will be referred to frequently, still existed.
[21] GdM and NEPAD (2017) confirm non-compliance with this goal though estimating slightly different budget allocations for the agricultural sector due to different classification criteria.

modernisation, there is, in fact, disagreement on how to promote agricultural development in practice.

In effect, there are two sides to this debate:

(i) One defends accelerated modernisation based on the industrialisation of agriculture and buying technology, with little attention paid to what it takes to transform small peasant farmers into commercial companies. The focus in this option is based on mechanical reading of experiences from elsewhere in combination with little attention to history and context. It is based in part on the belief that small family farmers do not really respond to economic stimuli, and that they are incapable of modernising without the intervention of the state. The other part of this perspective is that intervention should take place through projects and programmes where focus is on already established companies, whether agricultural, agro-industrial, state, cooperative, or private. It is systematically highlighted that medium-sized and large farms have higher yields than small farms (Mucavel 2018: 6, 10), to highlight the importance of prioritising the former to the detriment of the latter.

(ii) The other side argues that the modernisation of agriculture comes as a result of the modernisation of the entire society, and that it is not exclusively sectoral and depends on the political, social, and economic context of the country. It is not enough to buy technology, no matter how successful this may have been in other contexts. Put differently, this approach is based on small farmers being capable of modernising, by participating in the development and adoption of the most appropriate technology for each place and time, to the point of increasing their participation outside the agricultural sector, provided they have access to the resources and the rights needed for this.

The first perspective has been gaining ground during the last decade. While we noted the lack of success of the attempts at modernisation and agrarian transformation in the immediate post-independence years, there are, in fact, recent programmes and projects with positive impacts in terms of increasing productivity. They are, however, linked to specific geographic locations and groups involved. National indicators show that these interventions and the associated changes in policies and organisations do not seem to have influenced family farming, when it comes to their productivity, the generalized adoption of environmentally friendly technologies, or developments in the total volume of food production.[22]

---

[22] According to GdM and NEPAD (2017: 14), the value-added growth rate is estimated at, on average, 2.14 per cent (with MASA believing that this indicator was at risk of non-compliance at the time). There are also indications that the land productivity growth rate is increasing and may allow the goals to be met, considering the increase in the use of fertilisers to be an important step in this direction. No mention is made of quality seeds.

## C Low Quality and Quantity of Public Service Delivery

With all of the above organisational efforts, the aim was that the Mozambican government should be able to assume and perform in its assigned role, guiding and supporting agricultural development in an effective manner, including having the capacity to plan, implement, and negotiate with other agents in the sector. This was so at least for the principles adopted in 2003 in Maputo, by the African Union (AU) Summit, when it made its first declaration on the Comprehensive Africa Agriculture Development Programme (CAADP) as an integral part of the New Partnership for Africa's Development (NEPAD). The CAADP was established as Africa's policy framework for agricultural transformation, wealth creation, food security and nutrition, economic growth, and prosperity for all, and was adopted with the full support of the Mozambican government. This included the broad targets of 6 per cent annual growth in agricultural GDP and an allocation of at least 10 per cent of public expenditures to the agricultural sector. This was followed in 2014 with the Malabo Declaration on Accelerated Agricultural Growth, adopted by the AU.

In practice, under-budgeting, poor use of the budget, and the lack of a clear, long-term vision for the sector undermined the capacity of the state apparatus. This weakness became associated with the outsourcing of agricultural contracting schemes and development projects to NGOs and companies and agribusinesses whose participation was usually short in duration and with very limited geographic scope. In addition, the efforts made to support farmers' organisations so that they could have more bargaining capacity for negotiating prices and the terms and conditions of their production contracts were negligible.[23]

Assessing Mozambique's performance against the goals of the Malabo Declaration, it stands out that, as already noted, the state budget allocation was well below the 10 per cent goal. Moreover, funding has been insufficient to put in place the necessary internal capacity as well as staff able to provide even the most basic state services in support of agriculture development. This is so for plant and animal health, agricultural research and extension, statistics, supervision and quality control, protection and development of genetic material, enforcing the law and addressing market distortions. All of these areas have not received the necessary attention whereas responding to vested interests has been in focus.

---

[23] One example of the effects of this dependence is the weak development of a seed industry promoting more competition and less dependence of the farmer on the promoter. We find that the poor development of the national seed industry is mainly due to the (i) non-existence of a specific policy to promote the integrated development of the seed chain; (ii) poor technical and financial ability in public research and the non-existence of private research to develop productive varieties adapted to the different types of agriculture (mainly family farms); and (iii) the still very low demand on the certified seed market, given that the agricultural sector consists mainly of subsistence farming, unable to access improved seeds.

The distribution of ministry staff depends on the resources available at provincial and district levels, and Nova et al. (2019) note that Zambézia, Nampula, and Tete provinces, where 53 per cent of the country's cultivated land is farmed, only receive an allocation corresponding to 31 per cent of the operating budget. As to the public investment budget, this is distributed with around 24 per cent for production support, 24 per cent for extension and research, and 24 per cent for institutional support. The remaining 28 per cent is earmarked for forestry, livestock, irrigation, and land administration services (2019: 8).

The biennial assessment report on the implementation of the aforementioned Malabo Declaration goals (MASA 2017) assesses the level of CAADP progress in the country to be at 57 per cent.[24] Importantly, while noting some improvements, the report mentions that Mozambique is still far from reaching the goals of eradicating hunger and reducing poverty (2017: 32–34). More specifically, in relation to production assistance, the total number of extension staff was 2,025 in 2013 and 2,794 in 2018. This includes the public extension network – which increased from 1,137 to 1,863 – the network of companies – which went from 281 to 510 – and the NGO network, which fell from 607 to 421. The extension service currently provides assistance to around 20 per cent of farms in an irregular fashion and with few visits per farmer, for a goal of 100 per cent in 2018, according to the Malabo goals.

Overall, the poor ability to provide basic services to small farmers in the 'family sector' in a way that is reliable and focused on farmer needs stands out as a main shortcoming in the sector. Key associated weaknesses include a pronounced tendency to focus on the short term and rely on ad hoc, improvised restructuring at all levels rather than developing the longer-term vision and set of activities needed as part of a framework for sustained progress. The same can be said about the lack of attention to the needed decentralisation of public services, including services for development of appropriate technology with a view to increasing productivity, and the absence of appropriate credit systems for small farmers.

## D Unequal Access to Justice, Conflict Resolution, and Law Compliance

Generally speaking, the legislative framework concerning the agriculture sector is clear, but compliance is not assured. As already noted, the ten-year period between 1995 and 2005 was rife with approvals of reformed policies, strategies, and new laws. The ambition was that the legislative framework, in combination with the majority of customary regulations, whose application is enshrined in the constitution, would ensure adequate access to justice and

---

[24] Several indicators in the Biennial Report (MASA 2017) have not been calculated or their calculations are open to question. See, for example, the absence of data on post-harvest losses.

protection of farmers. Notable examples are the Land Act, frequently cited as one of the best in Africa (Tanner 2010: 105), and the Forest and Wildlife Act. However, as we shall see below access to justice is, in practice, unequal due to the structure and regulation of the system. In combination with the disproportionate power of the government and large private interests in influencing the decisions of the courts, this is a source of uncertainty for farmers.

The majority of land rights are not registered, which is not required by law, and non-registration does not per se undermine this right. Currently, around 24 million hectares (DINAT 2018), or 30 per cent of the land area, is registered, of which 12.3 million hectares, up to March 2019, were registered to rural communities (Topsøe-Jensen et al. 2019: 59). The majority of land conflicts are resolved by non-judicial bodies, through mediation and seeking reconciliation, promoted by the district authorities or by the Provincial Services of Geography and Cadastre (SPGC). When private companies and investors are involved, the resolution is more favourable to the communities when they are assisted by civil society organisations (Mandamule 2016: 24).

Many agricultural cases could be dealt with by the community courts, provided for in the constitution. While found in several districts, they lack guidance and regulation.[25] Given their position between the formal and the informal and their links with alternative ways and means of conflict resolution (Alfazema 2015: 8), extending their powers would facilitate the legal pluralism recognised by the constitution.[26]

Cases that have been through the local courts of mediation are normally sent to higher administrative bodies before being presented to the courts. This fact gives government bodies at various levels disproportionate power to determine the outcome of cases in which they are in conflict with citizens. Exceptionally, when the conditions are in place, cases can be taken to higher judicial courts. In some cases, when they have the support of the Mozambican Bar Association (OAM), they may get convictions, even against the government or the elite. Successful examples are the convictions against the global mining company VALE Moçambique and the Mozambican state in the case of forceful removal of local farmers from their land in Tete[27], as well as the conviction of the ProSAVANA Office[28], for engaging in secretiveness and lack of transparency regarding the plans for acquisition and use of land rights (OAM 2018).

Other cases, even with the support of the OAM, are faced with difficulties in being heard. An example is the case of the land irregularly attributed in Afungi,

---

[25] See http://opais.sapo.mz/muchanga-defende-regulamentacao-de-tribunais-comunitarios, 22 July 2019 (accessed 27 October 2019).
[26] Article 4 of the Constitution of the Republic (2004).
[27] Through Decision No. 09/TAPT/19 of the Tete Administrative Court (O País 2019).
[28] ProSAVANA implemented projects co-coordinated by the former Ministry of Agriculture and Food Security of Mozambique (MASA), the Japan International Cooperation Agency (JICA), and the Brazilian Cooperation Agency (ABC).

Palma District, to the Rovuma Basin gas project. This resulted in an illegal right to use and benefit from the land (*direito de uso e aproveitamento da terra*: DUAT), ultimately issued to the gas company two years after the legal opinion of its illegality was pronounced (Trindade et al. 2015). The OAM appealed against the DUAT, but one year later, the Administrative Court refused to hear the case, alleging that the communities had accepted it and could be adversely affected (OAM 2019) by an interruption of the activities. This example raises questions as to the independence of the courts, as does the fact that lots of land lies idle, especially along major roads and other infrastructure, where the DUATs are held by non-residents, who are not obliged to use the land or lose it as the law stipulates.

Finally, some areas in the agricultural sector are regularly inspected (Topsøe-Jensen et al. 2019: 72, list land use inspection instruments). The ministries responsible for the sector also have inspectors that deal with complaints from the public. In this way, officials who abuse their power may be penalised. A conflict management department was set up in land administration in 2015. In Forest and Wildlife administration, the law provides for a strategy for the participation of community inspectors, which was actually developed (Bila 2005). An inspection operation of national scope was implemented for monitoring timber harvesting ('operation trunk') and, occasionally, there has been news of combating poaching and trade in hunting trophies. The supervision of land use activities has resulted in the withdrawal of DUAT or rescaling of idle land. However, law enforcement powers are weak, partly due to the conflicts between legal regulations (Capaina 2019), the capture of the state by private interests, and the insufficiency of human and financial resources.

Thus, although the legislative framework is formally in place, some sub-sectors are subject to capture. This is more frequent for forestry plantations (Bruna 2017), livestock and game farms, and timber harvesting, where intensive logging is carried out (Afonso 2019: 9). The same goes for areas of interest to the elite with easy access to capital, who obtain land rights for areas where they only use a very small proportion and in conflict with the local population (JA and UNAC 2011: 58–59).

## E  Lack of Effective Voice, Participation, and Accountability (Weak Civil Society)

Community and public participation in decision-making is recognised in the legislation (OSISA 2009: 74 and following) and this extends to the agricultural sector. Turning to the right of association, it is governed by Law No. 8/91, of 18 July. However, the process of revising this law, in order to simplify it, with participation by civil society organisations, is not making progress.

Apart from public hearing mechanisms, where people can participate individually, there are also other types of participation through organisations. There are civil society organisations and consultation fora from community to central level.[29] Some have a wide membership base.[30] Others include product-oriented companies and/or institutions.[31] Some of these have local representation, taking part in consultations, work, and local assessment of policies (Topsøe-Jensen et al. 2015: 54 and following).

Some forms of participation are simply informational, opening up room for clarifications, others are for specific consultation on a topic or programmes, while others are for dialogue and working together, with operational results. Some operate independently, others are organized around topics or causes. Freedom of speech in the country favours the participation and accountability of the state and other formal organisations, as well as public assessment of their performance and the rules of the game that apply. However, public agricultural institutions have, in practice, shown little inclination to adopting accountability mechanisms open to their sector partners. For example, information on rights to use and benefit from the land is not available to the public.

On the positive side, community consultations in the application process for obtaining the DUAT might result in a record or document, such as a license or certificate, with legal value to the holder. Another example is the case of the Consultation Forum on Land or Forests. While any consensus is not binding, it is difficult to ignore, provided the consensus does not imply revision of the legislation. In addition, there are other consultation fora, which do not include representation of the state or the government, aimed at monitoring and advocacy, as is the case of the Budget Monitoring Forum (FMO), the Land Forum in Nampula, and the Women's Forum. Some of these are formally constituted and are the object of a legal instrument.[32]

Local organisations are also invited to take part in the formulation of policies, as well as the monitoring of their implementation. The favoured participation channels are the Community Councils, which can have specific names – for example, the Participatory Management Councils (COGEP) for land resources, forests, and fauna. However, in the agricultural sector, this has not been a systematic practice common to all the public institutions. There are cases where there was effective participation by civil society organisations (CSO) but, in the majority of cases, either there was no involvement or there

---

[29] For example, Law No. 19/97, of 1 October (on Land), Law No. 34/2014, of 31 December (on the Right to Information, the draft Agriculture Act, and the revision of Law No. 8/91, of 18 July (on Associations) had direct interaction from the parliament.

[30] The National Farmers' Union (UNAC), which came into being in 1987, is an example of a farmers' movement with provincial representation and support from the Farmers' Associations governed by Decree-Law No. 2/2006, of 3 May, on Farmers' Associations.

[31] Such as the Mozambican Association of Sugar Producers (APAMO), the National Forum for Cotton Producers (FONPA), the National Forum for Pulse Vegetables, the Mozambican Poultry Producers Association (AMA), the Mozambican Poultry Industry Association (AMIA), etc.

[32] For example, the Land Consultation Forum was set up by Decree No. 42/2010, of 20 October. The Tourism Forum was set up by Decree No. 25/2017, of 23 June.

were only poorly prepared soundings to no effect. Additionally, occasions for cooperation are systematically postponed.[33]

Overall, the complex network of organisations participating in the agricultural sector allows for attendance and participation at different levels and at different occasions for complaint, consultation, advocacy, supervision, etc. However, the examples presented in the previous section show that their voice is not always heard (Salomão et al. 2019a: 7) and they do not always fully represent the communities (Salomão et al. 2019b: 6). In spite of this, their participation is of intrinsic value in the transfer of information and knowledge of the general positions of the players involved. This value is also present in events at regional and national representation levels. It is from these consultations that alliances and agendas are structured and more effective actions are initiated.

In sum, consultations and participation, as well as the mechanisms established for this purpose, are present in the daily routines in the agricultural sector. However, the efficiency of such participation is not reliable, generating uncertainty among the farmers as to whether all the parties involved will stick to agreements arrived at. Put differently, the 'social contract' is still not binding.

## IV UNDERLYING FACTORS

The unsatisfactory performance of the agriculture sector and the institutional weaknesses reviewed above are due to a complex set of underlying factors. The political, economic, and social context within which Mozambique's agriculture sector has evolved since independence is tumultuous. The country has experienced several radical regime shifts and no sustained periods of peace and policy predictability. Such a context makes long-term nation-building and sustained agricultural development and transformation an exceedingly difficult challenge. Success is only feasible with coherent and determined leadership, promoting a sense of national unity, and giving priority to the agriculture sector and the many millions of farm households in accordance with the constitution, independent of private and outside interests.

In contrast, Mozambique has experienced extensive periods of war and conflict, with a vast and demanding geography and limited infrastructure. Lack of integration among the south, centre, and north of the country is characteristic, and policy directions have been fluid depending on interests of the elite and the role of donors, in a nation under construction. While these factors are not of exclusive importance to agriculture, they have had extensive impact on the sector, and agriculture has not received the priority stated in the constitution. This reflects the factors alluded to above, including that the attention of the state has been absorbed by imminent challenges to its authority, under pressure and systematic questioning of its legitimacy in connection with electoral cycles

---

[33] As an example, the last (9th) session of the Land Consultation Forum, which is supposed to be held twice a year, was held on 8 and 9 November 2017.

(Correia da Silva 2014). Moreover, attention has been absorbed by having to manage numerous emergency programmes to deal with the consequences of war, natural disasters, and hunger. To this comes, more recently, the extensive opportunities to invest in the exploration of mineral resources. We now turn to these different factors one by one, fully recognising they are interdependent.

## A  Political Instability, Violence, and Legitimacy of the State

Vast tracts of Mozambique have experienced a situation of political and military instability and violent conflict for 30–40 years. Peace was partially and temporarily restored for two decades, from 1992 to 2011, but political and military tensions returned to threaten peace and tranquillity. The impact on the agriculture sector has been devastating. Conflicts have caused people to abandon their areas of residence and production, generating pressure and situations of disputes over rights of use of resources and interrupting the provision of services to small farmers, delegated to medium-sized and large companies.

The war during the 1980s caused massive destruction of infrastructure and loss of human lives throughout the country. In addition, agricultural land was abandoned as millions of predominantly rural refugees sought shelter in neighbouring countries and urban areas. Furthermore, the war meant that resources were directed in very large measure to military purposes with long-term consequences. The war also undermined the Ministry of Agriculture preventing the creation of public services that are fundamental for a modern agriculture. Mozambique, in contrast to Zimbabwe, did not inherit rural extension services and the war broke down all marketing efforts.[34] Similarly, national capacity for agriculture research did not take off, and the weak production of seed and inadequate use of fertiliser are just two examples that have roots back to the destabilisation of the 1980s. A final example refers to local district administrators who, because of the war, became state representatives with a certain style of authoritarian governance in detriment to a process of focusing on the welfare of the people and seeing themselves serving for this purpose.[35] In addition, the turnaround in economic principles from the late 1980s led to an almost exclusive focus on getting prices right, market-based approaches, and the dismantling of state support for agriculture development in a country plagued by violent conflicts. Mozambique has not, so far, managed to escape from this heritage in any decisive manner, and population growth and its unbalanced territorial distribution have continued to generate conflict over scarce resources.

---

[34] Neighbouring Swaziland, with less than half a million people, had more rural extension workers than Mozambique.

[35] We acknowledge the former Minister of Finance, Magid Osman, for making this and other points in this paragraph.

The armed conflicts in Mozambique and the intermittent violence in recent years (2012–19)[36] involved and affected, due to their nature and location, rural communities and crop and livestock farmers, and also affected the sectors to which they were linked (Brück 1998: 1047–48). The main areas affected have been the provinces in the centre and north of the country, which are also the ones with the largest farming population, working the largest cultivated area, including the ones with the highest productivity, growing both food and cash crops. The main private commercial investments in land and natural resources are also in these regions, with impacts on the farming rights and conditions of the rural society. In addition, conflicts in the centre of the country have brought with them the risk of damaging cuts in terrestrial communications between north and south, and the coast and the hinterland.

Armed violence severed sales channels, worsened the already weak capacity for providing agricultural services, and affected activities related to jobs outside of farming and consumption of farm produce, including tourism. In 2014, the National Farmers' Union (UNAC) estimated that around 69,000 farming families had been affected by the war (UNAC 2014: 2). Political violence and the conflicts had an impact on people's movement and on women in particular (ASFC et al. 2019: 44–48), the main segment of the rural population, as well as on the environment.

It is also clear that the combination of widespread flooding and the Renamo insurgency in 2013 caused massive drops in food production as reflected in Table 4.1. Traditionally, rural households have turned to the sale of forest products, as well as wild food and medicinal products as a coping strategy when facing production shortfalls. However, the migration caused by the armed violence has disconnected the communities from their environment, limiting their access to these natural products.

Political, military, and social violence has in recent years had a deteriorating effect on the stability of the farming population and on food security (Jornal Notícias 2018; TVM – Redacção 2020). The attacks by groups assumed to have ethno-religious roots in the extreme northern coastal area in Mozambique began on 5 October 2017 (Maquenzi and Feijó 2019: 13), and are presently a major concern and security threat.

In sum, (a) faced with the existence of diverse armed groups, the state has no effective monopoly on the use of force; (b) local administrative structures have weakened; (c) the rural population, mostly farmers, have continued to be seriously affected by war and armed conflict; (d) the harshest hit regions are the ones with the highest agriculture and livestock production potential; and (e) these areas in the centre and northern part of the country are also those that have been affected most by extreme climate events during the recent episodes

---

[36] Some of the many documents giving the timeline and a description of the armed conflicts in Mozambique include those by Borges-Coelho (2010), Correia da Silva (2014) and Lucas (2016).

of armed violence. Moreover, the agreements between Frelimo and Renamo during the last decades have not led to the same sense of people's safety and a return to peace as was the case after the 1992 Treaty of Rome[37], which led to recovery of the agricultural sector in the 1990s.

Nation-building and building the legitimacy of the state is a long-term continuous process and certainly involves recognising the role of the state in assuring the safety of people and property, the protection of social rights, the structuring and provision of other public services and the promotion of development. In Mozambique, the inability of the state to assure the provision of agricultural public services and promote the development of a broad base in the sector, combined with growing spatial and group-based inequalities, has contributed to the erosion of the legitimacy of the state, facilitating the outbreak of violence with an impact on agricultural production and marketing.

## B Regional Divides and Lack of Market Integration

Mozambique has been a transit country since colonial days. Infrastructure was built to provide transport services for neighbouring countries with limited focus on integrating the national territory. Accordingly, and as summarized by Tarp et al. (2004), while the connections between east and west in Mozambique are relatively good, infrastructure is generally poor. Moreover, domestic transport between the northern and central parts of the country – the areas with highest agriculture potential – and the urban south is very costly and severely constrains agriculture development.[38]

Since 1992, major programmes have been implemented with donor support to develop the transport network, which have resulted in improvements in the primary and secondary road system, especially in the southern regions. However, rather limited attention has in practice continued to be paid to developing north–south integration and a badly needed rural roads network, and this is so in spite of the extensive geographic diversity already alluded to above. According to the World Bank (2016), only 17 per cent of the rural population lives within 2 km of the nearest road in good condition.

---

[37] See www.ipris.org/files/6/07_Documento_Acordo_Geral.pdf (accessed 14 July 2020).
[38] Heltberg and Tarp (2002) bring out the key importance of non-price factors such as risk, technology, and transport infrastructure for rural peasants' marketing decisions. They conclude that to achieve pro-poor rural growth it is essential to explicitly address the conditions of high-risk, low productivity, and low capital endowments of poor farmers. Arndt et al. (2012) use structural path analysis and compare the experiences of Mozambique and Vietnam – two countries with similar levels and compositions of economic growth but divergent poverty outcomes. They find that a given agricultural demand expansion in Mozambique will, ceteris paribus, achieve much less rural income growth than in Vietnam. Inadequate education, trade, and transport systems are more severe structural constraints to poverty reduction in Mozambique than in Vietnam.

Consequently, transaction costs are very high indeed, and markets for agricultural production are poorly integrated. This implies that improvements in agricultural technology alone are unlikely to be successful. Increasing production in local areas will be associated with falling prices if farmers do not have access to export markets and consumers in the south. This calls for coordinated investment in infrastructure and agriculture support services. This runs counter to the aspects discussed in Section B and the limited capacity of the state.

Summing up, it is clear that the above characteristics have over the years deepened the historical and socio-economic divides between southern Mozambique, on the one hand, and the central and northern regions, on the other (see Egger et al. 2020; DEEF 2016).

## C  Lack of Interest of the Elite

At independence the nation-building project of Frelimo was closely associated with attention to agrarian transformation and priorities were focused on the promotion of state farms and communal villages. The inherent investment strategy was capital-intensive and proved in the final analysis to be a failure. As Frelimo priorities started to shift towards small-scale peasant agriculture before the Fourth Congress in 1983, war was in the making, literally undermining attempts at agriculture advance. After peace in 1992, peasant agriculture seemed to rebound almost automatically due to recovery from a very low base and the interests of the elite were elsewhere.

The economic liberalisation programme led to a privatisation process and a merger of private and political powers, which became the focus of attention. Agriculture was, with prominent exceptions in forestry, wildlife, and land, largely ignored. Generally, the sector did not offer really major opportunities for rent-seeking and capital accumulation though cases of corruption associated with, for example, the forestry sector have attracted attention in the popular press. Moreover, the elite did not depend on agriculture progress in the midst of major inflows of foreign aid and their reliance on food and other imports from South Africa.

Towards the end of the 1990s, interests started shifting further towards the opportunities inherent in the extractive sector rather than to agriculture, which, as described above, continued to be affected by natural calamities and emergency management instead of long-term priorities and needs. This, in combination with the poor use of the state budget in the agriculture sector, meant that the share of the budget remained very low until the present. This has been further influenced by the weakness of civil society organisations as advocacy organisations for public concerns, a role that goes beyond their function as pressure groups.

## D  Donors (Lack of Agency in Strategic and Policy Formulation)

The lack of economic and financial resources has greatly constrained autonomy in economic policy decision-making in Mozambique ever since independence.

As stated by Mosca (2011: 452), agricultural policies and strategies were from the beginning imported and based on the assumption of external funding. To illustrate, in the agriculture sector this explains in large measure the adoption of capital-intensive technology and approaches to agrarian transformation in the immediate post-independence period, which proved unsuccessful. Another stark example of donor influence is the economic reform programme introduced after economic collapse in 1986. While the programme was evidently inappropriate in a context of war and destruction, its longer-term consequences are hard to exaggerate. This is certainly so in relation to the dismantling of state presence in the sector and the need for public intervention to address evident market failures in areas such as input supply, marketing, and access to credit.

In their review of aid and development in Mozambique from 1980 to 2004, Arndt et al. (2006: 79) highlight that:

... aid has not been without problems. The historical tendency of channelling external funding directly towards sectors, bypassing central review and management, has contributed to poorly coordinated policy interventions and fiscal imbalances. We also find that the staggering number of donor-supported endeavours continues to generate uneven and often unmanageable institutional pressures.

Put differently, the existence of numerous donors with competing interests and priorities contributed in the 1990s to a pronounced lack of strategic direction depending on which donor was the most influential at a particular point in time. Accordingly, aid agencies reinforced the lack of priority given to agriculture in sectoral budget allocations. We have referred above to the relative neglect of agriculture by the government in budgetary allocations. It should not be overlooked that the same was happening in the allocation of aid for agriculture development.

As emphasis shifted in aid modalities around the turn of the millennium from project and programme support to macroeconomic and budget support, an effort was made to ensure greater coherence and effectiveness. However, it is quite obvious that Mozambique's dependence on external finance has led to lack of agency and the practice of using donor-funded consultancies as a conditionality has weakened national policy coordination and ownership to the point where mutual trust between government and the donor community started breaking down from late 2000s. The most recent example of this appeared in relation to the hidden debts scandal where donors froze all budget support to the newly appointed government in 2015 with drastic socio-economic implications. Fortunately, relations have recovered, but the interests of donor countries have started to change with the discovery of large gas deposits.

In sum, donors have played a very significant and volatile role in Mozambique since independence. External interventions have not always been unproductive, sometimes contributing to the transfer of knowledge and the stabilisation of the conditions under which farmers make their decisions as economic and social agents. In addition, we find that the dependence on aid should not excuse the lack of ability to formulate and implement policies, whether on the part of the state or on the part of civil organisations.

## V LOOKING TO THE FUTURE

By way of conclusion, we have, in this chapter explored the agriculture performance of Mozambique, its institutional weaknesses and the underlying factors that help explain the present unsatisfactory situation. We have pointed to the role of systemic political instability and violence combined with challenges to state legitimacy. Regional divides and lack of market integration continue to influence in a critical and all-encompassing manner. Finally, the way in which the interests of the elite and the influence of donors have affected progress in the agriculture sector suggests the need for concerted reorientation in existing strategies, policies, and priorities. This is reinforced by a series of future challenges, discussed in Section A. They include:

(i)    Extractive industry;
(ii)   Population growth and internal migration;
(iii)  National and international markets;
(iv)   Climate change;
(v)    COVID-19.

Finally, we provide, in Section B, a set of policy considerations for priority actions to help improve future prospects and performance in terms of production of agriculture products and agro-industry. Our reflections are based on three fundamental principles: (i) peace will be consolidated and effective all over the country; (ii) governance will make the elimination of poverty and the reduction of social inequalities a priority; and (iii) the agricultural sector will be considered to be key for reducing poverty, achieving social stability, consolidating peace, and promoting socio-economic, endogenous, inclusive, and sustained development, and this will be reflected in future sectoral budget allocations once revenue from natural resource extraction becomes available. Furthermore, even if there are sweeping changes in the prevailing framework and priorities (especially with regard to economic and social public policies), it will be difficult for the economy as a whole to create enough employment at a pace that could absorb the increasing labour force. This suggests that agriculture development has to go hand in hand with structural transformation and employment generation more generally.

## A Challenges

### 1 *The Extractive Industry*
Huge investments are planned over the next ten years in the gas extraction industry, in areas 1 and 4 of the Rovuma Basin in the North of Mozambique. The estimated total investment in the projects in these areas is US$50.6 billion.

According to the MEF, the accumulated revenue generated for the government by these projects in the first twenty-five years may vary between US$31.3 billion, the worst-case scenario, and US$71.5 billion, the best-case scenario (MEF 2018). In either case, bearing in mind the other investments underway and planned for the extractive industry (gas in Inhambane, coal, heavy minerals, precious stones, etc.), there will be an increasing inflow of large amounts of foreign currency. This is associated with both risks and potentials, including an appreciation of the metical, which could have both positive and negative consequences for the Mozambican economy. For the agricultural sector, a stronger metical will, on the one hand, allow for reducing the cost of increasing production through intensification, given that the majority of production goods are imported. On the other hand, it will make domestic agricultural products more expensive and less competitive on national and international markets.

The broad expectation of different Mozambican political and civil society segments is that the revenue from the extractive industry will be channelled towards promoting more inclusive and sustainable socio-economic development, reducing dependence on the exploration of non-renewable resources, in line with the fundamental principles outlined above. The government has, at the highest level of authority, clearly manifested the intention and its readiness to adopt in practice policies that will make these expectations a reality and official discourse continues to consider the agricultural sector to be a priority in this diverse and sustained development perspective.[39] A study is underway on the constitution of a Sovereign Fund, which could be an essential instrument for the application of these policies and for avoiding undesirable fluctuations in the metical. These policies and instruments could be determining factors for the development of the agricultural sector in the long term. This is why it is fundamental that the public, private, and non-governmental institutions participating in the agricultural sector have the capacity to influence the formulation of development strategies and adoption of these policies.

## 2 Population Growth and Migration

The National Statistics Institute predicts that in 2050,[40] Mozambique will have a total population of around 60 million (around 2 times more than the estimated total population in 2019). It is also clear that the current population distribution of around 2/3 rural and 1/3 urban will change significantly due to migration to urban centres. Mozambique will experience a greater trend towards migration to the urban centres by younger and more resourceful

---

[39] According to the proposed Economic and Social Plan (PES) for 2020, submitted to parliament by the government (Council of Ministers 2020), 10.2 per cent of the state budget for 2020, excluding General State Expenditure, is earmarked for the Agriculture and Rural Development sector. Nevertheless, according to Mosca (2020: 11–12), the allocation to all the institutions of the new MADER and of the MTA is just 6.3 per cent.

[40] See www.ine.gov.mz/iv-rgph-2017/projeccoes-da-populacao-2017-2050/mocambique.xls/view.

people, which will result in a reduction of young people with some education working in agriculture unless significant progress takes place for education in rural areas.

Under these conditions, the trend will be towards inability of agricultural productivity to catch up with the growing consumption needs nationwide, particularly in urban areas, and an increase in the production of commodities for export. This tendency highlights the need for concerted efforts to promote technological progress and adaptation. At the same time, agriculture will in the foreseeable future have to absorb a sizeable share of the large numbers of new entrants into the labour market if major unemployment is to be avoided.

### 3 National and International Markets
When planning the future of the agricultural sector, there is a need for coming to grips with the changes and trends in the development of trade relations in these markets, increasingly determined by commodity exchanges and futures markets (Medeiros 2014). The demand for basic foodstuffs processed in the national market will increase, not only due to overall and urban population growth, but also due to the increase in family incomes if more inclusive public policies promoting economic diversification are adopted. Competition from imported food products is also likely to increase on the domestic market, whether due to the increase in domestic demand or due to the reduction in domestic prices of imported products resulting from the appreciation of the metical. This calls for effective exchange rate management and supply side economic policies to avoid Dutch disease. This will be critical, and it is unlikely going to be possible to completely neutralise the Dutch disease. However, much can be done by increasing capacity in non-tradable sectors and making a huge effort to increase productivity.[41]

There has been a huge increase in international transactions in agri-food products in the last fifty years – the value of international product flow increased fivefold (FAO 2018: 34) – and will very probably continue to increase exponentially with the increase in the world population and the improvement of the quality of life in densely populated countries like China and India. International markets for agri-food and other commodities will very probably continue to be dominated by the present leaders in these markets.[42] The tendency will be that the market leaders will continue to prefer sourcing primary and raw materials in a country like Mozambique due to the comparative advantage in agriculture

---

[41] See Cruz et al. (2020) for an illuminating review of the construction sector in Mozambique and its challenges.

[42] According to FAO data for 2018, the biggest importers and exporters of agri-food products are: (1) Importers: China, USA, Germany, Netherlands, Japan, France, Italy, Belgium, Canada, Spain, India, and Mexico; (2) Exporters: USA, Netherlands, Brazil, Germany, France, Spain, Canada, Italy, Australia, and Indonesia. In other words, eight of these countries are both the largest importers and exporters of agri-food.

discussed in Section I. However, in addition to developing agro-industry and building domestic value chains, pursuing increased processing of agricultural output must be incorporated into any long-term transformational development strategy. This is also in line with boosting the domestic supply side of the economy to avoid Dutch disease referred to above, and investing revenue from extractive industries to support such investment will be necessary.

## 4 Climate Change

Mozambique has always been affected by periodic droughts (especially in the southern and central regions) and by floods (all over the country, with greater incidence in the central and northern regions), as it is in an area at high risk of adverse climatic events. These risks are increasing due to climate change. An example of this is the violence of the recent cyclones, Idai and Kenneth. Brito and Holman (2012: 38) estimate that climate change will negatively impact productivity between 2046 and 2065 and the impact will be more severe in some regions.

Therefore, it is fundamental for the country to define a specific, long-term strategy to develop a form of agriculture that is less vulnerable to climate change.[43] This strategy should consider the costs and benefits for small farmers of incorporating concrete measures for the development and dissemination of agricultural technologies that are environmentally friendly and resilient to climate change, as well as appropriate infrastructures for mitigating the risks brought about by the negative impacts of climate change.

## 5 COVID-19

This chapter was completed in the context of COVID-19, which rapidly became a pandemic affecting public health and the economy all over the world, with a greater incidence in the countries that dominate the world market. The strategy adopted by these countries included total lockdowns in the circulation of people, public services, and economic activity, which is causing an accentuated contraction in their economies and turbulence in the financial markets, with negative socio-economic impacts worldwide.

There is a great deal of uncertainty as to what will happen in Mozambique. However, irrespective of how the pandemic plays out, given Mozambique's high dependence on foreign investment and the export of commodities, whose prices are trending downwards, Mozambique will experience an economic downturn, at least in the short term. This will reinforce budgetary constraints in a situation where there are urgent needs to increase allocations to the health sector (to deal with the effects of the pandemic) and the defence sector (due to the intensification and expansion of the armed conflicts in the central provinces and in Cabo Delgado). This obviously complicates the task of ensuring greater priority for agriculture development in state budget allocations.

---

[43] See Arndt et al. (2011) and Arndt et al. (2019).

## B Policy Considerations

### 1 Vision, Commitment, and Dialogue

Increasing agricultural productivity (essential for increasing market competitiveness) and reducing risk and vulnerability in the sector require the formulation of a broad structural reform agenda, not only in agriculture and agro-industry, but also in the secondary and tertiary sectors relevant to rural development. These transformations require integrated policies with a long-term outlook (at least ten years), as well as the ability and time to implement them effectively and efficiently. Sustained and inclusive development of agriculture is a long-term process, needing vision and stable public policies to promote compatibility and links between the various sectoral policies pursued by committed public institutions.

Finally, to ensure that policies are inclusive, adequate, and effective, non-governmental and private social and economic organisations must play a structured role both in their design and in the monitoring of their implementation. To this end, these organisations need specific training to improve the quality of their intervention in the policies through dialogue and advocacy. This would help offer an avenue for the development of an alliance between the state, the producers, especially the small farmers, their organisations, and other institutions to improve the performance in the sector.

### 2 Focus on the Small Family Farmers and the Creation of Jobs in Agriculture and Agro-industry

We have argued throughout this chapter that focus must be on promoting small-scale farming to contribute to inclusive development. Agriculture is, and will remain in the foreseeable future, the basis for the livelihood and well-being of the majority of rural families and over 95 per cent of agricultural production is small scale. Accordingly, small farmers in the family sector must be a target group for policies that are both conducive to productivity and environmentally friendly, recognising that trade-offs between equity and productivity may occur. Accordingly, policies should also consider promoting the transformation of family farms into commercial units. For this to happen, policies must, for example, further the integration of small farmers into value chains with high market potential and into goods and services markets, promoting their capacity to negotiate this integration under conditions that bring benefits to their income and living conditions. Clearly, these recommendations do not imply that medium- and large-scale commercial farms should be ignored. What is called for is a strategy that promotes a balanced approach where small farmers and their needs are taken into account, along the lines discussed in Berchin et al. (2019) for Brazil.

Furthermore, agro-industry, which adds value to agricultural commodities by processing them before marketing, can, as proposed by Benfica, Tschirley, and Sambo (2002), play a key role in agricultural development in Mozambique in sectors like maize, cotton, cashew, and sugar. Mozambique's comparative advantage in agriculture and some agro-industries must play a key role in any balanced development strategy focused on integrating networks of unorganised smallholder farmers with domestic and international markets along the supply chain. In this regard, the increase in productivity and productive efficiency through improved technology that is not harmful to the environment must be a main, specific aim of any future agricultural policy, to ensure the competitiveness of Mozambican producers.

These recommendations are in line with the analysis of the Mozambican labour market by Jones and Tarp (2012). They point to three jobs priorities. The first is to address existing low levels of agricultural productivity. Sustained poverty reduction requires transforming agricultural jobs. Secondly, the non-farm informal sector should be supported as they are a source of dynamism and entrepreneurship. Good jobs are not just formal sector jobs as noted by Jones and Tarp (2012). At present there is a tendency to perceive these firms in a negative light. Thirdly, government should, as already argued above, support labour intensive agro-industry with export potential.

### 3 Decentralisation and Improvement of Public and Private Services

Decentralisation and the improvement of the quality of agricultural services are necessary conditions to promote productive and environmentally friendly agriculture and agro-industry production. Decentralisation brings the services closer to the farmers, helping them increase their ability to respond to demand. However, for decentralisation to result in an increase in the quality of services, they must be provided with greater human, material, and financial capacity. Priority should be given to key services for technological development and productivity (agricultural research and extension, control of pests and diseases, seed production and certification, soil laboratories, etc.). The same goes for good management and preservation of natural resources (land, water, flora, fauna), which requires capacity for planning and monitoring the use of these resources and local resolution of conflicts about access to them and between social and economic players. Decentralisation of these key agricultural public services must take into account the fact that each one of them is an integrated national system, which includes their own internal organisation, their qualifications and technical and professional careers, their regulations and legal mandate for applying them, and their strategies or plans for increasing their scope and quality. These systems need to be improved and adapted to improve the response quality of the service providers to the needs on the demand side. They should avoid the tendency towards ad hoc, improvised restructuring, characteristic over the last two decades, with clear consequences for quality, effectiveness, and efficiency.

In parallel with the development of public services, there is a need to stimulate diversification, expansion, and an improvement in the quality of private services essential to production and productivity (supply of production goods, mechanisation, agricultural marketing, savings and credit, transport, communications, etc.). As Mozambican agriculture consists mainly of non-intensive family farms aimed at subsistence, there is still little actual market demand for these services. Therefore, it will be necessary to adopt policies and instruments which, on the one hand, stimulate small farmer demand for supplies and services and, on the other, promote the expansion of geographic coverage (to facilitate access by the farmers) and the quality of the supply.

In sum, future reforms must be conducive to productivity enhancement and must incorporate the development of productive infrastructures (to develop irrigated agriculture,[44] reduce post-harvest losses, and process and distribute products), as well as the expansion and improvement of the rural road, electricity, and communications networks. This in line with the jobs analysis by Jones and Tarp (2012), who conclude that spatial industrial policy and leveraging of natural resource revenues to substantially improve infrastructure and logistics services along key value chains offer great potential in addressing the present job challenges.

Finally, one more question for reflection: will it be possible to promote the development of Mozambican agriculture in the next 10–20 years in an essentially free market economic policy framework, or will specific economic policies and market interventions be needed to stimulate this development? We believe that to propel agricultural transformation and development that is socially inclusive and sustained, Mozambique will need to adopt suitable credit policies to stimulate investment in the intensification of agricultural production, subsidies aimed at promoting an increase in productivity, price and market policies that reduce the risk of negative impacts in the production sector caused by fluctuations and market downturns, and customs regulations that do not expose national farmers to very unequal competition from agricultural products whose export is promoted by their countries of origin through a variety of incentives and subsidies.

---

[44] According to the National Irrigation Programme 2017–42 (INIR 2017: 7), 181,000 hectares of land have irrigation infrastructures, of which only 90,000 hectares are operational, and there is an estimated total area of 3 million hectares that is potentially irrigable.

# 5

# Schooling without Learning

## Institutional Causes

Mouzinho Mário, Celso M. Monjane, and Ricardo Santos[1]

## I INTRODUCTION

Universal access to education, under the aegis of the international development agencies, is an educational policy objective, which has spread all over
the world, most particularly in the nations listed as 'developing countries'.
In this group of countries, the belief that education is one of the main factors in socio-economic development gave a certain impetus to the reforms in
education, many of them aimed at increasing school coverage rates (Birchler
and Michaelowa 2016). Mozambique is one of the countries that has been
implementing a set of reforms in its national education system, aiming at more
access to education.

In 1974, a year before its independence, Mozambique had an illiteracy rate
of around 97 per cent of the adult population (Mário and Nandja 2005: 3), the
result of a colonisation process characterised by social and political exclusion
of the majority of the population (Mondlane 1975). With the advent of independence in 1975, the new government of independent Mozambique decided to
nationalise education and expand the school network, with the aim of increasing
access for the majority of the population. This measure resulted in a significant
increase in the number of pupils. In only four years (1975–79) enrolment went
from 600,000 to 1.2 million, with an annual rate of increase of the primary
school population of around 22 per cent in Level 1 Primary Education (EP1)
and 43 per cent in Level 2 Primary Education (EP2) (Mário et al. 2002: 5).

[1] The authors would like to thank the EDI/MOZ project coordination team, Finn Tarp (project
leader), Ines A. Ferreira, Johnny Flentø, and António Cruz, for the availability and patience
they always had to monitor, support, and guide us through the different phases of the study.
We would also like to thank the MINEDH authorities for making all the documentation we
requested on the education sector available to us. Last, but by no means least, we would like to
express our appreciation to the reviewers for their dedication and professionalism.

In the framework of the reforms initiated in the early years of national independence, the parliament approved the first National Education System (SNE) in 1983, through Law No. 4/83, of 23 March. Originally, the SNE had the following main goals: the eradication of illiteracy through compulsory universal education for seven years; the assurance of access to professional education for schoolchildren aged fifteen or over; and the promotion of scientific and pedagogical education and training for teachers. However, the implementation of the SNE suffered major setbacks due to the spread of the armed conflict that broke out two years after independence (Abrahamsson and Nilsson 1995). During the conflict, around 68 per cent of the primary school network was destroyed or remained inactive. Due to the instability and destruction caused by the war, there was a significant decline in the education sector in relation to the gains achieved in the early years after independence.

When the conflict ended, in response to the new multiparty political context established in the Constitution of 1990, the SNE was readjusted. Law No. 4/83, of 23 March was repealed and the new SNE Act (Law No. 6/92, of 6 May) was approved, introducing some changes to the structure, organisation, and operation of the educational system, including the participation of players other than the state in the provision of formal education. These amendments were followed by the abolition of school fees and other direct costs in access to schools in 2005, as well as free distribution of schoolbooks to all seven years in primary schools. Since then, the path followed by the education sector has been one of increasing the supply, with the aim of ensuring that all school-age children have access to and remain in school until they have completed their primary school education.

Notwithstanding the significant increase in access to education, challenges remain in terms of keeping the pupils at school and in the quality of learning. On the one hand, the rate of concluding primary schooling is still under 50 per cent (UNICEF Mozambique 2016), which means that over half of the pupils enrolled do not complete their primary education. On the other hand, the assessment of school education showed that the percentage of 3rd class pupils able to read nationwide was only 6.3 in 2013, having fallen to 4.9 in 2016 (INDE 2017; UNESCO Mozambique 2017). These results indicate the existence of what Hossain and Hickey (2019) call an 'education crisis' or 'schooling without learning' to describe situations where governments are able to assure that a large part of the population have access to education without its quality showing any kind of improvement.

The factors behind this 'education crisis' that is being observed in developing countries have been extensively dealt with in the literature (e.g., Kingdon et al. 2014; Jones 2016; Masino and Niño-Zarazúa 2016; Hossain and Hickey 2019). A consensus is that while the reforms aimed at improving quality are not very appealing to politicians due to their lack of visibility for winning over voters, the reforms aimed at increasing access are relatively easy to implement and gauge. Thereby the latter reforms generate political gains for the incumbent, as instruments of distribution of benefits to the voters, namely: expansion of job opportunities for teachers, administrators, support staff, construction workers, book publishers, and producers of other school supplies (Ridell and Niño-Zarazúa 2016; Hossain et al. 2019; Kjaer and Muwaanga 2019; Williams 2019).

In this chapter, we aim to contribute to the analysis of the 'education crisis' using the tools of institutional theory. Thus, through an extensive review of the literature, documentary research, and carrying out semi-structured interviews with actors selected intentionally, we analyse how the different factors associated with *state capacity, external influence, and voice and participation* have influenced the quality of primary education in Mozambique. To this end, we have chosen to structure our contribution in four parts. This introductory section is the first of these parts. In the second part, we conceptualise the institutional dimensions that will serve as the basis for analysing aspects related to the quality of primary education in Mozambique. In the third part, we characterise the primary education system in Mozambique, with focus on the description of the material and pedagogical conditions of teaching and learning. In the fourth part, we relate the quality of learning with the institutional dimensions. Lastly, we draw our conclusions.

## II CONCEPTUAL FRAMEWORK

In the analysis carried out in this study, we used an Institutional Diagnostic Tool approach to the education sector in Mozambique, taking primary education as a support case.

We have identified three institutional dimensions (or conventional good governance principles), which will serve as the basis for the analysis of the quality of primary education in Mozambique, namely: *state capacity and independence from private interests; sovereignty and independence;* and *voice, participation, and political accountability.*

### A State Capacity and Independence from Private Interests

State capacity is a complex dimension with several inter-related components that are sometimes confused with other dimensions, such as the *rule of law* (Cingolani 2013; Hanson and Sigman 2013). Cingolani suggests the following components/capacities: coercive, fiscal, administrative, transformative, relational, legal, and political. Hanson and Sigman focus on three of these: *fiscal, coercive,* and *administrative.*

Fiscal capacity has to do with the efficiency and effectiveness of the state in acquiring the financial resources that will allow it to operate, and this efficiency could be extended to public expenditure, that is the state's capacity to do more with fewer resources.

Coercive capacity is centred on the state's capacity to be an agent for the defence of the *rule of law* (through the security forces, the judicial power but also, in this specific context, school administrative organs and structures in place within the education system). It is important to emphasise the role of state coercive capacity to enforce the rule of law in schools, in face of risks of possible child abuse, sexual harassment, gender-based violence, teacher absenteeism, corruption, and other offences.

Administrative capacity refers to the processes of policy implementation, the provision of public services, as in our example of education, and the regulation of private activities, pursuant to the law. The strength of this component of state capacity depends on a set of factors: the competence, independence, reliability, and professionalism of state officials; the existence and effectiveness of monitoring and coordination mechanisms; and effective territorial service coverage (presence of state infrastructures, sometimes used as in Acemoglu et al. (2015) as an instrument for measuring state capacity). We argue that the other capacities, reviewed by Cingolani (2013), while important, have less relevance in our case.

As the evidence is undeniable that the weaknesses in state capacity referred to above compromise the more fluid operation and growth of the economy, so too do they affect access to public services, such as health and education and human welfare (Halleröd et al. 2013). However, as Halleröd et al. have found, sometimes, and remarkably in the case of education, if the weaknesses in the capacities of the state are significant, they could themselves be caused by the low economic performance of countries. As previously mentioned, the lack of state capacity to capture resources, in this case because of the low fiscal base and low human capital, can be a decisive factor for the creation and reinforcement of other capacities of the state.

To sum up, the level of state capacity, particularly in its fiscal and administrative capacity and coercion capacity, is clearly reflected in the capacity of the education system to serve the entire population, without leaving no one behind. We believe it is evident that state capacity thus defined is a key factor with serious implications for the quality of education and keeping pupils at school.

## B Sovereignty and Independence

In the reality of cooperation for development, there is major discussion on the merits and limits of external intervention. In the education sector, the indisputable fact that international cooperation does not have a sovereign mandate, or even a partial one, over the countries where they operate, can delay the transformation processes they wish to contribute to. Focusing on the transitional administration period in East Timor by the United Nations (UNTAET) after independence, Millo and Barnett (2004) clearly illustrate how the mitigated legitimacy of UNTAET, as an external player temporarily tasked with managing the country's administration, delayed and weakened educational reform after independence. In this case, the Timorese were alienated by the transitional political and legal powers of UNTAET and the financial power of the World

Bank. Strutt and Kepe (2010) present a similar example in the context of the Ghana National Education Campaign Coalition (GNECC), which aimed at implementing the Education for All (EFA) agenda. Here too, the authors note in their analysis that the GNECC, a coalition begun through external initiatives, ended up operating only as a national NGO for implementing activities. It was linked to external donors but had very weak ties and funding at local level.

As added support for this, Miningou (2019) shows that, given the institutional weaknesses in the education sector nationwide, development aid loses its efficiency and this loss could well be total. The results of this study comparing technical efficiency between countries show that factors like good governance, political stability, and national commitment (which implies the existence of fiscal capacity) reinforce the efficiency of external support to the development of education.

In short, development support, due to the limited legitimacy of a sovereign mandate that is evidently external to the country supported, is insufficient for stimulating development in the education sector. It can, however, be damaging, whether through alienating the fundamental stakeholders at local and national level or by inverting the nexus of accountability of the initiatives promoted, of the citizens to the international cooperation players that finance the initiatives.

## C  Voice, Participation, and Political Accountability

As discussed by Gaventa (2002), the possibility of having a voice and participating actively in social processes and interaction with public service providers and companies is an essential component of citizenship. The existence of effective communication and accountability of national and local governments in response to the voices of citizens is one of the characteristics that defines 'good governance'. As stated by Paul (1992), political accountability processes are the set of approaches, mechanisms, and practices that allow the stakeholders to ensure performance and the correct level of public service provision. Of these stakeholders, Gaventa (2002) calls particular attention to the people who face economic hardship and marginalised people. Citizenship, whether in legal or sociological terms, is only experienced if the people feel they have the right to participate in social and political processes and if they are recognised as players who build and shape the services they use and are not just users or beneficiaries of these services. Gaventa (2002) stated that citizens' rights to health could not be exercised if the citizens cannot exercise their democratic right to take part in the decision-making process about the services that are provided. This principle applies naturally to education. The way participation space is given to citizens and the degree of inclusion of disadvantaged or marginalised people or those not necessarily belonging to social groups close to power determine the degree of voice, participation, and accountability that exists.

The actual agents of the educational system, with different levels and responsibilities, must feel that they are participants and that their voices are recognised (Smith and Benavot 2019). Regarding the concept of *structured democratic voice mechanisms*, Smith and Benavot discuss and illustrate the need for teachers, local leaders, and pupils to be able to state their position on political initiatives or reforms. If the democratic expression of the voice of the local community, that is the pupils or teachers, cannot be expressed directly, one alternative could be through independent representatives drawn from civil society (Mungiu-Pippidi and Dusu 2011; Smith and Benavot 2019). This voice can only be effective if the central and provincial government system of education and even the governing bodies of each school are open to relinquishing part of their decision-making power. An exercise in voice promotion that is merely consultative, without recognition of authority, weakens its effectiveness. However, if it is actually implemented, it allows for the intersection of the interests of the fundamental players in the education system.

What the citizens and players inside a system, for example the education system, do with the voice and participation they are allowed is also important. Véron et al. (2006) indicate that democratic decentralisation and community participation are often recommended as instruments for controlling corruption. However, reflecting on the case of a social protection mechanism in the rural areas of East Bengal and Bangladesh, they suggest that not only are the communities not homogenous, but key members of local communities can themselves be accomplices or perpetrators of corruption. In this case, rather than combating corruption, decentralisation can make it take on decentralised forms. This is perhaps an example of where weaknesses in the rule of law converge with weaknesses in the voice and participation mechanisms, making it difficult to respond to problems such as the corruption that can be seen in public service bureaucracy, thus undermining performance.

In short, voice, participation, and accountability mechanisms are necessary in the education system, not only to monitor its operation, but also to lead to improvements and adjust reforms through combining the contextualised perspectives of its players, including pupils, teachers, and local communities. However, the inequalities and dynamics of power and the fact that institutional weaknesses reinforce each other must not be forgotten: the weaknesses in the capacities of the state can reduce the effectiveness of measures for promoting voice and participation, corrupting the actual accountability mechanisms.

In the next section, we will present the case of primary education in Mozambique, which, after it has been described, will be discussed in the light of the interpretation key we have presented.

## III PRIMARY EDUCATION IN MOZAMBIQUE

Overcoming the negligence to which the Portuguese colonial administration consigned the education of Mozambicans, independent Mozambique quickly extended access to primary education. From little more than 30 per cent of

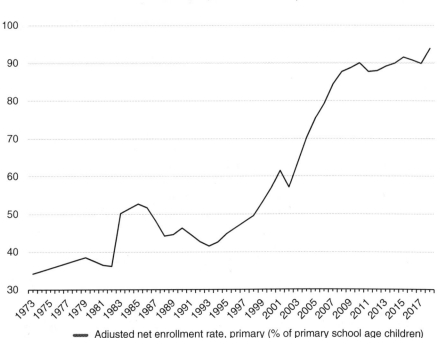

Adjusted net enrollment rate, primary (% of primary school age children)

FIGURE 5.1 Primary education enrolment 1973–2018 (%)
Source: Authors' illustration based on World Development Indicators (World Bank 2020).

school-age children in the year it gained independence, enrolment in primary school reached a rate of close to 100 per cent (Figure 5.1) in 2018. This remarkable expansion, particularly in the last 30 years, was the result of policies from successive governments of Mozambique that deliberately and systematically favoured the expansion of education.

Note that the efforts made to assure access to primary education for all children of school-going age were carried out at the same time as, and under pressure from, high population growth (around 2.8 per cent per year). This corresponded to an increase in the number of children in primary schools from 578,000 in 1973 to 6.6 million in 2018 (World Bank 2020), that is over ten times more. During the same period, the number of primary school teachers increased from 8,300 to 118,700. Moving out from under such a heavy colonial burden, with so few people able to read and write, it would have been practically impossible for the number of teachers to keep up with the pace of growth in the school-going population. This gave rise to tensions in the challenge to adjust the primary education available to the increasing demand, as is clear from the pupil–teacher ratios presented in Figure 5.2.

Such a high number of real and potential users, associated with the fact that education and schoolbooks were free in both cycles of primary education and

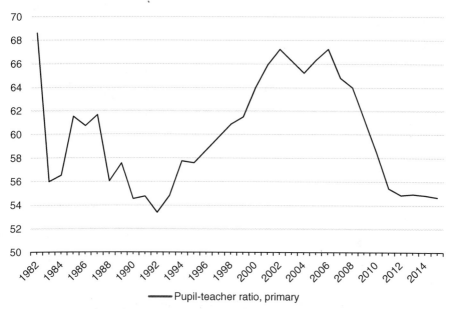

FIGURE 5.2 Pupil–teacher ratio 1982–2014 (%)
Source: Authors' illustration based on World Development Indicators (World Bank 2020).

the constant expansion of the school network, could not but put enormous pressure on the services provided by the education sector. There were also other challenges in terms of the sustainability and equity of the expansion, keeping pupils at school and quality of learning. We focus in particular on this last aspect.

There are worrying data regarding the quality of learning and evidence of a rate of concluding primary schooling of under 50 per cent (UNICEF Mozambique 2016), which means that over half of the pupils enrolled do not complete their primary education. Moreover, there are other strong indications of a low level of learning by primary school pupils, such as those shown in the results of independent research carried out in Mozambique by the Southern and Eastern Africa Consortium for Monitoring Education Quality (SACMEQ).

As is clear from the data in Table 5.1 and discussed in Magaia et al. (2011), in 2007, from a universe of structured questions at eight levels of numeracy, only 41.4 and 20.9 per cent of 6th class pupils achieved positive results in basic numeracy and beginning numeracy questions, respectively. In the reading test, only 22.0 and 17.9 per cent of pupils achieved positive results in basic reading and interpretive reading questions, respectively. Between 2000 and 2007, the quality of education deteriorated. Magaia et al. (2011: 3) attributed this fall to factors related to the rapid expansion of the education system.

TABLE 5.1 *Results of the SACMEQ II and III studies: proficiency of sixth class pupils*

| Mathematics | | | | | Reading | | | |
|---|---|---|---|---|---|---|---|---|
| Level | 2000 | 2007 | Δ | | 2000 | 2007 | Δ | Level |
| 1 Pre-numeracy | 0.4% | 5.1% | 4.6% | | 2.3% | 6.7% | 4.4% | Pre-reading | 1 |
| 2 Emergent numeracy | 12.6% | 27.7% | 15.1% | | 3.9% | 14.8% | 10.9% | Emergent reading | 2 |
| 3 Basic numeracy | 41.7% | 41.4% | -0.3% | | 11.2% | 22.0% | 10.8% | Basic reading | 3 |
| 4 Beginning numeracy | 32.1% | 20.9% | -11.2% | | 28.8% | 25.0% | -3.8% | Reading for meaning | 4 |
| 5 Competent numeracy | 11.4% | 3.9% | -7.5% | | 32.7% | 17.9% | -14.8% | Interpretive reading | 5 |
| 6 Mathematically skilled | 1.7% | 0.8% | -0.9% | | 16.1% | 10.7% | -5.4% | Inferential reading | 6 |
| 7 Concrete problem solving | 0.1% | 0.3% | 0.2% | | 5.0% | 2.7% | -2.3% | Analytical reading | 7 |
| 8 Abstract problem solving | 0.0% | 0.0% | 0.0% | | 0.1% | 0.3% | 0.2% | Critical reading | 8 |

*Source:* Authors' calculations based on data from the SACMEQ II and III studies published in (SACMEQ 2020).

TABLE 5.2 *Performance of third class pupils, %*

| Reading/Portuguese | | | | | | Mathematics | | |
|---|---|---|---|---|---|---|---|---|
| 2013 | | | 2016 | | | 2016 | | |
| Level 1 | Level 2 | Level 3 | Level 1 | Level 2 | Level 3 | Level 1 | Level 2 | Level 3 |
| 82.8 | 43.6 | 6.3 | 83.2 | 43.8 | 4.9 | 89.4 | 50.3 | 7.7 |

*Note:* Reading/Portuguese levels are: (1) recognising the alphabet; (2) reading words and sentences; (3) reading and text comprehension and analysis. Mathematics levels are: (1) counting numbers and identifying geometric figures; (2) reading numbers and basic arithmetic; (3) problem solving.
*Source:* Authors' illustration based on data from INDE (2017).

More recent data from a report on the assessment of 3rd class pupils (INDE 2017) confirm the previous indicators and once again show low levels of skills acquisition (Table 5.2). They also point to a deterioration in Portuguese learning between 2013 and 2016.

Given these results, it is important to bear in mind the facts behind them. Several factors can be pointed to as being the origin of the low levels reported. Considering the scope of this chapter, we will be focusing on the following:

## A Deficient Allocation of Time for Teaching and Learning Tasks

The reform of the basic education curriculum, whose implementation began in 2003 (INDE 2003), highlights the acquisition of reading and writing skills as the fundamental pillars on which the acquisition of skills in the other levels and classes in the education system are based. A large number of Mozambican schools teach three daily rounds of classes, which means that children are only in school doing teaching and learning tasks for three hours a day. This reality is quite common in public schools especially in rural areas, where the majority of the population lives. Considering the long distances most children have to travel between home and school allows us to understand that the time these children have for reading and writing tasks is very limited, both inside and outside of school.

## B Overcrowded Classes and Very High Pupil–Teacher Ratios

One of the direct consequences of the increase in numbers at primary schools and the absence of a sufficient number of teachers and facilities has been the need to extend the absorption capacity of the schools, which gave rise to overcrowded classes. Although the number of primary schools and teachers has shown a substantial increase, the first cycle EP classes and the pupil–teacher ratios remained practically unchanged between 2013 and 2018. In fact, a large number of EP2 schools are a result of the transformation of EP1 schools into full schools (EP1+EP2) without the addition of classrooms. Thus, in 2018, the average pupil–teacher ratio in full primary schooling (EP1+EP2) was around 55.27, compared to 64.2 in the beginners' classes (EP1). The highest ratios were in Zambezia, Nampula, and Cabo Delgado provinces (over seventy pupils per teacher). This fact, combined with the lack of time for learning tasks both inside and outside the classroom, shows how limited the capacity of teachers is to deal with the learning needs of all the pupils in the areas of reading, writing, and arithmetic, especially pupils with special needs.

## C  Deficient Preparation, Allocation, and Monitoring of the Work of Teachers

It is not enough to introduce curricular reforms and increase the number of teachers in schools while maintaining other basic characteristics unaltered and/or allowing these to deteriorate. The implementation plan for the Basic Education Course Plan (INDE 2003) points to the teacher as a factor in its success. Recent studies (e.g., Díaz 2003; Sheerens 2004; Makopa 2011) that examined the factors associated with the performance of the pupils highlight the importance of qualifications and the equitable distribution of teachers. Meanwhile, Darling-Hammond et al. (2005), McColskey et al. (2006), and Rice (2003) go further and defend the existence of a strong connection between teacher qualifications and pupil achievements. Moreover, there is a global consensus that 'to improve the quality of education, it is first necessary to improve the recruitment, training, social status and working conditions of the teachers' (Delors et al. 1996: 131). In practice, however, this reasoning is far from gaining the agreement of the majority of the political decision-makers and donors in the education sector.

It can be said, without doubt, that there is no other sector of education in Mozambique that has been subject to so many changes since independence as teacher training. In response to increasing pupil–teacher ratios, the government took the decision to reduce the number of years of training for primary teachers. This changed the training models in force (7th class + 3 years in Teacher Training Centres [CFPP] and 10th class + 2 years in Primary Teaching Institutes [IMAP]) and introduced a new model, called the 'fast track training model' (10th class + 1 year). With this alteration, the education sector was able to train 6,094 teachers between 2012 and 2018, around 80 per cent of whom were absorbed by the public sector (MINEDH 2018).

However, the introduction of the fast-track model is an example of how decisions on educational policy based almost exclusively on assumptions of a financial or economic nature can have devastating consequences for the quality of education of one or more generations, if not the entire nation. Sources that we contacted from the education sector, with long and proven experience in management at different levels, were unanimous in suggesting that the main motivation behind the introduction of this teacher training model was most likely the 'excessive burden of salaries' on the sector's operating expenses in comparison to other expenses. According to these sources, this fact caused some important international partners to put pressure on the Ministry of Education to reduce the number of years for primary teacher training from three to just one. This was a means to help provide the necessary teachers in a short space of time and stop the increasing salary expenses, given that the salary of a teacher with a 10+1 profile would be less than a 10+3 teacher.

Despite this effort, the decline in the quality of education has not stopped. The 10+1 training model contributed only to containing the increase in pupil–teacher ratios, but it was also shown to be totally incapable of providing primary teachers with the skills required in the areas of reading, writing, and arithmetic and preparing them for dealing with very large classes. In addition to the problem of the deficient training of teachers, we have the perception of generalised non-compliance with teachers' contractual obligations and a lack of monitoring during school hours by the school managers, which results in frequent tardiness and unjustified absences during school time, not only by the teachers, but also by a large number of school principals.

The phenomenon of chronic absenteeism among teachers has become a serious problem in many developing countries (Carron and Chau 1996). UNICEF Mozambique has revealed that in Mozambique in 2014, many 'pupils were losing more than 50 per cent of the potential learning time as a result of late start times, early closing and extended recesses' (2014: 68). In a study prepared for the USAID, it is also pointed out that teachers are between 10 and 40 minutes late and 'considering that the first class of the day is often Portuguese, where reading is taught, it is easy to see how teaching time is reduced by teachers being late' (Raupp et al. 2013: 4). Altogether, these anomalies mean that pupils have less daily instruction time, with negative effects on learning to read and write. All told, according to estimates made by UNICEF Mozambique (2016: 2), the absenteeism rate[2] for teachers is around 45 per cent, while for school principals, it is close to 44 per cent. If confirmed, these data indicate serious problems with school management and leadership and make us question the criteria for the selection and promotion of school principals and other holders of positions of responsibility at local and district levels.

## D Shortages of Teaching Materials

The available literature indicates that the availability of and access to basic school supplies in the classrooms has a positive impact on teacher motivation (Carron and Chau 1996; Díaz 2003) and the performance of pupils (INDE 2017; Makopa 2011). Material conditions include school infrastructures,

---

[2] In education, absenteeism accounts for unplanned absences of school workers (teachers, school directors,...) due to sickness or other causes. For instance, teacher absenteeism rate is measured as the share of teacher/pupil contact hours missed due to unplanned absence, as a percentage of total planned teacher/pupil contact hours.

classrooms, desks, schoolbooks, teachers' guides, the blackboard, chalk, teacher's table and chair, cupboards, maps, display cabinets for science materials, and other educational supplies. It is true that over the last twenty years, many schools and classrooms were built all over the country. However, there is no doubt that the construction of the schools and classrooms fell short of what had been planned and the expansion that took place in primary schools was at the expense of the 'adoption of three rounds of classes, an increase in the number of pupils per class and the existence of outdoor classes' (Duarte 2018: 41). In fact, the annual construction goal of 4,100 classrooms was later revised to 1,400 (CESO 2011: 11). This resulted in 'almost 56.6% of pupils studying in schools with no water and 72.8% in schools without electricity, while only 16% study in schools with a library. With the exception of Maputo Province, over 60% of pupils sit on the floor and only 25% of pupils have the same teacher until they finish 2nd class' (Duarte 2018: 42).

Similarly, data produced by the INDE (2017) reveal the existence of pupils who have classes outdoors. According to that study, the proportion of pupils having classes outdoors (outside the classroom) fell from 25 per cent in 2010 to 22.7 per cent in 2013. Despite this reduction, the situation is still worrying, given that, apart from studying outdoors, many of these children study sitting on the floor, with no physical support for their writing and arithmetic activities.

## E  Poor Involvement and Participation of Parents and the Community in School Management

A large portion of the anomalies already pointed to, particularly with regard to absenteeism by the teachers and school managers, could be prevented and minimised through the involvement of the local communities in school management, through school councils (CEs). Given the limited capacity of the state, through the ministry responsible for the area, for monitoring the activities carried out in all the schools, the CEs are still seen as a platform through which communities, parents, and guardians can demand accountability and put on some pressure for a change in direction towards the desired quality of education. However, there are indications that the performance of the CEs has fallen short of what was expected.

The education sector is structured in hierarchical levels. The Ministry of Education and Human Development (MINEDH) runs the sector at central level and below it are the provincial and district boards and, finally, the schools. However, between district level and the schools, there are so-called School Cluster Zones (ZIP), which are areas in the education sector that group together schools that are geographically close to each other in order to have pedagogical support between peers and promote teacher empowerment. At each one of the levels described above, there is a host of interested players, who mutually influence each other and are influenced by the system as a whole. At each one of the levels, the players develop specific dynamics because of the development of institutional practices or policies specific to the subsector they are attached to and because of institutionalised local practices.

At primary school level, which is at the centre of our analysis, the relevant players are the parents and guardians, the teachers, the school management body and the support service staff, pupils, and the community in general. There is a consensus that the greater the involvement of these players, the greater the degree of effectiveness of the practices in the schools, with positive effects on keeping pupils at school and improving the quality of education. This is an aspect formally recognised by the government, which is why the CEs have been revitalised as a participation platform for the different local players in school management.

As consultation bodies, the CEs are the main school body and their functions extend to monitoring and supervising school activities. The CEs, whose members are elected for two-year mandates, are made up of 13 to 19 members (according to the number of pupils in the school), representing the teachers, the administrative staff, parents and guardians, the pupils, and the community.

The list of powers of the CEs includes, but is not limited to, approval of plans, regulations, and projects, and the feasibility of their implementation in the schools; participation in financial decision-making and supervision; monitoring the execution of the budget (including Direct Support to Schools – ADE); monitoring the performance of teachers and the school management board; giving opinions on educational performance; and establishing mechanisms for resolving disputes, infractions, and the accountability of the offenders. In addition, it is also up to the CEs to propose the dismissal of school principals to the competent authority.

However, the idea according to which the CEs constitute a body that assures community participation in school management needs more scrutiny, given that there are cases where the CEs are taken over by local elite groups, based on the power relations characteristic of the communities where the schools are located. As an example, there are indications of the existence of a high number of cases where members of the CEs are co-opted by school principals without being elected by the community, which limits the pressure of accountability on the management body. According to this logic, once CEs are co-opted by some members of the school board with the aim of ensuring that these members remain in the positions they hold for an indefinite period, the CEs are no longer able to truly monitor teachers and the management body and hold them accountable. These practices raise questions as to the representative nature of the members of the CEs and their effectiveness in resolving school problems. Under these circumstances, the CEs serve only to rubber-stamp what has been previously decided by the school principal and his/her cronies without the CEs being involved in the decision-making process. This results in a lack of transparency in the use of the funds allocated to the school, bringing perceptions of misuse of the ADE (or lack of evidence as to its correct use) and of other public funds allocated to the school.

Interviews with staff of the District Education Services in Meconta (Nampula Province) led us to understand that they had been expecting the ADE to serve for paying subsidies to the members of the CEs also. As this did not happen, the CEs lost their motivation to effectively participate in the CE sessions because they could not see any material gain in this, particularly as there had been a general perception that the ADE would tend to benefit the managing body of the school and the President of the CE. In the same district, there were also situations where members of the CEs had to travel long distances to get to the school in order to take part in the CE meetings, which discouraged their participation.

Similarly, data collected in Meconta and Murrupula district (interviews conducted by one of the authors in 2017) showed how the communities sometimes present a series of complaints regarding teacher absences and tardiness. These complaints are then forwarded to the local CEs by the community leader or through the parents and guardians. However, little change has been seen because of these actions by the communities, which also discouraged their participation. In addition, as mentioned by the president of the CE at one of the primary schools in Murrupula District, very often, when the presidents of the CEs are not part of the school administrative staff, they are advised not to interfere in internal school issues. Thus, if on the one hand the lack of information on the actual role of the CEs works as an obstacle to their effectiveness, on the other hand there is an absence of an appeals body for CEs to turn to should a school principal carry out duties heavy-handedly. The net result of this situation is the lack of incentive for the members of the CEs to continue being involved in actively monitoring the school management activities. As a result, the problem of absences and tardiness of teachers and principals and the misuse of the scarce resources placed at the disposal of the schools, which could be resolved at local level, remain chronic and unaffected.

Cases of parents and pupils fearing reprisals from the teachers and school managers are frequently reported. On the one hand, pupil representatives barely have an active voice at CE meetings, given the power relations established, where the teacher has the educational authority the pupil does not have, hence the fear of reprisal. On the other hand, parents and guardians often fear that their children will suffer reprisals if they report cases of abuse of power by the management (in the cases where this happens) or the teachers (absences, tardiness, abuse, extortion, etc.) in a classroom context.

Thus, with regard to the involvement and participation of local players (parents and other community members) in school management, a kind of pseudo-participation is observed, as the CEs are very often used as tools, with their members being forced to accept what has already been decided by the school board. At best, community participation in school management is limited to participation in CE meetings only, but they have little power to influence decision-making processes. As a result, many schools are still facing chronic and apparently unsolvable problems, which include unjustified absences and tardiness of teachers and school principals, a lack of transparency in the use of the ADE funds to improve material conditions in the schools, a high number of school dropouts (especially girls) before completing the 2nd cycle of primary education.

## F  Weaknesses in External Support to Education

Mozambique's ambitions for education, given the budget difficulties it experiences as a low-income country, cannot be achieved without external support. With a view to coordinating the flow of external aid to the education programmes in Mozambique, in the context of the continued increase in school numbers, the international cooperation partners of the then Ministry of Education (MINED) proposed a funding mechanism known as FASE – Support Fund for the Education Sector to the government, as mentioned above. This paradigm shift came because of the idea put forward in 2001 of adopting the so-called Sector-Wide Approach – SWAp to the education sector. This can be defined as a 'process where a sector strategy is formulated and budgeted, aligned with the available resources through an iterative process, converted into a working plan and formalised in agreements between the implementing agency and the funding sources' (Mário and Takala 2003: 6). The implementation of this approach, through FASE, implied the need to involve the partners in the different stages of implementation of the education programmes. This includes the discussion and the development of the initial proposals for educational policy documents and the negotiation and harmonisation of the formal arrangements for the implementation of the programmes in Annual Review Meetings (RAR) and other support bodies (*ibidem*).

Through FASE, the Ministry of Education was able to cover a considerable volume of current expenses and investment in the education sector, which would otherwise have remained without coverage or would have had inadequate coverage. In fact, FASE has made the purchase of schoolbooks for free distribution feasible, as well as the acquisition of laboratory materials, teacher training, district and provincial supervision, and the construction of classrooms in the districts.

Notwithstanding these positive developments, the sector approach via FASE faced (and continues to face) serious constraints. For example, the delays seen in the release of funds from the State Budget (OE) by the Ministry of the Economy and Finance, particularly during the first three months of each financial year, seem to have reinforced the perception of the role of bilateral funding projects as sources of flexible or 'emergency' financial support, especially for the provincial boards, the district boards, and the schools, clearly going against the principles of SWAp (Mário and Takala 2003).

From 2014 to the present day, the amounts allocated to FASE by international partners have been decreasing steadily. For example, in 2014, the partners had committed to disburse US$149 million; in 2015, this had fallen to US$81 million and for 2016–18 disbursement commitments fluctuated between US$105 and 110 million per year (MINEDH 2015). However, in 2016, with the emergence of the 'hidden debt' crisis, the international partners found themselves confronted with the lack of measures to mitigate the risk of the flow of funds from FASE to the education sector, which is why they decided to suspend disbursements until the partnership instruments were revised and signed (MINEDH 2018). In 2017, disbursements to FASE were resumed but, that same year, a relatively low external investment budget was recorded (around 63 per cent), which was attributed to delays in contracting supervision for the construction work on classrooms (MINEDH 2018). Although it is a fact that the funds from FASE constitute the largest source of external resources available to the education sector, its contribution has never been able to break the 80 per cent barrier (MINEDH 2019).

Another point for reflection is how the reforms were implemented, clearly showing how dependence on external support can compromise the quality of the processes and the sustainability of the results. An example of this is the reform of the primary education curriculum (curricular plan for basic education) in 2003, which did not take into account the capacity to prepare, place, and supervise the qualified teachers needed to carry out the reforms set out in the new curriculum. Another example was the decision to abolish school fees and introduce free distribution of schoolbooks with the support of the FASE partners alone.

IV  INSTITUTIONAL DIMENSIONS AND LEARNING OUTCOMES

The description in Section III presents several instances in which factors acting in different ways have emerged as part of the institutional dimensions that shape primary education. Below, we attempt to systematise those instances.

A  State Capacity and External Influence

Throughout this subsection, we will attempt to show that, along with limited financial capacity to respond to the increasing demand and sustain the pace of increases in school numbers, the operation of the education sector is severely curtailed by its limited human and administrative capacity. Given these shortcomings, international support is fundamental, making the primary education system susceptible to external influence.

The demographic pressure on primary education revealed severe shortcomings in the *administrative capacity* of the state, which is particularly evident in the lack of the classrooms and, mainly, of the teachers that the system so badly needs. We believe these factors weaken the State's capacity, resulting in overcrowded classes, very high pupil–teacher ratios and pressure on the learning process.

However, as discussed conceptually, we must not forget that these shortcomings in administrative capacities are closely related to the shortcomings in the *fiscal capacity* of the state. As we have shown, the Mozambican State's focus on education is clearly seen in terms of the percentage of the budget it has been devoting to this sector, but it is also clear that there is a lack of financial resources in low-income countries like Mozambique.

This has led to pursuing options that compromise the *administrative capacity* of the state with regard to primary education, particularly an insufficient number of new classrooms built; an increase in the number of classes taught without any increase in the number of classrooms; teaching in three daily rounds of three hours/day; and reduction of the training time required to qualify as a primary school teacher (the fast track training model).

We also found evidence of factors that weaken the *coercive capacity* of the state, particularly in terms of administrative control and mitigation of absenteeism and other abuses by teachers. As we showed, this weak control of absenteeism suggests the existence of leadership and school management problems, which are also linked to other factors that weaken the *voice, participation and political accountability* of the institutional dimension. The combination of weaknesses in the coercive and administrative capacity of the state extends to the process of selecting and promoting school principals and other holders of local and district management positions as well.

Weaknesses in state capacities, which, like those we have found in primary education, can also be combined with other institutional dimensions. In particular, we have found clear interactions between weakened *state capacities* and the institution of *sovereignty and independence* in the way external support to the education sector operates. Given the limitations of the fiscal capacity of the Mozambican State, an initiative like FASE, as described above, is much needed and indeed admirable. Within the bounds of the limited legitimacy discussed in the conceptual framework, this initiative makes it possible to make up for financial shortcomings and even support the reinforcement of the administrative capacities of the educational system in the country.

However, the case of primary education reveals weaknesses too in the way external support can interact with central government structures. On the one hand, as mentioned above, the interaction with a weakened *fiscal/budget capacity* of central public administration in releasing funds to the provincial and district administrations in good time gives rise to dependency mechanisms and alienation of fundamental national governance structures.

On the other hand, by making financial support to the education sector conditional on political decisions with long-term and uncertain effects, the international partners risk exceeding the necessary limits that respect for Mozambican sovereignty should imply. This is clear in the influence of international partners on the decision to adopt the fast track teacher-training model in primary education. The discontinuity caused by the many teacher training models that have been introduced prevent the sector not only from learning about what works (or not), but also from building professional careers that will attract and retain the most talented young people in the teaching profession. As such, the imposition of giving financial criteria precedence over educational quality criteria by external partners fundamental for the actual funding of the education system proved to be problematic from the outset. Even more problematic is the imposition of a solution without others having been discussed openly and with the participation of players in the education system, in particular representatives of the school communities.

In the same way, the weaknesses that were probably behind the 'hidden debt' crisis were added to the imperative of being accountable to the external sovereignty entities that manage cooperation for development, creating problems for the support that FASE provides to education in Mozambique. Because Mozambique has ties to external sovereign entities, fundamental funds for reinforcing infrastructures, resources, and teacher training, aimed at improving the quality of learning, may then respond to the needs of the country in a disjointed manner.

To sum up, limitations and weaknesses in state capacities, sovereignty, and independence affect the epistemic quality of primary education. The scarcity of financial resources to make sector policies feasible, the small number of highly qualified professionals (whether teachers or technical or administrative staff), the problems of intra- and inter-sector coordination, and the limited capacity for monitoring, auditing, and inspecting the sector policies are just some of the aspects arising from the weak administrative capacity of the state, which have an impact on the quality of education.

Even though governments may choose educational reforms aimed at access to school because these generate immediate electoral gain, it is recognised that improving the quality of learning in school is more costly and difficult than increasing the number of schools (Nicolai et al. 2014, cited by Hossain and Hickey 2019: 2). As such, states with weak capacities tend to focus more on increasing access to education and less on its quality (Harding and Stasavage 2014). This is particularly so in countries like Mozambique where the exponential growth of demand for education outpaces by far the state capacity to offer quality education in schools. An issue worth raising is the fact that there may not be a trade-off between quantity and quality if one considers that universal access to schooling must be reached first, before improving quality. On the other hand, weak state capacity to fund its educational development plans exposes it to the priorities set by the donors.

## B Voice, Participation, and Political Accountability

Although systems for the promotion of voice and participation of the different players in the school community have been put in place, the evidence found reveals important weaknesses. The literature we reviewed states that voice, participation, and accountability mechanisms are necessary for monitoring the operation of the education system, but also for leading to improvements and adjusting reforms, through listening to the school community, including pupils, teachers, and local community representatives.

As we have seen, the CEs were set up and revitalised to be able to control and monitor the action of school management bodies, as well as teachers, with powers being assigned to them for resolving conflicts and holding them accountable. According to how they were designed, they should, in fact, be adequate voice, participation and political accountability mechanisms.

However, our study on primary education reveals clear evidence of factors that weaken these mechanisms, as is the case with other cases discussed in the literature. Cases where members of the CEs are co-opted by school principals or by other members, in the pursuit of their own personal interests, weaken the legitimacy and transparency of these bodies. The lack of clarity as to the duties of the members of the CEs, expectations of payment in some instances, and their lack of commitment to the public good undermine their operation. Consequently, the CEs do not fully carry out their duties of monitoring situations of absenteeism, the lack of punctuality of teachers and principals, and the misuse of school resources, which all have a tendency to be perpetuated.

Finally, concerns are reinforced through evidence of a lack of mechanisms for the CEs to appeal to district, provincial, or national bodies or the state or associations. This means that even those that operate correctly may not be able to exercise effective coercion over teachers or principals who are negligent or engage in abuses.

As mentioned above, Hanushek et al. (2013) suggest that voice and participation mechanisms at local level can contribute to reinforcing the capacities of the state. However, for this to happen, the institutional factors found lead us to recommend that attention should be paid to the actual voice and participation mechanisms implemented in primary schools, the CEs. Otherwise, the weaknesses they induce will only intensify the perceived weaknesses in the administrative and coercive capacities of the state under the scope of primary education.

## V CONCLUSION

Throughout this chapter, it has been observed that, since the early years of national independence, Mozambique opted for expansionary measures in education, with the aim of providing access to school to the majority of the population, without discrimination as to race, colour, ethnicity, religion, or social condition. To this end, a unified education system was set up and the school network extended to different parts of the country, both in the cities and in the countryside. Despite having suffered a huge blow in the 1980s because of a long and destructive armed conflict, over the last thirty years, the education sector has recovered and shown positive results in terms of school access and coverage. The net coverage rate for primary education (EP1+EP2) now stands at around 96.6 per cent. However, the expansionary measures implemented in the education sector have been at the expense of the quality of education. With less than 5 per cent of 3rd class pupils having developed reading skills and less than 8 per cent with the mathematical skills required for that level of education, the country is suffering from a chronic 'education crisis', characterised by a considerable increase in the number of primary school pupils and the reduction in the quality of learning over time. Behind this schooling without learning, there are factors related to the teaching conditions (absenteeism, poor preparation of the teachers, overcrowded classes, excessively high pupil–teacher ratios, etc.) and deficient material conditions for teaching and learning (not enough classrooms, desks, books, tables, etc.). In turn, these factors are also influenced by the institutional context in which the education sector operates. Limited state capacity, high dependence on external support, and deficient community participation in school life are the three factors in the institutional environment that have been shaping the characteristics of primary education.

The available data suggest that expansionary measures in a context of limited fiscal capacity, even with the support of donors, have had negative effects on the quality of education, on the lack of sufficient investment in building new classrooms, and/or on enlarging and equipping the existing ones. This is why there is still a high number of schools without water or electricity or a library and with over 60 per cent of pupils sitting on the floor. If on the one hand donors exercise enormous pressure towards a mass increase in access to primary education, making financial commitments to fund school infrastructures, on the other hand, donors do not fund a large part of the operating expenses that the expansionary measures involve, particularly staff salaries.

Given the scarcity of financial resources for the payment of the salaries for the primary teachers needed for the continuing increases in school numbers, the government's option, with the agreement of the donors, was to introduce the basic level (10+1) teacher training model in place of the one in force up to then (10+3). The net effect of this alteration was a proliferation of primary school teachers without the necessary skills to teach in essential curricular areas (including reading, writing, and arithmetic) and incapable of dealing with large classes.

In addition to the state's weak fiscal capacity, which justifies and drives external aid for education programmes, there is also its deficient administrative quality, which is very often associated with the lack of qualified staff in the sector. This situation becomes more evident as we move down to the lower levels of the structure of the education sector (i.e. from national to provincial and from there to district level). The state's poor administration capacity is also plainly seen in the almost non-existent control over teacher attendance and effectiveness. The creation and/or revitalisation of the CEs, as a mechanism for ensuring community involvement and participation in the management and improving the performance of school is not unrelated to this reality. However, a large number of CEs are lethargic, and there are many cases where school principals usurp the functions of the CEs, thus limiting the room for community participation in school management.

In short, we can conclude that some of the reforms introduced in the education sector since 1992 with support and supervision from MINEDH's international partners were either too ambitious/not very realistic, or no more than rhetoric from the political decision-makers, as human and financial resources were not assigned in sufficient quality for their implementation. In fact, as was already pointed out, some reforms did not even consider the possibility of the Mozambican State implementing them without recourse to aid from external partners. Involvement and participation by parents, community and religious leaders, and other stakeholders in school life is an important step. This involvement will, in part, allow for the prevention and removal of obstacles to keeping an increasingly higher number of schoolchildren, particularly girls, at school. Similarly, it will support the promotion of an effective improvement in the quality of learning, reporting, and fighting absenteeism by schoolteachers and principals, and the unlawful charges imposed on parents and guardians and gender-based violence, among other evils, as well as promoting the accountability of the leaders and school managers. The improvement in the quality of education also comes as a result of the reinforcement of state capacity, with the support of effective voice and participation mechanisms and external support mainly aimed at reinforcing this capacity, before moving on to new initiatives that put added pressure on the system.

# 6

# Obstacles to the Provision of Healthcare Services

Paulo Ivo Garrido

It always seems impossible until it's done

Nelson Mandela

## I OVERVIEW

### A Introduction

Mozambique is a country with a surface area of around 800,000 km², located in Southeast Africa. It became independent in 1975 after around five centuries of Portuguese colonisation. At the time of independence, Mozambique was one of the poorest countries in the world. Between 1976 (less than a year after the proclamation of independence) and 1992, the country was ravaged by a war that caused large-scale destruction of its economic and social infrastructure and affected over 5 million Mozambicans, of whom around 1 million lost their lives and 4 million were forcibly displaced from their homes (Pim and Kristensen 2007).

Thus, in 1992, when the war ended, Mozambique was the poorest country in the world, with a per capita GDP of only US$354 (2011 PPP) (Gradín and Tarp 2019). The economic growth seen in Mozambique from 1995 onwards led to a reduction in poverty levels, with the per capita GDP trebling in only twenty-five years (Gradín and Tarp 2019). Despite this economic growth, Mozambique remains one of the poorest and least developed countries in the world.

In Mozambique today, over half the population (estimated at around 29,000,000, 66 per cent of whom live in rural areas) lives below the poverty line (less than US$2 per person per day) (Gradín and Tarp 2019). According to data from 2017, Mozambique has a per capita GDP of US$1,136 and a Human Development Index of 0.442, putting it in 180th place out of 189 countries

(UNDP n.d.). According to data from 2019, Mozambique has a Sustainable Development index of 53 points out of 100, putting it in 136th place out of 162 countries (Sachs et al. 2019: 21).

The process of economic growth that is leading to a reduction in poverty has occurred and occurs at the same time as an increase in economic and social inequalities. These take place in a country with previous inequalities between urban and rural areas and between regions (North, Centre, and South).

## B Concept of Health and Social Determinants of Health

To study the topic of health in Mozambique, it is first necessary to understand the concepts of health and social determinants of health. According to the World Health Organization (WHO), 'Health is a state of complete physical, mental and social wellbeing and not merely the absence of disease or infirmity' (WHO 2006). This means that a person might not be sick in the normal opinion of people (i.e. not suffering from fever, diarrhoea, cough, or headaches and going to work every day) and even so not enjoy good health.

There is a consensus that the living and working conditions of individuals and groups in the population influence their health situation. In other words, most illnesses and health inequalities – which exist in every country – are derived from the conditions under which people are born, live, work, and grow old. This is where the concept of social determinants of health comes from. For the WHO, social determinants of health are the social conditions under which people live and work (WHO n.d.).

Some examples of social determinants of health are – apart from the quality and accessibility to healthcare and services – the quantity and quality of food a person ingests regularly and the quality of the water and sanitation to which they have access. The same goes for housing and transport conditions, the education level, the working environment, the consumption or not of tobacco, alcohol and other drugs, and the state of mental health of individuals and community.[1]

One of the most important social determinants of health are the institutions in a country or a community. Institutions are the rules of the game (formal or informal) that the political, economic, and social players in the country or community are expected to follow. Each society operates with a set of political, economic, and social rules created by the state and the citizens together. In this chapter, we focus on the role institutions have in the state of health of Mozambicans.

---

[1] The 1991 Dahlgren-Whitehead 'rainbow model' maps the relationship between the individual, their environment, and health. Individuals are placed at the centre, and surrounding them are the various layers of influences on health – such as individual lifestyle factors, community influences, living and working conditions, and more general social conditions (see ESRC 2021).

## C A Brief History of the Health Services in Mozambique before and after 1975

The history of the health services in Mozambique encompasses four different periods:

a)  the period prior to the independence of Mozambique (1975);
b)  the period immediately after independence (1975–80);
c)  the period from 1980 to 1993;
d)  the period from 1993 to the present day.


### *1  Period before Independence*[2]

Although the Portuguese arrived in Mozambique in the late fifteenth century, the organisation of health services by the colonial power in the then districts (now provinces) dates only from the nineteenth century, with the building of the first health infrastructures and the creation of rules for their operation. Around 1898, the colonial health system was organised in eleven health districts, with each district having a civil hospital and a military hospital.

The health system created by the Portuguese colonial government, which lasted until 1975, was concentrated in the cities and towns where the majority of the colonists lived. It was a fragmented system, based on hospitals and prioritising curative medicine (to the detriment of health promotion and disease prevention). Finally, it had a racist structure.

In rural areas, where 85 per cent of Mozambicans lived before 1975, the majority of the people lived more than 20 km away from the closest health facility. In the event of illness, this led to the vast majority of Mozambicans resorting almost exclusively to traditional medicine practitioners.


### *2  Period Immediately after Independence (1975–1980)*

Immediately after the formation of the Transitional Government, the Committee for the Restructuring and Reorganization of the Health Sector was set up. After 1975 – based on the findings and recommendations of the Committee for the Restructuring and Reorganization of the Health Sector – the first government of independent Mozambique defined and began implementing a health policy whose essential principles are enshrined in Decree-Law No. 1/75, of 29 July.

Article 37 of that decree-law states:

The essential aim of the Ministry of Health is to put the provisions of Article 16 of the Constitution into practice. It is up to the state to organize a health system that will benefit all Mozambican people.

This campaign will be guided by FRELIMO's policy to place health at the service of the people.

---

[2]  Gulube (1996).

A unified National Health Service will be created to serve all sectors of the population, irrespective of their ethnic group, economic or social level or religion.

Because rural areas were completely neglected in colonial times, efforts must be immediately focused on these areas.

Health is a right of the citizen and a duty of the state [author's underlining].

In the National Health Service, preventive action and curative action must be totally integrated at the base, but it must always be remembered that prevention should take priority over cure. Health education and environmental sanitation will play a major role in the actions of the Ministry.

On 24 July 1975, the government of Mozambique announced the abolition of private medicine practices. The five years after independence were characterised by substantial changes in the health sector. Along with the abolition of all types of private medicine, the process of creating and structuring the public health service, called the National Health Service, was begun. Significant steps were taken towards eliminating the fragmented and racist nature of the health services. Hundreds of new health units were built, the vast majority in rural areas. Implementation of a health policy began. This would essentially be enshrined by the WHO three years later under the name of Primary Health Care.

It should be noted that in these early days of independence, debate arose around health as a right versus the financial capacity of the state to assure this right. It was in the context of this debate that, in 1977 – when the Free Medicine Act was approved[3] – the government restricted free healthcare to disease prevention campaigns, while curative activities had to be paid for, albeit at very low prices.

During this process – and notwithstanding the immense enthusiasm of both the people and the healthcare workers – the greatest difficulty lay in the extreme lack of (a) human resources of all types and at all levels and (b) financial resources.

Apart from the National Health Service, the Military Health Service and the Paramilitary Health Service were also set up, under, respectively, the Ministry of National Defence and the Ministry of the Interior. In prisons, health units were and still are managed by the Ministry of Justice.

### 3 From 1980 to 1993

After 1980, the efforts to build a public health service to serve the entire population were seriously affected by the war. In all the provinces, over one hundred healthcare workers were killed, hundreds of health units and ambulances were totally or partially destroyed, and tonnes of medicine and medical supplies were destroyed or stolen. Over half of the health network in rural areas collapsed, with dramatic consequences for the health of millions of Mozambicans, especially children, women, and the elderly.

[3] Law No. 2/77, of 27 September 1977.

The political and military instability and subsequent economic crisis worsened when, in 1987, the so-called Bretton Woods institutions (the World Bank and the International Monetary Fund) imposed economic policies on the government of Mozambique that led to a drastic reduction in public spending, including the provision of free healthcare to the majority of the citizens.

At the same time – and due to the joint pressure of the Mozambican political and economic elite (on the one hand) and the imperatives of the policies imposed by the Bretton Woods institutions (on the other) – in 1992, the government of Mozambique reintroduced private for-profit medicine, which had been abolished in 1975 (Law No. 26/91, of 31 December[4]).

### 4 Period from 1993 to the Present Day

The war ended with the signing of the Rome Peace Accords in October 1992. In 1993, the process of building the health system began again, particularly the National Health Service. Over the last twenty-five years, hundreds of the health units that had been destroyed were rebuilt and hundreds of new health units were built.

The majority of these health units are health centres and facilities and are mainly located in rural areas. However, the construction of the National Health Institute, a central hospital (in Zambezia Province), a provincial hospital (in Maputo Province), and more than ten district hospitals and infrastructures aimed at providing training to human resources working in health and the logistics of medical supplies must be highlighted.

The National Council for the Fight against HIV/AIDS (CNCS), which is presided over by the Prime Minister, was also set up.

At the same time – and along with a small, but increasing, number of clinics, medical practices, laboratories, and private imaging services – dozens of non-governmental organisations (NGOs) appeared, almost all dedicated to vertical programmes in the health area.

However, it must be pointed out that due to the widespread poverty, the private medicine sector, including the NGOs, covers only 5 per cent of the population.

### D Description of the Health Sector

In Mozambique, the health sector is called the National Health System and is structured in the following subsystems:

1. a public subsystem run by the state and called the National Health Service;
2. a private subsystem;

---

[4] Law authorising the provision of healthcare by natural or legal persons under private law, for profit or not.

3. a military and paramilitary health subsystem;
4. socio-professional organisations such as the Medical Council, the Nursing Council, and the Medical Association of Mozambique, considered part of the National Health System.

The National Health Service is directly dependent on the Ministry of Health and is by far the largest provider of healthcare to the around 29 million Mozambicans. It includes four central hospitals (each one with over 600 beds), seven provincial hospitals (between 250 and 350 beds), two psychiatric hospitals, a little less than fifty district hospitals, and 1,585 health centres and facilities spread throughout the districts and communities in the country. It employs over 90 per cent of health workers in Mozambique.

The private subsystem is divided into (a) private for-profit; and (b) private not-for-profit medicine. The private for-profit sector is concentrated in the cities (mainly in the capital, Maputo) and includes two hospitals (both in Maputo City), a few dozen clinics, medical practices, pharmacies, laboratories, and imaging services. The for-profit private sector is devoted almost exclusively to curative activities.

The private not-for-profit subsystem includes religious organisations and non-governmental organisations (NGOs), mostly foreign and directly funded by the so-called cooperation partners (donors). It also includes health facilities in some large public and private companies and in educational establishments, such as the Eduardo Mondlane University.

The military and paramilitary health subsystem is in an early stage. Mozambique has no hospital to care specifically for paramilitary forces.

The National Health Institute (aimed at research) and the Traditional Medicine Institute are under the auspices of the Ministry of Health.

## E Traditional Medicine

Traditional medicine exists alongside the National Health System. According to the WHO, 'traditional medicine is the sum total of knowledge, skills and practices, used in the diagnosis, prevention or elimination of physical, mental and social illnesses, based exclusively on past experiences and observations handed down from generation to generation, orally or in writing' (Ministry of Health 2015).

According to the Ministry of Health, around 70 per cent of the people in Mozambique use traditional medicine to treat physical, as well as mental and social, illnesses. The activity engaged in by traditional medicine practitioners, estimated at a ratio of 1 practitioner per 200 inhabitants, has more coverage of primary health services than the National Health Service.[5] This explains why there are still people in Mozambique who are born, grow up, and die

---

[5] The ratios for doctor/inhabitant and nurse/inhabitant are, respectively, 1/15,000 and 1/2,000.

TABLE 6.1 *What is known about the practice of traditional medicine*

| Type | Coverage | Payment | Registration | Representativeness |
|---|---|---|---|---|
| Herbal medicine practitioners: those practitioners that treat patients with chemicals prepared from plants. Traditional midwives Healers who practice divination. | There are practitioners of traditional medicine all over the country, both in rural and in urban areas. | The provision of services by practitioners of traditional medicine is not free. | Patients often have recourse both to traditional medicine and so-called conventional medicine. | The Association of Traditional Healers of Mozambique (AMETRAMO) and the other associations of practitioners of traditional medicine do not represent all the practitioners. |

*Source:* Author's elaboration.

using only traditional medicine for their healthcare. This fact is due, on the one hand, to the still poor geographic coverage of the National Health Service and, on the other hand, to the intrinsic connection existing between traditional medicine and the defining traits of its users.

During colonial times, traditional medicine was perceived as associated with a lack of knowledge or superficial knowledge, superstitious, and based on folklore. Immediately after the proclamation of independence, the government of Mozambique recognised the importance of traditional medicine. In fact, Article 38(7) of the first decree-law of the government (Decree-Law No. 1/75, of 29 July), states: 'Boost medical and pharmacological research and, particularly, studies on traditional medicine'. Since then, traditional medicine has been gaining ground and consideration in government policies. In 1977, the Office of Traditional Medicine Studies was set up under the Ministry of Health. In 2010, the Office of Traditional Medicine Studies was closed and gave way to the Traditional Medicine Institute, also set up under the Ministry of Health.[6]

Despite these advances, the reality is that little is yet known about Mozambican traditional medicine (Tables 6.1 and 6.2).

## F The State of Health of Mozambican People

The state of health of the majority of Mozambicans is precarious. The burden of disease is high. Endemic infectious diseases predominate, such as malaria,

---

[6] Ministerial Order No. 52/2010, of the Ministry of Health, of 23 March 2010.

TABLE 6.2 *What is not known about the practice of traditional medicine*

| Statistics | Training | Relationships | Type of activities | Integration |
|---|---|---|---|---|
| The exact number of practitioners of traditional medicine per province, district, and place (total number and by type of practitioner). | The type, content, and duration of training for each one of the three types of practitioners of traditional medicine. | The relationship between practitioners of traditional medicine and their patients (and their families), including the means of payment for the work done. The relationship between practitioners of traditional medicine and the other traditional authorities. | If practitioners of traditional medicine limit themselves to curative activities or if they engage in other activities, whether in the health area or in other areas. | The best strategy for integrating traditional medicine into the Mozambican Health System. Specifically, should traditional medicine be considered as a subsystem or should it be integrated into the National Health Service? |

*Source:* Author's elaboration.

tuberculosis, AIDS, respiratory infections, diarrhoeal diseases (including cholera), and intestinal and bladder parasitosis, with the last three being very closely linked to access to drinking water and environmental sanitation.

Mozambique is one of the five countries in the world with the highest prevalence of tuberculosis (551 cases/100,000 inhabitants, compared to a world average of 140 cases/100,000 inhabitants) and among the 10 countries in the world with the highest prevalence of AIDS. Data for 2015 indicate that the overall prevalence of AIDS in people aged 15 to 49 was 13.2 per cent. Among women, it was 15.4 per cent versus 10.1 per cent for men, and AIDS is more prevalent in urban areas (16.8 per cent) than in rural areas (11.0 per cent) (Ministry of Health et al. 2013; Ministry of Health et al. 2018). Cholera is endemic, with outbreaks practically every year, varying only in the part of the country it appears. A study carried out between 2005 and 2007 and encompassing over 80,000 school-age children revealed a generalised occurrence of bladder infection caused by *Schistosoma haematobium* (national prevalence of 47 per cent) and intestinal helminths (national prevalence of 53.5 per cent) (Augusto et al. 2009). These diseases, related to lack of access to drinking water and basic environmental sanitation, are responsible for a higher number of deaths than malaria and AIDS combined. Mozambique is one of the few countries in the world where leprosy still exists.

At the same time – and as is the case in other African countries – an epidemiological transition is underway. Thus, the incidence and prevalence of non-communicable diseases, particularly high blood pressure and other cardiovascular diseases, diabetes, chronic respiratory diseases, cancer, and trauma (especially road traffic accidents) is increasing inexorably. A study on cardiovascular risk factors carried out in 2005 shows a high prevalence of high blood pressure (34.9 per cent).

Data from the UNICEF Annual Report 2019 entitled *The State of the World's Children 2019: Children, food and nutrition* (UNICEF 2019) indicate that Mozambique has one of the highest rates of child malnutrition in the world (43 per cent of children under five suffer from chronic malnutrition and 8 per cent from acute malnutrition). Chronic malnutrition increases the morbidity and mortality rate in children aged under five and reduces their cognitive abilities. The same report reveals that, for the first time in many years, Mozambique reported cases of pellagra, a disease linked to niacin (vitamin B3) deficiency.

Other indicators reflecting the deficient nutritional situation of Mozambicans are the following (Ministry of Health et al. 2013; Ministry of Health et al. 2018):

- Fourteen per cent of newborns (whose birth weight was registered) weighed less than 2.5 kg at birth (underweight);
- Sixty-four per cent of children under five, and 54 per cent of pregnant women, were suffering from anaemia;
- in 2011, only 45 per cent of the families questioned used iodised salt;
- in 2015, the exclusive breastfeeding rate was only 55 per cent.

Mozambique is among the countries in the world with the highest birth rates (five children per woman) and gross mortality (11.8/1000 inhabitants) and a low life expectancy (53.7 years). Maternal mortality (452/100,000 live births) and infant mortality (68/1,000 live births) are also very high (INE 2019).

## II INSTITUTIONAL FACTORS WITH AN IMPACT ON THE HEALTH SECTOR

The institutional factors that weaken the performance of the health sector can be structured according to five conventional areas.

### A Rule of Law and Judicial Independence

Despite it being enshrined in the constitution, Mozambique is still far from being a state under the rule of law.

With regard to the health sector, there are several factors – mainly related to non-compliance with the laws in force – which contribute to this:

- The process of contracting companies to carry out public works (such as building health centres, hospitals, human resource training centres and institutes, warehouses, housing for healthcare staff, etc.), as well as the acquisition of medicine, medical supplies, hospital equipment, and the like (such as ambulances), is very often done on the fringes of the law. There is frequent, abusive, and illegal recourse to what is called *private treaties* to the detriment of public tenders. This all leads to the construction of poor-quality buildings, the acquisition of medical supplies and equipment of inferior quality, and the unlawful siphoning of money to dishonest business people.

- In clear breach of the law, the processes of selecting people for jobs are frequently carried out without being offered for public tender. This gives rise to this selection being based on party political affiliation, nepotism, friendships, ethnic identity, and even the provision of sexual favours.
- With regard to promotions and career progression, it is common for the time periods provided for by law not to be complied with, allegedly due to budgetary restrictions.
- These practices are also contributed to by the fact that both trade union organisations (such as the Medical Association of Mozambique) and socio-professional organisations (such as the Medical Council and the Nursing Council) are weak and not very proactive.

The fact that these irregular situations persist – despite being frequently reported in the media and the repeated criticism in the annual report from the Administrative Court (Court of Auditors) to the National Assembly – gives citizens the feeling that the culprits can get away with anything because of the state's lack of political will, calling the legitimacy of that very state into question in the eyes of its citizens.

## B Voice, Participation, and Accountability

- Although it is provided for and heralded in the Constitution of the Republic[7] (Articles 89 and 116) and in the Charter of Patient Rights and Responsibilities,[8] the right of citizens to healthcare is not clarified or sufficiently protected.
  In the National Health Service – and in clear breach of Article 116(4) of the Constitution – citizens are discriminated against by the state on a socio-economic basis. All but one of the central and provincial hospitals have special clinics, special consultations, and private rooms that are off limits to anybody who cannot pay the prices stipulated. It should be noted that there is no legal basis for the existence and operation of these special clinics, special consultations, and private rooms. All attempts made to close these

---

[7] Constitution of the Republic of Mozambique, 2018.
[8] Approved by Resolution No. 73/2007, of the Council of Ministers, of 18 December 2007.

special clinics, special consultations, and other special services have been
thwarted due to resistance linked to the combined interests of the doctors,
on the one hand, and the political and economic elite on the other.

Even in the services considered to be free by law, citizens are frequently
subject to unlawful charges.

• The involvement of citizens and communities in the management and
monitoring of health sector activities is very poor. Despite there being
regulatory documents on the connection between the health sector and
the communities, it is the norm for there to be no accountability to
citizens regarding health activities. The citizens know little or nothing
about the annual budget for the health sector, from its preparation to
resource allocation priorities and how these resources are spent. This is
one of the reasons explaining why the Ministry of Health budget favours
allocations to:

    a)   central and provincial bodies to the detriment of district bodies,
where primary healthcare takes place;

    b)   spending mainly on curative actions to the detriment of health pro-
motion and disease prevention actions; and

    c)   money spent on needless bureaucracy (travelling abroad with the
corresponding travelling expenses, expensive meetings at hotels and
tourist resorts, acquisition of cars for leaders) to the detriment of
the acquisition of medicine and medical supplies and equipment and
ambulances that would improve the quality of healthcare.

• Particularly in rural areas – and because of fear of reprisal – citizens are afraid
to report any abuses by health workers, such as absenteeism, non-compliance
with schedules, ill-treatment, and unlawful charges.

## C Political Instability, Violence, and the Legitimacy of the State

Over forty years after the proclamation of independence, the National Health
Service still does not cover the entire country or respond to the basic needs of all
citizens, both in cities and towns and in rural areas. As previously mentioned,
there are three causes:

a)   the colonial legacy;

b)   the destruction of hundreds of health units during the war that ravaged
the country between 1976 and 1992; and

c)   the difficulty in moving forward more quickly, both in the replacement
of the infrastructures destroyed and in the building of new infrastructures, due to the lack of human resources and financial constraints.

After a twenty-year period of calm, political and military instability re-emerged
in the centre of the country in 2013. To further aggravate the situation, in
October 2017, a military conflict broke out in Cabo Delgado Province, the
cause of which is still not clear, and which is tending to spread.

The political and military instability:

- has negative repercussions on the lives of the people in towns and rural areas (where physical safety has been threatened and economic activities paralysed);
- negatively affects activities in the health sector and leads to stagnation or to setbacks in many health indicators. Two concrete examples of this negative impact are the temporary cessation of health promotion and disease prevention activities;
- ultimately calls the legitimacy of the state into question, either because the state cannot protect its citizens or because it does not assure the provision of basic health services, drinking water, basic sanitation, education, etc. in adequate quantity and quality.

## D State Capacity and Independence from Private Interests

Since 1975, the government of Mozambique has generally outlined appropriate policies for the health sector. The main problem lies in the weak capacity of the state to assure the implementation of these policies. There are many examples of this deficient implementation and the following are of particular importance:

### 1 Lack of Human Resources and Low Motivation of the Majority of Human Resources
The lack of human resources of all types – from doctors to orderlies, as well as nurses, pharmacists, laboratory and imaging professionals, management specialists, maintenance specialists, hospital administrators, etc., – is, alongside chronic underfinancing, the greatest weakness of the National Health Service.

No health facility (from the most modest health centre to the largest central hospital) has enough human resources. The doctor/inhabitant (1/15,000) and nurse/inhabitant (1/2,000) ratios do not allow for healthcare with even a minimum of quality.

The majority of the scarce human resources existing, particularly those working in the National Health Service, are unmotivated and demoralised, as they earn low salaries, lack basic working conditions (equipment, medicine, food, uniforms, etc.),and have to deal with a large (and always increasing) number of patients.

### 2 Chronic Underfinancing and Poor Financial Management
Since 1975, the health sector has faced the problem of not having enough funds to meet either operational expenses (salaries, fuel for transport, acquisition of medicine and other consumables, etc.) or investment expenses (building new health units, acquisition of equipment, etc.). In 2001, the WHO published the document *Macroeconomics and Health: Investing in Health for Economic Development*, in which it showed that the minimum required in any country

for the health sector to be able to ensure the provision of basic services stood at between US$30 and 40 per person per year. More recently, the WHO has set a recommendation of US$60, including both public and private spending (Jowett et al. 2016). This means that Mozambique should spend around 1.8 billion US dollars in order to ensure that the health sector could operate with a minimum of quality.[9] The reality is that, since 1975, the amount allocated to the National Health Service (which is responsible for healthcare for at least 90 per cent of Mozambicans) has never even reached a sum of US$25 per inhabitant per year. Thus, it is clear that Mozambique is facing a problem of chronic underfinancing of the health sector.

This chronic underfinancing calls into question the right of Mozambicans to health, as provided for in the constitution and has caused the government – under pressure from the World Bank – to opt for solutions relying on user fees and other forms of immediate co-payment that penalise the vast majority of Mozambicans. This is clearly described in the WHO document (2010) entitled *Health Systems Financing: The Path to Universal Coverage*, which emphasises that universal health coverage will only become a reality when, and where, the citizens have access to quality health services (promotion, prevention, treatment, rehabilitation, and palliative care) without the fear of being irretrievably drawn into poverty.

Even more tragic is the fact that the management of the scarce financial resources is deficient. It is very common for the financial resources allocated to a certain period not to be fully used, whether through incompetence or negligence of the managers. The most obvious example is the Global Fund to Fight AIDS, Tuberculosis, and Malaria.

## 3 Insufficient Geographical Coverage

One of the weaknesses of the Mozambican health system, and of its most important subsystem (the National Health Service) in particular, is insufficient geographical coverage, mainly in rural areas, where around 2/3 of Mozambicans live. Although the government has built over 1,000 health centres since 1975, mainly in rural areas, these remain insufficient for the demand. This explains why, to this day, there are Mozambicans who have to travel ten or more kilometres on foot to get to the nearest health facility.

In over 70 per cent of the 154 districts, there is no hospital with an x-ray machine and/or a laboratory and/or an operating theatre. At the same time, over 40 per cent of the districts do not have a pharmacy, either public or private.

This insufficient coverage explains, for example, the difficulty in (a) reducing the mother and child mortality rate and (b) increasing the vaccination coverage rates.

---

[9] This is based on a population of 30 million, and corresponds to around 12 per cent of GDP.

## 4 Deficient Implementation of the Primary Healthcare Policy

The primary healthcare policy prioritises health promotion and disease prevention over curative medicine. However, in Mozambique, healthcare is still predominantly curative and consists of medical interventions in hospitals and health centres.

Other aspects neglected by the primary healthcare policy are community involvement and inter-sector cooperation. It is well known that the greater the involvement of citizens and communities in the planning and monitoring of activities in the health sector, as well as current management of the activities of health units, the greater the satisfaction of these communities and the more careful and responsible the health workers. In Mozambique, the examples of community involvement are few and far between and consist essentially of sporadic meetings to listen to the views of patients at a minority of health units.

On the other hand – and as already mentioned – the state of health of a community depends on factors such as the quantity and quality of food available, a supply of drinking water, environmental sanitation, quality housing, access to quality education, and reliable transport at accessible prices, factors that are the responsibility of sectors other than the health sector. This is why improving the state of health of a community depends largely on cooperation between different government sectors at all levels and between the central government and local governance authorities. This is what is called inter-sector cooperation. In Mozambique – and despite regular meetings of the Council of Ministers – the ministries work in isolation from each other, like silos. The same situation is seen at provincial, district, and municipal levels. In addition, it is this practically non-existent inter-sector coordination that explains the fledgling state of initiatives such as school health, employee health, and the water and food hygiene area.

## 5 Health Inequities

Health inequities are health inequalities among population groups, which, apart from being systematic and relevant, are also unjust and avoidable. One of the main obstacles to improving the quality of healthcare in Mozambique has to do with the existence of health inequities.

Here are some examples of these inequities (Equity Observatory [Ministry of Health 2010]):

- the rates of infant mortality, maternal mortality, and malnutrition in children aged under five are higher in rural areas than in urban areas (urban–rural ratio of 1.6);
- children in the lowest wealth quintile are 1.8 times more likely to die before the age of five than children in the highest wealth quintile;
- a child in Cabo Delgado Province is around three times more likely to die before the age of five than a child in Maputo City;

- the rate of institutional births is slightly more than 40 per cent in Zambezia Province compared to over 90 per cent in Maputo City and Province;
- around 55 per cent of children in rural areas are vaccinated compared to 74 per cent in urban areas;
- Maputo City (with a population of around 1.1 million) has twice the number of doctors as Zambezia Province (with a population of over 5.5 million).

## 6 Inefficient Planning and Management

One of the weaknesses of the health system in Mozambique and particularly the National Health Service lies in the inefficient planning and management methods at all levels and in all sectors. Planning is carried out using rudimentary methodologies and the plans are rarely complied with in full. The quality of management of human resources, financial resources, medicine and medical supplies, transport, etc. is low, which generates a large number of inefficiencies. The same happens with maintenance of infrastructures and equipment.

Hospitals and other health units have very inefficient management and administration methods. Hospital administration practices are essentially the same as those that were in force at the time of independence. Although computers have been introduced in hospitals, they are mainly for the use of the executives and some employees. Not one single hospital has been completely computerised with the different sectors networked. The management of the clinical files of patients, outpatient consultations, the pharmacy, laboratories, kitchen, laundry, transport, etc. is all paper-based. The same happens with the maintenance of any hospital equipment. This archaic form of management and administration not only contributes to the poor quality of healthcare, but also to the corrupt practices engaged in by health workers.

## 7 Poor Regulation Capacity in the Other Service Providers

The Mozambican State has poor capacity to regulate the activities of the other providers of health services. Here are some examples:

- there are private clinics and practices that are set up and operate without authorisation from the competent authorities;
- several mandatory regulations issued by the Ministry of Health are not complied with by some service providers;
- control over the sale of medicine whether by state-licensed pharmacies or operators in the informal market is very deficient. It is common to see medicine acquired by the Ministry of Health on sale at markets and even on the streets. Mozambique is one of the few African countries and the only country in the Southern African Development Community (SADC) that does not have an operational regulatory authority for medicine;
- particularly at provincial level, priorities are frequently defined by the NGOs because they are the ones that fund the majority of health activities.

## 8 Corruption

Corruption is the misuse of the power entrusted to someone for private gain (Transparency International, n.d.[b]). Mozambique is among the countries considered the most corrupt in the world. According to the *Corruption Perceptions Index*[10] (which assesses the people's perception of corruption in the public sector), published by Transparency International, in 2019, Mozambique was in 146th place out of 180 countries, with an index of 26 (with 100 = *very clean* and 0 = *highly corrupt*). It should be noted that in 2013, Mozambique had an index of 30, which means the perceptions of corruption are increasing (Transparency International n.d.[a]). In Mozambique today, corruption is no longer seen as deviant behaviour, but rather has become something 'normal'.

The health sector is among those considered most corrupt, along with public works, education, the police, justice bodies, and others. In health, corruption is seen at all levels – from the central bodies of the Ministry of Health to health centres and maternity hospitals – and all over the country.

Corruption in the health sector takes a variety of forms, such as:

- unlawful charges both at the health units and in the Ministry of Health's management bodies;
- salary payments to 'ghost' employees;
- theft of medicine and medical supplies at all levels (from large warehouses to hospital pharmacies and wards);
- fraud in the tenders for the construction or renovation of infrastructures (such as hospitals, health centres, warehouses, etc.) and for the acquisition of equipment, medicine, and medical supplies;
- bribery to gain admission to the Ministry of Health's training centres;
- leaving work in the public sector to engage in private activities elsewhere;
- deliberate creation of difficulties in what is called normal service (free or almost free) to oblige patients to resort to what is called special service (much more expensive).

Corruption in the health sector has a particularly negative impact on poor patients and their families and contributes substantially to the increase in the dissatisfaction of the people with the health services. Unless corruption in the health sector is effectively, efficiently, and continuously combated, the goal of humanised and equal healthcare for all Mozambicans will never be achieved.

In conclusion, it should be noted that the failure in the fight against corruption is largely because in Mozambique, the judicial power is completely dependent on and subject to the executive power. This comes because of the constitution, according to which the members of the Supreme Court, the Constitutional Council, the Administrative Court, and the Office of the Attorney General are all appointed by the President of the Republic, and can

[10] Transparency International (2020).

be removed by the president at any time and without prior consultation with any state body.

## E Sovereignty and Independence

Now more than ever, it is clear that Mozambique needs help from the international community to improve the provision of quality healthcare to its citizens, especially the poorer ones. However, it is equally clear that this help must be given correctly to ensure that it does not have the opposite effect to what is intended.

Unfortunately, facts show that in the last thirty years, the government of Mozambique has not defined the public health policy independently. This applies both to the definition of priorities and particularly to the preparation of the budget for the health sector. The health policy is defined more by the international community (the cooperation partners or donors) than by the government of Mozambique.

This is the case because the international community (a) makes the largest financial contribution to the health budget and (b) orders and funds the 'consultations' where the diagnosis of the health sector is made and where health policy proposals are presented. It is based on these 'consultations' ordered and paid for by the international community that the government of Mozambique is pressured into prioritising selected strategies, programmes, and activities 'proposed' by the donors, not always coinciding with the strategies, programmes, and activities that are really a priority for improving the state of health of Mozambicans. We will cite examples of the negative role the cooperation partners play in the health sector in Mozambique.

First, human resources. Sufficient well-trained human resources are of vital importance for the correct operation of any health system. The shortage of human resources undermines the capacity of the health system to meet the health needs of the population. In Mozambique, the shortage of human resources is the biggest weakness of the National Health Service. Unfortunately, this shortage is aggravated by health workers (especially those more qualified and/or more experienced) leaving the National Health Service for work at embassies, NGOs, cooperation partner agents based in Maputo, and the private for-profit sector.

The main reason for this, but not the only one, is that these organisations pay higher salaries than the government. This is an internal brain drain, as opposed to the brain drain out of Mozambique. In Mozambique, the internal brain drain is at least three times higher than the brain drain out of the country. In other words, recruitment practices by the donor community in Mozambique undermine and weaken the National Health Service that this community claims it wants to strengthen.

At the same time, the macroeconomic policies imposed on Mozambique by the World Bank and by the International Monetary Fund mean there are tight limits to the contracting of human resources for the health and education sectors by the government. This is why, over the last fifteen years, the government has been unable even to hire and employ all of the doctors, nurses, and other health workers trained in Mozambique.

Secondly, almost all of the cooperation partners decided to channel the largest slice of their financial resources not into the National Health Service (which provides healthcare to over 90 per cent of the population), but rather to NGOs and other partners dedicated to the so-called vertical programmes for fighting diseases. While this is motivated in part by corruption, already discussed above, it leads to overlapping competencies adding another source of inefficiency.

These vertical programmes, dedicated at the most to three diseases or a specific segment of the population (such as mother and child health), and with bottom-up dynamics, contribute to the weakening of the public health sector due to the duplication of efforts, the distortion of national health plans, the 'theft' of scarce human resources, and the chronic underfinancing of the National Health Service.

In addition to the above – and because the ultimate causes of diseases are not properly taken into account – these vertical programmes for combating diseases have a limited impact on improving the health conditions of poorer citizens and communities, despite the hundreds of millions of US dollars invested each year by the international community in health in Mozambique.

Thirdly, it is important to mention another nefarious aspect of the World Bank's policy. From the 1980s, the World Bank began demanding that all developing countries should introduce user fees as an option for funding health services. It is now agreed that user fees punish the poor and constitute an obstacle to access to healthcare by citizens. According to the WHO, user fees are 'the most unequal way of funding health services' (OXFAM 2013: 11). Worldwide, around 150 million people incur financial catastrophe due to direct payments for healthcare, while 100 million are being pushed into poverty, the equivalent of 3 people per second (OXFAM 2013). Although the WHO has already taken a clear stance against user fees and the World Bank has issued a *mea culpa* (see the speech of the then president of the World Bank, Jim Yong Kim, at the World Health Assembly in 2013), the reality is that user fees persist in Mozambique.

Finally, it should be pointed out that the majority of the reforms and strategies proposed for the health sector by the so-called cooperation partners are unrealistic given the poor economic capacity of the country and because the cooperation partners are not willing to provide the necessary funds for the policies they themselves advocate as the most correct for Mozambique. There are many examples, the most important of which is the much-acclaimed **universal health coverage,** which is a constant in speeches by the World Bank, the WHO, UNICEF, and others in the United Nations and in other international forums. This is how a situation is created where a poor country like Mozambique is eternally 'plagued' by serious problems in terms of the credibility of the health sector arising from the poor quality of the healthcare provided.

The question that naturally arises is: what causes this state of affairs?

The starting point is that it is the political process, which determines the type of institutions existing, and that it is the institutions (mainly political), which influence how this process operates. It is the political institutions of a nation, which define the capacity of its citizens to control the politicians and influence their behaviour. In turn, this determines whether the politicians are representatives and defenders of the rights of the citizens who elected them or if they have the ability to abuse the power entrusted to them to achieve their own ends, even if this is to the detriment of the majority of the citizens.

Mozambican society is a profoundly unequal society, divided between a privileged minority that holds the reins of political and economic power and 'the others', that is a vast majority of poor, disadvantaged, and marginalised citizens, who have little capacity of controlling the actions of the political leaders and very little influence on the determination of the fate of the country.

The final cause explaining the weakness of the institutional factors with an impact on the health sector and, very particularly, on the poor capacity of the Mozambican state to prioritise the public health sector (which as we have seen is responsible for the healthcare provided to over 90 per cent of Mozambicans) lies in the lack of political will of the political leaders to put the satisfaction of healthcare needs in the poorer segments in first place. These leaders are part of, or have close connections with, the privileged minority groups in society, who relegated the public health sector to second place, largely because their own healthcare needs are met by going to organisations (such as hospitals, clinics, rehabilitation centres, etc.) abroad or, when this is not possible, the national private sector.

Another no less important aspect lies in the fact that in Mozambique there is limited and deficient understanding of the problems in the health sectors among political leaders, citizens, and the so-called civil society. There is confusion between the narrow concept of curative medicine and the broader concept of health and public health at all levels of Mozambican society. This results in the healthcare being predominantly curative and revolving around procedures in health centres and hospitals, with the consequent subordination of the promotion of health, the prevention of illness, community participation, and inter-sector cooperation. This is called medicalisation of healthcare. At meetings between the people and politicians, requests from the citizens revolve around the construction of more hospitals and maternity hospitals or at least requests for ambulances. This lack of knowledge results in there not being more interest or political merit in the promotion of public health on the part of political leaders.[11]

At the same time, both the opposition leaders and the majority of civil society organisations (including the media) do not give due priority to or show any

---

[11] It is also correct that in Mozambique the political leaders do not give priority to the prevention of diseases.

ability to present concrete solutions for the most pressing health problems for the majority of Mozambicans.

To give an example, a Mozambican opposition force has never presented a duly prepared document on (i) the deficient implementation of the primary healthcare policy, (ii) the chronic underfinancing of the health sector, (iii) the inequities in health, (iv) the discrimination that poorer Mozambicans are subject to, even in the public health sector, the problem of leprosy (whose elimination in Mozambique was proven by the WHO in 2009, only to resurge due to the negligence of the government), or, (v) finally, on a coherent policy for the relationship of the government with the foreign donor community for the health sector.

The disputes and 'contradictions' between the party in power, on the one hand, and the opposition forces, on the other, revolve mainly around the sharing of resources by the different factions of the privileged elite.

It is interesting to note that these 'contradictions' always disappear when, for example, parliament is discussing increases in salaries and the allocation of more privileges to different party representatives. On these occasions, unanimity is the rule that has never been broken.

Finally, in Mozambique, the executive power controls and dominates both the legislative power and the judicial power. Under these conditions, there are no checks and balances, which would perhaps make the elite in power take interests other than their own into account.

These are the institutional factors that ultimately explain the poor performance of the health sector, particularly in the quality of the healthcare provided to the majority of poor, disadvantaged, and marginalised citizens.

## III THE FUTURE: ACTION PROPOSALS

In the short and medium term, the main challenges for the health sector can be looked at from two points of view:

### A The Nosological Point of View

Over at least the next two decades, the burden of disease will continue to be very high in Mozambique. Although there is a trend towards a reduction in their incidence and prevalence, the infectious diseases referred to above (diarrhoeal diseases, respiratory illnesses, intestinal diarrhoeal diseases, schistosomiasis, tuberculosis, malaria, and HIV-AIDS) and child malnutrition will continue to predominate, all linked to the poverty that affects the majority of Mozambicans. At the same time, with the growth of the so-called middle class and the adoption of new and harmful lifestyles by an increasing number of Mozambicans (such as sedentarism, smoking, exaggerated and uncontrolled consumption of food high in fat, of alcohol, of soft drinks and sugary drinks, etc.) will continue to increase the incidence of non-communicable diseases.

If there is political will and better organisation, it will be possible to eliminate and then eradicate leprosy ad then substantially reduce the prevalence of
other diseases that are now neglected, such as trachoma, lymphatic filariasis,
scabies, and rabies.

## B The Institutional Point of View

As previously mentioned, the Mozambican state is characterised by the weakness
of its institutions, particularly political ones, which:

- on the one hand, make them vulnerable to the private interests of the
  privileged minority and the pressure from foreign organisations, whether
  international (the World Bank, the International Monetary Fund, etc.) or
  governmental, which, as we have seen, are commonly called cooperation
  partners; and
- on the other hand, they limit their capacity to respond adequately to the
  material and spiritual needs and desires of the majority of Mozambicans.

Ultimately, the aim is for there to be strong institutions in Mozambique, capable of outlining a health policy that puts the needs of the majority of its citizens
in first place, provided with effective regulatory capacity, capacity to suppress
all forms of crime, capacity to negotiate with the cooperation partners and
make the interests of Mozambicans prevail, and that contribute towards
balanced political, economic, and social development in the country.

With regard to the health sector, the ultimate aim is the provision of quality, **free** healthcare to all Mozambicans, without any economic, social, racial,
ethnic, sexual, religious, or geographic discrimination.

Even in a country as poor as Mozambique, it is possible to advance progressively towards quality, free healthcare at all levels, and not just basic healthcare. Obviously, this is a long-term process, but it all depends on political
will, **a clear definition of what the priorities are and what can be achieved in
health sector at each stage** and the sustained implementation of an economic
and social policy that will reduce poverty levels, as well as economic and social
inequalities.

The crucial question is: how can this goal, which is as noble as it is ambitious,
be achieved?

Our proposal focuses on six priorities:[12]

1 – Enshrining clearly in the constitution that: a) all Mozambicans have the
right to quality, free public healthcare at all levels of care, without any economic, social, racial, sexual, religious, or geographic discrimination; and b) it
is the responsibility of the government to progressively assure universal health
coverage in Mozambique.

---

[12] These priorities should be thought of as first steps to be taken along initiatives in other areas
such as the judicial sector and the rule of law.

2 – Based on the experience of other countries that made advances in political and administrative decentralisation, introducing changes to the structure and operation of the public health sector. One example that is a good source of inspiration is the Unified Health System (SUS) in Brazil, a country with social and anthropological characteristics similar to Mozambique.

Here, it is important at least to:

- Legislate the separation between the Ministry of Health (regulatory body) and the National Health Service (implementing body) with different budgets.
- Legislate the links between the National Health Service and the health services in municipalities and other local authorities.

All the aspects mentioned above should be contained in a law that defines a National Health Policy suitable for the next five decades, to be approved by the National Assembly (Parliament).

3 – Clearly defining how to progressively increase funding for the public health sector so that – as recommended by the WHO – the goal of at least US$60 per inhabitant per year for health sector expenses is achieved by 2050. To do this, the government must:

- Implement the Abuja Commitment (Nigeria) of allocating 15 per cent of the state budget to health instead of the present 8 per cent.
- Institute a *specific health tax* (for example, through an increase in current taxes on tobacco, alcoholic drinks, soft drinks, luxury products like jewellery, cosmetic, perfume and cars, and charge a percentage fee on each airline ticket sold in the country).
- Change the priorities in the health budget so that at least 50 per cent of the government's health expenditure is allocated to districts and 25 per cent to primary healthcare.
- Eliminate user fees and other forms of direct payment for the healthcare provided by the public sector.
- Harmonise the different mechanisms for funding health under a universal coverage framework.
- Be guided by austerity and strenuously fight against needless expenditure.
- Significantly improve budget management at all levels.

It is important to clarify here that a national health insurance system set up and run either by the state or by private entities is not presently a viable option for Mozambique. And the reason is simple: Mozambique is one of the poorest countries in the world and with over half the population living on less than US$2 per person per day, who would pay that insurance?[13]

---

[13] A proper national insurance system would require it (a) covers all the citizens; (b) covers all the diseases and treatments (including haemodialysis, organ transplants etc.); and (c) is funded domestically, with poor people being exempted from insurance fees.

On the other hand, we see no reason why private health insurance should not exist for the citizens who wish to have their healthcare provided by private health organisations.

4 – Implementing the primary healthcare policy nationwide, comprehensively and at all levels of healthcare. To do this, the government must:

- Progressively strengthen the National Health Service, which is the main subsystem of the National Health System.
- Give due priority to health promotion and disease prevention activities, rehabilitation, and palliative care, as well as curative activities.
- Implement effective coordination between the Ministry of Health and other sectors (Ministries, local authorities such as municipalities, NGOs, religious persuasions, unions, etc.) whose activities have an impact on the state of health of Mozambicans. As explained above, the health sector alone cannot assure an improvement in the state of health of Mozambicans. Many other sectors of governance and society play a crucial role in the improvement of living conditions – and, through this, the improvement of health conditions – of the people, through the provision of diversified food in quantity, drinking water, environmental sanitation, housing, transport, quality education, etc. The implementation of this inter-sector coordination should be inspired by the experiences in other countries.
- For inter-sector coordination to be effective and efficient, it must be institutionalised. It is under this framework that an Inter-Sector Health Coordination Council (CCIS) should be set up, a body whose mission will be to ensure inter-sector coordination, with the aim of taking concerted action on the social determinants of health at the different levels. It is important to specify the mission, the tasks, and the composition of the CCIS.
- Give priority to community participation. Community participation has two main aspects: (a) the right and duty of each citizen to participate individually and collectively in the planning and implementation of the healthcare aimed at them; and (b) the need for the entities responsible for the provision of healthcare to be accountable to the citizens (or their representatives) for their actions.

In this framework – and based on the experience of other countries, such as Brazil (Cornwall and Shankland 2008) and Thailand (Rasanathan et al. 2011) – community participation must be institutionalised through the set-up of bodies at all levels responsible for ensuring increasing involvement by the citizens and communities in health sector activities.

5 – Boosting the activities of the Traditional Medicine Institute.

Given the importance and the potential of traditional medicine in the provision of healthcare to Mozambicans, the government must further bolster the activities of the Traditional Medicine Institute, providing it with financial resources and qualified human resources at all levels. The Traditional Medicine Institute, working closely with the National Health Institute, must base itself on the experience of other African countries, as well as the experience in Asian countries (like China, Vietnam, North and South Korea, etc.) to define the best ways to stimulate research into traditional Mozambican medicine, seeking ultimately to make the most of its enormous potential.

6 – Engaging the international community in the efforts with the aim of improving the quality of healthcare in Mozambique.

Such engagement implies, first, progressively reducing interference from cooperation partners in the formulation of health policies and the implementation of sovereign decisions made by Mozambicans.

On the other hand, if the international community does in fact want to help improve the quality of healthcare in Mozambique – so that the much-heralded universal health coverage that enshrines the values of universality, equity, and solidary can be achieved – it should undertake the following actions:

- Allocate a larger proportion of closely monitored aid in the form of direct support for the National Health Service budget. Government-to-government aid through direct support for the state budget or the Ministry of Health budget is the best way of helping the government of Mozambique to achieve the aim of universal health coverage.
- Cease the promotion of inappropriate approaches in the name of universal health coverage, especially vertical programmes.[14]
- Help the government of Mozambique to make equity and universality explicit priorities from the outset. It is fundamental that poor people (i.e. the majority of Mozambicans) benefit at least in the same way as better-off citizens, at all stages.
- Help the government of Mozambique to measure and assess the progress and results of the actions aimed at universal health coverage, especially equity.[15]
- Take steps to combat the tax evasion that prevents Mozambique from having access to the financial resources that are so necessary in order to ensure quality healthcare for all Mozambicans.
- Honour their commitment to allocate at least 0.7 per cent of their gross domestic product (GDP) to official aid for the development and improvement of the effectiveness of aid to the health sector.

IV FINAL CONSIDERATIONS

Mozambique remains one of the poorest and least developed countries in the world. Here are some of the facets of poverty that directly influence the health of Mozambicans (INE 2019):

---

[14] An example is the Global Fund in Mozambique. Warren et al. (2017) conclude that the Fund should adapt grant implementation and monitoring procedures to the specific local realities.
[15] There is a clear need for evaluation with full publicity of the results involving independent reputed experts.

- Over 2/3 of Mozambicans do not have two balanced daily meals from the point of view of protein and calorie intake;
- Over half of Mozambicans do not have access to drinking water (only 5 per cent have running water in their homes and almost 60 per cent use water from wells, rivers, or lakes);
- Over 2/3 of Mozambicans do not have access to adequate basic sanitation (24 per cent do not have latrines and defecate outdoors and only 10 per cent have a toilet connected to a septic tank);
- Over 2/3 of Mozambicans do not live in decent housing (over 47 per cent live in grass-covered huts);
- Less than 25 per cent of Mozambicans have access to electricity in their homes;
- In 2017, the illiteracy rate (percentage of people aged fifteen or over that cannot read or write) was 39.0 per cent and the number of years of schooling for the people was 3.5 years. These figures conceal important gender inequities (the illiteracy rate is 27.2 per cent for men and 49.4 per cent for women and the number of years of schooling is 2.5 for women and 4.6 for men) and geographic inequities (the illiteracy rate in Cabo Delgado is almost twice that of Maputo City);
- The unemployment rate is high (24.9 per cent) (Sachs et al. 2019: 317).

Poverty blocks access to the benefits arising from economic growth. The differences between social groups, based on the place of residence, education level, and other social differentials, make the advantages arising from economic opportunities more accessible to certain groups.

Finally, economic inequality is frequently associated with worse results in the health area, not only for poor people, but also for the population in general (Wilkinson and Marmot 2003; Wilkinson and Pickett 2009). This is why the fight against poverty and economic and social inequality must be made a priority, so that economic growth in Mozambique can be seen through the achievement of the improvements recommended in the Sustainable Development Goals (SDGs).

## V CONCLUSION

All of the above makes it possible to conclude that the institutions – understood as the rules of the game (formal or informal) created jointly by the state and by citizens and that are expected to be followed by the political, economic, and social players – play an important role in the performance of the health sector and, through this, the economic and social development of Mozambique.

Of the institutional factors, the (in)capacity of the state and its (lack of) independence from private interests stand out negatively.

This (in)capacity and (lack of) independence of the state from private interests comes largely as a result of the state being under the control of a privileged minority who do not give due priority to the basic health needs of the vast majority of the population.

If there is really a desire to improve the provision of healthcare to *all* Mozambicans, changes absolutely must be made in the institutions with influence on the health sector.

The most important institutional measures are the revision of the Constitution of the Republic, the strengthening of the National Health System (particularly the National Health Service), and the reduction of poverty and economic and social inequality.

# 7

# The Political Stakes of Decentralisation

Salvador Forquilha

## I INTRODUCTION

In the context of the economic and political changes in the late 1980s, made visible through economic restructuring and pro-democracy movements, several countries in sub-Saharan Africa embarked on decentralisation reforms. The majority of these reforms can be seen as a response to state weakness (Olowu and Wunsch 1990; Osaghae 2007) in terms of political regulation and service delivery, particularly in the education, health, water, and sanitation sectors. Thirty years later, many scholars find that the successive decentralisation reforms in sub-Saharan Africa had little impact on the resolution of governance problems (Manor 1999; Crook and Manor 2000; Tilburg 2008; Bierschenk 2010; Booth 2010; Crook 2010; Olivier de Sardan 2011; Batley et al. 2012; Mohmand and Loureiro 2017). In fact, the extensive literature produced in recent years and the different instruments of governance measurement in Africa (Ibrahim Index of African Governance, Afrobarometer, Democracy Index) show not only the little progress made in terms of governance, but also the complexity of the dynamics and the institutional factors underlying the implementation of decentralisation reforms (Mattes and Bratton 2016; Mo Ibrahim Foundation 2016).

With the introduction of the economic reforms in the late 1980s, the opening up of the political space and the end of the war in the early 1990s, Mozambique embarked on decentralisation reforms, based essentially on two dimensions: administrative decentralisation, under the scope of the Local Government Act (Law No. 8/2003, of 19 May) and political decentralisation, in the context not only of establishment of local authorities (Law No. 2/97, of 18 February) but also of the approval of the so-called decentralisation package, which calls for the election of provincial governors (Laws Nos. 3/2019, 4/2019, 5/2019, 6/2019, and 7/2019, all of 31 May, and Decree No. 2/2020, of 8 January).

With strong support from international cooperation partners, through different programmes focusing not only on the districts but also on the municipalities (Weimer 2012), the decentralisation reforms in Mozambique, according to research carried out in recent years, are still far from promoting citizen participation in the solution of local problems and the broadening and consolidation of democracy. In fact, as is the case in other countries in sub-Saharan Africa, the impact of the decentralisation reforms in Mozambique has been modest in the resolution of governance problems (Forquilha 2008; Forquilha and Orre 2011; Weimer 2012; Weimer and Carrilho 2017). Indeed, data from the most recent rounds of Afrobarometer surveys, for example, show a significant reduction with regard to demand for democracy, having gone from 25 per cent in the 2011–13 round to 9 per cent in the 2014–15 round (Mattes and Bratton 2016). In addition, the democracy index for 2018 shows that Mozambique's classification has fallen significantly, going from a hybrid regime to an authoritarian regime (*The Economist* 2019).

How can the modest impact of the decentralisation reforms on the promotion of local development and the strengthening and consolidation of democracy in Mozambique be explained? Based on evidence collected from interviews, Afrobarometer data, assessment reports on support programmes/projects for decentralisation, and literature produced on decentralisation in Mozambique in recent years, this chapter aims to answer the question asked above by looking at institutional factors that constitute constraints to decentralisation reforms. It argues that the results of the decentralisation reforms are shaped by the nature of the political system and the way it operates, in the context of institutional dynamics. The chapter develops the argument exploring institutional dynamics by examining five institutional dimensions, namely (a) rule of law; (b) participation and political accountability; (c) political stability, violence, and the legitimacy of the state; (d) state capacity and independence from private interests; and (e) sovereignty and independence. The argument is looked at essentially in two parts. In the first part, the chapter analyses the process of formation of the Mozambican political system and the dynamics behind the decentralisation reforms. In the second part, the chapter focuses on the decentralisation reforms, seeking to analyse their results based on the way the political system operates, looking at the main institutional dynamics.

## II THE PROCESS OF FORMATION OF THE MOZAMBICAN POLITICAL SYSTEM

Mozambique won its independence from the Portuguese colonial power as a result of a lengthy armed struggle led by the Mozambique Liberation Front (FRELIMO). Transformed into a Marxist-Leninist political party in 1977, FRELIMO has been ruling the country since independence in 1975, first in a one-party context and later, following its successive re-elections, under the scope of the multiparty system in force since 1990. Despite its revolutionary discourse on the 'destruction of the colonial state', in the period following independence, FRELIMO maintained the centralising rationale and practices of the colonial state. Indeed, not only did the new organisation of the Mozambican state fail to bring autonomy to the subnational levels, but the national unity discourse in the one-party context also reinforced the rationale of a centralised state (Brito 2019). How can this centralisation be explained and why, at a certain time, were decentralisation reforms begun? The answer to this question will help us understand the way institutional dynamics shape the results of the reforms. We will be discussing this below.

## A  The Historical Trajectory of the Postcolonial State Building in Mozambique

The historical trajectory of postcolonial state building in Mozambique is largely confused with the internal dynamics of the constitution and the development of the anticolonial movement led by FRELIMO. These dynamics were marked by rifts, conflicts and violence, which became more acute particularly in the late 1960s and early 1970s, and structured the institution building process in the postcolonial period (Forquilha 2017). In fact, the internal crisis within FRELIMO[1] during the anticolonial struggle contributed significantly to the reinforcement of the rhetoric exalting national unity to the detriment of ethnic differences. These differences were very often regarded as tribalism or regionalism and therefore incompatible with the political project based on the idea of transformation of mentalities and social relations in the context of building the *Homem Novo*[2] and a new society (Cahen 1987; Brito 1991; Meneses 2015;).

With the advent of independence in 1975, the role of FRELIMO in the construction and transformation of Mozambican society was reinforced and enshrined in the Constitution of the Republic.[3] This fact contributed to the centralisation of the state, a process that soon gained consistency, particularly after 1977, when FRELIMO officially became a Marxist-Leninist party. In the programme presented for its 3rd party congress, FRELIMO's role in the materialisation of the revolution and the centralisation of state power were important aspects, as can be seen from the extract below:

With regard to the state, the party's task is to destroy the colonial state and create a new type of state apparatus that reflects the interests of the working classes in its structures

---

[1] In the late 1960s, during the anticolonial struggles, FRELIMO fell into a severe internal crisis. For an analysis of the crisis, see Brito (2019).

[2] Meaning New Man.

[3] Article 3 of the first Constitution of the People's Republic of Mozambique stated: 'The People's Republic of Mozambique is guided by the political lines defined by FRELIMO, which is the ruling force of the state and of society. FRELIMO outlines the basic guidelines of the state and directs and supervises the actions of the state bodies in order to ensure compliance with state policy and the interests of the people' (CRPM 1975).

and its activities. The state is the main instrument for the materialisation of the party's revolutionary politics. Therefore, the party directs and guides all state activities. The leadership role of the party in relation to the state is as follows: [...] b) the party outlines the fundamental guidelines for development in all walks of social life. These guidelines are reflected in the state laws. The state laws express the practical application of the party's directives; c) the party creates conditions for all state bodies to become party organisations so they can ensure the party's political line; d) the party mobilises and politically and technically trains staff loyal to the party to hold positions in the state apparatus [...]. The People's Republic of Mozambique is a revolutionary democratic dictatorship state of workers and peasants. It exercises its power against the enemies of the people, capitalists, against imperialism and its agents and in the interest of protecting and defending revolutionary conquests and territorial sovereignty and integrity. (FRELIMO 1977: 28–29)

In this context, the centralisation of state power arose due to a combination of two important factors, namely the inheritance of the centralising nature of the colonial state and FRELIMO's political project, culminating in the centralised Marxist-Leninist state at the service of the interests of the revolution. In the years that followed independence, the centralisation of state power significantly marked not only the functioning of the institutions, but also the operational practices and rationale of state employees and agents. This is an important aspect for understanding the result of the decentralisation process in the context of the market-oriented policy reforms underway in the county since the early 1990s.

## B The Origins of the Decentralisation Reforms in Mozambique: Actors and Dynamics

The economic and political reforms taking place in Mozambique in the late 1980s and early 1990s, including the switch to a market economy, the structural adjustment programme, and political liberalisation, brought important consequences from the point of view of the institutional set-up of the state, resulting in the decentralisation process.

In the literature, the concept of decentralisation refers to the transfer of power, authority, functions, and competencies from the central state to lower levels (Rondinelli et al. 1983; Adamolekun 1999; Manor 2011). However, it is important to point out that the concept has different meanings. There are at least three. In fact, when authority and resources are transferred to agents of the central state located at different levels (region, province, and district), this is administrative decentralisation, which is also known as 'deconcentration' (Rondinelli et al. 1983; Adamolekun 1999; Manor 1999). When power and resources are transferred to elected, independent subnational units with a legal personality separated from the central state, this is political decentralisation (Rondinelli et al. 1983; Adamolekun 1999; Manor 1999). This is the case of local authorities (and, more recently, provincial authorities) in Mozambique. Finally, decentralisation can also mean the transfer of responsibilities regarding budgets and financial decisions (Rondinelli et al. 1983; Adamolekun 1999; Manor 1999; Forquilha 2016). This is fiscal decentralisation. With regard to Mozambique, the Decentralisation Policy and Strategy (PED) states that 'in Mozambique, decentralization is carried out through local authorities, local state bodies and institutions with community participation and consultation' (Resolution No. 40/2012, of 20 December). According to the PED, the district development fund (known as 'the 7 million') is limited to the scope of the government's willingness to decentralise to empower the communities in the fight against poverty' (Resolution No. 40/2012, of 20 December). Therefore, when we speak of decentralisation in this chapter, we are referring primarily to the two main types of decentralisation, which are administrative decentralisation and political decentralisation.

If it is a fact that the centralised state model had a significant impact from an ideological point of view, namely in terms of associating the population with FRELIMO's political project, it is no less true that, from an administrative point of view, the results were modest. Indeed, the heavy centralisation of public administration, associated with the scarcity of financial, material, and human resources and the serious effects of the war of the 1980s, contributed to making the state distant from the citizens, particularly in rural areas, insofar that more and more difficulties arose in the provision of basic services, especially in the education, health, water, and sanitation sectors. In this context, in parallel to the process of implementation of the structural adjustment programme, which began in 1987, the Mozambican government took steps aimed at improving the functioning of public administration, underlining the need for less centralised management. That was how the law no. 2/87, of 30 January, on the general state budget for 1987 was approved. In fact, its preamble underlines the following:

The general state budget for 1987 reflects the economic and financial measures adopted by the government under the framework of the economic rehabilitation programme, whose aim is to reactivate production and the gradual reduction of the existing financial imbalances. It [the law] also reflects the concerns about introducing changes in the management mechanisms, particularly at companies and local levels, in order to make the management of the economy more streamlined and functional. (Law No. 2/87, of 30 January)

With regard to decentralisation, it is worth mentioning Article 8 of Law No. 2/87, of 30 January, as it establishes the following:

With the aim of promoting greater involvement and accountability of people's assemblies and executive councils at district level [...]. During 1987, in accordance with the working methods to be defined by the council of ministers, working closely with the provincial governments, in each province, a district will be selected to act as a 'pilot' where tests will be carried out on the administrative and financial autonomy measures to be gradually introduced. (Article 8 of Law No. 2/87, of 30 January)

At the institutional level, the law no. 2/87, of 30 January, in a way constitutes a break from the previous period in terms of the principle of administrative and financial management insofar as the aforementioned law uses expressions such as 'involvement', 'accountability', 'administrative and financial autonomy', which have little to do with the state centralism established in the Constitution of 1975. It is true that the law no. 2/87, of 30 January, does not create autonomous structures separated from the central state for local management and administration. Even so, it advances towards the gradual transfer of certain central responsibilities to subnational levels. To this end, the law no. 2/87, of 30 January, marks an important step towards the decentralisation process, whose fundamental bases would be launched later with the approval of the Constitution of the Republic in November 1990.

In the literature, decentralisation processes frequently appear as the result of a combination of internal and external factors (Olowu and Wunsch 2004). This aspect makes it relevant to the analysis in that there is a tendency to reduce decentralisation processes in Africa to merely external factors, particularly the 'demands' coming from donors, especially the World Bank and the International Monetary Fund. It is true that the 'good governance' component has played an important role in the implementation of decentralisation reforms in Africa, including Mozambique. However, it is important not to lose sight of the fact that for certain African states, particularly Mozambique, decentralisation is a relevant process of conflict management and state legitimacy in the context of bringing peace and democracy to the country (Faria and Chichava 1999).

This does not mean that decentralisation reforms in Mozambique are a consensual and peaceful process. In fact, over the last thirty years, the implementation of the main legislative and administrative measures in the context of decentralisation have proven to be contentious, resulting in political divisions not only between the main political players, namely FRELIMO and the Mozambican National Resistance (RENAMO), but also in the very heart of the ruling party. Indeed, in all discussions that led to the approval of several laws on decentralisation reforms[4], conflict has been one of the most significant features, playing an important role in the structuring of the results of the reforms, insofar as party political interests end up putting issues of consolidating democracy and local development on the back burner. We will return to this aspect below when discussing how institutional dynamics shape the results of the reforms in the context of decentralisation.

III DECENTRALISATION REFORMS IN MOZAMBIQUE:
THEIR RESULTS IN LOCAL DEVELOPMENT
AND STRENGTHENING DEMOCRACY

As mentioned above, the results of the decentralisation reforms in Mozambique are modest, as is the case in other countries in sub-Saharan Africa. An important part of this outcome can be explained by the context,

---

[4] This was the case of the following laws nos.: 3/94; 2/97; 8/2003; 3/2019; 4/2019; 5/2019; 6/2019; 7/2019; 2/2020.

that is the dynamics of the institutions in the process of implementation of the reforms. According to North, 'institutions are the rules of the game in a society or, more formally, are the humanly devised constrains that shape human interaction. Consequently, they structure the incentives in human exchange, whether political, social, or economic. Institutional change shapes the way societies evolve through time and hence is the key to understanding historical change' (North 1990: 3). Drawing on North's definition of institutions and the rich literature on institutional theory (March & Olsen 1989; Skocpol 1995; Peters 1996; Fusarelli 2003), we argue that institutions are fundamental elements that shape the incentives of the actors and policy outcomes, including decentralisation reforms. To analyse how institutions shape the results of the decentralisation reforms, we will focus on two key aspects: (a) institutional dimensions, in which there are different institutional dynamics that may shape the results of the reforms and (b) three important reforms: municipalisation, district development fund (the '7 million'), and decentralised provincial governance.

## A  Dimensions of Institutions

Institutional dynamics are analysed based on five dimensions of institutions against the backdrop of the nature and the functioning of the Mozambican political system. These dimensions of institutions are rule of law; voice, participation, and political accountability; political stability, violence, and state legitimacy; state capacity and independence from private interests; and sovereignty and independence. Below, we will be analysing some elements for each one of the mentioned dimensions of institutions. The dynamics, which exist in each of the five dimensions of institutions, will allow us to discuss the decentralisation reforms we chose for analysis in this chapter.

### 1  *Rule of Law*

Mozambique is, formally, a democracy that calls for the separation of powers and respect for the rule of law. However, political practices since the adoption of the democratic constitution in 1990 are still heavily influenced by the historical trajectory of the functioning of the institutions in the one-party state. In fact, the principle of separation of powers, although enshrined in the constitution, has been a challenge in the process of building democracy in Mozambique, where, in practice, the executive power has a strong influence on legislative and judicial powers, with a significant impact on the design, approval, and implementation of policies, including in the area of decentralisation. An example of this is the definition and creation of the local authority package and, more recently, the so-called decentralisation package, where the parliamentary debate did not significantly alter the initial proposals from the government on the subject, despite the controversies in many of the aspects approved.

## 2 Voice, Participation, and Political Accountability

Decentralisation is one of the most important aspects of the policy reforms in Mozambique in the last twenty years, insofar as not only did it significantly change the set-up of the state with the creation of autonomous political entities through the municipalisation process, but it also made political participation at local level more dynamic, holding regular local elections and lending viability to local political agendas.

Despite participation in local elections tending to increase, in comparison to what happens with general elections (Forquilha 2015), the decentralisation experience over the last twenty years has not necessarily extended the participation arenas. In fact, not only are the participation fora, particularly local councils and development observatories, still merely consultative in nature, where participation is more of a formality than a reality, but the debate on local issues at municipal assemblies has also been a limited, and often politicised, exercise (ANAMM and World Bank 2009). In addition, the experience of municipalising the country shows that the connection between the residents and the municipal representatives is tenuous (Forquilha et al. 2018, 2019), which negatively affects accountability. This tenuous connection comes mainly as a result of the proportional representation system in force in Mozambique. As pointed out by Brito:

The proportional representation system devalues the ties between the elected representatives and the voters. [...]. This is due to the fact that the election of representatives is not based on who they are but rather, in the Mozambican case, according to closed party lists. Therefore, the representatives are not individually dependent on the trust of the voters, but mainly, their possible re-election is dependent on their good relationship with the party structures or their party colleagues, who, in the midst of the party appa-ratus, can influence their inclusion on the lists and in a suitable position. To sum up, serving the interests of the party and its leaders prevails over any interests of the voters. (Brito 2009: 25)

In this context, municipal representatives are accountable more to party leadership than to the local residents. This explains, for example, the supposed resignation of the Mayors of Quelimane, Pemba, and Cuamba in 2011, in a process where FRELIMO played a crucial role in the decision of these mayors (Forquilha 2015). Indeed, the internal pressure coming from the FRELIMO party structures led the mayors of these municipalities to publicly resign from their functions.

## 3 Political Stability, Violence, and the Legitimacy of the State

Political violence has been a recurring factor in the last fifty years of the history of Mozambique (fight for national liberation; the war of the 1980s; post-election conflicts and, more recently, the conflict in Cabo Delgado Province). Since national independence in 1975, the nature of the state (the fact that the state is constitutionally defined as secular and not religious) has not been seriously questioned by any particular group, despite its absence in certain parts of the country, particularly the most remote rural areas. However, the fact that the Mozambican political system is founded on a democracy based on the 'winner takes all' principle, allied to the poor performance of the state in terms of providing basic services in a context of a divided society (Lijphart 2008), puts the country in a situation of high risk of the occurrence of politically motivated violence and political instability. Arguably, decentralisation could play an important role in integrating differences as a way of reducing the potential for conflict.

### 4 State Capacity and Independence from Private Interests
In Mozambique, the poor capacity of the state and the lack of independence from private interests have been some of the greatest challenges when it comes to the process of policy design and implementation. With regard to decentralisation, for example, state capture by the political interests of the ruling party has delayed the implementation of reforms and, in some cases, made it impossible. This is the case, for example, in the adoption of the principle of gradualism in terms of the municipalisation of the country, that is the gradual municipalisation of the entire country and the gradual transfer of functions and powers from the central state to local authorities. This explains why, twenty years after the beginning of municipalisation, the country still has only fifty-three local authorities, and many functions and powers have yet to be transferred from the central state to the municipalities.

### 5 Sovereignty and Independence
One of the recurring themes in the debates that led to the decentralisation reforms in Mozambique is the affirmation of the unitary nature of the Mozambican state and the idea of strengthening national unity, aimed at not calling the sovereignty[5] and independence of the country into question. In this context, for the more conservative circles in FRELIMO, the idea of creating autonomous entities through the municipalisation process should be approached cautiously. This partly explains the adoption of the principle of gradualism, its incorporation into the legislation on decentralisation, and the creation of the controversial figure of state secretary in the context of decentralised provincial government. It is important to mention that the municipalisation experience in the country has shown that gradualism and the creation of the figure of the state representative in municipal areas and, later, the creation of districts in the provincial capitals brought conflicts, which had an impact on the process of providing public services at the local level.

---

[5] Our definition of sovereignty follows the political science literature and refers to the holding of authority by the state within a territory and over its population. Sovereignty applies both domestically (the need for the state to exert authority within its territory and over its populations) and externally (in the context of international relations – non-acceptance of any interference from other states with regard to domestic affairs).

Since the late 1990s, the process of implementation of decentralisation reforms has had strong technical and financial support from donors in interventions such as the national planning and decentralised finance programme and the different municipal support programmes (Weimer 2012; Bunk 2018). In these programmes, the government is seeking to play a delicate game aimed at ensuring the support of donors on the one hand while, on the other, having room to manoeuvre independently as a sovereign state. This delicate game has sometimes affected the process of implementation of the programmes, with cases of programmes ending before their time, as happened with the Municipal Development Programme (PRODEM).

## B  Municipalisation, District Development Fund ('7 Million')[6] and Challenges of Decentralised Provincial Governance

In this section, three cases will be discussed to illustrate the institutional dynamics in the decentralisation reforms. These are the municipalisation, the district development fund ('7 million'), and the challenges of decentralised provincial governance. By taking these three cases, the aim is to analyse how institutional dynamics shape the results of decentralisation reforms from a political and economic point of view.

### 1  The Municipalisation Process: Between Breakthroughs and Setbacks

The first attempt at municipalisation in Mozambique after independence came in 1994 with the approval of the law no. 3/94, of 13 September, on municipal districts. Approved by the then People's Assembly, before the first multiparty election in the history of the country, the law no. 3/94, of 13 September, called for municipalisation of the entire country. In practice, it was a question of transforming all districts in the country into municipalised spaces with regular elections. But this law was repealed even before its implementation. In its place, three years later, the law no. 2/97, of 18 February, on local authorities, was approved, introducing functional and geographic gradualism into the process of municipalisation of the country. As a result, the first thirty-three local authorities were set up and the first local election was held in 1998. Obeying the principle of gradualism, twenty more local authorities were set up in the following years, making a total of fifty-three local authorities, with regular elections every five years. According to the legislation, more local authorities could be set up once the conditions for these were in place, based on the criteria established, namely:

a)  geographic, demographic, economic, social, cultural, and administrative factors;

b)  national interests or the interests of the place in question;

---

[6] In this chapter, 'district development fund', '7 million', and Local Initiative investment Budget (OIIL) are used interchangeably.

c)  reasons of a historical and cultural nature; and
d)  assessment of the financial capacity for engaging in the tasks assigned
    to them (article 5 of the law no. 2/97, of 18 February).

However, in practice, the criteria contained in the legislation for setting up new local authorities have, over the years, shown themselves to be vague, giving plenty of room for manoeuvre to the central government, which is responsible for proposing the list of new local authorities to parliament. In fact, a study of the ten years of municipalisation in Mozambique made reference to this aspect in the following terms:

The policy framework for decentralization has not been transparent. Despite gradualism being an essential principle of local authority reform in Mozambique, there has been little transparency in the analysis and discussion process for the selection of new municipalities. The technical basis for planning the continued expansion of the local governance system is not defined using a clear and repeatable methodology that establishes standards and goals for the creation of new municipal towns and introducing small, rural local authorities (*autarquias de povoação*). (ANAMM and World Bank 2009: 11)

The process of setting up the local authorities has been marked by conflicts in the context of space occupation and political influence from the main political players, namely FRELIMO, RENAMO, and the Mozambique Democratic Movement (MDM). But it is not only in geographic gradualism that there is little transparency and, through this, conflicts between the main political players. The same is true for functional gradualism, that is the transfer of functions and powers from the central state to local authorities. In fact, in 2006, the Government of Mozambique approved the decree no. 33/2006, of 30 August, which calls for the gradual transfer of functions and powers from the central state to local authorities. Article 5 of the decree provides the following:

The transfer of functions and powers from state bodies to local authorities should be gradual in order to allow for the creation and consolidation of the necessary technical, human and financial capacities in the local bodies; 3. The set of functions and powers established in this decree shall be progressively transferred to the local authorities in the three years subsequent to its coming into force. This may be extended for a further two years. (decree no. 33/2006, of 30 August)

More than ten years later, the implementation of this decree has been marked by huge conflicts insofar as the state has been reluctant to transfer functions and powers to the local authorities, arguing that the local authorities still do not have the capacity to receive the services to be transferred by the state, particularly in the areas of health and education.

Apart from territorial and functional gradualism, another aspect that significantly affects the implementation of the municipalisation process is funding for the local authorities. The historical trajectory of the process of political institution building in the country has been marked by a strong centralising rationale, erecting barriers to the funding mechanisms for the local authorities. In fact, the law no. 1/2008, of 16 January, which defines the financial, budget, and patrimonial arrangements for the local authorities and the local authority tax system, does not facilitate funding adjusted to the needs of the local authorities. Not only are the intergovernmental transfers provided for in the law a far cry from the reality. The local authority tax system also has severe limitations, which are a consequence of the highly centralised nature of the state tax system. To date, the main intergovernmental transfers to local authorities are: (a) the Municipal Compensation Fund (FCA); (b) the Investment Fund for Local Initiatives (FIIL); (c) the Fund for the Reduction of Urban Poverty (PERPU); and d) the Roads Fund (Weimer and Carrilho 2017; Schiller et al. 2018).

With regard to the FCA, article 43 of the law no. 1/2008, of 16 January, states that:

The Municipal Compensation Fund is a fund aimed at complementing the budgetary resources of local authorities; The amount of the Municipal Compensation Fund is subject to its own funding, which is presented in the state budget, and consists of 1.5% of the tax revenue provided for in the financial year in question. (article 43 of the law no. 1/2008, of 16 January)

In practice, however, the FCA and other state transfers represent the revenue with the heaviest weight on funding budgets of local authorities, particularly small- and medium-sized local authorities, namely Type D municipalities and towns,[7] which reveals high financial dependence of the local authorities on the central state. But it is important to mention that state transfers to local authorities have been marked by considerable variations over the years, as shown in Figure 7.1, which has put many local authorities into financial difficulties, given the low volume of own revenue in the funding of the budgets in question.

Contrary to what might have been expected, the local authority tax system has not been consistent and coherent enough to deal with the low volume of own revenue. In fact, when you look at the collection process for own revenue by local authorities, it becomes clear that:

The central powers in terms of taxation continue to lie with the central state. In certain cases, tax rates are set centrally, and the same is the case for the definition of the tax bases and other more general principles of taxation, established on the general principles and regulations of the Mozambican tax system. Along these lines, the degree of local autonomy in the definition of fiscal policy is much greater for tariffs and fees paid for services and for fines than for taxes. (Schiller et al., 2018: 36–37)

---

[7] Based on the classification of urban centres in Mozambique, Mozambican municipalities are divided into five types: A (Maputo), B (Matola, Beira, and Nampula), C (provincial capitals and cities whose economic importance is of national and regional interest), D (other urban centres), and towns (Schiller et al. 2018).

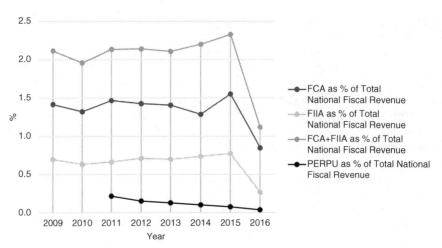

FIGURE 7.1 Transfers to local authorities as a percentage of national tax revenue (2009–2016) Source: Authors' calculation based on Ilal and Weimer (2018).

In this context, the lack of local fiscal autonomy puts a financial stranglehold on the municipalities, and this has a significant impact on the funding of local basic services and weakens the decentralisation reforms, particularly with regard to the municipalisation process.

What institutional dynamics are present in the case of the municipalisation, and what dimensions of institutions are these dynamics linked to? How do these dynamics affect the outcomes of municipalisation? Based on the implementation process described above, there are three dimensions of institutions, whose dynamics shape the results of municipalisation reform. These dimensions of institutions are: (a) rule of law; (b) state capacity and independence from private interests; and (c) sovereignty and independence.

Concerning the first dimension of institutions – rule of law – the process of municipalisation brings to light institutional dynamics, which show the way difficulties linked to separation of powers hamper policy design and implementation. In fact, as happens with other reforms, the debate on relevant aspects of the municipalisation process in the country is structured and dominated by the positions of the executive power, which ultimately represents the interests of the ruling party – FRELIMO. Since then, and because of the proportional electoral system in force, where the representatives are elected from a party list,[8] and the parliamentary majorities that FRELIMO has had since the first multiparty elections in 1994, parliament has taken on a minor role in the debate, very often limiting itself to 'rubber-stamping' the government positions in this matter. An example of this is the debate on the geographic and functional gradualism mentioned above and the process of creating new local authorities.

---

[8] For an in-depth analysis of the Mozambican electoral system, see Brito (2009).

As to the second dimension of institutions – state capacity and independence from private interests – institutional dynamics in this dimension show how the process of implementation of the reforms, in the context of municipalisation, is captured by party political private interests and, in some cases, delays the implementation of the reforms. This is the case, for example, with the delay in implementing the decree no. 33/2006, of 30 August, on the gradual transfer of functions and powers from the central state to local authorities. As mentioned above, this process is marked by conflict, which has been most visible in the municipalities that are ruled by political parties other than FRELIMO, namely the MDM and RENAMO (the cases of Beira, Quelimane, and Nampula municipalities). In this context, the political interests of the ruling party (FRELIMO) significantly structure the functioning of the state in terms of transfer of functions and powers to the local authorities, as also happens with the process of setting up new local authorities. This makes the process of implementation of the reforms more difficult and shape the outcomes of municipalisation, particularly when it comes to improving basic services (education, health, sanitation, transport) and strengthening democracy.

Finally, the dimensions of sovereignty and independence are probably the ones that stand out the most in the decentralisation reforms, particularly when it comes to municipalisation. It should be reiterated that the concept of sovereignty in this chapter draws on political science literature, and refers to the holding of authority by a state within a territory and over its population (Caramani 2017; Poggi 2017; Sørensen 2017). From this perspective, sovereignty applies both domestically (the need for the state to exert authority within its territory and over its populations) and externally (in the context of international relations – non-acceptance of any interference from other states with regard to domestic affairs). In a decidedly centralised state, as was mentioned above, institutional dynamics linked to sovereignty and independence show how the debate on the municipalisation process was very much structured around the idea of the need to preserve the unitary nature of the state, in accordance with the Constitution of the Republic (article 8 of the Constitution of the Republic, as amended by the law no. 1/2018, of 12 June). In this sense, the choice of territorial and functional gradualism (gradual creation of the local authorities and gradual transfer of functions and powers from the central state to the local authorities) comes essentially as a result of institutional dynamics linked to sovereignty and independence. The same can be said about the low fiscal autonomy of the municipalities, the creation of the figure of a state representative in the municipalities and the establishment of districts in all provincial capitals, leading to territorial overlaps (municipalities/districts) and, in some cases, conflicts between the mayors and district administrators (Forquilha 2016).

In addition, decentralisation is one of the areas that has had significant support from international cooperation partners, both in the area of deconcentration and the area of devolution (Borowczak and Weimer 2012; Weimer and Carrilho 2017; Bunk 2018). In fact, since the late 1990s, bilateral and multilateral partners have been supporting decentralised planning and finance programmes, as well as municipal development. This is the case, for example, of the National Programme for Decentralized Planning and Finance (PNPFD); Thirteen-City Support Programme (P 13); Decentralization and Municipalization Support Programme (PADEM); Support Programme for Districts and Municipalities (PADM), Local Authority Development Programme (PDA); PRODEM. In all of these decentralisation support programmes/projects, the government has been a key partner in the implementation process, playing a delicate game while at the same time ensuring technical and financial support and maximising any room for manoeuvre with a view to affirming country's sovereignty. In some cases, this delicate game has resulted in conflict between the government and the cooperation partners, significantly affecting the implementation process and the goals of the decentralisation support programmes.[9]

## 2 The District Development Fund ('7 Million'): Between Discourse and Practice

Introduced into governance practice two years after Armando Guebuza took office in his first term (2005–09), the district development fund is one of the most important reforms at district level in the context of administrative decentralisation. In fact, for the first time, with the approval of the law no. 12/2005, of 23 December, on the state budget for 2006, each district was given a district investment budget of 7 million meticais, the equivalent at the time of around US$250,000. This decision by the government of Armando Guebuza was warmly welcomed initially, particularly by the district governments, cooperation partners, civil society, and the local populations in general, insofar as the resources made available could be used for putting the District Strategic Development Plans (PEDD) and the District Economic and Social Plans and Budget (PESOD) into practice in the context of the decentralisation reforms, with the involvement of local councils – an institution set up under the scope of the Local Government Act (LOLE), approved in 2003 (Law No. 8/2003, of 19 May). Initially called the Local Initiative Investment Budget (OIIL), the 7 million later became known as the District Development Fund (FDD), with the approval of decree no. 90/2009, of 31 December.

For many stakeholders, the availability of a specific sum, the use of which was completely dependent on the decision of the districts, was an important step in making one of the main aims of decentralisation a reality, local development. However, in many cases, the lack of clarity as to the criteria for using these resources was visible. In fact, the first year of implementation of the reform was marked by disparity in terms of projects funded by the district governments, insofar as 'in some cases, there were administrators who renovated district palaces [...] and other cases where local police stations and Frelimo party headquarters were renovated' (Forquilha 2010b: 37). Given this lack of clarity in the use of the resources provided under the scope of the '7 million', President

---

[9] This was the case, for example, with the PNPFD and the PRODEM.

Guebuza began giving concrete guidelines in the country's provinces, underlining that the money had to be used for income generation, job creation, and food production. At the meeting of the council of ministers, extended to provincial governors, district administrators and FRELIMO officials, which took place in August 2006, President Guebuza once again insisted on the idea of creating wealth locally. After this, the guidelines for the preparation of PESOD for 2008, issued jointly by the Ministry of Planning and Development (MPD) and the Ministry of Finance (MF), gave instructions as to how the '7 million' was to be used, incorporating the will of the President of the Republic – income generation, job creation, and food production. Although these instructions were in line with the idea of local development, for many administrators this change was hard to manage, insofar as an important part of the PESOD planning activities was left without funding. This difficulty was plain to be seen, for example, in the words of the former administrator of Metarica, in Niassa Province. He said:

[...] now that the '7 million' is for food, income generation and jobs, I don't know how the district government will be able to pay for holding district consultative council sessions or how the projects approved by the consultative council for this year will be funded ... I think we'll have to go back to planning like we used to, without consulting the people, without the consultative councils [...]. (Forquilha 2010b: 37)

With the change in the guidelines on the use of the money, the '7 million' began operating along microcredit lines, managed by the district governments. Funding would be allocated to borrowers who presented projects in line with the goals of the fund, namely income generation, job creation, and food production. The borrowers would repay the amount allocated with interest. Initially, the interest rate varied from district to district, before the regulation introduced by the Ministry of State Administration (MAE) in 2011, when interest rates varied 'between 3% and 7% per month, i.e. 36%–84% per year' (Weimer and Carrilho 2017: 85). In theory, the money repaid should have gone back into the fund, with the aim of extending access to it to more citizens locally. But, in the early years of the initiative (i.e. 2006–08), the money repaid fell very short of contributing to the revolving nature of the fund (see Table 7.1).

In practice, there were enormous difficulties in that not only did the borrowers have trouble repaying as scheduled the amounts allocated, but also many of the projects approved and funded were not economically viable and did not have any clear connection to the district plans, namely the PEDD and the PESOD. In its debriefing regarding the early years of the implementation of the OIIL, the Mozambique government acknowledged that the process was facing constraints and challenges, namely:

(1) The non-formalisation of the procedures for the implementation of the OIIL is pointed to by almost all the participants as one of the main constraints to this process;

(2) The lack of full compliance with the decisions made at the 1st session of the council of ministers, extended to provincial governors, district

*Salvador Forquilha*

TABLE 7.1 *OIIL repayments up to the first half of 2008*

| N/O | Provinces | Ceiling in MZM | Paid in MZM | Repaid in MZM | % |
|---|---|---|---|---|---|
| 1 | Niassa | 110,632,870.00 | 81,452,030.00 | 1,782.67 | 2.2 |
| 2 | Cabo Delgado | 133,890,820.00 | 111,287,000.00 | 1,409.48 | 1.3 |
| 3 | Nampula | 166,679,180.00 | 139,834.980.00 | 3,533.27 | 2.5 |
| 4 | Zambezia | 172,272,600.00 | 130,640.800.00 | 4,394.25 | 3.4 |
| 5 | Tete | 139,696,240.00 | 73,903.000.00 | 1,500 | 0.002 |
| 6 | Manica | 96,058,850.00 | 62,898.500.00 | 199.2 | 0.3 |
| 7 | Sofala | 89,842,920.00 | 89,842.920.00 | 4,038.95 | 4.5 |
| 8 | Inhambane | 99,563,240.00 | 61,744.980.00 | 1,540.89 | 2.5 |
| 9 | Gaza | 85,308,880.00 | 85,308.880.00 | 1090.94 | 1.3 |
| 10 | Maputo | 53,817,000.00 | 27,127.300.00 | 15.75 | 0.6 |
| Total | | 1,147,772.600.00 | 864,040,390 | 19,524.65 | 1.8 |

*Source:* MPD (2008).
*Note:* The decimal separators used in the original have been maintained.

administrators, and other state and government officials, held on 11, 12, and 13 August 2006, considering that a large part of the process of prioritising and allocating resources had been concluded, particularly in 2006;

(3) The absence of systematic monitoring and following up on the projects funded, throughout the country, at central, provincial, and even district level;

(4) Lack of business management experience of the beneficiaries, linked to the poor design and feasibility of the projects submitted for approval;

(5) Limited capacity of the bodies involved in the process of selection and approval of projects;

(6) Absence of contracts between the districts and the borrowers, resulting in the absence of a repayment plan and disparity in the setting of interest rates and, where these exist, they are unclear as to the obligations of the borrowers;

(7) Difficulties with general repayments considering the nature (unprecedented and innovative) of the OIIL, allied to the local authorities' lack of experience in dealing with activities involving credit systems;

(8) Non-observance of connection elements, synergies, and consistency between projects, resulting in a weak production value chain and the subsequent underutilisation of the existing potential;

(9) Little or no involvement of local councils in the monitoring carried out in their areas of jurisdiction (MPD 2008: 14–16).

These constraints and challenges, on the one hand, and the administrators' difficulties in managing the change introduced by the President of the Republic, on the other, clearly show how institutional dynamics shape the results of the reforms. What institutional dynamics are present in the case of the '7 million', and what dimensions of institutions are these dynamics linked to? How do these dynamics affect the results of the '7 million'? Based on the implementation process described above, there are three institutional dimensions, whose dynamics shape the results of the '7 million' reform: (a) rule of law; (b) voice, participation, and political accountability; and (c) state capacity and independence from private interests.

With regard to the rule of law, institutional dynamics from this dimension show that although the separation of powers is enshrined in the constitution, there is a clear dominance of the executive power over the other two, particularly when it comes to designing and implementing reforms and policies. In many cases, the reforms are the sole initiative of the executive and, sometimes, of the actual President of the Republic, as is the case of the '7 million', without consultation and much less involvement of relevant actors. In this context, the ministers, who have to offer technical support to the reforms, limit themselves to finding mechanisms for making the reforms feasible, in the sense of making mere political guidelines a reality, entirely dependent on the President of the Republic. As a result, not only do the reforms become difficult to implement. They also become a mere political instrument for gaining ground and extending political influence, relegating issues of local development to second place. The '7 million' is a clear example of this. In fact, different research carried out on the subject shows that the '7 million' became an instrument for gaining ground locally, to the detriment of giving impetus to the local development process (Forquilha 2010b; Orre and Forquilha 2012; Sande 2011; Weimer and Carrilho 2017). In addition, the rules and regulations produced under the scope of the operationalisation of the '7 million' were not duly observed. Indeed, not only were there many cases where the allocation of money was not governed by any contractual ties between the state and the borrowers, but many of the procedures linked to management of the fund lacked formalisation, particularly in the early years of implementation of the initiative (MPD 2008). Consequently, the process of implementation was marked by differences in criteria and the treatment of the borrowers, particularly in terms of fund repayment, insofar as, throughout the country, there were differences in the interest rates set for repayments and few borrowers were able to repay the state for the funds received (MPD 2008), a fact that contradicted the goals and the role of the '7 million' in the context of local development.

With regard to the second dimension of institutions – voice, participation, and political accountability – the '7 million' implementation process brings to light institutional dynamics that show poor citizen involvement in the process of designing and implementing policies. Acclaimed as an important instrument for giving impetus to community participation in the local development process through the so-called local councils,[10] the '7 million' did not in fact broaden the local participation base. Indeed, not only were the local councils politically 'captured',

---

[10] On the local councils, see Forquilha (2010a); Forquilha and Orre (2011); Orre and Forquilha (2012).

reinforcing political and economic exclusion locally. They also failed to properly monitor the fund allocation process and the implementation of funded projects (MPD 2008). Moreover, the accountability dimension was practically absent from the process of implementation of the '7 million'. This was partly a result of the poor regulation and observance of the rules regarding the operationalisation of the fund, as mentioned above when speaking of the rule of law.

As to the third dimension of institutions – state capacity and independence from private interests – the case of the '7 million' brings to the fore institutional dynamics that make clear that poor state capacity, particularly when it comes to its poor institutionalisation and capture by party political interests, turned the reforms into an instrument for broadening FRELIMO's base of influence, particularly in the rural context (Orre and Forquilha 2012). Interviews held in Chimbunila District in Niassa Province in 2018, in a research project on social cohesion and political violence, for example, show how FRELIMO used the '7 million' to broaden their local base, in a clientelism rationale, setting issues of local development aside (Forquilha and Goncalves 2019).

### 3  The Challenges of Decentralised Provincial Governance

Following the results of the general election in 2014, where RENAMO won in some provinces in the centre and north, the country entered another political and military crisis and a lengthy negotiation process insofar as RENAMO claimed its right to govern in those provinces. In this context, decentralisation was one of the most important issues on the negotiating table. After attempts made by negotiating teams involving national and foreign personalities, President Filipe Nyusi, representing the Mozambique government, and President Afonso Dhlakama, representing RENAMO, decided to make more direct contact to negotiate the crisis on the facilitation of the so-called contact group, made up of representatives of some countries who are cooperation partners of Mozambique. After a long period of negotiation, marked by a certain amount of secrecy regarding the details of the issues discussed, particularly decentralisation, in February 2018 an understanding was reached between the government and RENAMO, which included a constitutional amendment and the subsequent production of legislation aimed at the introduction of Decentralized Provincial Governance Bodies (OGDPs).

In a process where parliament played only a minor role, insofar as it did not produce any profound or significant debate on the matter, limiting itself to 'rubber-stamping' the understandings that had been reached between the leaders (government and RENAMO), the new decentralisation package was approved before the October 2019 election. These are the Laws Nos. 3/2019, 4/2019, 5/2019, 6/2019, and 7/2019, all of 31 May, and the decree no. 2/2020, of 8 January, as mentioned above. In this context, the decentralisation package brings with it some important challenges, namely:

a)  Little clarity regarding fiscal decentralisation: how can OGDPs be assured of a tax base consistent and coherent with their duties and responsibilities in the context of a highly centralised state taxation system? How can it be assured that the allocation of state resources via intergovernmental transfers to OGDPs are in line with the decentralisation rationale and it does not reproduce what happens already in the municipalities and districts (few resources channelled locally)[11]?

b) Overlapping of some duties between the provincial directorates (OGDPs) and the state provincial services (OREPs);

c) Potential for conflict in the operation of OGDPs and OREPs;

d) Increase in the weight of the party machines on the functioning of OGDPs, making these more accountable to their political parties than to the voters.

Despite the challenges mentioned above, the new decentralisation package could have been not only an important means for improving public services and reinforcing democracy, but also a fundamental way of ensuring that the political institutions better reflected the heterogeneous nature of the country, its differences, thus reducing the potential for violent political conflict.

What institutional dynamics are at play in the case of decentralised provincial governance, and what dimensions of institutions are these dynamics linked to? How do these dynamics affect the outcomes of the reforms? Although the reforms regarding decentralised provincial governance in the country are recent, their implementation process brings to light two dimensions of institutions: (a) state capacity and independence from private interests and (b) political stability, violence, and the legitimacy of the state.

With regard to state capacity and independence from private interests, the process that led to the approval of the decentralisation package in 2019 shows once again how group interests, in this case political groups (FRELIMO and RENAMO), supersede the interests of the state in terms of development and the consolidation of democracy. In fact, although the issue of the election of provincial governors was raised following the claims from RENAMO in the context of the 2014 election results, it ended up becoming a potential instrument for pandering to the elite. By making the issue of the appointment of provincial governors a demand for its acceptance of the 2014 election results, RENAMO did not necessarily have in mind decentralisation as a mechanism for reinforcing local democracy and improving the provision of public services. Indeed, it is important to remember that before the demand for the appointment of provincial governors, one of RENAMO's conditions for accepting the election result was the formation of a 'caretaker government', a request that was rejected by the Mozambican parliament in November 2014, with the majority vote of FRELIMO (DW 2014).

It was after this rejection that RENAMO began demanding the appointment of governors in the provinces where it had won the election. Soon

---

[11] Municipalities are a different layer of decentralised entities within a province.

afterwards, this demand would be transformed into a draft bill on provincial authorities, rejected by the Mozambican parliament in April 2015 (RTP 2015). The months following the rejection of the draft bill on provincial authorities were marked by episodes of military tension, culminating in a return to armed violence, which continued until an understanding was reached between the leaders of the government and of RENAMO in February 2018, followed by the amendment to the constitution and the approval of the decentralisation package in 2019. In turn, FRELIMO, through the government, tried to ensure the reinforcement of its control and political influence locally, introducing provincial state representation bodies (OREPs) into the decentralisation package. In practical terms, these operate like parallel structures to the decentralised provincial governance bodies (OGDPs). In this way, the interests of RENAMO and FRELIMO ended up significantly conditioning not only how the debate on decentralised provincial governance was conducted, but also the process of implementation of the actual reforms, subordinating the issues of funding improvements in the provision of public services and local development associated with the decentralisation process.

As to political stability, violence, and the legitimacy of the state, institutional dynamics show that the historical trajectory of the process of political institution building in Mozambique has been marked by armed violence contesting the legitimacy of the state. This has significantly affected the process of designing and implementing policies, as is the case of the decentralisation package. As mentioned above, the debate and approval of the reforms regarding decentralised provincial governance took place in the context of finding a solution for the conflict between RENAMO and the Government of Mozambique following the 2014 election results. In this sense, rather than being a mechanism aimed at improving the provision of services and strengthening democracy, the decentralisation package acted as a way of accommodating political, social, and economic differences, minimising the potential for conflict and thus contributing to the stability of the country and the legitimacy of the state. However, the reforms approved and particularly their implementation process in the context of the decentralisation package fall very short of minimising conflict.

In fact, apart from being costly, insofar as the state budget will now be funding parallel provincial governance structures (OREPs and OGDPs), the decentralisation package contains contradictions and major potential for conflict, as mentioned above when speaking of some of the challenges of decentralised provincial governance. Indeed, the early days of operationalisation of this model, after the elected provincial governors and the provincial secretaries of state, appointed by the President of the Republic, had taken office, were marked by confusion regarding the operational scope of the elected provincial governors and the appointed provincial secretaries of state. Following this, on 29 January 2020, the Ministry of State Administration and Public Service found itself obliged to publish a circular entitled 'operationalization of state representation in the province and of the decentralized provincial governance bodies' (circular 9/MAEFP/GM-DNAL/214/2020), with a view to clarifying the operational scope of OREPs and OGDPs. This conflict would have been even greater if the 2019 election results had dictated victory for the opposition parties (RENAMO and MDM) in some provinces.

## IV CONCLUSION

More than twenty years on, how can the modest impact of the decentralisation reforms on the promotion of local development and the strengthening and consolidation of democracy in Mozambique be explained? Throughout this chapter, we have sought to answer this question based on institutional dynamics linked to the main dimensions of institutions identified above. The chapter underlines the idea according to which the results of the decentralisation reforms are shaped by the nature of the political system and the way it operates, in the context of institutional dynamics. From the cases of the district development fund ('7 million' fund), the municipalisation process and the challenges of decentralised provincial governance, on the one hand and, on the other, exploring institutional dynamics linked to five dimensions of institutions, with a particular emphasis on the rule of law, state capacity and autonomy from group interests, sovereignty and independence, the chapter sought to show how the institutions structure and shape the results of decentralisation reforms.

The analysis developed throughout the chapter showed that the five dimensions of institutions do not generate institutional dynamics that affect in the same way the results of the three reforms discussed. In fact, for the case of municipalisation, the process of implementation of the reforms in this area shows that the institutional dynamics that shape the results of the reforms are linked to three main dimensions of institutions. The first dimension is the rule of law, seen in the poor functioning of the system of checks and balances, placing the executive power (government) in a dominant position to the detriment of the legislative power (parliament) in the context of policies design and implementation. An example of this is the case of the adoption and implementation of territorial and functional gradualism, where parliament played a clearly minor role.

The second dimension of institutions, whose dynamics shape municipalisation reforms is state capacity and independence from private interests, which can be seen in the capture of the reforms with a view to promoting the interests of a political group. The process of implementation of the transfer of functions and powers from the central state to local authorities clearly shows how private interests of a political nature delay and, in a way, block the implementation of reforms. The third dimension of institutions with dynamics that affect the results of municipalisation is sovereignty and independence. In fact, the fear of autonomy of the local authorities that would affect the ideal of the unitary state significantly conditioned how the process of municipalisation is being implemented – gradually, from a territorial point of view and the transfer of functions and powers from the central state to the local authorities.

With regard to the district development fund ('7 million' fund), there are three dimensions of institutions, whose institutional dynamics are shown to be relevant. The first is the rule of law with an institutional dynamic marked by weak enforcement. As a result, the reforms became difficult to implement and were turned into a mere political instrument for gaining ground and extending political influence, relegating issues of local development to second place. The second dimension is voice, participation, and political accountability. Contrary to what might be thought, institutional dynamics show that the '7 million' did not broaden the participation base in local communities, due to the political capture of the local councils, which reinforced political exclusion. Not only did this fail to reinforce democracy. Issues of local development also became secondary. Finally, the third dimension is state capacity and independence from private interests. The dynamics analysed in this chapter show how the weak institutionalisation of the state led to the capture of the '7 million' by political party interests, which allowed FRELIMO to broaden its base of influence, particularly in rural areas.

Finally, concerning the case of decentralised provincial governance, the analysis suggests that there are two main dimensions underlying institutional dynamics that come from the implementation process. The first is state capacity and independence from private interests, which can be seen in the way the reforms were negotiated, approved and are being implemented. The second dimension is political stability, violence, and the legitimacy of the state. Indeed, the whole process of design and approval of the decentralisation package, which introduced decentralised provincial governance reforms, is deeply linked to the need of accommodating political differences, minimising the potential for violent conflict and increasing the legitimacy of the state.

Of the institutional dimensions mentioned above, state capacity and independence from private interests, particularly political groups, stand out in the three reforms analysed throughout this chapter, namely municipalisation, the district development fund ('7 million'), and decentralized provincial government. In this context, the reforms develop according to group interests, particularly political party interests, which capture the state and use the reforms as a mechanism for maintaining and bolstering political power. In this regard, rather than being a means of improving the provision of public services and strengthening democracy, decentralisation works more as an instrument for reinforcing state control and pandering to the elite. This is probably the biggest challenge decentralisation is facing in Mozambique, therefore making it a fundamental issue to be taken into account in any reform in this area, within the context of strengthening democracy and promoting local development.

# 8

## The Saga and Limits of Public Financial Management

António S. Cruz, Ines A. Ferreira, Johnny Flentø,
Finn Tarp, and Mariam Umarji

### I INTRODUCTION

Public financial management (PFM) comprises the laws, rules, and organisation, as well as systems and processes used by governments to secure, manage, and spend public funds in an effective manner (Allen et al. 2013; Lawson 2015). It incorporates the different activities of the budget cycle, including mobilising revenue, allocating funds, public expenditure, accounting and reporting, and auditing. Considering that the management of public finances affects the socio-economic costs and benefits of collecting and spending revenues (Haque et al. 2012), PFM is critical to all government activity and one of the principal tools of any political ideology. It is used to direct income and wealth in society and is therefore central to development and welfare.

A strong PFM system contributes to the effective delivery of public services and helps strengthen the ability to tax in a fair and efficient manner and to spend sensibly (Lawson 2015: 2). Three main broad goals have been proposed for an effective PFM (Lawson 2015: 2; Fritz et al. 2017: 1): (i) maintain aggregate fiscal discipline (i.e. ensure that targets for fiscal deficits are adhered to, and that levels of public borrowing are sustainable) and stability, as well as the appropriate management of public assets; (ii) promote both allocative and operational efficiency (i.e. that public resources are spent on agreed strategic priorities and that service delivery is optimized); and finally, (iii) ensure transparency and accountability for public resources and aid.

In contrast, a weak PFM system has a negative impact on fiscal discipline and macroeconomic stability and contributes to misalignment between the allocation of resources and the priorities in national policy (Fritz et al. 2017). Furthermore, PFM weaknesses can cause excessive annual fiscal deficits and unsustainable debt burdens, as well as disrupt the provision of public services and programmes (Guess and Ma 2015: 129), contributing to corruption and undermining development.

Fritz et al. (2017) highlight how ensuring a strong PFM system is crucial in low- and middle-income countries, given the pressures they face in terms of expenditure, namely from the provision of infrastructure and public services to respond to shocks (e.g., natural disasters or price volatility). Bearing this in mind, significant efforts have been made to reform existing PFM systems with a view to strengthening them and addressing existing challenges.

Given the importance of a well-functioning PFM system for sustainable and inclusive development, this chapter aims to identify institutional factors affecting the PFM system in Mozambique over the last forty-five years (Schick 1998; Fritz et al. 2017; Baland et al. 2020). In fact, Mozambique provides a telling case of the above general observations. Over the last almost half a century, the Mozambican governments have not always made the best use of PFM to help achieve the country's development goals. Its application changed over time with the political leadership and due to the external pressures and encouragement that the poor, young nation experienced. For a donor dependent country like Mozambique, the management of public funds has been one of the areas where development partners have been keen to assist and offer policy advice. Donors often legitimise their insistence on policy influence in relation to PFM with the need for technical efficiency in the management of funds as well as transparency to the electorate. The PFM system is, however, also a principal provider of evidence for donors to ascertain whether the government complies with reforms in other sectors and how reforms work.

Accordingly, PFM underwent a series of transformations in Mozambique since 1975. Until 1986, PFM was adapted to a top-down government system that enjoyed high legitimacy even though it had a low degree of transparency and public participation. In the transition to a market economy system from 1987 (PoM 1987a; GoM 1989) and multiparty democracy from 1994, PFM was substantially reformed with both technical and financial support from the international donor community, which supported PFM-reforms in their own right, and as a prerequisite to providing high levels of general budget support. The sequencing of reforms allowed the PFM reform to gain real ground and momentum, and high economic growth and gradual reduction of poverty can be seen as both a result and a driver of these reforms.

The high levels of donor funding came with widespread conditionality[1] that increasingly limited and challenged the Mozambican government's political choices. Wars on terror and post war stabilisation efforts increased in the 2000s and together with a world economic crisis this put aid budgets under

---

[1] We refer to Flentø and Simão (2020) for a comprehensive analysis of Mozambique's dependence on foreign aid and the ways in which the aid-based development model has evolved and created many key challenges of both political and institutional nature. Moreover, while Arndt et al. (2007) conclude that aid to Mozambique had a reasonable rate of return until the early 2000s, they cautioned that some features of the aid that Mozambique receives deepen rather than reduce dependency in the medium term.

pressure. Western donors grew less patient with progress on democracy and good governance in Mozambique, where a new president developed stronger ties to China. With the confirmation of significant natural gas reserves in the Rovuma Basin in 2010, the Government started focusing on large scale extraction of natural resources and external borrowing from other sources than Mozambique's traditional donors to bring the gas revenue forward.

PFM reforms slowed down and an international debt scandal erupted that undermined the credibility of the PFM system. The secret contraction of debt by top level government had little to do with the virtues of PFM reforms. No PFM system can discover top-secret letters, only the subsequent flows of funds, as was the case in Mozambique. The lacking disciplinary and legal action towards the top government people contracting the debt questioned the fundamental value of decades of sustained reform. Corruption became more widespread due to elite capture and rent-seeking, the lack of separation of powers, the merging of political and economic powers, and a weak opposition.

The rest of the chapter proceeds as follows: Section II reviews the evolution of the PFM system in Mozambique. Section III evaluates the PFM reform process, while Section IV tunes in on two key issues – lack of separation of powers and rule of law and decentralization. Section V concludes.

II EVOLUTION OF THE PFM SYSTEM[2]

A Independence and Central Planning and Management, 1975–1986

In 1975 the official public accounting system was based on the colonial framework[3], namely the Public Accounts General Regulations of 1881, the Finance Regulation (*Regulamento da Fazenda*) of 1901, and later legislation updates (*Portarias* dated 1947 and 1958). However, the exodus of Portuguese settlers and the very low level of education and experience with administration among Mozambicans at independence entailed significant challenges in managing the system. The point of departure for Mozambique in relation to PFM was a rather antiquated and little transparent system that had been managed by Portuguese bureaucrats, many of whom left the country at independence, not bothering to hand over or train their successors, sometimes even sabotaging the systems on their way out. Government accounts from the late 1970s were only reconciled and audited in the early 1990s with Swedish technical assistance.

During the first decade of independence, until the end of 1986, the PFM system was adjusted to serve Frelimo's objectives of dismantling the colonial

---

[2] See Figure A8.1 in the Appendix for a timeline of key events influencing the PFM system in Mozambique.

[3] The official public accounting system utilised the 'ordinary balance equilibrium' of Mozambican territory, which was a propaganda manoeuvre of the New State in Portugal to provide an appearance of quality and rigour in the PFM in Mozambique in 1946–73 (Madeira 2012). However, that system lacked transparency.

TABLE 8.1 *Public budget revenues (percentage of total current revenues)*

| Budget category | 1978–1979 (average) | 1985–1986 (average) |
|---|---|---|
| Total current revenues | 100 | 100 |
| Direct taxes | 26 | 33 |
| Indirect taxes | 60 | 40 |
| Other revenues | 14 | 27 |

*Source:* CNP (1985, 1987).

administration and promoting fast socio-economic development in the context of a Marxist-Leninist ideology (GoM 1981). At its 3rd Congress in 1977, Frelimo decided to implement an economic system of central planning and management (Frelimo 1977a, 1977b). The state planning system controlled the public financial system, the monetary system, wages and prices, and the material balance system. These institutional changes were driven by popular ideology distancing the new and sovereign Mozambique from its colonial past under a leadership that enjoyed widespread popular support. It involved the Mozambican population in a limited manner, but much more than any leadership had done before. Issues like transparency of public accounts were not at the centre of debate; it was about fuelling social transformation and increasingly how to finance the defence against an insurgency supported by the hugely superior neighbouring countries, Rhodesia and South Africa.

To improve internal revenue sources, the tax code was reformed[4] in 1978, increasing the weight of direct taxes, in line with a progressive system (Byiers 2005; Theodossiadis 2004: Table 8.1). Especially taxes on company profits increased. In the category of indirect taxes, which was the major component of revenue (Table 8.1), unessential goods were subject to higher taxes than essential goods. This reform was successful for a few years, when the share of total current revenues over the GDP increased from 11.1 per cent in 1978 to 14.2 per cent in 1983 (CNP 1985; Sulemane 2002).

Budget allocations served the purpose of promoting fast industrialisation, the collectivisation of agriculture, the expansion of state enterprises, and the expansion of primary education and health services. As the massive costs of the war in the 1980s aggravated,[5] a higher proportion of expenditures were allocated to military purposes ('other' expenditures in Table 8.2). The informal sector became gradually larger in the 1980s, reducing the share of revenue to GDP.

---

[4] As examples of reformed taxes: The National Reconstruction Tax was introduced as a progressive personal tax replacing various colonial-era income taxes, and the Circulation Tax was introduced as a consumption tax.

[5] We do not explore here the complex background (including domestic, regional, and global dimensions) for the military conflict and war in the 1980s, but refer to Cruz and Mafambissa (2020) and Flentø and Simão (2020).

TABLE 8.2 *Public budget expenditures (percentage of current and investment expenditures)*

| Budget category | 1979–1980 (average) | 1985–1986 (average) |
| --- | --- | --- |
| Current expenditures | 100 | 100 |
| Education | 18 | 17 |
| Health | 11 | 7 |
| Other | 71 | 76 |
| Investment expenditures | 100 | 100 |
| Agriculture | 18 | 19 |
| Industry and energy (mineral resources) | 10 | 16 |
| Transport, communications, construction | 53 | 46 |
| Education, and health | 4 | 4 |
| Other (including defence and security) | 15 | 15 |

*Source:* CNP (1985, 1987).

The share of total current revenues over the GDP declined from 14.2 per cent in 1983 to 8 per cent in 1986, and the overall deficit after grants as a percentage of GDP increased from 10.1 per cent in 1982 to 15.3 per cent in 1986 (CNP 1985: 40; World Bank 1989; Sulemane 2002: 50;). The public debt including arrears rose to US$3.2 billion in 1986 (World Bank 1987).

Overall, the centralised economic model, including its PFM component proved inefficient. Viable companies were subject to foreign exchange restrictions and many public companies were loss makers. The violent conflict was a huge burden on the economy and Mozambique became heavily indebted. After a few years, the economic system collapsed and forced the government to switch to a market-oriented economy in 1987 and to move towards a democratic political system in line with conditionality of the international creditors and donor community.

## B Economic Rehabilitation and the Market Economy, 1987–2009

We highlight three sub-periods in PFM reforms between the late 1980s and the discovery of natural gas reserves in 2010. The first started in 1987, when the government implemented a wide-ranging series of reforms aiming to shift the economy towards greater reliance on market mechanisms. Although the initial economic and PFM reforms were successful, in terms of reducing the public deficit as a share of GDP from 10.1 per cent in 1986 to 4.7 per cent in 1989 and recovering national production (8.1 per cent GDP annual average growth rate in 1987–89), the country remained at war under the one-party political regime opposed by Renamo. It was only after the multiparty and democratic elections in 1994 onwards – marking the beginning of the second sub-period – that the PFM reforms could proceed more systematically, in a more coherent and integrated manner.

The volume of internal revenue and foreign aid rose substantially, allowing for the creation of the State Financial Administration System (SISTAFE) in 2002, signalling the beginning of the third sub-period. Significant advances took place in the form of tax reforms, the creation of the Tax Authority (AT) in 2006 and the development of various budget cycle subsystems. However, the positive dynamics of PFM reforms, supported by foreign aid in the context of sustained economic growth and poverty reduction, changed when the existence of large reserves of natural gas was confirmed in the Rovuma Basin in 2010. Since then, government priorities have been focused on minerals and other natural resources. Before we discuss this shift, we describe the three stages in more detail.

### 1 *Economic Rehabilitation, 1987–1994*

In a war-torn country with administered prices and exchange rates, the principal tool of PFM, the state budget, shows a distorted picture of what is going on in the economy. One of the objectives with first generation stabilization and structural adjustment reform in the 1980s was to correct just that. Only when prices are no longer administered, the real economic cost of state financed activity, including implicit subsidies to loss making entities, becomes visible on the budget and can be addressed. The next step was calibrating the budget both in terms of quantity and quality of expenditures and income. With a view to achieving such prudent fiscal policy, the first step of a whole series of PFM reforms was undertaken during the period 1987–1994 (Figure A8.1 in the Appendix), addressing all areas of the PFM cycle, as summarised in Table A8.1 in the Appendix.

The revision of the Constitution of the Republic in 1990 (eliminating the monopoly of one political party and providing space for market economy and private sector activities) together with the general peace agreement signed with Renamo in 1992 facilitated access to support from the International Monetary Fund (IMF), the World Bank, other multinational organisations, and a broader range of bilateral donors. Public expenditures were scrutinised to reduce state enterprises deficits, and to restrain growth in the wage bill, price subsidies, and the purchase of goods and services. Investment expenditures were focused on priority maintenance and rehabilitation projects. The tax code was revised from 1987, increasing the turnover tax, other selected consumption and import taxes, income taxes for individuals and enterprises (PoM 1987c), and the basis for collecting business taxes was updated. The Administrative Court (TA), that is the Auditor General, was re-established[6] in 1992, creating conditions for re-launching external audits of public administration entities.

---

[6] The Administrative Court (n.d.) and Cistac (2009) mentioned that the Administrative Court was created in Mozambique in 1869. The Mozambican Constitution of 1975 did not mention the Administrative Court, but the Constitutions of 1990 and 2004 already mention the Administrative Court (Frelimo 1975).

Until 1987 the investment budget was prepared by the National Planning Commission (CNP) and the recurrent budget by the Ministry of Finance (MoF) (World Bank 1989). With the implementation of the PRE, MoF became responsible for preparing both budgets, but preparation continued separately. Due to low capacity in MoF, CNP continued to be involved in the investment budget preparation, which was mostly donor financed, while the recurrent budget was internally financed. A rolling three-year investment programme of core projects to monitor priority expenditures started in 1989 (IMF 2004b:33).

In reality, there was no popular demand for the above reforms; they were driven by donors and creditors. In Mozambique as elsewhere, this process entailed a myriad of knock-on effects between institutions as the adjustment to market prices sank through an economy that at the outset was entirely state run, except for small-scale farming. Inter-institutional debt evolved, and the relative importance and strength of institutions in society was affected.[7]

There was, however, no way around it for Mozambique. The reforms were at the core of the stabilisation programme, and, as such, a hard conditionality from IMF, creditors, and donors. Fundamentally, President Chissano had already decided to support the reform agenda demanded by Bretton Woods and donor countries as part of his strategy to lead the transformation of Mozambique that would necessarily happen after the collapse of the Soviet Block. The president installed a team of very competent technocrat ministers and vice-ministers in the key economic ministries dealing with donors and supported them against hard liners and die hard socialists, as long as reforms did not undermine Frelimo's popularity and domestic monopoly on economic management. Some of the reforms did test this strategy as reductions in the wage bill entailed lay-offs and pay cuts that turned the Frelimo-controlled labour unions against the government, which entailed strikes and manifestations and ensuing police brutality. Privatizations, lay-offs, and pay-cuts were politically difficult to handle, whereas restructuring the government's book-keeping and financial management system was not risky in this context. It was considered a technical reform, and it should be kept in mind that the clarity these reforms brought to economic management at large in the Mozambican economy was also useful to a president leading a very sensitive and complex reform agenda with many external and internal pressures.

---

[7] Not only state-run factories and commercial production were affected, also more core government entities. Army and hospitals must pay for electricity and water, the water companies must pay for electricity to pump water to the consumers. Government offices, cities, and towns must pay for electricity, including for street lights and traffic regulation. The electricity company builds arrears with the hydro dams and the petroleum importers etc. Many institutions could not pay and debt was pushed around until it found a political solution, via the budget or by mining the assets of government utilities.

## 2 Democratic and Multiparty Elections after the Peace Agreement, 1994–2002

The second sub-period of PFM reforms started in 1994 after the first democratic and multiparty elections. Until then, the management of state finance had not been public. During one party rule, there was no systemic reason for publication and, as for most countries at war, there was no appetite for publishing the details and real economic cost of the war effort, including debt to former Soviet Bloc countries. When the government budget was first published by the local press, it was leaked by a donor representative to a new fax newspaper, which printed it on the front page. It was a real sensation.

In the 1994–2002 sub-period, two laws and two policy documents are particularly relevant: the Budget and State General Account Framework Law, 15/1997, the Local Autarchies Basic Law, 2/1997, the 1997 Expenditure Management Reform Strategy and the first Poverty Reduction Strategy Paper, PARPA, 2001–2005 (PoM 1997a, 1997b; GoM 2001; McGill et al. 2004).

The Basic Law of Local Autarchies (*Lei Básica das Autarquias Locais*), 2/1997, was an important step for decentralisation. The Budget and State General Account Framework Law, 15/1997, and the 1997 Expenditure Management Reform Strategy established a new set of budget cycle and general accounts rules, as well as defined the main steps to reforming the public expenditure management, including investment in a computerised system (Lønstrup 2002). The first Medium-Term Expenditure Framework (MTEF) linked to the annual budget was prepared in 1998 (Fozzard 2002: 4). TA started issuing auditing reports and assessments and a new system of public accounting was prepared in 1999 to improve control and transparency in budget execution. The Finance General Inspection (IGF) statute was approved in 1999, creating the basis for the public finance internal auditing (GoM 1999). Finally, the Technical Unit of the State Finance Administration (UTRAFE) was created in 2001 to help ensure that the PFM reforms would continue to advance.

Importantly, Mozambique had at this stage to commit to implementing a strategy to reduce poverty to have access to international aid funds and debt cancellation. As a first step, the National Planning Commission was merged with the Ministry of Finance to create a new Ministry of Planning and Finance after the elections in 1994. This move was meant to address the need to better integrate the plan and the budget, to integrate the recurrent and investment budget, and to prepare a multi-year budget. As a next step, poverty reduction strategies were implemented and monitored. A Poverty Reduction Strategy was formulated in 1995 (IMF 2004b: 37). The first national household budget survey was carried out in 1996–97 and the first Poverty Reduction Strategy Paper (PARPA 2001–05) was approved in 2001, linking policy objectives and budgetary allocations (GoM 2001).

In the 1980s donor countries supported various government entities with financial and technical assistance on a bilateral basis. A handful of donors started to assist with multilateral debt relief and balance of payment support from the early

1990s which entailed wider conditionality, normally only imposed by Bretton Woods. Originally donors were looking for a peace dividend and demanded increased allocations to social sectors, preferably exceeding the domestic revenue or savings on the recurrent budgets resulting from their funding. Such conditionality on insight into the budget and influence on allocations increased as a wider 'like-minded' group of donors initiated attempts at coordinating budget support to the government (Batley et al. 2006: S2). The initial group of six donors grew to ten in 2002. The donor coordination process intended to reduce the coordination cost for the government, and also to provide opportunity for greater degree of 'ownership', and for participation of various actors, including civil society, in the planning, budgeting, monitoring, and evaluation process. Donors insisted on improving transparency and accountability in the budget cycle process to comply with aid financing rules and expectations from their headquarters.

As Mozambique continued to benefit from general budget support and the international debt cancellation initiatives, availability of funds increased significantly. So did donor dependency and conditionality, not only in relation to PFM itself, but to fiscal policy at large. When donors pledged un-earmarked funds to the budget, anything the government financed was supposedly of their concern, not least expenditure in the security sector, which donors endeavoured to seriously cap. Few donor countries understood the need for spending on security in Mozambique. Being surrounded by friendly countries, it had in their perspective little use of new security assets. At best, such assets would be useless, and in worst-case scenarios they could be used against the country's own civilian population. Only very few donor representatives saw the dangers in capping security expenditure too much. The European Commissioner for International Partnerships (1999–2004) and Danish Development Minister, Poul Nielson, was probably the only prominent donor representative alluding to this after studying events in West Africa.

Good PFM systems were the tools necessary to monitor how the money was spent, also the donor funds, now that they were co-mingled with the government's own resources. Half a dozen ministers of development cooperation in the donor countries were at times trying to co-manage the budget, and sometimes there was a real issue of direction of accountability for the government. Most fundamentally, however, the general budget support was based on a memorandum of understanding of the so-called underlying principles. These were supposed to reflect shared values in human rights, democracy, and good governance. The latter put PFM at the centre of conditionality for the general budget support that Mozambique was heavily dependent upon in the 1990s and early 2000s including for finance of recurrent costs and salaries.

### 3 New Financial Administration System and the Tax Authority, 2002–2009

The third sub-period of PFM reform was marked by the official creation of the State Financial Administration System (SISTAFE) in 2002. SISTAFE covered the following budget cycle subsystems: budget, public accounts, treasury, state procurement, and internal audit. In this sub-period, two other events and one policy decision had a noteworthy effect on PFM reforms in the long term:

- The local elections in 2003, when Renamo, the main opposition party, won in five municipalities for the first time (Brito 2008).
- The new Frelimo Government in 2005, switched party policy, gradually controlling more intensively the state bureaucracy and the armed forces (Hanlon and Mosse 2010; Orre and Rønning 2017).[8]
- The creation of the Tax Authority in 2006 became a significant signpost for tax reforms for about one decade.

In the 2000s, Mozambique received significant support in terms of financial aid and technical assistance from the international community. In 2001–02, the share of grants over the GDP, 13.3 per cent, was about the same size as the share of revenues over the GDP, 13.8 per cent (IMF 2004b: 28). The group of donors coordinating aid support to the state budget increased from 10 in 2002 to 15 donors in 2004, 17 in 2005, and 19 later on (Batley et al. 2006: S2). Not all donors joined the General Budget Support (GBS) for the noble reasons of aid effectiveness. Some bought the cheapest ticket to the table as the group increasingly became the way in which aid was coordinated and, more importantly, the format in which the policy dialogue between the government and donors was conducted. Considerable prestige and influence were attached to chairing the group, and many donors shared the belief that GBS could be used for coercive purposes.

Such coercion was not necessary in relation to PFM, where reforms generally got very positive assessments even publicly from IMF. The second PARPA was approved for the period of 2006–09 aiming at reducing poverty by better integrating the national economy and increasing productivity (GoM 2006a). However, an emerging donor concern at the time were non-transparent flows like contributions to the ruling party from businessmen and non-western countries. This invalidated the possibility for a level playing field at elections and was firmly believed to entail implicit cross-conditionality where the state would have to compensate for what the party had received. Furthermore, a key concern was the free run of drugs through Mozambique that would eventually help finance the war against western forces in and around Afghanistan as well as favourable commercial conditions to Chinese enterprises in public procurement of large-scale infrastructure and on distribution of concessions on land and limited business licenses.

Overall, PFM reforms did advance significantly in relation to both revenue and budget cycle components. Tax reforms aimed at reducing exemptions, simplifying procedures and tax codes, providing incentives to investments, and increasing revenue collection were implemented, and in 2009 Mozambique

---

[8] Hanlon and Mosse (2010:7–8) and Orre and Rønning (2017:29) analysed this party–state relationship.

submitted its candidature for membership of the Extractive Industries Transparency Initiative (EITI). Reference can furthermore be made to the reforms summarised in Table A8.2 in the Appendix.

In sum, donors were very content with progress of PFM reforms and in 2007, the IMF referred to Mozambique as a best practice example to be followed. Economic growth continued, and there was general agreement among donors that the areas on which to take issue with the government were democracy, human rights, including the rule of law. Macroeconomic management, including PFM, was considered a success and reforms were widely left to technical discussions. Donors increasingly directed their concern to the contacts the government kept, including businessmen whom the US-administration eventually named as drug kingpins and not least China's increasing involvement in Mozambique. Meanwhile, many other general and sector-specific reforms formed part of the at times feverish PFM effort. Finally, the process of greater autonomy of municipal and local state entities advanced in this period.[9]

## C Extraction of Natural Resources, 2010–Present

The period since 2010 saw a shift in the PFM reform effort with the confirmation of the existence of natural gas reserves in the Rovuma Basin[10]. The prospects of profiting from the extraction of hydrocarbon resources and other mineral resources prompted Frelimo and its governments to shift focus from PFM reforms and prioritise instead the quest for opportunities in mega projects related to mineral resources, especially oil and gas.

The inaugural message from donors to President Guebuza on the start of his second mandate was a freeze of general budget support, triggered by irregularities in the 2009 parliament and presidential elections. The decision came as a complete surprise and enormous disappointment to the government. The G19 had rarely been able to make radical decisions and the government found comfort in the fact that uniting 19 donors, some with very different agendas in Mozambique, on anything but status quo would be very difficult. The government also had informal observers in the G19 secretariat and some of the technical working groups who would catch any discords of significance. This time, however, a good handful of ambassadors knew that the geopolitical winds

[9] The state local entities law was approved in 2003 to update the legislation on local state structures and allow for legal relationship with local autarchies (PoM 2003). In 2006, state entities' functions and competencies were transferred to local autarchies (GoM 2006b). A legal framework for provincial assemblies was approved, in 2007 (PoM 2007a). The finance, budget, and state assets framework for local autarchies was approved, in 2008 (PoM 2008). Tax system for autarchies was approved in 2008 (GoM 2008).

[10] AMA1 (Anadarko) confirmed the existence of 75 trillion cubic feet (tcf) of natural gas reserves in Area 1 of the Rovuma Basin in 2010 (Crooks 2018; US-EIA 2018). In 2011, ENI confirmed the existence of natural gas reserves in Area 4 of the Rovuma Basin (ENI 2011). US-EIA reported that ENI natural gas reserves amount to 85 tcf.

had changed and headquarters would welcome a harder line, including possible savings that could be spent in fragile and post-conflict states. They acted quietly and without support staff during the big Mozambican holidays after the New Year in 2010, and skilfully organised the motion in a way that would leave softer donor voices behind in the policy dialogue with the government as well as with a problem explaining headquarters why they were lenient and not positioned where the action was.

The event exposed Mozambique's vulnerability to external shocks, and although ideas were certainly maturing already, the experience strengthened the Guebuza administration's resolve to reduce donor dependency and move future revenues from gas forward. Moreover, Frelimo tightened the control of the state apparatus, and allegiance to the party became central, sometimes at the cost of a law-abiding behaviour. A series of laws and regulations[11] were put in place from the 1980s through the 2000s to dissuade civil servants at all levels from abusing public goods or benefiting illicitly from using public goods. Furthermore, it was expected that the investment in 'sophisticated, modern and advanced' electronic and informatics systems, with international and advanced PFM models with the audit and report mechanisms would increase the efficiency of the system and make it easier to control the misuse/abuse or illicit use of public funds. A further reference can be made to the Probity law (PoM 2012, Law 16/2012), which explicitly forbids the abuse of party powers in relation to the functioning of the state entities. However, reality was that these laws were regularly ignored and the practice of asking for bribes in relation to public tenders started escalating.

The first consequence of the above change of priorities was the decision by the government to issue state guarantees for the so-called Proindicus and MAM loans, not included in the budget submitted to the parliament for approval, and which only became publicly known in April 2016 (Hanlon 2016a, 2016b; IMF 2016b; Wirz and Wernau 2016). They are widely referred to as the 'hidden debt' scandal and, together with the Embraer[12] case, reflect unlawful behaviour by high government officials (IMF 2018; Melo 2018; RM 2021).

A second consequence of the change of priorities was a neglect of the factors that could keep peace with Renamo and prevent the economic speculation on the coast of Cabo Delgado that fuelled the eruption of armed conflict in the North and the occurrence of various waves of high-profile kidnappings (Hanlon 2018, 2021a, 2021b; Orre and Rønning 2017; Pitcher 2020).

---

[11] They include EGFAE, State Civil Servants and Agents General Statute: Decree 14/1987, updated later through Law 14/2009, Decree 62/2009), as well as previous and complementary legislation, such as Decree 16/1978, Decree 4/1981, Law 8/1985, and various versions of the general labour law.

[12] A Minister, a CEO of a public company, and a third individual were accused of requesting commissions when dealing with the purchase of two airplanes from the Brazilian company Embraer.

A third consequence is a generalised lower quality of public services, and increasingly evident corruption. To illustrate, Mozambique fell to 149th position out of a total number of 180 countries in the 2020 corruption perceptions index (Transparency International 2020). VAT refund delays and the excessive bureaucracy and non-transparent procedures that taxpayers face when dealing with the tax authority created further opportunities for corruption and abuse of power (Cortez 2014; IMF 2019b).

Put differently, while the PFM reform programme continued in the 2010s and Mozambique was declared compliant with the EITI in 2012 (EITI 2020), this happened in a political environment that increasingly jeopardised both economic and institutional progress. As a result of the 2014 general and presidential elections, Filipe Nyusi replaced Armando Guebuza as the new President in 2015, becoming later in the year also President of Frelimo. The Ministry of Finance and the Ministry of Planning and Development were merged in the Ministry of Economy and Finance in 2015. Planning and Budget functions were merged again into the same directorate. As the public became aware of the 'hidden debt' decisions taken in 2013–14, the group of nineteen donors interrupted all budget support in 2016, and the IMF interrupted its policy assistance. Mozambican public and international partners lost confidence in the country and in the PFM reforms.

Contradictions between Frelimo and Renamo intensified, and the Constitution of the Republic was amended in 2018. The declared aim was to advance the decentralisation process (PoM 2018). However, introducing the position of provincial state secretary has also been interpreted as a move to take away key political and management functions from the elected provincial governor on the one hand, and as Frelimo's pre-emptive action should opposition parties win the provincial governors' positions on the other. Should Frelimo lose in local elections, the party would keep political control in provinces through the provincial state secretary.

While presidential, parliamentary, and provincial elections took place in 2019, they were controversial. In parallel, specific PFM reforms continued. The SISTAFE law was revised (PoM 2020) and a pilot planning and budget module and social and economic planning and state budget simulation were carried out in 2020.

## III EVALUATING THE PFM REFORM PROCESS

### A Building a PFM System: Successes and Constraints

Having outlined the main events that influenced the PFM system and marked its different periods, we now put this analysis in perspective and evaluate the PFM reform process. During the period 1975–86, the PFM system was adjusted to the purpose of national revolution, Marxist-Leninist ideology, and war, within a political framework of a one-party state. The government successfully managed the transition from the colonial period to post independence years and started implementing a development strategy based on the industrialisation model of the socialist countries led by USSR. Until 1980–81, the economy and state revenues were under control. There was popular support for the political and economic system adopted by Frelimo government, and political leaders were trusted. They were the national liberators and were adopting policies favouring rural and lower income families. Also, there was no evidence of private enrichment using public resources.

After 1981, Mozambican GDP and state revenue started declining each year, until 1986. The economic system based on central planning and management, the failure of the socialist countries to replace western countries and the rest of the world as commercial and investment partners, and the ongoing war were the main factors for the economic decline, and the PFM system started failing. The lack of separation of powers and non-transparent management prevented external and internal auditing, efficient budget management, effective revenue collection, and appropriate fiscal policy analysis. The Popular Assembly, Supreme Popular Court, CNP, the Ministry of Finance, sectoral ministries, and other public entities were unable to critically identify and correct the public financial system and management distortions for about a decade.

During 1987–94, the PFM system changed substantially, adapting to the market economy and becoming more efficient and transparent. Reforms took place through the approval of new legislation, the change in administrative structures and procedures, and training. Accordingly, this period saw key general reforms that contributed to overcome many PFM system constraints, a new 1990 Constitution, the peace agreement in 1992 and the first democratic and multiparty elections in 1994. However, reform efforts were initially constrained by the war, the lack of separation of powers, a weak rule of law, and the political system with a single party. Some of this was part of the underlying deal between Mozambique and western donor countries.

The sequencing of the reforms introduced by the Bretton Woods was less than optimal in economic terms, as the liberalisations of prices happened at a time where no supply response was possible due to the war. However, the early onset of economic reforms, before peace and armistice, allowed Frelimo to gain and maintain control of the reforms, including privatisations, before Renamo got demobilised and installed as opposition party. The protracted peace process from 1992 to 1994 also reduced the likelihood that Renamo could reject defeat at the first multiparty elections, as farmers, including Renamo supporters, and indeed Renamo's own rank and file combatants had settled and gotten used to a much more comfortable life than bush fighting and queuing for food in refugee camps.

The sequencing of reforms also meant that the government maintained control of the banking system during this first phase of fiscal reforms. Privatising the banking system was difficult and slow because the state banks were not commercially interesting to foreign banks. The same could be said for the

Mozambican market until a credible peace was achieved and economic growth had been sustained for some time. As the PFM-reforms progressed and subsidies were exposed and subsequently suppressed, much of the problem with subsidies to loss making state entities moved to the banking system through loans to companies that would never become viable entities in a market economy. The subsequent cost to the economy of this mining of the banking system has been felt for decades in Mozambique. Moreover, as the fiscal subsidies moved to the banking system as unrecoverable loans, it increased net credit to the economy just as much as it would have if handed out from the budget. This limited the expansion that otherwise could have been accommodated on the fiscal side, including in the social sectors, where expenditure, such as salaries to teachers and nurses in rural areas, was much more likely to generate strong multipliers than the loans to state corporations under privatisation.

## B A Feverish Frenzy of Initiatives

In 1994–2009, the PFM system started to change and systematically reform[13] in what can best be characterised as a feverish frenzy of initiatives. There was political commitment at the highest levels within Frelimo and Government, expressed through the main government programmes and budgets. The Ministry of Planning and Finance (1995–2004), and from 2005 onwards, the Ministry of Finance and the Ministry of Planning and Development were in charge of reforming the PFM system. The government was in agreement with international funding partners, bilateral and multilateral, such that aid financing was allocated to PFM reform programmes, technical assistance was provided, and formal and on-the-job training was carried out.

The tax administration body was reformed over time concluding in the establishment of the Tax Authority in 2006. Tax revenue collection capacity increased substantially (Figure 8.1). The budget reforms completed the cycle components, by improving the formulation, approval, execution, accounting, and external audit. Civil society gained access to budget information and had the opportunity to publish independent budget analyses. Internal audit and procurement improved.

The TA contributed to improving the recording of external funds entering the country for financing investment projects.[14] As a weakness, TA was auditing the State General Account (CGE) up to two years after the close of the

---

[13] Sub-periods 1994–2002 and 2002–09 are aggregated in this sub-section for simplification purposes.
[14] Hodges and Tibana (2005) analysed in detail the role of the general auditor (administrative court or TA), parliament and civil society in scrutinising the executive. They also wrote about the Labour Consultative Commission (CCT), business confederation (CTA), and poverty observatory and analysed the role of international partners in providing aid and technical assistance to the government, other public entities, civil society, and political parties.

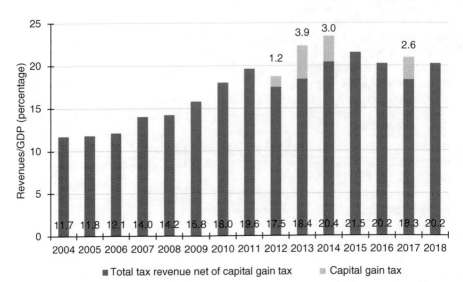

FIGURE 8.1  Tax revenues net of 'capital gains' increased from 2006 to 2011 (share of GDP)
Source: Authors' illustration based on IMF (2007, 2009, 2010, 2013, 2016a, 2019a).

fiscal year at the beginning, 1998–2002 (Hodges and Tibana 2005: 65). With the SISTAFE law this deadline was shortened, making parliamentary scrutiny of the budget execution more meaningful.

The multiparty composition of the parliament led the executive to respond to the public representatives about the management of public resources. However, the parliament remained quite weak in effectively overseeing the executive. Frelimo maintained absolute majority in parliament and most opposition politicians did not have experience with or technical insight to really scrutinise fiscal management and challenge the government. The limited parliamentary oversight was also in part due to the high proportion of external aid in the budget, combined with the fact that aid funded projects and programmes were discussed directly between donors and the executive. Moreover, big parts of the aid funds were regularly off-budget. Other limitations included the fact that tax rates were not part of the budget legislation submitted to the parliament, and by law, the executive had a wide latitude to reallocate the expenditure after parliament's approval of the budget (Hodges and Tibana 2005: 9–10).

Civil society gained more space for monitoring the executive within the multiparty democracy environment. Nevertheless, in the late 1990s and early 2000s civil society remained weak in demanding information on the management of public resources and in checking the legality of executive actions. One cause for this weakness was the lack of interest due to the narrow domestic tax base of the economy. Another factor was the low analytical capacity to analyse budget issues.

International partners played a significant role in the PFM reforms, investing resources, providing technical assistance and advice, as well as close monitoring. PARPAs, many public programmes and projects, and the respective reports were elaborated with close donor involvement. In 2004, fifteen aid partners signed a Memorandum of Understanding with the government to monitor government performance, decide their disbursements, and plan the application of funds in two annual joint sessions, the Midterm Review and the Joint Review (Batley et al. 2006).

The World Bank also collaborated to a certain extent with the government in preparing their credit programmes and projects and carrying out assessments and studies, like the Public Expenditure Review and the Country Policy and Institutional Assessment (CPIA). The IMF used to carry out at least three missions per year to Mozambique under the various programmes, like the Policy Support Instrument or the previous Poverty Reduction and Growth Facility, and also under the Article IV when an IMF team discusses with officials the country's economic developments and policies. In these missions, the IMF considered as structural benchmarks some of the PFM reforms, including the e-SISTAFE roll-out for all budgetary operations for goods and services to twenty-two additional ministries and organs in 2007 (IMF 2007). In many ways,these reforms were very successful, which can be seen not only from external technical evaluations, but also from the dynamics of political economy and relations with donors. When rent seeking and party finance moved away from public finance and donors increasingly focussed on the contacts the government and Frelimo kept, it was a sign that PFM reforms had progressed, at least to some extent. Some of the last areas covered were not surprisingly procurement audits, which were not mandatory and the patrimony (assets register) module in E-SISTAFE. However, even these areas advanced eventually.

The downside of the amount of aid was a high degree of donor dependency. Mozambique failed to integrate these resources, policies, and PFM procedures in the interests of local producers. Moreover, aid incentives were very generous but biased towards, for example, low quality investment in human resources. Some achievements were made, but in a fragile process (Cruz and Mafambissa 2020). An inclusive and sustainable productive environment remained lacking and difficulties in the donor–recipient relationship discussed by Flentø and Simão (2020) intensified. The overwhelmingly benign alliance for social transformation between western donors and the government of Mozambique started cracking in the mid-2000s as both parties changed their ways. One reason was a change of personalities and political line as Guebuza took over from Chissano, but there were strong underlying drivers pushing the divide.

On the donor side the re-securitisation of aid was significant after 9/11 and western military intervention in Afghanistan and Iraq. Aid budgets came under pressure and donors simply changed their yardstick in relation to the underlying principles guiding aid flows. As the unipolar world came to an end, donor countries wanted to spend more aid in fragile states, both post-conflict and the ones they were still bombing, as Afghanistan. Under such circumstances, where western security was on the line, donors would support any government regardless of its democratic and governance credentials. Large flows of harmonized aid to peaceful countries as prescribed in the Paris Declaration on effective aid management became an easy target for revenue collection. These programmes were not very popular with many politicians in donor countries, due to reduced visibility and low possibility of combining aid with commercial efforts. Mozambique was especially vulnerable as all aid was coordinated around GBS, which many donors had joined to get a seat at the dialogue table and not in true pursuit of aid effectiveness. All it took to reduce aid to countries like Mozambique was to interpret compliance with conditionality a little stricter and expose things that western security services had known for a long time about the ruling party's business finance.

In contrast to the governments in, for example, Kenya, Uganda, and Ethiopia, Frelimo did not comply with the new more or less explicit conditionality. Guebuza strengthened relations with China, did not respond to western concerns over piracy, and maintained friendly relations with private businessmen whom the west believed were drug lords. Realising that conditionality would only get tougher, top Frelimo leaders moved in the first half of the 2000s to strengthen the main party structures and their influence. Frelimo started to assert its dominance over state structures. This meant that policies were increasingly defined by Frelimo and not by foreign interests, which eventually led to tensions with the donor community. It also meant that activities to empower local producers would have to find their way through a centralised system of oligarchs who used their political influence in the executive to dominate the legislature and the judiciary. These oligarchs controlled positions in major public companies and obtained rents from large companies extracting natural resources.

Meanwhile, in the second half of the 2000s, PFM reforms did continue on the previously defined course, backed by aid resources. Mozambique had no star record on human rights and democracy, but in macro-economic management, including PFM, it was considered a very good performer as expressed by IMF in 2007. To keep the GBS and significant sector budget support flowing, the PFM reforms had to continue, even intensify. However, they concentrated on the management and transparency of flows and auditing of an ever-larger part of government entities and not least, the new priority of many donors, tax collection. In the medium term, few of these reforms would seriously reveal or hurt the way top party officials and oligarchs increasingly accumulated wealth. Elite accumulation had much more to do with acquiring land and other assets as well as exclusive licenses to team up with foreign partners in large scale infrastructure, extractive industries, power generation, and telecommunications. Some of these partners were from non-western countries like China and India, others were private corporations from the exact same countries that were providing the bulk of aid to Mozambique.

## C The Hope from Gas, but All That Glitters Is Not Gold

With the confirmation of large natural gas reserves in the Rovuma basin, and after a harsh reminder of donor dependency by the GBS-freeze after elections in 2010,[15] critical decisions were taken by the government to increase the use of commercial loans to finance a whole series of public investment projects and to provide hidden state guarantees to commercial investments in the Proindicus and MAM companies. Ematum became publicly known because a French shipyard gave interviews to their local press on new orders the company had received from Mozambique. Meanwhile, PFM reforms continued, but they became more tentative and fragile in light of the increase in the public deficit and debt. Roe (2018) characterises the process as one of 'bust before boom' and Henstridge and Roe (2018) discuss macroeconomic management of natural resources. Expectations of large natural gas revenues put pressure on the PFM system, but the system as such prevailed. When fiscal discipline was blatantly undermined, it was not by embezzlement, gross neglect, or mismanagement, which would be revealed by the system and the checks and balances built in during many years of reform. It took outright fraud committed secretly by the most senior government members to override the system, in an operation where the financial flows out of the system would only ensue several years after the crime had been committed. This is a kind of a hallmark for PFM reforms in Mozambique.

Even a good PFM system cannot discover three secret letters signed by senior ministers in breach of their mandate, but when such letters entail financial flows of public funds it will. Therefore, decisive rupture between the top party/government interests and the PFM reforms agenda only occurred in the first half of 2016 when the 'hidden debt' scandal became known by the public. That happened when the creditors announced they would call in the state guarantees signed by senior ministers in secret letters 3–4 years earlier.

The G19 group of international aid partners stopped all budget support (general and sector) and the IMF suspended its assistance to the government until 2019. When the Nyusi government took over in 2015, it inherited an economic crisis that was further deepened by a series of climatic and political shocks, and the mitigation measures taken came with a heavy cost to the economy. Expectations that economic progress could continue as in previous decades became an illusion and the GDP growth rate declined to very low levels.

---

[15] The irregularities in the 2009 general elections were not more serious than at previous elections. What made the donors call it breach of underlying principles was a combination of more rigid interpretation due to geo-political considerations and the appearance of a new political party in Mozambique. The Movement for Democratic Mozambique (MDM) was a Renamo offspring and held promise of changing the stereotype political environment in Mozambique, dominated by two former adversaries in armed conflict. The election commission, consisting of Renamo and Frelimo representatives knowing that they both would lose votes to the new party, made sure that MDM's lists of candidates were rejected in seven of Mozambique's eleven provinces. Donors froze GBS in response to this, but used the opportunity to draw up the long list of grievances that the government had to address in order to resume aid flows.

To understand why donors reacted so rigorously and relatively united, it is useful to understand how the guarantees issued by the Guebuza administration were conceived by many of Mozambique's partners.

Having believed they had practically full insight with the government's fiscal policy and budget and after several years of hardening of policy dialogue, the donors discovered that they had not had insight with state finances where it really counted. Especially IMF was disappointed, and logically questions were asked: 'How could we not know this, have we done a proper job?' Such questions trigger reactions from people whose career is in the balance and also questions the almost blind confidence donors have in IMF knowing what goes on in an aid dependent economy with large amounts of general budget support.

Originally, donors were not primarily concerned with the real crime of the secret guarantees – the fact that they were not disclosed to and approved by the Mozambican parliament. It was the case of misreporting to the IMF that concerned many donors most. Such misreporting occurs from time to time and although misreporting of this magnitude (almost 10 per cent of the GDP) is rare, it was not unprecedented (the Democratic Republic of Congo, for example, had known worse cases).

However, in Mozambique donors discovered that the government had contracted debt that would consume more funds than the entire G19 budget support would provide over the medium term. The government of Mozambique had secretly mortgaged the donors' confidence-based financial assistance for years to come. It was all possible because of the future gas revenues, but the extraction of gas was still too far away for those flows to service the debt. Some capital gain taxes from gas companies could probably be collected during the time the debt was to be serviced, but the really big financial flows from gas would only materialise after the loan were repaid.

This timing was probably not the initial intention of the government, which, together with many others, including IMF and donor countries, had very optimistic expectations in relation to how fast the gas fields could be operational. However, the Guebuza administration was sitting on its second and – according to the constitution – last mandate. Whether it was to finance an exit strategy and retirement or to swing constitutional reform in favour of a third mandate, waiting for the funds from the gas exploration was not an option. There was, however, also another reason the loans were urgent.

The loans were not just a bogus operation for personal enrichment of the elite, including foreign bankers and banks with little social conscience. What the government tried was fundamentally to finance its way into the security architecture that would surround the future gas and oil extraction in northern Mozambique. That was a significant additional concern to some donor countries.

By acquiring what looked like a fishing fleet and fast going inspection and patrol boats as well as shipyard service facilities for those vessels, the government of Mozambique, or rather the security sector of Mozambique's government, could be an important partner in future security operations around the extractives industries in the north. Such a Mozambican structure could arguably be strong enough to choose its foreign partner. That is relatively rare in Africa, where many governments, just like Mozambique's, lack the resources to do so, among other reasons because security expenditure had been restrained in highly donor-dependent countries.

When a government cannot guarantee the safety of extractive operations in its territory, there are only two other options. One is to let another country do it, which is often highly controversial and directly unthinkable in Mozambique. The other option is privatising the security operations, which is most often the outcome. Contracts for the services (often labelled security and logistics advice and training) are somehow overwhelmingly awarded to a handful of western companies.

All along, the PFM reform agenda continued to be pursued. There was a reform schedule to improve various procedures, correct more recent weaknesses (restructure MEF bodies, improve debt management, and public sector risk assessment), and roll out the system to all public entities and all spatial levels. Moreover, there were previously committed resources available, whether internal or external, and a sense of credibility by advancing with the reforms. In sum, the continuation of the reforms represented a professional commitment from those officials directly in charge and all those entities, both local and international partners, dedicated to the improvement of mechanisms and management of public financial resources.

Nevertheless, internal, and external trust in the state became very low. A former Minister of Finance and member of the Mozambican parliament has at the time of writing been in jail since 2018 in South Africa (Hanlon 2019).[16] Moreover, in the beginning of 2019, a former Treasury National Director and Deputy Minister of Finance was dismissed due to her links to the hidden debt. These and other events contributed significantly to demoralising civil servants working directly on improving the PFM system. More broadly, the 'hidden debt' scandal and its aftermath contributed to the decline in moral authority of high-ranking state officials. The quality of public services deteriorated and opportunities for corruption increased and became endemic. The continuing economic and political shocks that hit the country from 2015 onwards, including the insurgency in Cabo Delgado since 2017, have moved policy focus away from the more detailed needs of the PFM agenda, which has become less of a priority.

What we described above is reflected in a series of Public Expenditure and Financial Accountability (PEFA) reports.[17] Overall progress in PFM indicators

---

[16] South Africa jailed the former Mozambican finance minister at the request of the USA (Hanlon 2019). The US District Court of New York issued an indictment of this Mozambican citizen among other citizens for violating US financial and fraud laws. Curiously, the USA does not recognise the International Criminal Court, that is, violates the principle of reciprocity in the international relations, losing moral authority at international level.

[17] Together with the European Commission and four other bilateral donors, the IMF and the World Bank developed in 2001 the Public Expenditure and Financial Accountability (PEFA) assessment framework to measure the performance of the PFM system (www.pefa.org/about).

has deteriorated in recent years reflecting the reduction of available resources and the need to respond to urgent priorities, such as the natural disasters and since early 2020 COVID-19. Moreover, the enabling environment for PFM reform clearly deteriorated due to the abrupt stop to Budget Support in 2016.

## IV THREE KEY ISSUES IN PFM REFORM

### A The Role of Donors

The story of PFM in Mozambique shows that donor prompted reforms will only work in the long run, if they are truly owned and exercised by the host government. Even the best reforms from the technical point of view will not solve the fundamental challenges if they are imposed in exchange for amounts of aid so large that the government cannot afford to decline. As alluded to by Bourguignon and Gunning (2016), aid can be for pure finance or in exchange for reforms. In practice they overlap but conceptually they are very different. When aid is used to promote reforms, the fundamental difference in objectives between the government and donors is the key reason for conditionality. If there is no disagreement, conditionality is pointless, in the other extreme aid acts as a bribe.

The donor community applying GBS shared a belief that well-coordinated GBS could be used as a lever for almost any reform and starvation of the security sector. This has proven unrealistic in relation to reforms on governance and democracy that would entail severe risks to the holding power of sitting governments. The PFM reforms in Mozambique basically avoided this and were allowed to progress and improve fiscal management for more than two decades. When Mozambique's government no longer could pursue key priorities due to the PFM-reforms and donor dependency, they circumnavigated the PFM system by secret, illegal action.

This was possible because reforms were not comprehensive across sectors. Many laws and decrees had been passed, as well as procurement, installation, and training in new systems, in what had been a true and continuous upgrade of PFM during more than two decades. It looked good, also to donors, which believed they had assisted the reform-friendly parts of government against the hard-lines in Frelimo by providing generous amounts of aid, including GBS. But the fundamental anchorage was missing. Donors were to a large extent deceived by a phenomenon referred to by biologists as isomorphic mimicry. When a non-venomous snake looks like a very poisonous relative, it can help frighten enemies and predators. Yet it cannot hunt like a venomous snake if it has no poison. PFM reforms in Mozambique can be characterised as isomorphic mimicry. The reforms did help in directing the economy and provided the basis for critical scrutiny and exposure of mismanagement and embezzlement. But

---

This framework covers 31 key indicators across seven pillars of activity, which consider 94 dimensions of PFM performance.

without an independent legal system – state prosecutor and courts – to back it, the fundamental challenges could not be addressed. The snake had no venom.

## B The Separation of Powers and the Rule of Law

The necessary checks and balances for a democratic system to work were formally introduced in the 1990 Constitution of Mozambique but became gradually dysfunctional from 2005 onwards. In a presidential system, the role of the president in the government is key. In addition, in Mozambique, the president of the Frelimo party has also been the President of the Republic. The president appoints and dismisses the presidents of the Supreme Court, the Constitutional Council, the TA (external auditor), and the attorney general. As such, the incumbent holds significant power. Moreover, in parliament, Frelimo has had an absolute majority since 1994, and party members in parliament respond to centralised party instructions. In such a tightly controlled environment it is not surprising that when members of the elite decided to increase the demand for non-concessional credit, there was no effective mechanism to prevent systematic breach of the law and illegal actions.

The Mozambican parliament has a good track record in producing legislation and organising the legislatures, and the many PFM reforms have contributed significantly to this being possible. In the case of the hidden debt parliament could not exercise full oversight in the management of the budget, because senior ministers committed fraud secretly. In 2013–14, the government in effect bypassed parliament illegally and contracted direct liabilities by issuing state guarantees for debt. Subsequently, in 2016, when this information became public, parliament could have, but did not act upon it. There were no immediate or direct consequences for those responsible for violating the constitution and the budget laws. The lack of action in response to the infringement of key laws implies that the majority of the members of the parliament and the Budget Committee were either co-opted politically on this specific issue and did not aim to enforce the law, or lacked the effective power to do so, just as it was the case for the judiciary (Orre and Rønning 2017).

When it became clear to donors that no amount of withheld aid would make the Mozambican judiciary perform in this case, the US government acted to encourage the Mozambican judiciary to react by issuing international arrest mandates for the officials involved. Due to the risk of those arrested to enter plea-bargains with the US courts, the Mozambican state prosecutor acted in February 2018. Once legal action was finally taken against the culprits, the way was paved for declaring the guarantees and debt illegal. In May 2020, the Constitutional Court ruled on the secret debts, considering them 'null and void' (Hanlon 2020).

Similarly to the first historical phase in post-independence Mozambique, when political power was overly concentrated and the system of checks and balances was not operational, recent economic policy decisions can have large and lasting effects on the economic performance of the country and on the welfare of most citizens. In sum, Mozambique is a case where the party in power has held excessive political control, confronted by a weak opposition, a parliament and a judiciary that has been either unable or unwilling to act against obvious attempts to undermine the otherwise respectable progress during the 1990s and 2000s in the PFM system. Socio-economic consequences have been dire.

## C  Decentralisation

Principles of decentralisation were embedded in the legislation at the very beginning of the democratisation era in Mozambique. The new Constitution of the Republic of Mozambique in 1990, the Local Public Administration Reform Programme (PROL) in 1991, and the Constitution's Amendment through the Law 9/1996 allowed for the creation of municipalities composed of an executive organ, the Municipal Council, and a legislative organ, the Municipal Assembly (Fernandes 2007; Simione et al. 2018).

The decentralisation process did lead to greater autonomy in urban areas, thus giving more power to the local authorities responsible for improving the livelihoods of their citizens (Weimer 2012). The gradual increase in the number of municipalities has meant that decentralisation was understood as a process of expansion of urban structures to rural areas. However, the transformation of the rural areas into municipalities, as part of the decentralisation process, has been seriously lacking. There were only 33 cities and villages considered to be municipalities in 1997, 43 in 2008, and 53 in 2013 (Brito 2019), and this number has remained unchanged since. Rural areas that are not included in municipalities are governed by the government branches at provincial, district, administrative post, and locality level, meaning that Mozambique has effectively a highly centralised organisational system.

Since 1993, a pilot decentralised[18] planning and budgeting exercise was carried out through the Decentralized Planning and Finance Programme (PPFD), which was replicated in other provinces. Capacity building, including training, application of new procedures, and investment in equipment, has been provided for more than twenty years in this field. The results are positive, but the process is far from complete, and it is necessary to further develop the model of decentralisation suitable to the country.

A further dimension of the decentralisation process was the establishment of provincial assemblies in 2009 and the election of provincial governors in 2019 (Brito 2019). These are reforms of a primarily political nature, but their viability relies on a well-performing PFM system (PoM 2018). Political, military, and civil society activities have been leading to decentralisation reforms, including the PFM system. However, the success of these reforms will depend

---

[18] When we are dealing with state entities at local levels, it is considered 'de-concentration'. This is also valid for the PPFD.

on the allocation of quite large amounts of financial resources and current organisations in the state apparatus, elected assemblies, and political positions have been under severe budget constraints since 2015.

PFM reforms should help ensure that provinces and districts are entitled to decide over and manage public funds. Law 8/2003 of State Local Authorities and Decree 11/2005 established legal principles and norms for the decentralised levels of government (PoM 2003; GoM 2005a). This legislation allowed for greater budgetary autonomy at the provincial and district levels and has been implemented since then. However, the unequal distribution of the budget in per capita terms among provinces remains a core challenge (UNICEF 2017).

Political instability and military conflict are partially explained by the insufficient degree of decentralisation. This has been happening possibly due to a perceived risk by the party in power of losing political power at the local level and potentially at the national level. The political bottlenecks in the decentralisation process, the per capita inequalities in budget allocations, and the political interference in the budget execution criteria at local levels, in particular at district level, distorts the proper functioning of the PFM system.

## V CONCLUSION

Mozambique has since independence experienced several fundamental shifts in economic and political regimes. Consequently, development strategies have varied, and the role of PFM has changed from one decade to the next. Following the end of hostilities in 1992, a democratic political system was introduced, and a process of intensive PFM reform began supported by the international donor community with significant foreign aid combined with conditionality. This chapter brought out that Mozambique did indeed undertake an ambitious PFM reform programme (Andrews 2010; Renzio et al. 2011; CEDSIF 2015; IMF 2015, 2019b; MEF 2016; Table A8.1 in the Appendix). Many laws and norms were approved, management systems and tools were established and prepared, professionals were trained, and equipment and material were acquired. Accordingly, many of the building blocks of a modern democratic PFM system had by the end of the 2000s been put in place.

However, the degree of national ownership was an issue and when the prospects of large future natural resource revenues started to materialise, from 2010 onwards, the PFM system went into decay. Put differently, while a modern PFM system seemed to be evolving, the way in which resource allocation, programme monitoring, and auditing took place in reality started to diverge.[19] The lack of separation of powers and the merging of the political and executive power meant that critical decisions were taken by party structures bypassing parliament and a weak opposition. Elite capture and rent-seeking became

---

[19] See Andrews et al. (2017) for a general diagnosis of this type of situation and proposals for action.

widespread, as also experienced elsewhere. Fritz el al. (2017) and Andrews (2010) provide Africa region wide insight on the negative impact on PFM performance of a high share of revenues being obtained from natural resources, on the one hand, and the influence of stalling economic growth and stability, on the other. Andrews (2010) also highlights that countries where most revenues are collected domestically from citizens have stronger PFM systems than countries where revenues originate from external sources, such as natural resources and external donors.

Summing up, while significant efforts on putting in place a modern and proper functioning PFM system started happening in the 1990s, it largely was brought to a halt after 2010. Existing tools, such as the MTEF were increasingly neglected; VAT refunds were delayed or neglected for many years, and similarly for many laws, as illustrated by the 'hidden debt' scandal. The fundamental challenge for Mozambique is for the dominant party to fully recognise the critical importance of a well-functioning domestically owned PFM system for economic and social performance and advance and take the necessary steps to reenergise the process experienced until 2010. This will require that the dominant power finds it in its own interest. Arguably, these changes may not be necessary for Frelimo's hold on power, and there may be political resistance from elite groups. However, in the longer-run, the implications, including growing inequality, increasing fragmentation, and costly conflicts, already visible, are a forceful reminder of the need and incentive to act in the national interest.

APPENDIX

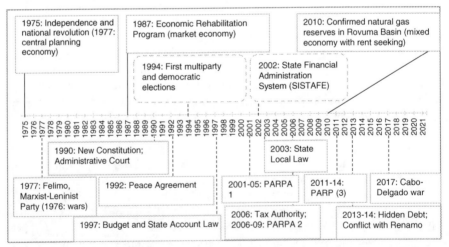

FIGURE A8.1 Public financial management timeline (main and secondary periods are indicated above the year axis)
Source: Authors' illustration.

TABLE A8.1 *Selected reforms in the PFM system*[1]

| PFM system | Reforms |
| --- | --- |
| Public finance policy documents and reform units | Economic Rehabilitation Programme legislation package, 1987 (PoM 1987a) |
| | Budget Reform Strategy approved, 1997 (Fozzard 2002) UTRAFE, 2001[a]; CEDSIF, 2010[b] |
| | State Financial Administration System (SISTAFE) (PoM 2002a) |
| | Public Finance Vision 2011–2015 (GoM 2012) |
| Revenue collection and management | Tax policy reform, 1987, 2002, 2007 (PoM 1987c, 2002a, 2002b, 2007b, 2007c) |
| | Crown Agents, 1996 (IMF 2004b) |
| | VAT introduced, 1999 (GoM 1998) |
| | Tax system basic law (PoM 1987c, 2002b) |
| | Tax Authority creation (PoM 2006) |
| Budget formulation and approval | State budget, 1987, 1997, 2002 (PoM 1987b, 1997b, 2002a) |
| | Three-year Medium Term Expenditure Framework, first version 1998 (Fozzard 2002) |
| Budget execution and internal audit | State Procurement decree (GoM 2005b, 2010) |
| | e-SISTAFE implementation |
| | Single treasury account (CUT) |
| | Finance General Inspection (IGF) |
| Accounting and reporting | Budget execution reports, quarterly, 2000 (IMF 2004b) |
| External audit | Administrative Court, 1992 (PoM 1992) |
| | State General Account, 1997 (PoM 1997) |
| | Planning and Budget Commission Reports, Parliament |

[1]This table reveals a large investment in terms of legislation and regulations, human skills to manage an increasingly complex system, and investment in computer, electronic, and information systems.
*Note:* [a]UTRAFE (Technical Unit of the State Finance Administration) was created in 2001; [b]CEDSIF (Development Centre of Finance Information Systems) was created in 2010.
*Source:* Authors' elaboration.

*António S. Cruz et al.*

TABLE A8.2 *Selected PFM reforms, 2003–2009*

| Year | Reforms |
|------|---------|
| 2003 | State bank accounts started being consolidated in commercial banks |
| 2004 | First external audit report issued by the TA |
|  | Approval of the Single Treasury Account system (CUT) regulation and introduction of virtual e-CUT |
|  | Direct payments via e-SISTAFE started |
|  | Approval of a new Constitution of the Republic |
| 2005 | Budget execution operations using e-SISTAFE started, pilot application was carried out in three ministries |
|  | Public Accounting system was introduced |
|  | Approval of the decree 54/2005 on public procurement, revising and consolidating previous sector specific legislation from 1996–1997 (ACIS 2011; Castro and Cerveira 2019) |
| 2006 | e-SISTAFE was rolled out to 22 ministries, a pilot budget preparation module was introduced, and procurement execution and supervision bodies were introduced |
|  | Preparation of an anti-corruption strategy |
| 2007 | Publication of the MTEF for 2007–2009 and preparation of a financial management handbook |
|  | Implementation of a pilot module on state assets management, salaries, revenues and a multi-currency CUT |
| 2008 | Introduction of the budget preparation based on programmes |
| 2009 | Approval of Law 26/2009 on public expenditure rules under supervision the TA and of two regulations, one on state assets investments and another on informatics systems purchase to be used for management of the state budget |
|  | The Government signed a Memorandum of Understanding with the group of 19 Donors for General Budget Support |
|  | A new legislation for civil servants, State Civil Servants and Agents General Statute (EGFAE), was approved with the intention to improve human resource management and performance evaluation (Simione 2014) |

*Source:* Authors' elaboration.

# 9

# Rule of Law and Judicial Independence

## *The Restricted Capacity of the Judicial System*

João Carlos Trindade

## I INTRODUCTION

This chapter deals with one of the most disturbing and controversial topics that states and democratic societies wrestle with, whatever their level of development or their place in the world system.[1]

The principles of the rule of law and the independence of the judiciary are values enshrined in the universal and regional declarations of human rights and the main pacts on civil, political, economic, and social rights, so their adoption by all countries – including those that have recently been through democratic transition processes – are a demand of the international community. This is so even accepting that the affirmation of these values presupposes a culture and a legal and cultural environment forged throughout lengthy processes of socialisation and acculturation (Canotilho 1999: 8).

On a worldwide scale, courts today are pressured by two movements with opposing interests: one coming from the top down, and the other from the bottom up (Lauris and Fernando 2010: 135). The first calls for a professional, efficient, and swift response from the judiciary, which is considered vital for achieving the aims of economic development and for the establishment of a climate of stability, predictability, and legal certainty to encourage new investments (Dakolias and Said 1999: 1; The World Bank 2004: 16). The second demands capacity, legitimacy, and independence from the judiciary so that it can take on its important role in the affirmation of constitutionally enshrined rights, freedoms, and assurances and the inclusion of the poorest segments of the population in the social contract (Santos 2014: 35).

[1] The concept of *world-systems* or *world-system*, based on the inter-regional and transnational division of labour, classifying countries as central, semi-peripheral, or peripheral, was developed by Fernand Braudel and added to by authors such as Immanuel Wallerstein, Giovanni Arrighi, and Samir Amin. For all of these, see Wallerstein (2004).

For either of these forces of pressure to see their goals attained, it is vital that the state political organisation is limited by the law and is provided with institutions, procedures for action, and ways of revealing the powers and competences that, as stated by Canotilho (1999: 21), permit the safeguarding of 'the *freedom* of the individual, individual and collective *security*, the *responsibility* and *accountability* of those in power, the *equality* of all citizens and the *prohibition* of discrimination against individuals and groups'.

The analysis we propose of the actual configuration of the rule of law and judicial independence in Mozambique begins by identifying the main problems persisting in the institutional framework of the legal authorities, as well as in the formulation and implementation of public policies in the sector. Next, it attempts to explain to what extent the inefficiency of the judiciary is negatively reflected in economic and social development, particularly in the areas of the economy that are more likely to generate conflict between private agents and between these and the state. Finally, it gives an indication of the most relevant challenge that justice administration is going to face in the near future and in the longer-term, so that the structural reforms proposed will not become just one more failed exercise but rather produce the results society is clamouring for.

## II CHARACTERISATION OF THE JUDICIAL SYSTEM[2]: WEAKNESSES AND POTENTIAL

The path followed by Mozambican justice since the first Judicial Organization Law[3] was approved has often been the subject of analysis and research work, more or less complete and wide-ranging, which allows us to be effectively aware now of the constraints and blockages that continue to affect its performance.

Of the different studies carried out over the last twenty years, two had a special impact. The first is the *Research project on the plurality of justice in Mozambique* (1997–2000), undertaken through a partnership between the Centre of African Studies at the Eduardo Mondlane University (CEA-UEM), the Centre for Judicial and Legal Training (CFJJ) and the Centre for Social Studies at the University of Coimbra (CES).[4] The second and more recent is the *Exploratory study on access to justice and the performance of the courts*

---

[2] Whenever the terms *justice system, judicial system*, or simply *administration of justice* are used in this chapter, we are referring to all the bodies, entities, institutions, or scopes of the state which directly or indirectly compete for the exercise of the jurisdictional duties exercised by the courts. This group includes, in addition to the actual courts, the Public Prosecutor, the criminal police, the Ministry of Justice, the Institute for Legal Representation and Assistance (IPAJ) and the Mozambican Bar Association, the National Prison Service (SERNAP), legal education and training institutions, Forensic Medicine services, social and community organisations, and other bodies involved in assisting with these duties.

[3] Law No. 12/78, of 2 December.

[4] See Santos et al. (2003).

*in Mozambique* (2018–19), a result of a cooperation agreement between the Mozambican Association of Judges (AMJ) and the CES.[5]

The conclusions of both studies show that there were no significant changes that would have affected the structure of the system in the time between them. The reforms carried out at different times – broadly following the constitutional developments in 1990 and 2004 – were always short-sighted and conjunctural, as a result of their partial, biased vision, under domestic and foreign influences in multiple senses. Three types of reforms can be identified, which are summarised below:

a) those whose aim was to increase the efficiency and response capacity of the courts and other judicial bodies in the requests put to them. These include the set-up of the higher courts of appeal and the sections specialising in commercial issues in the provincial courts, the introduction of new, alternative means of dispute resolution for commercial disputes[6] and computerised systems in the courts and prosecution units;

b) those that sought to increase the levels of probity and integrity in the system and assure the security and certainty of legal transactions, highlighting the fight against corruption and the consequent changes to the structure of the Public Prosecutor's Office and the current National Criminal Investigation Service (SERNIC);[7] and

c) those aimed at broadening access to the law and justice, through reinforcing the structure of legal and judicial assistance and conflict resolution and the extension of the network of courts (Fernando et al. 2019: 275).

## A The Creation of Higher Courts of Appeal and Commercial Sections in Provincial Judicial Courts

The most recent constitutional revision in 2004, as with the preceding reforms in 1990, brought important changes to the justice area, bringing renewed hope of a *qualitative leap in its operation*. We believe one should highlight the recognition of legal pluralism as an undeniable sociological reality; the redefinition of the categories of courts existing in Mozambique, including community courts, which would now be formally endowed with constitutional dignity; the opening of a space for rethinking the hierarchy of the courts and jurisdictional specialisation; the introduction, finally, of new management and disciplinary bodies for the judiciary – the Superior Council of the Judiciary of the Public Prosecutor's Office and the Superior Council of the Administrative Judiciary.

---

[5] See Fernando et al. (2019).
[6] See Resolution No. 1/CJ/2017, of 25 August, of the Judicial Council, which approves the Regulation on Mediation Services in Judicial Courts.
[7] Corresponding to the criminal police.

However, the new Judicial Organization Law (Law No. 24/2007, of 20 August)[8] fell very short of expectations. The slow and uncoordinated way in which its implementation happened shows, once again, some signs of lack of strategic sense in the management of the public policies of justice. It is enough to mention, for example, that, with the law having set a deadline of one year after publication for the higher courts of appeal to come into operation, these only began being set up in 2011, under extremely precarious conditions, and it was only in 2015 that they began operating at full capacity in three regions in the country.

The higher courts of appeal saw their response capacity constrained because they were suddenly being expected to deal with the overwhelming majority of the cases pending in the Supreme Court, thus becoming congested from the outset.[9] And as the changes to procedural law and the management and internal organisation of the courts were also unable to break down the existing barriers, it cannot be said that there were any substantial improvements, either in terms of speed or in the quality of the service provided.

If we look at Table 9.1, which compares the statistical data for the proceedings recorded in 2012 and 2013 (the first two years of operation of the higher courts of appeal) and the two most recent legal years (2018 and 2019), we see that, generally speaking, there is a constantly increasing trend in the number of cases handled. With regard to the higher courts of appeal, it was only in 2019 that a slight reduction happened. Even so, it remains significant that, after only seven years of operation, pending cases in these courts stand at around 5,000.

As to the commercial sections of provincial courts, they usually deal with enforcement procedures for consumer debts but, even so, they still face a progressive increase in pending cases. Around twenty years ago, the study undertaken by the partnership between the CEA-UEM, the CFJJ, and the CES had reached essentially identical conclusions (Santos et al. 2003, vol. I: 397). This is an indication that the more complex disputes could be settled by extrajudicial means (national and international arbitration, mediation, etc.) and that the confidence of investors in the quality of state justice remains very low.

A careful and attentive analysis of the information collected by the *Doing Business* programme by the World Bank (2019: 66) makes it possible to conclude, with no great surprise, that despite the extremely important role it plays in the actual volume of legal cases and the human and material resources

---

[8] This Law was later subject to two individual amendments, affecting some of its provisions, under the terms of Laws Nos. 24/2014, of 23 September, and 11/2018, of 3 October.

[9] Table 9.1, on the proceedings recorded in the courts, shows that, in 2012, the first year of actual operation of the higher courts of appeal, they received the weighty 'legacy' of 4,503 processes, which had previously been handled by the Supreme Court. Since then, despite all the efforts made, these pending cases have continued with little variation, reaching 4,901 cases in late 2019.

TABLE 9.1 *Proceedings in the courts*

| 2012 | | | |
|---|---|---|---|
| | Pending | Received | Closed | Ruled on |
| Supreme Court | 197 | 72 | 108 | 161 |
| Higher Court of Appeal | – | 4,503 | 479 | 4,024 |
| Provincial Judicial Court | 61,096 | 32,863 | 33,699 | 60,260 |
| District Judicial Court | 85,902 | 67,910 | 68,535 | 85,277 |
| TOTAL | 149,722 | 105,348 | 102,821 | 149,722 |

| 2013 | | | |
|---|---|---|---|
| | Pending | Received | Closed | Ruled on |
| Supreme Court | 161 | 42 | 117 | 86 |
| Higher Court of Appeal | 4,024 | 1,151 | 573 | 4,602 |
| Provincial Judicial Court | 60,260 | 30,943 | 30,605 | 60,598 |
| District Judicial Court | 85,277 | 72,576 | 73,060 | 84,793 |
| TOTAL | 149,722 | 104,712 | 104,355 | 150,079 |

| 2018 | | | |
|---|---|---|---|
| | Pending | Received | Closed | Ruled on |
| Supreme Court | 223 | 260 | 183 | 300 |
| Higher Court of Appeal | 4,998 | 1,165 | 1,100 | 5,063 |
| Provincial Judicial Court | 60,695 | 62,140 | 67,655 | 55,180 |
| District Judicial Court | 94,046 | 94,636 | 92,656 | 96,026 |
| TOTAL | 159,962 | 158,201 | 161,594 | 156,569 |

| 2019 | | | |
|---|---|---|---|
| | Pending | Received | Closed | Ruled on |
| Supreme Court | 300 | 338 | 257 | 381 |
| Higher Court of Appeal | 5,063 | 1,040 | 1,202 | 4,901 |
| Provincial Judicial Court | 55,180 | 63,020 | 55,236 | 62,964 |
| District Judicial Court | 96,026 | 91,213 | 86,442 | 100,797 |
| TOTAL | 156,569 | 155,611 | 143,137 | 169,043 |

*Source:* Statistics Department of the Supreme Court.

available to deal with them (quantitative data), it is the good or bad management and organisation practices and the quality of the work done by its agents (qualitative data) that the performance of the justice system depends on, whether in the commercial jurisdiction or in other jurisdictions.

## B The Introduction of New Alternative Means for the Resolution of Commercial and Labour Disputes

The transformations that took place in the country following the adoption of the market economy model and the intensification of international trade relationships in the late 1980s and early 1990s justified the approval of the first Law of Arbitration, Conciliation, and Mediation (Law No. 11/99, of 8 July), aimed at allowing legal subjects to use these different means and methods for conflict resolution, before, or as an alternative to, taking the case to court.

The law grants the freedom to set up and administer institutions for arbitration, conciliation, and mediation, as long as their articles of association provide for: (a) the representative nature of the institution responsible for the centre to be set up and (b) the reason for the constitution of the specialised centre of arbitration, conciliation, and mediation (Article 69).

Two centres of arbitration stand out in the national panorama, set up to intervene in two different areas of conflict: the Centre of Arbitration, Conciliation and Mediation (CACM) of the Confederation of Economic Associations of Mozambique (CTA), set up in 2002, and the Commission for Labour Mediation and Arbitration (COMAL), an institution under public law under the authority of the minister responsible for the labour area, in operation since 2011.[10]

In addition, the bodies operating in the area of legal and judicial assistance, such as the Institute for Legal Representation and Assistance (IPAJ), the Institute for Access to Justice (IAJ) of the Mozambican Bar Association, and the Centre for Legal Practices (CPJ) of the law faculty at Eduardo Mondlane University, have been carrying out, in practice, dispute resolution work using mediation and conciliation techniques, but on a much smaller scale and without very significant results because the actual agents of these institutions recognise that they are not duly qualified or equipped for using such techniques (Fernando et al. 2019: 72).

This is a factor that must not be neglected, as any initiatives for reducing judicial involvement that are not accompanied with the required assurances of quality and professional work run the risk of leading to the institutionalisation of justice of a lower quality for the economically and socially more vulnerable sectors and, what is worse, the 'enshrining of factual situations of repressive conciliation' (Fernando et al. 2019: 73).

## C The Fight against Corruption, the Public Prosecutor, and the Current SERNIC

The process of moving from a centrally planned to a free market economy, with the consequent process of privatisation of public companies and financial participation by the state, price liberalisation, monetary contraction, drastic cuts in social expenditure, and making labour relations more flexible, as well

---

[10] See Decree No. 50/2009, of 11 September, which approved the Regulation in question.

as other measures, paved the way to the progressive spread of the phenomenon of corruption in Mozambique.[11]

To deal with the problem, while at the same time promoting the transparency and integrity of the public sector, which is essential for achieving political, economic, and social stability and the reinforcement of legal security and certainty, the Anti-Corruption Unit was set up in 2002, under one of the specialised departments in the Office of the Attorney General. However, it was short-lived, as a result of not having foreseen an independent judicial-legal framework that would allow it to carry out its duties adequately. And so, following the restructuring measures from the Public Prosecutor's Office, determined by the constitutional revision in 2004, the GCCC – Central Office for Fighting Corruption (Law No. 6/2004, of 17 June) was set up, under the auspices of the Attorney General and with specific powers under the scope of criminal investigation and preparatory investigation of the crimes of corruption and unlawful economic participation.[12]

In its 2019 Corruption Perceptions Index,[13] the Transparency International organisation gave Mozambique 26 points, putting the country in 126th place (in 2018 it had been given 23 points and was in 158th place) on a list of 180 countries. According to the Public Integrity Centre (CIP) – an NGO set up in 2005 with the aim of contributing to the promotion of transparency and integrity in Mozambique – the fact that the GCCC had taken significant steps in the criminal proceedings related to 'hidden debts'[14] and, consequently, was able to make various arrests of the people accused in the case, decisively contributed to this improvement in results. In addition, there was also a positive change in the political anti-corruption discourse, given the fact that the President of

---

[11] Economist Toke Aidt summarises the three main conditions for the persistence of cases of corruption in the public sector as follows: '1. **Discretionary power**: the relevant public officials (bureaucrats, politicians, etc.) must possess the authority to design or administer regulations and policies in a discretionary manner. 2. **Economic rents**: the discretionary power must allow extraction of (existing) rents or creations of rents that can be extracted. 3. **Weak institutions**: the incentives embodied in political, administrative and legal institutions must be such that public officials are left with an incentive to exploit their discretionary power to extractor create rents' (Aidt 2011: 16 – bold text by the author).

[12] Currently, Law No. 4/2017, of 18 January, defines it as a body specialising in the prevention of and the fight against the crimes of corruption, embezzlement, and extortion (Article 78).

[13] The Corruption Perceptions Index (CPI) from Transparency International is a global barometer that seeks to assess the perception of citizens regarding the level of corruption in all the countries in the world. The assessment is carried out based on a table of points going from 1 to 100 – using different, previously defined criteria – with the countries with classifications closer to 100 being considered the least corrupt and, conversely, those that are furthest away from that figure deemed to be the most corrupt.

[14] Name by which the case is commonly known, beginning in mid-2015. It involved a set of loans contracted from some international banks based on sovereign guarantees issued by the government of former President Armando Guebuza, and aimed at financing the companies *MAM*, *Proindicus* and *EMATUM*, all linked to state security services, without authorisation from parliament, as determined by the Constitution Article 179(2)(p).

the Republic is apparently placing the problem of corruption at the top of his governance agenda (CIP 2020: 1).

But more must be done. The CIP has called attention to the fact that these arrests were neither accompanied by the recovery of the assets unlawfully diverted nor by the approval of a criminal policy to make the fight against this phenomenon more effective. This is recognised by the Attorney General herself as one of its weak points (Buchili 2020).

An essential instrument for supporting the investigation work and criminal prosecution by the Public Prosecutor's Office is its excellent auxiliary body, the criminal police, which was known in Mozambique for many years as the Criminal Investigation Police (PIC). The main judicial players – courts, Public Prosecutor's Office, Bar Association, IPAJ – and the civil society organisations interested in the prevention and repression of criminal groups – the CIP, human rights and women's human rights organisations, etc. – have been calling for sweeping reforms of the PIC that would return the institution to the 'dignity and grandeur of the Criminal Police' (Correia 2014: 86).

For a long time, one of the most hotly debated issues on this topic was the institutional inclusion and the internal organisation of the PIC. Some believed that:

> its subordination to the Public Prosecutor's Office is essential for it to be able to better carry out its auxiliary role. Its existence makes more sense as a criminal police force, with qualified human resources, led by a judge who is well-equipped and valued, and with agents who are regularly assessed. This is also relevant to the fight against crime, which we would all like to see being crowned with more success. (Timbane 2016)

In a text published in 2012, which analysed the implementation of the Strategic Policing Plan, Francisco Alar says that:

> the debate on whether the investigative branch should remain subordinate to the PRM or be transferred to the Public Prosecutor's Office or to the Ministry of Justice, as it was during the Portuguese era, has been dragging on for many years. The argument to remove it from the PRM[15] is that it does not enjoy the same independence as other administrative and legal institutions, leaving it exposed to operational interference from the police commissioner and the Ministry of the Interior (MINT). In 2002/2003, it seemed that the idea of separating the investigation branch from the PRM would be successful and that new investigators would be recruited. However, when discussions on the appropriate legislation began, the Minister of the Interior rejected the idea, arguing that there was no such separation in the other countries in the Southern African Development Community (SADC). This discussion on the subordination of the PIC adversely affects the relevant debate on policing resources and technical capacity.

[15] The police of the Republic of Mozambique includes the PIC and the following special operations and reserve branches and units: the Public Security and Order Police; the Border Police; the Coast, Lake and River Police; the Rapid Response Unit; the High-Level Protection Unit; the Counter-Terrorism Operations and Hostage Rescue Unit; the Canine Unit; the Mounted Police Unit; and the Bomb Disposal Unit (see Article 13 of Law No. 16/2013, of 12 August).

However, some changes are in force. At least internally, there have been reflections and studies on how investigation capacity can be improved. (Alar 2012: 181)

In 2017, with the approval of Law No. 2/2017, of 9 January, and in what seems to have been a political compromise solution, the PIC ended up being discontinued and gave way to a new structure, the SERNIC. Criminal investigation went from being a branch of the PRM to being a 'public service of paramilitary nature, an auxiliary of the administration of justice, endowed with administrative, technical and tactical autonomy, without prejudice to the authority of the Minister responsible for the area of public order, security and tranquillity, in matters that do not affect its autonomy' (Article 3 of Law No. 2/2017). It remained functionally subordinate to the Public Prosecutor's Office (Point 4 of the same law), as had been the case, but did not advance towards organic integration.

The main constraints to the operation of SERNIC in its three years of existence, despite the removal of criminal investigation as a branch integrated into the General Command of the PRM, were, and all indications point to these continuing, the lack of financial autonomy, the shortage of staff with the necessary qualifications, and the insufficiency of resources and instruments for adequately carrying out the duties they are responsible for.

## D The Widening of Access to Law and to Justice: Institutionalisation of Structures for the Administration of Justice and Legal and Judicial Assistance and Extension of the Network of Judicial Courts

If any doubts remained about the coexistence of different regulatory and conflict resolution systems in Mozambican society, they were dissipated by the constitutional recognition of legal pluralism. Therefore, any analysis of the administration of justice in Mozambique must take into account the two axes or dimensions it is divided into: *state*, including the courts, the Public Prosecutor's Office, the Bar Association, the IPAJ and other institutions in the judiciary, and *non-state*, involving community courts and other local dispute resolution tribunals.[16]

The development of state justice has had its ups and downs, on a winding road. In the year when the 45th anniversary of national independence (or, if preferred, the 42nd anniversary of the first Judicial Organization Law) was celebrated, it remained far from enjoying the confidence of society and achieving the level of performance that citizens and legal entities demand. Its coverage remains deficient, and the quality of the service provided is far from satisfactory for those who resort to it.

---

[16] See Article 4(212)(3) and Article 223 of the Constitution and Articles 5 and 6 of Law No. 24/2007, of 20 August.

In the last opening session of the legal year, the President of the Supreme Court did not refrain from admitting that 'we still have twenty-four districts in our country without courts operating locally, which means the citizens have to go to other nearby districts in order to resolve their disputes' (Muchanga 2020). For our part, we continue to argue that the problem is not the coverage of twenty-four districts that still do not have courts. More important is rethinking the legal map, providing more rational coverage of the country, taking into account the real needs of legal and judicial authority, the size of the population, the nature of the disputes and their degree of complexity, and not working from abstract criteria on the political and administrative organisation of the country. A careful study could lead to the conclusion that there are districts whose level of economic and social development, population density, infrastructures in place, etc., would justify the existence of more than one court with the powers due to the district courts in their geographic area, while others would only need a more organised and better distributed network of non-state or community tribunals.

The intense efforts that are being made by the managing bodies of other institutions in the judiciary in the task of concluding the slow process of physical establishment of the courts and support structures in the field are neither being ignored, nor are those of the entities charged with training the judges, court officials, and system managers. We know that there are now 157 courts, of different levels, operating all over the country and that the ratio of courts to 100,000 inhabitants has improved slightly, going from 1.1 in 2014 to 1.3 in 2019. The average time taken for dispute resolution fell from 17 months in 2014 to 12 months in 2019, and the resolution rate, which was 37.6 per cent in 2014, was always higher than 45 per cent in the following four years.[17] But these figures cannot hide the fact that there is still a lot to be done and consolidated so that the universal principles of the rule of law may be achieved.[18]

As to the provision of legal consultancy and assistance services, this is the responsibility of two bodies: the Mozambican Bar Association (OAM), constituted by Law No. 7/94, of 14 September, as a legal person under public law, representing the people holding law degrees and practising law, independent of the state bodies, having administrative, financial, and patrimonial autonomy and the Institute for Legal Representation and Assistance (IPAJ), set up by

[17] All the quantitative data referred to here are from Muchanga (2020: 8).
[18] The *World Justice Project* (https://worldjusticeproject.org), a self-proclaimed, independent, multidisciplinary, non-profit organisation that works for the advancement of the rule of law in the world believes that it is defined by four universal principles: **Accountability** – the government and private entities are accountable under the law; **Just laws** – laws must be clear, publicized and stable, applied evenly, and should protect fundamental rights, including the security of persons and contracts, property and human rights; **Open government** – the processes by which laws are enacted, administered and enforced are accessible, fair and efficient; and **Accessible and impartial dispute resolution** – justice must be delivered in good time, by competent, independent, ethical and neutral representatives who are accessible, have adequate resources and reflect the makeup of the communities they serve (*World Justice Project*, n.d.).

Law No. 6/94, of 13 September, as a state institute aimed at ensuring the right to defence, providing lower income citizens with the legal representation, and assistance they need.

Since it was set up in 1994, the OAM has grown exponentially. Ten years later, more precisely on 20 May 2005, 246 lawyers were registered with the bar association, with 226 of them having offices in Maputo, 9 in Beira, 6 in Nampula, 2 in Tete, 1 in Chimoio, 1 in Matola and 1 in Quelimane (OAM 2005). In late February 2020, the database on the Bar Association's webpage (www.oam.org.mz/advogados-inscritos/) had 1,856 lawyers, with around 73 per cent practising in Maputo. Despite the rapid growth in the list of lawyers practising in the provinces (Sofala, Nampula, and Tete have the highest figures), over recent years, one of the greatest challenges to the Bar Association has been to offer private legal services at district level, as well as in less populous urban centres.

The IPAJ in turn went through an initial period with enormous operating difficulties, whose main causes were the absence of political priority, poor management, and budget insufficiency (Santos et al. 2003, vol. II: 56). In 2007, when a survey was carried out on the IPAJ, this institute had 80 legal assistants and 400 other staff. It also had ten provincial offices and fifty-seven district offices (Bila 2008). The following year, the approval and establishment of the Strategic Plan for Legal Defence for Disadvantaged Citizens (PEDLCC) was decisive for the institution to be able to grow and consolidate itself, promoting organisational and institutional development and improving the efficiency and effectiveness of legal assistance and representation (Lauris and Araújo 2015: 94).

A new organic statute was adopted in 2013,[19] with the aim of making the operational structure adequate to the new conditions that had since been provided. However, the challenge of reaching the more disfavoured populations, mainly in the regions far from large urban centres, will require continued efforts towards institutional growth and consolidation.

But access to justice is not only through state mechanisms or institutions. In recent years, particularly since the early 1990s, some civil society organisations have assumed increasing importance in access to justice and the law, seeking to make up for the difficulties faced by the state. These are organisations that provide different kinds of support to citizens, in particular legal assistance and representation, legal information and advice, and conflict resolution. They have a wide field of intervention. Some are general in scope, while others specialise in certain rights or in providing support to more vulnerable citizens, or work in particularly problematic areas, such as cases of human rights, women's human rights, access to land and other natural resources.

With regard to community courts, it is worth mentioning that within the many non-judicial mechanisms for dispute resolution that interact in Mozambican society, they are the ones that appear to be best placed to promote local justice

---

[19] See Decree No. 15/2013, of 26 April.

and contribute to desirable links between state and non-state systems and for the administration of justice. They are different from all the others, fundamentally because they emanate from the actual state, through a formal regulatory act – Law No. 4/92, of 6 May – which was enacted to allow citizens to resolve minor disputes within the community, contribute to the harmonisation of different legal practices and to enriching the rules, habits, and customs that 'lead to a creative synthesis of Mozambican law' (see the Preamble to this act).

As it happens, although this law has been in force for thirty years, it has never been implemented through the necessary regulations. And there was no shortage of alerts from different sectors of society as to the risk of this lack of regulation and the unfeasibility of the application of the law without it. There is a set of related organisational issues, for example, with the procedure for electing the members of community courts (Article 9(2) and Article 13), with the establishment of these courts (Article 12) or the forwarding of the 'appeals' left unresolved to the district courts (Article 4). The incomprehensible legislative inertia of the government served, after all, as a pretext for the generalisation of the illegal practice of substituting elections for member (judge) co-option processes, with the involvement of agents of local authorities (heads of administrative posts, neighbourhood secretaries, village presidents, etc.), without the direct intervention of voters – the people.

We see this situation as highly problematic, with no explanation other than serving for the purpose of ensuring party political control of the community structures. This is controversial (and, from our point of view, unconstitutional), as is the current framework of the community courts under the authority of the Ministry of Justice, Constitutional, and Religious Affairs. This is so mainly because the Constitution of 2004 included them in the list of type of courts in the Republic of Mozambique (Article 223(2)), with all the guarantees of independence, impartiality, and objectivity these sovereign bodies should enjoy. It is unclear what legal basis the Civil Registry services use to organise and manage the establishment of the community courts when this responsibility is assigned to the district courts (Article 14 of Law No. 4/92).

These serious deviations from the spirit and the letter of the law, to which we could add disrespect for other regulations, such as articles 10 (on the mandate of the members of the community courts), 11 (on the payment of the members), and 12 (on the establishment of these bodies), contribute largely to their becoming discredited in the eyes of citizens and to the crisis of legitimacy that has taken over the system (Trindade and José 2017: 31).

## III IMPLICATIONS FOR SOCIAL AND ECONOMIC DEVELOPMENT

The blockages and dysfunctions in the performance of the Mozambican judiciary could not but affect, to a greater or lesser extent, the process of development in the country, both in economic and financial terms and in social terms. There seems to be no doubt of this. But its impact can be assessed from two different perspectives, corresponding to the top-down and bottom-up pressure groups referred to in the introduction.[20]

Thus, for those who favour the first perspective, a well-structured, independent judicial system enjoying the confidence of the legal and business community is the decisive factor for stimulating growth, protecting property rights, and maintaining control of free competition and the operation of the market economy.

Sherwood et al. (1994:104) point out that the good performance of the courts depends on a set of internal requirements (inputs), particularly:

- *A body of impartial and independent judges* – even though competence and impartiality are subjective criteria, the conditions for their existence can be identified objectively. Factors such as training, degree of specialisation, salaries, selection and recruitment criteria, and rules of prevention of conflicts of interests exercise a particular influence in this regard;
- *Adequate material and organisational conditions* – including, among others, physical infrastructure, equipment, and process management systems. Judicial precedents and collective actions might reduce the repetitive disputes and the accumulation of processes;
- *Procedural guarantees* – the balanced procedural guarantees include equity, institutionalised through the right of appeal of judicial decisions and of administrative decisions made in the first instance, the existence of rules regarding the discovery and production of proof and the 'due legal process' for those charged in criminal matters;
- *Wide public information* – it is important that information relative to the most relevant laws and judicial decisions is made public and disseminated. The World Bank itself, in some of its loans, has demanded that recipient countries not only revise certain laws but also make those concerned aware of their existence;
- *Well-conceived and clearly written laws* – the courts are frequently called to deal with ill-conceived and badly written laws. This fact constitutes a burden for the courts in addition to complicating the fair application of the relevant laws;
- *Widely shared knowledge of the role and competences of courts* – the understanding of the nature of the judicial power and the expectations around the performance of the courts in society should be widely shared. This refers, in large measure, to knowing the role that is reserved to them by the Constitution and how it can be distinguished from other state powers. This knowledge is essential for citizens and enterprises to have confidence in the

---

[20] Boaventura de Sousa Santos calls these two fields *hegemonic*, because they are essentially carried out by the World Bank, the International Monetary Fund, and large international development aid agencies, and *counter-hegemonic*, because they are led by citizens, organisations and social movements that progressively became more aware of their rights and the need for them to be defended and respected (Santos 2014: 33–35).

judicial system and to recognise in it an institution to which they can turn to safeguard their rights, even in cases against the actions of public powers.

It is not hard to observe that some of these requirements are yet to be fulfilled in the Mozambican judicial system.

In Brazil, Castelar (2009) highlights some of the virtues that characterise a 'good administration of justice':

- Favouring voluntary compliance by the parties to contracts under private law, reducing the costs of transactions and encouraging economic agents to increase the volume and distribution of their businesses;
- Permitting the accumulation of production factors, encouraging an increase in investment in physical and human capital, given that entrepreneurs will feel that their property rights are assured and protected;
- Reducing the risk of administrative arbitrariness, mainly in the cases of sustained, long-term private investment in public utility services, such as telecommunications, energy, etc.;
- Contributing to wider dissemination of knowledge, not only technological knowledge, but also knowledge of adequate management, marketing and financial practices, as the expansion of the market will bring stronger competition between companies, allowing them to make higher profits and sales and invest in innovation, whether through development of or the acquisition of technology (Castelar 2009: 15).

The basis for this line of thinking, according to Susana Santos (2014: 5), is the predominance of economic rationality, defined by criteria of effectiveness and efficiency that can be quantitatively measured. The author explains that according to this logic, the more rational the service in question is, the more productive it will be, in other words, the more gains it will make. In the justice sector, we are talking about the number of cases closed, the number of investigations, the number of hearings, etc., carried out by each system agent (judge, prosecutor, court official) or by each body in the system (court or tribunal or prosecution unit).

This is one of the principles of the *institutional re-engineering* that Hammergren (2006: 18) refers to as 'focusing on the results and not on the method'.

Taking different assumptions into account, those that highlight the importance of the bottom-up perspective, while recognising the central role of the judicial system in the development of democracy and in social and economic development, argue that structuring topics such as access to justice, recruitment, selection, training and career progression for judges, the quality and transparency of the legal acts cannot be planned or dealt with in purely economic or financial terms (Santos 2013). Here, the highest value to be preserved must be the jurisdictional authority over the civil, political, economic, and social rights enshrined by the constitution and whose enjoyment requires courts to be independent, the procedural law to be rapid, fair, and straightforward, and asymmetry in access to be eliminated.

Anyone subscribing to this line of thought is led to criticise the excessive focus on issues of productivity, the imposition of bureaucratic models based on scripts for 'good practices' and quality certification, insofar as this model produces a perverse effect on the organisational dynamics of legal institutions. In effect, we must not neglect the fact that the system is fuelled by a web of relationships between different players with different weights and powers inside the same structure, where attention is centred on economic growth and free market development, which can lead to latent conflicts between professionals who see their identity diminished in the face of standardised aims and irrespective of their position in the structure (Santos 2014: 7).

In addition, efficiency cannot be recognised as structuring and the courts will never engage in their duty to 'educate the citizens and public administration regarding voluntary, conscious compliance with the laws, establishing fair and harmonious social coexistence' (Article 213 of the Constitution) if the performance of the judiciary remains selective and if the view of the people and the community persists with the idea that 'justice is for the wealthy'.

## IV CHALLENGES FOR THE FUTURE

The diagnoses made of the performance of the justice administration system in different studies and research papers produced over the years show a clear persistence of problems that have long been identified.[21]

It is evident that the importance of these diagnoses must not be undervalued, in the same way that it is not a good idea to neglect the reports from international organisations and national business associations, concerned with improving the business environment and the performance of the economy. But, as Nuno Garoupa, a full professor at the University of Illinois says, 'there is no doubt that justice is important for economic and social development, but it is not a miracle solution. The quality of the judicial system, the courts or the judicature in China or in Central and Eastern Europe is catastrophic, but that does not stop these countries from attracting foreign investment or presenting enviable growth rates [...]' (Garoupa 2008: 1).

---

[21] According to Boaventura de Sousa Santos (2005: 77), there are three different ways of diagnosing justice problems. The first is the *sociological diagnosis*, based on sound, stringent assessment of the performance of the judicial system and the perception of the citizens as to the operation of the courts and related institutions. The second is the *political diagnosis*, made by political decision-makers and by analysts and commentators on social media. Diagnoses such as these are based on rules and assumptions that are very different from those used for the first way of diagnosing, and sometimes have very little to do with it. The third is *operational diagnosis*, made by participants in the judicial system: judges, lawyers, employees, professional associations and Superior Councils of the judiciary. They all have their own importance and reveal their own 'truth'.

As we have said, what the Mozambican judicial system needs is real structural reform, which it has never seen before. The political powers have already recognised this more than once, in the voice of their highest representative, the President of the Republic.[22]

But what should 'structural reform' consist of, from our point of view?

The topics we will be summarising below – given that the limits of a text of this nature do not allow for a more in-depth analysis – constitute some of the elements that we believe are the essential basis for this idea, without which we do not believe it will be possible to move on to another platform for debate on this topic and, thus, the desired paradigm shift.

## A Shared Strategic Vision

In the first place, the effectiveness, speed, and accessibility of justice can only be sustainable if the different entities in the sector share a systemic, integrated vision that permanently links the formal, professional judiciary, and the different non-judicial mechanisms for conflict resolution recognised by the State, under Article 4 of the Constitution. For this to happen, it will be necessary to pursue 'the committed quest for solutions so that justice in Mozambique will be predictable and accessible to all, administered within an economically and socially tolerable time and with standards that are more aligned with the collective conceptions of justice that are prominent in our society' (Correia 2014: 108).

As we have seen, there were successive attempts at judicial reform over the last thirty years. The worldwide reformist movement arrived in Mozambique through programmes and initiatives almost always focused on searching for solutions to solve the unfathomable problems of celerity and procedural simplification, providing the organisations with more human, material, and infrastructure resources and introducing alternative dispute resolution methods.

Nowadays, there seems to be some tacit recognition that the results did not live up to expectations. The complexity of litigation, the scarcity of resources, and the absence of this strategic vision superseded the greater or lesser desire for change, whether genuine or feigned.

---

[22] In two of his most recent speeches on topics of Justice, the Head of State spoke about the need for structural reforms: first, at a commemorative session for the Day of Legality, on 5 November 2019, stating that 'there is a need to ensure greater efficiency and credibility of the judiciary and this should include legal reform [...] The introduction of changes to the structure and organization of the judiciary will permit greater transparency and control over participants in the judiciary, whether by their peers or by society' (President of the Republic 2019). Then, at the ceremony for the opening of the 2020 Legal Year, he reiterated that 'the reform of the Law and Justice is a pressing need, in order to ensure the effectiveness of the rights and duties of citizens, making the system a factor in the promotion of citizenship, cohesion and social peace [...] Justice must facilitate the business environment and make the national market more attractive and competitive and safer for national and foreign private investment' (President of the Republic 2020). The only question is whether his understanding of 'structural reform' is the same as the one we are sharing here. We are rather doubtful about that.

Accordingly, it is necessary to definitively break this cycle; it is necessary to go beyond 'more of the same' measures (more courts, more judges, more resources ...) and look at the judicial system from another perspective.

Structural reform will only introduce greater efficiency, effectiveness, and quality in the administration of justice if it is looked at as a complex, integral system. The focus will have to be aimed at a gradual, but persistent, change in work methods, better, more streamlined management of human and material resources and processes and better coordination between all the participants in the system. This can only be achieved if, with every change that has to be made, we look at the various constituent components, as the system is distributed among different state bodies and the community and requires the definition of common medium- and long-term objectives.

As stated by Gomes (2018: 746), 'it is fundamental to lend substance to the idea that legal proceedings take place in a very broad, polycentric framework, with both internal judicial players (judicial magistrates and magistrates from the Public Prosecutor's Office, employees) and external players (police, social workers, experts, etc.) playing a part in them. Some of the time taken in court, indeed a significant amount in some proceedings, is the time of these latter professionals'.

## B Consensus between Relevant Players

This shared vision assumes the agreement to a broad consensus between the different state powers, the police forces, the judiciary, and society in general so that justice is understood as a public good of primary importance, the discussion and formulation of which should be above all the differences and private or corporate interests of each one.

This is a fundamental agreement that, in some cases, has been called a *Regime Pact* (Santos 2005: 77; Figueiredo 2017) and, in others, a *State Pact* (Representatives of the PP and PSOE-Spain 2007) and which, bearing in mind the scope and scale of the reform, will necessarily imply a specific revision of the constitution. This will have to be a constitutional revision broadly recognised as necessary, one that is patiently refined and not imposed by any de facto power for the benefit of private and conjunctural interests.

## C Central Role of the Judiciary in the Different Stages of Reform

The success of reform can only be attained if the participants from all the bodies, entities, or institutions in the justice administration system play a central role as active agents of change, as they are the main vehicle for conveying knowledge between the judicial reality and the common citizen (Garoupa 2008: 2). The commitment of these agents and the setting aside of a period of adaptation to the reform measures, accompanied by targeted training courses are of prime importance and should not be neglected (Gomes 2018: 747). One of the weaknesses pointed to in the case of the reform initiatives so far undertaken is, precisely, the lack of preparation of the conditions necessary for their later implementation, both in terms of training and in terms of technical and financial resources.

These weaknesses will make it difficult to break resistance, alter routines and change obsolete methods of work.

## D The Independence of the Judiciary as a Fundamental Right

Contemporary legal systems are broadly grouped around two fundamental models of organisation of the judiciary: the legal profession model seen in countries with an Anglo-Saxon tradition (common law)[23] and the judicial career seen in countries with a tradition of European continental law (Romano-Germanic family).[24]

Despite their differences, the conceptual framework regarding the independence of the judiciary, according to Carvalho (2016: 16), makes a distinction between substantial independence, personal independence, external independence, and internal independence. Substantial independence refers to the circumstance of judges, when acting in their judicial role, being subject only to the law and their conscience, free from any and all outside influence. Personal independence means the judges cannot be held accountable for their judgements and decisions, except in the cases where this is especially provided for by law, and they enjoy the assurance of their irremovability from office. External independence means the removal of executive control from the system management mechanisms and the preparation of their budgetary assumptions. Finally, internal independence assures judges of their freedom to directly or indirectly disregard pressure from other judges when making their judgements.

This conceptual framework helps to understand that only a judicial power with a high capacity for operation, free of excessive formalities, and endowed with functional autonomy from the other powers can meet the demands for greater efficiency, independence, impartiality, speed, and proximity that are required of them. Therefore, the right to have independent courts is also a fundamental human right, which should not be looked at as a privilege of judges, but rather as an assurance for society and a primary condition for citizens, organisations, and companies to be able to trust the judicial system, the law, and the state.

---

[23] According to Carvalho (2016: 12), this model is characterised by an extensive guarantee of the independence of judges, there being no distinction between judges and lawyers or a judicial career. The magistrates are removed from the civil liability mechanism, rather being subject to ethical rules and the application of the same disciplinary responsibility to all the professions in the legal community.

[24] Which, according to Carvalho (2016: 14), is characterised by a weak guarantee of the independence of judges, by the professional difference between judges and lawyers, by the existence of a judicial career, with judicial magistrates normally being subject to the rules of civil liability.

## E  Paradigm Shift in Legislative Production

Legislative production in Mozambique is also in need of substantial improvements. As is the case in other latitudes, whose model has served as an inspiration, and in the words of Garoupa (2008: 3), Mozambican legislators have shown themselves to be *frenetic* (legislating everything even when it is not necessary), *schizophrenic* (legislating erratically) and *sloppy* (legislating and repealing without regulating).

This impulse to legislate is followed without first assessing the existence of other legislation already in force and which might only need to be amended or have its application improved. Or without pondering another solution that does not include adding to the normative or regulatory burden.

Those who have the power to create regulations should, first of all, analyse the legislative framework in force and see if there are other solutions for achieving the desired aims, respecting the different phases of the legislative process. Charles-Albert Morand proposes that this process should be in seven stages: (i) identifying the problem; (ii) determining the aims; (iii) choosing the options; (iv) *ex ante* assessment; (v) adopting the legislation; (vi) implementation; and (vii) *ex post* assessment (Morand 1999).

The quality of the laws made depends on various factors and it is very true that there are no perfect laws. However, it is possible to improve the legislative process, provided those procedures and methodologies, which will certainly contribute to making the laws more comprehensive, less difficult to interpret and apply, more effective and suitable to the reality they are intended to regulate. Of these methodologies, *ex ante* and *ex post* assessment studies of the legislative impact and the participation of citizens, legal persons, and companies at the law preparation stage and in access to the elements that are the grounds for the political decision take on special importance. As stated by Sónia Rodrigues, 'if easy access to the law that regulates their daily lives is crucial for citizens, simplification and the reduction of context costs is vital for the economic competitiveness of companies' (Rodrigues 2017: 1038).

A step that we deem to be indispensable for assuring this methodological development includes the creation of a Law Reform Commission, not like the old Inter-Ministerial Law Reform Commission (CIREL),[25] but rather according to the model for the South African Law Reform Commission. It is presided over by a judge and is made up of law professors, magistrates, and lawyers with the power to carry out studies and research into all the branches of law, or have these carried out. These studies aim at presenting recommendations and projects for the improvement, modernisation, or reform of national and provincial legislation, including the repeal of obsolete or unnecessary provisions, the standardisation of laws all over the country, the consolidation or codification of any branch of the law and measures aimed at making the laws more readily available to the public. In short, the Law Reform Commission is

---

[25]  Created by Presidential Decree No. 3/2002, of 26 August.

an advisory body whose aim is the reform and the continued improvement of the legislation in South Africa.[26]

## F The Judicial Government: Fundaments and Management

In an interesting publication that discusses what should be understood by *judicial government*, Alberto Binder, a law professor at the University of Buenos Aires, argues that it is necessary to clearly differentiate the judiciary from other state powers, as well as from the different duties and tasks existing within judicial organisations, which are more or less diverse according to the country (Binder 2006: 12).

In his opinion, the true fundament that sustains the idea of *judicial government* is the need to preserve the independence of each one of the judges, taken individually. All the other reasons that might be invoked, such as assuring efficient management of the resources allocated, monitoring activity programmes, preparing budget proposals, planning campaigns, being answerable to society, etc., can only indirectly or tangentially justify the call for a judicial government. On the other hand, the implementation of the judicial government, like any other political institution, cannot be done in a vacuum, but rather under the scope of the historical setting of the specific judicial systems.

Therefore, Binder considers that any judicial government should be radically separated from the Supreme Courts, given that there is no reason for a judge from the higher courts to have the prerogative of acting and making decisions on behalf of the other members of the judiciary. In a judiciary with a democratic government, the president of the judiciary, apart from being completely separate from the President of the Supreme Court, should be an elected official. Each magistrate (irrespective of their seniority or the court they serve in, as these qualities do not give them special qualifications for administration or government) should have one vote and elect the president of the judiciary for a certain period of time. To those who raise the spectre of internal politicisation of the judiciary, he replies that this is not necessarily negative because, although politicisation is impossible to avoid, it is not harmful in itself,[27] it does exist, and it is better for it to be transparent and accountable. A democratically elected president of the judiciary has more power, legitimacy, room for manoeuvre, and a greater ability to defend the independence of the judges than any other person taking up the position merely because it is part of the job.

In short, the author proposes the following configuration of the judiciary:

a) A president of the judiciary without a judicial role, elected by all the judges, with no qualified votes and without excluding any judge, for a mandate lasting from four to five years, not coinciding with general elections (presidential, parliamentary, or local authority elections);

[26] See www.justice.gov.za/salrc/index.htm.
[27] The author points out that it is important not to confuse *politicisation* with *partisanship*.

b) A set of technical offices under the president, responsible for ordinary administration, planning, budget management, the internal disciplinary regime, the development of the information system, the management of human resources and infrastructures, etc., with sufficient scope to combine greater legitimacy with greater efficiency and feasibility;

c) A supervisory and monitoring body, also elected for the same mandate, of collegial composition, with the responsibility for approving accounts and managing and assessing complaints, in other words intervening in *ex post* situations. This monitoring board should consist of a certain number of judges (percentages can be established per areas, courts, etc., but never by categories), according to the characteristics of the judicial system.

In this context, the President of the Supreme Court will continue to be first among equals in the highest court of the land, but will no longer be the representative of the judiciary, unless democratically elected as the President of the Superior Council of the Judiciary, on the same footing and with the same opportunities as any other judge.

In general, we agree with this proposal. From what we have found in the literature and in judicial practices around the world, there is, to our knowledge, no more democratic configuration model that has better assurances of safeguarding the independence of the judiciary. The absence of an important mechanism can be mentioned, which is external control of the judiciary, but there too, this issue can be circumvented, allowing for some members of the monitoring board to be individuals outside of the judiciary, with a certain number of requirements and elected separately, while always maintaining a majority of judges on the judicial government bodies.

We are aware that in a country where the idea of centralisation and a tight hold on political power is widely predominant, it will not be easy to put a project like this into practice. But the idea is there, as our aim is to find innovative ways to ensure effective and sustainable judicial independence.

## G  A Democratic Judicial Culture

The conceptual underpinning on which this chapter draws refers to the aim of scrutinising the roads that could lead to positive institutional change, in other words, the way the institutions could contribute to growth and an improvement in economic and social results.

We have attempted to show that changes in the Justice area will only be possible with structural reform based on a systemic vision, shared and coordinated by the entire judiciary. But it is important to be aware that reform – any reform – cannot resolve the problems found if it is not based on a judicial and organisation culture that is open and receptive to innovation. A system where the main players resist change is doomed to isolate itself and protect itself from opinions and criticisms aimed at it from outside.

Around twenty years ago, the *Research Project on the Plurality of Justice in Mozambique* concluded that Mozambican courts 'are dominated by a regulatory, technical and bureaucratic culture, based on three main ideas: the autonomy of the *law* – an idea that the law is an autonomous phenomenon in relation to society; a restrictive view of what that law is or which proceedings the law applies to; and a bureaucratic or administrative view of the cases' (Trindade and Pedroso 2003: 64–65). Despite some developments since then, resulting from the initial and continuous training programmes set up by the Centre for Judicial and Legal Training, this kind of technical and bureaucratic culture still persists in many judges and others working in the system and it is seen in different and varied ways. One of these, perhaps the one with the most perverse effects, is confusing independence with self-sufficient individuality and, consequently, being extremely averse to teamwork, resisting the introduction of management by objectives in court, rejecting interdisciplinary cooperation and fuelling an idea of exclusivity that is not willing to learn and benefit from other abilities and areas of knowledge.

It is vital to oppose this idea through a democratic, political, and judicial culture that uses justice as a strategy. Justice must be at the service of social cohesion and democratic development. The complexity of the new duties will require a long learning process. The sociology of law has shown that, as new social relationships are given legal status – and this phenomenon is increasingly present in society – the gloss on the legal view of these relationships will get thinner and thinner and be released from dogmatic rigidity. Therefore, it is important to search in other areas – economics, psychology, anthropology, political science, etc. – for analytical tools that will help understand the reality, and this is part of the democratic culture.

## H Reinforcement of Training for Judicial Agents: Judges, Court Officials and Other Employees

In the context of the new democratic judicial culture, training can neither continue to have the same general profile, nor can it remain shackled to old, obsolete teaching methods. It needs to be differentiated. There is an increasing need for people engaging in activities in the courts requiring specialized skills to have specific training, with specific access conditions and specific examinations – this is the case of the criminal and supervisory courts, as well as administrative, maritime, commercial, arbitration and tax courts. Specialisation must then be accompanied by closer monitoring of the quality of the training process throughout all its phases.

Universities, which are where jurists, future agents of justice, are trained and graduate, will have to include this reality and undergo more or less in-depth transformations. Transformations of a political nature, which will make them look at law as a social phenomenon and the broadening and defence of human rights, as well as the transparency of democratic life, as the main objectives. Transformations of a sociological nature, which will allow knowledge of society as a constituent part of the law (*ubi societas ibi jus*) to be broadened. Practical transformations that will lead to their modernisation, so that part of the course programme – normally the last year or the last two years of degree courses – may be devoted to practical work, in the form of 'legal clinics' or similar initiatives, where the students are given the opportunity to experience and learn about social problems first hand. Then, these are transformations to the actual course structure and teaching and learning methods, covering not only the graduation phase, but also the post-graduation phase.

At the Centre for Judicial and Legal Training, it is necessary, on the one hand, to pursue – or resume in those areas where it has been lost – a multidisciplinary approach to the programme content, capable of revealing the social contexts underlying legal regulations and relationships and, on the other, to experiment with new working methods that will encourage the trainees to participate actively in the teaching and learning process, through teamwork, seminars and research activities.

It would also be a good idea for the main objectives of the training to be aligned with the particular learning or skills development needs of the students, whether they intend to go into the judiciary or any other legal profession. To this end, it is important to be aware, insofar as possible, of their training experiences, their interests and future specialisation projects, in order to bring about a *participatory reaction* in them and ensure that the 'results of the training were not acquired superficially or temporarily, but rather *have become* [...] *engrained* in the habits and learning abilities of the actual student' (Guadagni 2000: 8).

And, for this teacher/student interaction to occur, it is also a good idea to develop an environment conducive to their relationship being one of 'dialogue and cooperation, of equality where there is mutual respect, where opinions are consciously respected. Because they know more about and have more skills in certain areas, [teachers] have the role of supporting and facilitating the acquisition of new knowledge or perfecting the knowledge of others' (Cabral and Soares 2000: 4).

More than just absorbing knowledge about legislated law and becoming aware that they live in a reality that is plural in the sense that they come into contact and interact with the different regulatory systems within it, these future professionals must be prepared to take on the implementation of the ideal of justice, constantly updating this. To this end, training that values a structural understanding of the institutions of justice and legal institutes will serve to show them to be an integral part of a certain political project. Thus, each act, each procedure, each way of interpreting the rules, each decision, will not be limited to itself alone, it will not be neutral, rather it will be the practical implementation of an ideal of justice, in other words, the construction of a certain type of state.

## I Management of Alternative Conflict Resolution Mechanisms and Community Justice

We have already expressed our opinion on the current inclusion of community courts in the Ministry of Justice, Constitutional and Religious Affairs and the role the Civil Registry services have been playing in their management. We believe that this authority is, at the very least, illegal, because it is contrary to the provisions of Article 5 of Law No. 24/2007, of 20 August,[28] if not actually unconstitutional, as it violates the principle of separation of powers proclaimed in Article 134 of the Constitution.

Around fifteen years ago, the former Law Reform Technical Unit (UTREL)[29] asked the CFJJ for a set of legislative projects which had as its objective, precisely, to embody a broad reform of the administration of Justice. Among these, we highlight the preliminary proposals of the *Basic Law of Judicial Organization* and the *Organic Law of Community Courts*, as these have a more direct bearing on the point being analysed.

The first of these preliminary proposals defined a structure for the judicial system, according to which, without prejudice to the powers of the Constitutional Council, common justice would be assured by the Supreme Court and other courts, by community courts and, under the terms of that law, by courts of arbitration.[30] And it recommended the enshrining and materialisation of a principle of proximity and access to justice, through adequate coverage by legal institutions, in particular courts, community courts, agencies of the Public Prosecutor's Office, of the Public Institute for Access to Justice and the Law (which was replaced by the current IPAJ) and the entities that would be associated with compliance with their duties.

Community courts would deal with conciliation, processing, judging and implementing: a) cases arising from family relationships resulting from unions constituted according to traditional rules and not registered according to the Family Act; b) cases of other natures whose debt value, compensation requested or damages claimed were not greater than three times the national minimum wage; c) offences against property where the damage caused was not greater than two times the minimum wage and bodily injury, except in cases involving: i) a risk to life; ii) permanent disability; iii) temporary inability of the victim to work or to carry out their normal activities for longer than 15 days. Nor would they be permitted to decide on issues attributed by law to other courts, or cases

[28] Which states: 'Community courts are **independent** non-judicial, institutionalized tribunals for conflict resolution, whose judgements are in accordance with good sense and equity, informal, not professional in nature, privileging oral proceedings and bearing in mind the social and cultural values existing in Mozambican society, with respect for the Constitution' (bold text ours).
[29] UTREL, which worked as an operational instrument of CIREL (see Note 26), went into a technical partnership with the CFJJ to prepare a set of preliminary proposals for the law that was to embody a comprehensive reform of the administration of justice: the Preliminary Proposals for the *Basic Law of Judicial Organization*, the *Organic Law of Courts*, the *Organic Law of Community Courts* and the *Law of Access to Justice and the Law*. Only the second would be sent to parliament and approved, albeit with substantial alterations.
[30] The remaining courts (administrative, tax, customs, maritime, etc.) would certainly be part of the **jurisdictional power**, in terms of the bodies to which *jurisdictional duties* (of 'declaring the law of the case') are entrusted, but not **the judiciary**, which is more restrictive, referring only to *common justice*, provided with *general jurisdiction* (see Canotilho 2003: 661).

regarding people's ability, the validity or interpretation of wills, the dissolution of civil marriages or adoption.

The management and administration of community courts and the disciplining of their judges would be in the hands of the bodies entitled Provincial Councils for the Coordination of Community Justice, to be set up in each province in the country. These councils would be run by the presidents of the provincial courts and would have the following composition: a) a provincial prosecutor, appointed by the Superior Council of the Judiciary of the Public Prosecutor's Office; b) two district court judges, appointed by the Superior Council of the Judiciary; c) one representative of the legal assistance public service, appointed by the Director of the Public Institute for Access to Justice and the Law; d) eight representatives of the community courts, elected by their peers, with mandates of two years; and e) three representatives of the community authorities, elected by their peers, with mandates of two years.

The preliminary proposal for the *Basic Law* also enshrined the **principle of non-prohibition** of the remaining local conflict resolution mechanisms unless their actions or the type of penalties applied violated the principles, standards or values contained in the constitution.

Another important and innovative measure that this preliminary proposal included was a reform Monitoring Commission, which included representatives of the institutions with specific duties of monitoring the operation and quality of the system of administration of justice and the Centre for Judicial and Legal Training. The function of the commission – inspired by the British law commissions model – was to prepare the entry into force of the reform, and monitor and assess the degree of achievement of the aims and implementation of the measures established in the *Basic Law*.

Under the terms of the preliminary proposal for the *Organic Law*, the material powers of community courts would be defined bearing in mind the type of cases that these courts traditionally deal with, in conjunction with constitutional requirements and the need for jurisdictional effectiveness. Thus, these courts would deal with conciliation, processing, judging and implementing: a) cases arising from family relationships resulting from unions constituted according to traditional rules and not registered according to the Family Act; b) cases where the compensation requested or damages claimed were not greater than three times the national minimum wage; c) offences against property where the damage caused was not greater than two times the minimum wage and bodily injury not resulting in serious injuries.

Even though around a decade and a half has passed since these proposals were prepared and presented, it seems unquestionable that they are current and relevant. If they were to be adopted – irrespective of any improvements or updates to be introduced – we would have better justice as the basis for the judicial system, there, where the vast majority of Mozambicans live.

## V CONCLUSIONS

The rule of law and judicial independence are a project yet to be achieved in Mozambique. Their feasibility depends on the extent to which political decision-makers are capable of taking on the challenges that only a systemic, integrated and coordinated view among all the players can provide.

The different reform attempts made so far, mainly after the change in political and strategic direction, brought about by the Constitution of 1990, were always short-sighted and conjunctural in nature, under domestic and foreign pressure that was not always clear or well-intentioned. This 'baby steps technique', as Garoupa (2008) calls it, must be contrasted with structural reform capable of bringing about more drastic transformations in the institutional and regulatory frameworks that determine the operation of the legal authorities. The judiciary needs to assert itself as the real power, the system of checks and balances must be able to sustain itself in practice, in all its grandeur. This means the democratisation of the constituent methods and processes and the operability of the judiciary. And, as is well-known, more efficient, speedier performance by the courts and other legal institutions will ultimately be an important stimulus for the economy and for the balanced growth of companies, as it will help to increase productivity, investment, and employment.

On the other hand, from the point of view of citizenship, the defence of the rights and legitimate interests of individuals and social groups with fewer economic resources will tend to be more accessible and more effectively exercised.

Structural reform assumes a democratic judicial culture that will replace the current technical and bureaucratic culture that still prevails. For this to happen, it will be essential to focus on and invest seriously in sound training for citizenship, aimed at the relevant players in the system: judges, lawyers, court officials, the police, assistants, and others.

Although our analysis focused almost exclusively on the administration of common justice, the same concerns and the same sense of the measures that embody reform should apply, adapted as necessary, to the other branches of the judiciary, such as the Constitutional Council and the administrative, tax and customs courts, etc.

And, so that all of these ideas can make sense, there is a condition that Carlos Lopes[31] (2020) recently referred to during the ceremony to launch his book *Africa in Transformation: Economic Development in the Age of Doubt*, at the Polytechnic University in Maputo:

All African countries have the possibility to make structural changes, but they can only do this successfully if they have capable, disciplined leaders who have focus and the notion that they have to change the mentality and stop being lazy, rentier countries.

---

[31] Former executive secretary of the United Nations Economic Commission for Africa (2012–16) and adviser to the then Secretary-General Kofi Annan. He is currently a visiting professor at the Nelson Mandela School of Public Governance at the University of Cape Town.

10

# The Changing Dependence on Donor Countries

Johnny Flentø and Leonardo Santos Simão

## I INTRODUCTION

Mozambique has been receiving foreign aid for more than forty-five years since its independence from Portugal. It would be unrealistic to imagine that Mozambique could have no relations with donors and therefore no dependency. In fact, independence from colonial rule depended on international cooperation and solidarity, including support for its armed struggle. The interactions of the government and the ruling party with donors can be traced back to the early 1960s when the exiled FRELIMO (*Frente da Libertação de Moçambique*) embryo of diplomacy argued the case for independence with the world's leaders and nations. There is no doubt that donors have an influence on political and institutional development in poor countries including in Mozambique. This is often the purpose of their interventions, and, indeed, many donor-funded projects and programmes in Mozambique aim at strengthening or reforming the country's institutions.

How has the massive presence of donors in Mozambique since its independence in 1975 helped to shape key sovereign institutions in the country and how will this affect inclusive growth in the future?

This chapter studies Mozambique's donor relations and sovereignty. It is organised as follows: Section II provides an overview of the recent performance of donor relations, aid effectiveness, and sovereignty, drawing on available evidence and insights. Section III looks at institutional factors: What are the underlying drivers that influence how donor relations affect economic institutions and sovereignty? Finally, Section IV concludes and looks ahead: given the challenges foreseen for the future, which policy recommendations can be made about what to do to promote future inclusive development?

## II HOW AID INFLUENCES INSTITUTIONS

There is no generalised evidence that donor aid harms institution building. Although there may be situations where this happens, it is not an inherent feature of donor aid, as shown by Jones and Tarp (2016). They conclude that there is no evidence that aid has a systematic negative effect on political institutions.

Mozambique is, however, a rare case with extremely high donor dependency. It is therefore pertinent to enquire whether there are serious impacts arising from aid dependency and donor relations that significantly hamper sound and sustainable economic growth. Based on the data up to 2004, Arndt et al. (2007) concluded that aid to Mozambique works and has a reasonable rate of return. At the same time, they cautioned that some features of the aid that Mozambique receives might deepen rather than reduce dependency in the medium term. This evidence is solid and therefore important in the debate about the aggregate effects of aid. While the overall impact of aid seems positive, the debate about exactly how aid affects institutions is much less solid. Bourguignon and Gunning (2016) identified six possible channels of influence, grouped here into three clusters:

The first cluster relates to systemic efficiency, 'Dutch disease', and the cost of taxation. In a very donor-dependent country, Dutch disease is difficult to mitigate. However, we do not debate this aspect of donor relations further in this chapter as it is essentially one of appropriate macroeconomic management. The same is true in relation to the cost of taxation, and the majority of poor countries are comfortably on the safe side of the Laffer curve. Furthermore, distortive (and regressive) redistribution can be carried out in a variety of ways, not just through taxation.

The second cluster, as argued by Moss et al. (2006) and Birdsall (2007) among others, relates to the direction of accountability and government survival. It points to a view that donors may pervert institutional development and, in some cases, keep regimes afloat that would otherwise have given way to democratic change and more endogenous and sustainable institutional renewal. This belief is often built on the argument that the regime would have performed worse if it had not had access to donor funds, and this situation has created a more uneven playing field for local political opposition and other interest groups. The countries that have been able to raise large sums of donor support compared to their total government expenditure and income may be less concerned with accountability vis-à-vis their own populations and may be under less pressure to build and maintain domestic legitimacy. Such governments, it is argued, have less interest in building and investing in effective public institutions, and aid sometimes even helps to finance the tools of repression.

Similarly, rent seeking and corruption are sometimes claimed to be associated with, or even the result of, development aid. Not surprisingly, there is only anecdotal evidence of this, and the few solid empirical studies that exist point to different results, as highlighted by Bourguignon and Gunning (2016).

The issue here is that all economies experience rent seeking and corruption, particularly if institutions are weak. If aid is a significant source of funding for an economy, it will somehow help to feed rent seeking and sometimes corruption. This is typically the case in poor aid-dependent countries with few other large revenue flows. If they do have alternative large revenues to tap, such as from natural resources, such funds are probably more fungible due to donor conditionality and public expenditure reviews.

One frequently discussed feature of this cluster of arguments is that of taxation and nation-building. If governments can raise large sums of money from external donors, they do not need to tax their population, which can have an impact on their popularity and sometimes their legitimacy. If this is true, it is likely to apply primarily to direct taxes on income and holdings that people really feel and understand as their contribution to society. Also, the taxation argument assumes that in any country, public revenues, or significant amounts of them, will have to be raised eventually by taxing the broad population directly. To raise sufficient revenue, the tax base must go beyond indirect taxes and a narrow base of foreign companies, the local elite, and middle class in the formal sector.

This argument reflects European history rather than evidence from Africa.[1] Purely from a revenue point of view, the gas bonanza expected in the years to come may postpone the financial need for Mozambique to broaden the tax base to the population at large through direct taxes on income and holdings. What is at stake here is the basic contract of nation-building, and that is a much more complicated issue than finding ways to finance the budget.

There is ambiguity, to say the least, in the literature about the role of taxes in nation-building and democracy. Causality is thoroughly debated. Here only two arguments need to be remembered: The first relates to how European regimes extracted taxes in the eighteenth and nineteenth centuries, when their income levels were similar to those of poor African nations today. The second feature of taxation relevant to our study is the content of the nation-building contract in Europe and the USA at that time, which did not include the provision of social services to the broad population. The population paid taxes (and contributed their adult sons as conscripts to the army) in exchange for infrastructure and protection (security). The tax financing of education and health started much later, when countries were much richer (late nineteenth century even in the Nordic countries), and some rich countries are still fiercely debating whether it is a good idea (USA). In any case, it is almost impossible to tax finance the general provision of education and health[2] in countries with

[1] A number of the countries in Africa, that is Namibia, Zimbabwe, Botswana, Lesotho, Ghana, and indeed Mozambique raise relatively significant tax revenues (GDP/revenue comparable to Chile, USA, Ireland, and Turkey of 20–25 per cent) from quite narrow tax bases.

[2] US$2,00 per capita per year in its most basic version according to the UN.

income levels below US$2,000 per capita. Intriguingly, many donors promote this model when they give aid to very poor countries.

This brings us to the third cluster of arguments, which centres on the concept of conditionality. Bourguignon and Gunning (2016) introduce the distinction between aid for finance and aid for reform, and show that, theoretically, conditional aid is more efficient than unconditional aid when it comes to 'stopping the leakage' of funds aimed at the poor. They also argue, however, that true and enforced conditionality is very hard to come by.

When analysing donor relations and sovereignty, this channel of influence on institutions is highly relevant. If there is complete harmony and agreement about objectives and priorities between the donor and the recipient, conditionality can serve as a reinforcement to the receiving government vis-à-vis other interests (rent-seeking lobby or political opposition). More frequently though, conditionality is a means to align the interest and priorities of the receiving government to those of the donor, and this tampers with the nature of sovereignty.

There is no claim that there is inherent or embedded dysfunctionality in institutional development due to conditionality from donors. The claim is that reforms are much more likely to succeed if the recipient government truly believes in the reforms promoted by donors, internalises them, and takes responsibility for implementing them. Conditionality can be dysfunctional either because it cannot be implemented or because it is built around poor (unsuitable) policy advice and impatience. Failure to implement reforms without reprisals occurs when donors are unable to act on the non-fulfilment of the contract by the receiving government. This can be for various political reasons[3] and because of the so-called Samaritan problem. Even when conditionality is observed, it can be dysfunctional, simply because the reforms it supports are badly designed. This can have severe consequences for a poor country.

Donors are keen to promote development models that reflect international best practice and that often mirror their own efforts in sectors where they have been successful. Arguably, Denmark's health system, Finland's education sector, and the Netherlands' water management and ports administration appear to be very successful undertakings that a developing country could benefit from copying. The export of such systems may, however, be harmful and lead to overly optimistic policy choices in poor countries. When we want to understand the impact of donor relations on institutions, it is not a matter of considering how well or bad is the reform or institution suggested for copying. What matters is how recipient countries deal with donor-driven reforms that they are unable or unwilling to implement. One approach is to make believe, or to pretend, all is going well – a feature that is characteristic of Mozambique!

---

[3] Such as the commercial interests of powerful donors or unwillingness to expose aid failure to taxpayers.

In many other cases, the proposed systems may be necessary and appropriate for the recipient country. Yet, they seldom receive enough time to mature or to be fully assimilated and implemented due to budgetary considerations, or changes of government, relevant officials, and policies in the donor or recipient country. Whatever the reasons may be, the empirical evidence shows that donor-prompted reforms of institutions often happen too frequently, without sufficient time for them to consolidate and stabilise.

The literature uses a metaphor from biology called 'isomorphic mimicry' (Andrews 2009), which describes a situation where an animal looks like another animal that has capabilities it does not have (a non-venomous snake looking like a very poisonous relative). Such an animal can benefit from this similarity in some cases (to scare off enemies and predators), but it cannot develop the capability of the animal it looks like (it cannot hunt like a venomous snake if it is not one).

Isomorphic mimicry is attractive when an institution replicates the processes, systems, and outputs of other (often foreign) successful institutions without developing the capabilities of the institutions it seeks to replicate. When donors push for best-practice reforms, it can be difficult for institutions to develop the new skills needed in the local context. Arguably, donor requirements for agenda conformity close the path to novelty (Andrews et al. 2017, Chapter 2). The phenomenon relates to a rather blurred concept introduced by donors, referred to as 'ownership'. Ownership often equates the ability to control the formulation and outcome of policy and to act as a proxy for sovereignty. Recipient government ownership of reforms has become increasingly important to donors, at least formally. Consequently, if poor governments want donors to finance institutional development, they must ask for funding of programmes and reforms that donors believe in. This can still have positive outcomes, as mimicry can be an early part of learning.

Nevertheless, isomorphic mimicry becomes problematic when poor governments start asking donors what they would like them to pretend to do (to keep funds flowing). Then, it approaches institutional ventriloquism. This happens when best-practice reforms are articulated, planned, and implemented following external prompting with help from externally funded advisers and consultants. In its extreme form, reforms become fragmented and governments lose agency (Krause 2013). However, loss of agency is not equal to loss of sovereignty, though it may defeat its purpose.

Sovereignty is more than ownership (the capacity to control formulation and implementation) of policy. It is the right to rule and defines the ultimate location of authority. Sovereignty, as the right to rule, constitutes the very basis of the aid relationship and endows African states with the agency with which to contest the terms of aid deals. In Table 10.1, the first column represents the unavoidable loss of national control in the globalised world. The second and third columns represent policy choices that are influenced by the conditionality of aid, the latter being the politically most controversial. The fourth column

*Johnny Flentø and Leonardo Santos Simão*

TABLE 10.1 *Degrees of dependency*

| | External influences | | | |
|---|---|---|---|---|
| | *National control issues* | | | *Sovereignty issues* |
| Type | General external social, cultural and economic influence of societal development | External influence on state policy, particularly macroeconomic policy | External influence over constitutional structure | Sovereignty annulment |
| Examples | Foreign investment and trade, world markets, connectivity, information technology and communications | Aid conditionality, bilateral and multilateral agreements, lobbying, bribery | Political conditionality, state-building, post-conflict reconstruction | Occupation, colonization, military intervention, non-recognition |
| Impact | Implications for developmental, cultural, or economic purity | | Shape and foundation of internal authority | Forfeiture of political and legal independence |
| Is aid a factor? | Indirectly | Directly, various extents | Can be | No |

*Source:* Data from Brown (2013).

refers to the abrogation of sovereignty itself – the denial in one way or another of the politico–legal independence of the state.

When Mozambique won its independence, the location of ultimate authority over the Mozambican territory shifted from Portugal to Mozambique. The purpose of sovereignty is largely to be able to define and implement policy in one's own territory. As such, sovereignty becomes the legal base from which the Government of Mozambique (GoM) negotiates the terms and conditions of its international engagements, including its relations with donors.

## A Donor Characteristics

The rhetoric around donors and aid is strong. Donors like to be portrayed as do-gooders who administer funds in an attempt to alleviate poverty. They are concerned with the effectiveness of the aid they provide to help poor people. However, this is only a partial understanding of the true nature of donors.

To figure out what drives donors, we find good guidance from the Danish philosopher Søren Kierkegaard and former French President Charles de Gaulle.

According to Kierkegaard (1855, cited in Hong and Hong 2009), 'all true help-ing begins with a humbling':

> This is the secret in the entire art of helping. Anyone who cannot do this is himself under a delusion if he thinks he is able to help someone else. In order truly to help someone else, I must understand more than he—but certainly first and foremost understand what he understands. If I do not do that, then my greatest understanding does not help him at all. If I nevertheless want to assert my greater understanding, then it is because I am vain or proud, then basically instead of benefiting him I really want to be admired by him. But all true helping begins with a humbling. The helper must first humble himself under the person he wants to help and thereby understand that to help is not to dominate but to serve, that to help is not to be the most dominating but the most patient, that to help is a willingness for the time being to put up with being in the wrong and not understand what the other understands. (Hong and Hong 2009: 45)

The first thing to remember when studying donors and their behaviour is that they are foreign governments, or international institutions, which foreign gov-ernments influence and control. Some bilateral donor agencies are relatively independent institutions, separate from their government's foreign service, either as separate ministries or agencies (e.g., until recently the UK's Department for International Development and the United States Agency for International Development (USAID)). Others are integral parts of their government's foreign ministries (e.g., the Netherlands and Denmark). However, whatever the insti-tutional set-up is, or appears to be, development aid is an integral part of any donor country's foreign policy, though rarely the most important one. Security and commercial concerns normally far outweigh the aid considerations, and the question relates rather to the extent to which aid is instrumentalised in donor countries' pursuance of the other two.

The differences between countries' institutional set-ups of foreign policy formulation and management lie only in the level at which, and in how much detail, the co-ordination between aid and other foreign policy areas is pur-sued. To maintain the cash flow, donors must satisfy the interests, values, and incentives of their governments while at the same time providing them with the expected results. Therefore, one cannot understand donor behaviour and the institutional development around aid (instruments, architecture, conditional-ity, and volume) without analysing the evolution of donor countries' foreign policy concerns. For any country, foreign policy is a derivative of domestic policy. To understand donors, a good point of departure is to remember the words of President Charles de Gaulle: '*Les etats n'ont pas d'amis, ils n'ont que des intérets*' (translation: 'States do not have friends; they only have interests') (Haskew 2011: 187). Such interests may change from time to time, leading the same donor countries to adopt different policies over time. Their behaviour, but not always their narrative, will reflect this.

In the following, we discuss trends and defining moments in Mozambique's relations with its donors. What has driven the donor agenda, and how has

Mozambican society absorbed this? How has it mitigated and adapted to donor demands, and how has it influenced key institutions for economic development?

## III DONOR RELATIONS AND TRENDS IN UNDERLYING DRIVERS

The nature of relations between donor and recipient countries has evolved over time, but there is still fundamentally a lot of truth in the old saying: 'He who pays the piper calls the tune'. However, it sometimes happens in perfect disguise:

> The right to self-determination for the Mozambican people was the objective of the struggle for independence (from Portugal). The Lusaka Agreement is the internationally recognized legal instrument that grants this right to the Mozambican people. (Chissano 2019)[4]

Mozambique's independence from Portugal, and indeed the country's sovereignty, is the result of a persistent and successful diplomatic campaign supported by armed struggle. The creation of a sovereign Mozambique came about because FRELIMO's young diplomacy won the hearts and minds of countries of the world, which, with few exceptions, extended their diplomatic and sometimes economic and military assistance to the Mozambicans' struggle for the right to self-determination. According to Panguene (2019),[5] 'Mozambique is the result of international solidarity'. Being able to rally international solidarity and support around its struggle for independence was the first step and, in substance, what granted Mozambique sovereignty. The country's founders were united in FRELIMO, an institution, which by nature was dependent on international support and donations.

### A The First Decade after Independence – A True Alliance

After independence, Mozambique sought help from the socialist bloc, because its leaders believed in and wanted Mozambique to aspire to their development model. Mozambique served as a frontline player in the cold war, in exchange for which the Soviet bloc provided economic and military assistance. This was a true alliance founded on shared visions and foreign policy concerns. The donors exercised little coercion in political, economic, and social policy, and when some donors occasionally tried to impose military conditionality, Mozambique was able to resist it[6] (see Veloso 2007).

---

[4] Unpublished quote from Joaquim Chissano at Diplomatic Symposium in Homage of the 80th Anniversary of H. E. Joaquim Chissano, former President of the Republic, held on 22 November 2019 in Maputo, Katembe 3D Tent.
[5] Unpublished quote from Armando Panguene at Diplomatic Symposium in Homage of the 80th Anniversary of H.E. Joaquim Chissano, former President of the Republic, held on 22 November 2019 in Maputo, Katembe 3D Tent.
[6] Such as the Soviet Union wanting a large navy base in Nacala for its Indian Ocean fleet, which NATO and thus some of Mozambique's donors would consider as a game changer.

Mozambique's donors were few and, although they sometimes included co-founding programmes (especially the UN and the Nordic countries), they can be grouped into four clear groups: (i) the Soviet/Eastern bloc including Cuba, (ii) the UN agencies, (iii) non-governmental organisations (NGOs) from Europe and the USA (mostly left wing and faith based), and, increasingly, (iv) the Nordic countries, the Netherlands, and Switzerland (the like-minded group).

Socialist development models were dominant at the time. Although some of the policy choices in economic development and agricultural strategies followed in this period failed to produce positive results and prosperity, they were not seriously contested. The Soviet Union, GDR, Bulgaria, and the UN agreed with the GoM on the way forward for agriculture. Price controls (inherited from colonial rule), accelerated mechanisation, and state farms, including conscripted labour in some cases, were the recipe everyone agreed on in the policy circles in Maputo.

Extensive consultation and other forms of interaction with the peasants were common practice in the framework of a 'people's democracy'. Likewise, central planning was the norm at that time, but the State Central Plan was a harmonised set of sector policies and provincial plans created through exercises that started at the district level. These exercises were undertaken and predominantly led by Mozambicans. The plans, particularly at district level, included the contributions of communities and workers.

Up to 20,000 foreign technical advisers and volunteers, known as *cooperantes,* helped to implement the policies and strategies. Unlike donor-funded consultants and advisers decades later, they did not usually coordinate and prioritise policy. Policy was formulated and controlled by FRELIMO and the government, whereas implementation was heavily assisted by donors, as testified by Mutemba and Salomao.[7]

The policies and institutions of price controls (even on traded stables), mechanisation, and state ownership of the production apparatus developed under conditions of extremely high state legitimacy. There were no issues around voice, participation, and political accountability. President Samora Machel enjoyed extraordinary popular support (Newitt 1995). The high degree of political instability and violence, successfully attributed to foreign countries funding insurgencies, did not affect state legitimacy. The local media labelled the Mozambican National Resistance (MNR) insurgency as 'armed bandits', and donor countries knew that the MNR had been created and funded by elements from ex-colonial rule, Rhodesia, and South Africa, with a view to destabilising and eventually provoking regime change. Mozambique's very sovereignty and independence as a state were at risk, and the image of the enemy was clear. The war effort was justified, and low state capacity and lack of economic progress were explained by external destabilisation and colonial heritage.

---

[7] Recent interviews with former Ministers of Finance and Planning.

Even in the early 1980s, when the Nordic countries established embassies in Mozambique, there was little debate about legitimacy, accountability, and participation. Mozambique was a front-line state and important in the struggle against apartheid, which is probably the strongest and most resilient political solidarity project between Western Europe and Africa ever known. The anti-apartheid solidarity project at large commanded broad-based political backing in most European parliaments and populations as well as in the UN, and criticism of Mozambique was rare. The few concerns that did arise among donors typically related to human rights. The concept of judicial independence was not recognised by the socialist regimes, and when dissidents to the FRELIMO government were sentenced to death or long prison terms by executive order (or courts under direct instruction from the executive), Nordic donors were uncomfortable and faced questions. However, the brutality and cruelty of the MNR insurgency and the apartheid regime's brutality at home overshadowed this and were debated much more in European capitals. Gersony's account expressed the common understanding of donor countries about the insurgency in Mozambique:

Most significantly, RENAMO's[8] inward expansion into Mozambique required rapid recruitment, achieved overwhelmingly by the forced conscription of unwilling civilians.[iv] Direct killing of civilians, along with a myriad of human rights violations, manifested in murders, routine brutality, and large-scale massacres. In addition to using indiscriminate violence during military operations, RENAMO leveraged terror to enforce control over new recruits and the local population. New recruits were coerced to murder their family members, while other common acts ranged from facial and bodily mutilation to the use of land mines and burning people alive. (Morgan 1990: 49)

To understand where the Mozambican elite and FRELIMO come from as regards their relations with donors, it is important to remember the nature of the relationship. There was no explicit conditionality. The former Eastern bloc donors introduced no policy-based development contracts, no performance indicators, or no structural or quantitative benchmarks. It was an alliance built on shared ideology and shared foreign policy concerns that defined a common enemy as well as mutual security concerns. The relationship was much more than one of aid. Economic and technical assistance agreements were technical, not policy conditioned, and embedded in agreement on policy at a much higher level.

To understand the Mozambican elite's practices today, it is equally important to remember how this relationship changed and when. The spirit of the 'Decade of the Victory over Underdevelopment' was in trouble before Samora Machel died in 1986.

Although the peace agreement with RENAMO was still ten years away, and the structural adjustment programme only started in earnest in 1987,

[8] Mozambique National Resistance (MNR) changed its name to *Resistência Nacional de Moçambique* (RENAMO) in 1982.

the FRELIMO government was already beginning to lose its grit in the early 1980s. The combined effects of war, the second world economic crisis (a sharp increase in interest rates and oil prices), and a persistent drought lasting more than three years caused sharp declines in the economy, and Mozambique's sovereignty was increasingly being threatened.

Mozambique's joining the International Monetary Fund (IMF) and signing the Nkomati Accord with South Africa show that the FRELIMO government was already on its knees in 1984, despite a very different public rhetoric from Samora Machel. The Nkomati Accord, in particular, was regarded as a defeat in many circles and by some regional leaders as an outright treason. Mozambique had to make enormous diplomatic efforts to try to explain to its peers why a no-aggression pact with the apartheid regime was necessary.

The disillusionment and loss of grit already in the early 1980s influenced the strength of many government institutions. Civil servants experienced great difficulty in implementing the plans and projects they were supposed to manage due to an increasingly obvious discrepancy between means and ends (human and capital resources and policy objectives). The difficulties were explained by the armed insurgency (*por causa da guerra*), but it became increasingly clear that the war was not the only problem.

We know from mainstream management literature that staff motivation is a main driver of institutional efficiency. Staff need motivation to believe in what they do, feel that they have the confidence of their managers, and relate to clear performance criteria, that is understand their institution's mission and their own role in it. Remuneration is important insofar as it has to reach a certain level but, above that, salary can largely be taken off the table in terms of motivation.

When the World Bank and the IMF came to Mozambique in 1986 to formulate and help implement the structural adjustment programme (SAP), civil servants' self-esteem and confidence in the GoM were already low. Mozambique had become a demoralised country in many ways.

The traditions and approach of the Bretton Woods institutions did not make things better. The imposition, especially by the World Bank, of new working methods and the support of hordes of foreign consultants often led to weakening national institutions, turning them into rubber-stamping entities. The SAP itself caused public sector salaries to shrink significantly, often below the subsistence budget level for a family.

## B Structural Adjustment and Privatisations before Peace and Elections

The timing of the SAP from 1987 to 1995, the Rome Peace Agreement in 1992, and the multiparty elections in 1994 created an institutional framework where formal political power, but not economic power, was shared. Donor conditionality was introduced, and it changed the rules of the game, but the main players stayed the same.

By the mid-1980s, Mozambique was economically broke and faced increasing trouble with its creditors. The government, especially Joaquim Chissano, saw that Mozambique's sovereignty was threatened by the combination of domestic economic factors and geopolitical developments in the world, not least reduced support from the socialist countries, in particular the GDR whose intelligence had concluded that the war could not be won by military means (Wolf and McElvoy 1997).

Referring to Table 10.1, the constitutional reviews in 1986 and 1989 bear witness to externally prompted policy changes of the most fundamental calibre (Table 10.1, column 3). The first review was necessary to accommodate structural adjustment and privatisations, and the second in 1989 paved the way for multiparty democracy.

The sequence of policy changes shows that the FRELIMO government took the difficult decision to lead the institutional changes, although some powerful leaders in the party were not convinced that the capitalist model was better. However, Chissano's giving up control of policy formulation was necessary to defend sovereignty and FRELIMO's leadership in the long term. 'In the words of Luis Bernardo Honwana: "Chissano assured the preservation of the state and the continuation of the state without interruption".'[9]

The IMF and the World Bank introduced a much more direct contractual relationship with Mozambique as donors. The relationship with the IMF and the World Bank was the start of direct and explicit conditionality in development assistance. There was little *ex ante* belief that the former socialist GoM would wholeheartedly implement the SAP with fiscal austerity and privatisations as the main ingredients. It was evident from the start that the policy and institutional reforms embedded in the SAP would have negative effects on influential parts of Mozambican society and political costs for the government and ruling party. In exchange, Mozambique received loans, technical assistance, and, not least, rescheduling with the Paris Club of creditors.

Along with the introduction of capitalism, the most important institutional change in independent Mozambique was the adoption of multiparty democracy. This was not directly included in the agreements with the World Bank and IMF, but it was supported by a number of countries that were also Mozambique's main bilateral donors and creditors in the Paris Club, as well as by influential board members in the IMF and World Bank. Some of these countries were even in 'constructive engagement' with the apartheid regime underpinning the RENAMO insurgency. (The Reagan administration introduced only very limited sanctions in 1985).

Although somewhat controversial, it can be debated how conducive multiparty democracy is to economic growth (e.g., in the case of the 'Asian tigers' in the 1980s), especially in Mozambique's income level in the early 1990s.

[9] Unpublished quote from Luis Bernardo Honwana at Diplomatic Symposium in Homage of the 80th Anniversary of H. E. Joaquim Chissano, former President of the Republic, held on 22 November 2019 in Maputo, Katembe 3D Tent.

Particularly in a poor country like Mozambique, democracy itself constrains the ability of institutions to formulate and implement reforms. In a government's lifetime of five years, there will be two years with elections (municipal and parliamentary/presidential), which will divert efforts and drain resources from managing the country. This is caused to some extent by the incumbent government's abuse of public resources for campaign purposes, but it is by no means the only reason. Even in mature democracies where governments do not practise outright abuse of public resources, the waste of bureaucratic resources for short-lived campaign-motivated policy formulation and dissemination will drain resources (e.g., the preparation of two sets of policies and fiscal acts and Medium Term Expenditure Frameworks (MTEFs) in election years).

Short-lived governments, even from the same political party, will experience frequent changes of policy and of personnel in key positions. All politically headed institutions rely on personal networks, particularly when institutions are weak. Loyalty becomes more important than technical/professional ability, and high attrition, a sense of a lack of fairness, and insecurity of tenure undermine morale. The contribution of multiparty democracy has a negative effect on institutional efficiency.

In addition to the above, there is little doubt that the sequencing of the introduction of capitalism and multiparty elections in Mozambique has affected the country's current economic performance. It allowed the GoM (FRELIMO and the Mozambican elite) to create new rules of the game and to continue to occupy the economic sphere before political power sharing took place. Economic adjustment was carried out and state assets were sold to leading Mozambicans (allies or members of the government) while RENAMO was still a guerrilla force, rather than a political party, fighting or waiting in the bush to be demobilised – far away from the decisions about economic reforms being taken in Maputo. When successful elections finally took place, and the new parliament began work in earnest in 1995, the SAP was all but over and most state assets had been sold, often to people with sector knowledge from the defunct state companies. This is not remarkable as there was no private sector to recruit from or sell to, but it supported an understanding or underlying notion of entitlement in the elite, who claimed and possibly believed that they could make the companies viable in a liberal economy.

Until the SAP, the political leaders and the emerging middle class in general had been complying with the code of values and practices of probity and respect for public property. The privatisations that occurred started to change this with the emergence of an incipient business class, more affluent and dominated by former political leaders and civil servants who had benefited from the privatisations. Those who did not benefit felt excluded. Furthermore, the first and subsequent multiparty elections created, for the first time, the awareness that FRELIMO might eventually lose the elections with subsequent widespread purges to follow, as RENAMO would need to accommodate its members and sympathisers in the state apparatus. All of this brought growing levels of insecurity and fear and a sense of urgency to 'get something before it is too late'. It entailed corruption, compounded by a pervasive feeling and belief that FRELIMO members and sympathisers were more entitled to grab public assets than RENAMO members, who were portrayed as having colluded with external forces to destroy the country: 'Mozambique privatized more than 4000 companies, about 80% benefitting Mozambicans and on highly advantageous conditions' (Diogo 2013: 158).

There is speculation that the sequencing of the SAP was a deliberate tactic by FRELIMO to retain control of economic assets and that the Bretton Woods institutions accepted this – knowing that the economy would suffer in the medium term – to put the GoM in the driver's seat of reforms. While the deep motivation of either party is difficult to ascertain, there was at least one additional element in FRELIMO's motivation: The prospect for a lasting peace would be considerably better if demobilisation and reintegration happened before the elections. (See Appendix with separate note on peace process).

Contractual policy-based lending was not the only new feature in Mozambique's relations with donors. The IMF required negotiations to take place directly with Mozambique's Central Bank and Finance Ministry, whereas assistance from other donors was negotiated through the Ministry of Foreign Affairs and Cooperation. This separated the groups and privileged policy dialogue between the IMF and the Ministry of Finance as something all other donors depended on.

It had been intended that the SAP would address the structural imbalances in the de facto bankrupt Mozambican economy, introduce the fundamental institutional changes that capitalism entails, and succeed in implementing them. However, the whole operation was poorly timed and sequenced, and this had significant consequences for the way the Mozambican elite chose to mitigate and adapt to those changes. Even on its own isolated terms, sequencing of the SAP was unfortunate. While 're-installing' market-based prices (which had never been relied on in colonial times) was meant to reinvigorate Mozambique's comparative advantage, the economy was unable to produce a supply response to changes in relative prices.

There were a host of reasons for this, the most fundamental being that the programme went ahead in the middle of a devastating war, while Mozambique's main comparative advantage from factor endowments lay with agriculture and natural resources. The war kept the farmers away from their land, as most were waiting in refugee camps or in the suburbs of garrison towns. The war also made it impossible to transport and market coal and other natural resources, to get inputs and spares, and to market the little output farmers managed to produce in less war-affected areas. Even the distribution and sale of cheap power from Mozambique's dams crippled, as RENAMO sabotaged power lines. Few tourists dared visit the beautiful beach resorts and nature parks in the war-ravaged country.

Almost all the sectors where Mozambique could conceivably have a comparative advantage in a market-priced economy – except fisheries, which was already in Japanese and Spanish hands (through in-flagging and Mozambican silent partners) – were unable to respond to the changes in relative prices.

Therefore, while the expected positive effects of the SAP were late to arrive, the negative effects for previously established industries that had been protected by administered prices and exchange rates, on the other hand, took almost immediate effect. State enterprises across the manufacturing sector, which were overwhelmingly involved in import-substituting production, became unprofitable. The companies were subsidised by the government to avoid massive lay-offs and limit payroll cuts. However, once such subsidies became visible in the budget, they formed part of the fiscal equation in the IMF programme and were therefore short-lived. As the GoM still owned and controlled large sections of the banking sector, many subsidies were eventually moved to the banks, which were obliged to extend loans (e.g., under the heading of restructuring for viable commercial use) to unviable companies. This mining of the banking sector still affects the financial sector today.

At first, these companies could not make money, so they had to be subsidised in some way by the GoM until peace and foreign investors returned to favour their businesses. Eventually most companies' assets were used for other purposes and/or partly sold to foreign investors:

The case of cashew showed that the World Bank/IMF imposed reforms with a view to securing the best possible farm gate prices to farmers (privatise and remove export bans and tax). When the government resisted in an attempt to save the cashew processing industry, the World Bank blocked a US$50 million loan tranche. When the GoM finally agreed, it became clear that the people who had bought the industries from the GoM – claiming they would try to safeguard ten thousand jobs – had colluded with the bank and Indian traders and used the installations for storage and trade only, exporting only raw nuts. The industry died and no new trees were planted (see, e.g., Diogo 2013).

When contract aid in the form of policy-based lending was introduced into macroeconomic management and reforms in key industries, the GoM managed the legitimacy aspects of the situation in two ways. To the Mozambican population, the negative effects of the economic policy of the period were successfully attributed to the conditionality of the IMF. The GoM played the 'victim card'. It still controlled the press at home and took great care to protect other donors from bad press. In addition, in much of the international media, SAPs were reported to leave a trail of social havoc in Africa. This created the momentum for a group of countries and the UN to say that structural adjustment could be done with a human face. The same group of countries were the main bilateral donors to Mozambique. They found the IMF's policy recommendations and conditionality to be misguided and were optimistic about prospects for Mozambique.

In the mid-1990s, state legitimacy was still relatively intact in Mozambique. FRELIMO's election victory in 1994 was credible and accepted by RENAMO, although only after pressure from peers in the region (the ANC). Donors helped to convert Maputo's finest cinema to serve as the parliament, and opposition politicians started to appear in local media on a daily basis and in the streets and cafés of Maputo. Things were also opening up in terms of accountability. The budget, which had previously been a state secret, appeared on the front page of a new and popular daily publication, *Media Fax*. Most people witnessed a remarkable improvement in living standards compared to the times of war. Double-digit growth rates, including in family agriculture, made the GoM popular at home and abroad.

At the Consultative Group meeting in Paris in 1994, donors pledged almost US$1.4 billion in new investment projects (including technical assistance), against a gross domestic product (GDP) of around US$2.5 billion and a government budget of around US$1 billion. Clearly, the GoM was not able to absorb this money in any sustainable way, as it was unable to finance the ensuing recurrent costs.

These conditions led to a handful of donors (Swiss Development Corporation, USAID, EU, and Denmark) working successfully with the Central Bank and Ministry of Finance and Planning to make the Bretton Woods institutions accept a more expansionary fiscal policy, enabling faster growth of social sectors after the war. This limited group of donors financed the servicing of some of Mozambique's debt prior to the highly indebted poor countries' debt cancellation initiative and import support schemes, which generated counterpart revenue in Metical for the government, which the IMF agreed not to sterilise.

This all took place in a 'Marshall Plan' atmosphere, and it was believed that subsequent economic growth and the cancellation of HIPC[10] debt would enable medium-term sustainability. Mozambique was internationally recognised as a post-war rehabilitation success (OECD 2002). The real test for this to become a more sustained operation was whether donors in general would be prepared to finance recurrent costs, including salaries.

## C Scaling Up for a New Darling

This preparedness came from a strong international agenda at the time, which drove donors to provide higher volumes of aid and new instruments. It helped the GoM to expand services to the population but also maintained the country's dependency on donors even as GDP and domestic revenue grew. It created an aid architecture in the name of host country ownership that allowed and increasingly encouraged isomorphic mimicry, bordering on ventriloquism.

The World Summit for Social Development in Copenhagen in 1995, the largest gathering of world leaders at the time, reached a new consensus to put people at the centre of development. Its declaration and agreed programme of action made donors in all countries increase their volumes of aid especially towards social sectors. The summit cemented the discourse by UNICEF and

[10] Heavily indebted poor countries.

the Nordic countries of structural adjustment with a human face and obliged governments to formulate poverty eradication policies and plans (PRSPs), which became a condition for debt relief under HIPC.

Universal access to education and health was a tall order at the time, and pursuance of the '20/20 objective' faced particular obstacles. This objective required governments to allocate 20 per cent of their budget and donors to allocate 20 per cent of their support to social sectors. However, the Mozambican government established a budgetary regime of 20 per cent for education and 14 per cent for health (Diogo 2013: 157).

If most donors had one strong notion at the time, it was a narrow concept of sustainability, requiring Mozambique to meet future recurrent costs on the investments made by donors. Bilateral agreements between donors and the GoM usually included clauses about counterpart funds and promises by the GoM to staff and maintain the infrastructure created by donor-funded projects. At that time, few donors would get board approval for projects if this were not addressed.

Especially in the social sectors, the cost structure was heavily tilted towards recurrent costs. Unlike roads or power lines, where recurrent costs are closer to physical maintenance, the social sectors needed staffing and consumables on a completely different scale. The costs of the salaries of teachers, nurses, and doctors, and of drugs, which the GoM and most donors agreed were necessary for rapid social expansion, were impossible to finance given traditional conventions in development aid. Thus, the need to find a way to help the GoM finance the recurrent costs of rapid social expansion was a main driver of the establishment by bilateral donors of a new institution known as general budget support (GBS).

This drive by donors to increase absorption capacity by financing recurrent costs, including salaries, made Mozambique exceptionally dependent on donors. The GBS instrument also relocated the centre of dialogue between Mozambique and the donors from the Ministry of Foreign Affairs and Cooperation to the Ministry of Finance and Planning. In this way, one of the most important elements of Mozambique's foreign policy – its relations with donors – separated from other foreign policy elements in a different institutional frame. This compartmentalisation of the formulation and management of foreign policy was appropriate and worked at the time.

The GoM never formulated a full and coherent aid strategy, although donors encouraged it to do so. It was not required to and probably did not want to. Indeed, in 1994, when the Ministry of Cooperation and the Ministry of Foreign Affairs merged into the current Ministry of Foreign Affairs and Cooperation (MINEC), there were discussions about the need to formulate an international cooperation strategy. However, this was abandoned to make room for the flexibility that is always needed when dealing with different donors. Experience had shown that donors had different policies and procedures, and, quite often, it was difficult to predict the amount of funding the donors would pledge and actually disburse. Against this backdrop of uncertainty and sizeable challenges, it was felt that the broad objectives stated in the government's five-year plan were good enough to guide all stakeholders.

Given the overall context of the development challenges, the GoM had to be pragmatic and agree to meet the donors' essential objectives. At the same time, a government that is under pressure from donors to accept reforms, and from local interest groups to resist reforms, can manage the situation by avoiding taking (explicit) strategic decisions (Castel-Branco 2008).

The GoM embedded its priorities in the international aid effectiveness agenda, which was gaining strong momentum at the beginning of the century. The donor countries themselves were driving this agenda primarily through the UN, OECD, and the EU, which showed committed and competent leadership on the issue (e.g., by Poul Nielson, Richard Manning).

The Millennium Development Goals, New Economic Partnership for African Development, and the Paris Declaration, through which donor countries agreed to harmonise and increase aid/GDP ratios to get closer to the UN target of 0.7 per cent, were the main signposts for donors. Volume, ownership, and harmonisation through alignment and division of labour became the key elements in almost all donor countries' aid policies and their country assistance strategies in Mozambique.

The GBS and sector-wide approach (SWAP) became significant instruments for aid delivery, and the dialogue structure was built around them. Consequently, it became increasingly difficult and awkward for Western donors to be outside the group. The group all but monopolised policy dialogue with the GoM, and produced and shared important information only internally. A number of donors joined the GBS instrument for the wrong reasons, some with very small budgets both in absolute terms and relative to their total country budget. Aid effectiveness at the aggregate level may not have been their main concern, but a seat at the table conducting policy dialogue was. Free riding became a problem (Bourguignon and Platteau 2015). More importantly, though, there was – among most donors, including the pioneers of GBS – an underlying assumption that the instrument and broad co-ordination around it could be used for coercive purposes.

Since 2000, the government had been conducting half-yearly policy dialogue meetings with the EU, as agreed under Article 8 of the Cotonou Agreement. At these meetings, cooperation was evaluated and political issues were discussed. The GBS donors who were not members of the EU wanted to have a similar type of dialogue with the GoM. As the EU's own code of conduct obliged its Commission and member states to subscribe to the broadest-possible host country-led dialogue mechanisms, the solution adopted was to establish a forum for all GBS donors.

Donors organised themselves into sector working groups with common funds, each with a lead donor. The working groups reported to the deputy heads of missions (heads of agencies where these were outside the diplomatic missions), who reported to ambassadors and high commissioners. By 2009, donors had a dozen common funds and working groups reporting to the top two levels, where the 19 donors selected a rotating chair in a troika format that was entrusted to undertake policy dialogue with the government's key ministers. The donor troika was given a secretariat, paid for by donors with overseas development assistance (ODA). The GoM's troika was headed by the Minister for Finance and Planning for fifteen years and by the Minister for Planning and Development during President Guebuza's ten-year tenure, when the Ministry for Finance and Planning was split in two. The other members were the Governor of the Central Bank and the Minister of Foreign Affairs and Cooperation.

The whole machinery was based on a memorandum of understanding (MoU) between donors and the GoM, which set out the underlying principles, that is of democracy, good governance, and sound macroeconomic management (column 3 in Brown's model – see Table 10.1) for budget support. The MoU also described the main tasks for implementing sector reforms, plans and targets (column 2 in Table 10.1), joint reviews and assessment of progress (PAP), and financial pledges each year. The matrix contained more than forty indicators, often tied to different tranches of donor disbursements, but they were mostly output and process indicators rather than real outcome assessments. The indicator framework measured how many children were enrolled in primary school and how many legal cases were awaiting settlement in the courts. It said little about learning outcomes and access to justice. It allowed for isomorphic mimicry, sometimes even encouraged it, because meeting output indicators became the objective. The system was successful in increasing aid, which became a reference point at many international gatherings on aid efficiency and harmonisation.

Although many reforms remained shallow because of the high ambitions of donors and frequent changes of direction, and because GoM would not allow reforms to deepen (i.e. in agriculture and the justice sector), much of the institutional capacity building undertaken with donor assistance in the 2000s was solid.[11] This was the case with the strengthening of public financial management, including a strong tax authority and public budget and accounting system. According to the IMF (Dabàn and Pesoa 2007), 'Mozambique is a promising example of successful budget reform in Africa'.

Even where the reforms were shallow, there was little long-term systemic damage to the institutions due to isomorphic mimicry. Donor money and Mozambican human resources were wasted at times, but because the reforms remained shallow, they did little real damage. This occurs primarily when ill-conceived reforms and policies are implemented.

---

[11] It is beyond the scope of this chapter to evaluate the numerous reforms attempted with donor assistance. Other parts of this volume assess a number of reforms in detail. We merely discuss the institutional consequences of general donor conditionality and the way aid was delivered.

The GoM had few concerns about harmonisation, which was considered a win–win situation. The increased aid flow allowed the government to expand the social sectors and infrastructure, etc., which underpinned its legitimacy. The alignment with Mozambican procedures made the donors more anonymous and the GoM more visible. It also made the government a larger economic agent in the market (as a buyer of goods and services with donor money) helping to feed the bourgeoisie.

Aid dependency did not increase in nominal terms during the 2000s, as GDP and the government's domestic revenue picked up. However, more donor funds enabled the expansion of government spending in the social sectors and infrastructure, etc., above what would have been possible without increasing and more aligned assistance. More importantly for ownership, donors expanded policy-based granting and lending (which had previously been restricted to macroeconomic and strategic sectors imposed by the World Bank/IMF) to almost all sectors and main donors. Common funds and donor-financed technical advisers and consultants, embedded in Mozambican institutions to assist primarily with policy formulation, became an implicit part of conditionality. Policy formulation and dialogue, along with target setting and measurement of results, took place at sector level. As the whole aid architecture was organised around the group of donors providing GBS (and the USA), donors were able to influence policy formulation at the sector level at very early stages and to follow through with implicit conditionality in policy dialogue with the government all the way to the macro level, that is in discussion related to fiscal policy such as MTEFs, yearly budget allocations etc.

This had two profound effects: (1) it weakened the GoM's policy co-ordination efforts by strengthening the sectors vis-à-vis the Ministry of Planning and Development, enabling isomorphic mimicry and approaching ventriloquism and (2) it side-lined the Ministry of Foreign Affairs and Cooperation (to ceremonial duties) and compartmentalised foreign policy.

The government's policy-coordinating ministries, which are vital for ensuring true government agency (the ability to formulate and manage a central policy and plan), were not strong and were further weakened in terms of resources vis-à-vis sector ministries. At the same time, they were subject to unclear mandates that the donors could influence.

The international winds were favourable to Mozambique through most of the 2000s. The Paris Declaration came shortly after FRELIMO's and Guebuza's disputed election victory in 2004, and the aid effectiveness agenda remained alive, albeit weaker, with the Accra Agenda for Action in 2008. Although donors expressed increasing concerns about issues of democracy, human rights, and corruption, the aid kept flowing and even increased. The GoM got used to the donors 'barking but never really biting'.

Economic growth and aid flows continued strongly correlated throughout the 2000s. However, the Mozambican economy did not achieve structural transformation and became a consumption-driven economy where agriculture fed the rural population while the formal sector – urban elite and middle class – depended on the export of a few commodities, a handful of large foreign direct investments, and development aid. As much of the development aid was delivered as programme aid, it financed public salaries and procurement. This meant it was strongly focused on public servants and – via public procurement – the private sector, which supplied goods and services to the public sector, often through shallow trading companies owned by the Mozambican elite and dependent on foreign supplies.

The notion of entitlement in elite quarters thrived in this environment, and Mozambique's ranking in many international indexes of governance and corruption dropped. However, legal convictions in a few high-profile corruption cases (i.e. the Director of Airports) calmed things down. Donors agreed that Mozambique was heading in the right direction despite occasional setbacks:

## D The Thrill Is Gone

All this changed slowly but surely as the decade of the 2000s approached its end and donor countries faced a series of new challenges in the world. Mozambique lost its status as a donor darling as aid money was needed elsewhere for less altruistic purposes, while the GoM did not respond to Western governments' concerns about security and commerce. Donor assessments of Mozambique were carried out in a new light, and the attraction of isomorphic mimicry became more difficult. Contested elections, which were the norm, were no longer accepted. Donors evaluated reforms related to legitimacy and accountability as being too shallow, and the GBS ran into increasing trouble as an instrument of aid. At the same time, the aid architecture built around this institution remained intact.

The Western governments' war on terror became wider and costlier. Afghanistan and Pakistan, in particular, consumed enormous resources, but events in West Africa and the Horn of Africa also caused Western countries to reconsider their priorities. A worldwide economic crisis also strengthened critical voices in Western parliaments on aid spending and conditionality, including on migration. Donor budgets reduced and moved increasingly north in Africa.

The developments at the Horn of Africa spilled over and had repercussions in Mozambique. Somali piracy and human traffickers reached the shores of Inhambane, and Mozambique was unable to patrol its territorial waters – 200 nautical miles along 2,000 kilometres of coastline. This was also one of the reasons, why the smuggling of drugs from south Asia through northern Mozambique intensified, and it was almost risk free. At sea, there was no law enforcement and on shore, there was 'loosely governed territory' as the CIA put it.

Western shipping was threatened in Mozambican waters and the drug trade that ran almost unhindered through Mozambique helped to finance the Taliban and Al Qaeda killing of Western soldiers in Afghanistan. This was bad enough on its own, but Western governments were also thinking ahead about the safety of future gas operations in the Mozambican seas. Some of the major donor countries at the heart of the G19 structure now also had security and commercial concerns about Mozambique. (As one senior diplomat in Maputo put it at the time: 'There needs to be a roll-back of sovereignty'.)

President Guebuza and his government were insensitive to this. Guebuza forged ever-closer ties with China and Vietnam (awarded the third Global System for Mobile licence in Mozambique in 2010 along with enormous infrastructure contracts for a stadium, the Maputo circular road, and the bridge to Catembe). Furthermore, parts of the GoM, and Guebuza himself, openly supported a local business person, known to Western governments as a drug dealer.[12]

The Western governments' security and commercial concerns had little to do with the underlying principles of GBS. Nevertheless, they influenced the donor–GoM dialogue because this was where Western governments had leverage. Donors raised their commercial and security concerns in discussions under headings such as corruption, the Extractive Industries Transparency Initiative, state capacity, and independence from private interests. However, above all, the donors' new priorities and concerns influenced their assessments, and they became more determined to act together.

The GoM had plenty of opportunity during the 2000s to observe the donors' rising concerns about democracy, governance, and human rights elsewhere in Africa without cutting aid, but unlike Nigeria, Uganda, Ethiopia, and Tanzania, for example, the GoM did not address Western security concerns. Therefore, Mozambique was measured by another yardstick, and as the donors' list of critical issues grew, an increasing number of the G19 donors wanted to test the underlying assumption that GBS could be used for coercive purposes.

The opportunity to do so came with the troubled elections in 2009. A new political party, Mozambique's Democratic Movement, popular with intellectuals, NGOs, and donors, was prevented from running in seven of the country's eleven provinces. Donors delivered a démarche to President Guebuza on the issue prior to elections but to no avail. FRELIMO declared an enormous victory (with a qualified majority in parliament) and inaugurated President Guebuza's second term in office. All GBS was frozen shortly after. The decision followed many weeks of discussion between donors and was conveyed to the government in a short letter signed by all nineteen heads of missions, which claimed there had been a breach of the underlying principles in relation to democracy and governance. (See Table 10.1, column 3.)

This was a wake-up call for the GoM. A number of Mozambique's ambassadors in donor countries were called home to explain how this had surprisingly happened. The GoM concluded that donor agencies were highly decentralised

---

[12] Mohamed Bachir Suleman, who was officially declared a drug kingpin by the US administration in 2009.

and that ambassadors of donor countries in Maputo had been calling the shots. While this was partly true, many heads of missions had just been delivering what their governments wanted. The institutional factors that contributed to the GoM's poor assessment of the general donor drift was a more fundamental reason why the GoM was taken by surprise.

Donors discussed policy co-ordination and priorities primarily with the Ministry of Planning and Development (MPD), and the presidency took over an increasing number of the activities that the Ministry of Foreign Affairs and Cooperation (MINEC) had traditionally been tasked with. State protocol moved from MINEC to the president's office, and ad hoc consultations with resident ambassadors by the president without the participation of the Foreign Ministry began to occur along with a very busy calendar of international visits by heads of state. MINEC was sidelined from the aid dialogue and Mozambique made little use of its embassies abroad to understand the policy shift under way in most Western donor countries. Foreign policy co-ordination had been weakened.

The freezing of GBS hardened the relationship between the GoM and donors from then on. However, at the time, the GoM decided to please the donors, at least superficially, and initiated a series of reforms on transparency, participation, and state legitimacy (election law, EITI, etc.).

GBS resumed later the same year, but the policy dialogue became increasingly rigid and unproductive. If the GoM told donors about its fundamental challenges and troubles, these issues would soon become the subject of donor-prompted reforms and be measured in the joint indicator frameworks that guided GBS disbursements. Neither donors nor the GoM tried (in earnest) to change the dialogue architecture and ways of discussion to open the debate, separate policy debate from conditionality, and analyse issues in fora where they naturally belonged by people who knew what they were doing. Everything entered the policy dialogue in the G19. Donor-prompted reforms were formulated with the assistance of donor-funded consultancies and advisers and were presented to the MPD together with an already agreed financial pledge from donors.

In identifying institutional drivers, it is important to remember that development cooperation is by nature a very long-term endeavour, whereas politicians in Western democracies are elected for and often optimise their political capital over the medium term. There are of course exceptions to this but, generally speaking, bilateral donors are impatient by nature because ministers want to attract domestic attention. Thus, personally ambitious ambassadors and heads of aid agencies frequently mirror this and lack the courage to propose and design aid finance that reflects the true cost, in terms of time and money, of reforms and capacity building.

Very often, development ministers get attention by announcing new initiatives and funding to assist poor countries that have specific issues. This is often through vertical programmes (like support to combat HIV) rather than horizontal ones, as are often more called for (e.g., integrated support to primary healthcare). Such support programmes are much more complicated and difficult to explain, and GBS is only a front-page story when a development minister decides to stop it (showing resolve to taxpayers). This means that results achieved are not at the centre of the political debate about aid in Western democracies. Many aid agencies struggle to document their results and disseminate them to the broader public, but there is little uptake of this by journalists and politicians.

Almost all the successful cooperation programmes that have delivered good results are likely to have been initiated by the predecessors of current development ministers who are often from a different political party, as alternation of political parties holding power is common in Western democracies. No development minister dreams of extending the timescale and providing new funds for a support programme that was optimistically designed and approved by a predecessor from a different political party. As a result, there was constant pressure on the GoM to adopt and implement new reforms designed by donor-financed consultants in the image of donor countries themselves. This drive often led to isomorphic mimicry, either by default or by design, to keep the funds flowing.

Arrogance and urgency on the donor side (we need to discipline the GoM before it is too late) and on the GoM side (revenues from natural gas will soon outstrip donor assistance by far, so we do not need donors any more) made the atmosphere worse. Donors began to pay more attention to the household surveys and poverty assessments showing a very slow decline in poverty rates and no decline in the numbers of poor people (headcount), as well as marked regional differences that favoured the ruling party and discriminated against the opposition's heartlands.

Another contested election in 2014 proved to donors that the reforms initiated after the freezing of GBS in 2010 were shallow. Laws had been passed and procedures adopted. Nevertheless, they did not really change the state of democracy. The reforms were isomorphic mimicry – Mozambique was still not a multiparty democracy as defined and understood by Western governments. The main opposition party, RENAMO, gave up on democracy and went back to the bush to reinitiate insurgency to claim control over at least a part of the country. The GoM's legitimacy was seriously questioned, although irregularities were no more serious than at earlier elections and no more problematic than in other countries receiving GBS at the time, that is Burkina Faso, Uganda, and Ethiopia.

The drivers that had made the institutions of SWAPs and GBS a success and had pushed aid volumes to unprecedented heights had all but vanished. The international winds that had carried the agenda forward weakened even more during the 2010s as the Arab Spring, the success of ISIS, and the war in Syria created enormous security problems on the EU's doorstep and produced huge flows of refugees into Europe. This strengthened right-wing nationalist forces in the EU and the USA and put further pressure on aid budgets (cuts and re-direction to emergency aid in North Africa and the Levant).

Western donor countries were already starting to turn their backs on GBS at the beginning of the decade and would have abandoned the instrument no later than the early 2020s anyway (leaving such instruments to a few such as the EU and World Bank). The aid strategies, such as harmonisation, including GBS, that were formulated from around 2012/13 by countries, which had previously been stalwarts of aid effectiveness, clearly show that they were moving on and had new concerns and priorities. As international solidarity weakened, Western governments were clearly looking for more direct and endogenous reasons in recipient countries to justify reduced budgets and the move away from GBS and the Paris agenda at large towards results-based contracts and projects that could underpin their commercial and security interests.

The Guebuza government provided plenty of ammunition for this move – even a crash landing of donor relations – when it guaranteed three large commercial loans for partly fraudulent purposes to three state enterprises without informing parliament and donors. More than US$2 billion of new commercial debt was contracted in an attempt to create a maritime security infrastructure in Mozambican hands before the gas bonanza, when almost all security contracts would traditionally go to international companies with close links to foreign governments. A combination of incompetence and greed overwhelmed whatever good intentions there had been in the project, and Mozambique as a state was left with massive (defined as unsustainable by the IMF) levels of new debt that would inevitably be partly repaid by donor funds.

To Western donor countries, this was proof of further deception and mimicry. In partnership with the GoM and the IMF, they had promoted and financed what had been acknowledged as successful public financial management reform, and it was now clear that it had not solved the problem of accountability in any way. Donors acted swiftly and united around a single condition for resuming GBS: an international forensic audit showing what the money had been used for and by whom, along with appropriate legal follow-up of the findings. This condition was unmanageable for the GoM, as it would create decay in the ruling party. When the audit was finally carried out and revealed massive fraud and embezzlement, little or no action was taken by the Attorney General. After months of waiting and pressure from civil society and donors, lower-level officials were indicted and the legal processes crept forward very slowly.

Unlike the situation in the late 1980s, when Western donor countries had insisted on fundamental reforms (Brown's column 3 – see Table 1), Mozambique's sovereignty was not under threat in 2016. RENAMO's new armed insurgency was containable and the GoM knew that oil and gas revenues could replace donor aid within a decade. As it was not threatened, sovereignty served as FRELIMO's bulwark.

It was only when the British and South African courts complied with requests from the US courts and arrested former Finance Minister Manuel Chang and a number of foreign bankers involved in the scandal that the Mozambican Attorney General became busy. Although the Mozambican elite would not be threatened by withheld donor funds, high-ranking and centrally placed bankers and former members of the GoM who would cooperate with the US courts in a plea bargain could cause serious trouble.

While the freezing of funds by donors did not lead to change in the Mozambican leadership or its attitude, events in the justice sector in the region may well have influenced the mind-set in the ruling party, not least the indictment and order for preventive prisoning of former President Jacob Zuma. There is little doubt that these events inspired FRELIMO and the government to demonstrate stronger efforts to pursue corruption, although there still seemed to be some selectivity in deciding which cases to pursue.

Moreover, an often-ignored part of this phenomenon is the delays and the destruction of projects that infighting among the elite caused to programmes and projects financed by donors and foreign direct investment (FDI). When elements from different factions of the elite (FRELIMO) were destroying and stealing each other's projects (rent seeking or not), this helped to create a corrupt or 'do nothing' approach in key institutions that prioritised, coordinated, and approved vital investments for economic growth. It seems that the GoM was trying to use the greater caution of economic actors and the damage caused to FRELIMO's image by the debt scandal to reduce and control such infighting.

The political consequences of the debt scandal are far from over, but three things stand out:

1.  FRELIMO is still in government and has probably strengthened its position as compared to 2016. This has happened partly as a result of the manipulation of election results – intimidation, rigging voter lists, and direct ballot stuffing – but it is also the result of a completely disorganised political opposition and a new resolve within FRELIMO itself, to not lose power.
2.  Donors are coming back on stream, despite the lack of consequences for top party officials of the debt scandal and despite the election cheating that is incomparable to any previous elections.
3.  Donors have undermined their own previous institutional strengthening and capacity-building efforts by starving the government institutions of finance and choosing to finance NGOs, the UN, and standalone, vertical projects instead. The organisations pay good salaries (well above those paid by GoM) and have now hired a significant number of the best higher-level government officials and specialists in various sectors.

The donor's financial body language did not lead to any change of attitude in the FRELIMO leadership. Rather, it may have helped to strengthen the resolve of the party leadership, as the Mozambican economy proved remarkably resilient to the financial crisis that followed the loans and was made worse by freezing of donor funds. Events have proved that FRELIMO's sense of entitlement is still very strong, and it continues to be possible to equate Mozambique's sovereignty with the party's grip on power. Concessions were certainly given to some donor countries with large commercial investments, but not to the donor group at large.

Now, a few years later and after one much contested election since the non-declared state guarantees were revealed, many donors, including the largest and most intense defenders of the disbursement freeze, seem to have reviewed their standards for governance and democracy. The US Millennium Challenge Corporation has approved Mozambique for massive new financing and the IMF is finalising a new programme with the GoM, which will pave the way for the EU to re-engage. Most bilateral donors will follow, although their budgets have been reduced compared to the last decade (for other reasons) and their aid instruments have changed.

While the SWAPs in education and health may survive for some years in significantly reduced versions and with more strings attached, GBS is de facto dead for bilateral donors in Mozambique. No other known aid instrument can provide the volume of funds that GBS did, and Mozambique will have to raise revenue in other ways, including closing deals with foreign companies in the gas and natural resource sector. Most of these companies are from Mozambique's donor countries.

There will be new instruments and new players in combinations that cannot be assessed and dealt with in a narrow donor-recipient perspective. Investments from private foreign companies, pension funds, government guarantees, loans, and grants will be bundled and advanced under strategic international agendas like climate change and job creation to suit donor countries' interests.

When Mozambique begins to develop serious international commercial cooperation, it will with large and powerful foreign companies. They will use their governments to pave the way for general conditions for commercial exchange, sometimes even conditions for specific transactions. These foreign governments are Mozambique's main donors and there is an increased risk that Mozambique will be totally dependent on foreign governments and companies in the coming decades. As revenue from gas and coal depends on the operations of a handful of foreign companies from almost the same countries as the main donors, the risk to Mozambique of external shocks – political or market based – may be harder to mitigate than ever before.

It is interesting that many of the large contracts for oil and gas exploration were signed at the time of the crisis between the GoM and its donors. The same is the case for some of the security contracts for exploration, and foreign security companies are now openly operating in northern Mozambique.

## IV CONCLUSIONS AND LOOKING AHEAD

For more than three decades Mozambique's government nurtured donor relations in ways that allowed its partners to pursue the objectives, targets, and modalities set by the international development agenda and even make Mozambique a reference case in international aid. It allowed donors to challenge its ability, but never its authority. Consequently, the basic political fabric stayed the same, while the social and economic sectors were subject to ambitious donor-prompted reforms in exchange for high levels of external finance. Some reforms were shallow because donors were too ambitious or impatient, or because Mozambique's ruling party would not allow them to deepen. Nevertheless, much capacity has been built, which makes Mozambique comparable with many of its African peers, which had a thirty-year head start on Mozambique in independent development.

This changed over the last decade. Long-term, harmonised development aid fell out of fashion as Western countries became much more concerned with instrumentalising aid in pursuit of security and commercial interests. In this situation, it is detrimental to Mozambique's sovereignty to approach foreign countries primarily as donors. The loss of agency that Mozambique's government has experienced – and deliberately allowed in significant areas of the social and economic sectors in exchange for finance – must be rolled back. Development partners have changed their ways because their objectives have changed. The GoM is no longer dealing with a group of relatively well-coordinated donors, which are primarily pursuing effective development assistance and overwhelmingly playing transparently and by internationally agreed objectives and standards. Mozambique must prepare to no longer deal with donors pursuing poverty alleviation, but with foreign countries with a much more intertwined agenda of foreign policy concerns – security, commercial, and aid – that are bundled and labelled in tactical ways to serve each country's interests.

Mozambique's government would be well advised to revamp institutions (organisations and ways of working) used to dealing only with donors and to build institutions and structures suited to dealing with foreign countries. A holistic view of relations with foreign nations is now more relevant than a primary and overwhelming focus on the donor aspect of that relationship. A ministry of finance and planning should probably not be at the centre of dealing with foreign nations. It has other important functions (the plan, budget, and treasury) that deserve strong and persistent performance, including building coherence and discipline around national plans.

Mozambique would benefit from having a strengthened foreign service, which ensures that all aspects of foreign policy are (un)covered in relations with foreign countries. It would be advisable to create clear rules of the game for all foreign investments (public and private) through a solid public investment plan, with priorities based on clear objective criteria (internal rate of return). To do so, and indeed to police such plans and strategies, the government could establish strong interfaces between MINEC, MEF, and key sector ministries like the Ministry of Industry and Trade, the Ministry of Energy and Mineral Resources, and the Ministry of Agriculture and Rural Development under the leadership of the Prime Minister.

The proposed institutional arrangements could ensure better co-ordination and mutual understanding among the agencies and, most importantly, more coherent interaction with foreign countries and organisations to ensure that they support Mozambique's priorities rather than a rapidly changing kaleidoscope of their own ideas. The government should sometimes say 'no thank you' to aid money. If the government can align all foreign investments (ODA and FDI) to a coherent development strategy and investment plan, there is a chance that Mozambique can choose and receive the investments that will help finance inclusive growth, not just those that will ensure the greatest profit to foreign companies and sections of the Mozambican elite.

APPENDIX

## Note Regarding Peace Process

President Chissano believed that a lasting peace depended on RENAMO accepting a possible defeat in Mozambique's first multiparty elections. Many donor countries as well as the UN shared this belief. Few imagined that RENAMO could win the elections, and efforts had to be made to avoid an Angolan scenario where UNITA went back to war as soon as the election results were announced in 1992.

The main ingredients in this strategy were time and social and economic reintegration. Repatriation of the refugees and displaced people (including rank and file RENAMO fighters and families) took place to work the land and experience at least one good harvest. On demobilisation, combatants received a kit of hand tools, seeds, and a pension for two years to assist their social and economic reintegration, in addition to training through short skill-development courses.

As for the RENAMO leadership and cadres, temporary lodging was provided in hotels, as well as the allocation or facilitation of access to houses and cars in Maputo, provincial capitals, and some districts. Milling machines and agricultural tools were also distributed to some RENAMO leaders, to assist their economic reintegration (Manhenje).

Indirect evidence that the UN shared the GoM's analysis of critical moments in the peace process was that it took a very long time – even according to UN standards – to mobilise the UN peace keepers. Knowing that it would be impossible to sustain funding for more than a couple of years for what was, at the time, one of the world's largest peace-keeping operations, it was critical to time the operation right. As the blue helmets finally rolled into Mozambique during the spring of 1994 – more than 18 months after the Rome Agreement (October 1992) – farmers had already harvested one good crop and were witnessing the next one growing in the fields. People from both sides in the war were living and working together and the RENAMO leadership was enjoying a comfortable life in the better neighbourhoods of Maputo and Beira. Returning to fighting in the bush was not a very attractive alternative, and RENAMO's acceptance of defeat in the elections was *sine qua non* for any structural adjustment programme to succeed and indeed for economic growth in general.

# The Uncertain Development Impact of the Extraction Sector

José Jaime Macuane and Carlos Muianga[1]

## I INTRODUCTION

Until recently, the contribution of the extractive sector (mining and gas) to Mozambique's Gross Domestic Product (GDP) was below 4 per cent, on average. Agriculture is still regarded as the basis of the country's development, employing more than 70 per cent of the labour force and contributing over 20 per cent of GDP. This situation is set to change with the growing importance of the extractive industries, particularly the gas industry. The production of this commodity started in 2004 with the Pande and Temane projects of the South African company SASOL. The discovery of vast gas reserves in the early 2010s in the northern province of Cabo Delgado heralded the beginning of a new economic era, with prospects of foreign direct investment (FDI) that would dwarf the current US$14 billion GDP and make an estimated US$50 billion contribution to state revenues by 2050 (República de Moçambique 2018). The past decade and a half have also seen an upsurge of investment in the mining sector. Kenmare's heavy sands project in Moma began in 2007 (US$460 million), and the coal projects of Rio Tinto and Vale (US$1.3 billion) in the Tete Province and the Montepuez Rubi Mining gems project all started operations in 2011 (Deloitte and EITI 2018).

Recent developments in the gas sector, including the investment projected for the coming decades, have prompted significant changes in expectations over its contribution to the economy. The main gas projects in the Rovuma

[1] The authors would like to acknowledge the inputs to the research and to the study and the support throughout the process by the EDI and Copenhagen University teams: Finn Tarp, François Bourguignon, António Cruz, Inês Ferreira, and Johnny Flentø. We would also like to acknowledge the valuable comments and contributions made by Vasco Nhabinde, from the Ministry of Economy and Finance of Mozambique, and Tony Addison. These contributions notwithstanding, the authors are responsible for the content of the chapter.

basin (Areas 1 and 4) are expected to attract investment of over US$50 billion in the next few years (IMF 2019).

The Area 1 consortium, led by Total (formerly by Anadarko),[2] announced its final investment decision (FID) in June 2019. The consortium plans to invest about US$23 billion, and the project is expected to generate US$2.1 billion in state revenues over a twenty-five-year period. It is also expected that about 5,000 workers will be employed during the construction phase and US$2.5 billion will be devoted to the purchase of goods and services from Mozambican companies. In July 2020, Total signed all financing contracts, securing all the US$15.8 billion funding for its Rovuma project.[3] This followed a decision by the United States (US) EXIM Bank to secure a loan of about US$4.7 billion to finance American suppliers to liquefied natural gas (LNG) development in Mozambique. Additionally, it is said that the loan could support about 16,700 American jobs over the five-year construction period.[4] An additional US$1 billion from United Kingdom Export Finance is on track to be approved, and this would support about 2,000 jobs for British people.[5] These recent developments mark a turning point in the negotiations to start LNG production in the Rovuma basin, but they also show the limited leeway of the country in influencing these investments to have a more substantial impact at the national level, especially in job creation.

The ENI and Exxon Mobil-led Area 4 project announced its initial investment decision in October 2019. The FDI of about US$30 billion was to be announced in the same year but it was postponed to an unknown date.[6] Reports from June 2020, citing the National Petroleum Institute (INP) chairman, claimed that the ENI-led Coral-Sul Floating Liquefied Natural Gas project was on schedule, and production was expected to start in 2022.[7]

The combined gas projects are set to produce about 30 million tonnes of LNG per year – about '17 per cent of total global trade or 7.5 per cent of projected LNG global trade by 2026' (IMF 2019: 4).

Mozambique's resource abundance also prompted an upsurge of investment, especially FDI, in extractive resource-related projects and other auxiliary

---

[2] Area 1 LNG shareholders are Total E&P Mozambique Area 1 Ltd (26.5 per cent), ENH Rovuma Area 1, a subsidiary of the state company ENH (15 per cent), Mitsui E&P Mozambique Area 1 Ltd (20 per cent), ONGC Videsh Ltd (10 per cent), Beas Rovuma Energy Mozambique Ltd (10 per cent), BPRL Ventures Mozambique B.V. (10 per cent), and PTTEP Mozambique Area 1 Ltd (8.5 per cent).

[3] https://clubofmozambique.com/news/mozambique-lng-consortium-led-by-total-has-already-signed-all-financing-contracts-o-pais-164769/

[4] www.bloomberg.com/news/articles/2020-05-15/u-s-throws-down-gauntlet-to-china-with-mozambique-gas-mega-loan

[5] https://cartamz.com/index.php/politica/item/5533-emprestimos-de-5-7-bilhoes-de-usd-para-a-total-vao-garantir-18-700-empregos-nos-eua-e-no-reino-unido

[6] https://furtherafrica.com/2020/06/05/mozambique-expects-exxon-gas-fid-in-2021/

[7] https://allafrica.com/stories/202006040840.html

services, and the country became one of the most important destinations of FDI in sub-Saharan Africa. This investment upsurge lasted 2010–16, when the economy was hit by a crisis of commodity markets, which affected some of the main Mozambican export commodities, in particular coal. The investment decline was further aggravated by the discovery of undisclosed loans – known as 'hidden debts' – of about US$2.2 billion in 2016 to supposedly fund three government-related security companies on the assumption that they would profit from the new gas industry (Roe 2018).

The growth of the extractive sector has triggered discussions in various academic and political contexts over the prospects of natural resource exploitation in Mozambique and developing countries more generally. One of the issues in discussion is the country's prospects to reduce or even end its dependence on external resources – development aid and FDI – which dominated and drove the country's economy in most of the post-independence period (Vollmer 2013). Another point is the prospect of economic transformation, using natural resources to boost industrialisation, transfer technology, and knowledge to local companies, create economic linkages, and stimulate the diversification of the economy (Dietsche and Esteves 2018). Managing the macroeconomic dimensions is also crucial: These include the avoidance of 'Dutch disease' and other adverse consequences of a sudden increase in foreign exchange inflows linked to the natural resources boom. Henstridge and Roe (2018) suggest that governments can use macroeconomic policies – fiscal and monetary – to mitigate the risk of the disease. However, they warn that in low-income countries such as Mozambique, 'fiscal policy has to bear the brunt of responsibility, with monetary policy normally taking the stage as a supporting player' (Henstridge and Roe 2018: 165).

As the literature suggests, diversification of the economy and economic transformation require an industrial policy and a certain level of state capacity, which depend on the relations between and support of relevant political actors (Whitfield et al. 2015). Also important is understanding the political economy underlying a development strategy, and the issues arising from this, for example, the conflicting interests emerging from the implementation of the policy or strategy, the winners and losers in this process, and the ability of the state to manage such conflicting interests in a productive way (Chang and Andreoni 2020).

Since the turn of the twenty-first century, especially over the past decade, it has been widely argued that 'industrial policy is back', with new approaches, theories, and practices on the topic emerging. Most economists agree, however, that the reliance on 'perfect markets' has not brought about satisfactory economic and social outcomes in most of the developing world (Rodrik 2004; Stiglitz 2017; Chang and Andreoni 2020). With regard to sub-Saharan African economies (including Mozambique), for instance, it has been documented that, despite the high growth rates of the past two decades, these economies 'have experienced unsatisfactory productive transformation' and low job creation in manufacturing and services (Aiginger and Rodrik 2020: 1). Most of these countries' growth patterns are highly dependent on commodity production and exports, including minerals, gas, oil, and other agricultural commodities. These countries have failed to translate their resource endowments' 'comparative advantages' into structural transformation and significant poverty reduction. The case for industrial policy and its application in the extractives sector is built upon these and other issues related to concerns about avoiding the negative effects of resource dependence.

In the context of the growing extractives-led development agenda, Dietsche (2018b) argues that, despite its increasing importance, the contribution of industrial policies and strategies to structural transformation is not clear, especially regarding what positive institutional change they can bring about that can sustain the gains in economic transformation over time. The same is applicable to the promotion of local content strategies and policies as a way to link foreign investment to the local economy, as these are seen as having an equally narrow focus and lacking the facility to track the contribution they make in terms of productive knowledge and technologies. Amidst the lack of consensus on the contribution of industrial policy to economic transformation, the best that public authorities can do in this context, according to Dietsche (2018b), is to provide institutions that reduce transaction costs.

Buur et al. (2019) argue that for large-scale natural investments to attain their transformational goals, they need to create the proper conditions to prevent key actors from blocking their implementation. They analyse the relations between three main actors – ruling elites, investors (international and domestic), and local populations – and suggest that the way these actors negotiate their interests can affect the creation of conditions favourable for the implementation of large-scale investments in natural resources with positive development effects. In particular, they call attention to the importance of the relations between ruling elites and local populations, which have generally been neglected in studies in this area.

A World Bank study argues that countries that are successful in using natural resources – natural capital – to promote development are those that invest in other forms of capital, such as human and productive capital, and even in assets in other countries. The study further asserts that the appropriate use of natural capital depends on the quality of the governance and institutions of the country (World Bank 2014). This discussion is linked to the question of how much to save or spend when a country has a resource windfall, as in the case of Mozambique. A key issue is the creation of a sovereign wealth fund (SWF) from natural resources revenues and how this should be used, which has implications for the implementation of policies for structural transformation.

The insight of the above-mentioned scholarship is that a development strategy should link the exploitation of natural resources and the use of its revenues to the country's development goals. It should define a framework of relevant national and sectoral policies, and identify institutions for the articulation and coordination of different interests. In the case of Mozambique, the National Development Strategy (NDS) 2015–2035 highlights the role of natural resources in the structural transformation of the economy. Therefore, to some extent, the NDS has an extractives-led development component. The question is how this plays out in practice and what the prospects are for that contribution to be effective. In Mozambique, with its political patronage and clientelism, intra-ruling elite competition, limited productive base, weak state capacity, high level of poverty, and recurrent fiscal deficits, the prospects of the current resource boom leading to economic transformation, despite its considerable potential, are at best equivocal. The critical issue of how and when to use the resources was clouded by the debt crisis, when loans were contracted and then restructured on the assumption of future revenues from gas projects. This casts doubt on the willingness and ability of the political elites to use extractive resources for economic transformation.

This chapter analyses the prospects for the natural resources/extractive industries to contribute to economic transformation in Mozambique from an institutional perspective. For this purpose, we address the institutional dynamics of the resources sector, their effects on economic transformation, and the underlying causes.

The chapter is structured as follows: Section II presents the conceptual and analytical framework. Section III describes policies and institutions that are relevant to the process of structural transformation based on the development of the extractives sector. Section IV assesses how policies and institutions relate to the process of economic transformation in the context of the growing importance of natural resources. Section V explains the dynamics of economic transformation and institutional performance, looking at their underlying causes. The chapter closes with conclusions and an assessment of the opportunities for natural resources to play an effective role in economic transformation, taking into account the context of Mozambique.

## II CONCEPTUAL AND ANALYTICAL FRAMEWORK

In line with the objective of this chapter, it is important to understand the building blocks of the analytical framework – namely structural transformation, natural resources or extractive industries, and institutions – from a conceptual and theoretical perspective.

Structural transformation, as it is broadly understood, 'requires raising productivity across different sectors and achieving competitiveness in progressively higher value-adding sectors' (Khan 2018: 42). It is also understood as the reallocation of economic activity across the broad sectors of the economy, namely agriculture, manufacturing, and services (Herrendorf et al. 2013). It entails the reallocation of resources – including labour – from less to more productive sectors of the economy and involves changes in the level of productivity across sectors.

With regard to extractive industries or natural resources (we use the two terms interchangeably), we refer to mining and oil and gas (O&G). Whilst in some cases (e.g., revenues) the chapter will consider aggregate data on the two sectors, the analysis of the sectoral dynamics will focus on large-scale investments or megaprojects (investments of more than US$500 million), which are the dominant feature in the sector.

Here, institutions are considered as the political, social, and economic rules of the game – formal and informal norms – that are largely accepted and mediate the relations between individuals and collective actors in society (North 1990; North et al. 2009). In the economic realm, these institutions can be at different levels, such as belief systems and formal rules on the one hand, and the institutions responsible for putting the rules in place (governance) and allocating resources, as the market, on the other (Diestche 2018a). The analytical framework of the chapter is built on the concepts of new institutional theory and the role and effects of institutions on development (North 1990; Acemoglu and Robinson 2012).

We also assume that institutional performance is contingent on the context, and that similar institutions might perform differently in different contexts (North 1990; Khan 2010;). One explanation for this variable performance can be found in the interface between formal and informal institutions. As Khan (2018) argues, inclusive institutions – considered as having a positive effect on development everywhere (Acemoglu and Robinson 2012) – might have different outcomes in developing countries, where powerful groups constrain broad-based growth. Therefore, we do not adopt a normative vision of the 'best institutions' but rather use the theoretical categories to describe the institutional dynamics and their impact on development.

We also consider policies as a type of rule, although they are much easier to change than institutions (Khan 2018). As a complement to this analytical framework and to provide a more critical and nuanced view of institutions, we refer to more recent literature on the political economy of development in the context of Africa and Mozambique, based on the political settlement framework, applied to governance and large-scale natural resources investment (Weimer et al. 2012; Whitfield et al. 2015; Macuane et al. 2018; Buur et al. 2019; Macuane et al. forthcoming; Salimo et al. 2020;). Whilst we acknowledge that institutional analysis and political settlement analysis are different approaches (Behuria et al. 2017), we depart from the institutionalist analytical and conceptual framework to identify the analytical categories of our study. Additionally, we consider that outcomes depend on a combination of institutions and the context, among them the role of actors (groups and individuals) and their 'holding power' – the capacity to engage in conflict with other actors and survive, as well as the power to enforce the existing rules (Behuria et al. 2017; Dietsche 2018a). This approach is important if we are to identify specificities of the empirical reality we are analysing, where there is a high level of informality and where manifestations of a Weberian state and impersonal institutions are not the norm (North et al. 2009; Khan 2010). An example of the application of the political settlement framework to natural resources investment is the creation of pockets of effectiveness (PoE) – organisations with high performance in a context of a generally inefficient public sector (Roll 2014) – in the gas sector in Africa generally (Hickey and Izama 2017; Hickey 2019) and in Mozambique particularly (Macuane et al. forthcoming).

To operationalise the framework, we adopt Baldwin et al.'s idea that 'Institutional analysis comprises a suite of approaches for understanding the various ways in which formal laws and informal social or organisational norms shape policy actors' behaviour' (Baldwin et al. 2018: 2). A challenge of the institutional analysis is the difficulty in empirically operationalising its variables (Baldwin et al. 2018; Siddiki et al. 2019). In operational terms we adopt the multi-level institutional analysis proposed by two of the principal exponents of the field, Williamson and Ostrom (Williamson 2000; Ostrom 2005; Baldwin et al. 2018; Diestche 2018a; Siddiki et al. 2019), the levels being (i) the social level – socially embedded norms; (ii) the institutional environment or policy level – formal rules of the game; and (iii) the governance level – the operation of the rules of the game. This means that we will analyse the formal rules and policies, how they are implemented, their interface with the informal rules, and their outcomes. The analysis also has to be sensitive to the role of external actors. This is particularly relevant in the context of Mozambique, where high dependence on external resources is a key element in its political economy.

In the case of Mozambique, where the contribution of the recent boom in natural resources to economic transformation is yet to be seen, the argument will be forward looking. However, some past and present dynamics are important in building up the argument. In this regard, we look at the following elements: (i) institutional environment and performance – that is formal rules/ legislation, policies, their implementation, and outcomes in relation to the structural transformation of the economy; (ii) the history of the contribution of natural resources to the economy; (iii) the role of natural resources in economic transformation, namely policy and institutional choices and their effects; (iv) the underlying dynamics of policy and institutional choices and their economic transformation effects, with a focus on the relation between actors, institutions, and outcomes.

## III POLICIES AND INSTITUTIONS

In the last two decades, with the increasing importance of the extractive industries in the economy, Mozambique has passed extensive legislation in the extractives sector, with a focus on the mining and O&G sector and its respective tax regime. Concerns over the governance of the sector, along with demands for more accountability on the management of natural resources revenues, led Mozambique to join the Extractive Industries Transparency Initiative (EITI) in 2009 and become a compliant member in 2012.[8] Since then, Mozambique has produced eight reports, and improved its transparency, making the contracts of the natural resources' concessions publicly available. Reforms in the sector have included the creation and strengthening of the administrative (as the Extractive Industries Tax Unit within the Mozambique Tax Authority), regulatory (as the INP and the National Mining Institute – INAMI), and accountability institutions (as the Administrative Court), combined with the increasing participation of civil society in the debate on the contribution of natural resources to the country's development.

Whilst these reforms have improved the governance of the sector and responded to some of the challenges of its increasing importance, their effect on the country's economic transformation is more difficult to quantify. Not only is the importance of natural resources a relatively recent phenomenon in the economy, whose effects are still to be seen, but, as we have seen, economic transformation is underlain by a complex web of institutions, policies, actors, and dynamics. In this section, we describe some of these, as the background to assessing the role of institutions in the emerging resources economy of Mozambique, and the dynamics of economic transformation more broadly. In this regard, we analyse the NDS, which is the government's main instrument for presenting a vision of the contribution of natural resources at the macro level. We also assess the key structuring policies for economic transformation and the normative instruments of the extractives sector itself.

## A National Development Strategy

Mozambique has a set of long-term and mid-term instruments that are the framework of government policy and plans. The main long-term document is Agenda 2025 (Comité de Conselheiros 2013). The vision was originally defined in 2003 and revised in 2013 to align it with emerging challenges. According to Agenda 2025, development must be endogenous, prioritising the national market through the widening of the production base of small and medium enterprises (SMEs).

In 2014, the country adopted the NDS 2015–2035, based on the general lines of Agenda 2025. The main objective of the NDS is to improve the living conditions of the population 'through structural transformation of the economy [and] expansion and diversification of the production base' (República de Moçambique 2014b). Thus, industrialisation is at the core of the programme, and both agriculture and the extractive industries are aligned with the objective of structural transformation of the economy. The NDS acknowledges that

[8] The EITI is a global standard for the transparent and accountable management of natural resources, to which countries adhere voluntarily. To be considered compliant, a member country must complete steps defined in the Standard. For more details, see https://eiti.org/document/eiti-standard-2019 and https://eiti.org/mozambique.

the national economy generally and the rural economy particularly depend heavily on the exploitation and use of natural resources (land, agriculture, and forests). The strategy further includes the creation of an Investment and/ or Stabilisation Fund from the surplus revenues and resource windfalls resulting from the extraction of natural resources (República de Moçambique 2014b: 20). The linkage of the mineral resources sector with industry will be through vertical integration of minerals production – coal, gas, ore, and mineral sands – assuring their transformation into industrial goods for national and international markets. In the area of the extractive industries, the strategy includes (i) the establishment of a partnership between national and foreign enterprises in the exploitation of resources; (ii) the involvement of national enterprises in the provision of services; and (iii) the creation by the state of public–private partnerships (PPPs) for the provision of goods and public services (República de Moçambique 2014b: 37).

In the extractive industry – especially coal, gas, and heavy sands extraction – the main challenge posed by the NDS is the need for domestic transformation – a process, which, according to the strategy, may address the problems, related to primary commodity export dependency.

Considering natural resources as fundamental for economic growth and structural transformation, the NDS points out that sustainable management is, among other factors, key to their success. This strategic vision supports, at least partially, the established argument that 'resource-based accumulation is not an end in itself, but a means or stage(s) within a dynamic process of industrialization and economic transformation' (Castel-Branco 2011: 2). However, how resource-based accumulation should translate into industrialisation and economic transformation is not systematically explained in the strategy. Moreover, the NDS does not set out how the revenues generated from the country's natural resources will finance the policies for transformation.

The NDS does not mention explicitly the role of FDI, but inferences can be drawn about the role of FDI in development from the assertion of the need for the state to avoid investing in areas where the private sector can perform better, and from its encouragement of national companies to establish partnerships with foreign enterprises and, through them, potentially mobilise funding. The resources for the project of economic transformation will hypothetically come from the country's strategic and operational instruments of planning and budgeting, at the government and sectoral levels, and potentially from the above-mentioned Investment/Stabilisation Fund. Thus, for the NDS to attain its stated objectives, macroeconomic policies (fiscal and monetary), industrial policies, and relevant sector policies, especially related to the extractives, should define and determine the instruments for economic transformation. The following sections analyse the extent to which those instruments are consistent with the goals stated in the NDS with regard to the contribution of the extractives sector to structural transformation.

## B  Macroeconomic and Sector Policies

A set of policies creates an environment in which different economic and social actors can operate to generate structural transformation. These are the macroeconomic policies and key sector policies, but with a structural impact as the industrial policy. Macroeconomic policies (monetary and fiscal) play a central role in defining the conditions and directions of structural transformation. Their management is a major institutional factor determining the way the resources sector can effectively contribute to such a transformation. A major and widely discussed issue related to macroeconomic policy management in the context of extractives is how to avoid the adverse impacts of resource dependency, resulting, for instance, from a sudden increase in foreign exchange inflows – 'Dutch disease'. Mozambique is no exception, and major challenges regarding macroeconomic policy management are still to be addressed. These concern not only the role monetary and fiscal policy play in preventing Dutch disease but also, and fundamentally, their role in creating the conditions for structural transformation.

As argued in the most recent Industrial Policy and Strategy (2016–2025), productive linkages between domestic SMEs and megaprojects, particularly in the natural resources sector, are seen as a way to strengthen the domestic private sector (República de Moçambique 2016). These processes require commitment to the creation and improvement of institutional capabilities, in both the state and the private sectors, and at various levels (political, economic, organisational, and financial). These include coordination and investment capabilities, strengthening government financial capabilities through improved taxation, and a financial sector capable of financing productive investment. However, these commitments are set up, and whatever particular institutional and organisational capabilities are needed, the role of the state and the private sector in providing, through investment, the incentives to make them effective is central.

Complementary to the debate about industrial policy has been the discussion about local content (the participation of the national companies in the natural resources investment projects). This was initiated in 2007, but only in 2019 did the government approve a legislative proposal to be submitted for enactment by parliament. Discussions between the government and national private companies about how and to what extent Mozambican enterprises would benefit from the new developments in the extractive sector are the most contentious. Emphasis and interest, especially from the domestic private sector, have been particularly on the upstream sector of the resources industry (i.e. the supply of goods and services relevant to the operations of the gas projects).[9] The debate over the development of linkages is related

---

[9] There has been little discussion on the possibility of the development of the downstream sector, although, with respect to the O&G industry, policy discourse has emphasised the importance of this, especially in the NDS, discussed in the previous section, and the current industrial policy

to the fact that the main multinational corporations (MNCs) operating in the O&G sector in Mozambique have already approved their production plans for the next few decades, some of them including FIDs. FIDs for the projects in the northern Cabo Delgado province have created a set of expectations regarding the benefits of the gas exploitation to the country's development, including the business opportunities for domestic private enterprises (Muianga 2019a, b). However, most of these companies control global value chains (GVCs) within the industry and impose high international standards on their suppliers that local companies can hardly match. This poses the question as to how the natural resources projects can create opportunities for linkages that can contribute to the transfer of knowledge and technology for a sustainable diversification and structural transformation of the economy. The institutions and policies designed to respond to this question are described in the next section.

## C Policy and Institutional Environment of the Extractive Industries Sector

As mentioned before, the extractives sector considered here comprises large-scale mining and the O&G sector. Reforms in this sector have included the separation of the policy, commercial, and regulatory functions previously lumped together in one entity, such as the national oil company (NOC), a ministry, or agency. In the case of the gas sector, this was part of the so-called new institutional arrangements (NIA), following the Norwegian model, which was considered an example of good governance (Thurber et al. 2011). In Mozambique these reforms were reflected in the redefinition of the functions of the Hydrocarbons National Company (ENH), the NOC, which maintained the commercial functions but saw its former regulatory functions being allocated to the INP, as a result of pressure from the World Bank – Norwegian cooperation, the long-time donors to the sector (Macuane et al. forthcoming). The implementation of these reforms was more a strategic choice in a context of a country dependent on external resources than part of an internal agenda. In this regard, reforms were stimulated by increasing demands for the accountability of the sector in the international arena, embodied in the EITI, and by the need to attract FDI, which implied complying with international standards, to respond to pressures from donors and investors (Macuane et al. forthcoming). The disproportionate influence of external factors and actors' interests in the reforms to some extent explains the weak performance of above-mentioned commercial and regulatory institutions in this area, stemming from the limited

and strategy, 2016–2025 (República de Moçambique 2016). This may be explained by the fact that gas production has not yet started in the Rovuma basin. However, the possibilities of developing such downstream production appear to be very limited if we look at the structure of the gas industry, which consists essentially of primary commodity exporters.

commitment of the ruling elites to the process (Macuane et al. forthcoming). Specific reforms in the gas and mining sectors are presented below.

## 1 *Institutional Reform in the Gas Sector*

Well before these recent developments, Mozambique had set up new legislation and revised existing legislation, policies, and institutions for the 'promising' gas sector. The main policy instruments in the gas sector are the legal framework and the Natural Gas Master Plan (República de Moçambique 2014a), which regulate investment in and governance of the sector. Due to its specificity, this area has a specific legislation regime for investment, embodied in its core laws and regulations.

Recent legislative changes can be traced back to 2001, when the Oil Law was approved. Among its many initiatives, this introduced the direct participation of foreign enterprises and defined the mechanism of state participation in the sector. In 2004, the government approved the Regulations of the Oil Operations (Decree 24/2004) and, within this legal framework, a model concession contract was designed. In the same year, the INP was created. This took over the role of regulator (under Decree 25/2004). Two additional regulations were subsequently approved: for the licensing of premises for oil activities (Ministerial Diploma 272/2009) and the Environment Regulation for Oil Operations (Decree 56/2010).

This legal framework prevailed until the recent discoveries of gas, which made the existing laws obsolete. Under pressure from investors, the government proposed, and parliament approved, a new Oil Law, 21/2014, on 18 August 2014. Parliament also approved a law authorising the government to enact specific legislation on LNG in order to address the legal void for future investments in the Rovuma basin (Areas 1 and 4). Additional legislation was approved in 2014 and 2015, including regulations specific to the projects of the Rovuma basin (Law 25/2014 of 23 September 2014), the petroleum fiscal regime (Law 27/2014 of 23 September 2014, revised as Law 14/2017 of 28 December 2017), on the taxation and tax benefits of petroleum operations (Decree 32/2015 of 31 December 2015), and on the Environmental Impact Assessment (Decree 54/2015 of 31 December 2015). Subsequently, in 2017, additional legislation was approved. The fiscal legislation allows companies to recover part of the costs of their investments, and it is the responsibility of the INP to certify these costs to prevent companies from inflating them, hence reducing the revenues to be collected. The 2014 Petroleum Law includes provisions on local content, which consists of the participation of the ENH in all concessions and the involvement of local companies and markets in the procurement of goods and services for petroleum operations. The main concern relates to the weak capacity of the local companies to provide goods and services in terms of both scale and quality to meet the demands of the international companies involved in large-scale petroleum operations.

The Natural Gas Master Plan is consistent with the NDS concerning industrialisation and linkages. In this regard, it includes the development of an industrial zone with integrated support services in Nacala, Palma, and Pemba, a fertiliser plant, and a power plant. The Gas Master Plan promotes increased industrialisation of the country through the emergence of SMEs linked to the megaprojects.

A set of policy, regulatory, and administrative entities operate in this area: (i) the Ministry of Mineral Resources and Energy (MIREM), responsible for government policies; (ii) INP, the sector regulator; (iii) the public-owned company ENH, which participates in all O&G projects with a share ranging from 10 per cent to 25 per cent, and is the main shareholder of the Mozambican Hydrocarbons Company (CMH, a subsidiary of the ENH), which participates in the Pande and Temane gas ventures; (iv) Mozambique's Tax Authority (AT), responsible for fiscal revenues collection; and (v) the Administrative Court (TA), which plays the role of the auditor general and is responsible for the external audit (compliance and performance) of the whole public sector.

The INP is the entity responsible for coordinating the bidding process for the oil and gas concessions. It is therefore the main entry point for investments in this sector. The MIREM is responsible for policies related to natural gas (and mining) as well as the rest of the energy sector. It therefore coordinates the potential linkages between gas and coal extraction and power generation projects. The AT is the entity responsible for the taxation of gas operations, and in 2017, it created a specific unit to deal with extractive industries taxation. Finally, the TA is the entity responsible for auditing oil contracts and all operations related to revenues, including the revenues from natural resources received by public entities.

## 2 Legislation, Policies, and Institutions of the Mining Sector

The Strategy and Policy of Mineral Resources approved by the government in December 2013 states that mineral resources must above all benefit Mozambicans. Among its objectives is to make mineral resources one of the main contributors to industrialisation and country development, diversification, and economic transformation, as well as to the improvement of the balance of payments (Resolution 89/2013, article 4, a). It also aims to ensure the implementation of corporate social responsibility in the business sector involved in oil and mining activities and the attribution of benefits and special compensations to the communities where mineral extraction occurs.

As in the gas sector, investments in the mining sector are regulated through a specific law, the mining law (Law 20/2014 of 18 August 2014), which defines specific contracts for the different phases of the mining process, from prospection to exploitation. The law also regulates the different scales of mining (from big investments to artisanal mining) and licences for the trading of mineral products. Similar to the gas sector, there is a specific fiscal regime for the mining

TABLE 11.1 *Extractive sector main institutions*

| Type of institutions | Entities | Role |
|---|---|---|
| Legislative and accountability | Assembly of the Republic | Enacts legislation and oversees the extractive sector |
| Accountability | Administrative Court | Provide visa approvals regarding concession contracts and audits extractive related revenues |
| | Higher Authority for Extractive Industries (HAEI) | Controls extractive industries activities |
| Executive/policy/ Administrative | Government/Council of Ministers | Ensures the implementation of petroleum operations policy, approves regulations, and prepares legislative proposals |
| | MIREME | Policy development, implementation, and coordination |
| | Tax Authority (AT) – Extractive Industries Tax Unit (EITU) | Ensures the collection of fiscal revenues in the extractive sector |
| Regulatory | INAMI | Regulatory functions of the mining sector |
| | INP | Regulatory functions for upstream, downstream, and midstream operations |
| Commercial/Market | ENH | Commercial function and representing the state in petroleum operations |
| | EMEM | The public commercial branch and the represents the state in mining sector investments |
| | MNCs | Responsible for the main large-scale investments in natural resources |

*Source:* Authors' composition, sourced from various extractive sector legislation.

sector approved on 23 September 2014 (Law 28/2014) and revised on 28 December 2017 (Law 15/2017). AT and the Administrative Court also exert the same mandates regarding taxation and auditing for mining as in the gas sector.

The 2014 mining law created two entities, namely the High Authority for the Extractive Industry (HAEI) and the INAMI. The HAEI is a mixture of a regulatory and oversight body, comprising representatives of government, the National Assembly, and civil society. In the commercial area there is a state-owned (85 per cent) company, the Mozambican Company for Mineral Exploration (EMEM), created in 2009 with the objective of defending the interests of the state in the mining sector, managing the state's shares in mining investments, ensuring the participation of local companies, and promoting local content in the sector.

The institutions of both the mining and the petroleum sectors, apart from the HAEI, are under the tutelage of the MIREM, which plays the coordination and policy role. A summary of the main institutions of the extractive sector is presented in Table 11.1.

This institutional setting, comprising a set of legislation and policies, and the actors – MNCs, donors, public entities, organisations, and political actors – operating within it is key to understanding the contribution of natural resources to structural transformation. Consequently, it is important to analyse the performance of these institutions in interaction with the actors that operate within them, to understand their role in the process of economic transformation.

## IV NATURAL RESOURCES, INSTITUTIONAL FRAMEWORK, AND ECONOMIC TRANSFORMATION

The institutional setting (policy and legislation) of the extractives includes various elements with the potential to promote economic transformation, among them the involvement and promotion of local companies and markets and the promotion of national industrialisation. However, despite the existence of a supposedly clear vision in the NDS, there is no instrument that brings all the relevant elements together at the operational level. Moreover, the instruments that do exist provide neither a clear plan of resources mobilisation for the diversification of the economy, nor broad and structuring macroeconomic and strategic sectoral policies linked to the demands of structural transformation. This section shows how the institutions identified in the previous section are performing in the context of the natural resources economy and the implications of that performance for structural transformation.

### A Macroeconomic Policies

Macroeconomic policy is key to setting the conditions for and directing structural transformation. Mozambique's high level of external dependence in a context of an emerging resources economy poses a challenge to macroeconomic management – namely, how to avoid Dutch disease. The challenge is due to the inconsistency between fiscal and monetary policies, which is manifested in the way they have been addressed over the past two decades.

On the one hand, monetary policy in Mozambique has been geared towards achieving a stable, low, and single digit inflation. Until 2017, the main instrument of monetary policy was based on a quantitative variable, the control of money supply, or the monetary base. This goal has been set in an economy that is highly dependent on imports for the majority of consumer goods (especially food) and suffers from a chronic current account deficit, and where the major sources of foreign exchange are concentrated and volatile – about 90 per cent of exports are concentrated in few primary products, including mining and other natural resources (Castel-Branco 2017; Chivulele 2017). Given this, the focus of monetary policy is on managing liquidity to guarantee the value of the national currency relative to the main global currencies and thus maintain the capacity to import basic goods and services. The Central Bank therefore also defines the direction of monetary policy in terms of the exchange rate and the level of foreign capital inflows and international reserves. From April 2017, a monetary policy interest rate, the Mozambique Interbanking Money Market (MIMO), was introduced as the main monetary policy instrument to achieve the ultimate goal of stable and low inflation. This has not prevented the Central Bank from using other instruments such as the exchange rate, through operations in the interbanking exchange rate market and other forms of controlling international reserves as the country continues to depend highly on imports of basics.

On the other hand, fiscal policy in the context of the natural resource boom has become geared towards expanding public expenditure, especially public investment in infrastructures to support the growing extractives sector of the economy.[10] These investments have been funded essentially by external and domestic debt, which puts more pressure on the state budget to service the debt (Massarongo 2016). For example, between 2014 and 2019, external debt financed more than 20 public investment projects accounting for almost US$6 billion (see Table 11.2). Of these public investments, 10 were major infrastructure projects in the energy, transport, and communications sectors (see highlighted projects in Table 11.2). Domestic public debt has also increased, having been intensively used to finance short-term public expenditure over the past decade. Domestic debt servicing has increased continuously between 2009 and 2019, from almost less MT1 billion (US$14 million) in 2009 to more than MT150 billion (US$2 billion) in 2019 (Ibraimo 2020).

Chivulele (2017) noted that, given the current dynamic of the economy, which has shaped policy management, macroeconomic policies had become inconsistent, both among themselves and consequently with the objective of structural transformation. Such inconsistences are present within monetary policy, between monetary policy and the real economy, and between monetary

---

[10] It is worth noting that despite a large proportion of debt was towards financing infrastructure development, which in the case of the extractive industry may be seen as temporary, in the past decade public debt has become a central strategy to promote private domestic capital accumulation, without necessarily benefiting the broader economy. The case of the hidden debts is of particular interest.

TABLE 11.2 *Public investment projects financed by external public debt (2014–2019)*

| Public investment project | US$ million |
| --- | --- |
| Maputo Ring Road Project and Maputo–Katembe Bridge | 982 |
| Development and expansion of Nacala Port-Phase II, Nacala Special Economic Zone, Nacala Free Trade Industrial Zone and Beluluane Industrial Park | 868 |
| Road constructions: Mueda–Negomano, Nampula–Nameti; construction and rehabilitation of road infrastructures; Rovuma River bridge; management and maintenance of roads and bridges | 727 |
| Upgrade and extension of the national electricity power network in the northern region; power transmission line Chimuara–Nacala; Temane; Niassa rural electrification, Phase II; improvement of power network in Maputo and Matola and peripheral zones | 687 |
| Moamba major dam study and construction | 329 |
| Maputo gas project, technical assistance for large scale power and gas investment; Ressano Garcia thermal power plant | 237 |
| Digital migration project | 156 |
| Beira and Angoche fishing port construction and rehabilitation | 152 |
| Acquisition of carriages, wagons, locomotives, and railway equipment for Mozambique Railway Company (CFM) and Beira container terminal | 126 |
| Maputo International Airport rehabilitation and navigation infrastructure improvement | 79 |
| EMATUM – Mozambican Tuna Fish Company | 850 |
| Rural water supply for Manica, Sofala, Zambézia, Nampula, and Maputo provinces | 216 |
| Financial assistance for emergencies in the central and northern regions of Mozambique | 178 |
| Drainage system project in Maputo city and construction of Maputo and Matola landfills | 120 |
| Construction of the Department of Geology of Eduardo Mondlane University; Nampula Agrarian Polytechnic Institute; Maputo Health Sciences Institute | 115 |
| Olympic Games Infrastructures | 100 |
| Lumbo Hospital construction, Quelimane (supplementary area); emergency ambulance acquisition; tuberculosis and health system support | 59 |
| Combined cycle development project | 44 |
| Forestry investment | 28 |
| Aquaculture and artisanal fishing | 12 |
| Acquisition of equipment for the Public Rescue Services (SENSAP) | 5 |
| Total | 6,060 |

*Source:* Adapted from Ibraimo (2020: Figure 7).

policy and fiscal policy. The inconsistencies between monetary and fiscal policy and the real economy are principally due to the weak responsiveness by the financial sector to expansionary and restrictive policies such as the significant reductions in reference interest rates by the central bank. For example, between the period 2011 and 2015, the permanent lending facility (FPC) was reduced by 55 per cent and the permanent deposit facility (FPD) by 70 per cent.[11] These reductions were followed by a timid reduction of interest rates charged by commercial banks – from 24 per cent to 21 per cent in the same period. However, when the Central Bank increases interest rates, commercial banks react more quickly. The increase by the Central Bank of the FPC rate between 2015 and 2016 from 7.5 per cent to 23.25 per cent was immediately responded to by an increase in the commercial interest rate of about 50 per cent. Although the percentage change of the reference rate is higher than that of the commercial interest rates charged by commercial banks, the important aspect to highlight is how quickly commercial banks react to an increase in reference rates as compared to a decrease.

The continual resort by the state to treasury bills, associated with a relatively small and highly speculative financial market, has created pressure to increase commercial interest rates, making it difficult for monetary policy to stimulate the economy (Ibraimo 2020). Expansionary monetary policies, which are supposed to expand credit for financing the productive sector towards a more diversified economy, are abruptly interrupted by these dynamics of reliance of the government on domestic public debt (Castel-Branco 2014). The activity of the financial sector is then geared towards financing the infrastructure supporting the extractive core of the economy, and the issuance of public debt, consumption of durable goods, and the real estate sector with speculative prices. This tendency to speculation is partly explained by the higher demand and short-term profitability of these assets, as the increasing investment in extractives has prompted an emergence of a middle-income strata with access to higher salaries from the extractive sector. By concentrating its financing capacity in such activities, the financial sector diverts resources that should be used to finance productive investment in the country, a process that may allow the achievement of a more diversified productive domestic capacity and hence build the basis for the structural transformation of the economy.

---

[11] According to the Bank of Mozambique Monetary Policy Framework, FPC and FPD are the rates through which the operational variable of the monetary policy in Mozambique, MIMO rate is determined. On the one hand, FPC is the rate through which the Central Bank provides overnight loans to the commercial banks that present liquidity deficits, against the presentation of collaterals. On the other hand, FPD is the rate through which commercial banks deposit their excess liquidity by overnight maturity against a remuneration provided by the central bank. The gap between these rates is defined in order to maintain the interbanking market interest rates close to the MIMO and prevent their volatility (see www.bancomoc.mz).

## B Dependence and Structural Economic Transformation

The past and recent history of Mozambique is that of a highly and structurally dependent economy, which has implications for its economic transformation. In the economic and social dimensions, dependence on foreign capital inflows – both public (foreign aid) and private (FDI, concessional, and commercial loans from the international financial system) – is, along with resource extraction, the main structural feature of the country's dependence.

With respect to private capital inflows, the dependence on FDI, especially in the extractives sector and related activities, is the dominant feature of the pattern of economic growth and one of the fundamental elements of the 'dominant political economy of Mozambique' (Castel-Branco 2010, 2014).[12] Over the past two-and-a-half decades, Mozambique has presented a pattern of dependence on natural resources extraction similar to those of several resource-dependent developing countries. Between 2000 and 2009 (the period before gas discoveries in the Rovuma Basin in Cabo Delgado), the resources sector, especially mining, represented 43 per cent of total FDI inflows, followed by the manufacturing sector with 28 per cent (of which 92 per cent corresponded only to the Mozambique Aluminium Smelter Company MOZAL). From a total FDI of US$1.4 billion that the sector received over this period, megaprojects in the extraction of heavy sands and coal contributed 53 per cent (US$580 million and US$171 million, respectively). In terms of exports, the resources/extractives sector in general or the mineral energy complex (aluminium, gas, coal, and energy) represented, on average, about 64 per cent of the total value of exports between 2000 and 2016 (Langa 2017). By 2012, after the gas discoveries, the sector had increased its share to 72 per cent. It continued to do well until 2014, despite lower commodity prices after 2012 (Roe 2018). The effect of the dependence on natural resources hit hard in 2015, when prices of Mozambique's main export commodities (especially coal, gas, and aluminium) fell drastically, affecting the country's economy, with GDP growth decelerating to 6.6 per cent and subsequently dropping as low as 2.2 per cent, after a mean value of over 7 per cent in most of the period since 2000. Figure 11.1 shows the growth of the extractives sector in relation to GDP growth between 2009 and 2018.

As Figure 11.2 shows, the contribution of the extractives sector to GDP increased from 1.2 per cent in 2009 to 13.6 per cent in 2018, and it is expected to contribute substantially more over the next few years, as the production of gas in northern Mozambique starts. Manufacturing declined

---

[12] 'The dominant political economy of Mozambique is focused on three fundamental and interlinked processes, namely the maximisation of inflows of foreign capital – FDI and commercial loans – without political conditionality; the development of linkages between these capital inflows and the domestic process of accumulation and the formation of national capitalist classes; and the reproduction of a labour system in which the workforce is remunerated at below its costs of subsistence' (Castel-Branco 2014: S29).

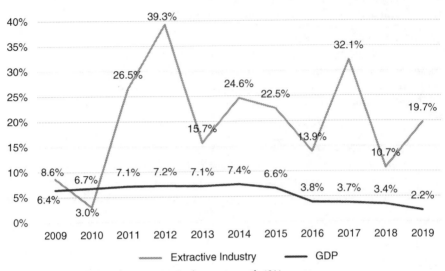

FIGURE 11.1 GDP and extractive industry growth (%), 2009–2019
Source: Data from National Statistics Institute (INE).

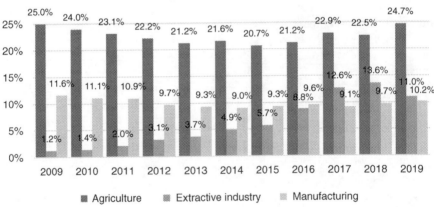

FIGURE 11.2 Contribution of agriculture, manufacturing, and extractive industry to
GDP (%), 2009–2019
Source: Authors' illustration; data from INE.

over 2009–14 when it started a slight increase up to 2019, but it is still
below its 2009 share of the GDP. Agriculture remains the main sector, contributing 24.7 per cent in 2019 to GDP, but the extractives sector has been
the fastest growing sector over the past decade.

Current economic dynamics, supported by the discoveries and recent FIDs in the gas sector, and the set of expectations over future FDI, revenues, and linkages, point to an increasing dependence of the country's economy on natural resource exploitation, consolidating the country's structural dependence. As Langa (2017: 165) argues, under such conditions 'Mozambique is following an opposite trajectory to economic [structural] transformation', in the sense that the dependence on primary commodities has been expanding, at the same time that 'a process of premature deindustrialization [defined as the increasing underdevelopment of the existing manufacturing sector] has been underway, constraining the possibilities of multiplication and intensification of productive linkages within the economy'.

Tendencies towards deindustrialisation are confirmed by research on the manufacturing sector, which shows that from 2011 to 2017 there was a reduction in the number of companies in the sector, of the labour force, and of turnover (CEEG, Ministério de Economia e Finanças, University of Copenhagen, and UNU-WIDER 2018). Whilst there has been some mobility of the labour force from agriculture to other sectors (services and manufacturing), the productivity of the labour force in these areas has been lower (Jones and Tarp 2015). These results cannot be directly linked to the emerging resources economy, but the consistency of the downward trend in manufacturing as well as in its employment suggests that economic growth is heading in the opposite direction to structural transformation.

Despite the government's approval of the local content bill in 2019 (for submission to parliament for its enactment as an Act), prospects of local companies making linkages with the gas projects of the Rovuma basin are still uncertain. National companies lack the capacity to match the quality standards of the O&G industry and the national business class poses a high reputational risk to international companies due to its excessive reliance on political lobbying.[13] These factors are contributing to the resistance to local content policies from the international companies leading the investments in the gas sector.[14] Total's signing of all financing contracts in July 2020, following EXIM Bank's decision to back American suppliers to LNG development in Mozambique, together with the imminent approval of US$1 billion from UK Export Finance (see Introduction) may mark a turning point towards the start of the LNG production, but at the same time they signal the difficulties national companies will have in establishing linkages with the gas projects. Despite the provisions in the local content policy to promote linkages with national companies, this

---

[13] See interviews with the Head of Local Content of the National Business Association (CTA) https://macua.blogs.com/moambique_todos/2019/02/h%C3%A1-um-l%C3%B3bi-contra-a-lei-do-conte%C3%BAdo-local-em-mo%C3%A7ambique.html, and www.rfi.fr/pt/mocambique/20190823-lei-de-conteudo-local-tem-de-ser-atractiva-para-o-investimento.

[14] www.africaintelligence.fr/petrole-et-gaz_strategies-etat/2020/07/16/contenu-local--total-eni-et-exxonmobil-font-de-la-resistance,109243877-ar1.

will be a more complex issue than expected. Power dynamics have played a central role in providing the conditions and the direction of public policy for local content. More specifically, the power that MNCs have in controlling the GVCs of their production, including the suppliers of goods and services to their industry, may define the possibilities and outcomes of local content initiatives. In fact, the dynamics and structure of natural resources extraction reflect the dependence of the natural resources sector upon FDI for financing development projects, thus justifying the relative power that MNCs have in influencing local content policies and resource extraction in a capital and (industrial) capability scarce economy. This puts MNCs in a position to determine the direction of policy.

Internal actors will more likely support policies that promote structural transformation through diversification of the economy and the establishment of linkages between local companies and the natural resources projects than by FDI. This makes domestic resource mobilisation an alternative to external resources – which is in fact the idea of using natural resources revenues to promote the diversification and economic transformation presented in the NDS.

## C The Contribution of the Extractives Sector to Revenue Mobilisation

As mentioned, the natural resources area has experienced a set of reforms in the last two decades, which were accelerated by the increasing importance of natural resources in the Mozambican economy. Most of these institutional reforms have been either directly or indirectly linked to the generation of natural resources revenues, and they have led to the creation of regulatory agencies in the petroleum sector (INP), in 2004, and mining (INAMI), in 2014. Besides, in response to the growing importance of the extractive industries in the economy, the AT created in 2017 a specific unit to deal with the sector. The results of these reforms are mixed, with implications for revenue generation.

There has not been a systematic assessment of the performance of key institutions related to natural resources. The most relevant is the Resource Governance Index (Natural Resource Governance Institute 2017), which covers three indicators: value realisation, revenue management, and enabling environment. Scores range from zero to 100, higher values referring to higher performance. In the last assessment, carried out in 2017, Mozambique's overall score on resources governance was 50 (average) and on value realisation 66 – which is satisfactory due to good performance in taxation – but its scores on revenue management and enabling environment were poor: 42 and 43, respectively. The enabling environment is related to governance indicators, voice and accountability, government effectiveness, regulatory quality, rule of law, control of corruption, political stability, and absence of violence.

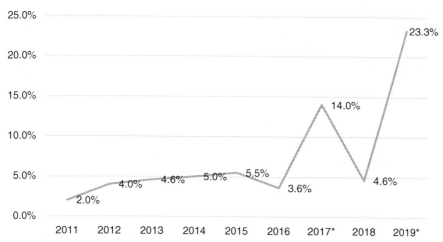

FIGURE 11.3 Fiscal contribution of megaprojects in the mining and oil sector to total state revenues, 2011–2019
Note: *includes capital gains taxes.
Source: Authors' illustration based on State General Accounts 2014–19.

Revenues from natural resources derive from a series of standard taxes and fees, including value-added tax (VAT), income tax (corporate (IRPC) and individual (IRPS)), royalties, and production taxes (República de Moçambique 2018). Specific revenues are collected by the regulatory agencies, INP and INAMI, including for their capacity development. Public-owned companies (ENH, CMH, EMEM) in the sector must provide dividends to their shareholders when they are profitable.

Figure 11.3 shows the share of fiscal revenues from megaprojects in the mining and oil sectors in total state revenues. The fiscal contribution of extractives increased over the first half of the last decade, from 2 per cent of total revenues in 2011 to more than 5 per cent in 2015. This increase reflects the boom in production – especially of mineral coal, as prices were high. However, the commodity prices drop since the end of 2014 has prompted a decline in regular extractives revenues.

The higher contribution of the sector in 2017 and 2019 is explained by the extraordinary revenues – capital gains taxes (CGT) of about US$350 million and US$880 million, from oil asset transactions between ENI and Exxon Mobil, and between Occidental (which took over the concession and assets of Anadarko) and Total, respectively. Without CGT, the contribution of the extractives would fall to 5 per cent and 3.7 per cent of the total revenues in 2017 and 2019, respectively. This would confirm the downward trend that began in 2015. Despite the fact that the legislation is clear about the rate of 32 per cent and the mandate of the AT to collect CGT, this revenue has been embroiled in intense debate and 'interpretations' of its calculation, with suspicions that MNCs have negotiated politically to pay less than what is due. Presidents Guebuza and Nyusi were directly involved in the ENI and Total deals, respectively, to some extent bypassing the existing institutions, especially the AT (Macuane et al. forthcoming). In the case of the negotiations with ENI, part of the payment agreed was in kind – the construction of a coal power plant, which was never delivered, fuelling suspicions of corruption (Macuane et al. 2018).

Despite progress in creating capacity to implement the tax regime, there are still institutional weaknesses in revenue collection, among them the capacity to audit companies to define the taxable amount and, in the case of oil and gas projects, the recoverable costs. Moreover, discrepant information on natural resources for revenue collection purposes is an institutional inefficiency that has been persistent over time and systematically reported by the Administrative Court analysis of public accounts. The successive country EITI reports show discrepancies in the revenues declared by the companies and by the Revenue Authority, although the differences are reducing and in 2018 were of 1% (Tribunal Administrativo 2017, 2018; EITI Mozambique/ I2A Consultoria e Serviços 2020). Part of this improvement is due to the increasing scrutiny that the sector has been subject to from civil society organisations, which also participate in the secretariat of the EITI. To some extent, demand for transparency in the sector is contributing to the increasing collection of revenues.

Despite the growing importance of the extractives in total state revenues and the institutional reforms made to strengthen institutions of revenue collection, the contribution of the sector (when CGT is not included) is low. It is therefore not an alternative to foreign aid for public investment in areas to stimulate structural transformation. The regular bypassing of the institutions where CGT is concerned also suggests that natural resources revenues are vulnerable to appropriation by political leaders and use for clientelist purposes.

The gas sector has been the principal source of another revenue stream, dividends paid to the government by the natural resources public enterprises (ENH and its subsidiary CMH), INP, and companies with state shares (Mozambique Gas Pipeline Company (CMG)), but this has accounted for less than 1.5 per cent of state revenues in most of the 2014–19 period (Figure 11.4).

The contribution of the extractives sector's public enterprises to public revenues is still modest. However, in the case of the gas sector, specifically in the SASOL projects of Pande and Temane, these companies have been a source of rents for national business elites linked to the ruling party, in down- and midstream projects such as gas distribution and electricity generation (Salimo et al. 2020). The participation of the public companies in these gas projects did not make a visible contribution to the promotion of linkages with local companies, and the lead company SASOL has been criticised for its limited contracting

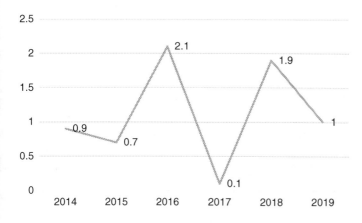

FIGURE 11.4 Extractives dividends as % of total revenues
Source: Authors' illustration based on State General Accounts 2014–19.

of local companies in its supply chain. In sum, the model so far adopted, of participation by public companies in the extractives, has neither been a good source of revenues to public coffers nor visibly contributed to the structural transformation of the economy.

Extractives revenues, apart from the extraordinary CGT payments, have not played any significant or transformational role in public expenditures. This is partially attributable to the size of the revenues so far, but it is also due to the lack of a specific regime to earmark its contribution for broader or defined economic goals. The discussion over creating a SWF, which would go some way in that direction, has so far been restricted to a limited group. To some extent, this is a continuation of the uncertainty and lack of transparency that have characterised the use of CGT revenue so far. The use of CGT to cover budget deficits has been recurrent (e.g., in the last transaction of assets between Occidental and Total in 2019, the President announced that part of the revenues would be used to finance the deficit resulting from the elections), but there is no specific mechanism of accountability for this.

## V UNDERLYING CAUSES

The NDS is a resource-led economic transformation strategy, whose main objective is to promote industrialisation for the diversification of the economy, using the country's natural resources as the catalysers of this process. However, despite the growing importance of the extractives' dynamics in the economy and institutional reforms to improve the sector's governance, both its impact and its prospects for structural transformation are limited. Two underlying factors explain these dynamics: the nature of the NDS as a coordination policy instrument and the country's structural dependence. These factors are developed below.

Since its elaboration, the NDS has never been formally adopted as the country's strategy by a broad-based coalition or legitimised by the key decision-making institutions, such as parliament. This renders its implementation less binding and its role as a coordination mechanism of the various actors towards structural transformation limited. Despite being referred to in many sector programmes and strategies, there is no explicit integration of this instrument with a broader framework of structural transformation. Fragmented decisions and responsibility for implementation across uncoordinated organisational mandates have created a weak context for the effectiveness of the economic transformation strategies embodied in the NDS. Strategic decisions about the use of natural resources revenues have not been implemented continuously and are vulnerable to changes in the leadership of the country.

The lack of broad-based participation in key decisions of the sector is another critical factor. For example, the discussion about the role of the local content policy in promoting industrialisation has been undermined by the disproportionate power dynamics and interests, including those of foreign investors, which do not have incentives to contribute to national long-term goals and would rather favour the use of their GVCs, which are more efficient. Moreover, the existence of an economically weak entrepreneurial class, undercapitalised and very much prone to use its political influence for rent seeking, prevents the creation of a strong coalition of national actors pushing for institutions that can enable a sustainable economic transformation.

There is no acknowledged set of ideas informing institutional choices and actions, which is reflected in the fragmentation of interventions and the lack of linkages between ideas and actions to make natural resources contribute to broader economic and social change. From an institutional point of view, this means that the NDS does not have the status of a widely accepted set of norms that can intermediate relations between and influence the behaviour of the key actors in the sector and those that might contribute to structural transformation. This is clear from the limited impact that the increasing contribution of the extractives to the GDP and of the natural resources revenues have had on the fiscal policy. The way natural resources revenues, especially through CGT, have been negotiated and managed is a good example. The country's top political leadership taking over the process and bypassing existing institutions and processes denotes the existence of inconsistencies between the objectives of economic transformation and policy actions, which affects fiscal policy management. It also denotes the weakness of the existing policy instruments in influencing political actors' behaviour with respect to broader development goals.

The recent developments related to the FIDs in the gas sector have created new expectations and pointed to an even greater dependence of the country's economy on natural resource exploitation. It is therefore important to bear in mind that dependence should not be reduced only to the inflows of FDI that the country has received over the past decades and might receive in the decades to come. Instead, the ability of these foreign capital inflows to effectively structure the general dynamics and conditions of production and reproduction (or sustainability) of the economy should be acknowledged. Particularly important here is how the country's economic policy and macro-policy management in general are set through, and shaped by, the dynamics of foreign dependence at various levels (investment, production, and consumption). This includes, for instance, the development of productive linkages and the role of macroeconomic and sectoral policies in addressing relevant questions of economic transformation.

A fundamental problem in the case of Mozambique is that the dependence of the economy on resource extraction and the corresponding foreign capital inflows has become a dilemma, since domestic capital accumulation is strategically promoted through these capital inflows, which at the same time provide the main opportunities for industrialisation and diversification of the economy. Hence, diversification of the economy cannot be conceptualised outside the aforementioned core dynamics of dependence. However, in the context of dependence it cannot be expected that Mozambique will receive significantly large FDI into the manufacturing and agricultural sectors compared with what it currently receives in the extractives sector, which is much more attractive to the foreign investors. In fact, given that external financing of the non-resources sector is limited, it is expected that the country will have to rely on its own domestic savings to finance diversification. However, so far, productive domestic investment has usually been crowded out by a debt-financing government expenditure policy, through the issuance of treasury bills, which are more attractive and less risky for the domestic financial sector (Castel-Branco 2014; Massarongo 2016). This creates limitations for the implementation of a sustainable industrial policy that can stimulate diversification and create linkages with the natural resources projects that promote the transfer of technology and knowledge to the broader economy. However, with the potential increase of state revenues stemming from gas projects in future, there can be, hypothetically, more space for public investment in non-resource sectors to stimulate economic transformation. Recently (September 2020), the Central Bank made available the Proposal of the SWF Model for Mozambique, which includes a more inclusive governance setting, for wider public discussion. The opportunities created by this new development are discussed in the final section.

VI CONCLUSIONS AND PERSPECTIVES

Mozambique's NDS hinges on the structural transformation of the economy through industrialisation and diversification, catalysed by the growing importance of the extractives sector. In this context, the country has carried out institutional reforms to respond to the increasing importance of the natural resources sector in its economy. These reforms are resulting in the growing contribution of the resources sector to the economy. However, underlying dynamics undermine the prospects of the resources sector contributing to economic transformation, namely: (i) the absence of a strong institutional setting expressed in a resource-based strategy that plays the role of a binding set of norms and references for coordination of the various actors; (ii) the different strategies pursued by the political and economic actors, especially the political leadership and the government, the national entrepreneurial class (undercapitalised and more reliant on its political linkages), and the MNCs with less incentive to invest in other areas than the extractives; and (iii) the structural dependence of the country on external resources, particularly FDI and its role in shaping the relations between international and domestic actors and influencing macroeconomic policies, especially monetary and fiscal policies, in ways that contradict the objectives of economic transformation.

To contribute to structural transformation, the sector needs to influence institutional and policy dynamics in two ways.

The first is to activate relevant policy actors, especially the government and the private sector, and improve coordination, as defined in the NDS and reflected in its various policy instruments. Activating such relevant policy actors and processes implies the mobilisation and alignment of the agendas of the government and the domestic entrepreneurial class in the context of the increasing role of the extractives sector in the economy. In this regard, there must be a clear alignment between the industrialisation strategy and the relevant sector policies, particularly the local content policy, in which the domestic private sector has to play a role. One way to improve coordination is through a fiscal regime and institutional mechanism that define the scope of public expenditure in areas related to structural transformation, especially industrial policy, and domestic and human capability development. This could be combined with a mechanism to aggregate sector policies – for example local content and industrial policy – as part of a broader development strategy.

The second way in which the sector needs to influence institutional and policy dynamics is to confront the conditions of dependence that influence macroeconomic policy management. This implies, for instance, addressing the existing conflicts and tensions between fiscal and monetary policies with the objective of structural transformation. In other words, this implies untying macroeconomic policy management from the logic of dependence, and subordinating it to the agenda of economic transformation, as a central instrument for the promotion of industrialisation and economic diversification. Thus, fiscal policy must clearly define strategically how natural resources revenues must be used within a broader development framework that addresses central aspects of economic transformation. This means that, instead of financing recurrent public deficits indiscriminately, as has been the case so far, these resources must selectively finance public expenditures directly linked to industrialisation and the diversification of the economy. Among them are those related to the promotion of local content in the extractive industries and beyond. It also demands the existence of more effective rules to bind and influence behaviour of relevant political and economic actors, which can be attained through the approval of a more consensual resource-led economic transformation strategy by parliament.

Such a strategy has to be defined through a broad consultation process, involving different government sectors, the private sector, civil society, and parliament. This is important to allow the instrument to be more binding – not only because it is enacted by the legislature, but also because it has been approved by a broader coalition that will contribute to its continuous scrutiny throughout the implementation process. The operationalisation of such a strategy must also demand a reform or at least the strengthening of the budgetary institutions and processes, within the logic of inclusion of the various actors. This means that the budget elaboration, enactment, and oversight must be aligned with the priorities defined in the fiscal policy. In this regard, the Parliament, the Administrative Court, the private sector, and the civil society, through the existing mechanisms of control, participation and dialogue, must be able to follow up on the implementation of the fiscal policy through the budgetary process and hold the relevant actors accountable. The discussion of the SWF model recently initiated can be a good entry point to propose and introduce relevant reforms to address the above-mentioned challenges.

Regarding monetary policy, it must be ensured that it is more aligned with the challenges of mobilising resources for the domestic financing of a strategy of economic transformation, in a context of limited financial resources. This means a more coordinated approach between the monetary authorities, the domestic private financial sector, and the government. Such a coordination approach should aim not only to avoid adopting policies that crowd out productive investment from the domestic private sector but also to promote flexible access to financial resources to fund initiatives in line with the strategy of industrialisation and diversification of the economy, inherent in the NDS.

PART III

SYNTHESIS

# 12

# A Country at a Fork in the Road

António S. Cruz, Ines A. Ferreira, Johnny Flentø, and Finn Tarp

## I INTRODUCTION

We now proceed to bringing together the different elements of previous chapters with the aim of presenting the essence of this country study of Mozambique. In the next section, we take stock and revisit our points of departure from Chapters 2 and 3. This background work culminated in the identification of eight thematic areas, subsequently subjected to individual in-depth studies in Chapters 4–11. We end the section by summarising the core findings from these chapters. Next, in Section III we present our integrated assessment of key institutional weaknesses and go a decisive step further, and analyse and discuss their proximate causes and deep factors. We end in Section IV with a series of ideas for reform, as an input to national reflection, debate, and action.

Before we start, we would like to add a word of caution on four aspects.

The first aspect is the uniqueness of the Mozambican case. As highlighted throughout this volume, Mozambique's historical and more recent development experience has been exceptional in many aspects, including for example that Mozambique became independent much later than nearly all other African countries. This creates analytical challenges in terms of untangling the complexity of the links between institutions and economic development and the broader regional and global context. So, and to be clear, even though we included a brief comparison between Mozambique and its neighbouring and peer countries in terms of their performance in international institutional indicators in Chapter 3, our goal is not to assess whether/how Mozambique deviates from some kind of norm. The institutional weaknesses and underlying causes and mechanisms may not be unique in the sense that they might also apply to other countries. Yet the focus of our study is on understanding the relationship between institutions and development in the specific case of Mozambique.

The second aspect is the direction of causality in the relationship between institutions and economic development. The perspective adopted in this volume assumes that the link is from institutions to economic development. However, this relationship is in reality more complex. The level of development also affects institutional performance (e.g., Chang 2011). Accordingly, low development hampers institutional improvement. This is also true in the case of Mozambique. For example, Mozambique emerged from a particularly dramatic history in 1975 when it achieved independence with extremely low levels of education among the indigenous population. Financial resources were exceedingly scarce and only available from external sources, and therefore dependent on political and other conditions with wide-ranging consequences (including the last phase of the Cold War, which affected how donors treated a strategically located country next to apartheid South Africa). Similarly, distorted economic structures clearly influenced the formation of the institutional set-up and subsequent developments, and the same goes for the institutions put in place under wartime conditions in the 1980s and more recently.

The third word of caution relates to the proposals for reform put forward at the end of this synthesis. Arguably, some of them are ambitious in the sense that they would not necessarily gather political consensus, specifically when they do not speak favourably to all groups in society. Given that the analysis uncovers both deep factors and proximate causes for the institutional weaknesses and their economic consequences, some of the proposals are difficult to implement and require fundamental changes. Yet we believe that this study would be incomplete if we were to shy away from making concrete proposals aimed at overcoming current obstacles.

The final point refers to the consequences of COVID-19, which remains unfolding throughout the world and in Mozambique as well (Addison et al. 2020). While it has become clear that the social and economic consequences of the pandemic for development in Mozambique are serious, at the time of finalising the thematic studies and writing this synthesis, it is too early to assess in detail the dynamic implications of the pandemic for development in the coming years. However, we will reflect on this dimension in the last section.

## II TAKING STOCK

We now briefly revisit the history and socio-economic context of Mozambique and refer to the performance of the country according to different institutional indicators, also drawing on the assessment of perceived institutional constraints. We then provide an overview of the main take-away messages from the thematic chapters.

## A Troubled History

Historical roots go deep in Mozambique, including ethnic and regional diversity, interaction and conflict among Bantu tribes, and Arab influence from around 1100 CE. After the arrival of Vasco da Gama in 1498, the Portuguese gradually extended their control over the territory. The colonial system developed over centuries and deepened significantly from the mid-1880s, relying on investment by foreign capital and companies, especially British, Rhodesian, and South African.

Before 1960, Mozambique mainly supplied cheap raw materials to Portugal and labour and transport services to neighbouring countries (the hinterland). Whatever infrastructure existed ran east–west, and the vast country remained economically disintegrated in the north–south dimension, with the capital – then Lourenço Marques – in the far south very close to South Africa. In fact, the southern part of the country was more integrated economically with South Africa than with the centre and northern regions. Moreover, the local, mainly agriculture-based, economy continued to be underdeveloped. Both of these fundamental characteristics remain very much in place to this day.

The last twenty years of the colonial period saw large inflows of Portuguese settlers, some agricultural and industrial progress, and the liberation struggle, initiated by the Front for the Liberation of Mozambique (FRELIMO). Originally constitutionalist and non-violent, FRELIMO opted for armed struggle in 1964. A decade of violent conflict followed until independence suddenly happened, after the Carnation Revolution in 1974 in Portugal.

The assassination of the first president of Frelimo, Eduardo Mondlane, in Dar es Salaam in 1969 led to an internal power scuffle along ideological lines, which resulted in the expulsion (and subsequent execution) of the heir apparent, Uria Simango (see Pitcher 2020).[1] Samora Machel took over as party chair, and formal independence and the foundation of the People's Republic of Mozambique as a one-party socialist state was achieved on 25 June 1975 under the leadership of Frelimo and President Samora Machel.

The struggle-hardened Frelimo 'comrades', who took over government, originally enjoyed a high degree of legitimacy and quite extensive public support, built around a socialist-inspired social contract. To date this has arguably provided the only credible unifying development vision for the country. As was the case in Vietnam in the mid-1970s (after Vietnam's defeat of US forces), the atmosphere in Mozambique was at the time 'upbeat'. Frelimo optimistically declared that the coming decade would see 'victory over under-development'. While this was naïve in retrospect, it appeared at the time self-evident to many.

Yet post-independence challenges and ruptures quickly mounted. Key factors include:

- The exodus of some 80 per cent of the Portuguese settlers, involving several hundred thousand people. This devastated the public administration and led to an almost total collapse of commercial agriculture, with millions of peasants left without inputs, supplies, or market access. Institutions disintegrated

---

[1] Dissidents from Frelimo came to play an important role in the establishment of MNR, later renamed Renamo, which has opposed Frelimo politically and militarily since the late 1970s.

with the departure of the Portuguese. Thus, living and educational/managerial standards were dismal to begin with in the newly independent state.

- As already alluded to, independence in Mozambique came suddenly as well as late as compared with other African countries, and regional anti-apartheid (Rhodesia and South Africa) and global (Cold War) conflicts left the new country with very little room for manoeuvre, politically or economically. This turned out to be very costly indeed, illustrated by the massive economic and military costs associated with Mozambique's decision to enforce United Nations sanctions against Rhodesia.[2]

- Misguided economic choices were made during the years following the Third Frelimo Congress in 1977. Frelimo declared itself a Marxist-Leninist vanguard party and pursued policies including state farms, forced mechanisation of agriculture, and resettlement of large numbers of people. Rather than winning increasing support among the peasantry, Frelimo was losing it. At the Fourth Congress in 1984, Frelimo openly recognised the neglect of small peasant farmers, but by then the country was at war. Also relevant throughout is the fact that many influential members of the Frelimo leadership opposed private sector development due to their political outlook.

- The development, with Rhodesian and South African support, of the Mozambican National Resistance (MNR) (renamed Renamo in 1980) as an effective military force (that became the main political opposition party from 1994 onwards). Renamo incorporated people with roots in central Mozambique (where religious and ethnic grievances were both common and deep), and gradually absorbed others who had become increasingly critical of Frelimo. In addition, a significant number of people were kidnapped and forced into Renamo ranks. With the independence of Zimbabwe in 1980, hopes were high that a turnaround might be possible. Yet, backed by South Africa, Renamo slowly but surely undermined Frelimo's nation-building efforts. On the other side, Frelimo cadres remained steadfast in criminalising the insurgents and their supporters.

A brief glimmer of renewed optimism occurred with the signing of the Nkomati Accord between Mozambique and South Africa in 1984. Yet large-scale destruction of infrastructure and killings continued with support from South Africa, though rather more covertly, and a political settlement was not on the cards before the end the Cold War and subsequently of apartheid in 1992. In October of that year, Frelimo and Renamo signed the Rome General Peace Accords that ended more than a decade of gruesome destruction, including more than one million dead.

---

[2] It can be added that, notwithstanding gaining independence very late and the availability of several other earlier experiences in the region, Mozambique did not manage to exploit the advantages of being a late starter, learning from and avoiding the pitfalls suffered by other countries in terms of rent seeking and elite capture.

Thus, when Mozambique introduced multiparty elections in 1994 and went to the polls with Frelimo and Renamo as the key contenders and a voter turnout of 88 per cent, the country had been at war for two and a half out of the previous three decades. Joaquim Chissano, who took over from Samora Machel after his death in a plane crash in South Africa in 1986, was elected president, and Frelimo gained majority control of the Assembly of the Republic. It has maintained this control ever since.[3]

In this context, and in spite of the significant economic recovery that took place in the second part of the 1990s and first years of the 2000s, a sustainable political settlement would have required at least some degree of political and economic power-sharing. This did not come about. In fact, quite the opposite happened, and the country, its people, and the economy have since then experienced increasing rather than decreasing fragmentation economically and politically.

The international donor community responded with significant amounts of foreign assistance in the form of humanitarian and grant aid and soft loans following peace in 1992; foreign aid remains a crucial factor in the modern history of Mozambique. Economic recovery took place in the 1990s, supported by aid, but a growth engine for sustained inclusive development remained lacking. In spite of its rhetoric, Frelimo failed in these years to implement the measures necessary for agricultural development, which is critical for structural transformation, poverty reduction, and inclusive development, both vertically and horizontally between different groups of people and different regions of the country. The same goes for the two first decades of the twenty-first century.

As is clear, Mozambique has experienced violent conflict at different stages of its history. The most recent is the military insurgency in Cabo Delgado since mid-2018. The causes of this conflict are subject to debate, but likely include local discontent caused by limited socio-economic development and the activities of both local and international Islamic groups in an area where illegal trade is widespread. Critically, these tensions have the potential to spill over to other parts of northern and central Mozambique if not addressed effectively.

This will require that the country both adopts and implements an inclusive and coherent growth and development strategy, which, as noted, has been lacking for decades. It will also require continued progress in terms of decentralisation. As noted in Chapter 2, the Nyusi government chose to negotiate in 2018 and give in to some of Renamo's main demands in this regard. This included the election of provincial governors, a move sustained after the death of Renamo's leader Afonso Dhlakama. However, the introduction of a provincial secretary of state nominated by the president of the republic alongside the elected governor illustrates the continuing juggle.[4]

[3] President Guebuza succeeded Chissano in 2005; Filipe Nyusi took over in 2015 and in the 2019 elections won a second term in a disputed landslide victory (Pitcher 2020).
[4] This is described in detail by Kössler (2018).

## B  Socio-economic Strategy and Context

The collapse of former allies in Eastern Europe and elsewhere in the global arena, the ongoing war, and an economic state of affairs that reached a historical low point in Mozambique in 1986 forced Frelimo to change economic course from 1987 onwards. Negotiations for support from the Bretton Woods institutions and a range of Western donors (in addition to the Nordic countries, which were present from very early on) began after the signing of the Nkomati Accord. Subsequently, the government agreed a comprehensive deal with the Bretton Woods institutions and the Paris Club creditors in 1987. This introduced a five-year Economic Rehabilitation Programme (PRE), which meant a drastic U-turn in economic policy.

In retrospect, the misfortune for Mozambique is that the Structural Adjustment Programme (SAP) was as inadequate for a country at war, as the ten-year development plan had been. Both short-run and longer-term consequences were dismal. In the short run, no supply response from agriculture was possible due to the overwhelming effects of the war; and in the longer term, the PRE introduced a deep-seated structural economic and political imbalance between Frelimo and Renamo. Put differently, while Cramer (2001) argues that the privatisation inherent in the adopted programme was both hasty and careless, it also sowed a seed of political fragility that led to continued polarisation and instability with frequent outbursts of violent conflict. Unequal economic and power relations added to pre-existing regional, ethnic, and religious tensions.

To be clear, Pitcher (2002, 2020) notes: 'the first democratic elections of 1994 ideally placed [Frelimo] party members and their families to take advantage of most policies regarding privatisation and the creation of a market economy'. Renamo associates were in no position to benefit, as they were still fighting in the bush when assets and opportunities were privatised. Frelimo also treated them with suspicion, and they have since found it very difficult to establish themselves in the evolving legal and economic environment. What this means is that political and economic power merged in the hands of the former socialist FRELIMO elite.

The linkages between the Frelimo party and business are intricate (see Pitcher 2017; Cortês 2018) and the extent of Frelimo party member participation in key business activities and interests across the economy and its sectors stands out. Pitcher (2017) further argues that, 'as might be expected in a locale where the private sector is fragile, they rely on state-party connections to secure and protect business opportunities'. Accordingly, the lack of effective separation of state and party that had existed under Frelimo's one-party rule remained in place. Moreover, this opened up possibilities for rent-seeking and elite capture.

Meanwhile, Mozambique continued to receive very significant inflows of foreign aid that financed public expenses and major infrastructure investments.

Aid dependence became a key characteristic and has been hugely important for the funding of public expenditure, including critical investment in human capital and infrastructure and much-needed humanitarian relief. However, aid has also been associated with the side effects of aid dependence, including Dutch disease, lack of agency, and undermining of local institutions. Arguably, the pressure for the country to be more productive and develop the much-needed private sector, including the rural economy as a priority, appeared less pressing to policy-makers.

In parallel, the public sector grew significantly, in large measure due to the inflow of foreign aid. Yet public efficiency and effectiveness are well below capacity. Social spending is comparable to that of neighbouring countries, but outcomes in Mozambique are inferior, and geographically uneven investments in public services have contributed to increasing inequality between the regions of the country.

The weakness of both the domestic political system and the private sector referred to above, including extensive links between the holders of political office (also the most educated cohort) and owners of private firms, is now embedded in Mozambique. One consequence is the almost complete absence of an independent non-political capitalist class. Another linked characteristic is the lack of contestation in political and economic life. To illustrate, the current electoral system relies on closed party candidate lists, which means that while party members are in principle accountable to the people, they are in reality foremost accountable to the party, both for their election and in their ability to access business opportunities.

This dynamic has manifested itself in a variety of ways, and it intensified considerably in 2006 when international companies were granted exclusive rights to explore and exploit oil and gas off the coast of Cabo Delgado (and especially after the confirmation of the existence of massive deposits of natural gas in the Rovuma Basin in 2010). It became apparent that the distribution of income and assets in Mozambican society for generations to come were in play, so the political and economic stakes of maintaining control multiplied manifold. President Guebuza, who came to power in 2005, strengthened the hold on state institutions and replaced many technocrats in leading government positions with politicians. He also used the extensive powers allotted to the president by the Mozambican Constitution to secure loyalty to the party in all three pillars of the state. We give two examples of elite control and corruption to illustrate the many-faceted effects of these unfolding dynamics.

The first is the 'hidden debt scandal' that erupted in 2016, and which has deeply affected both the economic and political climate in Mozambique and the country's relations with the international community over the past five years.[5] The second example is that industrial policy formulation has since the

---

[5] See Cortez et al. (2019) for an account of the different costs and consequences of the hidden debts.

PRE followed a mixed and piecemeal approach, with no clearly articulated and commonly agreed vision. Among the successes, the sugar rehabilitation strategy stands out. Whitfield and Buur (2014: 131) largely associate this success with three political factors: first, sustained political support from a faction of the Frelimo ruling elite with mutual interests with a group of foreign sugar companies; second, the ability of that faction to overcome resistance to implementation inside and outside the ruling coalition; and third, the ability of the state agency implementing the strategy to enforce the rules structuring the sugar companies' access to rents. Such successes are, however, far from standard across the board.[6]

Solid macroeconomic management played a key role in addressing the economic crisis that erupted following the hidden debt scandal in 2016 and will also be crucial looking forward when gas revenues start flowing, with a particular focus on developing the supply side of the economy. Most of the population continues to be highly dependent on low-productivity informal activities, such as smallholder agriculture, and is vulnerable to economic, political, and environmental shocks. It is becoming increasingly evident, as witnessed by the 2019 Cyclones Idai and Kenneth, that Mozambique is among the countries most prone to the effects of climate change, including weather shocks and natural disasters.

The vulnerability of Mozambique and its population is also evident in the ongoing COVID-19 pandemic. While the consequences of the crisis are still unfolding, it is clear that there have been serious repercussions for both the economy and the Mozambican people. Negative spillovers from the global economic downturn will no doubt be sizeable; restrictions to domestic movement have further affected economic activity; and significant increases in the poverty rate, food insecurity, and the number of poor people are likely over the short and medium term. This is reinforced by the overwhelming imperatives of the demographic dynamics, which imply that hundreds of thousands of young people will enter the labour market each year. This represents a very high number of people who need to find jobs to secure their livelihoods, and this stands out as a critical priority in avoiding increased poverty, inequality, and social unrest.

---

[6] Examples of success include the sugar-processing companies, a tobacco leaf company, rehabilitated cement factories, the rehabilitation of the hydropower plant of Cahora Bassa, a natural gas power plant in Maputo province, an electric power line linking the Cahora Bassa hydropower plant to the south of the country, electric grid lines linking district headquarters, the Mozal aluminium smelter, and new or rehabilitated hotels in most major cities. In terms of failed investments, one can highlight Mabor vehicle tyres, steel producers Companhia Siderúrgica de Moçambique (Cifel) and Companhia Moçambique de Trefilaria (Trefil), and various textile and clothing factories (Sutton 2014: 7, 137, 149). Lastly, the Moamba Major dam, the Mphanda Nkuwa dam and hydro-power plant, and the Ncondezi coal power plant, and various processing plants based on coal and natural gas raw materials can be pointed out as cases of delayed investments.

Summing up, the above developments, combined with Frelimo's continuing inability to promote agriculture and broad-based private sector growth, help to explain why Mozambique lacks a consistent domestic engine of inclusive growth and remains close to the bottom of the scale in terms of GDP and human development, in a context where rent-seeking is on the rise and the polarisation between Frelimo and Renamo remains tense. Returning to the fork in the road, in terms of development strategy Mozambique faces a choice. Remaining on the present path would lead to increasing inequality, further regional imbalances, and possibly armed conflict. The alternative is to use the expected gas revenues effectively for poverty reduction, in a process in which agricultural development and agro-industry, as well as labour-intensive private sector advance, are central.[7] The added bonus of the alternative strategy is that should gas revenues disappoint due to the global energy transition and a glut of gas, then a more dynamic and poverty-reducing agriculture would have been built.

## C  Institutional Performance: International Datasets, Quantitative Survey, and Key Informants

### 1  *International databases*

Having laid out the historical, political, and economic context, and to help identify the main institutional weaknesses, we started compiling insights from selected available data (Worldwide Governance Indicators, World Economic Forum, the Transformation Index of Bertelsmann Stiftung, and Varieties of Democracy) on different institutional dimensions. We compared the performance of Mozambique with that of neighbouring countries (Tanzania, Malawi, and Zambia) and with peers (Uganda, Ethiopia, Vietnam, and Lao PDR), selected based on geographic criteria as well as level of income and similarity in terms of historical factors and economic characteristics either past or present. Bearing in mind the caveats of this type of analysis,[8] we drew up a list of observations.

Overall, Mozambique's comparative performance deteriorated between 2005 and 2018. We uncovered more detail by focusing on broad institutional dimensions and describing either the differences between two points in time (2005/06 and 2018/19/20) or the trend over the period 2005/07–19. More specifically:

- focusing on the most recent period, Mozambique showed particular weaknesses in terms of rule of law and judicial independence when compared with the other countries;

---

[7] See Jensen and Tarp (2004) for model-based insights about the importance of ADLI in the Mozambican context.

[8] Resulting from wide confidence intervals and from variations in the databases from year to year.

- the declining trend was also striking when looking at indicators of political participation in comparison with the performance of neighbouring countries, although Mozambique still outperforms peer countries in this indicator;
- Mozambique's performance declined in terms of the monopoly of the use of force as well as political stability and absence of violence;
- while we observed a weakening in government effectiveness, Mozambique's score in political corruption remained relatively stable, with an increase in 2017, probably reflecting the hidden debts scandal;
- finally, and unsurprisingly in light of the events alluded to in the previous sections, the position of Mozambique in terms of international cooperation fell between 2006 and 2020, even though it retained good performance in terms of regional cooperation.

## 2 *Quantitative Questionnaire and Key Informant Interviews*

In Chapter 3 of this volume, we then combined these observations with an analysis of the perceptions of institutional constraints to economic development in the country, based on the results of a quantitative questionnaire and insights from our interviews with key informants. The quantitative questionnaire covered 149 individuals, affiliated with different sectors (from public administration to the business sector and non-governmental organisations/NGOs). We complemented the quantitative analysis with qualitative evidence obtained from over 50 hours of interviews with key people in the country, including politicians, business-people, academics, and liberal professionals. We highlight the main issues that emerged, which are broadly in line with the analysis of the data provided in international datasets, as elaborated in the previous section.

In the first part of the quantitative questionnaire, we asked respondents to select what they thought were the main obstacles to economic development in the country. The key areas that emerged as the most selected choices were human capital, poverty, and inequality, as well as management of public administration and a common vision of national strategy.

Respondents in the key informant interviews agreed that low state capacity and lack of independence from private interests are major reasons why institutions are not performing well in Mozambique. Low capacity is partly associated with widespread corruption, regularly believed to have roots in the co-mingling of business and politics but also in the complexity of laws and frequent changes to institutional arrangements related to regulation and enforcement. There is also a perception that the state has never gained full capacity to finance its costs, since it has been too dependent on aid. Low levels of education hamper law enforcement, exacerbated by the fact that recruitment and promotion in the public service reflect not professional merit but alliances and loyalty.

Personnel selection and promotion are neither transparent nor based on the merits of professional qualifications and results. Many qualified professionals leave state institutions due to low wages or a non-motivating work environment. To illustrate, criteria for promotions at the level of the national director no longer include experience as provincial director. Moreover, at the district and local levels state representatives often do not have sufficient qualifications to carry out their duties. This is highly problematic: The role of the district administrator is essential, as the individual ability to plan and implement at the district level affects the lives of many people. Yet district administrators, who have an ambiguous mission, are appointed with reference to political loyalty, and most of them are not properly trained. This, combined with a chronic mismatch between resources and plans, leads to district administrators not being assessed on results, so the entire public planning exercise becomes of secondary importance.

While there was disagreement as to whether the number of civil servants is too high, there was almost consensus that Mozambique has too many ministries and related institutions, and that there is too much remodelling of the government structure. The competencies between sectoral ministries and their subordinate institutions are often changed for short-term political gains. The lack of clarity in competencies confuses responsibility and exerts a heavy weight on the budget. For many respondents, the state apparatus serves the purposes of offering jobs to acquaintances, family members, and 'comrades' and of creating a politically loyal group. The consequence is an ineffective and expensive state that fails to meet the need to provide public services to the population.

The second part of the quantitative questionnaire elicited detailed information by asking participants to state their degree of agreement with 156 statements organised into 18 thematic areas that covered different institutional dimensions. The answers failed to provide a consensus of opinion on a specific group of constraints. Still, they highlighted the importance attributed to issues related to legal and constitutional matters, public protection, and provision of public goods and services. A closer look at the respondents' opinions also emphasised the resolution of land issues and corruption in the business environment and public administration as important problems in Mozambique.

Weak law enforcement and dispute resolution reflects the fact that the judicial apparatus is heavy, dispersed in the territory, and inefficient. While much investment has taken place in palaces of justice, not much has gone to the efficient management of the different entities that operate in these buildings. There is also huge inequality in the resources available to the courts in the national and provincial capitals compared with the resources in the districts.

Respondents shared the perception that there is no independence of the judiciary from the executive. Some believe that this dependence stems from the fact that the president of the republic appoints the judges, who lead the Supreme, Administrative, and Constitutional Courts, as well as the attorney general of the republic. This, in their assessment, creates an opportunity to demand loyalty, and some serious criminal cases are not brought to court.

On the theme of low levels of education, key informants noted that there has been a high level of investment in education since independence. Mozambique has achieved significant results in the number of people who have been educated. However, there is a lack of quality in education at all levels: primary, secondary, higher, and technical-professional. The practice of allowing all students to move to higher education levels without having achieved minimum quality standards represents a major failure of the education system. The proliferation and subdivision of universities and other institutions of higher education are opposed to the objective of improving the quality of education.

At the same time, there is a demand for training and qualification of personnel in new areas, such as cybersecurity, robotics, and artificial intelligence. Universities must also invest in these areas. Unfortunately, national policies continue to focus on traditional fields, neglecting the new areas of science and technology.

One particular area in which there seemed to be less consensus based on the results of the quantitative questionnaire relates to external cooperation. While there was some indication that respondents find events in neighbouring countries to have negative effects on Mozambique, they also identified the degree of collaboration with these countries as an institutional strength. We delve more deeply into this theme in the synthesis in the next section of this chapter.

## D  Summary of Thematic Studies

Together with the background information on the history and socio-economic development of Mozambique, the insights from the above analysis pointed us to the selection of the areas addressed in our series of thematic studies. More specifically, *agriculture* and *natural resources* are clearly crucial sectors for achieving sustained growth and tackling poverty and inequality. The issues raised in terms of state capacity, and a lack of common vision are covered in the different chapters dealing with *public financial management* and *decentralisation*, as well as *education* and *health*. Both the quantitative questionnaire and the key informant interviews revealed legal and constitutional matters as an important area, which led us to include a chapter on the *legal sector*. Finally, we dedicated a chapter to *relations with donors* given the manifest relevance of this topic in the context of Mozambique, as revealed from the background analysis, quantitative questionnaire, and interviews with key informants.

We asked a carefully selected group of experts, who have first-hand experience from work in policy-making and research, to uncover the main institutional weaknesses and their underlying causes in these thematic areas. We summarise key insights from these studies (included as Chapters 4 to 11) in what follows.

## 1 *Agriculture*

The agriculture study (Chapter 4) by Carrilho et al. brings out clearly that the peasantry and the development of agriculture and the rural sector have over the years remained *de facto* a low priority in development efforts, and that much-needed productivity growth has been both slow and unsatisfactory. Incapacity to implement strategies and plans that have been formally announced has been evident. In parallel, the organisational framework for planning and the support of the agriculture and rural sector has suffered from frequent changes responding to short-run political convenience rather than long-term fundamental needs for inclusive growth and poverty reduction. This is reinforced by the existing lack of consensus over a broad range of issues about how to confront the agriculture and rural challenges in support of sustained growth.

For future progress, it is essential that political violence and armed conflict end and that the government ensures that the sector gets the precedence it requires in national plans to effectively contribute to the reduction of poverty and inequality, and that this is both in rhetoric and in practice. A laissez faire approach will not unleash the productive potential of the sector. What is required instead is a comprehensive and consistent set of public sector interventions and support to address the many externalities and co-ordination issues associated with agricultural production and transformation. Also looming is the need for agricultural development to address effectively the existing regional imbalances.

While pertinent legal regulations exist in many cases, they are often not adhered to and only some 30 per cent of the land is registered with user rights. Peasants' needs, including the need for secure access to land, are quite well understood, but low state capacity in delivering services and inputs and lack of access to the legal system are severe constraints. Furthermore, agriculture is a potential victim if the gas economy is allowed to undermine Mozambique's comparative advantage in agriculture, while population growth, climate change, and the dynamic effects of the COVID-19 pandemic no doubt provide compelling arguments for action in support of agriculture in both the short, medium, and long term, keeping in mind that should the gas windfall disappoint, a dynamic agriculture (an area in which Mozambique has a well-recognised comparative advantage) will have been built.

## 2 *Education*

As described by Mário, Monjane, and Santos (Chapter 5), despite the impressive increase in the schooling rate, significant problems remain in terms of the quality of education. For instance, less than 5 per cent of the students in the third class achieved a developed reading competence and less than 8 per cent fulfil the requirements for their level in terms of maths skills. The analysis highlights different pedagogical deficiencies, such as absenteeism, very high student–teacher ratios, and poor preparation and control of teachers' work, as well as shortages in teaching materials and lack of classrooms.

The key line of argument indicates three underlying institutional dimensions to the low-quality levels of learning. The first relates to weak state capacity in the provision of education services. The demographic pressure on primary education brings out weaknesses in terms of the number of classrooms and teachers. While the education sector receives an important share of the state budget (17.2 per cent of the entire 2018 state budget, according to UNICEF 2018), this is still insufficient to fulfil the needs in terms of the equipment, human capacity, and skills required.

The second institutional dimension relates to international support. While the financial support of international partners has been necessary, given the aforementioned financial shortages, it has also created dependence mechanisms and meant that decisions reflect conditionality from these partners, including over-ambitious policies and targets. Additionally, even if external donors provide financial support in terms of creating infrastructure, they do not finance a significant part of maintenance and other recurrent costs, including salaries, which account for the lion's share of the budget.

The final dimension relates to the weaknesses in the accountability of the public school system, which should enable the involvement of parents and the community in school management.

## 3 Health

Despite the investment in infrastructure and the progress since peace in 1992, current health indicators show a precarious health status for most Mozambicans. In Chapter 6, Garrido highlights different problems and argues that the deficiencies and inefficiencies in the functioning of the health sector are not least a result of a minority of privileged people controlling the main institutions in the health sector and not *de facto* prioritising the basic health needs of the majority of the population. Thus, there is weak state capacity to prioritise the health sector due to lack of political will, as well as lack of autonomy from private interests.

The problems include several instances of irregularities in legal compliance and enforcement (e.g., selection of people to healthcare positions without public tender) and the fact that the citizens' right to healthcare is neither clear in the Constitution nor sufficiently protected. Additionally, the healthcare system does not yet cover the entire territory and does not meet the basic needs of citizens either in urban or in rural areas, with political instability and violent conflict creating further challenges.

While policies and plans in the health sector have been adequate, there have been several problems with their implementation. The international community has heavily influenced health policies in Mozambique not only in terms of priorities, but also in terms of budget allocation decisions, some of which were not feasible given the capacity constraints in the country, undermining the quality of the services provided and the credibility of the sector.

## 4 *Decentralisation*

Forquilha stresses in Chapter 7 that while the process of decentralisation is potentially an important means for democratic consolidation and for 'good governance', the impact of the decentralisation reforms on governance in Mozambique has so far been very modest. The comprehensive overview of the links between the formation of the political systems in Mozambique and the emergence of decentralisation reforms shows how the results of the latter have been conditioned by the political system.

During the period after independence, the centralisation of the state resulted from the legacy of state control from the colonial times and the Marxist-Leninist orientation adopted by Frelimo. The political and economic reforms in the late 1980s and early 1990s were central to the decentralisation process. Even if external pressure was important (within the realm of the good governance agenda), decentralisation was also part of a process of conflict management and re-legitimisation of the state at a time of peace-building and democratisation. Still, the implementation of the reforms has not been a pacific process or one based on consensus.

Decentralisation has been a way to occupy political space to reinforce state control and to benefit the elite, rather than a means to improve public service provision and strengthen democracy. This can be seen as a form of elite capture, in this case of the decentralisation law. Three different reforms are used to illustrate this argument, and they show that while different institutional dimensions have had distinct effects on the implementation of these reforms, state capacity and autonomy from private interests have been a pervasive conditional factor in all three.

## 5 *Public Financial Management*

As is clear throughout this volume, Mozambique is a country case that has seen fragile socio-economic change since independence in 1975. In Chapter 8, Cruz et al. provide a detailed account, and put this in perspective with reference to the impact on public financial management (PFM). Their historical record is both detailed and insightful as regards achievements and the complex process of policy-making that Mozambique has undergone. More specifically, they describe the successes and limitations of building a PFM system during the period since independence until the end of 1986, list and discuss the plethora of reforms that were taken from the late 1980s to around 2010, and examine the implications of the discovery of the gas reserves for the period since then.

The PFM system (including both its objectives and its procedural aspects) was indeed reformed and improved significantly during the period before and after the turn of the millennium. However, the PFM system weakened markedly during the 2010s. Against this background, attention is given to three themes that cut across several of the thematic chapters in an integrative manner.

- The detailed account of the evolution of PFM in Mozambique reveals the importance of the role of donors and the fact that the success of donor-prompted reforms depends on their ownership by the host government and its ability to exercise them.
- While the implemented reforms had positive effects in improving fiscal management for more than two decades, the lack of an independent legal system meant that fundamental challenges remained. The chapter highlights the socio-economic consequences of the lack of separation of powers and the merging of the political and executive power, which allowed for critical decisions to be made by party structures, without action by the parliament and a weak opposition.
- The insufficient degree of decentralisation has distorted the functionalities of the PFM system, leading to a system that does not deliver on declared priorities.

The current growth strategy relying on the exploitation of natural resources seems to be failing, and an alternative balanced growth strategy is put forward in the context of an effective democratic political system where the policy priorities required to foster sustainable and inclusive development are clearly identified. The PFM system needs to be reformed accordingly.

## 6 Dispute Resolution

Trindade's thorough account of the judicial system in Mozambique (Chapter 9) highlights weaknesses in terms of rule of law and judicial independence. While there have been different attempts at reforming the judicial system, mainly after the Constitution of 1990, they were of an immediate and cyclical nature and were a result of internal and external pressures that were not always clear or convergent. Additionally, some indicators point to poor performance in the sector. For instance, comparing the movement of court lawsuits between 2012/13 and 2018/19, one observes an increase in the number that were carried out. Nevertheless, there is still a significant number of pending cases.

There is a need to implement structural reform, which will be viable only if there is a systemic, integrated, and co-ordinated view among all actors and willingness from policy-makers. The different elements that this structural reform would entail point to two main institutional weaknesses. On the one hand, they relate to a lack of state capacity applied to this sector. Structural reform would require a shared strategic vision and a degree of consensus between the relevant actors, and the judicial operators should play a central role in its different stages. The reforms should also proceed with reference to the democratisation of the constitutional and operational methods and processes of the judiciary. Two additional suggestions emphasise the need to strengthen the training of judicial agents and to restructure the alternative mechanisms for conflict resolution and community justice. On the other hand, they point to the need to ensure the independence of the judicial power and to change the paradigm of legislative production.

## 7 *Donor Relations and Sovereignty*

A key chapter in this volume is the study on donor relations and sovereignty (Chapter 10) by Flentø and Simão. The point of departure is the observation that during the struggle for independence from Portugal and the first three decades as a sovereign country, Mozambique relied on international solidarity and managed donor relations well. Against a background of an extraordinarily favourable international environment regarding development cooperation, and in a setting where donor countries had little or no other interest in Mozambique than aid effectiveness, the Mozambican government adapted to donor-prompted reforms and mitigated the associated loss of agency. The government allowed the donors to challenge its capacity but never its authority.

This has changed in the last decade. Donor countries started to express increasing disappointment with the reform process and began to openly challenge the government's legitimacy. This change is not only associated with developments in Mozambique. Donor countries have become much less enthusiastic about long-term, and especially harmonised development cooperation. Aid budgets are under pressure and development finance has become much more linked to other donor-country foreign policy concerns, especially those related to security and commerce. This has changed donor yard-sticks and their modus operandi. Accordingly, Mozambique should expect increasing and significant instrumentalisation of aid budgets by donor countries, meaning that in the coming years it will have to be able to access and address other concerns of its partners than those of poverty alleviation, human rights, and democracy.

This is a challenge because the aid architecture and institutions Mozambique developed to deal with donors are not well suited for these new challenges. They separate and focus on a part of the relationship with foreign countries that is becoming less relevant and often serves as a vehicle for other agendas. Reforms should, probably, start with a strengthening of Mozambique's Foreign Service as genuine co-ordinator of foreign relations and the establishment of more discipline around national plans and strategies to improve state capacity.

A domestic, political dimension, and an often-ignored part, of external finance is the delays and destruction of projects that elite infighting and rent-seeking cause to programmes and projects financed by donors and foreign direct investment (FDI). When elements from different factions of the elite (Frelimo) are poisoning and stealing each other's projects (rent-seeking or not), this helps to create corrupt or 'do nothing' overcautious behaviour in vital institutions prioritising, co-ordinating, and approving vital investments for economic growth.

In sum, the 'donors' financial body language' used during the past decade has not provoked regime change or a change of attitude in the Frelimo leadership. Rather to the contrary, it may have helped to strengthen the resolve of the party leadership, as the Mozambican economy proved remarkably resilient to the financial crisis that followed when donors and investors froze loans and aid funds. Events illustrate that the sentiment of entitlement remains very strong in Frelimo, where many continue to equate sovereignty with the party's grip on power.

## 8 Natural Resources

Chapter 11 moves into the unfolding and necessarily forward-looking role of natural resources in Mozambique, especially large-scale investments in mining, oil, and gas. Macuane and Muianga bring us up to date with what is happening in the sector and make an assessment from an institutional perspective of the prospects of the natural resources/extractive industries to contribute to economic transformation.

Mozambique's wealth of natural resources is widely expected to generate new revenue streams in the medium and longer term. This could stimulate the economy, turning assets under the ground into assets above the ground, and allow for more investment in infrastructure and key social sectors, as well as agriculture. Nevertheless, there is reason to sound notes of caution and allude to the significant risks and constraints associated with major resource booms, which carry with them both potential pitfalls and benefits. The pitfalls include increased reliance on income from natural resources, depending on a few large foreign companies, and the observation that Mozambique has experienced a 'bust before the boom', reflected in the hidden debt (corruption) incurred during the era of President Guebuza.

Mozambique has indeed carried out institutional reforms to respond to the increasing importance of natural resources in the economy. They include passing extensive legislation with a focus on the mining, oil, and gas sector and its respective tax regimes, joining the Extractive Industries Transparency Initiative,[9] and the creation and strengthening of administrative regulatory and accountability institutions, combined with increasing participation of members of parliament and civil society in policy debates. While these reforms have improved the governance of the resources sector, their impact on economic transformation is harder to establish, and issues of state capacity remain.

Long term, Mozambique will be affected by the global energy transition now underway, which will significantly weaken the market for coal and, eventually, natural gas – thereby potentially 'stranding' the country's fossil fuel assets. Proper public expenditure management and systems are essential to ensure that investments yield adequate returns. Accordingly, one way to improve co-ordination is through a fiscal regime and institutional mechanism that define the scope of public expenditure in areas related to structural transformation, especially sectoral policy, and domestic and human capability development. This could be combined with initiatives regarding local content and industrial policy as part of a broader development strategy. Local procurement

---

[9] Mozambique joined in 2009 and became a compliant member in 2012.

regulations have largely failed to increase participation by local firms in value chains. Training can raise the capabilities of local firms and allow them to enter the value chains, but government and the resource extraction companies must agree on the design of training and the qualification processes for local firms to achieve 'approved vendor' status.

## III THE INSTITUTIONAL DIAGNOSTIC

We turn now to the institutional diagnostic illustrated in Table 12.1, where we bring together the material accumulated so far. Starting from the column of basic institutional weaknesses, the table can be read from left to right, with the right-hand column showing the major economic and social consequences of these institutional weaknesses. It can also be read from right to left, with a column showing the main proximate causes of the institutional weaknesses and a left-hand column displaying the deep factors that ultimately determine the feasibility of reforms that could correct the proximate causes, improving the institutional weaknesses and supporting socio-economic development.

An important caveat is that logical implications go from column to column, not from one item in a column to the item in the same row in another column. In other words, it is sometimes the case that several or all items in a column depend on, or jointly determine, the items in another column. It should also be kept in mind that the relationships between the items in different columns, and within a column, may be circular.

Moreover, we make no claim that the dividing lines between deep factors and proximate causes, on the one hand, and between proximate causes and basic institutional weaknesses, on the other, are beyond discussion. The reason for this juxtaposition is that the identified weaknesses are often more the symptoms than they are the causes of an institutional problem. A diagnostic must therefore start from the symptoms in order to go to the root of the problems, and then to the possible remedies, which themselves depend on which deep factors are at play.

We begin by briefly reviewing the basic institutional weaknesses as they emerge from preceding sections. They are common to several of the areas subjected to thematic studies, and they were also the subject of attention in previous chapters. Next, we address their proximate causes, which are themselves related to several deep factors described afterwards. Our final reflections and policy recommendations follow in the last subsection.

## A Basic Institutional Weaknesses (IW)

### 1 IW1: Incapacity to Implement Strategies and Plans That Have Been Formally Announced

At first glance, Mozambique is pursuing inclusive economic policies. The official policies and strategies have been formulated with the assistance of donors and approved by all relevant authorities, including the parliament. However,

TABLE 12.1  *A synthetic ordering of the institutional factors impeding Mozambique's long-term development*

| Deep factors | Proximate causes | Basic institutional weaknesses | Economic consequences |
|---|---|---|---|
| Physical and human geography<br>Colonial and socialist legacies<br>Neighbourhood with South Africa<br>Distribution of political power and weak political opposition (dominance of Frelimo, competition within Frelimo, and lack of voice)<br>Armed conflicts and political violence<br>Critical dependence on external finance (role of donors)<br>Contemporaneous: dominance of the natural resources sector and role of foreign companies and FDI | Lack of integration and diminished sense of unity<br>Lack of skills<br>Merging of political and economic powers (incipient entrepreneurial class and lack of market competition)<br>Lack of separation of executive and legislative powers<br>Instability of development strategies<br>Lack of agency in strategic and policy formulation<br>Elite capture and rent-seeking | Incapacity to implement strategies and plans that have been formally announced<br>Low state capacity (service delivery, decentralisation, control over the territory, administrative capacity)<br>Dependence of the judicial power on the executive<br>Corruption, lack of transparency, and ineffective auditing | Lack of an inclusive growth engine<br>Slow reduction of poverty<br>Increasing inequality (horizontally and vertically and by gender)<br>Non-inclusive and inefficient financial sector<br>Low quality of education<br>Non-inclusivity of health services<br>Lopsided spatial (regional) development<br>Absence of business dynamics<br>Low level of domestic savings<br>Vulnerability to external shocks |

*Source:* Authors' construction.

there are challenges in terms of their implementation. This goes for plans both at national and sector levels.

A case in point with regard to the latter is the agriculture sector, which is blessed with well-conceived sector strategies and policies but receives low priority in practice. To give an example, Filipe and Norfolk (2017) point out that Mozambique already has many reasonable policies and legal frameworks for land administration, land use planning, and environmental management. However, they highlight the 'need for greater political will and stronger institutional capacity and commitment to the implementation of the legal framework for land, particularly to recognise land rights acquired in law and the role of traditional and community authorities in the management of the land use and other resources' (Filipe and Norfolk, 2017: 103). Similarly, while financial inclusion is well established as an aim, the necessary measures to promote bank lending to the rural poor and MSEs are not yet in place. Finally, influence from the donor community has led to over-ambitious and non-sustainable plans for social sectors including education and health.

## 2 IW2: Low State Capacity (Service Delivery, Decentralisation, Control over the Territory, Administrative Capacity)

A related institutional weakness is low state capacity. This comes across in many different dimensions. Efforts at reforming the structure of the public sector have not been sustained, and there are important problems in relation to frequent rotations of staff (e.g., following changes in government) and in its spatial distribution. In many of the more remote parts of the country, government entities are simply not present. Additionally, large parts of the public administration are over-staffed with low-skilled and poorly motivated personnel lacking quality leadership.

The co-ordination of state functions leaves much to be desired, and while exceptions exist, the general situation remains one of low-capacity administration at both central and decentralised levels. Recruitment reform has been implemented to secure better-skilled personnel, but inertia and significantly better remuneration in the private sector continue to be challenges. Absenteeism is high, and many public servants are chasing fringe benefits like travel allowances and are involved in other economic activities in the private sector. At the decentralised level, the special double role of the district administrators (as politicians as well as technical supervisors and co-ordinators) is challenging technical professionalism in a system already struggling with the impact of Mozambique's geography. To this must be added mandatory postings, far from large cities where career opportunities for spouses and education for children are much better.

Moreover, the low quality of education and non-inclusivity in access to health and financial services are symptoms of poor delivery of public services. The provision of electricity also illustrates weakness in the delivery of infrastructure. The public electricity company (EdM) fundamentally runs at a loss in spite of significant donor finance especially during the first two decades after the war. The company is recognised as an efficiently run entity from a technical point of view, with both technical and non-technical losses well below those of most of its sister companies in the region. The company's cost structure is unique, as Mozambique is home to one of Africa's largest hydro dams. Although EdM is obliged to pay transmission fees to ESKOM, South Africa's public electricity company, this has endowed EdM with an exceptionally low unit cost for generation and very high fixed costs to finance power lines in a huge and sparsely populated country. Yet only a tiny fraction of the Mozambicans living below the poverty line has a power supply. Access to electricity in rural areas is practically non-existent, and the potential of solar power remains unexploited.

Additionally, and as is clear from Chapter 2 and previous sections in this chapter, the Mozambican government has not fully controlled the national territory since independence. This is associated with both geographic characteristics (Mozambique is a vast country in which guerrilla activity is relatively easy) and socio-economic factors. More specifically, the country remains poorly integrated in terms of economic and physical infrastructure.

This is linked also to the inability of the state to ensure security, as illustrated by the events in the northern province of Cabo Delgado, where a combination of looming domestic conflicts and external factors has erupted into significant military activity. It is noteworthy that while Mozambique's armed conflicts have traditionally been politically motivated and internationally backed and sponsored, none has been about religion. Intriguingly, the armed insurgency in Cabo Delgado is reported to be both 'home-grown' and religious – a war fought by a movement started by a group of young local Muslims with the sole purpose of installing a more fundamentalist practice of Islam. But there is much more than religion driving this powerful insurgency, and it has become a major challenge for the Mozambican government and army and strains state capacity to the very limit, if not beyond.

### 3  IW3: Dependence of the Judicial Power on the Executive

The formal separation of powers, especially the independence of the judiciary, is relatively recent in Mozambique, introduced in 1990 as a part of the constitutional reform package paving the way for peace and increased aid from the Western democracies. The process of implementing these institutional reforms is far from complete. There is still no independence of the judiciary and no effective separation of party and state, reflecting that the democratic institutions in Mozambique are young and weak.

Donor-prompted reforms in governance institutions have remained shallow primarily because the Mozambican elite has been reluctant to fully implement them. This is compounded by the fact that the Constitution gives the president extensive powers of appointment, with a systemic trickle-down effect in the justice sector. Strong affiliation with the dominant party is decisive for the careers and livelihood for judges, sometimes as much as their professional ability and integrity. This situation compromises peaceful conflict resolution and weakens fundamentals of society, from basic human rights to the business environment.

### 4  IW4: Corruption, Lack of Transparency, and Ineffective Auditing

Corruption has been sharply on the increase in Mozambique since the mid-1980s. This institutional weakness relates not only to political grand corruption, illustrated by the case of the hidden debt scandal.[10] It also includes

---

[10] Other examples are described in Shipley (2019).

cases of petty corruption and embezzlement of public funds. Cases of Frelimo members, their families, and highly positioned civil servants – who happen to receive commissions in the economic deals involving public entities – obtain privileged access to land use rights, and provide politically motivated cheap electricity to urban families illustrate this.

Turning to the lack of transparency, this is discussed in detail in IMF (2019), where it is highlighted that many critical databases, such as the company registry, the land registry, the movable property registry, and the notarial database, are either entirely or partially manual and are difficult to access and search. In addition, information remains in general fragmented among different government ministries, with the result that policies and regulations end up being contradictory.

The institutions combatting corruption remain weak and lack independence from political influence. Moreover, their technical and financial resources are limited. Audit controls are, as recognised in IMF (2019), not effective, opening up the possibility for both criminal acts (that might not be discovered) and misallocation and misuse of funds as a result of lack of information. While recent improvements have been noted in terms of transparency and the capacity to implement the tax regime in the natural resource sector, challenges remain – for example, in terms of the capacity to audit companies. Moreover, discrepancies continue to be reported between the revenues declared by companies and those declared by the Revenue Authority.

## B Proximate Causes (PC)

Seven proximate causes stand out from our analysis (see Table 12.1). We discuss them in turn.

### *1 PC1: Lack of Integration and Diminished Sense of Unity*
Since colonial days, Mozambique has been a transit country, with backbone transport infrastructure that was built primarily to serve mining and farming in the much larger economies of South Africa and Rhodesia. Thus, the rail and main road networks run east–west. Little infrastructure serves north–south traffic and national integration, and rural roads serving farmers are few and far between.

Over the last three decades, donors have supported the government programme of investing in rehabilitating roads, bridges, and railways, or building new roads and bridges. However, the main investments were directed to serve landlocked countries. Only a smaller share of the investments was allocated to the north–south connection. This reflects the fact that projects undertaken had to meet established criteria as regards the internal rate of return, in which vehicle operation costs are a key determinant. Consequently, the large trunk roads in the east–west corridors serving the much larger economies of South Africa and Zimbabwe take priority, as there is much less traffic going north–south (due to the colonial economic model and the fact that Renamo split the country in two and interrupted traffic south of the Zambézia river for fifteen years). The bridge over the Zambézia in Caia was built only in 2009, and small rural roads to serve farmers have received only a small share of the road funds budget.

While the government has clear priorities in relation to overall connectivity in the country, including for security reasons, its own contribution to the transport sector, especially to maintenance, has not been sufficient. The collection of road users' fees in the form of vehicle registration taxes, import duties, and not least fuel levy has also been insufficient to cover expenditure. A further characteristic is that the government has subsidised fuel consumption to protect urban transport from strikes and riots.

The overall result is that the fundamental layout of infrastructure inherited from colonial days remains in place and that road maintenance is very expensive. Routine maintenance is deferred and migrated from the recurrent to the investment budget, where donors are more inclined to help finance major rehabilitations once the infrastructure has degraded substantially. This is a much more costly solution both in terms of the civil work itself and in terms of vehicle operation costs. The dynamic effects also include lack of capacity-building among the smaller local contractors that would normally compete for, and grow on, a portfolio of smaller works, not least routine maintenance. This is the segment of civil work contractors that a country like Mozambique needs for the maintenance of its rural roads network.

The modal split is heavily tilted towards roads. The public railways are running at a loss, and have been largely neglected since the days of the SAP. One reason is that the golden egg in the railway business is actually the ports owned by the Mozambique railway company (CFM). Prominent figures of the elite are involved with foreign companies operating the three deep-sea ports on concessions from CFM. There is much less interest in the rail lines, and the only real rehabilitations of railways in Mozambique during the last twenty-five years relate to and are financed by the foreign coal companies in Tete. However, the coal trains running through some of Mozambique's most fertile land do not carry other cargo than coal, and that only one way.

Importantly, the poor state of physical capital stock and infrastructure, in combination with a weakly Integrated Public Investment Plan (Plano Integrado de Investimentos Públicos), substantially constrain private sector development. This happens due to very high transaction costs, inherent in expensive and unreliable transport and communications.

An important undercurrent has been that, while the sense of unity of the population of Mozambique was high at independence, this has gradually waned over the years. The continued polarisation between Frelimo and Renamo is an integral element thereof, and the same goes for the deepening imbalance in development between the south, on the one hand, and the centre and north, on the other.

## 2  PC2: Lack of Skills

A true institutional disruption happened at independence when the overwhelming majority of educated and trained people (Portuguese settlers)
left Mozambique and sabotaged assets on their way out. This meant that
Mozambique (and other Portuguese colonies) started from a much lower point
in 1974 than most former British and French colonies did in the early 1960s.
While Frelimo prioritised education in the early post-independence years, little
was possible during sixteen years of war. Notable progress has undoubtedly
taken place since the early 1990s. However, the lack of skills and educated
people does continue to hamper socio-economic progress. This is especially so
when account is taken of the existing lack of attention to the need for a functioning meritocratic system in appointments and promotions. Similar issues
reverberate through the legal and judicial system.

## 3  PC3: Merging of Political and Economic Powers (Incipient
## Entrepreneurial Class and Lack of Market Competition)

In the socialist system after 1977, the economic and political powers were
merged by design. The SAP was meant to separate them, but this failed. The
underlying assumptions behind large-scale liberalisation and privatisation to
arrive at a competitive economy were simply not in place. Privatised enterprises were taken over by party members, civil servants, and army officers.
Consequently, most public companies were either substituted by private
monopolies or closed down.

Mozambique's first post-independence private entrepreneurs were overwhelmingly government officials and public servants who acquired public assets (sometimes at very low prices) in the privatisation drive in the late
eighties and early nineties. Since there were practically no private businesses in
Mozambique during the socialist area, the new entrepreneurial class had to be
recruited from public institutions, including the security forces and the government itself. For the liberation struggle to be meaningful at all, it was necessary
to make sure that Mozambicans got the privatised state assets and not foreign
capitalists, including Portuguese and South African business constellations that
were very much reminiscent of colonial times. Furthermore, Mozambique was
still a one-party state when the economic reforms were rolled out. RENAMO
was not yet a political party but a guerrilla army fighting in the bush or waiting
to be demobilised.

In short, Frelimo privatised the assets and, more importantly, the business
opportunities to its own members. Some of the new Mozambican business
people had technical knowledge, but they rarely had the skills and mind-set
of an entrepreneur. Most were started off in private business with a public
asset including some sort of exclusivity (licence, quota, geographic position,
or contract for supplies to government) and continued to depend on government protection of their monopolistic position. Some of the new entrepreneurs
went broke or liquidated the assets, but others continued and some arranged

for foreign partners with capital and knowledge. Whether it was in fisheries, tourism, transport, export of primary products, or just general import trade business, regulations controlled by the government would be the key to profitable business. This is in part a logical consequence of the forces of liberal markets and in part a consequence of the deliberate and persistent exclusion of entrepreneurs with ties to the opposition.

The economic consequences are similar to those of state capture; the cure is not. In contrast to a political system where political parties are owned or significantly influenced by big business (e.g., as in Benin), the big business in Mozambique is organised by politicians[11] in a powerful structure where business owners cannot hedge their bets and finance the campaigns of various political parties (as seen in some former Eastern European countries and Russia).[12] If Frelimo loses elections, it is likely to be 'game over' for many of Mozambique's business owners and entrepreneurs in an environment where politics and business are closely intertwined. Everyone knows that their best and maybe only bet to stay in power and continue to harvest rent is to protect the party's interests.[13] Thus, the business owners oil the party machine, competition is kept internal, and the party has its own rules and referees, not depending much on (or needing) the dispute resolution institutions of the state.

Frelimo knows that it can win elections (be declared winner) with almost any presidential candidate. As the incumbent party, it can and does abuse state assets in the campaign, and more importantly, it has access to campaign finance in a completely different league to the opposition. Most of this money is raised from the business people in the party, often with funds from their foreign business partners and associates. Campaign funding is raised in exchange for business relations with the state that are supposed to influence not only the general conditions of the exchange, that is the business environment at large or

---

[11] Mozambique is not a case of capture of government by a business elite, but of capture of business by the political elite. Moreover, the oligarchs had only limited experience to begin with. Furthermore, the primary organiser of business owners in Mozambique is not the employers' associations or their confederation (CTA). It is the governing party.

[12] See also Addison (2003).

[13] This is visible, for example, in relation to the business environment at large and related laws, licences, permits, etc. Much of the business in real estate is deeply dependent on the way the land law is administered, as land cannot be owned (the principle of 'use it or lose it' is not applied, and many hold land for speculation). Licences to do business in the import–export sector are heavily regulated, including customs tariffs, sometimes providing negative protection to help importers over farmers and local industry. Additionally, transport business (people and goods) is heavily regulated and many operators would be put out of business if the laws were applied. Coincidentally, Frelimo members or their families co-share the capital participation in various companies in the private sector. This indicates an overuse of political power to obtain economic power. In many public tenders to purchase equipment or participate in investment projects, companies have to pay a commission to government officials, which is not foreseen in the law. One justification for these commissions is that they are used to finance Frelimo.

in a sector but also specific deals. As such, conflict of interest at best, and more often corruption, is embedded within the system.

Moreover, as foreign trade liberalised and competition from much more efficient foreign companies commenced, the easiest profit and best business opportunities for Mozambican entrepreneurs were in trade in imported consumer goods and exports of primary products, tourism, and, not least, construction related to land development and privatised real estate. The government continued as a very large player in a small market for goods and services and as the regulator of all duties, licences, and permits. Combined with the effects of the revolving door, where business people and officials enter and leave government frequently, the ties between the government and entrepreneurs become exceptionally tight.

Associated with the intertwining of political and business interests and the characteristics of the Mozambican geography and economy, there is absence of genuine market competition in the economy. There is competition among different groups in the party, but this does not translate into making market mechanisms work.

## 4 PC4: Lack of Separation of Executive and Legislative Powers

Frelimo, as the dominant party, commands a majority – sometimes even a qualified majority – in the parliament, and the party can thus vote almost all policy it requires through the legislative process. This logically weakens the separation of the legislative from the executive mandate, but such is part and parcel of democracy if elections are free and fair. A weak opposition leaves democracy wanting.

Manipulations of elections have taken place in Mozambique, where most observers agree that few elections have been free and fair (see, e.g., Human Rights Watch 2019). The practices of manipulation of the list of candidates and voters register, limitation of observers' access, intimidation during campaign and on the day of election, and manipulations of results including ballot box stuffing and tinkering with the final tabulation have been reported by reputable observers at various elections in Mozambique (Human Rights Watch 2019). Disagreement has centred on the significance of these phenomena – whether the irregularities were substantial enough to have changed the bottom-line outcome, that is, the majority in parliament or who becomes president. It seems, however, that most observers agree that things are not changing for the better.

## 5 PC5: Instability of Development Strategies

Few countries have experienced as many chaotic political and economic changes as Mozambique both before and since independence in 1975, with frequent changes in strategy and the organisation of key economic sectors.

After independence, Frelimo aimed at a drastic change in economic policy, adopting Marxist-Leninist principles. This proved unsuccessful, and the incipient attempt, at the Fourth Party Congress in 1984, at reorientation to focus on peasant needs sank in the middle of war. The SAP of 1987, including liberalisations and privatisations, represented another fundamental shift in strategy in almost all corners of Mozambique's society and economy. This shift happened only around a decade after independence and attempted not only to roll back the protectionist policies introduced by socialism but also to reorganise many of the basic institutions of the economy.

While Frelimo has remained in power, fragmentation within the party led to strong regime changes at presidential elections. The resulting instability of development strategies has been characteristic, as illustrated in the quite different approaches to policy and reform pursued by presidents Chissano and Guebuza. The lack of continuity in strategic plans has led to redirection of policy and frequent changes of personnel in government and leading positions of public administration, which has weakened state capacity and the capacity to implement strategies and plans in a coherent manner.

## 6  PC6: Lack of Agency in Strategic and Policy Formulation

Donor assistance and international solidarity were never enough to make up for the devastation of war and bad economic policy in the first half of the 1980s. As debt mounted and key allies in the socialist camp fell, Mozambique was forced to seek assistance elsewhere and adopt new economic policies in exchange for aid and debt relief. Those policies were standard recipes for former socialist regimes joining the Bretton Woods institutions. They made Mozambique pursue fiscal austerity, market-based reforms, and privatisations in a wartime environment where the economy was incapable of responding to market incentives.

What did happen when the SAP was introduced was that the Frelimo-government lost agency to donors. It was no longer in charge of policy formulation in macroeconomic management and key sectors. It concentrated its efforts on surviving and adapting to new rules of the game. The survival of Frelimo became dependent on satisfying the donors, implicitly by selling donor-prompted policies to the electorate by winning elections.

More recently, the decline in the importance of donor funding has opened up space for more independent agency on the part of the Mozambican government. However, Mozambique still remains highly dependent on external finance, increasingly in the form of FDI. This means that the country will in the coming years be dealing with foreign governments that will be driven by other concerns than those inherent in the aid process, that is poverty alleviation, human rights, and democracy. The lack of agency will therefore continue in a different form unless concerted action is taken.

## 7  PC7: Elite Capture and Rent-Seeking

Mozambique was moving in the direction of strengthened governance institutions for around twenty years, from 1994, as many international indicators show (see Chapter 3). One could have hoped that this development would continue, but this trend reversed due *inter alia* to the onset of the extractive industries and the pre-boom curse, which started in the early 2000s, including hidden debts and economic crises. The fundamental curse of the pre-boom phase of extractive economies is exactly that they are characterised by huge opportunities for rents, which necessarily arise before extraction starts.[14]

Moreover, as there is no effective separation between party and state and big business, the stakes in politics were raised considerably after 2006 when international companies were granted exclusive rights to explore and exploit oil and gas off the coast of Cabo Delgado (especially after the confirmation of the existence of massive reserves of natural gas in the Rovuma Basin in 2010). It became apparent that the distribution of income and assets in the Mozambican society for generations to come could be determined in the coming decade. This has been detrimental to the furthering of democratic and legal reform.

With a view to better competing with foreign interests for the rents of the oil and gas extraction, President Guebuza strengthened the party's hold on state institutions and replaced many technocrats with politicians in leading government positions. He managed to get an almost completely loyal polit-buro, and the extensive powers allotted to the president by the Mozambican Constitution were used extensively and secured loyalty to the party in all three pillars of the state.

Originally, this process created opportunities for rent and related earnings that kept the politically affluent segments of society satisfied.[15] However, the consequence for Frelimo of staying in power and managing the forced radi-cal change of policy (and loss of agency to donors) was, as described above, that it became deeply intertwined with the leading domestic business commu-nity and public servants. The 'new' elite that emerged accepted capitalism and started using state control as a means of economic accumulation. This process intensified in the early years of the new millennium with the advent of natural resources, associated rent opportunities, and the centralist approach to gover-nance pursued by President Guebuza.

Accordingly, the non-inclusive traits of the Mozambican economy ampli-fied, and this explains – at least in part – why economic growth in Mozambique slowed down. A growth strategy based on mega-projects in infrastructure and energy will reinforce the underlying drivers of exclusion unless extreme care is taken in policy formulation and implementation. While FDI in extractive industries led to some infrastructure investments in the northern provinces, massive amounts of (loan) finance went towards infrastructure in the south, especially in and around the capital.[16] Both developments dramatically

---

[14] See Roe (2018) for an illuminating overview of international experiences of relevance in Mozambique.

[15] These groups are heavily concentrated in southern Mozambique, especially in the capital, and to a lesser extent in a couple of large cities in the centre and north of the country.

[16] The major infrastructure investments in the south are not justified by economic use, but rather by the massive rents (increases in land and real estate values) they would bring and the monu-mental effects on the president's legacy. Finance was not hard to come by due to creditworthi-ness from gas reserves and other barter trading with China and a few other countries.

increased the value of land overwhelmingly owned by the elite and the urban middle class. A limited number of people made fortunes, at the expense of many. The public financing of infrastructure to benefit the private sector in general is not a phenomenon special to Mozambique. In fact, it is the rule of the game in most capitalist countries and part of the reason why people pay taxes. What matters is the quality of the infrastructure investments, or rather whom they benefit. Good infrastructure investments raise productivity in the economy. That does not happen with infrastructure development designed to create rent opportunities.[17]

The largest cost of rent-seeking and corruption is not the money stolen or assets appropriated. It is the summarised cost to the economy of all the bad (economically ineffective) decisions taken to create, or to avoid eliminating, opportunities for profits without production. Rent-seeking and elite grabbing seriously distort allocative efficiency in the economy at large. The much-needed possible alternative investment in true productivity growth is forgone, which is very damaging to a poor country where investment resources are scarce. Especially when large, public projects benefitting private elite business are loan-financed, this policy can drain a small economy and halt sustainable growth. Changing this dynamic stands out as a major challenge.

## C  Deep Factors (DF)

We now proceed to presenting the deep underlying factors that condition the viability of reforms that could correct the proximate causes, improving the institutional weaknesses and underpinning future socioeconomic development. We identify seven deep factors and aim in what follows to integrate them with the findings in previous sections, bringing out the correspondence across columns so as to ensure maximum consistency.

### 1  DF1: Physical and Human Geography

As described in Chapter 2, Mozambique is a large, sparsely populated country with twenty-five main rivers crossing into the Indian Ocean and physically dividing the country, bordering Tanzania in the north, Malawi, Zimbabwe, Zambia, and Eswatini to the west, and South Africa to the south. The country is well endowed with natural resources, including the recent finds of major gas reserves in the north.

The high investment and transaction costs resulting from the vastness of the territory and its characteristics have always been a barrier to economic

---

[17] One could consider the Catembe bridge over Maputo Bay and the road to Ponta d'Ouro close to South Africa, costing together around US$1 billion (financed mainly from China), as an example. To put the cost into perspective, it would be possible to almost rehabilitate the north–south trunk highway N1 from Maputo to Nampula with the same money. Alternatively, one could get 1,800 km of good roads from the farmland to the towns and cities.

integration. We alluded above to the fact that infrastructure runs mainly east–west (an inheritance from colonial times) and that while some improvement has been made (with the support of donors) in terms of rehabilitating or building new roads and bridges, the north–south connection has received only a minor share of the investment. This had a further effect on the capacity of the state not only in terms of controlling and administering the territory but also in terms of implementing the approved development plans and strategies.

Moreover, as evidenced by the 2019 cyclones Idai and Kenneth, Mozambique is among the countries most prone to the effects of climate change, including weather shocks and natural disasters. Weather shocks have been a recurring feature in Mozambique over the centuries, and their costs to the economy are massive. This has, since the independence, been the motivation for significant amounts of humanitarian aid to Mozambique.

Regional and ethnic fractionalisation in the country have deep historical roots that go back to the time when different Bantu-speaking tribes were established in the territory. Subsequently, the Arabs began to have an influence from approximately 1100 CE. The effects of the encounter between the tribes and Arab traders turned out differently among different tribes. However, the resulting ethnic diversity and the Arab influence remain present to this day alongside the colonial legacy and post-independence development experiences, including the drastic transformation of relations between certain ethnic groups due to the liberation war and postcolonial experience. This diversity has also resulted in economic fragmentation and is an underlying factor explaining differences in access to political power. The different ethnic power balances of the main political parties also come into play here, contributing to challenging the sense of unity in present times.

## 2 DF2: Colonial and Socialist Legacies

When assessing economic development in Mozambique today, especially in relation to its African peers, it is fundamental to reiterate when and how Mozambique started as a sovereign country. It happened well over a decade later than in most other sub-Saharan African countries and from an incredibly low point in terms of human development and governance capacity, due to an especially crippling colonial legacy.

Moreover, victory and independence came suddenly because of events in Portugal, at a time where the Portuguese security forces were still largely in control of 90 per cent of the Mozambican territory. Frelimo governed only a small fraction of rural Mozambique along the borders with Tanzania and in Tete province, and it consisted of an international lobby group and a guerrilla army hosted in Dar es Salaam and Nachingwea. Frelimo moved into this space and, almost overnight, had a huge country to rule after the departure of hundreds of thousands of settlers and the colonial exploitation and extraction of resources, combined with top-down management and distorted political economic structures. The almost complete dismantling of colonial institutions with the flight of the Portuguese left the country in a very difficult situation.

Frelimo made a concerted effort at nation-building, within a unified socialist vision of the nation. However, the introduction of a socialist-style planned economy was a shock to economic institutions, albeit in some areas less so than socialist propaganda might lead us to believe. Controlled prices, including on staples, were simply continued from the colonial system, just as many parastatals were continued with new, inexperienced leaders combined with upbeat rhetoric. Importantly, rural trade was not carried out by parastatals in colonial times. It was done by private traders who left in huge numbers, leading to total collapse in marketing and trade.

In sum, Mozambique has had precious little time to develop a modern state and society, and this helps to explain its ranking at the bottom of the scale in terms of GDP and the Human Development Index (HDI). This links to the continued lack of skills and low state capacity. Moreover, the fact that Frelimo ruled Mozambique as a one-party state for almost two decades has impacted on the present biased distribution of political power and the merging of political and economic powers, including the lack of separation of the executive, legislative, and judicial powers.

### 3 DF3: Neighbourhood with South Africa

Mozambique's location as a neighbour of South Africa has throughout history impacted very significantly on both institutional and economic trends in the country, and it continues to do so to this day. It determined how the economy was built during the colonial period, how the liberation struggle evolved, how the first fifteen years of independence turned out, and the fact that southern Mozambique interacts with its neighbour in a very different way from the rest of the country. To illustrate, hundreds of thousands of migrant labourers from southern Mozambique have for many decades worked in the mines of South Africa and played a key role in transferring resources back to southern Mozambique.

Moreover, at the time when Mozambique gained its independence in 1975 (some ten to fifteen years later than most other African former colonies), the apartheid regime's strategy of destructive engagement with the region caused havoc and economic destruction. Put differently, Frelimo did not have the same opportunities as other African governments did at the time of their independence. To this can be added the fact that RENAMO was supported by external forces (from South Africa and Rhodesia) as a guerrilla movement, skilfully exploiting domestic differences and contradictions (Pinto 2008).

Of particular importance, multiparty elections and universal suffrage were conditions for peace in 1992 not only in Mozambique, but also in South Africa. As the Cold War came to an end, and the African National Congress was no longer seen as a possible Soviet ally, Western countries mounted more pressure on the apartheid regime and the first free elections were held almost simultaneously in Mozambique and South Africa. This meant that borders and trade flows between the two countries were reopened, leading to increasing economic integration between southern Mozambique and South Africa.

Economic and social power was already concentrated in the south before independence, because of the South African economy. The moving of the capital from Ilha to Lourenço Marques[18] in the early twentieth century was due to the gold economy in South Africa. This move of the capital to the extreme south of a very large country because of important economic links with another, much larger economy cannot be overemphasised.

Most of the modern-day elite and urban middle class live in southern Mozambique, benefitting from the neighbourhood with South Africa. They are not dependent on domestic agriculture for their produce, or on their export earnings and foreign currency to finance imports of consumer goods. Donors and a handful of large foreign companies in the energy sector provide for the currency, while South African and to a lesser extent Asian farmers feed the urban middle class and elite in Mozambique.

South Africa is a formidable competitor, with its advanced manufacturing sector and mechanised agriculture enjoying high levels of protection and subsidy. Maputo is much closer to the agricultural heartland of South Africa than to its own rich farmland in the central and northern provinces. Infrastructure is better and tariffs are low due to economic integration in the SADC (Southern African Development Community) area and massive corruption in the customs services. Mozambique has not only been buying agricultural goods from South Africa but also purchasing all sorts of consumer goods (durable goods, garments, medicines, etc.), construction goods, and other services to enterprises; tourist services (hotels and restaurants); and houses, as well as using medical services (combining medical and tourism services in many cases). Mozambique has contributed to South Africa's economy since 1993, in particular in the Mpumalanga region, rather than prioritising its own industries and services.

South African supermarket chains have expanded into all provincial capitals and cater overwhelmingly for the middle class, with products imported from South Africa and Asia. Even the staple food of most city dwellers is imported. White bread is the staple of choice of the urban population, rich and poor. Mozambique produces no wheat (for climatic reasons), and bread is heavily subsidised.[19] This de-linking of the urban middle class from its own agriculture

---

[18] Ilha became the capital because of economic links with India (Goa), where Portugal ruled for 451 years until 1961. It was the declining importance of the Indian trade and increasing importance of South Africa (when it discovered gold in 1860) that moved the centre of economic gravity southwards.

[19] The key point here is that the urban population is not buying and eating what the farmers produce. Moreover, the wheat import and milling industry allows for rent-seeking because it is a profitable business depending on licences and administered prices.

is a fundamental problem for inclusive development in Mozambique, and it is a growing one. As the infrastructure developments especially around Maputo are the start of a new corridor to Durban, they will have significant dynamic effects by connecting southern Mozambique and Maputo even more closely to South Africa and not to the central and northern provinces. This will not help the rural–urban exchange in Mozambique; on the contrary, it will increase land rents and opportunities for tourism and real estate development in southern Mozambique. That will attract foreign investment that the elite can joint venture with and create jobs in construction and subsequently some few white-collar jobs in the industries themselves.

In our assessment, the integration of southern Mozambique with South Africa is connected with some of the most fundamental issues and challenges Mozambique faces. Northern products are more expensive because of transport costs. However, north–south infrastructure and regional integration has not received the necessary priority in public investment plans. It would appear that this is linked to both the distribution of political power and the donor focus on investment projects in the south.

## 4 DF4: Distribution of Political Power and Weak Political Opposition (Dominance of Frelimo, Competition within Frelimo, and Lack of Voice)

Leadership matters in nation-building and development. The liberation struggle, as well as the first decade as a sovereign state, promoted and shaped hardy leaders in Mozambique, with lots of resolve, who initially enjoyed very high levels of legitimacy and popular support. However, while the overall objectives and principles driving Mozambique's first leaders were both noble and humane, the circumstances also provided for a ruling party that gradually became more paternalistic, centralist, rather relentless, and hard-handed. Violence was always present and considered a way to solve controversies. There are strong indications that well-known political opposition leaders have been killed since 1975, and Frelimo has in effect remained in power with no real contestation or opposition from domestic political movements (Ncomo 2003: 17–18).

Moreover, what had begun as a revolutionary political party to unite and promote peasants and workers began to change during the implementation of the SAP. The sense of unity started to diminish, and when Mozambique was finally able to embark on peaceful economic development in 1992, some thirty years after most of its African peers, it was the poorest country in the world measured by per capita income. The country's infrastructure was devastated and its leadership disillusioned but still very convinced of its entitlement to rule. The notion of entitlement came from the fact that it had led the struggle for independence from colonial rule and made Mozambique a sovereign country. Meanwhile, the farmers who were returning to their land from refugee camps and garrison towns after the war experienced bumper crops and significant improvement in living conditions compared with war. It was therefore relatively easy for Frelimo to round up the majority of the rural vote by promising education, health, and seeds that donors were prepared to pay for and by portraying the opposition party as foreign collaborators that had destroyed the country.

In sum, Frelimo departed from the need to engage in a fair nation-building contract with the peasantry that represents the majority of the population. It did not need the farmers' produce for consumption, and it could safely count on enough rural votes to win elections – if not as cast then as counted. Consequently, the importance of agriculture for inclusive development went out of sight. Meanwhile, the opposition party, Renamo, has remained weak and unable to establish itself as a credible alternative.

While the merging of the political and economic powers has clearly undermined market competition, competition among different groups within Frelimo remains, as reflected in the challenging transition from President Guebuza to President Nyusi, who was not Guebuza's preferred candidate. This competition in the party obstructs market competition in the economy, as the issues are settled between the business people members in relation to their political strength. The competition is not economic in the sense that the more efficient or economically competitive company will win the market. Elite rivalry in Frelimo is not enough to create meaningful change. Only a few groups benefit from the connection between political and business interests. It generally distorts incentives and creates barriers to companies.

Who rises to power internally in the party depends to a large extent on financial strength. Coming to power in the Frelimo party brings with it, as noted by Cortês (2018: 7):

... opportunities for the reconfiguration of the main beneficiaries in the process of capital accumulation. This fact aggravates the disputes and tensions between the political elites of the Frelimo party because state control allows privileged access to capital accumulation opportunities, but to control the state, one must first have control of the party, since it is the Party controlling the state.

The central committee of Frelimo consists of 180 full members and 18 candidate members. Moreover, all provincial first secretaries sit on the committee *ex officio* together with the general secretaries of the Mozambican Women's Organisation, the Mozambican Youth Organisation, and the Association of Veterans of the National Liberation Struggle, which select its politburo of just ten people and, every five years, its president. The president of Frelimo almost automatically becomes president of the republic. In addition, the party's candidates for parliament are appointed based on blocked party lists. Political competition within the party happens at different levels. As further explained in Cortês (2018), there is dispute not only among different party patrons but also within their own networks of clients, which compete for visibility or to be a part of the networks that are currently dominant.

Thus, it is internally within the party, at the primaries, that business owners can enter alliances and hedge their bets to reduce future risks for their business. Vote-buying in the primary elections is common. Therefore, elite grabbing is no longer just an opportunity for the elite in the party (because it is protected and has privileged access) but is in fact almost necessary for those who want to stay in central party organs and compete for high offices in government. They must raise funds to finance the party and to capture votes at the primaries. Such governance is only possible if corruption goes largely unpunished, which has – at least until recently – been the case in Mozambique. The basic requirement here is that the elite is untouchable by the courts and the electorate. In other words, certain fundamental institutions of effective governance must be weak.

The context of manipulation of elections alluded to in the previous subsection leads to lack of transparency and a situation in which Frelimo is not accountable to the people. The internal weakness of the main opposition party, Renamo, with its strong and centralised leadership, alienating much of the younger talent in the party, has made things easier for Frelimo. The evident lack of voice in society and the externally driven rather than 'home-grown' nature of NGOs reinforce this.

Mozambique's legal system recognises in principle the right of citizens to participate in the political, economic, and social development issues of the country. Yet a widespread lack of knowledge of who can engage in what processes and how leads to ordinary people not having much voice in decision-making in practice. Weak accountability, at both national and local levels, for ensuring opportunities for ordinary people to have a voice is therefore a critical weakness. Moreover, while formally the principles of freedom of the press are assured, several observers argue that press freedom is under pressure (Human Rights Watch 2019).

## 5 DF5: Armed Conflicts and Political Violence

Throughout Mozambique's history, armed conflict and political violence have been regular and widespread phenomena, and they continue to this day. Armed conflicts have been one of the recurring factors that prevented the country from building up the right institutions. After only a few years of independence from colonial rule, the armed insurgencies began to provoke disruptions in a very direct way. Lives were lost, as well as economic and social services, as infrastructure was sabotaged by Mozambique's National Resistance Movement and Rhodesian armed forces operating almost at will in Mozambique. At various occasions, entire sector strategies had to be abandoned and reformulated as the economic assets and infrastructure in the sector were no longer there or were reduced to ruins, with long-term consequences.

Other consequences included the abandoning of agricultural land by millions of predominantly rural refugees who fled to neighbouring countries and urban areas. The war also meant that public resources were absorbed in very large measure for military purposes, which have had long-term consequences. In parallel, the conflict undermined the creation of public services that are critical to the performance of the agriculture sector. This includes the provision of inputs as well as rural extension and marketing services. Finally, continuing instability and conflict reinforced the role of, for example, district administrators as representative of the State with all the associated symbols of authority rather than as a public civil servant accountable to the people.

The armed conflict in the 1980s happened mainly because Mozambique was caught up in the Cold War during the second scramble for Africa. However, in Mozambique, the Cold War was hot: a real and brutal armed conflict driven by an insurgency trained and supported by two of Mozambique's neighbours, commanding what were probably the most powerful armies and security forces in sub-Saharan Africa at the time. Armed conflict has continued to erupt on different occasions to the present due to the continued polarisation between Renamo and Frelimo. This is illustrated with the violence associated with the 2019 elections.

## 6 DF6: *Critical Dependence on External Finance (Role of Donors)*

Mozambique has always been fundamentally dependent on outside forces and agents. We have already alluded to the colonial legacy and the relations with South Africa. The circumstances under which Mozambique was born also created a regime that was extraordinarily dependent on external assistance in terms of finance and technical know-how. Moreover, the country's vulnerability to natural calamities has motivated food aid and large amounts of humanitarian aid.

Mozambique's stand in the struggles against apartheid made it a favoured nation among many Western European governments and NGOs. It also made it heavily dependent on external finance from Western donors. This dependency has continued to the present, though donor dependence measured as aid as a share of GDP has gone down. Importantly, donor dependence entails instability, as donors' objectives and modus operandi change over time and provoke different conditionality for aid finance. Most donor agencies are fronted by diplomats, who know that aid effectiveness ranges below security and commerce in the foreign policy hierarchy. Even on their own terms, aid agencies can be rather paternalistic and compete for influence over policy formulation.

The agriculture sector provides an example of the influence of donors. Agriculture is decisive for Mozambique's growth, and donors have competed for influence in policy development. Numerous new subsector strategies were developed, and policies changed over time and according to which donor formation was the most influential. Foreign assistance helped to build technical capacity in government institutions to research and regulate agriculture, but much of this consisted of white-collar jobs in government institutions that made their presence count for farmers in only a limited way.[20]

---

[20] One of the most disastrous pieces of advice from donors was to privatise the country's well-functioning and solid seed institute. Foreign investors bought it, and soon after, it closed.

This dependence on external finance has led to lack of agency (as described in the previous subsection), which is in turn reflected in the lack of ability to implement strategies and plans and in weak state capacity, in terms of co-ordination of state function. The SAP was the most brutal example of this, but even after the introduction of the Poverty Alleviation Strategies and Paris Agenda of the early 2000s, stressing the importance of host-country ownership of policy, aid delivery fragmented policy formulation in Mozambique. As Sector-Wide Approaches became the preferred instrument among donors, the deep implanting of donor-funded consultancies to assist in policy development became an implicit condition for aid from donor groups interacting directly with line ministries, circumnavigating the government's co-ordination ministries, that is Foreign Affairs, Finance, and Planning. This weakened national policy co-ordination and ownership to the point where it contributed to the breaking down of mutual trust between the government and the donor community that followed from late 2000.

Recently, aid to Mozambique has been increasingly instrumentalised by donor countries for their own security and commercial interests, a trend that will intensify as Mozambique's largest donors will be foreign governments that also represent its largest private investors. China and the USA are the most prominent examples of donor countries that have important commercial interests in Mozambique, but one could also mention France, Italy, India, and Brazil – countries with large companies involved in resource extraction and sales of arms and drugs to Mozambique that are not necessarily pursuing goals of poverty reduction.

## 7 DF7: Contemporaneous: Dominance of the Natural Resources Sector and Role of Foreign Companies and FDI

While for many countries in Africa the discovery of natural resources is in theory a great opportunity, it is not without risks. An extensive literature links natural resource dependence to poor economic performance (see Page and Tarp 2020). One cause is that resource-abundant economies tend to have highly concentrated economic and export structures and find it difficult to break out of this dependence. Mozambique fits in this category. It also responded to inflated expectations of forthcoming resource revenues by increasing public expenditure and accumulating debt (including the hidden debt) well ahead of the income coming on stream.

What this implies is that the fiscal situation is much less favourable than would otherwise have been the case, and that Mozambique will remain severely capital-constrained for quite some time to come. Consequently, turning capital under the ground into capital above the ground will have to be the guiding principle in policy-making. The key caveat here is that attention must focus both on the bringing the international debt under control and on building a pipeline of economically viable investment projects and improving the capacity effectively to manage these.

In addition to the institutional weaknesses associated with corrupt behaviour and lack of transparency associated with the above outcomes, three failures of decision-making in public investment are at the core of the present situation. They include 'a failure to select public investments by reference to sound economic criteria, a systematic tendency to use overly optimistic predictions of prices, costs, and impacts, and a serious lack of information at the time of implementation on the likely rates of return on investments and their impact' (Page and Tarp 2020: 10).

The above developments mean that Mozambique is also about to experience a shift from development aid to FDI in the extractives sector as the prime mover of growth. This shift presents risks, and so far, the large inflows of FDI into the extractive industries have also not created many linkages to the rest of the economy. First, the domestic role of large foreign savings is very limited and can be damaging for the local economy, through Dutch disease effects and the risk of neglecting agriculture. Moreover, it may replace one kind of (donor) dependency with another, potentially more risky dependency on the export of a few commodities and a handful of large foreign companies. Natural resources or primary commodities rarely provide exporters with a stable long-run engine of development, and they may make Mozambique very vulnerable to external shocks, from both market and political risks, and create little employment.

However, this shift also presents an opportunity; natural resources will bring revenues that can be used to pursue inclusive development, as evidenced by cases of success in natural resource management (e.g., Chile, Malaysia, or Indonesia). The fork in the road is between pursuing this trajectory and continuing on the current path along an Angola-style scenario. It is vital that the natural resource boom does not deepen and aggravate the existing lack of linkages between the urban and rural sectors in Mozambique. At present, foreign savings are not benefitting the rural economy and livelihoods but are largely used for large-scale investment or siphoned off in imported consumption by the elite and middle class overwhelmingly living in southern Mozambique.

IV  RECOMMENDATIONS FOR REFORM

We began this volume in Chapters 1 and 2 by laying out the exceptional historical, political, and economic context of Mozambique. While much progress has been achieved, it is clear that the country is a long way from meeting the expectations of its people. Moreover, a consistent domestic engine of inclusive growth remains absent. We proceeded in Chapter 3 to map out the country's institutional performance as it transpires from available international data and a quantitative survey of key opinion leaders and decision makers. This was supplemented by a series of qualitative interviews with key informants. On this basis, we identified eight core thematic areas for further study in Chapters 4 to 11. They were carried out by a carefully selected group of authors, who have first-hand experience from work in policy-making and research during different stages of contemporary Mozambique. The core topic pursued throughout has been the role and importance of institutional weaknesses behind this lagging performance, on the one hand, and the underlying proximate causes and deep factors, on the other. We brought these elements together in our institutional diagnostic presented in this chapter and now proceed to distil a series of suggested reforms to address existing institutional constraints as they emerge from both the accumulated insights from the thematic chapters and the institutional diagnostic.

We fully recognise that proposals for institutional reform should be appropriate for addressing the economic and political challenges that the country faces. They should also take into account the feasible governance capabilities that the particular country has, or can feasibly develop. Accordingly, the design of institutional reforms has to consider the specific economic, political, and historical conditions that determine these capabilities. While we aim to be as specific as possible, the reforms presented in what follows are envisaged at a rather general level. Greater specificity would require getting into design and practical particulars that are beyond the scope of this volume. Therefore, our proposals are put forward with a view to stimulating further informed national debate, reflection and in due course action, not as a comprehensive master plan.

## A Proposals

### 1 *Growth Strategy*

We concluded in Chapter 2 that there has been no single engine of growth and that the Mozambican economy remains fragmented and highly dependent on external resources. This vicious circle must be broken. Political leadership at the highest levels is key in this regard. To develop a unifying vision should be a core activity of, for example, the Ministry of Economy and Finance. A planning commission could be established and tasked with the duty of developing such a vision, including identifying strategic public investments required to diversify the economy (including agriculture) and address spatial inequities.

This approach to reform needs to be grounded not only within the context of a unified development vision, but also in a transparent process of identifying, formulating, selecting, and monitoring major investment programmes. A pertinent requirement in this regard is the strengthening of existing project appraisal units relying on proper professional evaluation criteria. Close interaction with the relevant committees of parliament would help to ensure national buy-in, and annual monitoring reports should be presented to the highest levels of government and to parliament.

More specifically, fiscal rules must be established to sustain public investment and guarantee spatial equity in public sector spending. There is a strong argument for creating a Ministry of Infrastructure Development, taking away this task from separate ministries such as Health, Education, Transport and Communications, Agriculture, Public Works, Mineral Resources and Energy, etc. This would help to bring the more coherent and unified approach to infrastructure development that will have to be at the core of any meaningful growth strategy. It could also help to create the conditions for the success of the agriculture and agro-industry recommendations below, and make it easier to avoid donor-driven projects that disregard national priorities and correct historical imbalances.

Core elements of the above strategy would focus on agriculture and agro-industry, industrial policy and private sector dynamics, and natural resources. This is so because the level of increasing poverty in both relative and absolute numbers must be brought down. The same goes for the need to change existing trends in inequality and to address the challenge of generating jobs for hundreds of thousands of new entrants to the labour market every year, reflecting in-built demographic dynamics. Without decent jobs and livelihoods, regional divides will deepen and undermine social stability.

## 2 Agriculture and Agro-industry

Within the context of a unified vision of development, agriculture and agro-industry must be at the core. We have already alluded to the clear socio-economic benefits of following an Agricultural Development Led Industrialisation (ADLI) strategy in the case of Mozambique. Jensen and Tarp (2004) also bring out that primary sector export-oriented progress represents an important set of complementary actions. Taking into account both supply- and demand-side factors, Sørensen et al. (2020) confirm that priority should be given to agriculture, agro-industry, and metal products. Furthermore, agro-industry could play a key role in agricultural development in sectors like maize, cotton, cashew, and sugar where Mozambique has strong comparative advantages (Benfica, Tschirley, and Sambo 2002). Agriculture and agro-industries must be central in any balanced development strategy focused on integrating networks of unorganised smallholder farmers with domestic and international markets along the supply chain.

This would include a strengthened set of institutions for the delivery of agriculture services, support for the development of technologies for agricultural processing, and the dissemination of more efficient production, storage, and distribution technologies. Moreover, it would require a competent national and regional apparatus for project identification and appraisal, which would focus on the wider synergies from agriculture for the national economy, including a non-farm economy, local manufacturing, etc. In a longer-term perspective and given the risks of climate change for agricultural production, it is imperative to develop clear adaptation strategies and technologies that are environmentally friendly and resilient to climate shocks.

Public resources should not be allocated based on a mechanical fixed-rates criterion. Debates about budget shares to be allocated to different sectors are often reduced to references to various international declarations, such as the 2003 Maputo Declaration and the 2014 Malabo Declaration. According to these declarations, 10 per cent of the total state budget should be allocated to agriculture.[21] However, the allocation of the budget should be based on explicit socio-economic criteria and analysis demonstrating ability to reach targeted outcomes and should have an impact in the real economy in line with established policy goals. Moreover, it is critical to come to grips with the fact that expenditure in education, health, energy, roads, bridges, transportation, communications, rural commercialisation, and many other sectors all interact with and impact on agriculture.

We furthermore stress that it is critical for the development of a dynamic private sector that reforms are put in place for it to play a more active role in promoting domestic savings and investments. Developing financing and insurance organisations dedicated to supplying services for smallholder producers, whether agriculture or small- and medium-scale enterprises, would increase the access to resources and reduce risk. Recommendations to be considered include creating a lower-risk agricultural bank. Such a bank could also promote the use of secure digital platforms. The ongoing programme 'One district, one bank' provides an example of credit provision to smallholder producers to expand crop areas, hire seasonal labour, develop cash crops, purchase improved seeds and fertilizers, and purchase agricultural tools.

Loan guarantee funds are another example of a mechanism that applies lower interest rates than the market interest rates, which could expand through a dedicated National Guarantee Fund. Although controversial, a real game-changer would be if the central bank could be requested to keep mandatory reserves as a proportion of the money lent to MSEs. Finally, attention should be given to changing existing laws in such a way that the state-granted land use right (DUAT) could be used as collateral, making it possible to increase the access of peasant farmers to financial resources in support of much-needed development in the agriculture sector.

## 3 Industrial Policy and Private Sector Dynamics

Industrial policy has moved away from the arid debate on 'picking winners' versus 'levelling the playing field'. Today, there is growing understanding internationally that the market imperfections on which the theoretical arguments for industrial policy rest are pervasive, especially in low-income countries. Moreover, increasing the amount of industry is key to creating decent jobs, a fundamental requirement for development progress in Mozambique. Similarly, both researchers and policymakers increasingly recognise that policy interventions to promote industry development and transformation cut across many areas of public policy. Thus, industrial policy must form an integral part of the overall growth and development strategy discussed above and further elaborated on by Monga and Lin (2019).

---

[21] It was 5.7% in 2018, according to OMR (2019).

At the same time, it stands out in the Mozambican case that there is a strong need to promote change in the existing relationship between the government and the private sector. On the one hand, there is need to curtail the existing licensing procedures that ensure that selected interests linked to the ruling government are in a controlling position. This marginalises potential local entrepreneurs from business opportunities in industry (see Cruz et al. 2016). On the other hand, relations with the largely small-scale private sector must change into an effective public–private partnership where dialogue and effective feedback mechanisms are in focus to ensure orderly coordination.

The relationship between the government and the private sector is typically fraught with complications everywhere in the world, and this is certainly so in Mozambique. To illustrate, almost half of the Mozambican SMEs fear closing down by the authorities (Berkel et al. 2018), the main reason being difficulties in conforming to laws of different kinds. Moreover, company owners generally exhibit risk aversion and low levels of trust. The institutions that shape government–business relations are a key element of industrial policy, and it will require concerted action to change the present state of affairs.

There is no single model of success of business–government coordination or industrial policy. Yet, experiences from elsewhere provide inspiration on how to develop a dynamic relationship between the state and the private sector (see Page and Tarp 2017). These experiences show that success requires a high level of commitment of senior government officials to the dialogue and coordination agenda, sharply focusing policy decisions and actions on specific constraints to firm performance combined with a willingness to experiment and careful attention to feedback.

Many of the reforms pursued in Mozambique over the past two decades focused on reforms of the investment climate. Continued efforts to reform regulations and promote efficient fora for coordination and information exchange is obviously important for the reasons noted. At the same time, it should not be overlooked that firm level studies from Mozambique and elsewhere (see Newman et al. 2016) highlight infrastructure as a significant constraint to enterprise growth, and the same goes for production skills (i.e. capabilities). To compete in the global market for manufactures, which is indispensable for future progress, Mozambique needs to develop a range of policies to promote industrial exports, build the capabilities of domestic firms, foster industrial clusters, and develop growth corridors. These are important areas for action and reform as discussed elsewhere in this volume.

Moreover, industrial policy would have to focus on developing competitive labour-intensive companies that would deliver much-needed jobs and gradually upgrade from low to high value-added products (Rasiah 2017). A complementary aspect of this would be to identify non-smokestack industries to compete in the international market. These industries would focus on the transformation of products such as fruits and vegetables (baby corn, green beans, citrus fruits, bananas, and mangos), cereals (maize and related products, sesame), and cut flowers, and promote tourism, electricity from hydropower and natural gas plants, and transportation services (Newfarmer et al. 2018).

### 4 Natural Resources

The current fragmented approach to the extraction of natural resources is a dead end. What is required is a deliberate and coherent supply-side approach aimed at using the natural resources industry as an important opportunity to support agriculture and business sector growth, as well as the integration and development of the economy more generally. Put differently, the future revenue from natural resources should be used to crowd-in private activity and be a positive force for stimulating enhanced rates of growth. However, crowding-in effects will work only if the government manages well-known macroeconomic challenges (Roe 2020). Reforms that need to be put in place therefore include a high-quality capacity in economic analysis, modelling, and forecasting that can provide informative forward-looking information to guide fiscal policies.

Furthermore, macroeconomic management of the natural resources will require strong commitment from senior policymakers, and the same goes for the establishment of a public company based on best international experiences to exploit and extract hydrocarbons on a large scale, or grant a concession to the National Hydrocarbon Company (Empresa Nacional de Hidrocarbonetos – ENH).[22] A competitive and transparent policy in line with best international practices should be developed to hire managers, engineers, and other professionals. The public company would have to be managed with autonomy and independently from direct political interference. It should be supervised by an administrative board, which in turn operates under a transparent management system. The operation of such a company would not exclude the participation of other international competing companies in Mozambique in exploring and producing hydrocarbons.

Another recommendation for reform is to promote linkages between natural gas projects in the Rovuma Basin and local companies, which would bring domestic business opportunities. Cruz et al. (2020) identify lack of planning and management capacity as well skilled labour as major constraints to the growth of local construction firms in Mozambique. Specialised technical services for large projects must be imported. Similarly, only about 15 per cent of the upstream construction value chain originates in Mozambique, and limited

---

[22] ENH is a Mozambican public company holding a 15 per cent interest in the Mozambique liquid natural gas (LNG) project in Area 1 of Rovuma Basin (Total 2019). This company also holds a 10 per cent interest in another LNG project consortium operating in Area 4 of Rovuma Basin (ExxonMobil 2020; Galp 2020). ENH is not a leading company in any of the large natural gas projects in the Rovuma Basin. It has been granted exclusive rights on a concession to explore and produce hydrocarbons in a relatively small project of the Mazenga Onshore Block, which is estimated to have reserves of 223 billion cubic feet of gas (Esau 2019). See also Roe (2020).

access to credit is a major constraint. This draws attention to the fact that while Mozambique has identified several areas in which resource extraction firms are required to make special efforts to increase local participation, the legal framework is at an early stage and in need for further development. According to Cruz et al. (2020), there is also a range of laws that remain in place that helps political elites and politically connected domestic entrepreneurs benefit from existing local content requirements. Regulatory reform in this area is therefore called for alongside reforms regarding PFM and investment planning.

In sum, when Mozambique starts to export natural gas from the Rovuma Basin and the inflow of foreign revenues increases substantially, macroeconomic policies must focus on developing the absorptive capacity of the country and curtail the distortions imposed on the domestic economy by an appreciating real exchange rate (Henstridge and Roe 2018). Mozambique will also have to carefully consider the pros and cons of establishing a sovereign wealth fund and a stabilisation fund to benefit future generations and insulate the economy from short- to medium-term volatility in commodity prices (see Otto 2018), though it will take time to build up the fund.[23] Critical in this regard will be the formulation of binding guidelines for the management and operation in a transparent and predictable manner.

## 5 Social Sectors

We have throughout this volume argued the case for striving for a more equitable Mozambican society. A key aim in this context is to ensure that citizens are healthy enough to produce their own means of survival and well-being. Central priorities for reform are the need to:

- legislate the separation between the Ministry of Health (normative and regulatory body) and the National Health Service (implementing agency), with different budgets;
- legislate the articulation between the National Health Service (on the one hand) and the health services of the municipalities and other local authorities (on the other).

These aspects should be contained in a law that sets out the appropriate national health policy for the longer term, to be approved by parliament.

The investment in education that has taken place over the years has supported progress in economic development. However, quality is limited (see Jones 2017). Accordingly, there is a need to assess and monitor quality and to promote systematic standards in education, both for teachers and for students. Education practices should be separated from political interests. These interests represent an attempt to obtain parents' votes by allowing students to graduate at higher levels without satisfying minimum required standards. Moreover, within the framework of the agreed national vision of development, education

---

[23] See also Roe (2020) for a succinct list of pros and cons.

must focus on fields that the Mozambican economy requires – for example, agronomy, fisheries, and tourism, and new areas in science and technology.

Finally, social safety nets must be developed, including expanding social protection. This could be, for example, by leveraging the current roll-out of COVID-19 emergency funds to cover an increasing number of households (similar to a universal basic income). Tax-financed social sectors providing universal access to basic health and education have so far been unrealistic for Mozambique given its present income level. However, if the projections of future income from natural resources materialise, Mozambique will have the financial means to pursue such a policy in the foreseeable future.

## 6 Political Power and Participation

In a well-functioning multiparty democratic system, political parties have equal opportunities to access financial resources from the state and from all those who wish to contribute. It is important that the party in power and its members do not use public funds or resources for campaigning purposes, beyond those stipulated by law. This is a fine line to draw and is challenging also for richer and more developed democracies, but in Mozambique there is much room for improvement. Both legislation and legal practices should make sure that political actors do not abuse their office or intimidate enterprises or individuals to finance the party under the threat of not providing licences, imposing fines, or firing individuals from public sector positions. Creating a level playing field is critical.

Another key reform area would be to pursue the effective separation of the executive, judicial, and legislative powers. Focusing on the judicial power, an important first step would be to create an additional post of president of the judiciary. Instead of being appointed by the president of the republic, the president of the judiciary should be elected by all judges. Their votes would have equal weights, such that no one would have special voting powers. The president of the judiciary would not have the jurisdictional function of the courts, and would be in charge for four to five years, not coinciding with the years of the presidential and parliamentary elections, and if possible, also not coinciding with municipal elections. A body for oversight and control would be elected for the same period as the president of the judicial power. This body would be composed of judges as collegial members with the role of approving the budget and managing complaints. Members would represent a percentage of areas or courts, but not judge categories.

Following this recommendation, the president of the Supreme Court would keep the position as '*primus inter pares*' but would not represent the judicial power. The only exception would be if the president of the Supreme Court were democratically elected as president of the Magistrate Superior Council, on an equal footing with any other candidate judge.

After lengthy negotiations, the parliament approved the introduction of the election of the provincial government and the creation of a secretary of state for each province. Consequently, in April 2019 the parliament approved three bills on decentralised governance, provincial assembly organisation and functioning, and the provincial assembly elections. The stated goal of these initiatives is to further democratise and empower local levels. It is critical that these reforms do not result in the provincial position of state secretary offsetting the political power of provincial governors (elected in local elections), which potentially increases instability in the institutional set-up. The core requirement is that accountability to the people becomes embedded.

Finally, lack of transparency has wide-ranging implications for how the Mozambican society operates. It opens up possibilities for corruption and misuse of public funds and deepens existing imbalances when it comes to political power. A first set of reforms would include effective monitoring and enforcement of public probity and conflict of interest legislation, including public registries of the wealth of members of parliament and senior government officials. While lack of transparency is also associated with low state capacity, focused reform should be feasible. Moreover, massively heightened transparency around all forms of government contracts and beneficiaries must be enforced.

## 7 Foreign Relations

As alluded to above, Mozambique must prepare to face not donors in pursuit of poverty alleviation but foreign countries with a much more intertwined agenda of foreign policy concerns – security, commercial, and aid – bundled and labelled in tactical ways to serve each country's interests. Accordingly, Mozambique should expect increasing and significant instrumentalisation of aid budgets by donors. The government must be able to access and address the concerns of its partners and indeed balance the conflicting interests of different foreign countries (as different as China and the USA) carefully against Mozambique's long-term goals. This is especially so in making sure that Mozambique preserves sovereignty and national unity and that its government truly holds agency. It entails saying 'no thanks' at times to aid proposed by donors, when such aid is not in line with national policy and plans.

Mozambique would therefore be well advised to revamp the entities (organisations and ways of working) dealing with donors and to put in place a structural framework and set of institutions suited to dealing with foreign countries. A holistic view of relations with foreign nations is now more relevant than a primary and overwhelming focus on the donor part of that relationship.

Mozambique would benefit from a strengthened Foreign Service, making sure that all aspects of foreign policy are covered in relations with foreign countries. Importantly, it would be indispensable to create clear and transparent rules of the game for all foreign investments (public and private), with reference to a carefully elaborated investment plan with priorities based on clear, objective criteria. To do so, and indeed to monitor such plans and strategies, the government should establish strong interfaces between key co-ordinating ministries and sector ministries, such as the Ministry of Industry and Trade (MIC), Ministry of Energy and Mineral Resources (MEMR), and the Ministry of Agriculture and Rural Development (MADR), chaired by the prime minister.

Finally, we strongly recommend that government align all foreign investments (official development assistance and FDI) with reference to the coherent development strategy and investment plan referred to above. We reiterate that development takes time. Therefore, once adopted, policy recommendations should be given enough time to bear fruit, irrespective of changes of government. We conclude by suggesting that the parliament should approve not only the development plans, but also the timeframe needed for their implementation, review, or change. This would help to ensure stability and coherence, and shelter them from changes motivated by short-term political gains.

## B Final Reflections

There is no single set of institutional fixes or master plan that can guarantee that Mozambique will avoid an Angola-type development scenario. The fundamental issue, then, is which kinds of institutional innovations might contribute to building a social contract for national development and curbing the worst excesses of rent-seeking and corruption.

In this regard, it is fundamental to recognise that political power and authority in Mozambique continue to be almost exclusively vested in Frelimo. This is a deep factor in our diagnostic. Leadership matters in nation-building and development. President Nyusi is in his second term, and potential successors will soon begin to strategise on how to become Frelimo's next leader and candidate for president. It takes visionary and brave leaders with strong economic backing to take on the necessary reforms to put Mozambique back on a favourable institutional and socioeconomic trend. There are definitely people meeting such criteria in Frelimo who understand that short-run personal or group-based gain may well be in contradiction with the requirements for longer term socio-economic progress.

Continuing on the existing economic, political, and social trajectory, Frelimo, and indeed Mozambique, will miss a unique opportunity to take agency and set a forward-looking agenda, pursuing policies of its own choice for inclusive and sustained growth. The uniting capabilities that the party at least once possessed are exactly what is needed at this point to prevent the balkanisation of Mozambique, both geographically and economically. Currently, there is no Cold War, no donor-prompted policy choices to implement or mimic, and Mozambique's natural resources can help to finance high and inclusive rural and spatially balanced growth if governed properly. While one may argue that these changes are not necessary for Frelimo's hold on power and that there is likely to be political resistance, the implications of increasing inequality, fragmentation, and conflict, which are already visible, serve as a strong warning sign and incentive to act in the national interest.

Peace and development are two sides of the same coin. Consequently, the events in Cabo Delgado are a wake-up call when it comes to assessing what sustainable development will require. The ongoing conflicts and military insurgency show where exclusion and extractive policies lead, even when it is possible to control almost all of the secular political opposition. Transnational networks promoting radicalism exist, and the social conditions in areas they reach will determine whether armed conflict ensues and possibly escalates in different forms to other parts of the country. Zambézia province is another case pointing to the need for political leaders to engage with the rural population in central and northern parts of the country. Its young population of more than 5 million people, almost all rural, will be difficult to control if they feel excluded from the development process. Existing poverty, inequality, and lack of inclusion will generate frustration, which must be addressed rather than suppressed.

The need for indispensable national resolve has become increasingly clear over the past decade where donors have finally proven unable to make conditionality work for poverty alleviation. Lately, donors have reduced their influence because aid is declining in size and importance in the government's finances. At the same time, Mozambique will, in the coming years, have to manage foreign governments with their own security and commercial interests, which are different from the traditional donor focus on poverty reduction, democracy, and human rights. Moreover, Mozambique must draw on international experiences in shaping the role of foreign companies and FDI in such a way that it benefits the national economy.

Finally, we conclude with a couple of points related to the COVID-19 pandemic. Although it is difficult to predict the medium-longer term dynamic economic impact of the pandemic in Mozambique, one can anticipate some of the potential challenges. As described in the first section of the chapter, there has been improvement in the living conditions since the mid-1990s. Yet, the levels of access to basic services are still relatively low, especially in rural areas, and access to, and the capacity of, healthcare also remain limited (Jimenez and Daniel 2020). The pandemic and the policy-measures adopted did lead to a slowdown in economic activity (Jimenez and Daniel 2020), which will also be affected by ongoing events in the international markets, for example via a likely decline in the demand for exports of goods and services (United Nations in Mozambique 2020). Finally, it is important to consider the vulnerability of the people, and the possibility that they may have fallen back into poverty. A significant part of the Mozambican population work in the informal sector and/or depend on agriculture for their livelihood.

A critical point of uncertainty at this point is how long it will more precisely take to overcome the pandemic. It will undoubtedly take time for the global economy to recover and readjust, so Mozambique will in the meantime face the challenge of handling this severe shock, while minimising the social and economic costs, and preparing to achieve quick economic recovery. The constraints caused by the institutional weaknesses highlighted in this synthesis may be even more severe in the light of the COVID-19 situation described. Thus, it is important to note that the recommendations made above were formulated with regard to a pre-COVID-19 scenario. We remain convinced that their relevance is even greater than before and that the way in which the present institutional challenges are dealt with might affect the capacity of the state to overcome the present crisis and continue on the path to achieving sustainable and inclusive development.

# References

Abbas, M. (2017). 'Segurança alimentar. Auto-suficiência alimentar: mito ou realidade?'. Observador Rural, (55). Maputo: Observatório do Meio Rural (OMR).

Abrahamsson, H. and A. Nilsson (1995). *Mozambique: The Troubled Transition – From Socialist Construction to the Free Market Capitalism*. London: Zed Books.

Acemoglu, D. and J. Robinson (2012). *Why Nations Fail: The Origins of Power, Prosperity, and Poverty*. New York: Crown Business.

Acemoglu, D., C. García-Jimeno, and J. A. Robinson (2015). 'State Capacity and Economic Development: A Network Approach'. *American Economic Review*, 105(8): 2364–409. https://doi.org/10.1257/aer.20140044

ACIS (2011). 'O Quadro Legal para a Contratação de Empreitada de Obras Públicas, Fornecimento de Bens e Prestação de Serviços ao Estado em Moçambique.' Edição II, com GIZ. www.acismoz.com/wp-content/uploads/2017/06/Procurement-Edicao-II-Portugues-vf.pdf

Adamolekun, L. (1999). 'Decentralization, Subnational Governments, and Intergovernmental Relations'. In: L. Adamolekun (ed.), *Public Administration in Africa. Main Issues and Selected Country Studies*, pp. 49–67. Boulder and Oxford: Westview Press.

Addison, T. (2003). *From Conflict to Recovery in Africa*. Oxford: Oxford University Press.

Addison, T., V. Pikkarainen, R. Rönkkö, and F. Tarp (2017). 'Development and Poverty in sub-Saharan Africa'. WIDER Working Paper 2017/169. Helsinki: UNU-WIDER. https://doi.org/10.35188/UNU-WIDER/2017/395-0

Addison, T., K. Sen, and F. Tarp (2020). 'COVID-19: Macroeconomic Dimensions in the Developing World'. WIDER Working Paper 2020/74. Helsinki: UNU-WIDER. Available at: www.wider.unu.edu/sites/default/files/Publications/Working-paper/PDF/wp2020-74.pdf (accessed 28 July 2020).

Adelman, I. (1984). 'Beyond Export-Led Growth'. *World Development*, 12(9): 937–49. https://doi.org/10.1016/0305-750X(84)90050-0

Administrative Court (n.d.). 'O Tribunal Administrativo: Breve Historial'. (Administrative Court: Brief History). Maputo: Administrative Court. Available at: www.ta.gov.mz/Pages/BreveHistorial.aspx (accessed 24 August 2021).

AfDB and OECD (2004). *Mozambique: African Economic Outlook*. Available at: www.oecd.org/countries/mozambique/32430193.pdf (accessed 28 September 2020).

Afonso, C. (2019). *Dinâmicas do sector florestal em Moçambique*. Slides, Direcção Nacional de Florestas (DINAF), presented at the Dialogue on Agrarian Development and Climate Change in Mozambique, Universidade Eduardo Mondlane (UEM), 23, 24 and 26 September 2019, Maputo.

Afrobarometer (2020). 'The Quality of Democracy and Governance in Mozambique, Afrobarometer'. Available at: http://afrobarometer.org/online-data-analysis (accessed 23 June 2020).

Aidt, Toke S. (2011). 'The Causes of Corruption'. CESifo DICE Report, *Journal for Institutional Comparisons*, 9(2): 15–19. Munich: Institute for Economic Research (IFO).

Aiginger, K. and D. Rodrik (2020). 'Rebirth of Industrial Policy and an Agenda for the Twenty-First Century'. *Journal of Industry, Competition and Trade*, 20: 189–207. https://doi.org/10.1007/s10842-019-00322-3

Alar, Francisco Inácio (2012). 'O Plano Estratégico da Polícia e sua Implementação'. In: Helene Maria Kyed, João Paulo Borges Coelho, Amélia Souto and Sara Araújo (orgs.), *A Dinâmica do Pluralismo Jurídico em Moçambique*, pp. 176–96. Maputo: Centro de Estudos Sociais Aquino de Bragança (CESAB).

Alfazema, A. (2015). *Os Desafios dos Tribunais Comunitários na Administração de Justiça em Moçambique*. Available at: Academia.edu, www.academia.edu/10809756/Os_Desafios_dos_Tribunais_Comunitários_na_Administração_de_Justiça_em_Moçambique (accessed 25 October 2019).

Allen, R., R. Hemming, and B. H. Potter (eds.) (2013). *The International Handbook of Public Financial Management*. Hampshire and New York: Palgrave Macmillan. https://doi.org/10.1057/9781137315304

Amaral, C., B. Mouzinho, D. Villisa, G. Matchaya, S. Nhlengethwa, D. Wilson, and C. Nhemachena (2020). 'Analysis of Maize Production and Yield in Mozambique (2000–2018): Trends, Challenges and Opportunities for Improvement', unpublished. Available at: www.agricultura.gov.mz/wp-content/uploads/2020/02/Analysis-of-maize-production-and-yield-in-Mozambique-2000-2018.pdf (accessed 18 December 2020).

ANAMM and World Bank (2009). *Desenvolvimento Municipal em Moçambique: Lições da Primeira Década*. Maputo: ANAMM.

Andersson, P.-Å. (2002). 'Impacto dos megaprojectos na economia Moçambicana'. In: C. Rolim, A. S. Franco, B. Bolnick, and P.-Å. Andersson (eds.), *A Economia Moçambicana Contemporanea: Ensaios*. Maputo: Gabinete de Estudos, Ministério do Plano e Finanças.

Andrews, M. (2009). 'Isomorphism and the Limits to African Public Financial Management Reform'. HKS Faculty Research Working Paper Series RWP09-012. Cambridge, MA: John F. Kennedy School of Government, Harvard University. https://doi.org/10.2139/ssrn.1404799

Andrews, M. (2010). 'How Far Have Public Financial Management Reforms Come in Africa?' Working Paper RWP10-018. Cambridge, MA: John F. Kennedy School of Government, Harvard University. https://doi.org/10.2139/ssrn.1724741

Andrews, M., L. Pritchett, and M. Woolcock (2017). *Building State Capability: Evidence, Analysis, Action*. Oxford: Oxford University Press. https://doi.org/10.1093/acprof:oso/9780198747482.001.0001

Andrews, M., L. Pritchett, and M. Woolcock (2017). *Building State Capability: Evidence, Analysis, Action*. Oxford and New York, NY: Oxford University Press. https://doi.org/10.1093/acprof:oso/9780198747482.003.0003 (Chapter 2).

Arndt, C., P. Chinowsky, C. Fant, S. Paltsev, C. A. Schlosser, K. Strzepek, F. Tarp, and J. Thurlow (2019). 'Climate Change and Developing Country Growth: The Cases of Malawi, Mozambique, and Zambia'. *Climatic Change*, 154(3–4): 335–49. https://doi.org/10.1007/s10584-019-02428-3

Arndt, C., A. F. Garcia, F. Tarp, and J. Thurlow (2012). 'Poverty Reduction and Economic Structure: Comparative Path Analysis for Mozambique and Vietnam'. *Review of Income and Wealth*, 58(4): 742–63. https://doi.org/10.1111/j.1475-4991.2011.00474.x

Arndt, C., M. A. Hussain, E. S. Jones, V. Nhate, F. Tarp, and J. Thurlow (2012). 'Explaining the Evolution of Poverty: The Case of Mozambique'. *American Journal of Agricultural Economics*, 94(4): 854–72. https://doi.org/10.1093/ajae/aas022

Arndt, C., S. Jones, and F. Tarp (2006). Aid and Development: The Mozambican Case DISCUSSION PAPERS 06-13. Available at: www.economics.ku.dk/research/publications/wp/2006/0613.pdf/ (accessed 18 December 2020).

Arndt, C., M. A. Hussain, S. Jones, V. Nhate, F. Tarp, and J. Thurlow (2012b). 'Explaining the Evolution of Poverty: The Case of Mozambique'. *American Journal of Agricultural Economics*, 94(4): 854–72. https://doi.org/10.1093/ajae/aas022

Arndt, C., S. Jones, and F. Tarp (2007). 'Aid and Development: The Mozambican Case'. In: S. Lahiri (ed.), *Theory and Practice of Foreign Aid (Frontiers of Economics and Globalization, Vol. 1)*. Amsterdam: Elsevier. https://doi.org/10.1016/S1574-8715(06)01014-1

Arndt, C., K. Strzepek, F. Tarp, J. Thurlow, C. Fant, and L. Wright (2011). 'Adapting to Climate Change: An Integrated Biophysical and Economic Assessment for Mozambique'. *Sustainability Science*, 6(1): 7–20. https://doi.org/10.1007/s11625-010-0118-9

ASFC, MULEIDE and CEEI/ISRI (2019). *Impacto dos conflitos armados na vida das mulheres e raparigas em Moçambique: Relatório das pesquisas de campo nas Províncias de Zambézia, Nampula, Sofala e Gaza*. Maputo: Advogados Sem Fronteiras Canadá (ASFC). Available at: www.asfcanada.ca/site/assets/files/7636/icavmm_13022019_web.pdf (accessed 27 October 2019).

AU/NEPAD (2017). Document for preparing country Biennial Review report on progress made for achieving the Malabo Declaration Goals and Targets: Technical Guidelines. Addis Ababa: AU/NEPAD. Available at: https://au.int/sites/default/files/documents/32377-doc-technical_guidelines_for_reporting_on_malabo_rev2_eng.pdf (accessed 25 October 2019).

Augusto, G., R. Nalá, V. Casmo, A. Sabonete, L. Mapaco, and J. Monteiro (2009). 'Geographic Distribution and Prevalence of Schistosomiasis and Soil-transmitted Helminths among Schoolchildren in Mozambique'. *American Journal of Tropical Medicine and Hygiene*, 81(5): 799–803. https://doi.org/10.4269/ajtmh.2009.08-0344.

Baland, J.-M., F. Bourguignon, J. P. Platteau, and T. Verdier (2020). *The Handbook of Economic Development and Institutions*. Princeton: Princeton University Press. https://doi.org/10.1515/9780691192017

Baland, J.-M., F. Bourguignon, J.-P. Platteau, and T. Verdier (2020). *Handbook of Institutions and Development*, Princeton: Princeton University Press.

Baldwin, E., T. Chen, and D. Cole (2018). 'Institutional Analysis for New Public Governance'. *Public Management Review*, 21(6): 890–917. https://doi.org/10.1080/14719037.2018.1538427

Banco Mundial (2019). *Doing Business in Mozambique 2019*. Washington, DC: Banco Mundial. License: Creative Commons Attribution CC BY 3.0 IGO. Available at: www.doingbusiness.org/content/dam/doingBusiness/media/Miscellaneous/SubNational/Doing-Business-em-Mo-ambique-2019_Pt.pdf (accessed on 12 January 2020).

Batley, R., L. Bjornestad, and A. Cumbi (2006) 'Avaliação Conjunta do Apoio Orçamental Geral 1994–2004: Relatório de Moçambique'. Birmingham: The University of Birmingham, IDD. Available at: www.iese.ac.mz/lib/PPI/IESE-PPI/pastas/governacao/geral/artigos_cientificos_imprensa/relatorio.pdf (accessed 24 August 2021).

Batley, R., W. McCourt, and C. Mcloughlin (2012). 'The Politics and Governance of Public Services in Developing Countries'. *Public Management Review*, 14(2): 131–44. https://doi.org/10.1080/14719037.2012.657840.

Behuria, P., L. Buur, and H. Gray (2017). 'Studying Political Settlements in Africa'. *African Affairs*, 116 (464): 508–25. https://doi.org/10.1093/afraf/adx019

Behuria, P., L. Buur, and H. Gray (2017). 'Research Note: Studying Political Settlements in Africa'. *African Affairs*, 116(464): 508–25. https://doi.org/10.1093/afraf/adx019

Benfica, R., D. Tschirley, and L. Sambo (2002). 'Agro-industry and Smallholder Agriculture: Institutional Arrangements and Rural Poverty Reduction in Mozambique', *flash* ..., 33E: 1–8.

Berchin, I. I., N. A. Nunes, W. Silva de Amorim, G. A. A. Zimmer, F. Rodrigues da Silva, V. H. Fornasari, M. Sima, J. B. Salgueirinho, and O. A. Guerra (2019). 'The Contributions of Public Policies for Strengthening Family Farming and Increasing Food Security: The Case of Brazil'. *Land Use Policy*, 82: 573–84. https://doi.org/10.1016/j.landusepol.2018.12.043

Berkel, H., M. Cardona, P. Fisker, J. Rand, R. Santos, and F. Tarp (2018). 'Survey of Mozambican Manufacturing Firms 2017: Descriptive Report'. Helsinki: UNU-WIDER, University of Copenhagen, University of Eduardo Mondlane.

Bierschenk, T. (2010). *States at Work in West Africa: Sedimentation, Fragmentation and Normative Double-binds*. Mainz: Johannes Gutemberg Universität.

Bila, A. (2005). *Estratégia para a Fiscalização Participativa de Florestas e Fauna Bravia em Moçambique*. Maputo: Direcção Nacional de Florestas e Fauna Bravia (DNFFB)/FAO. Available at: www.fao.org/forestry/12931-0dbfeb0710acca6eca be61e7ae746d135.pdf (accessed 26 October 2019).

Bila, Josué (2008). 'Pessoas desfavorecidas: Assistência Jurídica custará cerca de 8,6 milhões de USD'. *Bantulândia* (blog), 12 November 2008. Available at: https://bantulandia.blogspot.com/2008/11/pessoas-desfavorecidas-assistncia.html (accessed on 14 February 2020).

Binder, Alberto (2006). 'Gobierno Judicial y Democratización de la Justicia – Observaciones a las propuestas de Juan Enrique Vargas'. Revista *Sistemas Judiciales*, (10): 11–13. Santiago, Chile: Centro de Estudios de Justicia de las Américas (CEJA).

Birchler, K. and K. Michaelowa (2016). 'Making Aid Work for Education in Developing Countries: An Analysis of Aid Effectiveness for Primary Education coverage and quality'. *International Journal of Educational Development*, 48: 37–52. https://doi.org/10.1016/j.ijedudev.2015.11.008.

Birdsall, N. (2007). 'Do No Harm: Aid, Weak Institutions, and the Missing Middle in Africa'. Center for Global Development, Working Paper 113. Washington, DC: Center for Global Development.

Booth, D. (2010). *Towards a Theory of Local Governance and Public Goods' Provision in Sub-Saharan Africa*. London: Africa Power & Politics.

Borges-Coelho, J. P. (2010). A *'Literatura Qualitativa' e a interpretação do Conflito armado em Moçambique (1075–1992)*. Coimbra: Centro de Estudos Sociais da Universidade de Coimbra. Available at: www.ces.uc.pt/ces/estilhacos_do_imperio/ comprometidos/media/Moçambique 20e 20a 20LQ 20pdf 20(2).pdf (accessed 25 October 2019).

Borowczak, W. and B. Weimer (2012). 'Andar com Bengala Emprestada Revisitado: O Apoio Internacional à Descentralização em Moçambique'. In B. Weimer (org.), *Moçambique: descentralizar o centralismo. Economia política, recursos e resultados*, pp. 103–61. Maputo: IESE.

Bourguignon, F. and J.-P. Platteau (2015). 'The Hard Challenge of Aid Coordination'. *World Development*, 69: 86–97. https://doi.org/10.1016/j.worlddev.2013.12.011

Bourguignon, F. and J. W. Gunning (2016). 'Foreign Aid and Governance: A Survey'. EDI Working Papers WP16/10. Oxford: Economic Development & Institutions.

Brito, L. (1991). 'Le Frelimo et la construction de l'État national au Mozambique. Le sens de la référence au marxisme (1962–1983)'. Thèse de Doctorat. Paris: Université Paris VIII – Vincennes.

Brito, L. (2008). 'Uma Nota Sobre Voto, Abstenção e Fraude em Moçambique'. IESE Discussion Paper 04/2008. Maputo: Institute of Social and Economic Studies. www .iese.ac.mz/wp-content/uploads/2017/05/Brito-L.-de-2008_Uma_Nota_Sobre_o_ Voto_Abstencao_e_Fraude_em_Mocambique.-DiscussionPaper.pdf

Brito, L. (2009). 'O Sistema Eleitoral: Uma Dimensão Crítica da Representação Política em Moçambique'. In: L. Brito, C. N. Castel-Branco, S. Chichava and A. Francisco (orgs.), *Desafios para Moçambique 2010*, pp. 17–29. Maputo: IESE.

Brito, L. (2019). 'Multipartidarismo, Geografia do Voto e Descentralização em Moçambique'. In: S. Chichava (ed.), *Desafios para Moçambique 2019*. Maputo: Institute of Social and Economic Studies.

Brito, L. (2019). A *Frelimo, o Marxismo e a Construção do Estado Nacional, 1962–1983*. Maputo: IESE.

Brito, R. and Holman, E. (2012). 'Respondendo as mudanças climáticas em Moçambique. Tema 6: Agricultura'. In *INCG, Respondendo às mudanças climáticas em Moçambique. Fase II*. Maputo: INGC.

Brown, W. (2013). 'Sovereignty Matters: Africa, Donors, and the Aid Relationship'. *African Affairs*, 112: 262–82. https://doi.org/10.1093/afraf/adt001

Brück, T. (1998). 'Guerra e Desenvolvimento em Moçambique'. *Análise Social*, XXXIII (5.º) (149): 1019–51. Available at: http://analisesocial.ics.ul.pt/documentos/ 1221844645N4pCJ4pyoBk4oIF4.pdf (accessed 26 October 2019).

Bruna, N. (2017). 'Plantações Florestais e a Instrumentalização do Estado em Moçambique'. *Observador Rural*, (53), Maputo: Observatório do Meio Rural (OMR).

BTI (2020). 'Bertelsmann Stiftung's Transformation Index'. Available at: www.bti-project.org/en/index/political-transformation.html (accessed 23 June 2020).

Buchili, Beatriz (2020). Intervenção da Procuradora-Geral da República na Abertura do Ano Judicial de 2020. Maputo. Available at: www.ts.gov.mz/images/ Intervenc%C3%A30_da_Procuradora-Geral_da_Rep%C3%BAblica_na_abertura_ do_Ano_Judiucial_2020.pdf (accessed on 14 February 2020).

Bunk, B. (2018). 'The Dynamics of Donors and Domestic Elite Interaction in Mozambique. Formal Decentralization and Informal Power Structure'. *Conflict, Security & Development*, 18(4): 321–46. https://doi.org/10.1080/14678802.2018.1483555.

Buur, L., R. H. Pedersen, M. Nystrand, and J. J. Macuane (2019). 'Understanding the Three Key Relationships in Natural Resource Investments in Africa: an Analytical Framework'. *The Extractive Industries and Society*, 6: 1195–204. https://doi.org/10.1016/j.exis.2019.11.009

Byiers, B. (2005). 'Tax Reforms & Revenue Performance in Mozambique since Independence'. DNEAP Discussion Paper 12E. Maputo: Ministry of Planning and Development. www.iese.ac.mz/~ieseacmz/lib/saber/fd_19.pdf (accessed 24 August 2021).

Cabral, Zaida and M. do Carmo Soares. (2000). *Formação Jurídica e Educação de Adultos em Moçambique*. Communication presented at the 'Jornadas sobre Formação Profissional na Área da Justiça'. Maputo: CFJJ.

Cahen, M. (1987). *Mozambique. La révolution implosée. Études sur 12 ans d'indépendance (1975–1987)*. Paris: L'Harmattan.

Canotilho, J. J. Gomes (1999). *Estado de Direito*. Lisboa: Gradiva.

Canotilho, J. J. Gomes (2003). *Direito Constitucional e Teoria da Constituição. 7.ª Edição*. Coimbra: Almedina.

Capaina, N. (2019). 'Titulação e Subaproveitamento da Terra em Moçambique: Algumas Causas e Implicações'. *Observador Rural*, (73). Maputo: Observatório do Meio Rural (OMR).

Caramani, D. (2017). (ed.). *Comparative Politics*. Oxford: Oxford University Press.

Carrilho, J., M. Abbas, A. Júnior, J. Chidassicua, and J. Mosca (2016). *Desafios para a Segurança Alimentar e Nutrição em Moçambique*. Maputo: Observatório do Meio Rural (OMR).

Carrilho, J. Z. and R. N. Ribeiro (2020). 'Influence of institutional factors on the performance of the agricultural sector in Mozambique'. WIDER Working Paper 2020/128. Helsinki: UNU-WIDER. https://doi.org/10.35188/UNU-WIDER/2020/885-6

Carron, G. and T. N. Chau (1996). *The Quality of Primary Schools in Different Development Contexts*. Paris: UNESCO.

Carvalho, António Santos (2016). 'A independência dos tribunais e dos juízes'. *Revista Oriente Ocidente*, (33) II Série: 12–17. Macau: Instituto Internacional de Macau.

Castelar, Armando (org.) (2009). *Judiciário e Economia no Brasil*. Rio de Janeiro: Centro Edelstein de Pesquisas Sociais. Available at: www.precog.com.br/bc-texto/obras/castelar-9788579820199.pdf (accessed on 19 January 2020).

Castel-Branco, C. (2008). 'Aid Dependency and Development: A Question of Ownership'. IESE Working Paper. Available at: www.iese.ac.mz/lib/saber/ead_34.pdf (accessed on 11 November 2019).

Castel-Branco, C. N. (2009). 'Indústrias de Recursos Naturais e Desenvolvimento: Alguns Comentários'. *Ideias*, 10. Available at: www.iese.ac.mz/lib/publication//outras/ideias/Ideias_10.pdf (accessed 17 August 2020).

Castel-Branco, C. N. (2010). 'Economia Extractiva e Desafios de Industrialização em Moçambique'. In: L. de Brito, C. N. Castel-Branco, S. Chichava, and A. Francisco (eds.), *Economia Extractiva e Desafios de Industrialização em Moçambique* (pp. 19–109). Maputo: IESE.

Castel-Branco, C. N. (2011). 'Political Economy of Resource Extraction and Taxation in Mozambique'. Presentation in the 'Governance for Development in Africa' workshop. Maputo. IESE.

Castel-Branco, C. N. (2014). 'Growth, Capital Accumulation and Economic Porosity in Mozambique: Social Losses, Private Gains'. *Review of African Political Economy*, 41(sup1): S26–48. https://doi.org/10.1080/03056244.2014.976363

Castel-Branco, C. N. (2017). 'Crises Económicas e Estruturas de Acumulação de Capital em Moçambique'. In: L. de Brito, C. Castel-Branco, S. Chichava, S. Forquilha, and A. Francisco (eds.), *Desafios para Moçambique 2017* (pp. 203–32). Maputo: IESE.

Castel-Branco, C. N., C. Cramer, and D. Hailu (2001). 'Privatization and Economic Strategy in Mozambique'. WIDER Working Paper 2001/064. Helsinki: UNU-WIDER.

Castigo, F. and V. Salvucci (2017). 'Estimativas e Perfil da Pobreza em Moçambique, Uma Análise Baseada no Inquérito sobre Orçamento Familiar – IOF 2014/15'. Inclusive Growth in Mozambique Working Paper.

Castro, A. M. and e R. M. Cerveira (2019). 'Public Procurement 2019: Mozambique'. In: T. Kotsonis (ed.) (2019). *Public Procurement 2019*. London: Lexology. www .vda.pt/xms/files/05_Publicacoes/2019/Livros_e_Artigos/PP2019Mozambique.pdf (accessed 24 August 2021).

CEDSIF (Centro de Desenvolvimento de Sistemas de Informação de Finanças) (2015). *Plano Estratégico do CEDSIF 2015–2019*. Maputo: Ministry of Economy and Finance.

CEEG, Ministério de Economia e Finanças, University of Copenhagen, and UNU-WIDER (2018). *Survey of Mozambican Manufacturing Firms 2017*. Maputo, Copenhagen, Helsinki: UNU-WIDER.

CESO (2011). *Avaliação do Plano Estratégico para a Educação e Cultura 2006–2010/11*. Relatório de Avaliação, Volume II. Available at: www.mined.gov.mz/ POEMA/Biblioteca/MA-S5-Volume_IIA_Ensinos_Primario_e_Secundario.pdf (accessed on 20 February 2020).

Chang, H.-J. (2011). 'Institutions and Economic Development: Theory, Policy and History'. *Journal of Institutional Economics*, 7: 473–98. https://doi.org/10.1017/ S1744137410000378

Chang, H.-J. and A. Andreoni (2020). 'Industrial Policy in the 21st Century'. *Development and Change*, 51(2): 324–51. https://doi.org/10.1111/dech.12570

Chivulele, F. M. (2017). 'Política Monetária e Estrutura Produtiva da Economia de Moçambique'. In: L. de Brito, C. Castel-Branco, S. Chichava, S. Forquilha, and A. Francisco (eds.), *Desafios para Moçambique 2017* (pp. 99–164). Maputo: IESE.

Chiziane, E. (2015). 'Legislação sobre os recursos naturais em Moçambique: convergências e conflitos na relação com a terra'. *Observador Rural*, (28). Maputo: Observatório do Meio Rural (OMR).

Cingolani, L. (2013) 'The State of State Capacity: a review of concepts, evidence and measures'. UNU-MERIT Working Paper, Working Paper Series on Institutions and Economic Growth: IPD WP13 (October).

CIP – Centro de Integridade Pública (2020). Moçambique registou melhorias no Índice de Percepção da Corrupção da Transparência Internacional-2019, mas tem que fazer mais. Available at: https://cipmoz.org/wp-content/uploads/2020/01/ Percepc%CC%A7a%CC%830-da-Corrupc%CC%A7a%CC%830-3.pdf (accessed on 30 January 2020).

Cistac, G. (2009). 'O Direito Administrativo em Moçambique'. Maputo: Konrad Adenauer Foundation. www.sislog.com/ta/IMG/pdf/Direito_Administrativo_em_ Mocambique.pdf (accessed 24 August 2021).

Cistac, G. (2012). *Moçambique: Institucionalização, organização e problemas do poder local*. Lisboa: Jornadas de Direito Municipal Comparado Lusófono.

CNP (1987). 'Informação Estatística: 1986'. Maputo: DNE.

Comissão Nacional do Plano (CNP) (1985). '*Informação Estatística: 1973–1983*'. Maputo: DNE.

Comité de Conselheiros (2013). *Agenda 2025: Visão e Estratégias da Nação* (revised). Maputo: Comité de Conselheiros.

Coppedge, M., J. Gerring, S. I. Lindberg, S.-E. Skaaning, J. Teorell, D. Altman, F. Andersson, M. Bernhard, S. M. Fish, A. Glynn, A. Hicken, K. H. Knutsen, K. Marquandt, K. McMann, V. Mechkova, P. Paxton, D. Pemstein, L. Saxer, B. Seim, R. Sigman, J. Staton et al. (2020). 'V-Dem [Country–Year/Country–Date] Dataset v10'. Varieties of Democracy (V-Dem) Project. Available at: www.v-dem.net/en/data/data-version-10/ (accessed 24 June 2020).

Cornwall, A. and A. Shankland (2008). 'Engaging Citizens: Lessons from Building Brazil's National Health System'. *Social Science & Medicine*, 66(10): 2173–84. https://doi.org/10.1016/j.socscimed.2008.01.038.

Correia da Silva, G. (2014). 'Doze momentos-chave do cónflito entre a RENAMO e o Governo de Moçambique' [*Online*]. DW Made for Minds, 5 August 2014. Available at: www.dw.com/pt-002/doze-momentos-chave-do-conflito-entre-a-renamo-e-o-governo-de-moçambique/a-17822725 (accessed 26 October 2019).

Correia, Gilberto (2014). *Pontos de Ordem. Compilação de Intervenções sobre Advocacia, Justiça, Estado de Direito, Direitos Humanos e Cidadania*. Maputo: W Editora.

Cortês, E. (2018). 'Velhos Amigos, Novos Adversários: As Disputas, Alianças e Reconfigurações Empresariais na Elite Política Moçambicana'. PhD dissertation. Lisbon: University of Lisbon. Available at: http://hdl.handle.net/10451/32314 (accessed 21 July 2020).

Cortez, E. (2014). 'Reembolso do IVA: Burocracia Excessiva, Corrupção e Abuso de Poder'. Maputo: Centro de Integridade Pública (CIP). Available at: https://cipmoz.org/wp-content/uploads/2018/08/319_Servic%CC%A7o_de_Partilha_de_Informacao_n%C2%BA08_2014_pt.pdf (accessed 24 August 2021).

Cortez, E. et al. (2019). 'Custos e consequências das dívidas ocultas para Moçambique'. Maputo and Bergen: Centro de Integridade Pública and Chr. Michelsen Institute. Available at: www.cipmoz.org/wp-content/uploads/2021/05/Custos-e-consequencias-das-dividas-ocultas.pdf (accessed 25 March 2022).

Council of Ministers (2020). *Proposta do Plano Económico e Social para 2020*. Maputo: Assembleia da República.

Cramer, C. (2001). 'Privatisation and Adjustment in Mozambique: A "Hospital Pass"?' *Southern African Studies*, 27(1):79–103.

Crook, R. (2010). 'Rethinking Civil Service Reform in Africa: "Islands of Effectiveness" and Organisation Commitment'. *Commonwealth & Comparative Politics*, 48(4): 479–504. https://doi.org/10.1080/14662043.2010.522037.

Crook, R. and Manor, J. (2000). *Democratic Decentralization*. Washington, DC: The World Bank.

Crooks, E. (2018). 'Mozambique to Become a Gas Supplier to World'. Financial Times, 27 June. Available at: www.ft.com/content/d34685b2-7995-11e8-bc55-50daf11b720d (accessed 29 February 2020).

Cruz, A. S., D. Guambe, C. P. Marrengula and A. F. Ubisse (2016). 'Mozambique's Industrial Policy: Sufficient to Face the Winds of Globalization?' Chapter 5, In: C. Newman, J. Rand, A. Shimeles, M. Söderbom, F. Tarp and J. Page (eds.), *Manufacturing Transformation: Comparative Studies of Industrial Development in Africa and Emerging Asia*. Oxford: Oxford University Press.

Cruz, A. S., F. Fernances, F. J. Mafambissa, and F. Pereira (2020). 'The Construction Sector in Mozambique'. Chapter 9. In: J. Page and F. Tarp (eds.), *Mining for Change: Natural Resources and Industry in Africa*. Oxford: Oxford University Press. https://doi.org/10.1093/oso/9780198851172.003.0009

Cruz, A. S., I. Ferreira, J. Flentø, S. Jones, and F. Tarp (2020). 'Economic Development of Mozambique in Perspective: Background'.

Cruz, A., F. Fernandes, F. Mafambissa, and F. Pereira (2018). 'The Construction Sector in Mozambique: An Overview'. WIDER Working Paper 2018/117. Helsinki: UNU-WIDER. https://doi.org/10.35188/UNU-WIDER/2018/559-6

Cruz, A. S. and F. Mafambissa (2020). 'Economic Development and Institutions in Mozambique: Factors Affecting Public Financial Management'. WIDER Working Paper 2020/133. Helsinki: UNU-WIDER. https://doi.org/10.35188/UNU-WIDER/2020/890-0

Dabàn, T. and M. Pesoa (2007). 'IMF Survey: Budget Reform Holds Promise in Mozambique'. IMF News [Online]. Available at: www.imf.org/en/News/Articles/2015/09/28/04/53/socar1126c (accessed on 11 November 2019).

Dakolias, Maria and J. Said (1999). *Judicial Reform – A Process of Change through Pilot Courts*. Washington, DC: The World Bank Legal Department.

Darling-Hammond, L., D. J. Holtzman, S. J. Gatlin, and J. V. Heilig (2005). 'Does Teacher Preparation Matter? Evidence about Teacher Certification: Teach for America, and Teacher Effectiveness.' *Education Policy Analysis Archives*, 13(42): 1–51. https://doi.org/10.14507/epaa.v13n42.2005.

DEEF (2016). Poverty and Well-Being in Mozambique: Fourth National Poverty Assessment. In Portuguese. Executive Summary in English. Maputo: Directorate of Economic and Financial Studies, Ministry of Economics and Finance. Available at: www.wider.unu.edu/sites/default/files/Final_QUARTA%20AVALIA%C3%87AO%20NACIONAL%20DA%20POBREZA_2016-10-26_2.pdf (accessed 18 December 2020)

Deloitte and EITI (2018). *Relatorio Final, ITIE Moçambique*. Maputo: EITI Mozambique.

Delors, J., I. Al-Mufti, I. Amagi, R. Carneiro, F. Chung, B. Geremek, W. Gorham, A. Kornhauser, M. Manley, M. P. Quero, M. A. Savané, K. Singh, R. Stavenhagen, M. W. Suhr, and Z. Nanzhao. (1996). *Educação: Um Tesouro a Descobrir. Relatório para a UNESCO da Comissão Internacional sobre Educação para o Século XXI*. Porto: UNESCO/Edições Asa.

Díaz, A. S. (2003). *Avaliação da qualidade das escolas*. Porto: Edições ASA.

Diestche, E. (2018a). 'Political Economy and Governance'. In: T. Addison, and A. Roe (eds.), *Extractive Industries: The Management of Resources as a Driver of Sustainable Development* (pp. 114–36). Oxford University Press. https://doi.org/10.1093/oso/9780198817369.003.0006

Dietsche, E. (2018b). 'New Industrial Policy and the Extractive Industries'. In: T. Addison and A. Roe (eds.), *Extractive Industries: The Management of Resources as a Driver of Sustainable Development* (pp. 137–57). UNU-WIDER Studies in Development Economics. Oxford: Oxford University Press. https://doi.org/10.1093/oso/9780198817369.003.0007

Dietsche, E. and A. M. Esteves (2018). 'What Are the Prospects for Mozambique to Diversify Its Economy on the Back of "Local Content"'? WIDER Working Paper 2018/113. Helsinki: UNU-WIDER. https://doi.org/10.35188/UNU-WIDER/2018/555-8

DINAT (2018). Balanço dos registos activos no SIGIT. [Map]. Documento de Trabalho. Maputo: Direcção Nacional de Terras (DINAT).

Diogo, L. (2013). *Soup Before Sunrise: From the Reforms to Economic and Social Transformation in Mozambique: 1994–2009.* Lisbon: Porto Editora.

Duarte, S. M. (2018). 'A avaliação por ciclos de aprendizagem no ensino básico em Moçambique: entre tensões e desafios'. *Práxis Educativa, Ponta Grossa*, 13(1): 33–47.

DW (2014). 'Proposta da RENAMO de 'Governo de Gestão' Recusada pelo Parlamento de Mocambique'. [*Online*]. *DW.* Available at: www.dw.com/pt-002/proposta-da-renamo-de-governo-de-gest%C3%A30-recusada-pelo-parlamento-de-mo%C3%A7ambique/a-18090844 (accessed on 30 May 2020).

Economic and Social Research Council (ECRS) (2021). 'The Dahlgren-Whitehead Rainbow'. Available at: https://esrc.ukri.org/about-us/50-years-of-esrc/50-achievements/the-dahlgren-whitehead-rainbow/.

EDI (2020). 'Mozambique Institutional Diagnostic Overview'. Available at: https://edi.opml.co.uk/wpcms/wp-content/uploads/2019/06/Mozambique-Institutional-Diagnostic-June2019.pdf (accessed 23 June 2020).

Egger, E.-M., V. Salvucci, and F. Tarp (2020). 'Evolution of Multidimensional Poverty in Crisis-ridden Mozambique'. WIDER Working Paper 2020/69. Helsinki: UNU-WIDER. https://doi.org/10.35188/UNU-WIDER/2020/826-9

EITI (Extractive Industries Transparency Initiative) (2020). 'EITI Timeline: Mozambique'. Available at: https://eiti.org/mozambique#validation (accessed 9 March 2020).

EITI Mozambique/I2A Consultoria e Serviços (2020). *8th Report: Years 2017 and 2018.* Maputo: Extractive Industries Transparency Initiative.

ENI (2011). 'ENI Announces a Giant Gas Discovery Offshore Mozambique', 20 October. Milan: ENI. Available at: www.eni.com/en-IT/media/press-release/2011/10/eni-announces-a-giant-gas-discovery-offshore-mozambique.html (accessed 9 March 2020).

Esau, I. (2019). 'Duo Set Sights on Wildcats at Mozambique Onshore Tract'. Upstream, 6 November. Available at: www.upstreamonline.com/exploration/duo-set-sights-on-wildcats-at-mozambique-onshore-tract/2-1-702124 (accessed 29 July 2020).

ExxonMobil (2020). 'Rovuma LNG Project in Mozambique Awards Onshore EPC Contract'. Available at: www.exxonmobillng.com/About-us/Trending-topics/Rovuma-LNG-Project-in-Mozambique-Awards-Onshore-EPC-Contract?gclid=EAIaIQobChMIzvvl_qPy6gIVRZnVChobFQyZEAAYASAAEgIUyfD_BwE (accessed 29 July 2020).

FAO (2016). *AQUASTAT Country Profile – Mozambique.* Rome: Food and Agriculture Organization of the United Nations (FAO).

FAO (2018). *World Food and Agriculture Statistical Pocketbook 2018.* Rome: FAO. Available at: www.fao.org/3/CA1796EN/ca1796en.pdf (accessed 26 January 2020).

Faria, F. and Chichava, A. (1999). *Descentralização e Cooperação Descentralizada em Moçambique.* Maastricht: European Centre for Development Policy Management.

Fernandes, T. M. (2007). 'Descentralizar é fragmentar? Riscos do pluralismo administrativo para a unidade do Estado em Moçambique'. *Revista Crítica de Ciências Sociais*, 77: 151–64. https://doi.org/10.4000/rccs.795

Fernando, P., A. José, C. Soares, and C. Gomes (2019). *Estudo exploratório sobre o acesso à justiça e o desempenho funcional dos tribunais em Moçambique,* study carried out by the Permanent Observatory of Justice of the Centre of Social Studies of the University of Coimbra, at the request and in conjunction with the Mozambican Association of Judges. Coimbra: CES.

Figueiredo, Guilherme (2017). 'Bastonário dos advogados pede 'pacto de regime' para Justiça'. Jornal *Diário de Notícias*, edition of 20 May. Lisboa.

Filipe, E., and S. Norfolk (2017). *Understanding Changing Land Issues for the Rural Poor in Mozambique*. London: IIED (International Institute for Environment and Development). Available at: https://pubs.iied.org/pdfs/17594IIED.pdf (accessed 21 July 2020).

Flentø, J. and L. S. Simão (2020). 'Donor Relations and Sovereignty'. WIDER Working Paper 2020/135. Helsinki: UNU-WIDER. https://doi.org/10.35188/UNU-WIDER/2020/892-4

Forquilha, S. (2008). '"Remendo Novo em Pano Velho": O Impacto das Reformas de Descentralização no Processo de Governação Local em Moçambique'. In L. Brito, C. N. Castel-Branco, S. Chichava and A. Francisco (orgs.), *Cidadania e Governação em Moçambique*, pp. 71–89. Maputo: IESE.

Forquilha, S. (2010a). 'Governação Distrital no contexto da Reformas de Descentralização Administrativa em Moçambique. Lógicas, Dinâmicas e Desafios'. In: L. Brito, C. N. Castel-Branco, S. Chichava and A. Francisco (orgs.), *Desafios para Moçambique 2010*, pp. 31–49. Maputo: IESE.

Forquilha, S. (2010b). 'Reformas de descentralização e redução da pobreza num contexto de Estado neo-patrimonial. Um olhar a partir dos conselhos locais e OIIL em Moçambique'. In L. Brito, C. N. Castel-Branco, S. Chichava and A. Francisco (orgs.), *Pobreza, desigualdade e vulnerabilidade em Moçambique*, pp. 19–48. Maputo: IESE.

Forquilha, S. (2015). 'Sector privado no contexto da implementação das reformas no sector agrário. Uma análise a partir de experiências locais'. In C. N. Castel-Branco, N. Massingue and C. Muianga (orgs.), *Questões sobre o desenvolvimento produtivo em Moçambique*. Maputo: IESE.

Forquilha, S. (2016). 'Democracia e municipalização em Moçambique'. In L. Brito, C. N. Castel-Branco, S. Chichava and A. Francisco (orgs.), *Desafios para Moçambique 2016*, pp. 73–91. Maputo: IESE.

Forquilha, S. (2017). 'Descentralização e Conflito em Moçambique. O Desafio da Construção do Estado'. In: L. Brito, C. N. Castel-Branco, S. Chichava, S. Forquilha and A. Francisco (orgs.), *Desafios para Moçambique 2017*, pp. 35–59. Maputo: IESE.

Forquilha, S. (coord.) et al. (2018) *Barómetro da Governação Municipal 2017*. Relatório de Dados Quantitativos. Maputo: IESE.

Forquilha, S. (coord.) et al. (2019) *Barómetro da Governação Municipal 2018*. Relatórios de Dados Quantitativos. Maputo: IESE.

Forquilha, S. and E. Gonçalves (2019). *Social Cohesion and Political Violence in Northern Mozambique: A View from Chimbonila, Chiure and Mossuril*. Maputo: IESE.

Forquilha, S. and A. Orre (2011). '"Transformações sem Mudanças?' Os Conselhos Locais e o Desafio de Institucionalização Democrática em Moçambique. In L. Brito, C. N. Castel-Branco, S. Chichava and A. Francisco (orgs.), *Desafios para Moçambique 2011*, pp. 35–53. Maputo: IESE.

Fozzard, A. (2002). 'How, When and Why Does Poverty Get Budget Priority: Poverty Reduction Strategy and Public Expenditure in Mozambique. Case Study 5'. Working Paper 167. London: Overseas Development Institute (ODI).

Franco, A. S. and L. Katiyo (2017). *Business Environment Reform Facility: BER Scoping Assessment for DFID Mozambique Economic Governance Programme*. Department of International Development, UK Government. Available at: www.gov.uk/dfid-research-outputs/business-environment-reform-scoping-assessments-for-dfid-mozambique-economic-governance-programme (accessed 28 September 2020).

FRELIMO (1977). *Programa e estatutos*. Maputo: Departamento do Trabalho Ideológico da FRELIMO.

Frelimo (1977a). 'Relatório do Comité Central ao 3º Congresso da Frelimo'. Maputo: Frelimo.

Frelimo (1977b). '3º Congresso da Frelimo: Directivas Económicas e Sociais'. Maputo: Frelimo.

Frelimo (Frente de Libertação de Moçambique) (1975). 'Constituição da República Popular de Moçambique de 20 de Junho de 1975'. Maputo: Assembleia da República.

Fritz, V. M., M. Verhoeven, and A. Avenia (2017). *'Political Economy of Public Financial Management Reforms: Experiences and Implications for Dialogue and Operational Engagement'*. Washington, DC: World Bank Group. https://doi.org/10.1596/28887

Fusarelli, L. D. (2003). 'Institucional Dynamics: The Power of Structure'. In *The Political Dynamics of School Choice*. pp. 39–70.

Galp (2020). 'Upstream in Mozambique'. Available at: www.galp.com/corp/en/about-us/what-we-do/upstream/e-p-in-mozambique (accessed 29 July 2020).

Garoupa, Nuno (2008). 'Reforma da Justiça e Reformas na Justiça'. *Iprisverbis*, newsletter of the Instituto Português de Relações Internacionais e Segurança, (3). Lisboa: Instituto Português de Relações Internacionais e Segurança (IESE).

Gaventa, J. (2002). 'Exploring Citizenship, Participation and Accountability'. *IDS Bulletin*, 33(2): 1–14. https://doi.org/10.1111/j.1759-5436.2002.tb00020.x.

GdM and NEPAD (2017). *Trend Report of the Malabo Declaration Biennial Evaluation. [Online]*. Trend Report. Maputo: GdM and NEPAD. Available at: www.masa.gov.mz/wp-content/uploads/2018/05/MalaboTrend-Report.pdf (accessed 21 September 2019).

Gisselquist, R. M. (2014). 'Developing and Evaluating Governance Indexes: 10 Questions'. *Policy Studies*, 35(5): 513–31. https://doi.org/10.1080/01442872.2014.946484

GoM (1989). 'Decreto 21/1989'. Maputo: Conselho de Ministros (Privatization of state enterprises)

GoM (1998). 'Decreto 51/1998'. Maputo: Conselho de Ministros (Value added tax code)

GoM (1999). 'Decreto 40/1999'. Maputo: Conselho de Ministros (Finance General Inspection organic statute)

GoM (2001). 'Plano de Acção para a Redução da Pobreza Absoluta, 2001–2015 (PARPA)'. Maputo: Conselho de Ministros (Poverty reduction strategy paper)

GoM (2005a). 'Decreto 11/2005'. Maputo: Conselho de Ministros (State local entities regulation)

GoM (2005b). 'Decreto 54/2005'. Maputo: Conselho de Ministros (State procurement)

GoM (2006a). 'Plano de Acção para a Redução da Pobreza Absoluta, 2006–2009 (PARPA II)'. Maputo: Conselho de Ministros (Poverty reduction strategy paper)

GoM (2006b). 'Decreto 33/2006'. Maputo: Conselho de Ministros (transfer of state entities' functions and competencies to local autarchies)

GoM (2008). 'Decreto 63/2008'. Maputo: Conselho de Ministros (Tax system for local autarchies)

GoM (2010). 'Decreto 15/2010'. Maputo: Conselho de Ministros (State procurement)

GoM (2012). 'Visão das Finanças Públicas 2011–2025'. Maputo: Conselho de Ministros (Public Finance Vision 2011–2025)

GoM (Government of Mozambique) (1981). 'Linhas Fundamentais do Plano Prospectivo Indicativo para 1981–1990'. Maputo: Imprensa Nacional de Moçambique.

Gomes, Conceição (2018). 'Tribunais e transformação social: desafios às reformas da Justiça'. In: Maria de Lurdes Rodrigues, Nuno Garoupa, Pedro Magalhães, Conceição Gomes and Rui Guerra Fonseca (org. e coord.), *40 Anos de Políticas de Justiça em Portugal*, pp. 733–51. Coimbra: Almedina.

González, S., L. Fleischer, and M. Mira d'Ercole (2017). 'Governance Statistics in OECD Countries and Beyond: What Exists, and What Would Be Required to Assess Their Quality?'. OECD Statistics Working Paper 2017/03. Paris: OECD Publishing. https://doi.org/10.1787/cod45b5e-en

Government of Mozambique (2020). 'Covid-19 #Fica Atento'. Available at: https://covid19.ins.gov.mz (accessed 21 July 2020).

Government Spending Watch (2020). Available at: www.governmentspendingwatch.org (accessed 28 September 2020).

Gradín, C. and F. Tarp (2019). 'Investigating Growing Inequality in Mozambique'. *South African Journal of Economics*, 87(2): 110–38. https://doi.org/10.1111/saje.12215.

Granheim, S. I. (2013). Análise de Políticas Nacionais: Impacto dos sistemas agrícolas e alimentares na Nutrição – Moçambique. Estudo de Caso, Agosto de 2013. Maputo: UNS-SCN.

Grobbelaar, N., and A. Lala (2003). 'Managing Group Grievances and Internal Conflict: Mozambique Country Report'. Working Paper 12. The Hague: Netherlands Institute of International Relations Clingendael.

Growth Lab at Harvard University (2020). *The Atlas of Economic Complexity*. Available at: www.atlas.cid.harvard.edu (accessed 5 October 2020).

Guadagni, Marco (2000). Monitorização e avaliação para o planeamento: estratégias institucionais e percursos individuais. Communication presented at the 'Jornadas sobre Formação Profissional na Área da Justiça'. Maputo: CFJJ.

Guess, G. M. and J. Ma (2015). 'The Risks of Chinese Subnational Debt for Public Financial Management'. *Public Administration and Development*, 35: 128–39. https://doi.org/10.1002/pad.1712

Gulube, A. (1996). Breve Historial da Medicina em Moçambique (Mimeo).

Halleröd, B., B. Rothstein, A. Daoud, and S. Nandy (2013). 'Bad Governance and Poor Children: A Comparative Analysis of Government Efficiency and Severe Child Deprivation in 68 Low- and Middle-Income Countries'. *World Development*, 48: 19–31. https://doi.org/10.1016/j.worlddev.2013.03.007.

Hammergren, Linn (2006). 'Apuntes para Avanzar en el Debate sobre cómo Mejorar el Gobierno Judicial.' *Revista Sistemas Judiciales*, (10): 14–21. Buenos Aires: Centro de Estudios de Justicia de las Américas (CEJA).

Hanlon, J. (2016a, 2019, 2020, 2021a, 2021b). 'Mozambique News Reports & Clippings', editions 330, 430, 487, 537, 538. Available at: www.open.ac.uk/technology/mozambique (accessed 11 July 2016 to 24 May 2020).

Hanlon, J. (2016b). 'Following the Donor-Designed Path to Mozambique's $2.2 Billion Secret Debt Deal'. *Third World Quarterly*, 38: 753–70. https://doi.org/10.1080/01436597.2016.1241140

Hanlon, J. (2018). 'The Uberization of Mozambique's Heroin Trade'. LSE Working Paper 18-190. London: LSE. Available at: www.lse.ac.uk/international-development/Assets/Documents/PDFs/Working-Papers/WP190.pdf (accessed 23 March 2020).

Hanlon, J. and M. Mosse (2010). 'Mozambique's Elite – Finding Its Way in a Globalized World and Returning to Old Development Models'. Helsinki: UNU-WIDER. Working Paper 2010/105. www.wider.unu.edu/sites/default/files/wp2010-105.pdf

Hansine, R. and Arnaldo, C. (2019). 'Natureza Demográfica e Consequências do Crescimento Urbano em Moçambique'. In S. Chichava (org.), *Desafios para Moçambique 2019*, pp. 297–318. Maputo: IESE.

Hanson, J. K. and R. Sigman (2013). 'Leviathan's Latent Dimensions: Measuring State Capacity For Comparative Political Research'. APSA 2011 Annual meeting paper.

Hanushek, E. A., S. Link, and L. Woessmann (2013). 'Does School Autonomy Make Sense Everywhere? Panel Estimates from PISA'. *Journal of Development Economics*, 104: 212–32. https://doi.org/10.1016/j.jdeveco.2012.08.002.

Haque, T. A., D. S. Knight, and D. S. Jayasuriya (2012). 'Capacity Constraints and Public Financial Management in Small Pacific Islands' Policy Research Working Paper 6297. Washington, DC: World Bank. https://doi.org/10.1596/1813-9450-6297

Harding, R. and D. Stasavage (2014). 'What Democracy Does (and doesn't do) for Basic Services: School Fees, School Inputs, and African Elections'. *The Journal of Politics*, 76(1): 229–45. https://doi.org/10.1017/s0022381613001254.

Haskew, M. E. (2011). *De Gaulle. Lessons in Leadership from the Defiant General*. New York: Palgrave Macmillan.

Hausmann, R., D. Rodrik, and A. Velasco (2005). 'Growth Diagnostics', Growth Lab, Harvard University, www.tinyurl.com/y3y5zksu.

Hausmann, R., D. Rodrik, and D. Velasco (2005). *Growth Diagnostics*. Cambridge, MA: John F. Kennedy School of Government, Harvard University. Available at: http://ksghome.harvard.edu/~drodrik/barcelonafinalmarch2005.pdf (accessed 28 September 2020).

Heltberg, R. and F. Tarp (2002). 'Agricultural Supply Response and Poverty in Mozambique'. *Food Policy*, 27(2): 103–24. https://doi.org/10.1016/S0306-9192(02)00006-4

Henstridge, M. and A. Roe (2018). 'The Macroeconomic Management of Natural Resources. In T. Addison and A. Roe, *Extractive Industries: The Management of Resources as a Driver of Sustainable Development* (pp. 161–78). UNU-WIDER Studies in Development Economics. Oxford: Oxford University Press. https://doi.org/10.1093/oso/9780198817369.003.0008

Henstridge, M. and A. Roe (2018). 'The Macroeconomic Management of Natural Resources'. Chapter 8, In: T. Addison and A. Roe (eds.), *Extractive Industries: The Management of Resources as a Driver of Sustainable Development*. Oxford: Oxford University Press.

Herrendorf, B., R. Rogerson, and Á. Valentinyi (2013). 'Growth and Structural Transformation'. NBER Working Paper 18996. Cambridge, MA: National Bureau of Economic Research. https://doi.org/10.3386/w18996

Hickey, S. (2019). 'The Politics of State Capacity and Development in Africa: Reframing and Researching "Pockets of Effectiveness"'. ESID Working Paper 117. Manchester: University of Manchester. https://doi.org/10.2139/ssrn.3430432

Hickey, S. and A. Izama (2017). 'The Politics of Governing Oil in Uganda: Going against the Grain?'. *African Affairs*, 116(463): 163–85. https://doi.org/10.1093/afraf/adw048

Hodges, T. and R. Tibana (2005). *A Economia Política do Orçamento em Moçambique*. Lisbon: Principia.

Hong, H. V. and E. H. Hong (eds. and trs.) (2009). *The Point of View of My Work as an Author. Søren Kierkegaard*. Princeton, NJ: Princeton University Press.

Hossain, N. and S. Hickey (2019). 'The Problem of Education Quality in Developing Countries'. In: S. Hickey and N. Hossain (eds.), *The Politics of Education in Developing Countries: From Schooling to Learning* (1st ed.: 1–21). Oxford: Oxford University Press.

Hossain, N., M. Hassan, M. Rahman, K. Ali, and M. Islam (2019). 'The Politics of Learning Reforms in Bangladesh'. In: S. Hickey and N. Hossain (eds.), *The Politics of Education in Developing Countries: From Schooling to Learning* (1st ed.: 64–85). Oxford: Oxford University Press.

Human Rights Watch (2019). 'Mozambique: Events of 2019'. Available at: www.hrw.org/world-report/2020/country-chapters/mozambique (accessed 21 July 2020).

Ibraimo, Y. (2020). 'Tensões, conflitos e inconsistências nas relações entre as políticas monetária e fiscal'. In: S. Forquilha (ed.), *Desafios para Moçambique 2020* (pp. 207–33). Maputo: IESE.

Ilal, A. and B. Weimer (2018). 'Urbanização, Serviços Públicos e Recursos Fiscais. Os Principais Desafios para as Autarquias Moçambicanas'. In Salvador Forquilha (org.), *Desafios para Mocambique 2018*, pp. 65–107. Maputo: IESE.

IMF (2016b). 'Transcript of African Department Press Briefing', 15 April. Washington, DC: IMF. Available at: www.imf.org/external/np/tr/2016/tr041516a.htm (accessed 2 June 2016).

IMF (2018). 'Republic of Mozambique: Selected Issues'. IMF Staff Country Report 18/66. Washington, DC: IMF. https://doi.org/10.5089/9781484345634.002

IMF (2018). 'World Economic Outlook Database'. Washington, DC: International Monetary Fund. Database updated on 12 April 2017 (accessed 21 April 2017).

IMF (2020). 'Policy Responses to Covid-19: Mozambique', Washington, DC: IMF. Available at: www.imf.org/en/Topics/imf-and-covid19/Policy-Responses-to-COVID-19#M (accessed 21 July 2020).

IMF (International Monetary Fund) (2001, 2004a, 2004b, 2007, 2009, 2010, 2013, 2015a, 2015b, 2015c, 2016a, 2019a, 2019b, 2020). *Republic of Mozambique, Country Reports: 01–25, 04–51, 04–53, 05–311, 07–262, 09–49, 10–174, 13–01, 15–12, 15–32, 15–223, 16–09, 19–136, 19–276, 20–141*. Washington, DC: IMF. Available at: www.imf.org (accessed 1 June 2016 to 26 April 2021).

IMF (International Monetary Fund) (2019). '*Republic of Mozambique: Diagnostic Report on Transparency, Governance and Corruption*'. Washington, DC: IMF. Available at: www.imf.org/en/Publications/CR/Issues/2019/08/23/Republic-of-Mozambique-Diagnostic-Report-on-Transparency-Governance-and-Corruption-48613 (accessed 25 September 2020).

IMF (International Monetary Fund) (2019). *Republic of Mozambique: Selected Issues*. IMF Country Report 19/167. https://doi.org/10.5089/9781498320009.002

INDE (2003). *Plano Curricular do Ensino Básico*. Maputo: Instituto Nacional do Desenvolvimento da Educação, MINEDH.

INDE (2017). *Relatório do 20 Estudo da Avaliação Nacional da 3a Classe 2016.* Maputo: Instituto Nacional do Desenvolvimento da Educação, MINEDH.

INE – Instituto Nacional de Estatística (2019). *IV Recenseamento Geral da População e da Habitação 2017.* Available at: www.ine.gov.mz/iv-rgph-2017/mocambique/ apresentacao-resultados-do-censo-2017-1/at_download/file.

INE (2017). *Anuário Estatístico 2016.* Maputo: Instituto Nacional de Estatística (INE), República de Moçambique. Available at: www.ine.gov.mz/estatisticas/publicacoes/ anuario/nacionais/anuario-estatistico-2016 (accessed 27 October 2019).

INE (2019). *IV Recenseamento Geral da População e Habitação 2017: Resultados Definitivos – Moçambique.* Maputo: Instituto Nacional de Estatística (INE), República de Moçambique. See Censo 2017 Brochura dos Resultados Definitivos do IV RGPH – Nacional.pdf (accessed 20 December 2020).

INIR (2017). *Programa Nacional de Irrigação.* Maputo: INIR-MASA.

Intellica (2015). *Sexto Relatório da ITIEM – Anos de 2013 e 2014. Iniciativa de Transparência na Indústria Extractiva (ITIE) MOÇAMBIQUE.* Available at: https:// eiti.org/sites/default/files/documents/2013-2014_mozambique_eiti_report_portugese .pdf (accessed 7 September 2018).

JA and UNAC (2011). *Os senhores da terra.* Maputo: Justiça Ambiental; UNAC.

Jansson, J. and C. Kiala (2009). 'Patterns of Chinese Investment, Aid and Trade in Mozambique'. Center for Chinese Studies Briefing Paper with Stellenbosch University for the WWF. Available at: http://assets.wwf.org.uk/downloads/ccs_mozambique_ briefing_paper_october_2009.pdf (accessed 15 April 2020).

Jensen, H. T. and F. Tarp (2004). 'On the Choice of Appropriate Development Strategy: Insights Gained from CGE Modelling of the Mozambican Economy', *Journal of African Economies*, 13(3): 446–78. https://doi.org/10.1093/jae/ejh026

Jimenez, M. A. and E. Daniel (2020). 'Mozambique's Response to COVID-19: Challenges and Questions'. International Growth Centre blog, 5 May. Available at: www.theigc.org/blog/mozambiques-response-to-covid-19-challenges-and-questions (accessed 17 July 2020).

Jones, S. (2016). 'How Does Classroom Composition Affect Learning Outcomes in Ugandan Primary Schools?'. *International Journal of Educational Development*, 48: 66–78. https://doi.org/10.1016/j.ijedudev.2015.11.010.

Jones, S. (2017). 'Has the Quality of Mozambique's Education Been Sacrificed at the Altar of Access?' UNU-WIDER blog, November. Available at: www.wider.unu .edu/publication/has-quality-mozambique%E2%80%99s-education-been-sacrificed- altar-access (accessed 29 May 2020).

Jones, S. and F. Tarp (2012). *Jobs and Welfare in Mozambique: Country Case Study for the 2013 World Development Report.* Washington, DC: World Bank. Available at: https:// openknowledge.worldbank.org/handle/10986/12136 (accessed 18 December 2020)

Jones, S. and F. Tarp (2016). 'Mozambique: Jobs and Welfare in an Agrarian Economy'. Chapter 2 (pp. 20–61), In: G. Betcherman and M. Rama (eds.), *Jobs and Development: Challenges and Solutions in Different Country Settings.* Oxford: Oxford University Press.

Jones, S. and F. Tarp (2013). 'Jobs and Welfare in Mozambique'. WIDER Working Paper 2013/045, UNU-WIDER.

Jones, S. and F. Tarp (2015). 'Priorities for Boosting Employment in Sub-Saharan Africa: Evidence for Mozambique'. *African Development Review*, 57 (S1): 56–70. https://doi.org/10.1111/1467-8268.12139

Jones, S. and F. Tarp (2015). 'Understanding Mozambique's Growth Experience through an Employment Lens'. WIDER Working Paper 2015/109. Helsinki: UNU-WIDER. https://doi.org/10.35188/UNU-WIDER/2015/998-5

Jones, S. and F. Tarp (2016). 'Does Foreign Aid Harm Political Institutions?'. *Journal of Development Economics*, 118: 266–81. https://doi.org/10.1016/j.jdeveco.2015.09.004

Jornal Notícias (2018). 'Falta de alimentos agrava-se em zonas atacadas na província de Cabo Delgado'. *Notícias online*, 1 October 2018. Available at: www.jornalnoticias.co.mz/index.php/sociedade/82237-falta-de-alimentos-agrava-se-em-zonas-atacadas-na-provincia-de-cabo-delgado (accessed 19 de Abril de 2020).

Jowett, M., M. P. Brunal, G. Flores, and J. Cylus. (2016) 'Spending Targets for Health: No Magic Number'. WHO/HIS/HGF/HF WorkingPaper/16.1; Health Financing Working Paper No. 1. Geneva: World Health Organization. Available at: http://apps.who.int/iris/bitstream/10665/250048/1/WHO-HIS-HGFHFWorkingPaper-16.1-eng.pdf

Kaufmann, D. and A. Kraay (2007). 'On Measuring Governance: Framing Issues for Debate'. Issues paper for 11 January 2007 Roundtable on Measuring Governance. Washington, DC: The World Bank. https://doi.org/10.2139/ssrn.961624

Khan, M. (2010). 'Political Settlements and the Governance of Growth-Enhancing Institutions'. Working Paper (unpublished). London: School of Oriental and African Studies, University of London. Available at: http://eprints.soas.ac.uk/9968/ (accessed 17 August 2020).

Khan, M. (2018). 'Political Settlements and the Analysis of Institutions'. *African Affairs*, 117(469): 636–55. https://doi.org/10.1093/afraf/adx044

Kingdon, G., A. Little, M. Alsam, S. Rawal, T. Moe, H. Patrinos, T. Beteille, R. Banerji, N. Parton, and S. Sharma (2014). *A Rigorous Review of the Political Economy of Education Systems in Developing Countries*. Final Report. Education Rigorous Literature Review. London: Department for International Development.

Kjaer, A. M. and N. Muwanga (2019). 'The Political Economy of Education Quality Initiatives in Uganda'. In: S. Hickey and N. Hossain (eds.), *The Politics of Education in Developing Countries: From Schooling to Learning* (1st ed.: 152–71). Oxford: Oxford University Press.

Kössler, K. (2018). 'Conflict and Decentralization in Mozambique: The Challenges of Implementation'. Constitutionnet, 20 December. Available at: http://constitutionnet.org/news/conflict-and-decentralization-mozambique-challenges-implementation (accessed 8 October 2020).

Krause, P. (2013). 'Of Institutions and Butterflies: Is Isomorphism in Developing Countries Necessarily a Bad Thing?'. ODI Background Note. Available at: www.odi.org/sites/odi.org.uk/files/odi-assets/publications-opinion-files/8353.pdf (accessed on 08 November 2019).

Langa, E. (2017). 'Dependência de Megaprojectos e Desindustrialização Prematura em Moçambique'. In: L. C.-B. de Brito, S. Chichava, and S. Forquilha (eds.), *Desafios para Moçambique 2017* (pp. 165–83). Maputo: IESE.

Lauris, É. and S. Araújo(2015). 'Reforma Global da Justiça, Pluriversalismo e Ilegalidade Subalterna: Reflexões Teóricas e Empíricas a Partir de uma Ecologia de Justiças no Brasil, em Moçambique e em Portugal'. *Cronos – Revista do Programa de Pós-Graduação em Ciências Sociais da UFRN*, 16(2): 87–113. Natal: Universidade Federal do Rio Grande do Norte (UFRN).

Lauris, É. and P. Fernando (2010). 'A dupla face de Janus: as reformas da justiça e a lei tutelar educativa'. *Revista Julgar*, (11): 135–46. Lisboa: Associação Sindical dos Juízes Portugueses (ASJP).

Lawson, A. (2015). 'Public Financial Management' Professional Development Reading Pack 6. Birmingham: GSDRC, University of Birmingham. Available at: http://gsdrc .org/docs/open/reading-packs/pfm_rp.pdf (accessed 24 August 2021).

Leite, J. P. (1989). 'Pacte Colonial et Industrialisation : Du Colonialisme Portugais aux Réseaux Informels de Sujétion Marchande – 1930/1974'. PhD Thesis, Vols. I and II. Paris: École des Hautes Études en Sciences Sociales.

Lijphart, A. (2008). *Thinking about Democracy. Power Sharing and Majority in Theory and Practice.* London; New York: Routledge.

Lledó, V. (2007). 'Strengthening Mozambique's Business Environment: Diagnostics, Strategies, and Outcomes'. In: J. A. P. Clément and S. J. Peiris (eds.), *Post-Stabilization Economics in Sub-Saharan Africa: Lessons from Mozambique.* Washington, DC: International Monetary Fund.

Lønstrup, E. (2002). 'Status of Public Financial Management in Mozambique: Fiduciary Risk Assessment'. Maputo: DFID. Available at: http://gsdrc.org/docs/open/pf14.pdf (accessed 24 August 2021).

Lopes, Carlos (2020). Intervention at the Launching of the Work *Africa in Transformation: Economic Development in the Age of Doubt*, Universidade Politécnica. News from the onnline newspaper Mediafax, no. 7014, of 26 February 2020, p. 4. Maputo.

Lucas, L. (2016). 'Análise da Guerra em Moçambique'. *ISRIANOS* (blog), 3 December 2016. Available at: http://isrianos.blogspot.com/2016/12/analise-da-guerra-em-mocambique.html (accessed 26 October 2019).

Macuane, J. J., L. Buur, and C. Monjane (2018). 'Power, Conflict and Natural Resources: the Mozambican Crisis Revisited'. *African Affairs*, 117(468): 415–38. https://doi.org/10.1093/afraf/adx029

Macuane, J. J., L. Buur, and C. Monjane (forthcoming). 'Institutional Reform and Pockets of Effectiveness in the Mozambique Gas Sector'.

Madeira, L. F. (2012). 'As Finanças Públicas de Moçambique após a Segunda Guerra Mundial: Mitos e Realidades'. IICT – JBT/Jardim Botânico Tropical. Lisbon, 24–26 October. Available at: https://2012congressomz.files.wordpress.com/2013/08/to3c04.pdf (accessed 24 August 2021).

Magaia, F., A. Passos and T. Nahara (2011). *Trends in Achievement Levels of Grade 6 Pupils in Mozambique.* 1. SACMEQ Policy Brief. SACMEQ.

Makopa, Z. (2011). The provision of the basic classroom teaching and learning resources in Zimbabwe primary schools and their relationship with the grade 6 pupils' achievements in the SACMEQ III Project. Memoir presented within the framework of the IIEP 2010/2011 Advanced Training Programme in Educational Planning and Management. Paris: IIEP. Available at: www.sacmeq.org/sites/default/files/sacmeq/research/Masters%20and%20Doctoral%20Theses/the_provision_of_the_basic_classroom_-_makopa.pdf (accessed on 26 May 2020).

Mandamule, U. (2019). 'Gestão e Administração de Terras em Contexto de Riscos Climáticos: Desafios e Cenários Futuros'. *Destaque Rural*, (67): 5. Available at: https://omrmz.org/omrweb/wp-content/uploads/DR-67-Questo%CC%83es-de-terra-vs-IDAI.pdf (accessed 10 July 2019).

Mandamule, U. A. (2016). 'Tipologia dos Conflitos sobre Ocupação da Terra em Moçambique'. *Observador Rural*, (37). Maputo: Observatório do Meio Rural (OMR).

Manor, J. (1999). *The Political Economy of Democratic Decentralization*. Washington, DC.: The World Bank.

Manor, J. (2011). *Perspectives on Decentralization*. Washington, DC.: The World Bank.

Maquenzi, J. and J. Feijó (2019). 'Pobreza, desigualdades e conflitos no norte de Cabo Delgado'. *Observador Rural*, (76). Maputo: Observatório do Meio Rural (OMR).

March, J. and J. P. Olsen (1989). Rediscovering Institutions. *The Organisational Basis of Politics*. New York: The Free Press.

Mário, M. and D. Nandja (2005). 'Literacy in Mozambique: Education for All Challenges'. Paper commissioned for the EFA Global Monitoring Report 2006, 'Literacy for Life'. Paris: UNESCO.

Mário, M. and T. Takala (2003) *Evaluation of the Implementation Process of the Education Sector Strategic Plan (ESSP) 1999–2003*. Commissioned by the Ministry of Education of Mozambique. Maputo: Ministry of Education.

Mário, M., M. Buendia, W. Kowenhoven, C. Waddington, and A. Alberto (2002). *Review of Education Sector Analysis in Mozambique, 1990–1998*. ADEA Working Group on Education Sector Analysis. Paris: UNESCO Press.

MASA (2012). *Anuário de Estatística Agrárias 2002–2011*. Maputo: Ministério da Agricultura e Segurança Alimentar (MASA), República de Moçambique.

MASA (2015). *Agricultural Statistics Yearbook 2012–2014*. Maputo: Ministério da Agricultura e Segurança Alimentar (MASA), República de Moçambique.

MASA (2016). *Agricultural Statistics Yearbook 2015*. Maputo: Ministério da Agricultura e Segurança Alimentar (MASA), República de Moçambique.

MASA (2017). *Relatório Bienal das Metas da Declaração de Malabo. [Slides. Online]*. Maputo: Ministério da Agricultura e Segurança Alimentar (MASA). Available at: www.agricultura.gov.mz/instituicional/ministerio/arquivo/apresentacoes/ (accessed 14 July 2020 – see note 6).

MASA (2018). *Plano Nacional de Investimentos para o Sector Agrário – PNISA (2018–2019)*. Ministério da Agricultura e Segurança Alimentar – MASA. República de Moçambique, Maputo. Available at: www.agricultura.gov.mz/instituicional/ministerio/arquivo/politicas-e-estrategias/ (accessed 14 July 2020 – cf. note 6).

Masino, S. and Nino-Zarazúa, M. (2016). 'What Works to Improve the Quality of Student Learning in Developing Countries?' *International Journal of Educational Development*, 48: 53–65. https://doi.org/10.1016/j.ijedudev.2015.11.012.

Massarongo, F. (2016). 'Estrutura da dívida pública em Moçambique e a sua relação com as dinâmicas de acumulação'. In: L. de Brito, C. Castel-Branco, S. Chichava, S. Forquilha, and A. Francisco (eds.), *Desafios para Moçambique 2016* (pp. 113–39). Maputo: IESE.

Mattes, R. and M. Bratton (2016). 'Do Africans Still Want Democracy?'. Afrobarometer Policy Paper n.º 36.

McColskey, W., J. H. Stronge, T. J. Ward, P. D. Tucker, B. Howard, K. Lewis, and J. L. Hindman (2006). Teacher effectiveness, student achievement and National Board of Certified Teachers. *A Comparison of National Board Certified Teachers and Non-National Board Certified Teachers: Is there a difference in teacher effectiveness and student achievement?* Arlington, VA: National Board for Professional Teaching Standards.

McGill, R., P. Boulding, and T. Bennett (2004). 'Mozambique State Financial Management Project (SFMP)'. Sida Evaluation 04/29. Stockholm: Sida, Department for Democracy and Social Development and Department for Africa. Available at: www.sida.se/en/publications/mozambique-state-financial-management-project-sfmp (accessed 24 August 2021).

Medeiros, M. C. (2014). 'A Geografia do Mercado Mundial de Produtos Agroalimentares e o Papel do Brasil'. *Raega – O Espaço Geográfico em Análise*, 31: 260–79. https://doi.org/10.5380/raega.v31i0.32943

MEF (2018). *Projected Government Revenues from Gas Projects*. Junho de 2018. Maputo: Ministério da Economia e Finanças.

MEF (Ministry of Economy and Finance) (2016). 'Plano Estratégico das Finanças Públicas 2016–2019'. Maputo: MEF. Available at: www.cedsif.gov.mz/cedsifportal/wp-content/uploads/2018/08/Plano-Estrategico-de-Financas-Publicas-2016-2019.pdf (accessed 18 February 2020). (Public finance strategic plan 2016–19)

MEF/DEEF (2016). 'Poverty and Well-Being in Mozambique: Fourth National Poverty Assessment'. Research Report. Maputo: Ministério da Economia e Finanças/Direcção de Estudos Económicos e Financeiros. Available at: www.wider.unu.edu/report/poverty-and-well-being-mozambique-fourth%C2%Aonational-poverty-assessment (accessed 6 October 2020)

Melo, T. (2018). 'Moçambique: Acusação no caso Embraer é 'uma luz no fim do túnel', diz CIP'. Deutsche Welle (DW), 28 February. Available at: www.dw.com/pt-oo2/mo%C3%A7ambique-acusa%C3%A7%C3%A30-no-caso-embraer-%C3%A9-uma-luz-no-fim-do-t%C3%BAnel-diz-cip/a-42775969 (accessed 24 August 2021).

Meneses, M. P. (2015). 'Xiconhoca, o inimigo: Narrativas de violência sobre a construção da nação em Moçambique'. *Revista Crítica de Ciências Sociais*, (106): 9–52. https://doi.org/10.4000/

MIC (2013). *Plano integrado da comercialização agrícola para 2013–2020*. Maputo: Ministério de Indústria e Comércio (MIC), República de Moçambique.

MICOA (2007). *Programa de Acção Nacional para a Adaptação às Mudanças Climáticas (NAPA)*. Maputo: Ministério para Coordenação da Acção Ambiental (MICOA), Direcção Nacional de Gestão Ambiental. Available at: www.preventionweb.net/files/16411_planonacionalparaadaptaoasmudanascl.pdf (accessed 19 February 2020).

Millo, Y. and J. Barnett (2004). 'Educational Development in East Timor'. *International Journal of Educational Development*, 24(6): 721–37. https://doi.org/10.1016/j.ijedudev.2004.04.005.

MINAG (2011). *Plano Estratégico de Desenvolvimento do Sector Agrário (PEDSA) 2011–2020*. Maputo: Ministério da Agricultura (MINAG), República de Moçambique. Available at: www.agricultura.gov.mz/instituicional/ministerio/arquivo/politicas-e-estrategias/ (accessed 14 July 2020 – cf. note 6).

MINAG (2013). *Plano Nacional de Investimentos para o Sector Agrário PNISA 2013–2017*. Maputo: Ministério da Agricultura (MNAG), República de Moçambique. Available at: www.agricultura.gov.mz/instituicional/ministerio/arquivo/politicas-e-estrategias/ (accessed 14 July 2020 – cf. note 6).

MINEDH (2015). *Desempenho do Sector da Educação*. Relatório. Documento número 1.02/RAR15. Maputo: MINEDH.

MINEDH (2018). *Desempenho do Sector da Educação*. Relatório. 19.ª Reunião Anual de Revisão. Maputo: MINEDH.

MINEDH (2019). *Análise do Sector da Educação (ESA)*. Relatório Final. Maputo: MINEDH.

References

Miningou, E. W. (2019). 'Effectiveness of Education Aid Revisited: Country-Level Inefficiencies Matter'. *International Journal of Educational Development*, 71. https://doi.org/10.1016/j.ijedudev.2019.102123.

Ministério da Saúde (2010). *Observatório da Equidade 2010*. Ministério da Saúde, Governo de Moçambique.

Ministério da Saúde (2015). *Medicina Tradicional em Moçambique, 40 anos Pós-Independência. Da Proibição à Coordenação Entre as Duas Medicinas: Tradicional e Convencional*. Maputo: Ministério da Saúde.

Ministério da Saúde, INE – Instituto Nacional de Estatística and ICFI – ICF International (2013). *Moçambique Inquérito Demográfico e de Saúde 2011*. Calverton, Maryland, USA: Ministério da Saúde; INE; ICFI. Available at: https://dhsprogram.com/pubs/pdf/FR266/FR266.pdf.

Ministério da Saúde, INE – Instituto Nacional de Estatística and ICF (2018). *Inquérito de Indicadores de Imunização, Malária e HIV/SIDA em Moçambique (IMASIDA) 2015*. Maputo, Moçambique; Rockville, Maryland, EUA: Ministério da Saúde, INE and ICF. Available at: https://dhsprogram.com/pubs/pdf/AIS12/AIS12.pdf.

Minot, N. (2007). 'Chapter 3. Contract Farming in Developing Countries: Patterns, Impact, and Policy Implications.' In: P. Pinstrup-Andersen and F. Cheng (eds.), *Case Studies in Food Policy for Developing Countries*. Ithaca: Cornell University Press.

MITSS (2020). *Labour Force in Mozambique*. Maputo: Ministério do Trabalho e Segurança Social. Available at: www.mitess.gov.mz/sites/default/files/documents/files/Desdobravel%20forca%20de%20trabalho.pdf (accessed 5 January 2021).

MNRC (2017a). Mozambique News Reports and Clippings 367, 17 April. Available at: bit.ly/mozamb (accessed 11 August 2020).

MNRC (2017b). Mozambique News Reports and Clippings, 372, 2 June. Available at: bit.ly/mozamb (accessed 11 August 2020).

MNRC (2019). Mozambique News Reports and Clippings, 429, 5 January. Available at: bit.ly/mozamb (accessed 11 August 2020).

Mo Ibrahim Foundation (2016). *2016 Ibrahim Index of African Governance. Mozambique insights*. London: Mo Ibrahim Foundation.

Mohmand, S. and M. Loureiro (2017). 'Introduction: Interrogating decentralization in Africa'. *IDS Bulletin*, 48(2)): 1–14.

Mondlane, E. (1975). *Lutar por Moçambique*. Lisboa: Sá da Costa.

Monga, C. and J. Y. Lin (eds.) (2019). *The Oxford Handbook of Structural Transformation*. Oxford: Oxford University Press.

Morand, Charles-Albert (1999). *Légistique formelle et matérielle*. Aix-en-Provence: Presses Universitaires d'Aix-Marseille (PUAM).

Morgan, G. (1990). 'Violence in Mozambique: Towards an Understanding of Renamo'. *Journal of Modern African Studies*, 28(4): 603–19. https://doi.org/10.1017/S0022278X00054756

Morier-Genoud, E. (2007). 'Shaping Democracy: Frelimo, Liberalism and Politics in Contemporary Mozambique'. Unpublished Paper, African History and Politics Seminar, University of Oxford.

Mosca, J. (2011). *Políticas agrárias de (em) Moçambique (1975–2009)*. Maputo: Editora Escolar.

Mosca, J. (2020). 'Orçamento de Estado para 2020: Uma Caixa de Pandora'. *Destaque Rural*, (87): 12. Available at: https://omrmz.org/omrweb/publicacoes/dr-87/ (accessed 9 May 2020).

Mosca, J. and N. Bruna (2016). 'Metodologia de estudo dos impactos dos megaprojec-tos'. *Observador Rural*, (41). Maputo: Observatório do Meio Rural (OMR).

Mosca, J. and Y. Nova (2019). 'Agricultura: Assim, não é possível reduzir a pobreza em Moçambique'. *Observador Rural*, (80). Maputo: Observatório do Meio Rural (OMR). Available at: https://omrmz.org/omrweb/publicacoes/or-80/ (accessed 9 May 2020).

Moss, T., G. Pettersson Gelander, and N. Van De Walle (2006). 'An Aid-Institutions Paradox? A Review Essay on Aid Dependency and State Building in Sub-Saharan Africa'. Center for Global Development, Working Paper Number 74. Washington, DC: Center for Global Development. https://doi.org/10.2139/ssrn.860826

MPD (2008). *Relatório Balanço de Actividades no Âmbito do Orçamento de Investimento de Iniciativa Local*. Maputo: MPD.

Mucavel, C. (2018). Sobre Agricultura e Segurança Alimentar. Slides of the Ministry of Agriculture and Food Security (MASA), presented at Universidade Eduardo Mondlane (UEM), at the Symposium on Agriculture, X Scientific Conference of UEM, 28 September 2018. Maputo: MASA.

Muchanga, Adelino (2020). *Opening Speech of the Judicial Year*. Maputo. Available at: www.ts.gov.mz/images/Discurso_de_Abertura_do_Ano_Judicial_-_2020.pdf (accessed on 14 February 2020).

Muianga, C. (2019a). 'Investimento, recursos naturais e desafios para Moçambique'. In: S. Chichava (ed.), *Desafios para Moçambique 2019* (pp. 147–64). Maputo: IESE.

Muianga, C. (2019b). *'Decisões de investimento para a exploração de gás e os limites do 'realismo' sobre o 'progresso dos moçambicanos"*. *IDeIAS 110*. Maputo: IESE. Available at: www.iese.ac.mz/wp-content/uploads/2019/11/Ideias-119_CM.pdf (accessed 17 August 2020).

Mungiu-Pippidi, A. and Dusu, A. E. (2011). 'Civil Society and Control of Corruption: Assessing Governance of Romanian Public Universities'. *International Journal of Educational Development*, 31(5): 532–46. https://doi.org/10.1016/j.ijedudev.2010.03.016.

Natural Resource Governance Institute (2017). *Resource Governance Index: Sub-Saharan Africa Highlights*. Available at: https://resourcegovernanceindex.org/country-profiles/MOZ/oil-gas (accessed 27 July 2020).

Ncomo, B. L. (2003). *Uria Simango: Um homem, uma causa*. Maputo: Edições Novafrica.

Newfarmer, R., J. Page, and F. Tarp (eds.) (2018). *Industries without Smokestacks: Industrialization in Africa Reconsidered*. Oxford: Oxford University Press.

Newitt, M. (1995). *A History of Mozambique*. Hong Kong: Indiana University Press.

Newman, C., J. Rand, A. Shimeles, M. Söderbom, F. Tarp and J. Page (eds.) (2016). *Manufacturing Transformation: Comparative Studies of Industrial Development in Africa and Emerging Asia*. Oxford: Oxford University Press.

Nhate, V., C. Massingarela, and V. Salvucci (2014). 'The Political Economy of Food Price Policy in Mozambique'. In: P. Pinstrup-Andersen (ed.), *Food Price Policy in an Era of Market Instability: A Political Economy Analysis*. Oxford: Oxford University Press. https://doi.org/10.1093/acprof:oso/9780198718574.003.0010

Nicolai, S., L. Wild, J. Wales, S. Hine, and J. Engel (2014). 'Unbalanced Progress'. ODI Development Progress Working Paper 5. London: Overseas Development Institute.

North, D. C. (1990). *Institutions, Institutional Change, and Economic Performance. The Political Economy of Institutions and Decisions*. Cambridge, New York: Cambridge University Press.

North, D., J. Wallis, and B. Weingast (2009). *Violence and Social Orders: A Conceptual Framework for Interpreting Recorded Human History*. New York: Cambridge University Press. https://doi.org/10.1017/CBO9780511575839

North, Douglass (1990). *Institutions, Institutional Change and Economic Performance*, Cambridge: Cambridge University Press.

Nova, Y., Y. A. Dadá, and C. Mussá (2019). 'Agricultura em Números: Análise do Orçamento do Estado, Investimento, Crédito e Balança Comercial'. *Observador Rural*, (74). Maputo: Observatório do Meio Rural (OMR).

O País (2019). 'Mineradora Vale e Estado moçambicano condenados'. *O País*, 17 October 2019. Available at: http://opais.sapo.mz/mineradora-vale-e-estado-mocambicano-condenados# (accessed 27 October 2019).

OAM – Ordem dos Advogados de Moçambique (2005). *Relação dos Advogados*. Maputo: OAM.

OAM (2018). Comunicado de Imprensa: Condenação do Gabinete de Coordenação do Prosavana, do Ministério da Agricultura e Segurança Alimentar (MASA). 28 September 2018. Available at: www.oam.org.mz/comunicado-de-imprensa-condenacao-do-gabinete-de-coordenacao-do-prosavana-do-ministerio-da-agricultura-e-seguranca-alimentarmasa/ (accessed 26 October 2019).

OAM (2019). Comunicado de Imprensa: Primeira Secção do Tribunal Administrativo nega julgar o mérito da causa sobre a declaração de nulidade do DUAT atribuído à exploração exclusiva, pela ANADARKO, no contexto do projecto de Gás em Palma. 16 September 2019. Available at: www.oam.org.mz/comunicado-de-imprensa-primeira-seccao-do-tribunal-administrativo-nega-julgar-o-merito-da-causa-sobre-a-declaracao-de-nulidade-do-duat-atribuido-a-exploracao-exclusiva-pela-anadarko-no-contexto-do/ (accessed 26 October 2019).

OECD (2002). 'Mozambique'. Available at: www.oecd.org/countries/mozambique/1825790.pdf (accessed on 8 November 2019).

Olivier de Sardan, J.-P. (2011). 'The Eight Modes of Local Governance in West Africa'. *IDS Bulletin*, 42(2): 22–31. https://doi.org/10.1111/j.1759-5436.2011.00208.x.

Olowu, D. and J. Wunsch (1990). *The Failure of the Centralized State: Institutions and Self-Governance in Africa*. Boulder: Westview Press.

Olowu, D. and J. Wunsch (2004). *Local Governance in Africa. The Challenges of Democratic Decentralization*. Boulder; London: Lynne Rienner Publishers.

OMR (Observatório do Meio Rural) (2018) 'Agricultura e Desenvolvimento Rural na Proposta de OE 2019'. Maputo: OMR. Available at: https://omrmz.org/omrweb/wp-content/uploads/Analise-_-FMO-_-OE-2018-_-Agricultura-_-draft-3.pdf (accessed 28 July 2020).

Orre, A. and S. Forquilha (2012). 'Uma Iniciativa Condenada ao Sucesso. O Fundo Distrital dos 7 Milhões e suas Consequências para a Governação em Moçambique'. In: B. Weimer (org.), *Moçambique: Descentralizar o Centralismo. Economia Política, Recursos e Resultados*, pp. 168–96. Maputo: IESE.

Orre, A. and H. Rønning. (2017). *Mozambique: A Political Economy Analysis*. Oslo: Norwegian Institute of International Affairs. Available at: www.cmi.no/publications/file/6366-mozambique-a-political-economy-analysis.pdf (accessed 27 February 2020).

Osaghae, E. (2007). 'Fragile States'. *Development in Practice*, 17(4–5): 691–99. https://doi.org/10.1080/09614520701470060.

OSISA (2009). *Moçambique: Democracia e Participação Política.* Johannesburg: AfriMAP. Open Society Initiative of Southern Africa – OSISA. Available at: https://agora-parl.org/sites/default/files/pt-mocambique_-_democracia_e_participacao_politica-open_society_initiative_for_southern_africa.pdf (accessed 26 October 2019).

Ostrom, E. (2005). *Understanding Institutional Diversity.* Princeton University Press. Available at: http://wtf.tw/ref/ostrom_2005.pdf (accessed 27 July 2020).

Otto, J. M. (2018). 'The Taxation of Extractive Industries: Mining'. Chapter 14, In: T. Addison and A. Roe (eds.), *Extractive Industries: The Management of Resources as a Driver of Sustainable Development.* Oxford: Oxford University Press.

OXFAM (2013). *Universal Health Coverage.* Available at: www-cdn.oxfam.org/s3fs-public/file_attachments/bp176-universal-health-coverage-091013-en__3.pdf.

Oxford Policy Management (2019). *Economic Development Institutions: Institutional Diagnostic Tool.* Available at: https://edi.opml.co.uk/wpcms/wp-content/uploads/2019/06/Mozambique-InstitutionalDiagnostic-June2019.pdf.

Page, J. and F. Tarp (eds.) (2017). *The Practice of Industrial Policy: Government–Business Coordination in Africa and East Asia.* Oxford: Oxford University Press.

Page, J. and F. Tarp (eds.) (2020). *Mining for Change: Natural Resources and Industry in Africa.* Oxford: Oxford University Press. https://doi.org/10.1093/oso/9780198851172.001.0001

Paul, S. 1992. 'Accountability in Public Services: Exit, Voice and Control'. *World Development,* 20 (7): 1047–60. https://doi.org/10.1016/0305-750X(92)90130-N.

Pemstein, D., K. L. Marquardt, E. Tzelgov, Y.-t. Wang, J. Medzihorsky, J. Krusell, F. Miri, and J. von Römer (2020). 'The V-Dem Measurement Model: Latent Variable Analysis for Cross-National and Cross-Temporal Expert-Coded Data'. V-Dem Working Paper 21. 5th edition. University of Gothenburg: Varieties of Democracy Institute. https://doi.org/10.2139/ssrn.3595962

Peters, B. G. (1996). 'Political Institutions. Old and New'. In: *A New Handbook of Political Science.* New York: Oxford University Press, pp. 205–2020.

Pim, J. E. and Kristensen, B. (2007). 'Globalizing Understanding of Nonkilling Capabilities'. In: G. D. Page and J. E. Pim (eds.), *Global Nonkilling Leadership: First Forum Proceedings.* Honolulu, Hawaii: Center for Global Nonviolence.

Pinstrup-Andersen, P. (2014). *Food Price Policy in an Era of Market Instability: A Political Economy Analysis.* Oxford: Oxford University Press. https://doi.org/10.1093/acprof:oso/9780198718574.001.0001

Pinto, J. N. (2008). 'A Guerra dos Quinze Años', in J. N. Pinto, *Jogos Africanos.* Lisbon: Esfera dos Livros. Available at: https://macua.blogs.com/files/guerra15anos.pdf (accessed 5 July 2020).

Pitcher, A. (1996). 'Recreating Colonialism or Reconstructing the State? Privatisation and Politics in Mozambique'. *Journal of Southern African Studies,* 22: 49–74. https://doi.org/10.1080/03057079608708478

Pitcher, A. (2002). *Transforming Mozambique: The Politics of Privatization, 1975–2000.* Cambridge: Cambridge University Press (reprinted 2009). https://doi.org/10.1017/CBO9780511491085

Pitcher, A. (2017). 'Party System Competition and Private Sector Development in Africa'. *Journal of Development Studies,* 51(1): 1–17. https://doi.org/10.1080/00220388.2016.1171848

Pitcher, M. A. (2020). 'Mozambique Elections 2019: Pernicious Polarization, Democratic Decline, and Rising Authoritarianism'. *African Affairs*, 119(476): 468–86. https://doi.org/10.1093/afraf/adaa012

Poggi, G. (2017). 'The Nation-State'. In: D. Caramani (ed.), *Comparative Politics*. Oxford: Oxford University Press. pp. 67–112.

PoM (1987b). 'Lei 2/1987'. Maputo: Assembleia Popular. (State budget).

PoM (1987c). 'Lei 3/1987'. Maputo: Assembleia Popular. (Tax system)

PoM (1990). 'Constituição da República de Moçambique', 2 November. Maputo: Assembleia Popular. (1990 Constitution).

PoM (1992). 'Lei 5/1992'. Maputo: Assembleia da República. (Administrative Court organic law)

PoM (1997a). 'Lei 2/1997'. Maputo: Assembleia da República. (Municipalities basic law)

PoM (1997b). 'Lei 15/1997'. Maputo: Assembleia da República. (Budget and State General Account framework law)

PoM (2002a). 'Lei 9/2002'. Maputo: Assembleia da República. (Creation of the state financial administration system)

PoM (2002b). 'Lei 15/2002'. Maputo: Assembleia da República. (Tax system basic law)

PoM (2003). 'Lei 8/2003'. Maputo: Assembleia da República. (State local entities)

PoM (2006). 'Lei 1/2006'. Maputo: Assembleia da República. (Establishment of the revenue authority)

PoM (2007a). 'Lei 5/2007'. Maputo: Assembleia da República. (Legal framework for provincial assemblies)

PoM (2007b). 'Lei 32/2007'. Maputo: Assembleia da República. (Value added tax code)

PoM (2007c). 'Lei 33/2007'. Maputo: Assembleia da República. (Personal income tax code)

PoM (2008). 'Lei 1/2008'. Maputo: Assembleia da República. (finance, budget and state assets framework for local autarchies)

PoM (2012). 'Lei 16/2012'. Maputo: Assembleia da República. (Public probity law)

PoM (2018). 'Lei 1/2018'. Maputo: Assembleia da República. (Constitution amendment)

PoM (2020). 'Lei 14/2002'. Maputo: Assembleia da República. (Revision of the state financial administration system)

PoM (Parliament of Mozambique) (1987a). '1° e 2° Suplementos do Boletim da República', I Série 4, de 30 de Janeiro. Maputo: Assembleia Popular. (Legislation on the Economic Rehabilitation Programme)

Presidente da República (2019). 'PR moçambicano defende reformas estruturais para credibilidade do poder judicial'. News published by the Lusa agency on November 5th. Available at: www.sapo.pt/noticias/atualidade/pr-mocambicano-defende-reformas-estruturais_5dc1a8134090fe02a6b1ceb8 (accessed on 7 November 2019).

Presidente da República (2020). Speech Given at the Opening Ceremony of the Judicial Year. Available at: www.ts.gov.mz/images/Discurso_do_Presidente_da_Rep%C3%BAblica_de_Mocambique_proferido_na_abertura_do_Ano_Judicial_2020_VF.pdf (accessed on 18 February 2020).

Rádio Moçambique (RM) (2021). 'Tribunal Judicial da cidade de Maputo retoma julgamento do Caso Embraer'. RM website, 23 February 2021. Maputo. Available at: www.rm.co.mz/rm.co.mz/index.php/component/k2/item/15011-tribunal-judicial-d a-cidade-de-maputo-retoma-julgamento-do-caso-embraer.html (accessed 24 August 2021).

Rasanathan, K., T. Posayanonda, Birmingham, M. and Tangcharoensathien, V. (2011). 'Innovation and Participation for Healthy Public Policy: The First National Health Assembly in Thailand'. *Health Expectations*, 2011, 15(1): 97–96. https://doi.org/10.1111/j.1369-7625.2010.00656.x.

Rasiah, R. (2017). 'The Industrial Policy Experience of the Electronics Industry in Malaysia'. Chapter 7, In: J. Page and F. Tarp (eds.), *The Practice of Industrial Policy: Government–Business Coordination in Africa and East Asia*. Oxford: Oxford University Press.

Raupp, M., Newman, B. and Reves, L. (2013) *Avaliação do impacto do projecto 'USAID/Aprender a Ler' em Moçambique*. Baseline Report. Designed for USAID/Mocambique. Maputo, 19 June 2013.

Renzio, P. de, M. Andrews, and Z. Mills. (2011). 'Does Donor Support to Public Financial Management Reforms in Developing Countries Work? An Analytical Study of Quantitative Cross-Country Evidence'. Working Paper 329. London: Overseas Development Institute (ODI). Available at: www.odi.org/sites/odi.org.uk/files/odi-assets/publications-opinion-files/7098.pdf (accessed 9 August 2019).

Representantes do PP e do PSOE (2007). 'Pacto de Estado para a Reforma da Justiça (Espanha)'. *Revista Julgar*, (1): 183–92. Lisboa: Associação Sindical dos Juízes Portugueses (ASJP).

República de Moçambique (2014a). *Plano Director do Gás Natural* (Natural Gas Master Plan). Maputo: Government of Mozambique.

República de Moçambique (2014b). *Estratégia Nacional de Desenvolvimento 2015–2035*. Maputo: Government of Mozambique.

República de Moçambique (2016). *Proposta da Política de Emprego (Versão Final)*. Maputo: Ministério do Trabalho, Emprego e Segurança Social.

República de Moçambique (2018). *Projected Government Revenues from Gas Projects*. Maputo: Ministério de Economia e Finanças.

Rice, J. K. (2003) *Teacher Quality: Understanding the Effectiveness of Teacher Attributes*. Washington DC: The Economic Policy Institute.

Ridell, A. and M. Niño-Zarazúa (2016). 'The Effectiveness of Foreign Aid to Education: What Can be Learned?'. *International Journal of Educational Development*, 48: 23–36. https://doi.org/10.1016/j.ijedudev.2015.11.013.

Rodrigues, Sónia (2017). 'Análise quantitativa da produção legislativa'. *In 40 Anos de Políticas de Justiça em Portugal*. Unpublished version. Available at: https://ial-online.org/wp-content/uploads/2019/03/SoniaRodrigues_40anosJustica_vers%C3%A30-n%C3%A30-publicada.pdf (accessed on 17 February 2020).

Rodrik, D. (2004). *Industrial Policy for the Twenty-First Century*. Cambridge, MA: John F. Kennedy School of Government. Available at: https://drodrik.scholar.harvard.edu/files/dani-rodrik/files/industrial-policy-twenty-first-century.pdf (accessed 17 August 2020).

Roe, A. (2018). 'Extractive Industries and Development: Lessons from International Experience for Mozambique'. WIDER Working Paper 2018/56. Helsinki: UNU-WIDER. Available at: www.wider.unu.edu/sites/default/files/Publications/Working-paper/wp2018-56.pdf (accessed 21 July 2020).

Roe, A. (2018). 'Mozambique – Bust before Boom: Reflections on Investment Surges and New Gas'. WIDER Working Paper 2018/140. Helsinki: UNU-WIDER. https://doi.org/10.35188/UNU-WIDER/2018/582-4

Roe, A. (2020). 'Mozambique – Bust before Boom: Reflections on Investment Surges and New Gas'. Chapter 8, In: J. Page and F. Tarp (eds.), *Mining for Change: Natural Resources and Industry in Africa*. Oxford: Oxford University Press.

Roe, A. R. (2018). 'Extractive Industries and Development: Lessons from International Experience for Mozambique'. WIDER Working Paper 2018/56. Helsinki: UNU-WIDER. https://doi.org/10.35188/UNU-WIDER/2018/498-8

Roe, A. R. (2018). 'Mozambique – Bust Before Boom: Reflections on Investment Surges and New Gas'. WIDER Working Paper 140/2018. Helsinki: UNU-WIDER. https://doi.org/10.35188/UNU-WIDER/2018/582-4

Roll, M. (2014). 'Introduction'. In: M. Roll (ed.), *The Politics of Public Sector Performance: Pockets of Effectiveness in Developing Countries* (pp. 1–21). London: Routledge. https://doi.org/10.4324/9781315857718-1

Rondinelli, D., Nellis, J. and Cheema, G. S. (1983). *Decentralization in Developing Countries. A Review of Recent Experience*. Washington, DC: The World Bank.

RTP (2015). Lei de Autarquias Provinciais da Renamo Chumbada no Parlamento Mocambicano. [*Online*]. RTP. Available at: www.rtp.pt/noticias/mundo/lei-de-autarquias-provinciais-da-renamo-chumbada-no-parlamento-mocambicano_n825002 (accessed on 30 May 2020).

Saad-Filho, A., and J. Weeks (2013). 'Curses, Diseases and Other Resource Confusions'. *Third World Quarterly*, 34(1): 1–21. https://doi.org/10.1080/01436597.2012.755010

Sachs, J., G. Schmidt-Traub, C. Kroll, G. Lafortune, and G. Fuller (2019). *Sustainable Development Report 2019*. New York: Bertelsmann Stiftung; Sustainable Development Solutions Network (SDSN). Available at: https://s3.amazonaws.com/sustainabledevelopment.report/2019/ 2019_sustainable_development_report.pdf.

SACMEQ (2020). SACMEQ Reading & Math Achievement Scores. 2020. www.sacmeq.org/ReadingMathScores (accessed on 3 May 2020).

Salazar-Espinoza, C., S. Jones, and F. Tarp (2015). 'Weather Shocks and Cropland Decisions in Rural Mozambique', *Food Policy*, 53: 9–21. https://doi.org/10.1016/j.foodpol.2015.03.003

Salimo, P., L. Buur, and J. J. Macuane (2020). 'Deal-Making between Revenues and Rents: the Political Economy of the Sasol Natural Gas Projects in Mozambique'. *The Extractive Industries and Society*, 7(4): 1219–29. https://doi.org/10.1016/j.exis.2020.05.017

Salimo, P., L. Buur, and J. J. Macuane (forthcoming). 'The Politics of Domestic Gas: The Sasol Natural Gas Deals in Mozambique'. *The Extractive Industries and Society* (available online). https://doi.org/10.1016/j.exis.2020.05.017

Salomão, A., T. V. Mário, and C. Tanner (2019a). *Consultas Comunitárias. Nota Técnica*, April 2019. Maputo: SPEED+; USAID.

Salomão, A., T. V. Mário, and C. Tanner (2019b). *Representação Comunitária na Gestão de Terras e Recursos Naturais. Nota Técnica*, April 2019. Maputo: SPEED+; USAID.

Sande, Z. (2011). '"7 Milhões'. Revisão do Debate e Desafios para Diversificação da Base Produtiva'. In L. Brito, C. N. Castel-Branco, S. Chichava and A. Francisco (orgs.), *Desafios para Moçambique 2011*, pp. 207–28. Maputo: IESE.

Santos, Boaventura de Sousa (2005). 'A justiça em Portugal: diagnósticos e terapêuticas'. *Revista Manifesto*, (7): 76–87, Lisboa.

Santos, Boaventura de Sousa (2013). 'A Justiça Armadilhada.' Revista *Visão*, 14 November, Lisboa.

Santos, Boaventura de Sousa (2014). *Para uma Revolução Democrática da Justiça.* Coimbra: Almedina.

Santos, Boaventura de Sousa and Trindade, João Carlos (orgs.) (2003). *Conflito e Transformação Social: uma Paisagem das Justiças em Moçambique*, 2 vols. Porto: Afrontamento.

Santos, Susana (2014). 'Novas Reformas, Velhos Debates: Análise das Políticas de Justiça e dos Seus Impactos no Sistema Judicial.' *Configurações – Revista de Sociologia* [*Online*], (13). https://doi.org/10.4000/configuracoes.2364

Schick, A. (1998). *A Contemporary Approach to Public Expenditure Management.* Washington, DC: World Bank Institute. Available at: http://documents.worldbank.org/curated/pt/739061468323718599/pdf/351160REVoContemporaryoPEM1book.pdf (accessed 31 October 2019).

Schiller, A., S. Forquilha, S. Bunk, D. Klawonn, J. Krull, A. Sennewald, C. Steinhilber, and J. Boeselager (2018). 'Aptos para Alcançar os seus Objectivos? Obstáculos de Ordem Administrativa a Mobilização da Receita Local nos Municípios Moçambicanos'. In S. Forquilha, *Desafios para Moçambique 2018*, pp. 33–64. Maputo: IESE.

Sheerens, J. (2004). *Melhorar a eficácia das escolas.* Porto: ASA.

Sherwood, R. M., G. Shepherd, and C. M. de Souza (1994). 'Judicial Systems and Economic Performance'. *The Quarterly Review of Economics and Finance*, 34, Special Issue, 101–16. www.sciencedirect.com/science/article/abs/pii/1062976994900388

Shipley, T. (2019). 'Grand Corruption and the SDGs: The Visible Costs of Mozambique's Hidden Debts Scandal'. Berlin: Transparency International. Available at: www.transparency.org/en/publications/grand-corruption-and-the-sdgs-the-visible-costs-of-mozambiques-hidden-debts (accessed 25 September 2019).

Siddiki, S., et al. (2019). 'Institutional Analysis with the Institutional Grammar'. *Policy Studies Journal* (available online). https://doi.org/10.1111/psj.12361

Simão, L. (2020). 'Some Important Dates in the History of Mozambique'. Unpublished.

Simione, A. A. (2014). 'A Modernização da Gestão e a Governança no Setor Público em Moçambique'. *Rev. Adm. Pública*, 48(3):551–70. https://doi.org/10.1590/0034-76121425

Simione, A. A., F. Matos, and I. B. Ckagnazaroff (2018). 'A História da Municipalização em Moçambique: Atores, Estratégias e Implicações para a Gestão Pública Local'. *Revista de Administração de Roraima-UFRR*, 8(2): 526–49. https://doi.org/10.18227/2237-8057rarr.v8i2.5049

Skocpol, T. (ed.) (1995). *Vision and Method in Historical Sociology.* Cambridge: Cambridge University Press.

Smith, W. C. and A. Benavot (2019). 'Improving Accountability in Education: The Importance of Structured Democratic Voice'. *Asia Pacific Education Review*, 20(2): 193–205. https://doi.org/10.1007/s12564-019-09599-9.

Sørensen, B. B., C. Estmann, E. F. Sarmento and J. Rand (2020) 'Economic Complexity and Structural Transformation: The Case of Mozambique'. WIDER Working Paper 2020/141. https://doi.org/10.35188/UNU-WIDER/2020/898-6

Sørensen, G. (2017). 'The Impacto of the Nation-State'. In: D. Caramani (ed.), *Comparative Politics.* Oxford: Oxford University Press. pp. 422–36.

Sousa, G. (2018). 'Ngungunhane, o rei moçambicano que lutou contra a ocupação portuguesa'. *Deutsche Welle: História de África*, 6 July. Available at: www.dw.com/pt-002/ngungunhane-o-rei-mo%C3%A7ambicano-que-lutou-contra-a-ocupa%C3%A7%C3%A3o-portuguesa/a-44177023 (accessed 18 September 2020).

Stifel, D., and T. Woldehanna (2016). 'Poverty in Ethiopia, 2000–11: Welfare Improvements in a Changing Economic Landscape.' In: C. Arndt, A. Mckay and F. Tarp (eds.), *Growth and Poverty in Sub-Saharan Africa*: 43–68. Oxford University Press. https://doi.org/10.1093/acprof:oso/9780198744795.003.0003

Stiglitz, J. (2017). 'Industrial Policy, Learning, and Development'. In: J. Page and F. Tarp (eds.), *The Practice of Industrial Policy: Government–Business Coordination in Africa and East Asia* (pp. 23–39). Oxford: Oxford University Press. https://doi.org/10.1093/acprof:oso/9780198796954.003.0002

Strutt, C. and Keep, T. (2010). 'Implementing Education for All – Whose Agenda, Whose Change? The Case Study of the Ghana National Education Campaign Coalition'. *International Journal of Educational Development*, 30(4): 369–76. https://doi.org/10.1016/j.ijedudev.2009.12.008.

Sulemane, J. (2002). 'Dados Básicos da Economia Moçambicana'. In: C. Rolim, A. S. Franco, B. Bolnick, and P.-A. Andersson (eds.), *A Economia Moçambicana Contemporânea: Ensaios*. Maputo: Gabinete de Estudos, Ministério do Plano e Finanças.

Sumich, J., and J. Honwana (2007). 'Strong Party, Weak State? Frelimo and State Survival through the Mozambican Civil War: An Analytical Narrative on State-Making'. Working Paper 23, Crisis State Working Paper Series 2. London: LSE Destin.

Sutton, J. (2014). *Mapa Empresarial de Moçambique*. London: International Growth Centre and London Publishing Partnership. Available at: www.theigc.org/wp-content/uploads/2014/06/An-Enterprise-Map-of-Mozambique-Portuguese.pdf (accessed 17 July 2020).

Tanner, C. (2010). 'Land Rights and Enclosures: Implementing the Mozambican Land Law in Practice'. In: W. Anseeuw and C. Alden (eds.), *The Struggle over Land in Africa: Conflict, Politics and Change*: 105–130. Cape Town: HSRC Press. Available at: www.researchgate.net/publication/262010411_Land_rights_and_enclosures_Implementing_the_Mozambican_land_law_in_practice (accessed 25 October 2019).

Tarp, F. (1993). *Stabilization and Structural Adjustment: Macroeconomic Frameworks for Analysing the Crisis in Sub-Saharan Africa*. London and New York: Routledge. https://doi.org/10.4324/9780203309285

Tarp, F., C. Arndt, H. T. Jensen, S. Robinson, and R. Heltberg (2004) *Facing the Development Challenge in Mozambique: An Economywide Perspective*. Washington, DC: International Food Policy Research Institute. Available at: http://ebrary.ifpri.org/utils/getfile/collection/p15738coll2/id/87288/filename/87289.pdf (accessed 18 December 2020)

Tarp, F., et al. (2002). 'Facing the Development Challenge in Mozambique: an Economy-Wide Perspective'. Research Report 126. Washington, DC: International Food Policy Research Institute (IFPRI).

Teka, K., A. Van Rompaey, and J. Poesen (2013). 'Assessing the Role of Policies on Land Use Change and Agriculture Development since 1960s in Northern Ethiopia'. *Land Use Policy*, 30: 944–51. http://dx.doi.org/10.1016/j.landusepol.2012.07.005

The Economist (2019). *Democracy Index 2018: Me too? Political Participation, Protest and Democracy*. London; New York; Hong Kong: The Economist Intelligence Unit.

Theodossiadis, L. (2004). 'Tax Reforms and Macroeconomic Stabilisation in Mozambique'. Master thesis. Lund: School of Economics and Management, Lund University. Available at: https://lup.lub.lu.se/luur/download?func=downloadFile&recordOId=1337665&fileOId=1646463 (accessed 24 August 2021).

Thurber, M., D. Hults, and P. Heller (2011). 'Exporting the "Norwegian Model": The Effect of Administrative Design on Oil Sector Performance'. *Energy Policy*, 39: 5366–78. https://doi.org/10.1016/j.enpol.2011.05.027

Tilburg, P. V. (2008). 'Decentralization as a Stabilising Factor in Rwanda'. In: G. Crawford and C. Hartmann (eds.), *Decentralization in Africa: A Pathway out of Poverty and Conflict?*, pp. 213–31. Amsterdam: Amsterdam University Press.

Timbane, Tomás Luís (2016). Speech of the President of the Bar Association at the Opening of the 2016 Judicial Year. Maputo. Available at: www.ts.gov.mz/images/pdf_files/Interven%C3%A7%C3%A3o_do_Baston%C3%A1rio_da_Ordem_dos_Advogados_na_abertura_do_Ano_Judicial_de_2016.pdf (accessed on 23 November 2019).

Topsøe-Jensen, B., E. Ainadine, A. S. Calane, and C. J. Macia (2019). *Final evaluation of GESTERRA capacity building programme on Land Management and Administration within DINAT*. First Draft. Maputo: NIRAS Sweden AB.

Topsøe-Jensen, B., A. Pisco, P. Salimo, and J. Lameiras (2015). *Estudo de Mapeamento das Organizações da Sociedade Civil em Moçambique*. Maputo: Altair Asesores and Agriconsulting SL. Comissão Europeia. Available at: www.eeas.europa.eu/archives/delegations/mozambique/documents/news/mappingsco/20151020_estudomapea mento_onlineversion3.pdf (accessed 25 October 2019).

Total (2019). 'Total Closes the Acquisition of Anadarko's Shareholding in Mozambique LNG'. Total.com, 30 September. Available at: www.total.com/media/news/press-releases/total-closes-acquisition-anadarkos-shareholding-mozambique-lng (accessed 29 July 2020).

Transparency International (2020). 'Corruption Perceptions Index: 2020'. Available at: www.transparency.org/en/cpi/2020/index/nzl.

Transparency International (2020). *Corruption Perceptions Index 2019*. Available at: www.transparency.org/en/publications/corruption-perceptions-index-2019.

Transparency International (n.d.[a]) 'Corruption Perceptions Index'. Data for 2013. *Transparency International*. Available at: www.transparency.org/en/cpi/2013/results/moz

Transparency International (n.d.[b]). 'What Is Corruption?' *Transparency International*. Available at: www.transparency.org/en/what-is-corruption.

Tribunal Administrativo (2017). *Relatório Sobre a Conta Geral do Estado de 2016* (Chapter 6: Extractive Industries). Maputo: Tribunal Administrativo.

Tribunal Administrativo (2018). *Relatório e Parecer Sobre a Conta Geral do Estado 2017* (Chapter 5). Maputo: Tribunal Administrativo.

Trindade, J. C., L. Cruz, and A. C. José (2015). *Avaliação Jurídica Independente aos Processos de Licenciamento dos Projectos Minerais e de Hidrocarbonetos. Parecer Jurídico*. Maputo: Centro Terra Viva – CTV.

Trindade, João Carlos and André Cristiano José (2017). *Os Sistemas (Des)integrados de Justiça na Província de Cabo Delgado*. Maputo: Ministério da Justiça, Assuntos Constitucionais e Religiosos; Fundación Internacional y para Iberoamérica de Administración y Políticas Públicas (FIIAPP).

Trindade, João Carlos and João Pedroso(2003). 'A caracterização do sistema judicial e do ensino e formação jurídica'. In Boaventura de Sousa Santos and João Carlos Trindade (orgs.), *Conflito e Transformação Social: uma Paisagem das Justiças em Moçambique*, vol. I, pp. 259–317. Porto: Afrontamento.

TVM – Redacção (2020). '162 mil pessoas afectadas por insegurança alimentar devido aos ataques de malfeitores' [*Online*]. *TVM*, 20 de Abril de 2020. Available at: www

.tvm.co.mz/index.php?option=com_k2&view=item&id=6743:162-mil-pessoas-afectadas-por-inseguranca-alimentar-devido-aos-ataques-de-malfeitores&Itemid= 277 (accessed 9 May 2020).

UN (1976). 'United Nations Security Council Resolution on Assistance to Mozambique during Its Application of Sanctions Against Southern Rhodesia'. *International Legal Materials*, 15(3): 718–19. doi:10.1017/S0020782900034550

UNAC (2014). *Comunicado de Imprensa: Os Impactos da Situação Política e Militar no Desenvolvimento da Agricultura em Moçambique*. 13 February 2014. Available at: www.universidadepopular.org/site/media/Campanha_dos_movimentos_sociais/ Comunicado_de_Imprensa_UNAC012014_(1).pdf (accessed 26 October 2019).

UNDP (2018). *Human Development Report 2018*. New York: United Nations Development Programme, Human Development Report Office.

UNDP (n.d.). 'Table 2: Human Development Index trends, 1990–2018'. *United Nations Development Programme: Human Development Reports*. Available at: http://hdr.undp .org/en/content/table-2-human-development-index-trends-1990%E2%80%932018.

UNESCO Moçambique (2017). *Relatório anual de 2016*. Available at: http://unesdoc .unesco.org/images/0026/002603/260351POR.pdf (accessed on 17 November 2019).

UNICEF (2017). 'Budget Brief 2017: Health'. Co-publication with Fórum de Monitoria do Orçamento and ROSC. Available at: www.unicef.org/esaro/UNICEF_ Mozambique_--_2017_--_Health_Budget_Brief.pdf (accessed 29 May 2020).

UNICEF (2018). *Mozambique. Budget Brief 2018: Education Sector*. Maputo: UNICEF, ROSC (Civil Society Forum for Child Rights in Mozambique), and Forum de Monitoria do Orcamento. Available at: www.unicef.org/esa/sites/unicef.org.esa/files/2019-04/ UNICEF-Mozambique-2018-Education-Budget-Brief.pdf (accessed 28 July 2020).

UNICEF (2019). *A Situação Mundial da Infância 2019: Crianças, Alimentação e Nutrição*. New York UNICEF.

UNICEF (2020). UNICEF Data. Available at: https://data.unicef.org/country/moz/ (accessed 5 October 2020).

UNICEF Mozambique (2014). *Situation Analysis of Children in Mozambique 2014*. Available at: www.unicef.org/mozambique/media/1961/file/Situation%20of%20 Children%20in%20Mozambique%202014.pdf (accessed on 17 November 2019).

UNICEF Mozambique (2016). *Education in the New Country Programme 2017– 2020: Strategy note*. Available at: http://files.unicef.org/transparency/documents/ Mozambique%20CPD%20-%20Education%20Strategy%20Note%20%20-%20 28%20March%202016.pdf (accessed on 17 November 2019).

United Nations in Mozambique (2020). *Unpacking the Potential Socioeconomic Impact of the Coronavirus Pandemic in Mozambique: A United Nations Situation Analysis and Policy Recommendations*. Maputo: United Nations in Mozambique. Available at: www.undp.org/content/dam/rba/docs/COVID-19-CO-Response/Socio-Economic-Impact-COVID-19-Mozambique-UN-Mozambique-March-2020.pdf (accessed 17 July 2020).

US-EIA (US-Energy Information Administration) (2018). 'Mozambique: Natural Gas', May. Washington, DC: US-EIA. Available at: www.eia.gov/international/analysis/ country/MOZ (accessed 9 March 2020).

Veloso, J. (2007). *Memórias em Voo Rasante: Contributos para a História Política Recente da África Austral*. Lisbon: Papa-Letras.

Véron, R., Williams, G., Corbridge, S. and Srivastava, M. (2006). 'Decentralized Corruption or Gorrupt Decentralization? Community Monitoring of Poverty-Alleviation

Schemes in Eastern India'. *World Development*, 34(11): 1922–41. https://doi.org/
10.1016/j.worlddev.2005.11,024.

Vollmer, F. (2013). 'The Changing Face of Africa: Mozambique's Economic
Transformation and Its Implications for Aid Harmonisation'. *Irish Studies in
International Affairs*, 24: 137–64. https://doi.org/10.3318/ISIA.2013.24.6

Wallerstein, Immanuel (2004). *World-Systems Analysis: An Introduction*. Durham;
London: Duke University Press. https://doi.org/10.1215/9780822399018

Warren, A., R. Cordon, M. Told, D. de Savigny, I. Kickbusch, and M. Tanner (2017).
'The Global Fund's Paradigm of Oversight, Monitoring, and Results in Mozambique'
*Globalization and Health*, 13(89). https://doi.org/10.1186/s12992-017-0308-7.

Weimer, B. (2012). *Descentralizar o Centralismo. Economia Política, Recursos e
Resultados*. Maputo: IESE.

Weimer, B. (2012). *Moçambique: Descentralizar o Centralismo*. Maputo: IESE.

Weimer, B. and J. Carrilho (2017). *A Economia Política da Descentralização em
Moçambique*. Dinâmicas, Efeitos, Desafios. Maputo: IESE.

Weimer, B., J. J. Macuane, and L. Buur (2012). 'A Economia Política do Political
Settlement em Moçambique: Contexto e Implicações da Descentralização'. In: B.
Weimer (ed.), *Moçambique: Descentralizar o Centralismo – Economia Política,
Recursos e Resultados* (pp. 31–75). Maputo: Instituto de Estudos Sociais e Económicos.

Whitfield, L., and L. Buur (2014). 'The Politics of Industrial Policy: Ruling Elites and
Their Alliances'. *Third World Quarterly*, 35: 126–44. https://doi.org/10.1080/0143
6597.2014.868991

Whitfield, L., O. Therkildsen, L. Buur, and A. M. Kjaer (2015). *The Politics of African
Industrial Policy: A Comparative Perspective*. Cambridge University Press. https://
doi.org/10.1017/CBO9781316225509

WHO (2001). Macroeconomics And Health: Investing in Health for Economic
Development. Report of the Commission on Macroeconomics and Health. Available
at: https://apps.who.int/iris/handle/10665/42463.

WHO (2006). 'INDICADORES DE SAÚDE: Elementos Conceituais e Práticos (Capítulo
1)'. *World Health Organization – Regional Office for the Americas*. Available at: www
.paho.org/hq/index.php?option=com_content&view=article&id=14401:health-
indicators-conceptual-and-operational-considerations-section-1&Itemid=0&
showall=1&lang=pt.

WHO (2010). *Health Systems Financing: The Path to Universal Coverage*. Available at:
www.who.int/whr/2010/en/.

WHO (n.d.). 'Social determinants'. *World Health Organization – Regional Office
for Europe*. Available at: www.euro.who.int/en/health-topics/health-determinants/
social-determinants/social-determinants.

Wilkinson, R. and Marmot, M. (eds.) (2003). *Social Determinants of Health: The Solid
Facts*, 2nd ed. Geneva: World Health Organization.

Wilkinson, R. and K. Pickett (2009). *The Spirit Level: Why More Equal Societies
Almost Always Do Better*. London: Allen Lane.

Williams, A., and J. Isaksen (2016). 'Corruption and State-Backed Debts in Mozambique:
What Can External Actors Do?'. U4 Anti-corruption Resource Centre. Available at:
www.cmi.no/publications/file/6024-corruption-and-state-backed-debts-in-mozambique
.pdf (accessed 10 August 2020).

Williams, T. (2019). The Downsides of Dominance: Education Quality Reforms and
Rwanda's Political Settlement. In: S. Hickey and N. Hossain (eds.), *The Politics of*

*Education in Developing Countries: From Schooling to Learning* (1st ed.: 86–104). Oxford: Oxford University Press.

Williamson, O. E. (2000). 'The New Institutional Economics: Taking Stock, Looking Ahead.' *Journal of Economic Literature*, 38(3): 595–613. https://doi.org/10.1257/jel.38.3.595

Wirz, M., and J. Wernau (2016). 'Tuna and Gunships: How $850 Million in Bonds Went Bad in Mozambique'. *Wall Street Journal*, 3 April. Available at: www.wsj.com/articles/tuna-and-gunships-how-850-million-in-bonds-went-bad-in-mozambique-1459675803 (accessed 5 April 2016).

Wolf, M., with A. McElvoy (1997). *Man Without a Face: The Autobiography of Communist's Greatest Spymaster*. New York, NY: Public Affairs.'

World Bank (1987). 'People's Republic of Mozambique: Second Rehabilitation Credit'. Report P-4608-Moz. Washington, DC: World Bank. Available at: http://documents.worldbank.org/curated/en/832571468057846532/pdf/multi-page.pdf (accessed 4 June 2018).

World Bank (1989). 'Mozambique: Public Expenditure Review'. Report 7615-MOZ. Washington, DC: World Bank. Available at: http://documents.worldbank.org/curated/en/793871468323993746/pdf/multi-page.pdf (accessed 17 February 2020).

World Bank (2004). *Initiatives in Legal and Judicial Reform*. Legal Vice Presidency: Washington, DC: World Bank.

World Bank (2014). 'How Wealthy Is Mozambique after the Discovery of Coal and Gas? Measuring Wealth in Mozambique Using the Wealth Accounting Framework'. World Bank Mozambique Policy Note. Washington, DC: The World Bank.

World Bank (2016). *Accelerating Poverty Reduction in Mozambique: Challenges and Opportunities*. Washington, DC: World Bank. Available at: https://openknowledge.worldbank.org/handle/10986/25757 (accessed 18 December 2020)

World Bank (2016). *Mozambique – Systematic Country Diagnostic*. Washington, DC: World Bank Group.

World Bank (2017). *Governance and the Law*, World Economic Report, Washington DC: World Bank.

World Bank (2019). *Republic of Mozambique – Agriculture Public Expenditure Review: Assessment and Result-Focused Expenditure Management*. Washington, DC: World Bank. https://doi.org/10.1596/32534

World Bank (2020). 'World Development Indicators'. http://data.worldbank.org/data-catalog/world-development-indicators/ (accessed on 3 May 2020).

World Bank (2020). 'Worldwide Governance Indicators (WGIs)'. Available at: http://info.worldbank.org/governance/wgi/#home (accessed 23 June 2020).

World Bank (2020). *World Development Indicators (WDI)*. Available at: https://datacatalog.worldbank.org/dataset/world-development-indicators

World Economic Forum (2020). 'The Global Competitiveness Report'. Available at: http://reports.weforum.org/global-competitiveness-index-2017-2018/downloads/, https://reports.weforum.org/global-competitiveness-report-2018/downloads/, http://reports.weforum.org/global-competitiveness-report-2019/downloads/ (accessed 23 June 2020).

World Justice Project (n.d.). 'What Is the Rule of Law?'. *World Justice Project*. Available at: https://worldjusticeproject.org/about-us/overview/what-rule-law (accessed on 8 February 2020).

## Legislation and Regulations

Circular 9/MAEFP/GM-DNAL/214/2020 (n.d.)MAEFP.

Constitution of the Republic of Mozambique, 2018.

Constitution of the Republic, of 25 June 1975, Official Gazette.

Decree No. 2/2020, of 8 January, Official Gazette, Series I, No. 5, of 8 January 2020.

Decree No. 33/2006, of 30 August, Official Gazette, Series I, No. 35, of 30 August 2006.

Decree No. 90/2009, of 31 December, Official Gazette.

Decree-Law No. 1/75, of 29 July. Official Gazette of 29 July 1975.

Law No. 1/2008, of 16 January, Official Gazette, Series I, No. 3, of 6 January 2008.

Law No. 1/2018, of 12 June, Official Gazette, 2nd Supplement, Series I, No. 115, of 12 June 2018.

Law No. 12/2005 of 23 December, Official Gazette, Series I, No. 51, of 23 December.

Law No. 2/77, of 27 September. Official Gazette, Series I, No. 112, of 27 September 1977.

Law No. 2/87, of 30 January, Official Gazette, Series I, 1st Supplement, No. 4, of 30 January 1987.

Law No. 2/97, of 18 February, Official Gazette, Series I, 2nd Supplement, No. 7, of 18 February 1997.

Law No. 26/91, of 31 December. Official Gazette, Series I, No. 52, of 31 December 1991.

Law No. 3/2019, of 31 May, Official Gazette, Series I, No. 105, of 31 May 2019.

Law No. 3/94, of 13 September, Official Gazette, Series I, No. 37, of 13 September.

Law No. 4/2019, of 31 May, Official Gazette, Series I, No. 105, of 31 May 2019.

Law No. 5/2019, of 31 May, Official Gazette, Series I, No. 105, of 31 May 2019.

Law No. 6/2019 of 31 May, Official Gazette, Series I, No. 105, of 31 May 2019.

Law No. 7/2019 of 31 May, Official Gazette, Series I, No. 105, of 31 May 2019.

Law No. 8/2003, of 19 May, Official Gazette, Series I, No. 20, of 19 May.

Ministerial Order No. 52/2010, of the Ministry of Health, of 23 March 2010. Official Gazette, Series I, No. 11, of 23 March 2010.

Resolution No. 40/2012, of 20 December, Official Gazette, Series I, No. 51, of 20 December.

Resolution No. 73/2007, of the Council of Ministers, of 18 December. Official Gazette, Series I, No. 50, of 18 December 2007.

# Index

Footnotes are indicated by n. after the page number.

Printed in the United States
by Baker & Taylor Publisher Services